NEW VENTURE CREATION:
Entrepreneurship for the 21st Century

Jeffrey A. Timmons

Stephen Spinelli

Prescott C. Ensign

McGraw-Hill Ryerson
Connect. Learn. Succeed.

McGraw-Hill Ryerson
Connect. Learn. Succeed.

New Venture Creation: Entrepreneurship for the 21st Century
Canadian Edition

ISBN-13: 978-0-07-071995-8
ISBN-10: 0-07-071995-0

1 2 3 4 5 6 7 8 9 10   TCP   1 9 8 7 6 5 4 3 2 1 0

Statistics Canada information is used with the permission of Statistics Canada. Users are forbidden
to copy this material and/or redisseminate the data, in an original or modified form, for commercial
purposes, without the expressed permission of Statistics Canada. Information on the availability of the
wide range of data from Statistics Canada can be obtained from Statistics Canada's Regional Offices, its
World Wide Web site at http://www.statcan.ca and its toll-free access number 1-800-263-1136.

Printed and bound in Canada

Care has been taken to trace ownership of copyright material contained in this text; however, the
publisher will welcome any information that enables them to rectify any reference or credit for
subsequent editions.

VICE PRESIDENT, EDITOR-IN-CHIEF: Joanna Cotton
SENIOR SPONSORING EDITOR: Kim Brewster
MARKETING MANAGER: Cathie Lefebvre
DEVELOPMENTAL EDITOR: Tracey Haggert
SENIOR EDITORIAL ASSOCIATE: Christine Lomas
PERMISSIONS EDITOR: Shelley Wickabrod
SUPERVISING EDITOR: Graeme Powell
COPY EDITOR: Erin Moore
PRODUCTION COORDINATOR: Lena Keating
COVER DESIGN: Michelle Losier
COVER IMAGE: © Gary Pearl/Getty Images
INTERIOR DESIGN: Michelle Losier
PAGE LAYOUT: ArtPlus Ltd.
PRINTER: Transcontinental Gagne

Library and Archives Canada Cataloguing in Publication

Timmons, Jeffry A.

   New venture creation : entrepreneurship for the 21st century / Jeffrey A. Timmons,
Stephen Spinelli, Prescott C. Ensign. — Canadian ed.

ISBN 978-0-07-071995-8

   1. New business enterprises — Handbooks, manuals, etc.   2. Entrepreneurship — Handbooks,
manuals, etc.
I. Spinelli, Stephen   II. Ensign, Prescott C.   III. Title.

HD62.5.T54 2009   658.1'141   C2009-905401-9

DEDICATION

Dedicated to our families—to our children, and grandchildren.
Thank you for propelling our dreams.

ABOUT THE AUTHORS

Jeffry A. Timmons (December 7, 1941–April 8, 2008)

Franklin W. Olin Distinguished Professor of Entrepreneurship and director, Price-Babson College Fellows Program at Babson College. AB, Colgate University; MBA, DBA, Harvard University Graduate School of Business.

Days before he dies Jeff submitted the last few revisions for the U.S. edition of this text. He was never more engaged intellectually then when he was translating research and experience into coursework. He worked on the belief that deep thinking could motivate decisive action and provide dedicated students of entrepreneurship a competitive advantage.

Beginning his career in the late 1960s, Jeff was one of the pioneers in the development of entrepreneurship education and research in America. He is recognized as a leading authority internationally for his research, innovative curriculum development, and teaching in entrepreneurship, new ventures, entrepreneurial finance, and venture capital.

A prolific researcher and writer, he wrote nine books, including this textbook first published in 1974. *New Venture Creation* has been rated by *INC., Success*, and *The Wall Street Journal* as a "classic" in entrepreneurship. Timmons authored over 100 articles and papers, which appeared in numerous leading publications, such as *Harvard Business Review* and *Journal of Business Venturing*, along with numerous teaching case studies.

Dr. Timmons received his MBA and DBA from Harvard Business School, where he was a National Defense Education Act fellow, and is a graduate of Colgate University, where he was a Scott Paper Foundation Scholar. He served as a trustee of Colgate from 1991 to 2000.

Stephen Spinelli, Jr.

Director, Arthur M. Blank Center for Entrepreneurship, and chairman, Entrepreneurship Division at Babson College.
Vice provost for Entrepreneurship and Global Management at Babson College.
Paul T. Babson Chair in Entrepreneurship at Babson College.
Alan Lewis Chair in Global Management.

The majority of Dr. Spinelli's professional experience has been in entrepreneurship. He was a founding shareholder, director, and manager of Jiffy Lube International. He was also founder, chairman, and CEO of American Oil Change Corporation. In 1991, he completed a sale of Jiffy Lube to Pennzoil Company. Although Dr. Spinelli led the Entrepreneurship Division at Babson and taught full-time, he did not abandon his business roots. He continues to consult with regional, national, and international companies; serves as a director at several corporations and participates as an angel investor with investments in more than a dozen start-ups.

Dr. Spinelli has been a strong voice for entrepreneurship outside the Babson community as well. He has been a keynote speaker for Advent International's CEO Conference, the MCAA National Convention, and Allied Domecq International's Retailing Conference, the Entrepreneur's Organization at MIT and many others; has been called to testify before the U.S. Senate Subcommittee on Small Business and Entrepreneurship; and is often quoted as an expert in the field in such leading publications as *The Wall Street Journal, Forbes, Financial Times*, and *Inc. magazine*.

Prescott C. Ensign, Ph.D

Associate Professor Telfer School of Management University of Ottawa Ontario, Canada

Dr. Ensign has served on the faculties of several universities in Canada as well as state universities in California and Ohio. He is a recipient of a Fulbright Scholarship and has been honoured for both his teaching and research. With a background in industrial engineering and management, Ensign's research has focused on innovation and technology development. His research has also examined the strategy and structure of enterprises as they internationalize. Recently, Ensign has investigated entrepreneurship in remote locations as well as economic development and change in emerging markets. His research has been funded by the Carnegie Bosch Institute, Carnegie Mellon University; Canadian International Development Agency; Export Development Canada; Indian and Northern Affairs Canada, and repeatedly by the Social Sciences and Humanities Research Council, for which he serves as a grant proposal reviewer.

He is the author of *Knowledge Sharing Among Scientists* (2009), which explores social interaction and innovative behaviour among R&D workers. Most recently Ensign has co-edited *Demography at the Edge* (2010), which considers economic and social development in remote regions—such as the far North. Ensign has authored or co-authored over 25 journal articles, 10 book chapters, 20 case studies, and given more than 50 conference presentations. His case studies have been translated into French, Korean, and Spanish.

Ensign has supervised undergraduate, M.Sc., and Ph.D. students. Much of this involves the study of market entry and expansion. Projects have included: commercialization of green/clean technologies; integration of scientific know-how when company cultures merge; social networks of entrepreneurs; small firm-large firm cooperation vs. competition; and social entrepreneurship.

Dr. Ensign has presented workshops on new venture creation to Aboriginal, immigrant, and visible minorities, and is a supporter of several national and international organizations that foster entrepreneurial behaviour. He is also a frequent coach and judge for business plan competitions.

BRIEF CONTENTS

TABLE OF CONTENTS

PART III   The Founder and Team   151

PREFACE

A BOOK FOR THE NEXT GENERATION OF ENTREPRENEURIAL LEADERS

The evolution of entrepreneurship over the years has had an extraordinary impact on the cultural and economic landscape in Canada and worldwide. While there will always be opportunities for improvement and innovation, the present entrepreneurial revolution has become a model for business people, educators, and policymakers around the globe.

People in every nation have enormous entrepreneurial qualities and aspirations, and that spirit is finding its way into nearly all world markets. Entrepreneurship is exploding in countries like India, China, and in the former Soviet bloc—and affecting positive social and economic change in such diverse countries as Korea, Mexico, South Africa, El Salvador, and Ireland.

In our roles as student, teacher, researcher, observer, and participant in this revolution, we can honestly say that global adoption of the entrepreneurial mind-set appears to be growing exponentially larger and faster. That mind-set, while informed by new venture experiences, affects larger corporations and the not-for-profit world as well. In our assessment, we are at the dawn of a new age of entrepreneurial reasoning, equity creation, and philanthropy, whose impact in the coming years will dwarf what we experienced over the last century.

AN EDITION FOR AN ERA OF EXTRAORDINARY UNCERTAINTY AND OPPORTUNITY

Current business times are being defined as much by worldwide challenges and uncertainty as from the enormous opportunities afforded by technology, global communications, and the increasing drive to develop socially, economically, and environmentally sane and sensible new ventures. As with past generations, entrepreneurs in this arena face the ultimate and most demanding juggling act: how to simultaneously balance the insatiable requirements of marriage, family, new venture, service to community, and still have time for one's own pleasure and peace.

A BOOK ABOUT THE CANADIAN ENTREPRENEURIAL PROCESS

New Venture Creation is about the actual process of getting a new venture started, growing the venture, successfully harvesting it, and starting again.

There is a substantial body of knowledge, concepts, and tools that entrepreneurs need to know—before taking the start-up plunge—if they are to get the odds in their favour. Accompanying the explosion in entrepreneurship has been a significant increase in research and knowledge about the entrepreneurial process. Much of what was known previously has been reinforced and refined, while some has been challenged. Numerous new insights have emerged. *New Venture Creation* continues to be the product of experience and considerable research in this field, rooted in real-world application and refined in the classroom.

The design and flow of this book are aimed at creating knowledge, skills, and awareness. In a pragmatic way—through text, case studies, and hands-on exercises—students are engaged to discover critical aspects of entrepreneurship, and what level of competencies, know-how, experience, attitudes, resources, and networks is required to pursue different entrepreneurial opportunities. No doubt about it: There is no substitute for the real thing—actually starting a company. But short of that, it is possible to expose students to many of the vital issues and immerse them in key learning experiences, such as critical self-assessment and the development of a business plan.

This book is divided into five parts, which detail the driving forces of entrepreneurship—the entrepreneurial mind, the opportunity, the founder and team, financing entrepreneurial ventures, and the start-up and beyond. Part I explores the entrepreneurial revolution and addresses the mind-set required to tackle this tremendously challenging and rewarding pursuit. Part II lays out the process by which real opportunities—not just ideas—can be discovered and selected. This section examines the type of opportunity around which higher potential ventures can be built (with acceptable risks and trade-offs), and how such opportunities can profitably be shaped, recognized, and seized. Part III concerns entrepreneurial leadership, team creation, and personal ethics. Part IV addresses marshalling resources, entrepreneurial finance, and fund-raising—including structuring and striking a deal. The book concludes in Part V with sections dealing with strategies for success, leading rapid growth, franchising as an entrepreneurial vehicle, family enterprise, and harvest issues.

Once the reader understands how winning entrepreneurs think, act, and perform, he or she can then establish goals to practise emulating those actions, attitudes, habits, and strategies. *New Venture Creation* challenges readers to think about the process of becoming an entrepreneur, and seeks to enable entrepreneurs to immerse themselves in the dynamics of launching and growing a company. The book addresses practical issues such as the following:

- What are my real talents, strengths, and weaknesses, and how can I exploit those talents and strengths, and minimize my weaknesses?
- How can I recognize when an opportunity is more than just another good idea, and whether it is one that fits with my personal mind-set, capabilities, and life goals?
- Why do some firms grow quickly to several million dollars in sales, but then stumble, never growing beyond a single-product firm?
- What are the critical tasks and hurdles in seizing an opportunity and building the business?
- How much money do I need, and when, where, and how can I get it—on acceptable terms?
- What financing sources, strategies, and mechanisms can I bring to bear throughout the process—from pre-start, through the early growth stage, to the harvest of my venture?
- What are the minimum resources I need to gain control over the opportunity, and how can I do this?
- Is a business plan needed? If so, what kind is required and how and when should I develop one?
- Who are the constituents for whom I must create or add value to achieve a positive cash flow, and to develop harvest options?
- What is my venture worth, and how do I negotiate what to give up?
- What are the critical transitions in entrepreneurial leadership as a firm grows from $1 million, to $5 million, to over $25 million in sales?
- What are some of the pitfalls, minefields, and hazards I need to anticipate, prepare for, and respond to?
- What are the contacts and networks I need to access and develop?
- Do I know what I do and do not know, and do I know what to do about it?
- How can I develop a personal "entrepreneurial game plan" to acquire the experience I need to succeed?
- How critical and sensitive is the timing in each of these areas?

The textbook also exposes the reader to the well-known paradoxes that characterize entrepreneurship and challenge entrepreneurial leaders, such as:

- Ambiguity and uncertainty versus planning and rigour
- Creativity versus disciplined analysis
- Patience and perseverance versus urgency
- Organization and management versus flexibility
- Innovation and responsiveness versus systemization
- Risk avoidance versus risk management
- Current profits versus long-term equity

The *New Venture Creation* models are useful not only as a comprehensive textbook for a course in entrepreneurship, but may also serve as a roadmap for a curriculum in entrepreneurship. This textbook may also be successfully deployed for training and workshops offered by economic development offices. The real-world applications and exercises can be blended with theory to provide a solid basis for nascent entrepreneurs and would-be entrepreneurs.

WHAT TO EXPECT FROM THE CANADIAN EDITION

This edition is a significant update: Canadian cases, exercises, Web sites, and textual material have been added to capture the current financial, economic, technological, and globally competitive environment. A special effort has been made to include cases that capture the dynamic ups and downs new firms experience over an extended period of time. By grappling with decisions faced by entrepreneurs—from start-up to harvest—this textbook offers a broad and rich perspective on the often turbulent and unpredictable nature of the entrepreneurial process.

This Canadian edition features major changes and additions:

- *Tailored for Canadian institutions.* There has been a restructuring and reordering of the flow of the book, which now begins with a focus on the reader as the aspiring entrepreneur. The table of contents has been designed to reflect the subjects taught in Canadian higher learning institutions, and the 15-chapter format has been tailored to accommodate the length of the Canadian semester.
- *Written for a Canadian business context.* Based on extensive feedback and input from Canadian instructors, the new venture creation process has been grounded squarely in a Canadian context. The text teaches the universal applicability of many entrepreneurial and new venture creation tasks by focusing on the latest updates, and yet remains directly and deeply linked to the Canadian experience through examples of entrepreneurs in action coping with the post-Internet bubble era and grappling with the global economic crisis.
- *Refinements to the Timmons Model of the entrepreneurial process.* We have included a dynamic financial planning model that can be a breakthrough tool for entrepreneurs evaluating or planning a venture. Plus, the textbook includes the addition of social, economic, and environmental sustainability factors.
- *The family as entrepreneur.* Chapter 14 outlines the significant economic and entrepreneurial contribution families make to communities and countries worldwide, and examines the different roles families play in the entrepreneurial process. The chapter describes the Six Dimensions for Family Enterprising, and provides a dynamic model to assess a family's relative mind-set for enterprising, and to identify key issues for family dialogue. The running example in the chapter is Canadian (Backerhaus Veit of Toronto).
- *Canadian examples, data, and visuals.* Canadian examples are woven seamlessly throughout the chapters, and data, in the form of clear, easy-to-follow figures and tables, is derived from Canadian sources and Canadian industries whenever appropriate. Readers can expect to see the latest Canadian data and updates on the significant changes in the brave new world of capital markets, the economy, and the banking environment that are relevant to entrepreneurs.

- *In-chapter and online exercises.* In keeping with the practical focus of the text, both text chapters and the corresponding online material contain hands-on exercises to help reinforce the theory in the chapter or help the future entrepreneur assess his/her readiness for the next step in the new venture creation process. These exercises will challenge students to research, brainstorm, and identify what are likely to be the upcoming "sea changes" that will drive the next growth industries.
- *Canadian end-of-chapter and end-of-text cases.* Every chapter concludes with a short case featuring a Canadian company or individual that relates directly to the chapter content. The text also features eight end-of-text cases of varying lengths that relate more broadly to the concepts covered in the new venture creation process.
- *Business plan chapter and sample plan.* Chapter 4 presents a complete business plan guide along with tips, practical advice, and know-how from successful entrepreneurs and investors on the development and presentation of the plan. The guide has been updated to reflect current trends and includes material on social and environmental sustainability. The sample business plan, positioned as an appendix to Chapter 4, features the plan from an actual Canadian start-up and is modelled on the guide found in the chapter.

Acknowledgments

The Canadian edition of this book celebrates many years of intellectual capital acquired through research, case writing, course development, teaching, and practice. The latter has included a wide range of ventures, involving both former students and others. It has also been made possible by the support, encouragement, thinking, and achievements of many people: academic colleagues, former professors and mentors, entrepreneurs, former students, and our many friends who till this soil. A special thanks and debt of appreciation is due to all of our current and former students from whom we learn, and by whom we are inspired with each encounter. We marvel at your accomplishments!

Cases in this edition could not have been generated without the collaboration and support of sharing entrepreneurs. We wish to thank the case authors for their efforts in bringing these stories forward. The cases greatly enrich the educational experience of our students. Our case authors are:

Zeina Farhat, *University of Windsor*

Lisa Giguere, *Wilfrid Laurier University*

Sean M. Hennessey, *University of Prince Edward Island*

Gordon Lucyk, *Grant MacEwan University*

Ken Mark, *University of Western Ontario*

Josephine McMurray, *Wilfrid Laurier University*

Daniel Mireault, *Grant MacEwan University*

Aydin Y. Mirzaee, *chide.it Inc.*

Eric Morse, *University of Western Ontario*

Hugh Munro, *Wilfrid Laurier University*

Elspeth J. Murray, *Queen's University*

Lukas Neville, *Queen's University*

Detlev Nitsch, *Wilfrid Laurier University*

Nicholas P. Robinson, *McGill University*

David Rose, *Wilfrid Laurier University*

Francine K. Schlosser, *University of Windsor*

Maria Scopelliti, *European School of Economics, Milan, Italy*

Don B. Smith, *Wilfrid Laurier University*

Dan Thompson, *Thompson Rivers University*

Stewart Thornhill, *University of Western Ontario*

Mary Weil, *University of Western Ontario*

Anthony A. Woods, *Incoho Inc.*

We would like to extend a special thanks to those professors who reviewed *New Venture Creation*, as they have surely helped to shape the direction of the text.

James Beatty, *George Brown College*

James Bowen, *University of Ottawa*

Victoria Calvert, *Mount Royal College*

Terri Champion, *Niagara College*

Anthony Goerzen, *University of Victoria*

Jim Higginson, *University of Guelph-Humber*

Robert Jago, *Northern Alberta Institute of Technology*

Knud Jensen, *Ryerson University*

Ariff Kachra, *University of Western Ontario*

Jay Krysler, *Northern Alberta Institute of Technology*

Reg Litz, *University of Manitoba*

Geoffery Malleck, *University of Waterloo*

Tom O'Connell, *Concordia University*

Barbara Orser, *University of Ottawa*

Eben Otuteye, *University of New Brunswick*

Jason Perepelkin, *University of Saskatchewan*

Michael Robertson, *Brock University*

Martine Spence, *University of Ottawa*

Lloyd Steier, *University of Alberta*

Keith Wallace, *Kwantlen University*

Taras Wasyliw, *Red River College*

A number of individuals and organizations also deserve accolades for their contributions:

Orinn Benn, Canadian Aboriginal and Minority Supplier Council

Stephen Daze, Entrepreneurship Centre

Nicholas P. Robinson, Merchant Law Group

Baffin Business Development Corporation

Business Development Bank of Canada

Canadian Association of Family Enterprise

Canadian Federation of Independent Business

Canadian Venture Capital & Private Equity Association

Industry Canada

Kitikmeot Economic Development Commission

A debt of gratitude is due to the Social Sciences and Humanities Research Council of Canada for providing a portion of the financing for this venture. They bought me the most precious commodity—time; and their support for case development was instrumental in producing this Canadian edition.

We are truly indebted to Jeffry Timmons and Stephen Spinelli who saw promise in this venture and gave us the "green light" to pursue it!

This Canadian edition came to fruition because of the tremendous effort of Developmental Editor Tracey Haggert who took charge of seeing this project from beginning to end. All of this was accomplished on schedule and with a most cheerful disposition. Extreme gratitude is due to Senior Sponsoring Editor Kim Brewster for believing in this venture, who at the outset envisioned a Canadian edition of *New Venture Creation*, and placed her confidence in this endeavour. Finally, we wish to express a special thank-you to a very capable array of individuals at McGraw-Hill Ryerson who showed great pride and professionalism in producing the finished product you see before you.

Prescott C. Ensign

CHAPTER WALKTHROUGH

In-chapter Pedagogy

The in-chapter pedagogy has been designed to facilitate learning and take the concepts from the Timmons Model and apply them to real-word situations. Whether a practical example of entrepreneurship in action, a trip to the Web, or highlighting relevant data through a figure or a table, these features reinforce chapter material and keep students focused on what is important in each chapter.

RESULTS EXPECTED. To help students identify key concepts, each chapter opens with a list of objectives related to the key topics in the chapter.

FIGURES AND TABLES. The most up-to-date charts and diagrams are included to illustrate relevant ideas and concepts. Canadian data is used where appropriate.

TEXT BOXES FEATURING CANADIAN ENTREPRENEURS. To tie the chapter concepts more directly to the Canadian experience, most chapters include at least one textbox featuring the trials and tribulations of a Canadian company or individual entrepreneur.

INTERNET IMPACT. There is no question that the Internet has fundamentally changed the business landscape forever, and these brief, focused reports extend the reach of the Timmons Model out to the Internet. These are concrete, current examples of how entrepreneurs can and should use the Internet to their advantage in every aspect of their venture from launch to growth and renewal.

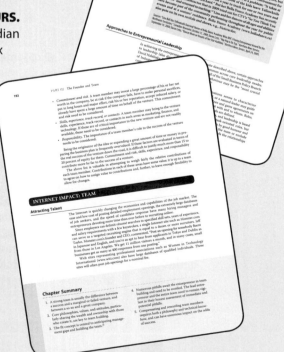

End-of-chapter Pedagogy

Chapters conclude with a series of features that provide a tie-in to the chapter-opening features or reinforce chapter concepts through additional experiential material.

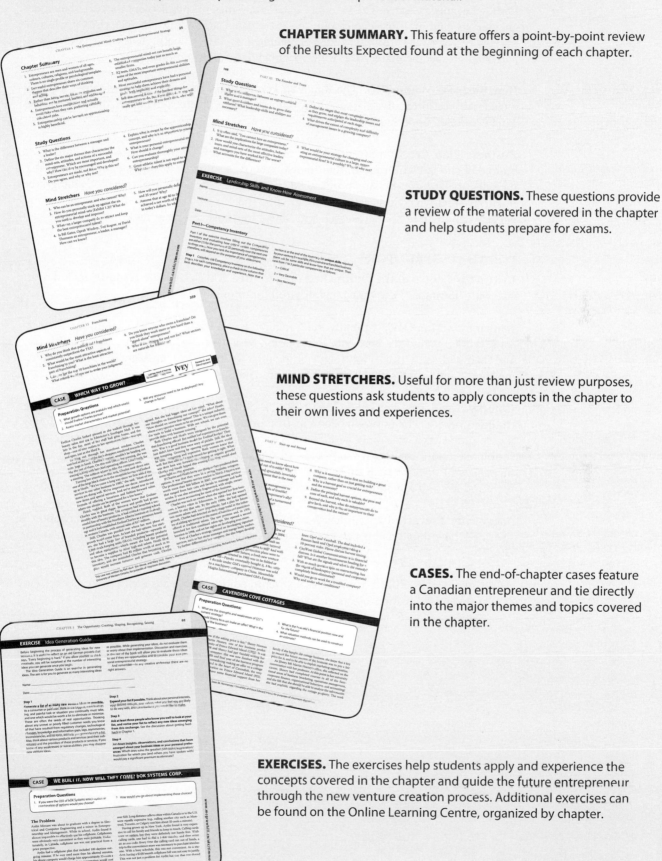

CHAPTER SUMMARY. This feature offers a point-by-point review of the Results Expected found at the beginning of each chapter.

STUDY QUESTIONS. These questions provide a review of the material covered in the chapter and help students prepare for exams.

MIND STRETCHERS. Useful for more than just review purposes, these questions ask students to apply concepts in the chapter to their own lives and experiences.

CASES. The end-of-chapter cases feature a Canadian entrepreneur and tie directly into the major themes and topics covered in the chapter.

EXERCISES. The exercises help students apply and experience the concepts covered in the chapter and guide the future entrepreneur through the new venture creation process. Additional exercises can be found on the Online Learning Centre, organized by chapter.

Supplements

FOR THE STUDENT:

Online Learning Centre. The Student Centre is designed to complement the text. It includes chapter-specific multiple-choice quizzes, extra cases, and additional exercises (including the very popular Venture Opportunity Screening Exercises (VOSE)). Access both the general and chapter-specific material at: www.mcgrawhill.ca/olc/timmons.

New Business Mentor CD. The Kaufman Foundation's "New Business Mentor" CD that includes several interactive planning tools, sample business plans, and links to online resources can be bundled upon request.

Business Plan Pro. We are providing the opportunity for instructors and students to bundle Business Plan Pro with their new textbook, a valuable business planning tool that includes an easy step-by-step process, 68 sample plans for guidance, complete, integrated financials, real-world forecasting tools, grading sheet, a white paper on business plan competitions, built-in industry research data, and a free business plan book.

FOR THE INSTRUCTOR:

Instructor Centre of the Online Learning Centre. This all-in-one resource includes the following, located at: www.mcgrawhill.ca/olc/timmons.

Instructor's Manual. Written by the Canadian text author Prescott Ensign, the Instructor's Manual includes a wealth of information to assist instructors in presenting this text and their course to its best advantage. It includes lecture notes, answers to end-of-chapter questions, and useful suggestions for presenting key concepts and ideas.

Computerized Test Bank. McGraw-Hill's EZ Test is a flexible and easy-to-use electronic testing program. The program allows instructor's to create tests from book-specific items. It accommodates a wide range of question types and instructors may add their own questions. Multiple versions of the test can be created and any test can be exported to use with course management systems such as WebCT, BlackBoard, or PageOut. The program is available for Windows and Macintosh environments.

Microsoft© PowerPoint© Slides. A complete set of PowerPoint slides for each chapter is provided, including graphics and key chapter material to aid in illustrating and explaining concepts.

Additional Cases. Pulled from the U.S. seventh edition, these cases can serve as excellent in-class exercises, team projects, or exam questions.

PART

I

THE ENTREPRENEURIAL MIND

At the heart of the entrepreneurial process is the founder: the opportunity seeker, the creator and initiator; the leader, problem solver, and motivator; the strategizer and guardian of the mission, values, and culture of the venture. Without this human energy, drive, and vitality, the greatest ideas—even when they are backed by an overabundance of resources and staff—will fail, grossly underperform, or simply never get off the ground. Brilliant musical, scientific, or athletic aptitude and potential do not equal the great musician, the great scientist, or the great athlete. The difference lies in the intangibles: creativity and ingenuity, commitment, tenacity and determination, a passion to win and excel, and leadership and team-building skills.

Think of the number of first-round draft picks who never made the grade in professional sports—even without suffering a career-ending injury. Then consider the many later-round picks who became superstars. Another curiosity is the athlete who languishes with one team and then thrives when traded to another team.

So what is it that an aspiring young entrepreneur needs to know, and what habits, attitudes, and mind-sets can be learned, practised, and developed—and thereby improve the odds of success? We begin this first Canadian edition with a focus on you—the lead entrepreneur. We examine the mind-sets, the learnable and acquirable attitudes and habits that lead to entrepreneurial success—and failure. By examining patterns and practices of entrepreneurial thinking and reasoning, and the entrepreneurial mind in action, you can begin your own assessment and planning process to get you headed where you want to go. This personal entrepreneurial strategy will evolve into your personal business plan—a blueprint to help you learn, grow, attract mentors who can change your life and your ventures, and pursue the opportunities that best suit you.

Survival odds for a venture go up once you reach the benchmark of $1 million in sales and 20 employees. Launching or acquiring and then building a business that will exceed these levels is more fun and more challenging than being involved in the vast majority of small one- or two-person operations. But perhaps most important, a business of this magnitude achieves the critical mass necessary to attract good people and, as a result, significantly enhances the prospects of realizing a harvest. An entrepreneur isn't simply creating a job; he or she can build a business that can lift a community.

A leader who thinks and acts with an "entrepreneurial mind" can make a critical difference as to whether a business is destined to be a traditional, very small lifestyle firm, a stagnant or declining large one, or a higher potential venture. Practising certain mental attitudes and actions can stimulate, motivate, and reinforce the kind of zest and entrepreneurial culture whose self-fulfilling prophecy is success.

It is almost impossible to take a number of people, give them a single test, and determine those who possess entrepreneurial minds and those who do not. Rather, it is useful for would-be entrepreneurs and others involved in entrepreneurship to study how successful entrepreneurs think, feel, and respond and how those factors that are significant can be developed and strengthened—as a decathlete develops and strengthens certain muscles to compete at a certain level.

Entrepreneurs who create or recognize opportunities and then seize and shape them into higher potential ventures think and do things differently. They operate in an entrepreneurial domain, a place governed by certain modes of action and dominated by certain driving forces.

Take for example, Mike Lazaridis, the founder and co-CEO of Research In Motion (RIM). An immigrant to Canada, Lazaridis took science courses in high school with an eye toward future university studies and shop courses that allowed him hands on experience. While a student at the University of Waterloo he and several classmates formed an electronics and computer science consulting business and landed a $600,000 contract from General Motors. According to Lazaridis, "I've always been entrepreneurial. In fact, I paid for a lot of my tuition through consulting. It used all the skills that I learned. I had a contract with General Motors that was very exciting. You get an opportunity and it absorbs your time."[1] In 1992, with fewer than 10 RIM employees, Jim Balsillie came onboard as co-CEO to handle the business affairs leaving Lazaridis to develop the technology vision that later turned into the BlackBerry. Lazaridis remarked, "We're not in this for an IPO to get rich. We've proven to the world that we want to run and build a company. We're going to put in the time. We're going to make the sacrifices and investments we need to provide an environment where we can make products and meet customer demands."[2]

It makes a lot of sense for entrepreneurs to pay particular attention to picking partners, key business associates, and managers with an eye for complementing the entrepreneurs' own weaknesses and strengths and the needs of the venture. As will be seen, they seek people who fit. Not only can an entrepreneur's weakness be an Achilles' heel for a new venture, but also the whole is almost always greater than the sum of its parts.

Finally, ethics are terribly important in entrepreneurship. In highly unpredictable and fragile situations, ethical issues cannot be handled according to such simplistic notions as "always tell the truth." It is critical that an entrepreneur understands, develops, and implements an effective integrity strategy for the business.

1

THE ENTREPRENEURIAL MIND: CRAFTING A PERSONAL ENTREPRENEURIAL STRATEGY[1]

If you're going to lick the icing off somebody else's cake you won't be
nourished and it won't do you any good.
You will have to experiment and try things out for yourself.

Emily Carr

Upon completion of this chapter, you will be able to:

1. Determine whether being an entrepreneur gives sustaining energy, rather than takes it away.

2. Explore the entrepreneurial mind—the strategies, habits, attitudes, and behaviours that work for entrepreneurs who build higher potential ventures.[2]

3. Describe the characteristics of various entrepreneurial groups.

4. Appreciate the benefits of an apprenticeship and an entrepreneur's creed.

5. Develop a personal entrepreneurial strategy; initiate a self-assessment and goal-setting process that can become a lifelong habit of entrepreneurial thinking and action.

ACHIEVING ENTREPRENEURIAL GREATNESS

One of the most extraordinary success stories of our time is that of serial entrepreneur Terry Matthews. His first start-up with fellow British Isle immigrant Michael Cowpland was Mitel, an abbreviation for Mike and Terry's Electric Lawnmowers. Those responsible for delivering the goods to the partners for later resale lost the container. The lawnmowers arrived in winter; with the ground covered in snow there was little hope of sales. Matthews recalled, "That taught me a key lesson—the importance of timing. The shipping company lost the lawnmowers! By the time they showed up no-one wanted them, as you can't cut grass when it's covered with snow."[3] Terry and Mike rebounded with a profitable and popular two-tone, multi-frequency receiver in the telephone voice communications market. The telephony device, which hastened the demise of rotary-dial phones was inspired by Cowpland's Ph.D. thesis and allowed them to sell a better product than competitors at a fraction of the cost while garnering returns of 1,000 percent. The pair purchased a silicon chip foundry and moved to newer technologies—microprocessors and semiconductor devices. Mitel went public on the New York Stock Exchange and the company was later acquired by British Telecom. Cowpland went on to found the software company Corel and Matthews transitioned from voice to data networking with the launch of Newbridge Networks, which he subsequently turned over to Alcatel for $7.1 billion.

With some irony, Matthews bought back the Mitel name and PBX business from British Telecom. Mitel's manufacturing was spun off as Breconridge. Later, Matthews' March Networks became the first successful Canadian IPO in the tech industry after the bubble burst and high-tech crashed.

Matthews has founded 65 different ventures and remains active in about 20 of them. Successes include Celtic House Venture Partners, an early stage technology venture capital firm with interests in telecom, storage, networking, and Internet infrastructure. Matthews is also founder and chairman of Wesley Clover, a private equity firm with assets in telecom, real estate, and leisure industries. Matthews' words of determination and drive: "Don't be boring, do something… make a mark, don't be part of the living dead."[4] "I don't think I'm stubborn, I just focus on the task at hand and do what it takes. Persistence is the single most important thing for success."[5] "I've always been a big believer in the early-mover advantage."[6] When the 65-year-old is pushed on the subject of retirement—why someone who doesn't need to work chooses to work and is not sitting on a beach or hot-air ballooning around the world—Matthews' reply is brief. "It's fun."[7]

On a smaller scale, Tom Heintzman and Greg Kiessling with both conviction and an array of relevant experience made the leap and founded Bullfrog Power in 2004. Bullfrog delivers environmentally responsible electricity to the powergrids in Ontario and Alberta. Electricity consumers (residential, commercial, and government) can elect Bullfrog Power as their provider. Bullfrog and its partners then inject electricity derived from renewable sources into the system. On August 1, 2008 in Kingston, Ontario, 160 Queen's University students elected to have their housing complex get on the green grid. "While students won't be saving any money with Bullfrog Power, it is a conscious decision they made to assist the environment. On the contrary, it's going to cost them each $65 extra a year to reduce their carbon footprint by 56 tonnes."[8] Boyd Cohen of the University of Victoria observes that "young, entrepreneurial firms can contribute towards a more sustainable society through innovation."[9] Research conducted by Richard Hudson of Mount Allison University and Roger Wehrell of Saint Francis Xavier University shows that socially responsible investors have two goals: to obtain a market-based return and make others act in a more socially responsible way.[10] Bullfrog's founders are hoping to do just that—to turn a profit and improve the planet.

The ultimate message is clear: Great companies can be built and all the capital, technology, and latest information available cannot substitute for hard work and determination. An entrepreneur creates the culture in his or her own new venture. These ideals are at the very heart of the difference between good and great entrepreneurs and the enterprises they create.

LEADERSHIP AND HUMAN BEHAVIOUR

People don't want to be managed, they want to be led.

Ewing Marion Kauffman

A single psychological model of entrepreneurship has not been supported by research. However, behavioural scientists, venture capitalists, investors, and entrepreneurs share the opinion that the eventual success of a new venture will depend a great deal upon the talent and behaviour of the lead entrepreneur and of his or her team.

A number of myths still persist about entrepreneurs. Foremost among these myths is the belief that leaders are born, not made. The roots of much of this thinking reflect the assumptions and biases of an earlier era, when rulers were royalty and leadership was the prerogative of the aristocracy. Fortunately, such notions have not withstood the tests of time or the scrutiny of scientific investigation of leadership and management. Consider studies, which distinguish managers from leaders, as summarized in Exhibit 1.1. It is widely accepted today that leadership is an extraordinarily complex subject, depending more on the interconnections among the leader, the task, the situation, and those being led than on inborn or inherited characteristics alone.

There are numerous ways of analyzing human behaviour that have implications in the study of entrepreneurship. For example, for over 35 years David McClelland of Harvard University and John Atkinson of the University of Michigan and their colleagues sought to understand individual motivation.[11] Their theory of psychological motivation is a generally accepted part of the literature on entrepreneurial behaviour. People are motivated by three principal needs: (1) the need for achievement, (2) the need for power, and (3) the need for affiliation. The *need for achievement* is the need to excel and for measurable personal accomplishment. A person competes against a self-imposed standard that does not involve competition with others. The individual sets realistic and challenging goals and likes to get feedback on how well he or she is doing in order to improve performance. The *need for power* is the need to influence others and to achieve an "influence goal." The *need for affiliation* is the need to attain an "affiliation goal"—the goal is to build a warm relationship with someone else and/or to enjoy mutual friendship. The prototypical entrepreneur has a high need for achievement and power and a low need for affiliation.

RESEARCH

Other research focused on the common attitudes and behaviours of entrepreneurs. One study found a relationship between attitudes and behaviours of successful entrepreneurs and various stages of company development.[12] Another study found that entrepreneurs were unique individuals and that those motives do influence later performance of the venture.[13] A study of entrepreneurs revealed that "those who like to plan are much more likely to be in the survival group than those who do not."[14] Clearly, the get-rich-quick entrepreneurs are not the company builders, nor are they the planners of successful ventures. Rather it is the visionary who participates in the day-to-day routine to achieve a long-term objective and who is generally passionate and not exclusively profit-oriented.

EXHIBIT 1.1   Comparing Management and Leadership

	Management	Leadership
Creating an Agenda	Planning and budgeting—establishing detailed steps and timetables for achieving needed results, and then allocating the resources necessary to achieve these results	Establishing direction—developing a vision of the future, often the distant future, and strategies for producing the changes needed to achieve that vision
Developing a Human Network for Achieving the Agenda	Organizing and staffing—establishing some structure for accomplishing plan requirements, staffing that structure with individuals, delegating responsibility and authority for carrying out the plan, providing policies and procedures to help guide people, and creating methods or systems to monitor implementation	Aligning people—communicating the direction by words and deeds to all those whose cooperation may be needed to influence the creation of teams and coalitions that understand the vision and strategies, and accept their validity
Execution	Controlling and problem solving—monitoring results versus plan in some detail, identifying deviations, and then planning and organizing to solve these problems	Motivating and inspiring—energizing people to overcome major political, bureaucratic, and resource barriers to change by satisfying very basic, often unfulfilled human needs
Outcomes	Producing a degree of predictability and order, and having the potential of consistently producing key results expected by various stakeholders	Producing change, often to a dramatic degree, and having the potential of producing extremely useful change

Source: John P. Koter, *A Force for Change: How Leadership Differs from Management* (New York, NY: Free Press, 1990).

Academics have continued to characterize the special qualities of entrepreneurs. (See Exhibit 1.2 for a summary of this research.) In this quest to understand the entrepreneurial mind, researchers spoke with 60 practising entrepreneurs. One finding was that entrepreneurs felt they had to concentrate on certain fundamentals: responsiveness, resiliency, and adaptiveness in seizing new opportunities.[15] These entrepreneurs spoke of other attitudes, including an ability "to activate vision" and a willingness to learn about and invest in new techniques, to be adaptable, to have a professional attitude, and to have patience. They talked about the importance of "enjoying and being interested in business," as well as the business as "a way of life."

Many of the respondents recognized and endorsed the importance of human resource management; one entrepreneur said that one of the most challenging tasks was playing "a leadership role in attracting high-quality people, imparting your vision to them, and holding and motivating them." Other entrepreneurs focused on the importance of building an organization and teamwork. For example, the head of a manufacturing firm with $10 million in sales said, "Understanding people and how to pull them together toward a basic goal will be my main challenge in five years." The head of a clothing manufacturing business with 225 employees and $6 million in sales shared a view of many that one of the most critical areas where an entrepreneur has leverage and long-term impact is in leading employees. He said, "Treating people honestly and letting them know when they do well goes a long way."

A number of respondents believed that the ability to conceptualize their business and do strategic planning would be of growing importance, particularly when thinking five years ahead. Similarly, the ageless importance of sensitivity to and respect for employees was stressed by the CEO of a firm with $40 million in sales and 400 employees: "It is essential that the separation between management and the average employee should be eliminated. Students should be taught to respect employees all the way down to the janitor and accept them as knowledgeable and able persons." One company that took this concept to heart was Ben & Jerry's Homemade Ice Cream Inc. The company began operations with a covenant that "no boss got more than five times the compensation, including both pay and benefits,

EXHIBIT 1.2   Characteristics of Entrepreneurs

Date	Authors	Characteristics
1848	Mill	Risk bearing
1917	Weber	Source of formal authority
1934	Schumpeter	Innovative; take initiative
1954	Sutton	Desire for responsibility
1959	Hartman	Source of formal authority
1961	McClelland	Risk taking; need for achievement
1963	Davids	Ambitious; desire for independence; self-confidence
1964	Pickle	Drive; communication ability; technical knowledge
1971	Hornaday and Aboud	Need for achievement; autonomy; aggression; power
1973	Winter	Need for power
1982	Casson	Risk; innovation; power; authority
1985	Gartner	Change and ambiguity
1987	Begley and Boyd	Risk taking; tolerance and ambiguity
1988	Caird	Drive
1998	Roper	Power and authority
2000	Thomas and Mueller	Risk; power; internal locus of control; innovation
2001	Lee and Tsang	Internal locus of control
2007	Stewart and Roth	High achievement motivation
2009	McCluskey and Ensign	Social network astuteness

of the lowest-paid worker with at least one year at the company."[16] Since its inception, the covenant was modified to seven to one, while the company reported $63.2 million in revenue in the first half of 1992.[17] By 2000 the ratio had reached 17 to 1. In 2004 and after four consecutive years of workforce reductions, Ben & Jerry's stopped reporting this number.

A consulting study by McKinsey & Co. of medium-size growth companies confirms that the CEOs of winning companies were notable for three common traits: perseverance, a builder's mentality, and a strong propensity for taking calculated risks.[18]

CONVERGING ON THE ENTREPRENEURIAL MIND

The entrepreneur is one of the most intriguing and at the same time most elusive characters.

William Baumol

Desirable and Acquirable Attitudes, Habits, and Behaviours

Many successful entrepreneurs have emphasized that while their colleagues have initiative and a take-charge attitude, are determined to persevere, and are resilient and able to adapt, it is not just a matter of personality. It is what they *do* that matters most.[19]

While there is an undeniable core of such inborn characteristics as energy and raw intelligence, which an entrepreneur either has or does not, it is becoming apparent that possession of these characteristics does not necessarily an entrepreneur make. There is also a good deal of evidence that entrepreneurs are born and made better and that certain attitudes and behaviours can be acquired, developed, practised, and refined through a combination of experience and study.[20]

While not all attitudes, habits, and behaviours can be acquired by everyone at the same pace and with the same proficiency, entrepreneurs are able to significantly improve their odds of success by concentrating on those that work, by nurturing and practising them, and by eliminating, or at least mitigating, the rest. Painstaking effort may be required, and much will depend upon the motivation of an individual to grow, but it seems people have an astounding capacity to change and learn if they are motivated and committed to do so.

Testimony given by successful entrepreneurs also confirms attitudes and behaviours that successful entrepreneurs have in common. In an examination of 21 well-known entrepreneurs, all mentioned the possession of three attributes as the principal reasons for their successes: (1) the ability to respond positively to challenges and learn from mistakes, (2) personal initiative, and (3) great perseverance and determination.[21]

"Themes" have emerged from what successful entrepreneurs do and how they perform. Undoubtedly many attitudes and behaviours characterize the entrepreneurial mind, and there is no single set of attitudes and behaviours that every entrepreneur must have for every venture opportunity. Further, the *fit* concept argues that what is required in each situation depends on the mix and match of the key players and how promising and forgiving the opportunity is, given the founder's strengths and shortcomings. A team might collectively show many of the desired strengths, but even then there is no such thing as a perfect entrepreneur—as yet.

Six Dominant Themes

Nothing that sends you to the grave with a smile on your face comes easy. Work hard doing what you love. Find out what gives you energy and improve on it.

Betty Coster

A consensus has emerged around six dominant themes, shown in Exhibits 1.3 and 1.4.

EXHIBIT 1.3   Six Themes of Desirable and Acquirable Attitudes and Behaviours

Theme	Attitude or Behaviour
Commitment and Determination	Tenacious and decisive, able to recommit/commit quickly
	Intensely competitive in achieving goals
	Persistent in solving problems, disciplined
	Willing to undertake personal sacrifice
	Immersed
Leadership	Self-starter; high standards but not perfectionist
	Team builder and hero maker; inspires others
	Treats others as you want to be treated
	Shares the wealth with all the people who helped create it
	Honest and reliable; builds trust; practises fairness
	Not a lone wolf
	Superior learner and teacher; courage
	Patient and urgent
Opportunity Obsession	Has intimate knowledge of customers' needs and wants
	Market driven
	Obsessed with value creation and enhancement
Tolerance of Risk, Ambiguity, and Uncertainty	Calculated risk taker
	Risk minimizer
	Risk sharer
	Manages paradoxes and contradictions
	Tolerates uncertainty and lack of structure
	Tolerates stress and conflict
	Able to resolve problems and integrate solutions
Creativity, Self-Reliance, and Adaptability	Non-conventional, open-minded, lateral thinker
	Restless with status quo
	Able to adapt and change; creative problem solver
	Quick learner
	No fear of failure
	Able to conceptualize and "sweat details" (helicopter mind)
Motivation to Excel	Goal-and-results oriented; high but realistic goals
	Drive to achieve and grow
	Low need for status and power
	Interpersonally supporting (versus competitive)
	Aware of weaknesses and strengths
	Has perspective and sense of humour

Commitment and Determination   Commitment and determination are seen as more important than any other factor. With commitment and determination, an entrepreneur can overcome incredible obstacles and also compensate enormously for other weaknesses.

Total commitment is required in nearly all entrepreneurial ventures. Almost without exception, entrepreneurs live under huge, constant pressures—first for their firms to survive start-up, then for them to stay alive, and, finally, for them to grow. A new venture demands top priority for the entrepreneur's time, emotions, and loyalty. Thus, commitment and determination usually require personal sacrifice. An entrepreneur's commitment can be measured in several ways—through a willingness to invest a substantial portion of his or her net worth in the venture, through a willingness to take a cut in pay because he or she will own a major piece of the venture, and through other major sacrifices in lifestyle and family circumstances.

The desire to win does not equal the will to never give up. This is a critically important distinction. Countless would-be entrepreneurs (and lots of other types of people for that matter) say that they really want to win. But few have the dogged tenacity and unflinching perseverance to make it happen. Take a young entrepreneur we shall call Stephen. One of the authors

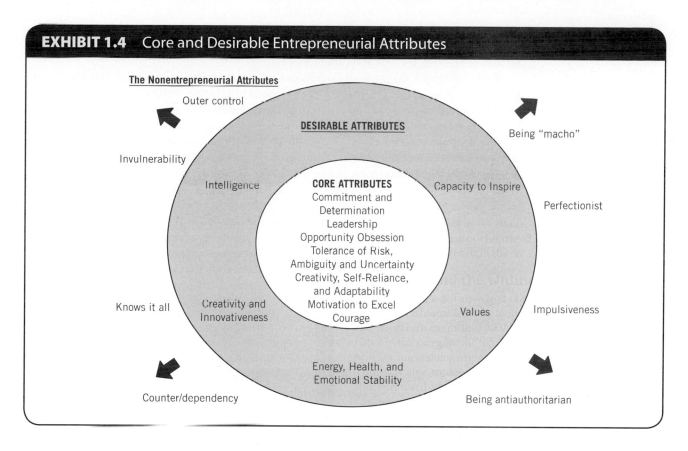

EXHIBIT 1.4   Core and Desirable Entrepreneurial Attributes

introduced him to a potentially invaluable lead—a brain trust prospect and mega-angel investor. Stephen placed several phone calls to the investor, but none were returned. He made a few more calls, each time leaving a message with the referral information. Still, no response.

Over the next week the young entrepreneur made yet another series of over two dozen calls that once again received no response. At that point, what would you have done? Have you ever called anyone that many times and not gotten any sort of reply? Would you keep trying, or decide to move on and not waste any more time? Feeling that this individual was a potentially invaluable contact, Stephen refused to give up. He would make 12 more calls before finally getting a response. In the luncheon meeting that followed soon after, the mega-angel agreed to invest $1 million in Stephen's start-up, and serve as chairman of the board. The company became successful, and was sold four years later for $55 million.

Entrepreneurs are intensely competitive: they love to win and love to compete—at anything! The best of them direct all this competitive energy toward the goal and toward their external competitors. This is critical; founders who get caught up in competing with peers in the company invariably destroy team cohesion and spirit and, ultimately, the team.

Entrepreneurs who successfully build new enterprises seek to overcome hurdles, solve problems, and complete the job; they are disciplined, tenacious, and persistent. They are able to commit and recommit quickly. They are not intimidated by difficult situations; in fact, they seem to think that the impossible just takes a little longer. However, they are neither aimless nor foolhardy in their relentless attack on a problem or obstacle that can impede their business. If a task is unsolvable, an entrepreneur will actually give up sooner than others. Most researchers share the opinion that while entrepreneurs are extremely persistent, they are also realistic in recognizing what they can and cannot do, and where they can get help to solve a very difficult but necessary task.

Leadership   Successful entrepreneurs are experienced, possessing intimate knowledge of the technology and marketplace in which they will compete, sound general management skills, and a proven track record. They are self-starters and have an internal locus of control with high standards. They are patient leaders, capable of instilling tangible goals, and managing for the longer haul. The entrepreneur is at once a learner and a teacher, a doer and a visionary. The vision of building a substantial enterprise that will contribute something lasting and relevant to the world while realizing a capital gain requires the patience to stick to the task for 5 to 10 years or more.

Work by Alan J. Grant lends significant support to the fundamental "driving forces" theory of entrepreneurship that will be explored in Chapter 3. Grant surveyed 25 senior venture capitalists to develop an entrepreneurial leadership paradigm. Three clear areas evolved from his study: the lead entrepreneur, the venture team, and the external environment influences, which are outlined in further detail in Exhibit 1.5. Furthermore, Grant suggested that to truly understand this paradigm, it should be "metaphorically associated with a *troika*, a Russian vehicle pulled by three horses of *equal* strength. Each horse represents a cluster of the success factors. The troika was driven toward success by the visions and *dreams* of the founding entrepreneurs."[22]

Successful entrepreneurs possess a well-developed capacity to exert influence *without* formal power. These people are adept at conflict resolution. They know when to use logic and when to persuade, when to make a concession, and when to exact one. To run a successful venture, an entrepreneur learns to get along with many different constituencies—the customer, the supplier, the financial backer, the creditor, as well as the partners and others on the inside—often with conflicting aims. Success comes when the entrepreneur is a mediator—a negotiator rather than a dictator.

EXHIBIT 1.5   The Entrepreneurial Leadership Paradigm

The Lead Entrepreneur	
Self-concept	Has a realist's attitude rather than one of invincibility
Intellectually honest	Trustworthy, his/her word is his/her contract
	Admits what and when he/she does not know
Pace maker	Displays a high energy level and a sense of urgency
Courage	Capable of making hard decisions: setting and beating high goals
Communication skills	Maintains an effective dialogue with the venture team, in the marketplace, and with other venture constituents
Team player	Competent in people management and team-building skills
The Venture Team	
Organizational style	The lead entrepreneur and the venture team blend their skills to operate in a participative environment
Ethical behaviour	Practises strong adherence to ethical business practices
Faithfulness	Stretched commitments are consistently met or bettered
Focus	Long-term venture strategies are kept in focus but tactics are varied to achieve them
Performance/reward	High standards of performance are created and superior performance is rewarded fairly and equitably
Adaptability	Responsive to rapid changes in product/technological cycles
External Environmental Influences	
Constituent needs	Organization needs are satisfied, in parallel with those of the public the enterprise serves
Prior experience	Extensive prior experiences are effectively applied
Mentoring	The competencies of others are sought and used
Problem resolution	New problems are immediately solved or prioritized
Value creation	High commitment is placed on long-term value creation for backers, customers, employees, and other stakeholders
Skill emphasis	Marketing skills are stressed over technical ones

Source: Adapted from Alan Grant, "The Development of an Entrepreneurial Leadership Paradigm for Enhancing Venture Capital Success," *Frontiers of Entrepreneurship Research* (Babson Park, MA: Babson College, 1992).

Successful entrepreneurs are interpersonally supporting and nurturing—not interpersonally competitive. When a strong need to control, influence, and gain power over others characterizes the lead entrepreneur, or where he or she has an insatiable appetite for putting an associate down, the venture usually gets into trouble. Entrepreneurs should treat others as they want to be treated; they should share the wealth with those who contributed. A dictatorial, adversarial, and domineering management style makes it very difficult to attract and keep people who thrive on a thirst for achievement, responsibility, and results. Compliant partners and managers often are chosen. Destructive conflicts often erupt over who has the final say, who is right, and whose prerogatives are what.

Entrepreneurs who create and build substantial enterprises are not lone wolves and super-independent. Neither do they need to collect all the credit for the effort. But rather they actively build a team recognizing the reality that it is rarely possible to build a substantial business working all alone. They have an uncanny ability to make heroes out of the people they attract to the venture by giving responsibility and sharing credit for accomplishments.

In the corporate setting, this "hero-making" ability is identified as an essential attribute of successful intrapreneurs.[23] These hero makers, of both the independent and corporate varieties, try to make the pie bigger and better, rather than jealously clutching and hoarding a tiny pie that is all theirs. They have a capacity for objective interpersonal relationships as well, which enables them to smooth out individual differences of opinion by keeping attention focused on the common goal to be achieved.[24]

Opportunity Obsession   Successful entrepreneurs are obsessed first with opportunity—not with the money, the resources, the contacts and networking, and not with image or appearances. While some of these latter items have a place and time in the entrepreneurial process, they are not the source and driver for new ventures. Entrepreneurs, in their best creative mode, are constantly thinking of new ideas for businesses by watching trends, spotting patterns, and connecting the dots to shape and mould a unique enterprise.

Take Tom Stemberg, for example. After business school—and after over 15 years in the supermarket business—he began to look for major new opportunities. He researched and rejected many decent ideas that were either not good "big" opportunities, or not the right fit for him. He then noted a recurring pattern with profound economic implications; every Main Street shop was selling ballpoint pens (wholesale cost: about 30 cents) for $2, $3, and more. He soon learned that these very large gross margins were common for a wide range of products used by small businesses and the self-employed: copy paper, writing and clerical supplies, calculators, and other electronics. Stemberg believed there was a new business model underlying this opportunity pattern—which, if well-developed and executed, could revolutionize the office supply business and become a major enterprise. He and Leo Kahn founded Staples, and they were certainly right.

Entrepreneurs realize good ideas are a dime a dozen, but good opportunities are few and far between. Fortunately, a great deal is now known about the criteria, the patterns, and the requirements that differentiate the good idea from the good opportunity. Entrepreneurs rely heavily on their own previous experiences (or their frustrations as customers) to come up with their breakthrough opportunities.

In Chapters 2 and 3, we will examine in great detail how entrepreneurs and investors are "opportunity obsessed." We will see their ingenious, as well as straightforward, ways and patterns of creating, shaping, moulding, and recognizing opportunities that are not just another good idea, and then transforming these "caterpillars into butterflies." These practices, strategies, and habits are part of the entrepreneurial mind-set, and are skills and know-how that are learnable and acquirable.

The entrepreneur's credo is to think opportunity first and cash last. Paul Kedrosky points out that Flickr took no venture capital. By not having all that money "the Flickr folks were forced to compete smarter... They came up with many dandy ideas, and then cheerfully borrowed the best of everyone else's."[25] Time and again—even after harvesting a highly successful venture—lead entrepreneurs will start up another company. They possess all the money and material wealth anyone would ever hope for, yet it is not enough. Like the artist, scientist, athlete, or musician who, at great personal sacrifice, strives for yet another breakthrough discovery, new record, or masterpiece, the greatest entrepreneurs are similarly obsessed with what they believe is the next breakthrough opportunity.

An excellent example of this is Maynard Freeman Schurman who in 1896 advertized in the Summerside, Prince Edward Island, newspaper that he was taking over a local company and would now be serving local residents. This family-controlled enterprise grew and became the prominent player in the Island's lumber and construction business. M. F. Schurman Co. Ltd. grew in the retail space and moved into steel fabrication, concrete, trusses, cartage, rentals, and property management. The legacy of the Schurman family was felt Island-wide and the family in 2004 sold their empire—10 separate companies— to J. D. Irving Ltd., the namesake of another legendary tycoon on the Atlantic coast.

Entrepreneurs like Stemberg, Schurman, and Irving think big enough about opportunities. They know that a mom-and-pop business can often be more exhausting and stressful, and much less rewarding, than a high-potential business. Their opportunity mind-set is how to create it, shape it, mould it, or fix it so that the customer/end-user will respond: Wow! Their thinking habits focus on what can go right here, what and how can we change the product or service to make it go right? What do we have to offer to become the superior, dominant product or service?

Tolerance of Risk, Ambiguity, and Uncertainty   Because high rates of change and high levels of risk, ambiguity, and uncertainty are almost a given, successful entrepreneurs tolerate risk, ambiguity, and uncertainty. They balance paradoxes and contradictions.

Entrepreneurs risk money, but they also risk reputation. Successful entrepreneurs are not gamblers; they take calculated risks. Like the parachutist, they are willing to take a risk; however, in deciding to do so, they calculate the risk carefully and thoroughly and do everything possible to get the odds in their favour. Entrepreneurs get others to share inherent financial and business risks with them. Partners put up money and put their reputations on the line, and investors do likewise. Creditors also join the party, as do customers who advance payments and suppliers who advance credit. For example, one researcher studied very successful entrepreneurs who initiated and orchestrated actions that had risk consequences.[26] It was found that while they shunned risk, these entrepreneurs sustained their courage by the clarity and optimism with which they saw the future. Entrepreneurs limited the risks they initiated by carefully defining and strategizing their ends and by controlling and monitoring their means—and by tailoring them both to what they saw the future to be. Further, they managed risk by transferring it to others.

One proposed concept of motivation-organizational fit contrasts a hierarchic (managerial) role with a task (entrepreneurial) role.[27] This study of motivational patterns showed that those who are task oriented (i.e., entrepreneurs) opt for the following roles because of the corresponding motivations:

Role	Motivation
1. Individual achievement.	A desire to achieve through one's own efforts and to attribute success to personal causation.
2. Risk avoidance.	A desire to avoid risk and leave little to chance.
3. Seeking results of behaviour.	A desire for feedback.
4. Personal innovation.	A desire to introduce innovative solutions.
5. Planning and setting goals.	A desire to think about the future and anticipate future possibilities.

Entrepreneurs also tolerate ambiguity and uncertainty and are comfortable with conflict. Ask someone working in a large company how sure they are about receiving a paycheque this month, in two months, in six months, and next year. Invariably, they will say that it is virtually certain and will muse at the question. Start-up entrepreneurs face just the opposite situation; there may be no revenue at the beginning, and if there is, a 90-day backlog in orders would be quite an exception. To make matters worse, lack of organization, structure, and order is a way of life. Constant changes introduce ambiguity and stress into every part of the enterprise. Jobs are undefined and changing continually, customers are new, co-workers are new, and setbacks and surprises are inevitable. And there never seems to be enough time.

Successful entrepreneurs maximize the good "higher performance" results of stress and minimize the negative reactions of exhaustion and frustration. Two surveys have suggested that very high levels of both satisfaction and stress characterize founders, to a greater degree than managers, regardless of the success of their ventures.[28]

Creativity, Self-Reliance, and Ability to Adapt   The high levels of uncertainty and very rapid rates of change that characterize new ventures require fluid and highly adaptive forms of organization that can respond quickly and effectively.

Successful entrepreneurs believe in themselves. They believe that their accomplishments (and setbacks) lie within their own control and influence and that they can affect the outcome. Successful entrepreneurs have the ability to see and "sweat the details" and also to conceptualize (i.e., they have "helicopter minds"). They are dissatisfied with the status quo and are restless initiators.

The entrepreneur has historically been viewed as an independent, highly self-reliant innovator, and champion (and occasional villain) of the free enterprise economy. More modern research and investigation have refined the agreement among researchers and practitioners alike that effective entrepreneurs actively seek and take initiative. They willingly put themselves in situations where they are personally responsible for the success or failure of the operation. They like to take the initiative to solve a problem or fill a vacuum where no leadership exists. They also like situations where personal impact on problems can be measured. Again, this is the action-oriented nature of the entrepreneur expressing itself.

Coralie Lalonde is such an example. She was born in Calgary and grew up in a middle-class family. After graduate school she started a product design and research company. Lalonde leveraged that success into an investment in Sybarus Technologies, which was purchased by Lucent for over $100 million. Able to retire at age 33 she then turned to helping start-ups and social causes. Providing seed funding and expertise to both groups she expects strong returns on her efforts. Lalonde and her fellow angel investors have placed bets on Softv.net, Quake Technologies, Galazar Networks, and several venture capital funds. Her philanthropic bets have paid hefty dividends as well. Coralie Lalonde's charitable endeavours include Junior Achievement (for which she serves as regional chairwoman), Community Foundation, Women in Technology mentoring program, Social Innovation Challenge, and Tech Venture Challenge.

"If we want to have a strong community we have to get involved in that community, and that means not just putting money in, but putting in time and energy and skills."[29] "I love working with people, being engaged, having to make decisions, the anxiety. I just like to spend time with entrepreneurs."[30]

Successful entrepreneurs are adaptive and resilient. They have an insatiable desire to know how well they are performing. They realize that to know how well they are doing and how to improve their performance, they need to actively seek and use feedback. Seeking and using feedback is also central to the habit of learning from mistakes and setbacks, and of responding to the unexpected. For the same reasons, these entrepreneurs often are described as excellent listeners and quick learners.

Entrepreneurs are not afraid of failing; rather, they are more intent on succeeding, counting on the fact that "success covers a multitude of blunders," as George Bernard Shaw eloquently stated. People who fear failure will neutralize whatever achievement motivation they may possess. They will tend to engage in a very easy task, where there is little chance of failure, or in a very difficult situation, where they cannot be held personally responsible if they do not succeed.

Further, successful entrepreneurs learn from failure experiences. They better understand not only their roles but also the roles of others in causing the failure, and thus are able to avoid similar problems in the future. There is an old saying to the effect that the cowboy who has never been thrown from a horse undoubtedly has not ridden too many! The iterative, trial-and-error nature of becoming a successful entrepreneur makes serious setbacks and disappointments an integral part of the learning process.

Motivation to Excel   Successful entrepreneurs are motivated to excel. Entrepreneurs are self-starters who appear driven internally by a strong desire to compete against their own self-imposed standards and to pursue and attain challenging goals. This need to achieve

PART I The Entrepreneurial Mind

has been well established in the literature on entrepreneurs since the pioneering work of McClelland and Atkinson on motivation in the 1950s and 1960s. Seeking out the challenge inherent in a start-up and responding in a positive way, noted by the entrepreneurs mentioned earlier, is achievement motivation in action.

Conversely, these entrepreneurs have a low need for status and power, and they derive personal motivation from the challenge and excitement of creating and building enterprises. They are driven by a thirst for achievement, rather than by status and power. Ironically, their accomplishments, especially if they are very successful, give them power. But it is important to recognize that power and status are a result of their activities. Setting high but attainable goals enables entrepreneurs to focus their energies, be very selective in sorting out opportunities, and know what to say no to. Having goals and direction also helps define priorities and provides measures of how well they are performing. Possessing an objective way of keeping score, such as changes in profits, sales, or stock price, is also important. Thus, money is seen as a tool, and a way of keeping score, rather than the object of the game by itself.

Successful entrepreneurs insist on the highest personal standards of integrity and reliability. They do what they say they are going to do, and they pull for the long haul. These high personal standards are the glue and fibre that bind successful personal and business relationships and make them endure.

A study involving 130 participants in a small business training program at Harvard Business School confirmed how important this issue is. Most simply said it was the single most important factor in their long-term successes.[31]

The best entrepreneurs have a keen awareness of their own strengths and weaknesses and those of their partners and of the competitive environment surrounding and influencing them. They are coldly realistic about what they can and cannot do and do not delude themselves; that is, they have "veridical awareness" or "optimistic realism." It also is worth noting that successful entrepreneurs believe in themselves. They do not believe that fate, luck, or other powerful, external forces will govern the success or failure of their venture. They believe they personally can affect the outcome. This attribute is also consistent with achievement motivation, which is the desire to take personal responsibility, and self-confidence.

This veridical awareness often is accompanied by other valuable entrepreneurial traits—perspective and a sense of humour. The ability to retain a sense of perspective, and to "know thyself" in both strengths and weaknesses, makes it possible for an entrepreneur to laugh, to ease tensions, and to get an unfavourable situation set in a more profitable direction.

ENTREPRENEURIAL REASONING: THE ENTREPRENEURIAL MIND[32] IN ACTION

How do successful entrepreneurs think, what actions do they initiate, and how do they start and build businesses? By understanding the attitudes, behaviours, management competencies, experience, and know-how that contribute to entrepreneurial success, one has some useful benchmarks for gauging what to do. Exhibit 1.6 examines the role of opportunity in entrepreneurship.

Successful entrepreneurs have a wide range of personality types. Most research about entrepreneurs has focused on the influences of genes, family, education, career experience, and so forth, but no psychological model has been supported. Studies have shown that an entrepreneur does not need specific inherent traits, but rather a set of acquired skills.[33] Individual learning leads to group learning which leads to enterprise-level learning.[34] Start-up intentions and venture-creation decisions depend upon cognitive processes, social context, cultural values, and characteristics of the entrepreneur. One study asserts that an entrepreneurial way of thinking is universal. Like culture, it is a common characteristic of entrepreneurs regardless of national origin.[35]

"There is no evidence of an ideal entrepreneurial personality. Great entrepreneurs can be either gregarious or low key, analytical or intuitive, charismatic or boring, good with details or terrible, delegators or control freaks. What you need is a capacity to execute in

EXHIBIT 1.6   Opportunity Knocks—Or Does It Hide? An Examination of the Role of Opportunity Recognition in Entrepreneurship

Opportunities of Various Sources and Types		
Sources of Opportunities	**Entrepreneurs**	**Non-entrepreneurs**
Prior work	58%	48%
Network	22%	30%
Thinking by analogy	11%	22%
Partner	9%	—
Types of Opportunities	**Entrepreneurs**	**Non-entrepreneurs**
Niche expansion/underserved niche	25%	29%
Customer need	30%	25%
Own firm's need	5%	4%
Better technology	40%	42%

Source: Charlene Zietsma, "Opportunity Knocks—Or Does It Hide? An Examination of the Role of Opportunity Recognition in Entrepreneurship," *Frontiers of Entrepreneurship Research* (Babson Park, MA: Babson College, 1999).

Note: Numbers equal total people in the sample allocated to each category.

certain key ways."[36] Successful entrepreneurs share common attitudes and behaviours. They work hard and are driven by an intense commitment and determined perseverance; they see the cup half full, rather than half empty; they strive for integrity; they thrive on the competitive desire to excel and win; they are dissatisfied with the status quo and seek opportunities to improve almost any situation they encounter; they use failure as a tool for learning and eschew perfection in favour of effectiveness; and they believe they can personally make an enormous difference in the final outcome of their ventures and their lives.

Those who have succeeded speak of these attitudes and behaviours time and again.[37] For example, David Large of the University of Ottawa, himself a founder or co-founder of several ventures and investor in others, knows the intense commitment and perseverance of entrepreneurs. He defines an entrepreneur as "someone who stands up and says I'm going to make that happen!" Other phrases that capture the spirit of the entrepreneur include: "seeing opportunities where others see problems," "never accepting no for an answer," "freedom to soar or sink," and "biting off more than you can chew."

Successful entrepreneurs possess not only a creative and innovative flair, but also solid management skills, business know-how, and sufficient contacts. Exhibit 1.7 demonstrates this relationship.

Inventors, noted for their creativity, often lack the necessary management skills and business know-how. Promoters usually lack serious general management and business

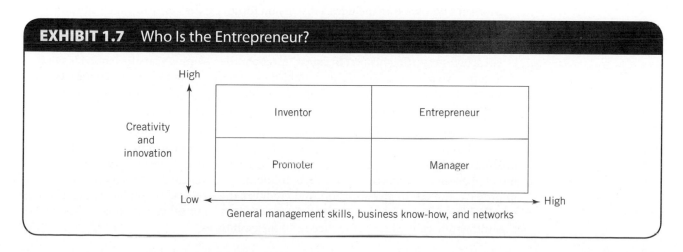

EXHIBIT 1.7   Who Is the Entrepreneur?

skills and true creativity. Managers govern, police, and ensure the smooth operation of the status quo; their management skills, while high, are tuned to efficiency as well, and creativity is usually not required. Although the management skills of the manager and the entrepreneur overlap, the manager is more driven by conservation of resources and the entrepreneur is more opportunity-driven.[38]

THE CONCEPT OF APPRENTICESHIP

It occurred to me how much knowledge I have gained in the short time I have worked as the "apprentice." Much of what I've learned can't be recorded... In my first week, I was off to the races with piles of reading material... The advantages of working with a small group of people are that I remain in "the loop" and have a greater opportunity to explore various roles within the company. The challenges of growing quickly with such a small team are the increasing demands... This position requires a high level of confidentiality with a strong focus on business ethics. My experiences in the first few months have varied from attending a precious metals conference with fund managers and analysts to travelling to the Amazon for a mine opening... However, the most exciting and challenging event so far has been working on a hostile takeover!

Melanie Pilon
"The Apprentice" to Ian Telfer, CEO Goldcorp

Shaping and Managing an Apprenticeship

When one looks at successful entrepreneurs, one sees profiles of careers rich in experience. Time and again there is a pattern among successful entrepreneurs. They have all acquired 10 or more years of substantial experience, built contacts, garnered the know-how, and established a track record in the industry, market, and technology niche within which they eventually launch, acquire, or build a business. Frequently, they have acquired intimate knowledge of the customer, distribution channels, and market through direct sales and marketing experience. The more successful ones have made money for their employer before doing it for themselves. Consider the following examples:

- Apple Computer founders Steve Jobs and Steve Wozniak were computer enthusiasts as preteens and had accumulated a relatively lengthy amount of experience by the time they started the company in their mid-20s. In entirely new industries such as micro-computers, a few years can be a large amount of experience.

- Tim Morgan, a former WestJet Airlines executive and co-founder is taking his experience to launch a new airline and tour company that promises "a refreshing new way to travel." He is also leveraging what he learned as founder and president of Morgan Air. In this social-network era, even before painting planes and getting them in the air, Morgan's new venture includes a discussion forum on the company Web site and even a presence on Facebook.

- Frank Stronach apprenticed as a tool and die maker and worked for others for 10 years before starting his first business. After another 10-plus years he landed his first automotive parts contract. From humble beginnings he has gone on to create a colossal empire in auto parts manufacturing—including the ability to now produce and assemble entire vehicles.

Tens of thousands of similar examples exist. There are always exceptions to any such pattern, but if you want the odds in your favour, get the experience first. Successful entrepreneurs are likely to have at least 8 to 10 years of experience. They are likely to have accumulated enough net worth to contribute to funding the venture or to have a track record impressive enough to give investors and creditors the necessary confidence. Finally, they usually have acquired and nurtured relevant business and other contacts and networks that ultimately contribute to the success of their ventures.

The first 10 or so years after leaving school can make or break an entrepreneur's career in terms of how well he or she is prepared for serious entrepreneuring. Evidence suggests that the most durable entrepreneurial careers, those found to last 25 years or more, were begun across a broad age spectrum, but the person had selected prior work and experiences to prepare specifically for an entrepreneurial path.

Having relevant experience, know-how, attitudes, behaviours, and skills appropriate for a particular venture opportunity can dramatically improve the odds for success. The other side of the coin is that if an entrepreneur does not have these, then he or she will have to learn them while launching and growing the business. The tuition for such an approach is often greater than most entrepreneurs can afford.

Since entrepreneurs frequently evolve from an entrepreneurial heritage or are shaped and nurtured by their closeness to entrepreneurs and others, the concept of an apprenticeship can be a useful one. Much of what an entrepreneur needs to know about entrepreneuring comes from learning by doing. Knowing what to prepare for, where the windows for acquiring the relevant exposure lie, how to anticipate these, where to position oneself, and when to move on can be quite useful.

As Howard Stevenson of the Harvard Business School reminds us:

> You have to approach the world as an equal. There is no such thing as being supplicant. You are trying to work and create a better solution by creating action among a series of people who are relatively equal. We destroy potential entrepreneurs by putting them in a velvet-lined rut, by giving them jobs that pay too much, and by telling them they are too good, before they get adequate intelligence, experience, and responsibility.

Windows of Apprenticeship

Exhibit 1.8 summarizes the key elements of an apprenticeship and experience curve and relates these to age windows. Age windows are especially important because of the inevitable time it takes to create and build a successful activity, whether it is a new venture or within another organization.

There is a saying in the venture capital business that the "lemons," or losers, in a portfolio ripen in about two and one-half years and that the "pearls," or winners, usually take seven or eight years to come to fruition. Therefore, seven years is a realistic time frame to expect to grow a higher potential business to a point where a capital gain can be realized. Interestingly, presidents of large corporations, presidents of universities, and self-employed professionals often describe years as the time it takes to do something significant.

The implications of this are quite provocative. First, time is precious. Assume an entrepreneur spends the first five years after college, university, or graduate school gaining relevant experience. He or she will be 25 to 30 years of age (or maybe as old as 35) when launching a new venture. By the age of 50, there will have been time for starting, at most, three successful new ventures. What's more, entrepreneurs commonly go through false starts or even a failure at first in the trial-and-error process of learning the entrepreneurial ropes. As a result, the first venture may not be launched until later (i.e., in the entrepreneur's mid- to late 30s). This would leave time to grow the current venture and maybe one more. But there are always exceptions. Aydin Mirzaee, for example, hit the ground running in his early 20s. And many others gained experience in their childhood through lemonade stands, babysitting, etc. Recently, its common for aspiring entrepreneurs to launch multiple ventures even before the first succeeds or fails.

Reflecting on Exhibit 1.8 will reveal some other paradoxes and dilemmas. For one thing, just when an entrepreneur's drive, energy, and ambition are at a peak, the necessary relevant business experience and leadership skills are least developed, and those critical elements, wisdom and judgment, are in their infancy. Later, when an entrepreneur has gained the necessary experience in the "deep, dark canyons of uncertainty" and has thereby gained wisdom and judgment, age begins to take its toll. Also, patience and perseverance to relentlessly pursue a long-term vision need to be balanced with the urgency and realism to make it happen. Flexibility to stick with the moving opportunity targets and to abandon some and shift to others is also required. However, flexibility and the ability to act with urgency disappear as the other commitments of life are assumed.

EXHIBIT 1.8   Windows of Entrepreneurial Apprenticeship

Elements of the Apprenticeship and Experience Curve	Age			
	20s	30s	40s	50s
1. Relevant Business Experience	Low	Moderate to high	Higher	Highest
2. Management Skills and Know-How	Low to moderate	Moderate to high	High	High
3. Entrepreneurial Goals and Commitment	Varies widely	Focused high	High	High
4. Drive and Energy	Highest	High	Moderate	Lowest
5. Wisdom and Judgment	Lowest	High	Higher	Highest
6. Focus of Apprenticeship	Discussing what you enjoy; key is learning business, sales, marketing; profit and loss responsibility	General management Division management Founder	Growing and harvesting	Reinvesting
7. Dominant Life-Stage Issues*	Realizing your dream of adolescence and young adulthood	Personal growth and new directions and ventures	Renewal, regeneration, reinvesting in the system	

*Source: Daniel J. Levinson, *The Seasons of a Man's Life* (New York, NY: Random House, 1986).

The Concept of Apprenticeship: Acquiring the 50,000 Chunks

During the past several years, studies about entrepreneurs have tended to confirm what practitioners have known all along: that some attitudes, behaviours, and know-how can be acquired and that some of these attributes are more desirable than others.

Increasingly, research studies on the career paths of entrepreneurs and the self-employed suggest the role of experience and know-how is central in successful venture creation. Many successful entrepreneurs do not have prior industry experience. More critical to the entrepreneur is the ability to gain information and act on it.[39] Evidence also suggests that success is linked to preparation and planning.[40] This is what getting 50,000 chunks of experience is all about.

Although formal market research may provide useful information, it is also important to recognize the entrepreneur's collective, qualitative judgment must be weighted most heavily in evaluating opportunities. One study found that entrepreneurs view believing in the idea, and experimenting with new venture ideas that result in both failures and successes as the most important components of opportunity recognition.[41]

Many successful entrepreneurs follow a pattern of apprenticeship, where they prepare for becoming entrepreneurs by gaining the relevant business experiences from parents who are self-employed or through job experiences. They do not leave acquisition of experience to accident or osmosis. As one entrepreneur said, "Know what you know and what you *don't* know."[42]

Role Models

Numerous studies show a strong connection between the presence of role models and the emergence of entrepreneurs. For instance, more than half of those starting new businesses had parents who owned businesses. Likewise, 70 percent of MIT graduates who started technology businesses had entrepreneurial parents.[43] The authors summarized it this way:

Family firms spawn entrepreneurs. Older generations provide leadership and role modeling. This phenomenon cuts across industries, firm size, and gender.

MYTHS AND REALITIES

Folklore and stereotypes about entrepreneurs and entrepreneurial success are remarkably durable, even in these informed and sophisticated times. More is known about the founders and the process of entrepreneurship than ever before.

However, certain myths enjoy recurring attention and popularity, in part because while generalities may apply to certain types of entrepreneurs and particular situations, the great variety of founders tend to defy generalization. Exhibit 1.9 lists myths about entrepreneurs that have persisted and realities that are supported by research.

EXHIBIT 1.9   Myths and Realities about Entrepreneurs

Myth 1— Entrepreneurs are born, not made.

Reality— While entrepreneurs are born with certain native intelligence, a flair for creating, and energy, these talents by themselves are like unmoulded clay or an unpainted canvas. The making of an entrepreneur occurs by accumulating the relevant skills, know-how, experiences, and contacts over a period of years and includes large doses of self-development. The creative capacity to envision and then pursue an opportunity is a direct descendant of at least 10 or more years of experience that lead to pattern recognition.

Myth 2— Anyone can start a business.

Reality— Entrepreneurs who recognize the difference between an idea and an opportunity, and who think big enough, start businesses that have a better chance of succeeding. Luck, to the extent it is involved, requires good preparation. And the easiest part is starting. What is hardest is surviving, sustaining, and building a venture so its founders can realize a harvest. Perhaps only one in 10 to 20 new businesses that survive five years or more results in a capital gain for the founders.

Myth 3— Entrepreneurs are gamblers.

Reality— Successful entrepreneurs take very careful, calculated risks. They try to influence the odds, often by getting others to share risk with them and by avoiding or minimizing risks if they have the choice. Often they slice up the risk into smaller, quite digestible pieces; only then do they commit the time or resources to determine if that piece will work. They do not deliberately seek to take more risk or to take unnecessary risk, nor do they shy away from unavoidable risk.

Myth 4— Entrepreneurs want the whole show to themselves.

Reality— Owning and running the whole show effectively puts a ceiling on growth. Solo entrepreneurs usually make a living. It is extremely difficult to grow a higher potential venture by working single-handedly. Higher potential entrepreneurs build a team, an organization, and a company. Besides, 100 percent of nothing is nothing, so rather than taking a large piece of the pie, they work to make the pie bigger.

Myth 5— Entrepreneurs are their own bosses and completely independent.

Reality— Entrepreneurs are far from independent and have to serve many masters and constituencies, including partners, investors, customers, suppliers, creditors, employees, families, and those involved in social and community obligations. Entrepreneurs, however, can make free choices of whether, when, and what they care to respond to. Moreover, it is extremely difficult, and rare, to build a business beyond annual sales of $1 million single-handedly.

Myth 6— Entrepreneurs work longer and harder than managers in big companies.

Reality— There is no evidence that all entrepreneurs work more than their corporate counterparts. Some do, some do not. Some actually report that they work less.

Myth 7— Entrepreneurs experience a great deal of stress and pay a high price.

Reality— Being an entrepreneur is stressful and demanding. But there is no evidence that it is any more stressful than numerous other highly demanding professional roles, and entrepreneurs find their jobs very satisfying. They have a high sense of accomplishment, are healthier, and are much less likely to retire than those who work for others. Three times as many entrepreneurs as corporate managers say they plan to never retire.

Myth 8— Start a business and fail and you'll never raise money again.

Reality— Talented and experienced entrepreneurs—because they pursue attractive opportunities and are able to attract the right people and necessary financial and other resources to make the venture work—often head successful ventures. Further, businesses fail, but entrepreneurs do not. Failure is often the fire that tempers the steel of an entrepreneur's learning experience and street savvy.

Myth 9— Money is the most important start-up ingredient.

Reality— If the other pieces and talents are there, the money will follow, but it does not follow that an entrepreneur will succeed if he or she has enough money. Money is one of the least important ingredients in new venture success. Money is to the entrepreneur what the paint and brush are to the artist—an inert tool that in the right hands, can create marvels.

(continued)

EXHIBIT 1.9 Myths and Realities about Entrepreneurs *(continued)*

Myth 10—Entrepreneurs should be young and energetic.

Reality— While these qualities may help, age is no barrier. The average age of entrepreneurs starting high potential businesses is in the mid-30s, and there are numerous examples of entrepreneurs starting businesses in their 60s. What is critical is possessing the relevant know-how, experience, and contacts that greatly facilitate recognizing and pursuing an opportunity.

Myth 11—Entrepreneurs are motivated solely by the quest for the almighty dollar.

Reality— Entrepreneurs seeking high potential ventures are more driven by building enterprises and realizing long-term capital gains than by instant gratification through high salaries and perks. A sense of personal achievement and accomplishment, feeling in control of their own destinies, and realizing their vision and dreams are also powerful motivators. Money is viewed as a tool and a way of keeping score, rather than an end in itself. Entrepreneurs thrive on the thrill of the chase; and, time and again, even after an entrepreneur has made a few million dollars or more, he or she will work on a new vision to build another company.

Myth 12—Entrepreneurs seek power and control over others.

Reality— Successful entrepreneurs are driven by the quest for responsibility, achievement, and results, rather than for power for its own sake. They thrive on a sense of accomplishment and of outperforming the competition, rather than a personal need for power expressed by dominating and controlling others. By virtue of their accomplishments, they may be powerful and influential, but these are more the by-products of the entrepreneurial process than a driving force behind it.

Myth 13—If an entrepreneur is talented, success will happen in a year or two.

Reality— An old maxim among venture capitalists says it all: The lemons ripen in two and a half years, but the pearls take seven or eight. Rarely is a new business established solidly in less than three or four years.

Myth 14—Any entrepreneur with a good idea can raise venture capital.

Reality— Of the ventures of entrepreneurs with good ideas who seek out venture capital, only 1 to 3 out of 100 are funded.

Myth 15—If an entrepreneur has enough start-up capital, he or she can't miss.

Reality— The opposite is often true; that is, too much money at the outset often creates euphoria and a spoiled-child syndrome. The accompanying lack of discipline and impulsive spending usually lead to serious problems and failure.

Myth 16—Entrepreneurs are lone wolves and cannot work with others.

Reality— The most successful entrepreneurs are leaders who build great teams and effective relationships working with peers, directors, investors, key customers, key suppliers, and the like.

Myth 17—Unless you attained 700-plus on your GMAT and have an "A" average, you'll never be a successful entrepreneur.

Reality— Entrepreneurial IQ is a unique combination of creativity, motivation, integrity, leadership, team building, analytical ability, and ability to deal with ambiguity and adversity.

Studies have indicated that 90 percent or more of founders start their companies in the same marketplace, technology, or industry they have been working in. Others have found that entrepreneurs are likely to have role models, have 8 to 10 years of experience, and be well educated. It also appears that successful entrepreneurs have a wide range of experiences in products/markets and across functional areas. Studies also have shown that most successful entrepreneurs start companies in their 30s. One study of founders of high-tech companies showed that the average age of the founders was 40.

Entrepreneurs work both more and less than their counterparts in large organizations, that they have high degrees of satisfaction with their jobs, and that they are healthier.[44] Another study showed that nearly 21 percent of the founders were over 40 when they embarked on their entrepreneurial career, the majority were in their 30s, and just over one-quarter did so by the time they were 25.

WHAT CAN BE LEARNED?

For nearly 40 years, the authors have been engaged as educators, cofounders, investors, advisors, and directors of new, higher potential ventures. Many of these have been launched by former students, and the cases in this book are about such founders. A vivid image is when the Texas real estate tycoon Trammel Crow said, "Perfesser, do you mean to tell me you think you can actually teach someone to be an on-tree-pre-newer!" My response was straightforward, "Mr. Crow, what I think you are really asking me is, 'Am I preposterous enough to believe that in 35 to 40 hours of class time, during a single semester, I can convert the average student into the economic equivalent of a Picasso or a Beethoven!?' Mr. Crow, I think we both know the answer to that question." Canada's own Henry Mintzberg has been on a tirade over business school education for years. His assertion is that "MBA classrooms overemphasize the science of management while ignoring its art."[45] Practising managers should be learning from their own experiences—from each other. Ed McMullan and Vance Gough join in the assertion that entrepreneurs learn from seeing the successes and innovations of others. The University of Calgary implemented an MBA in enterprise development in 1993 that combined entrepreneurs and managers in the same classroom.[16]

New Venture Creation immerses you in the dynamics and realities of launching and growing lifestyle to higher potential ventures. Throughout the text are cases and examples about real, young entrepreneurs, including students and recent graduates. You will face the same situations these aspiring entrepreneurs faced as they sought to turn dreams into reality. The cases and text, combined with other online resources, will enable you to grapple with all of the conceptual, practical, financial, and personal issues entrepreneurs encounter. This book will help you get the odds of success in your favour. It will focus your attention on developing answers for the most important of these questions, including:

- What does an entrepreneurial career take?
- What is the difference between a good opportunity and just another idea?
- Is the opportunity I am considering the right opportunity for me now?
- Why do some firms grow quickly to several million dollars in sales but then stumble, never growing beyond a single-product firm?
- What are the critical tasks and hurdles in seizing an opportunity and building the business?
- How much money do I need and when, where, and how can I get it—on acceptable terms?
- What financing sources, strategies, and mechanisms can I use from pre-start, through meaningful careers in new and growing firms, and in the early growth stage to the harvest of my venture?
- What are the minimum resources I need to gain control over the opportunity, and how can I do this?
- Is a business plan needed? If so, what kind is needed and how and when should I develop one?
- Who are the constituents for whom I must create or add value to achieve a positive cash flow and to develop harvest options?
- What is my venture worth and how do I negotiate what to give up?
- What are the critical transitions in entrepreneurial management as a firm grows from $1 million to $5 million to $25 million in sales?
- What is it that entrepreneurial leaders do differently which enables them to achieve such competitive breakthroughs and advantages, particularly over conventional practices, but also so-called best practices?
- What are the opportunities and implications for 20th century entrepreneurs and the Internet, and how can these be seized and financed?
- What do I need to know and practise in entrepreneurial reasoning and thinking to have a competitive edge?
- What are some of the pitfalls, minefields, and hazards I need to anticipate, prepare for, and respond to?
- What are the contacts and networks I need to access and to develop?
- Do I know what I do and do not know, and do I know what to do about it?
- How can I develop a personal "entrepreneurial game plan" to acquire the experience I need to succeed?
- How critical and sensitive is the timing in each of these areas?
- Why do entrepreneurs who succeed in the long term seek to maintain reputations for integrity and ethical business practices?

We believe that we can significantly improve the quality of decisions students make about entrepreneurship and thereby also improve the fit between what they aspire to do and the requirements of the particular opportunity. In many cases, those choices lead to self-employment or meaningful careers in new and growing firms and, increasingly, in large firms that "get it." In other cases, students join larger firms whose customer base and/or suppliers are principally the entrepreneurial sector. Still others seek careers in the financial institutions and professional services firms that are at the vortex of the entrepreneurial economy: venture capital, private equity, investment banks, commercial banks, consulting, accounting, and the like.

Our view of entrepreneurship is that it need not be an end in itself. Rather, it is a pathway that leads to innumerable ideas and opportunities, and opens visions of what young people can become. You will learn skills, and how to use those skills appropriately. You will learn how to tap your own and others' creativity, and to apply your new energy. You will learn the difference between another good idea and a serious opportunity. You will learn the power and potential of the entrepreneurial team. You will learn how entrepreneurs finance and grow their companies, often with ingenious bootstrapping strategies that get big results with minimal resources. You will learn the joy of self-sufficiency and independence. You will learn how entrepreneurial leaders make this happen, and give back to society. You will discover anew what it is about entrepreneurship that gives you sustaining entrepreneurial reasoning and thinking in order to fuel your dreams.

A WORD OF CAUTION: WHAT GRADES, IQ TESTS, GMATS, AND OTHERS DON'T MEASURE

Never, never, never give up.

If you are going through hell, keep going.

Success is going from failure to failure without losing enthusiasm.

Every day you may make progress. Every step may be fruitful. Yet there will stretch out before you an ever-lengthening, ever-ascending, ever-improving path. You know you will never get to the end of the journey. But this, so far from discouraging, only adds to the joy and the glory of the climb.

Winston Churchill

The following data about Harvard Business School alumni whose careers were followed for nearly 25 years has surprised many. Regardless of the measure one applies, among the very top of the class were graduates who were both highly successful and not very successful. At the bottom of the class were alumni who became outrageously successful, and others who accomplished little. The middle of the class achieved all points on the continuum of success. How could this be? "One of the little secrets of higher education is that conventional A students often end up working for creative and entrepreneurial C students."[47] One medical trade journal reports:

> "A" students often lack the personality skills essential when working with the public. There are delightful exceptions, but there is some truth to this cliché. The discipline and attention to detail necessary to do well on academic tests can be barriers to "connecting" with patients and building the rapport necessary for successful practice.[48]

In short, there are many different kinds of intelligence, a much greater bandwidth than most researchers and test architects ever imagined. The dynamic and subtle complexities of the entrepreneurial task require its own special intelligences. How else would one explain the enormous contradiction inherent in business and financially failed geniuses?

One only need consider the critical skills and capacities that are at the heart of entrepreneurial leadership and achievement, yet are not measured by the IQ tests, GMATs, and the like that rank and sort young applicants with such imprecision. Consider the skills and capacities not measured by these tests:

✓ Leadership skills.

✓ Interpersonal skills.

✓ Team building and team playing.

✓ Creativity and ingenuity.

✓ Motivation.

✓ Learning skills (versus knowledge).

✓ Persistence and determination.

✓ Values, ethics, honesty, and integrity.

✓ Goal-setting orientation.

✓ Self-discipline.

✓ Frugality.

✓ Resourcefulness.

✓ Resiliency and capacity to handle adversity.

✓ Ability to seek, listen, and use feedback.

✓ Reliability.

✓ Dependability.

✓ Sense of humour.

It is no wonder that a number of excellent colleges and universities eliminated these measures or placed them in a proper perspective. Obviously, this should not be construed to mean entrepreneurship is for dummies. Quite the opposite is true. Indeed, intelligence is a very valuable and important asset for entrepreneurs, but by itself is woefully inadequate.

Clearly, just being very smart won't help much if one doesn't possess numerous other qualities (see Chapters 5, 6, and 7: "The Entrepreneurial Leader," "The New Venture Team," and "Ethical Decision Making and the Entrepreneur," respectively, for an elaboration on these other qualities). A fascinating article in *Maclean's*, "Do Grades Really Matter: Why A+ Students Often End Up Working for C+ Students," is well worth reading to get some powerful insights into why it is often *not* the class genius who becomes most successful.[49]

A PERSONAL STRATEGY

An apprenticeship can be an integral part of the process of shaping an entrepreneurial career. One principal task is to determine what kind of entrepreneur he or she is likely to become, based on background, experience, and drive. Through an apprenticeship, an entrepreneur can shape a strategy and action plan to make it happen. The "Crafting a Personal Entrepreneurship Strategy" exercise found in this chapter addresses this issue more fully. For a quick inventory of your entrepreneurial attributes, do the "QuickLook: The Personal Entrepreneurial Strategy" exercise available online at www.mcgrawhill.ca/olc/timmons.

Despite all the work involved in becoming an entrepreneur, the bottom line is revealing. Evidence about careers and job satisfaction of entrepreneurs all points to the same conclusion: If they had to do it over again, not only would more of them become entrepreneurs again, but also they would do it sooner.[50] They report higher personal satisfaction with their lives and their careers than their managerial counterparts. Nearly three times as many say they plan never to retire. Numerous other studies show that the satisfaction from independence and living and working where and how they want to is a source of great satisfaction.[51] Financially, successful entrepreneurs enjoy higher incomes and a higher net worth than career managers in large companies. In addition, the successful harvest of a company usually means a capital gain of several million dollars or more and, with it, a new array of very attractive options and opportunities to do whatever they choose to do with the rest of their lives.

ENTREPRENEUR'S CREED

So much time and space would not be spent on the entrepreneurial mind if it were just of academic interest. But they are, entrepreneurs themselves believe, in large part responsible for success. When asked an open-ended question about what entrepreneurs believed are the most critical concepts, skills, and know-how for running a business—today and five years hence—their answers were very revealing. Most mentioned mental attitudes and philosophies based on entrepreneurial attributes, rather than specific skills or organizational concepts. These answers are gathered together in what might be called an entrepreneur's creed:

- Do what gives you energy—have fun.
- Figure out what can go right and make it.
- Say "can do," rather than "cannot" or "maybe."
- *Illegitimi non carborundum:* tenacity and creativity will triumph.
- Anything is possible if you believe you can do it.
- If you don't know it can't be done, then you'll go ahead and do it.
- The cup is half-full, not half-empty.
- Be dissatisfied with the way things are—and look for improvement.
- Do things differently.
- Don't take a risk if you don't have to—but take a calculated risk if it's the right opportunity for *you.*
- Businesses fail; successful entrepreneurs learn—but keep the tuition low.
- It is easier to beg for forgiveness than to ask for permission in the first place.
- Make opportunity and results your obsession—not money.
- Money is a tool and a scorecard available to the right people with the right opportunity at the right time.
- Making money is even more fun than spending it.
- Make heroes out of others—a team builds a business; an individual makes a living.
- Take pride in your accomplishments—it's contagious!
- Sweat the details that are critical to success.
- Integrity and reliability equal long-run oil and glue.
- Accept the responsibility, less than half the credit, and more than half the blame.
- Make the pie bigger—don't waste time trying to cut smaller slices.
- Play for the long haul—it is rarely possible to get rich quickly.
- Don't pay too much—but don't lose it!
- Only the lead dog gets a change of view.
- Success is getting what you want: Happiness is wanting what you get.
- Give back.
- Never give up.

Chapter Summary

1. Entrepreneurs are men and women of all ages, colours, cultures, religions, and backgrounds. There is no single profile or psychological template.

2. Successful entrepreneurs share six common themes that describe their ways of thinking and acting.

3. Rather than being innate, these six attitudes and behaviour can be nurtured, learned, and encouraged.

4. Entrepreneurs love competition and actually avoid risks when they can, preferring carefully calculated risks.

5. Entrepreneurship can be learned; an apprenticeship is highly beneficial.

6. The entrepreneurial mind-set can benefit large, established companies today just as much as smaller firms.

7. IQ tests, GMATs, and even grades do not measure some of the most important entrepreneurial abilities and aptitudes.

8. Most successful entrepreneurs have had a personal strategy to help them achieve their dreams and goals, both implicitly and explicitly.

9. Self-assessment is one of the hardest things for entrepreneurs to do, but if you don't do it, you will really get into trouble. If you don't do it, who will?

Study Questions

1. What is the difference between a manager and a leader?

2. Define the six major themes that characterize the mind-sets, attitudes, and actions of a successful entrepreneur. Which are most important, and why? How can they be encouraged and developed?

3. Entrepreneurs are made, not born. Why is this so? Do you agree, and why or why not?

4. Explain what is meant by the apprenticeship concept, and why is it so important to young entrepreneurs?

5. What is your personal entrepreneurial strategy? How should it change?

6. Can you evaluate thoroughly your attraction to entrepreneurship?

7. Great athletic talent is not equal to a great athlete. Why? How does this apply to entrepreneurship?

Mind Stretchers   *Have you considered?*

1. Who can be an entrepreneur, and who cannot? Why?

2. How do you personally stack up against the six entrepreneurial mind-sets (Exhibit 1.3)? What do you need to develop and improve?

3. What can a larger company do to attract and keep the best entrepreneurial talent?

4. Is Bill Gates, Oprah Winfrey, Ted Rogers, or David Thomson an entrepreneur, a leader, a manager? How can we know?

5. How will you personally define success in 5, 10, and 25 years? Why?

6. Assume that at age 40 to 50 years, you have achieved a net worth of $25 million to $50 million in today's dollars. So what? Then what?

EXERCISE   Crafting a Personal Entrepreneurial Strategy

If you don't know where you're going, any path will take you there.

From The Wizard of Oz

Crafting a personal entrepreneurial strategy can be viewed as the personal equivalent of developing a business plan. As with planning in other situations, the process itself is more important than the plan.

The key is the process and discipline that put an individual in charge of evaluating and shaping choices and initiating action that makes sense, rather than letting things just happen. Having a longer-term sense of direction can be highly motivating. It also can be extremely helpful in determining when to say no (which is much harder than saying yes) and can temper impulsive hunches with a more thoughtful strategic purpose. This is important because today's choices, whether or not they are thought out, become tomorrow's track record. They may end up shaping an entrepreneur in ways that he or she may not find so attractive 10 years hence and, worse, may also result in failure to obtain just those experiences needed in order to have high-quality opportunities later on.

Therefore, a personal strategy can be invaluable, but it need not be a prison sentence. It is a point of departure, rather than a contract of indenture, and it can and will change over time. This process of developing a personal strategy for an entrepreneurial career is a very individual one and, in a sense, one of self-selection.

Reasons for planning are similar to those for developing a business plan (see Chapter 4). Planning helps an entrepreneur to manage the risks and uncertainties of the future; helps him or her to work smarter, rather than simply harder; keeps him or her in a future-oriented frame of mind; helps him or her to develop and update a keener strategy by testing the sensibility of his or her ideas and approaches with others; helps motivate him or her; gives him or her a "results orientation"; helps him or her be effective in managing and coping with what is by nature a stressful role; and so forth.

Rationalizations and reasons given for not planning, like those that will be covered in Chapter 4, are that plans are out of date as soon as they are finished and that no one knows what tomorrow will bring and, therefore, it is dangerous to commit to uncertainty. Further, the cautious, anxious person may find that setting personal goals creates a further source of tension and pressure and a heightened fear of failure. There is also the possibility that future or yet unknown options, which actually might be more attractive than the one chosen, may become lost or be excluded.

Commitment to a career-oriented goal, particularly for an entrepreneur who is younger and lacks much real-world experience, can be premature. For the person who is inclined to be a compulsive and obsessive competitor and achiever, goal setting may add gasoline to the fire. And, invariably, some events and environmental factors beyond one's control may boost or sink the best-laid plans.

Personal plans fail for the same reasons as business plans, including frustration when the plan appears not to work immediately and problems of changing behaviour from an activity-oriented routine to one that is goal-oriented. Other problems are developing plans that are based on admirable missions, such as improving performance, rather than goals, and developing plans that fail to anticipate obstacles, and those that lack progress milestones, reviews, and so forth.

A Conceptual Scheme for Self-Assessment

Exhibit 1.10 shows one conceptual scheme for thinking about the self-assessment process called the Johari Window. According to this scheme, there are two sources of information about the self: the individual and others. According to the Johari Window, there are three areas in which individuals can learn about themselves.

There are two potential obstacles to self-assessment efforts. First, it is hard to obtain feedback; second, it is hard to receive and benefit from it. Everyone possesses a personal frame of reference, values, and so forth, which influence first impressions. It is, therefore, almost impossible for an individual to obtain an unbiased view of himself or herself from someone else. Further, in most social situations, people usually present self-images that they want to preserve, protect, and defend, and behavioural norms usually exist that prohibit people from telling a person that he or she is presenting a face or impression that differs from what the person thinks is being presented. For example, most people will not point out to a stranger during a conversation that a piece of spinach is prominently dangling from between his or her front teeth.

EXHIBIT 1.10   Peeling the Onion

	Known to Entrepreneur and Team	Not Known to Entrepreneur and Team
Known to Prospective Investors and Stakeholders	Area 1 *Known area:* (what you see is what you get)	Area 2 *Blind area:* (we do not know what we do not know, but you do)
Not Known to Prospective Investors and Stakeholders	Area 3 *Hidden area:* (unshared—you do not know what we do, but the deal does not get done until we find out)	Area 4 *Unknown area:* (no venture is certain or risk free)

Source: James McIntyre, Irwin M. Rubin, David A. Kolb, *Organizational Psychology: Experiential Approach*, 2nd ed., © 1974. Adapted by permission of Pearson Education, Inc., Upper Saddle River, NJ.

The first step for an individual in self-assessment is to generate data through observation of his or her thoughts and actions and by getting feedback from others for the purposes of (1) becoming aware of blind spots and (2) reinforcing or changing existing perceptions of both strengths and weaknesses.

Once an individual has generated the necessary data, the next steps in the self-assessment process are to study the data generated, develop insights, and then establish apprenticeship goals to gain any learning, experience, and so forth.

Finally, choices can be made in terms of goals and opportunities to be created or seized.

Crafting an Entrepreneurial Strategy

Profiling the Past

One useful way to begin the process of self-assessment and planning is for an individual to think about his or her entrepreneurial roots (what he or she has done, his or her preferences in terms of lifestyle and work style, etc.) and couple this with a look into the future and what he or she would like most to be doing and how he or she would like to live.

In this regard, everyone has a personal history that has played and will continue to play a significant role in influencing his or her values, motivations, attitudes, and behaviours. Some of this history may provide useful insight into prior entrepreneurial inclinations, as well as into his or her future potential fit with an entrepreneurial role. Unless an entrepreneur is enjoying what he or she is doing for work most of the time, when in his or her 30s, 40s, or 50s, having a great deal of money without enjoying the journey will be a very hollow success.

Profiling the Present

It is useful to profile the present. Possession of certain personal entrepreneurial attitudes and behaviours (i.e., an "entrepreneurial mind") has been linked to successful careers in entrepreneurship. These attitudes and behaviours deal with such factors as commitment, determination, and perseverance; the drive to achieve and grow; an orientation toward goals; the taking of initiative and personal responsibility; and so forth.

In addition, various role demands result from the pursuit of opportunities. These role demands are external in the sense that they are imposed upon every entrepreneur by the nature of entrepreneurship. As will be discussed in Chapter 4, the external business environment is given, the demands of a higher potential business in terms of stress and commitment are given, and the ethical values and integrity of key actors are given. Required as a result of the demands, pressures, and realities of starting, owning, and operating a substantial business are such factors as accommodation to the venture, toleration of stress, and so forth. A realistic appraisal of entrepreneurial attitudes and behaviours in light of the requirements of the entrepreneurial role is useful as part of the self-assessment process.

Also, part of any self-assessment is an assessment of management competencies and what "chunks" of experience, know-how, and contacts need to be developed.

Getting Constructive Feedback

A Scottish proverb says, "The greatest gift that God hath given us is to see ourselves as others see us." One common denominator among successful entrepreneurs is a desire to know how they are doing and where they stand. They have an uncanny knack for asking the right questions about their performance at the right time. This thirst to know is driven by a keen awareness that such feedback is vital to improving their performance and their odds for success.

Receiving feedback from others can be a most demanding experience. The following list of guidelines in receiving feedback can help:

- Feedback needs to be solicited, ideally, from those who know the individual well (e.g., someone he or she has worked with or for) and who can be trusted. The context in which the person is known needs to be considered. For example, a business colleague may be better able to comment upon an individual's leadership skills than a friend. Or a personal friend may be able to comment on motivation or on the possible effects on the family situation. It is helpful to chat with the person before asking him or her to provide any specific written impressions and to indicate the specific areas he or she can best comment upon. One way to do this is to formulate questions first. For example, the person could be told, "I've been asking myself the following question . . . and I would really like your impressions in that regard."

- Specific comments in areas that are particularly important either personally or to the success of the venture need to be solicited and more detail probed if the person giving feedback is not clear. A good way to check if a statement is being understood correctly is to paraphrase the statement. The person needs to be encouraged to describe and give examples of specific situations or behaviours that have influenced the impressions he or she has developed.

- Feedback is most helpful if it is neither all positive nor all negative.

- Feedback needs to be obtained in writing so that the person can take some time to think about the issues, and so feedback from various sources can be pulled together.

- The person asking for feedback needs to be honest and straightforward with himself or herself and with others.

- Time is too precious and the road to new venture success too treacherous to clutter this activity with game playing or hidden agendas. The person receiving feedback needs to avoid becoming defensive and taking negative comments personally.

- It is important to listen carefully to what is being said and think about it. Answering, debating, or rationalizing should be avoided.

- An assessment of whether the person soliciting feedback has considered all important information and has been realistic in his or her inferences and conclusions needs to be made.

- Help needs to be requested in identifying common threads or patterns, possible implications of self-assessment data and certain weaknesses (including alternative inferences or conclusions), and other relevant information that is missing.

- Additional feedback from others needs to be sought to verify feedback and to supplement the data.

- Reaching final conclusions or decisions needs to be left until a later time.

Putting It All Together

Exhibit 1.11 shows the relative fit of an entrepreneur with a venture opportunity, given his or her relevant attitudes and behaviours and relevant general leadership skills, experience, know-how, and contacts, and given the role demands of the venture opportunity. A clean appraisal is almost impossible. Self-assessment just is not that simple. The process is cumulative, and what an entrepreneur does about weaknesses, for example, is far more important than what the particular weaknesses might be. After all, everyone has weaknesses.

Thinking Ahead

As it is in developing business plans, goal setting is important in personal planning. Few people are effective goal setters. Perhaps fewer than 5 percent have ever committed their goals to writing, and perhaps fewer than 25 percent of adults even set goals mentally.

Again, goal setting is a process, a way of dealing with the world. Effective goal setting demands time, self-discipline, commitment and dedication, and practice. Goals, once set, do not become static targets.

A number of distinct steps are involved in goal setting, steps that are repeated over and over as conditions change:

- Establishment of goals that are specific and concrete (rather than abstract and out of focus), measurable, related to time (i.e., specific about what will be accomplished over a certain time period), realistic, and attainable.

- Establishment of priorities, including the identification of conflicts and trade-offs and how these can be resolved.

- Identification of potential problems and obstacles that could prevent goals from being attained.

- Specification of action steps that are to be performed to accomplish the goal.

- Indication of how results will be measured.

- Establishment of metrics for reviewing progress and tying these to specific dates on a calendar.

- Identification of risks involved in meeting the goals.

- Identification of help and other resources that may be needed to obtain goals.

- Periodic review of progress and revision of goals.

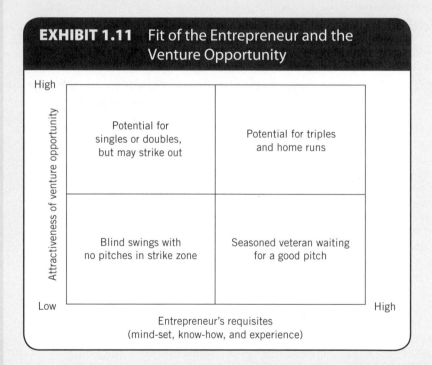

EXHIBIT 1.11   Fit of the Entrepreneur and the Venture Opportunity

CASE   TRAVELHANGAR.COM

Preparation Questions

1. What should Jason and Alex do?
2. How could Jason and Alex have avoided this current situation?
3. Assuming the crisis is resolved, how would you grow the venture in the future?
4. What lessons can be learned from this case about starting your own company? How do you best manage a company with limited or no resources?
5. Can you effectively start/maintain a venture if it is a part-time focus?
6. How do you manage personal relationships while maintaining business ones?

Present Situation

With the recent explosion in Facebook—a start-up that began as a student's class project—two budding entrepreneurs were looking to cash in. They had been up and running for about two and a half years and it was now November 2007; bouncing along packed in with all the other commuters on the GO Train heading out of downtown Toronto, Jason turned to Alex and remarked, "We're backed into a corner, I can't believe Brett is holding us hostage like this." "I know," replied Alex, "we've been working on expansion of the business and now it may have no future—my first reaction is to spite Brett—even shutting this thing down! But we're going to have to confront him—I bet the three of us won't all be standing by the end of this."

Background

In July 2005, two young and completely inexperienced entrepreneurs founded an Internet travel company while in their final year of university. The major Internet brands were reasonably established, but another household name was only a Super Bowl commercial away. Jason and Alex believed that they had identified a business model with strong revenue potential.

They had discussed many business ideas to begin a Web company, including Internet groceries (at the time it had only begun in San Francisco) and providing portal services, but acknowledged that these ideas were beyond their ability to execute. How, for example, could two guys who had never run a grocery business, which operates on 2-percent margins, start an Internet grocery company, add a delivery expense, and expect to be a success? Worse yet, if they did succeed what would stop one of the major grocery chains from leveraging natural advantages (existing inventory, capital, distribution channels) from replicating their success and forcing them into bankruptcy?

Instead, the team decided to move towards providing student travel. The target market was group travel, specifically graduation trips and/or spring break trips. The model was to sell to the key influencer (sorority president, captain of the marching band, head of the engineering society, etc.) within an educational facility (university, college, or high school) and have them organize travel for themselves and of course bring 30 or 40 of their friends. With the volume, the margin justified more effort aimed at selling.

As their strategic advantage, the TravelHangar team had decided to leverage the Internet to facilitate the organization of the travel for their customers. Basically, a trip organizer would have all the information for the trip, including trip details, who had committed to go, legal agreements, waivers, etc., online and could point potential travellers to it to join the trip. The thought was also to leverage the Internet to create buzz for the trip by allowing the organizer to post notes about the vacation along with photos after the event.

One of the other appealing things about the business model was that neither Jason nor Alex would be required to refuse full-time employment after they graduated—and preliminary talks with recruiters suggested they both would land good jobs next year. They would then use those stable jobs to fund the development of TravelHangar, and manage the business as a hobby on the side.

First Hurdle. Without any direct contacts in travel, the team tried to figure out the process of actually executing on the business they planned on generating. They reviewed several models, including becoming a travel agency in their own right. This ultimately though was rejected as it required a level of commitment to complete legal requirements and a fairly substantial financial outlay, including perhaps establishing a bricks-and-mortar operation.

In mid-August 2005, while discussing the issue with one of their friends, they discovered that they knew someone who was executing on a fairly similar model providing sports team training camp travel. This individual had forged a relationship with Avenue Travel, a Carlson Wagonlit travel agency, based in Toronto, Ontario, to provide the agency infrastructure.

Jason and Alex approached their friend, Allen Reed, who agreed to introduce them to his contact at Avenue Travel. The catch though was that Allen wanted to be part of the business. His value to the team was experience, and a partnership was eventually formed where Allen would retain 30 percent of the equity, and Jason and Alex would each maintain 35 percent respectively. Alex recalled, "The deal was done quickly and without properly managing expectations."

Jason continued, "The team was able to create the partnership with Avenue Travel. We would share a small percentage of the revenue generated from the travel with Avenue Travel, and in exchange be allowed to use the Carlson Wagonlit brand

This case was written by Anthony A. Woods and Prescott C. Ensign for purposes of classroom discussion.

for legitimacy, as well as leverage an experienced agent at Avenue Travel to assist setting up the travel and getting quotes on potential trips. We also benefited from the immediate ability to take credit card payments by running them through the Avenue Travel accounts."

Jason and Alex discovered in the process they had made a significant mistake. Allen Reed did not have time or energy to spare. He had a profitable business booking exotic trips—many of which he joined in on. Jason and Alex had traded 30 percent of their company for an introduction that they probably could have done on their own with some diligence. They quickly realized their mistake and found a way to reclaim that equity and remove Mr. Reed as a partner—but it had been a costly blunder.

Second Hurdle. The team had no experience on how to build a Web site or for that matter find a technology partner. They did a search and located a few potential companies, but in the end found only one that would complete the project within the $5,000 budget that had been allocated. They selected TechLogic, a small company of two individuals working from their respective homes in Gatineau, Québec. One was a programmer and the other a designer—providing TravelHangar with the combination of skills they thought necessary for success.

The TravelHangar team realized two separate issues with the approach. First was that they had not laid out the specifications for the site in coding terms, and that the direction they provided TechLogic was not as straightforward as they had suspected. The site, for example, was programmed in a language that provided very little flexibility (updates/changes would be costly) and looked different on every browser. Second, Alex sputtered, "Working with two individuals with very little experience was also a serious mistake. We simply did not understand the nuances of Web site construction and needed a partner who could provide us that guidance." Jason added, "Sometimes cheaper isn't better."

After several months of frustrating interactions, the TravelHangar site went live at the end of summer 2005. Jason acknowledged, "It lacked almost all the identified functionality and essentially was just a basic brochure site with a half-working homepage."

The First Year—Spring Break 2006

Despite the lack of functionality on the Web site, the team had begun to market the ease of use of their Internet presence and were quickly getting good leads on business. Jason and Alex focused on two main areas—the universities that they knew and private high schools in Toronto. Initially they were concerned as most of the leads seemed genuinely excited about the functionality, so the team waited for the expected complaints to come in while desperately working with TechLogic to try to fix the "hobbled and rather ugly Web site."

After a few months though, the team noticed something. They had not received a single complaint or comment about the Web site's functionality. Not even a comment about the Web site's clear lack of promised functionality. Alex elaborated, "Most of the 'click here' icons did nothing and we were riddled with dead links." The team acknowledged an interesting truth; the selling features of their virtual company were enough to peak the interest of potential clients and sway their business, but that none of these clients actually cared to use this functionality. They were winning business more on their proactive approach in making trip organization easy for these students (no need for the organizers to visit an agency several times to get their trip organized—the team was coming to them) than anything else.

This solved one problem but caused another. The lack of functionality of the site was not an issue with customers and the situation with TechLogic was also no longer problematic. Jason indicated, "Without any real hard feelings we finally had to cancel them and move on." He continued, "We didn't have to deal with those two any longer, but the lack of functionality meant no efficiency." Alex chimed in, "That automation cost us, the issue was that our online, Web-based travel business required a lot of manual work and we were not leveraging the scalability of the Internet to make this thing really take off."

Despite the rocky start, the team had several triumphs in their first year. They managed to generate 172 trips, which provided $14,500 in revenue for the team. They also thoroughly solidified a relationship with Avenue Travel, along with the processes necessary to work well together. Finally, "every trip had been pulled off without a hitch, customers had been pleased with their accommodations and there were no real complaints—I think only one group encountered some rain," remarked Alex. Jason added, "It was then that we realized we had established a recognizable brand on campus."

The team also came to the realization that they had built an extremely cyclical business. As they were providing "Spring Break" travel, their trips were all executed in February and March 2006. This created an extremely busy time in November and December 2005 setting up the travel, but otherwise a relatively easy business to manage while maintaining schoolwork and their personal lives.

In May 2006, the pair, Jason Steels and Alex Cremoni, graduated from Queen's School of Business with Bachelor of Commerce degrees and both found employment with Mercer Management Consulting Services, though each in separate workgroups. The consulting work and jet-set lifestyle had provided the two with amazing learning opportunities that leveraged their skills and ambitions. The Internet market was rebounding and they wanted to participate as it was heating up this time. Within a short while, Jason in fact, decided to leave that steady paycheque and moved to California to join a promising Internet start-up. Overnight riches eluded him, and another handful of months later, he was back in Toronto picking up where he left off.

The Second Year—Spring Break 2007

The team still faced a nagging issue; the process involved in selling travel was very manual. The team also had to solve another growing issue. They were both successful in their respective careers that were taking up more and more time. It had them on the road at least four days a week, so their sales approach—hands-on involvement with their sales agents (classmates still at Queen's and former high school friends elsewhere) that they tried to groom over the summer—was increasingly difficult.

They decided that the best approach would be to start leveraging additional existing students, particularly ones still a few years from graduation, to act as their local agents. To do this, they would find as many key students involved with clubs and social organizations at various schools and recruit them to be part of their team. They would then train these individuals on how to execute on the business directly with Avenue Travel and make them self-sufficient revenue generators. They also pushed for a variable cost model—giving the agent a share of the revenue generated from their travel portfolio.

Jason noted, "This model didn't solve the issue though—Alex and I didn't have time to sell travel and we equally didn't have time to build and maintain a team." Alex piped in, "We were able to establish one good agent at our old alma mater who then in turn was successful in generating the same amount of business as we had the prior year, our other agents fell through."

In its second season, TravelHangar did 168 trips, but focusing on selling higher margin products, including travel insurance, had generated $19,000 in revenue. The student involved picked up $6,000 of this revenue.

The Third Year—Spring Break 2008

Although year two had been a success, their key student graduated once again leaving a void that they needed to fill. Leveraging their contacts they once again found a student who would run the business at Queen's University. Their core business was becoming established, their brand was respected and intact—it clearly meant something on campus. The new representative, Brett, was a student in multiple disciplines and very active in student organizations. Additionally, he had two more years to go prior to graduation, providing the team with some assurances of continuity.

Jason and Alex went back to recruiting students at other post-secondary institutions. They ended up identifying three other individuals, but were not successful in providing these new team members with the guidance and leadership required to execute on the business. These new relationships slowly but surely all died.

In the end, all of the business was once again coming through one agent, which caused an unforeseen issue. In October 2007,

when it was clear that over 200 students would be travelling with TravelHangar that year, Brett approached Jason and Alex to renegotiate the commission structure as he was doing all the work for the company. Jason and Alex were in an awkward position; they had no legal contracts established with Brett to prevent him from leaving their company with all the clients, and he was the only person with business that year for TravelHangar. Alex recounted, "We shifted the commission structure so that Brett would keep half of the fees. Sadly, the issue has now reappeared in November." Jason interjected, "With a strong leverage position, Brett is again asking for an increase in the commission structure. I just don't know how to manage this second request, or how to avoid a third one if we agree to this one."

Decisions/Opportunities

The team determined that they were at an inflection point and needed to make decisions about their business before heading into 2008. Several opportunities were being discussed on that GO Train ride, including:

- Sell the business to Brett in exchange for future revenue.
- Fix the multiple-agent model, generating the necessary scale from a manual process.
- Close up the business.

The team struggled to discern the most appropriate course of action. Alex remarked, "In my gut, my first reaction is to scuttle TravelHangar and stick it to Brett, but would that be the most logical thing to do?" Jason felt, "We have expanding careers and personal lives and either need to commit to success or move on."

Find more great exercises and additional study tools on the Online Learning Centre at **www.mcgrawhill.ca/olc/timmons**

PART

II

THE OPPORTUNITY

One often hears, especially from younger, newer entrepreneurs, the exhortation: "Go for it! You have nothing to lose now. So what if it doesn't work out. You can do it again. Why wait?" While the spirit this reflects is commendable and there can be no substitute for doing, such itchiness can be a mistake unless it is focused on a solid opportunity.

Most entrepreneurs launching businesses, particularly the first time, run out of cash quicker than they bring in customers and profitable sales. While there are many reasons for this, the first is that they have not focused on the *right* opportunities. Unsuccessful entrepreneurs usually equate an idea with an opportunity; successful entrepreneurs know the difference!

Successful entrepreneurs know that it is important to "think big enough." They understand that they aren't simply creating a job for themselves and a few employees; they are building a business that can create value for themselves and their community.

While there are boundless opportunities for those with entrepreneurial zest, a single entrepreneur will likely be able to launch and build only a few good businesses—probably no more than three or four—during his or her energetic and productive years. (Fortunately, all you need to do is grow and harvest one quite profitable venture whose sales have exceeded several million dollars. The result will be a most satisfying professional life, as well as a financially rewarding one.)

How important is it, then, that you screen and choose an opportunity with great care? Very important! It is no accident that venture capital investors have consistently invested in no more than 1 or 2 percent of all the ventures they review.

As important as it is to find a good opportunity, even good opportunities have risks and problems. The perfect deal has yet to be seen. Identifying risks and problems before the launch while steps can be taken to eliminate them or reduce any negative effect early is another dimension of opportunity screening.

CHAPTER

2

THE ENTREPRENEURIAL PROCESS

I don't make movies to make money. I make money to make movies.

Walt Disney

Upon completion of this chapter, you will be able to:

1. Articulate a definition of entrepreneurship and the entrepreneurial process—from lifestyle ventures to high-potential enterprises.

2. Understand the practical issues and explore the complex map of requirements necessary to launch; including an appreciation that no one works alone—an array of stakeholders play a role.

3. See how entrepreneurs and their financial backers get the odds for success in their favour by defying the pattern of disappointment and failure experienced by many.

4. Explain the Timmons Model of the entrepreneurial process, how it can be applied to your entrepreneurial career aspirations and ideas for businesses, and how recent research confirms its validity.

DEMYSTIFYING ENTREPRENEURSHIP

Entrepreneurship is a way of thinking, reasoning, and acting that is opportunity obsessed, holistic in approach, and leadership balanced. Entrepreneurship results in the creation, enhancement, realization, and renewal of value, not just for owners, but for all participants and stakeholders. At the heart of the process is the creation and/or recognition of opportunities,[1] followed by the will and initiative to seize these opportunities. It requires a willingness to take risks—both personal and financial—but in a very calculated fashion in order to constantly shift the odds of success, balancing the risk with the potential reward. Typically, entrepreneurs devise ingenious strategies to marshal their limited resources. Take for example Tom Jablonski, who started ShoeGuru, the subject of this chapter's case, a new venture formed to deliver stylish shoes combined with a slick Web site experience.

Today, entrepreneurship has evolved beyond the classic start-up notion to include companies and organizations of all types, in all stages. Thus, *entrepreneurship can occur—and fail to occur—in firms that are old and new; small and large; fast and slow growing; in the private, not-for-profit, and public sectors; in all geographic points; and in all stages of a nation's development, regardless of politics.*

Entrepreneurial leaders inject imagination, motivation, commitment, passion, tenacity, integrity, teamwork, and vision into their companies. They face dilemmas and must make decisions despite ambiguity and contradictions. Very rarely is entrepreneurship a get-rich-quick proposition. On the contrary, it is one of continuous renewal, as entrepreneurs are never satisfied with the nature of their opportunity. The result of this value creation process is that the total economic pie grows larger and society benefits.

CLASSIC ENTREPRENEURSHIP: THE START-UP

The classic expression of entrepreneurship is the raw start-up company, an innovative idea that develops into a high growth company. The best of these become entrepreneurial legends: Virgin Group, Netscape, Amazon.com, Sun Microsystems, Home Depot, Tim Hortons, Compaq Computer, Canadian Tire, and hundreds of others are now household names. Success, in addition to the strong leadership from the main entrepreneur, almost always involves building a team with complementary talents. The ability to work as a team and sense an opportunity where others see contradiction, chaos, and confusion are critical elements of success. Entrepreneurship also requires the skill and ingenuity to find and control resources, often owned by others, in order to pursue the opportunity. It means making sure the upstart venture does not run out of money when it needs it the most. Most highly successful entrepreneurs have held together a team and acquired financial backing in order to chase an opportunity others may not recognize.

ENTREPRENEURSHIP IN POST-BRONTOSAURUS CAPITALISM: BEYOND START-UPS

The upstart companies of yesterday and today have had a profound impact on the competitive structure of North American and global industries. Giant firms, such as IBM (knocked off by Apple, then Microsoft, and recently Lenovo acquired IBM's once strong PC division), Digital Equipment Corporation (another victim of Apple and acquired by Compaq Computer, which was in turn absorbed by HP), the music recording industry (hobbled by Napster and then legally by Apple's iTunes), or Eaton's and Kmart (entirely disappearing from Canada) once thought invincible, have been dismembered by the new wave of entrepreneurial ventures. The resulting downsizing during the 1980s returned in waves; economic downturns, rising fuel prices, and shifting consumer preferences were responsible for restructuring in the auto industry. While large companies, like Nortel Networks, shrink head count, new ventures add jobs. As autopsy after autopsy was performed on failing large companies, a fascinating pattern emerged, showing, at worst, a total disregard for the winning entrepreneurial approaches of their new rivals and, at best, a glacial pace in recognizing the impending demise and the changing course.

"People Don't Want to Be Managed. They Want to Be Led!"[2]

These giant firms can be characterized, during their highly vulnerable periods, as hierarchical in structure with many layers of reviews, approvals, and vetoes. Their tired executive blood conceived of leadership as *managing and administering* from the top down, in stark contrast to Ewing M. Kauffman's powerful insight, "People don't want to be managed. They want to be led!" These stagnating giants tended to reward people who accumulated the largest assets, budgets, number of plants, products, and head count, rather than rewarding those who created or found new business opportunities, took calculated risks, and occasionally made mistakes, all with bootstrap resources. While very cognizant of the importance of corporate culture and strategy, the corporate giants' pace was glacial: Research on these dinosaurs concludes that it typically took six years for a large firm to change its strategy and 10 to 30 years to change its culture. Meanwhile, the median time it took start-ups to accumulate the necessary capital was one month, but averaged six months.[3]

To make matters worse, these corporate giants had many bureaucratic tendencies, particularly arrogance. They shared a blind belief that if they followed the almost sacred best-management practices of the day, they could not help but prevail. Previously, these best-management practices did not include entrepreneurship, entrepreneurial leadership, and entrepreneurial reasoning. If anything, these were considered dirty words in the corporate world. Chief among these sacred cows was staying close to your customer. What may shock you is the following conclusion of a study of disruptive technologies:

> One of the most consistent patterns in business is the failure of leading companies to stay at the top of their industries when technologies or markets change. ... But a more fundamental reason lies at the heart of the paradox: Leading companies succumb to one of the most popular, valuable management dogmas. They stay close to their customers.[4]
>
> When they do attack, the [new] entrant companies find the established players to be easy and unprepared opponents because the opponents have been looking up markets themselves, discounting the threat from below.[5]

One gets further insight into just how vulnerable and fragile the larger, so-called well-managed companies can become, and why it is the newcomers who pose the greatest threats. This pattern also explains why there are tremendous opportunities for the coming e-generation even in markets that are currently dominated by large players.

> The problem is that managers keep doing what has worked in the past: serving the rapidly growing needs of their current customers. The processes that successful, well-managed companies have developed to allocate resources among proposed investments are incapable of funnelling resources in programs that current customers explicitly don't want and whose profit margins seem unattractive.[6]

Coupled with the number of new innovations, firms, and industries have been created in the past 30 years, it is no wonder that brontosaurus capitalism has found its ice age.

Signs of Hope in a Corporate Ice Age

Fortunately, for many giant firms, the entrepreneurial revolution may spare them from their own ice age. One of the most exciting developments of the decade is the response of some large, established corporations to the revolution in entrepreneurial leadership. After decades of experiencing the demise of giant after giant, corporate leadership, in unprecedented numbers, is launching experiments and strategies to recapture entrepreneurial spirit and to instill the culture and practices we would characterize as entrepreneurial reasoning. The e-generation has too many attractive opportunities in truly entrepreneurial environments. They do not need to work for a brontosaurus that lacks spirit.

Increasingly, we see examples of large companies adopting principles of entrepreneurship and entrepreneurial leadership in order to survive and to renew. Researchers document how large firms are applying entrepreneurial thinking, in pioneering ways, to invent their futures, including companies such as GE, Corning, Motorola, PotashCorp of Saskatchewan, Bombardier, and EnCana.[7] Most large brontosaurus firms could learn valuable lessons on how to apply entrepreneurial thinking from companies such as these.

Metaphors

Improvisational, quick, clever, resourceful, and inventive all describe good entrepreneurs. Likewise, innumerable metaphors from other parts of life can describe the complex world of the entrepreneur and the entrepreneurial process. From music it is jazz, with its uniquely impromptu flair. From sports many metaphors exist: LeBron James's agility, the broken-field running of Pinball Clemons, the wizardry on ice of Sidney Crosby, or the competitiveness of Silken Laumann. Even more fascinating are the unprecedented comebacks of athletic greats such as Mario Lemieux, Picabo Street, and Lance Armstrong.

Perhaps the game of golf, more than any other, replicates the complex and dynamic nature of managing risk and reward, including all the intricate mental challenges faced in entrepreneuring. No other sport, at one time, demands so much physically, is so complex, intricate, and delicate, and is simultaneously so rewarding and punishing; and none tests one's will, patience, self-discipline, and self-control like golf. Entrepreneurs face these challenges and remunerations as well. If you think that the team concept isn't important in golf, remember the 2004 American Ryder Cup "dream team," which failed to work together and lost to the Europeans. And what about the relationship between the caddy and golfer?

An entrepreneur also faces challenges like a symphony conductor or a coach who must blend and balance a group of diverse people with different skills, talents, and personalities into a superb team. On many occasions it demands all the talents and agility of a juggler who must, under great stress, keep many balls in the air at once.

The complex decisions and numerous alternatives facing the entrepreneur also have many parallels with the game of chess. As in chess, the victory goes to the most creative player, who can imagine several alternate moves in advance and anticipate possible defences. This kind of mental agility is frequently demanded in entrepreneurial decision-making. Mike Chiasson and Chad Saunders both of the University of Calgary find that entrepreneurial actions are driven as well as constrained by mental processes. Recognizing and formulating entrepreneurial opportunity is a cyclical yin and yang where restrictions and possibilities must be reconciled.[8]

Regardless of the metaphor or analogy you choose for entrepreneurship, each is likely to describe a creative, even artistic, improvised act. The outcomes are often either highly rewarding successes or painfully visible misses. Always, urgency is on the doorstep.

ENTREPRENEURSHIP = PARADOXES

One of the most confounding aspects of the entrepreneurial process is its contradictions. Because of its highly dynamic, fluid, ambiguous, and chaotic character, the process's constant changes frequently pose paradoxes. A sampling of entrepreneurial paradoxes follows. Can you think of other paradoxes that you have observed or heard about?

✓ *An opportunity with no or very low potential can be an enormously big opportunity.* One of the most famous examples of this paradox is Apple. Founders Steve Jobs and Steve Wozniak approached their employer, Hewlett-Packard, with the idea for a desktop, personal computer and were told this was not an opportunity for HP. Hence, Jobs and Wozniak started their own company. Frequently, business plans rejected by some venture capitalists become legendary successes when backed by another investor. In addition to quite a few instances where some now famous and successful entrepreneurs had their ideas initially turned down, there are a growing number of cases where some entrepreneurs said 'no' to investment money—despite indications from many that it is getting harder to find venture capital in Canada. One such individual is Albert Lai. He turned down offers of funding and it turned out to be the right move—he later sold BubbleShare for $3 million… and didn't have to share his winnings. In his blog Albert Lai writes:

> Lack of entrepreneurial support systems for students (and recent grads): students are not given the a) role models & motivation, b) knowledge & encouragement, c) support systems & funding, d) education/network, to enable them to succeed. Many of the most innovative start-ups/products on the net that you use everyday today were started in dorm rooms of university students—especially in the B2C space (i.e., Netscape, Napster, Yahoo, Google, Facebook, etc.). Virtually none of them are from Canadian university dorm rooms. The above points can really be boiled down to two things a) lack of funding, b) lack of entrepreneurial culture/encouragement.
>
> How do we solve this? We need to provide Canadian students with more exposure to "what's possible" and a real support system.

✓ *To make money you have to first lose money.* It is commonly said in the venture capital business that the lemons, or losers, ripen in two-and-a-half years, while the plums take seven or eight years. A start-up, venture-backed company typically loses money, often $10 million or more, before sustaining profitability and going public, usually at least five to seven years later.

✓ *To create and build wealth one must relinquish wealth.* Among the most successful and growing companies, the founders aggressively dilute their ownership to create ownership throughout the company. By rewarding and sharing the wealth with the people who contribute significantly to its creation, owners motivate stakeholders to make the pie bigger. A recurring theme on the popular CBC television show, *Dragons' Den*, is that the investors must relinquish some equity but the value of bringing a Dragon on board is worth the price.

✓ *To succeed, one first has to experience failure.* It is a common pattern that the first venture fails; yet the entrepreneur learns and goes on to create a highly successful company. Joseph Smallwood grew up in abject poverty in St. John's, Newfoundland. He finished day school but was unable to complete studies at Bishop Field College and at age 15 became a printer's apprentice. He spent a number of years gaining experience as a reporter with various newspapers, including five years in New York City. He moved back to Newfoundland and his first venture in politics was a flop. He did go on to serve as Newfoundland's premier for nearly 25 years and brought the island into Confederation.[9] A recent study finds those entrepreneurs who have previously failed increase their odds of success compared to those who are first time entrepreneurs. Of course those with a track record of success do even better![10]

✓ *Entrepreneurship requires considerable thought, preparation, and planning, yet is basically an unplannable event.* The highly dynamic, changing character of technology, markets, and competition make it impossible to know all your competitors today, let alone five years from now. Yet great effort is invested in attempting to model and envision the future. The resulting business plan is inevitably obsolete when it comes off the printer. This is a creative process—like moulding clay.[11] You need to make a habit of planning and reacting as you constantly re-evaluate your options, blending the messages from your head and your gut, until this process becomes second nature.

✓ *For creativity and innovativeness to prosper, rigour and discipline must accompany the process.* For years, hundreds of thousands of patents for new products and technologies lay fallow in government and university research labs because there was no commercial discipline.

✓ *Entrepreneurship requires a bias toward action and a sense of urgency, but also demands patience and perseverance.* While his competitors were acquiring and expanding rapidly, one entrepreneur's management team became nearly outraged at his inaction. This entrepreneur reported he saved the company at least $50 million to $100 million during the prior year by just sitting tight. He learned this lesson from a case study in *New Venture Creation.*

✓ *The greater the organization, orderliness, discipline, and control, the less you will control your ultimate destiny.* Entrepreneurship requires great flexibility and nimbleness in strategy and tactics. One has to play with the knees bent. Overcontrol and an obsession with orderliness are impediments to the entrepreneurial approach. As the great racecar driver Mario Andretti said, "If I am in total control, I know I am going too slow!"

✓ *Adhering to management best practice, especially staying close to the customer that created industry leaders in the 1980s, became a seed of self-destruction and loss of leadership to upstart competitors.* We discussed earlier the study of "disruptive technologies."

✓ *To realize long-term equity value, you have to forgo the temptations of short term profitability.* Building long-term equity requires large, continuous reinvestment in new people, products, services, and support systems, usually at the expense of immediate profits.

The world of entrepreneurship is not neat, tidy, linear, consistent, and predictable, no matter how much we might like it to be that way.[12] In fact, it is from the collisions inherent in these paradoxes that value is created as illustrated in Exhibit 2.1. These paradoxes illustrate just how contradictory and chaotic this world can be. To thrive in this environment, one needs to be very adept at coping with ambiguity, chaos, and uncertainty, and at building management skills that create predictability.

EXHIBIT 2.1   Entrepreneurship IS a Contact Sport

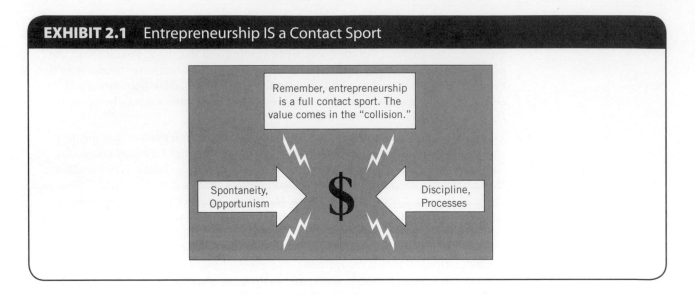

The Higher Potential Venture: Think Big Enough

One of the biggest mistakes aspiring entrepreneurs make is strategic. They think too small. Sensible as it may be to think in terms of a very small, simple business as being more affordable, more manageable, less demanding, and less risky, the opposite is true. The chances of survival and success are lower in these small, job-substitute businesses, and even if they do survive, they are less financially rewarding. As one founder of numerous businesses put it: Unless this business can pay you at least five times your present salary, the risk and wear and tear won't be worth it.

Consider one of the most successful venture capital investors ever, Arthur Rock. His criterion for searching for opportunities is very simple: *look for business concepts that will change the way people live or work.* His home-run investments are legendary, including Intel, Apple, Teledyne, and dozens of others. Clearly, his philosophy is to think big. Today an extraordinary variety of people, opportunities, and strategies characterize the millions of proprietorships, partnerships, and corporations in the country. Remember, high potential ventures become high impact firms that often make the world a better place!

Nearly 10 percent of the Canadian population is actively working on a new venture.[13] More than 95 percent of start-ups have revenues of less than $1 million annually. Statistics Canada reports about 150,000 new businesses enter the playing field annually and nearly as many exit each year. Harry Bowen of Queen's University and Dirk De Clercq of Brock University find that entrepreneurial effort toward high-growth activities is related to financial conditions and educational factors that vary from place to place as well as over time.[14]

Not only can nearly anyone start a business, but also a great many can succeed. While it certainly might help, a person does not have to be a genius to create a successful business. As Nolan Bushnell, founder of Atari, one of the first desktop computer games in the early 1980s, and Pizza Time Theater, said, "If you are not a millionaire or bankrupt by the time you are 30, you are not really trying!"[15] It is an entrepreneur's preparedness for the entrepreneurial process that is important. Being an entrepreneur has moved from cult status in the 1980s to rock star infamy in the 1990s to become de rigueur at present. Amateur entrepreneurship is over. The professionals have arrived.

A stunning number of mega-entrepreneurs launched their ventures during their 20s. While the rigours of new ventures may favour the "young at start," age is *not* a barrier to entry. Most studies show that about 25 percent of founders were over 40 when they embarked on their entrepreneurial careers, half were in their 30s, and just over one-quarter did so by the time they were 25. The Global Entrepreneurship Monitor finds that 25 to 34-year-olds are most active in entrepreneurship and that entrepreneurial activity declines after the age of 35.[16] However, numerous examples exist of founders who were over 60 at the time of launch, including one of the most famous seniors, Colonel Harland Sanders, who at 65 started franchising KFC with his first old-age pension cheque.

SMALLER CAN MEAN HIGHER FAILURE ODDS

Unfortunately, the record of survival is not good among all firms started. Most estimates place the failure rate for start-ups at 50 percent in the first few years. While government data, research, and business mortality statisticians may not agree on the precise failure and survival figures for new businesses, they do agree that failure is the rule, not the exception.

Complicating efforts to obtain precise figures is the fact that it is not easy to define and identify failures, and reliable statistics and databases are not available. One study reports after one year, 71 percent of new ventures are still in business, the number drops to 58 percent by year two and 49 percent by year three. At the five-year mark 37 percent are still in business and going into the tenth year only 23 percent of those original start-ups remain in business (see Exhibit 2.2).

Exit rates vary widely across industries, but so too do entry rates. For instance, retail and services accounted for the majority of all failures. Restaurants come and go like clockwork, everybody thinks they have a better idea or menu. Chances of success also differ for other factors.

The likelihood that start-ups will survive their initial year differs dramatically across provinces. Firms in their initial year of life exhibit a much higher success rate in Ontario (75 percent) than in the Atlantic Provinces (59 percent). Business start-ups in British Columbia (75 percent), Québec (74 percent), and Alberta (72 percent) are more likely to survive their first year than those in Saskatchewan or Manitoba (63 percent) (see Exhibit 2.3).

The following discussion provides a distillation of a number of failure-rate studies over many years. These studies illustrate that (1) failure rates are high, and (2) although the majority of the failures occur in the first two to five years, it may take considerably longer for some to fail.[17]

EXHIBIT 2.2   Start-up Survival Rates by Firm Size

Firm Size	Number of Years (Percent)								
	1	2	3	4	5	6	7	8	9
Small (1–4)	71	57	49	42	36	31	27	24	22
Medium (5–99)	74	61	53	47	42	38	34	31	29
Large (100+)	81	68	63	58	54	52	50	49	45
All	**71**	**58**	**49**	**42**	**37**	**32**	**28**	**25**	**23**

Source: *Longitudinal Employment Analysis Program (LEAP)*, Small Business Research and Policy, Industry Canada. Start-ups tracked from 2003 to 2008. Statistics based on firm size at start-up: 1 to 4 employees 130,021 observations; 5 to 99 employees 18,255 observations; 100+ employees 184 observations.

EXHIBIT 2.3   Start-up Survival Rates by Firm Location

Region	Number of Years (Percent)								
	1	2	3	4	5	6	7	8	9
Atlantic Canada	58.9	43.6	36.0	30.7	26.8	23.8	21.3	19.3	17.1
Quebec	74.2	56.0	46.8	40.7	36.3	32.6	29.6	27.1	24.8
Ontario	74.7	57.8	49.0	42.8	38.2	34.4	31.2	28.5	25.6
Prairies	63.2	49.4	41.6	35.9	31.7	28.5	25.7	22.9	20.2
Alberta	72.3	56.8	48.8	42.9	38.2	34.6	31.5	28.6	25.7
British Columbia	74.7	57.7	48.7	42.1	37.0	32.9	29.6	26.7	24.0
Canada	**71.3**	**54.8**	**46.1**	**40.1**	**35.5**	**31.9**	**28.9**	**26.3**	**23.7**

Source: Small Business Research and Policy, Industry Canada, July 2008.

Finally, "failure" may not always be the most appropriate term. There are instances where an entrepreneur chooses to get out—either to close it or sell it off. Further, an idea may have run its course and no longer be viable, even after only one year—such as a product or service tied to an event like a music festival or a Winter Olympics. A better opportunity may come along and the entrepreneur may have to abandon the current venture for that more attractive one. Entrepreneurs that hop from one opportunity to another have been described as having a high churn rate. The serial entrepreneur is one who goes from venture to venture in succession, but there is also evidence of the portfolio entrepreneur, an individual who can't concentrate his or her efforts on a single venture—perhaps even counting on some falling off along the way. Often data are unable to capture businesses that de-register or change name.

Failure rates across industries vary as well. The real estate industry, with a 37-percent rate of start-up failure, is the lowest. The technology sector has a high rate of failure at 54 percent. The software and services segment of the technology industry has an even higher failure rate; 55 percent of start-ups tracked closed their doors. Unfortunately, the record of survival is not good among all firms started.

To make matters worse, most people think the failure rates are actually much higher. Since actions often are governed by perceptions rather than facts, this perception of failure, in addition to the dismal record, can be a serious obstacle to aspiring entrepreneurs.

Still other studies have shown significant differences in survival rates among industry categories: retail trade, construction, and small service businesses accounted for 70 percent of all failures and bankruptcies. One study calculates a risk factor or index for start-ups by industry, which sends a clear warning signal to the would-be entrepreneur.[18] "The fishing is better in some streams versus others," is another favourite saying of the authors. Further, the vast majority of these failed companies had fewer than 100 employees. Through observation and practical experience one would not be surprised by such reports. The implications for would-be entrepreneurs are important: Knowing the difference between a good idea and a real opportunity is vital. This will be addressed in detail in Chapter 3. Monica Diochon of St. Francis Xavier, Teresa Menzies of Brock University, and Yvon Gasse of the Université Laval point out that opportunity identification is not the same as opportunity pursuit. Factors that may help in identifying opportunities, such as education and experience, may even hamper pursuing opportunities.[19]

A certain level of failure is part of the "creative destruction" described by Joseph Schumpeter in his writings. It is part of the dynamics of innovation and economic renewal, a process that requires both births and deaths. More important, it is also part of the learning process inherent in an entrepreneurial apprenticeship. Businesses fail, but entrepreneurs survive and learn.

The daunting evidence of failure poses two important questions for aspiring entrepreneurs. First, are there any exceptions to this general rule of failure, or are we faced with a punishing game of entrepreneurial roulette? Second, if there is an exception, how does one get the odds for success in one's favour?

Getting the Odds in Your Favour

Fortunately, there is a decided pattern of exceptions to the overall rate of failure among the vast majority of small, marginal firms created each year. Most smaller enterprises that cease operation simply do not meet our notion of entrepreneurship. They do not create, enhance, or pursue opportunities that realize value. They tend to be job substitutes in many instances. Undercapitalized, undermanaged, and often poorly located, they soon fail.

Threshold Concept

Who are the survivors? The odds for survival and a higher level of success change dramatically if the venture reaches a critical mass of at least 10 to 20 people with $2 million to $3 million in revenues and is currently pursuing opportunities with growth potential. Survival rates for new firms increase steadily as the firm size increases. The survival rates at the three-year mark jump from approximately 49 percent for firms having up to five employees to approximately 63 percent for firms with over 100 employees.

Empirical evidence supports the *liability of newness* and *liability of smallness* arguments and suggests that being new and small make survival difficult. The authors of one study inferred, "Perceived satisfaction, cooperation, and trust between the customer and the organization [are] important for the continuation of the relationship. High levels of satisfaction, cooperation, and trust represent a stock of goodwill and positive beliefs which are critical assets that influence the commitment of the two parties to the relationship."[20] The authors of this study noted, "Smaller organizations are found to be more responsive, while larger organizations are found to provide greater depth of service. ... The entrepreneurial task is to find a way to either direct the arena of competition away from the areas where you are at a competitive disadvantage, or find some creative way to develop the required competency."[21]

Although any estimates based on sales per employee vary considerably from industry to industry, this minimum translates roughly to a threshold of $50,000 to $100,000 of sales per employee annually. But highly successful firms can generate much higher sales per employee.

Promise of Growth

The definition of entrepreneurship implies the promise of expansion and the building of long-term value and durable cash flow streams as well. It is perhaps not surprising that time frames and growth aspirations are idiosyncratic. Dev Dutta of the University of New Hampshire and Stewart Thornhill of the University of Western Ontario find that entrepreneurs vary in their cognitive styles. This outlook combined with their assessment of the competitive environment influences the growth intentions for their enterprise.[22]

However, as will be discussed later, it takes time for enterprises to become established and grow. Historically, two of every five small firms founded survive four years but few achieve growth during those first few years. Odds of survival increase substantially for those enterprises that grow, and the earlier in the life of the business that growth occurs, the higher the chance of survival.[23] The 2008 INC. 500 exemplify this, with a median three-year growth rate of 334 percent.[24] Profit's Hot 50 for 2008 achieved average two-year revenue growth of 756 percent, but 26 percent of them were not yet profitable in their most recent fiscal year.[25] Of Canada's hottest 50 home-grown enterprises, 54 percent are headed by CEOs that have started ventures in the past.[26] The 2008 list of enterprises includes a wide range of products and services offered: model train manufacturer (Rapido Trains), organic food ingredient distributor (N2 Ingredients), oilfield construction (CerPro Energy Services), designer doggy wear (FouFou Dog), Web systems integrator (Spheric Technologies), custom 'skins' for electronics (MyTego.com), cosmetics (Bleu Lavande), and online auction management (Auctionwire).

Some of the true excitement of entrepreneurship lies in conceiving, launching, and building firms such as these.

Venture Capital Backing

Another notable pattern of exception to the failure rule is found for businesses that attract start-up financing from successful private venture capital companies. As Exhibit 2.4 shows venture-backed firms account for a very small fraction of the population each year.

Venture capital is not essential to a start-up, nor is it a guarantee of success. Of the companies making the 2001 INC. 500, only 18 percent raised venture capital and only 3 percent had venture funding at start-up.[27] Consider, for instance, that even in the dot-com heyday of 2000 only 1,300 Canadian enterprises received venture capital. However, companies with venture capital support fare better overall. Perhaps as few as 1 percent of the venture-backed companies declare bankruptcy or become defunct.[28]

These compelling data have led some to conclude a threshold core of 10 to 15 percent of new companies will become the winners in terms of size, job creation, profitability, innovation, and potential for harvesting (and thereby realize a capital gain).

EXHIBIT 2.4   Canadian Venture Capital Activity

Year	Amount invested	Number of deals	Average deal
1998	1.5 billion	850	$1.8 million
1999	2.75 billion	900	3.1 million
2000	5.9 billion	1300	4.5 million
2001	3.7 billion	925	4 million
2002	2.75 billion	790	3.5 million
2003	1.7 billion	680	2.5 million
2004	1.85 billion	600	3 million
2005	1.82 billion	630	2.9 million
2006	1.7 billion	408	4.2 million
2007	2.1 billion	412	5.1 million
2008	1.3 billion	371	3.5 million

Source: Courtesy of CVCA—Canada's Venture Capital and Private Equity Association and Thomson Reuters.

Private Investors Join Venture Capitalists

Entrepreneurs that have cashed out, harvesting their enterprises, by the tens of thousands have become "angels" as private investors in the next generation of entrepreneurs. Many of the more successful entrepreneurs have created their own investment pools and are competing directly with venture capitalists—such as Skypoint Capital, Garage Technology Ventures, Golden Opportunities Fund, TriWest Capital, AVAC, or Ventures West—for deals. Their operating experiences and successful track records provide a compelling case for adding value to an upstart company. Take, for example, Purple Angel, a Canadian group of former high-tech executives who came together in 2001 to give back—to support technology start-ups by investing resources: time, money, and effort. Some of their chosen projects have required business acumen (e.g., help with market identification or making an introduction to a key contact); others have needed technological expertise. While Purple Angel's mission explicitly mentions the goal of fun, generating wealth is a stated objective too.

Private investors and entrepreneurs have very similar selection criteria to the venture capitalists: They are in search of the high potential, higher growth ventures. Unlike the venture capitalists, however, private investors are not constrained by having to invest so much money in a relatively short period that they must invest it in minimum chunks of $3 million to $5 million or more. Angel investors, therefore, are prime sources for less capital-intensive start-ups and early-stage businesses.

This overall search for higher potential ventures has become more evident in recent years. The new e-generation appears to be learning the lessons of these survivors, venture capitalists, private investors, and founders of higher potential firms. Hundreds of thousands of students now have been exposed to these concepts over the years, and their strategies for identifying potential businesses are mindful of and disciplined about the ingredients for success. Unlike 20 or more years ago, it is now nearly impossible not to hear and read about these principles whether on television, in books, on the Internet, or in a multitude of seminars, courses, and programs for would-be entrepreneurs of all types.

Find Financial Backers and Associates Who Add Value

One of the most distinguishing disciplines of these higher potential ventures is how the founders identify financial partners and key team members. They insist on backers and part-ners who do more than bring just money, friendship, commitment, and motivation to the venture. They surround themselves with backers who can add value to the venture through their experience, know-how, networks, and wisdom. Key associates are selected because they are smarter and better at what they do than the founder; and they raise the overall average of the entire company. This theme will be examined in detail in later chapters.

Option: The Lifestyle Venture

For many aspiring entrepreneurs, issues of family roots and location take precedence. Accessibility to a preferred way of life, whether it is access to skiing, hiking, music, surfing, canoeing, a rural setting, the mountains, can be more important than how large a business one has or the size of one's net worth. Others vastly prefer to be with and work alongside their family or spouse. They want to live in a non-urban area that they consider very attractive or even pursue a noble cause. Maria Panínguakí Kjærulff (www.mariagreenland.com) is a full-time artist that, for now, calls Nuuk, Greenland home. After graduating from Nova Scotia College of Art and Design with a Bachelor of Fine Arts, including a semester at Cooper Union School of Art in New York City, she chose her hometown. Though she has spent time in Minnesota and Denmark, she returned to comfortable surroundings, family, and friends. Despite the relative isolation of Greenland—a large island with low population, primarily within the Arctic Circle—Maria's art is exhibited in Denmark, Canada, Korea, Iceland, Finland, Sweden, and Norway.

Yet, couples who give up successful careers in Toronto to buy a bed-and-breakfast in cottage country to avoid the rat race generally last only six to seven years. They discover the joys of self-employment, including seven-day, 70- to 90-hour workweeks, chefs and day help that do not show up, roofs that leak when least expected, and the occasional guests from hell. The grass is always greener, so they say.

Methods of financing often separate ventures. Jean-Etienne de Bettignies of Queen's University finds that equity-type contracts are prevalent for high-growth ventures whereas debt-type contracts are typical of lifestyle ventures.[29]

THE TIMMONS MODEL: WHERE THEORY AND PRACTICE COLLIDE IN THE REAL WORLD

How can aspiring entrepreneurs—and the investors and associates who join the venture—get the odds of success on their side? What do these talented and successful high potential entrepreneurs, their venture capitalists, and their private backers do differently? What accounts for their exceptional record? Are there general lessons and principles underlying their successes that can benefit aspiring entrepreneurs, investors, and those who would join a venture? If so, can these lessons be learned?

These are the central questions of our lifetime work. We have been immersed as students, researchers, teachers, and practitioners of the *entrepreneurial process.* As founding shareholders and investors of several high potential ventures (some of which are now public), advisors to ventures, and mentors to entrepreneurs—including many former students, we have each applied, tested, refined, and tempered academic theory as fire tempers iron into steel: in the fire of practice. Chances are that your instructor for this course has considerable background in entrepreneurship, perhaps advising government on policy matters or local/regional economic development agencies. Much of the wisdom we have gained, whether from activities such as judging and coaching business plan and elevator pitch competitions or a seat on a board of directors, comes from you—the student.

Intellectual and Practical Collisions with the Real World

Throughout this period of evolution and revolution, *New Venture Creation* has adhered to one core principle: In every quest for greater knowledge of the entrepreneurial process and more effective learning, there must be intellectual and practical collisions between academic theory and the real world of practice. The standard academic notion of something being all right in practice but not in theory is unacceptable. This integrated, holistic balance is at the heart of what we know about the entrepreneurial process and getting the odds in your favour.

Value Creation: The Driving Forces

A core, fundamental entrepreneurial process accounts for the substantially greater success pattern among higher potential ventures. Despite the great variety of businesses, entrepreneurs, geographies, and technologies, central themes or driving forces dominate this highly dynamic entrepreneurial process.

- It is *opportunity* driven.
- It is driven by a *lead entrepreneur* and an *entrepreneurial team*.
- It is *resource parsimonious* and *creative*.
- It depends on the *fit* and *balance* among these.
- It is *integrated* and *holistic*.
- It is *sustainable*.

These are the controllable components of the entrepreneurial process that can be assessed, influenced, and altered. Founders and investors focus on these forces during their careful due-diligence process to analyze the risks and determine what changes can be made to improve a venture's chances of success.

First, we will elaborate on each of these forces to provide a blueprint and a definition of what each means. Then using the early years of Mitel as an example, we will illustrate how the holistic, balance, and fit concepts pertain to a start-up.

Change the Odds: Fix It, Shape It, Mould It, Make It

The driving forces underlying successful new venture creation are illustrated in Exhibit 2.5. The process starts with opportunity, not money, strategy, networks, team, or the business plan. Most genuine opportunities are much bigger than either the talent and capacity of the team or the initial resources available to the team. The role of the lead entrepreneur and the team is to juggle all these key elements in a changing environment. Think of a juggler bouncing up and down on a trampoline that is moving on a conveyor belt at unpredictable speeds and directions, while trying to keep objects of various shapes, weights, and sizes all in the air. That is the dynamic nature of an early-stage start-up. The business plan provides the language and code for communicating the quality of the three driving forces of the Timmons Model and of their fit and balance.

In the entrepreneurial process depicted in the Timmons Model, the shape, size, and depth of the opportunity establishes the required shape, size, and depth of both the resources and the team. We have found that many people are a bit uncomfortable viewing the opportunity and resources somewhat precariously balanced by the team. It is especially disconcerting to some because we show the three key elements of the entrepreneurial process as circles, and thus the balance appears tenuous. These reactions are justified, accurate, and realistic. The entrepreneurial process is dynamic. Those who recognize the risks better manage the process and garner higher returns.

The lead entrepreneur's job is simple enough. He or she must carry the deal by *taking charge of the success equation*. In this dynamic context, ambiguity and risk are actually your friends. Central to the homework, creative problem solving and strategizing, and due diligence that lies ahead is analyzing the fits and gaps that exist in the venture. What is wrong with this opportunity? What is missing? What good news and favourable events can happen, as well as the adverse? What has to happen to make it attractive and a fit for me? What market, technology, competitive, management, and financial risks can be reduced or eliminated? What can be changed to make this happen? Who can change it? What are the

EXHIBIT 2.5   The Timmons Model of the Entrepreneurial Process

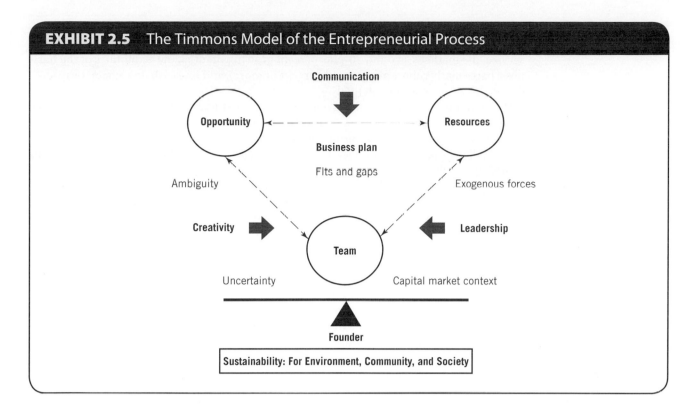

least resources necessary to grow the business the farthest? Is this the right team? By implication, if you can determine these answers and make the necessary changes by figuring out how to fill the gaps and improve the fit and attract key players who can add such value, then the odds for success rise significantly. In essence, the entrepreneur's role is to manage and redefine the risk–reward equation—all with an eye towards **sustainability**. Since part of the entrepreneur's legacy is to create positive impact without harming the environment, the community, or society, the concept of sustainability appears as the underlying foundation in the model.

The Opportunity   At the heart of the process is the opportunity. Successful entrepreneurs and investors know that a good idea is not necessarily a good opportunity. For every 100 ideas presented to investors in the form of a business plan or proposal, usually fewer than four get funded. More than 80 percent of those rejections occur in the first few hours; another 10 to 15 percent are rejected after investors have read the business plan carefully. Less than 10 percent attract enough interest to merit a more thorough review; that due diligence can take several weeks or months. These are very slim odds. Countless hours and days have been wasted by would-be entrepreneurs chasing ideas that are going nowhere. An important skill for an entrepreneur or an investor is to be able to quickly evaluate whether serious potential exists, and to decide how much time and effort to invest. Many give the aspiring entrepreneur the advice to visit a bank to ask for a loan even if you do not need the money. The rigour of the assessment is worthwhile and often the banker delivers medicine that others cannot see or friends will not share.

One senior partner at a prominent venture capital fund asserted, "There's never been a better time than now to start a company. In the past, entrepreneurs started businesses. Today they invent new business models. That's a big difference, and it creates huge opportunities."[30] Even after a big stock market crash, when financing often dries up, those words still ring true. In fact, of those enterprises that started during the toughest times and survived, most go on to thrive.

Another venture capitalist stated, "After the irrational exuberance of the late 90s, it is again a great time to start a business. Venture capital is plentiful, valuations make sense and venture capitalists are anxious for high potential ventures."[31]

Exhibit 2.6 summarizes the most important characteristics of good opportunities. Underlying market demand—because of the value-added properties of the product or service, the market's size and 20-plus percent growth potential, the economics of the business, particularly robust margins (40 percent or more), and free cash flow characteristics—drives the value creation potential.

We build our understanding of opportunity by first focusing on market readiness: the consumer trends and behaviours that seek new products or services. Once these emerging patterns are identified, the aspiring entrepreneur develops a service or product concept and, finally, the service or product delivery system is conceived. We then ask the questions articulated in the exhibit.

These criteria will be described in more detail in Chapter 4 and can be applied to the search and evaluation of any opportunity. In short, the greater the growth, size, durability, and robustness of the gross and net margins and free cash flow, the greater the opportunity. The more *imperfect* the market, the greater the opportunity. The greater the rate of change, the discontinuities, and the chaos, the greater is the opportunity. The greater the inconsistencies in existing service and quality, in lead times and lag times, and the greater the vacuums and gaps in information and knowledge, the greater is the opportunity.

Resources: Creative and Parsimonious   One of the most common misconceptions among untried entrepreneurs is that you first need to have all the resources in place, especially the money, to succeed with a venture. Thinking money first is a big mistake. Money follows high potential opportunities conceived of and led by a strong management team. Investors have bemoaned for years that there is too much money chasing too few deals. Some insist that there is a shortage of quality entrepreneurs and opportunities, not money. Successful entrepreneurs devise ingeniously creative and stingy strategies to marshal and gain control of resources (Exhibit 2.7). Surprising as it may sound, investors and successful entrepreneurs often say one of the worst things that can happen to an entrepreneur is to have *too much money too early*. This flies contrary to the most common advice from entrepreneurs: Get enough capital; then get some more.[32] These seemingly clashing perspectives will be reconciled in due course.

EXHIBIT 2.6   The Entrepreneurial Process Is Opportunity Driven*

Market demand is a key ingredient to measuring an opportunity:
- Is customer payback less than one year?
- Do market share and growth potential equal 20 percent annual growth and is it durable?
- Is the customer reachable?

Market structure and size help define an opportunity:
- Emerging and/or fragmented?
- $50 million or more, with a $1 billion potential?
- Proprietary barriers to entry?

Margin analysis helps differentiate an opportunity from an idea:
- Low cost provider (40 percent gross margin)?
- Low capital requirement versus the competition?
- Break even in 1–2 years?
- Value added increase of overall corporate P/E ratio?

*Durability of an opportunity is a widely misunderstood concept. In entrepreneurship, durability exists when the investor gets his or her money back plus a market or better return on investment.

EXHIBIT 2.7   Understand and Marshal Resources, Don't Be Driven by Them

"Bootstrapping"

Minimize and **Control**
versus
Maximize and **Own**

Resources

Relationships

Unleashing creativity

Financial resources
Assets
People   Think cash last!
Your business plan

Howard Head is a wonderful example of succeeding with few resources. He developed the first laminate, metal-edged ski, which became the market leader, and then the oversize Prince tennis racket—developing two totally unrelated technologies is a rare feat. Head left his job at a large aircraft manufacturer during World War II and worked in his garage on a shoestring budget to create the modern ski. It took more than 40 iterations before he developed a ski that worked and could be marketed. He insisted that one of the biggest reasons he finally succeeded is that he had so little money. He argued that if he had complete financing he would have blown it all long before he evolved the ski into something that weighed half as much as solid wood skis and had better performance. Within a few years the Head Ski company was making the majority of skis in use. The company went on to diversify into tennis and other racquet sports and manufactured an aluminium honeycomb tennis racquet. Howard Head sold his venture and retired. Head played more tennis in retirement with the aid of a tennis ball machine (built by Prince Manufacturing). Howard Head became the majority shareholder and chairman of the board of Prince. While he worked to improve the ball machine, his own game of tennis never got better. He went on to patent the oversize racquet and develop graphite composites—changing the game of tennis forever.[33]

Bootstrapping is a way of life in entrepreneurial companies and can create a significant competitive advantage. Doing more with less is a powerful competitive weapon. The necessary approach is to minimize and control the resources, not necessarily own them. Whether it is assets for the business, key people, the business plan, or start-up and growth capital, many successful entrepreneurs *think cash last*. Such strategies encourage a discipline of leanness, where everyone knows that every dollar counts, and the principle "conserve your equity" becomes a way of maximizing shareholder value.

The Entrepreneurial Team   There is little dispute today that the entrepreneurial team is a key ingredient in the higher potential venture. Investors are captivated "by the creative brilliance of a company's head entrepreneur. . . and bet on the superb track records of the management team working as a group."[34] French-born Georges Doriot's dictum was: I prefer a grade A entrepreneur and team with a grade B idea, over a grade B team with a grade A idea. "In the world today, there's plenty of technology, plenty of entrepreneurs, plenty of money, plenty of venture capital. What's in short supply is great teams. Your biggest challenge will be building a great team."[35]

"If you can find good people, they can always change the product. Nearly every mistake I've made has been I picked the wrong people, not the wrong idea."[36] Finally, as we noted earlier, ventures with more than 20 employees and $2 million to $3 million in sales are much more likely to survive and prosper than smaller ventures. In the vast majority of cases, it is very difficult to grow beyond this without a team of two or more key contributors.

Clearly, a new venture requires a lead entrepreneur that has personal characteristics described in Exhibit 2.8. But the high potential venture also requires interpersonal skills to foster communications and, therefore, team building.

EXHIBIT 2.8   An Entrepreneurial Team Is a Critical Ingredient for Success

An entrepreneurial leader
- Learns and teaches—faster, better
- Deals with adversity, is resilient
- Exhibits integrity, dependability, honesty
- Builds entrepreneurial culture and organization

Quality of the team
- Relevant experience and track record
- Motivation to excel
- Commitment, determination, and persistence
- Tolerance of risk, ambiguity, and uncertainty
- Creativity
- Team locus of control
- Adaptability
- Opportunity obsession
- Leadership and courage
- Communication

Team

"Passion"

Exhibit 2.8 summarizes the important aspects of the team. These teams invariably are formed and led by a very capable entrepreneurial leader whose track record exhibits both accomplishments and several qualities that the team must possess. A pacesetter and culture creator, the lead entrepreneur is central to the team as both a player and a coach. The ability and skill in attracting other key management members and then building the team is one of the most valued capabilities investors look for. The founder who becomes the leader does so by building heroes in the team. A leader adapts a philosophy that rewards success and supports honest failure, shares the wealth with those who help create it, and sets high standards for both performance and conduct. We will examine in detail the entrepreneurial leader and the new venture team in Chapters 5 and 6.

Importance of Fit and Balance   Rounding out the model of the three driving forces is the concept of fit and balance between and among these forces. Note that the team is positioned at the bottom of the triangle in the Timmons Model (Exhibit 2.5). Imagine the founder, the entrepreneurial leader of the venture, standing on a large ball, balancing the triangle over her head. This imagery is helpful in appreciating the constant balancing act since opportunity, team, and resources rarely match. When envisioning a company's future, the entrepreneur asks: What pitfalls will I encounter to get to the next boundary of success? Will my current team be large enough, or will we be over our heads if the company grows 30 percent over the next two years? Are my resources sufficient (or too abundant)? Vivid examples of the failure to maintain a balance are everywhere, such as when large companies throw too many resources at a weak, poorly defined opportunity. For example, Lucent Technologies' misplaced assumption and slowness to react to bandwidth demand resulted in an almost 90-percent reduction in market capitalization.

Exhibit 2.9 shows how this balancing act evolved for Mitel from inception through the initial public offering to British Telecom's purchase and later sell-off. While the drawings oversimplify these incredibly complex events, they help us to think conceptually—an important entrepreneurial talent—about the company building process, including the strategic and managerial implications of striving to achieve balance and the inevitable fragility of the process.

A telephony tone receiver was Mitel's first product to hit the market. Following Michael Cowpland's and Terry Matthews' success with the tone receiver, the founders saw the potential of microprocessors to revolutionize telephone equipment. The opportunities were huge in this rapidly growing field and they quickly expanded into semiconductors. Though short on significant capital or other resources, the team had big ideas. Such a mismatch of ideas, resources, and talent could quickly topple out of the founder's control and fall into the hands of someone who could turn it into a real opportunity. Visually, the process can be appreciated as a constant balancing act, requiring continual assessment, revised strategies and tactics, an experimental approach. By addressing the types of questions necessary to shape the opportunity, the resources, and the team, the founder begins to mould the idea into an opportunity, and the opportunity into a business, just as you would mould clay from a shapeless form into a piece of artwork.

At the outset, founders Michael Cowpland and Terry Matthews would have seen something like the first figure, Exhibit 2.9(a), with the huge opportunity far outweighing the team and resources. The gaps were major. Seeing the size and potential of the opportunity they were able to double in size every year for quite a few years. With great faith and many promises they knew they could fill the resource gaps and build the team, both with inside management and outside directors. This new balance in Exhibit 2.9(b) creates a justifiable investment. The opportunity is still huge and growing, and competitors are inevitable (see Exhibit 2.9(c)). To fully exploit this opportunity, attract a large and highly talented group of managers and professionals, and create even greater financial strength than competitors, an influx of cash is often necessary. British Telecom purchased a controlling 51 percent of Mitel in 1985 and Cowpland and Matthews were out. Strategic investors can greatly enhance the balance of the driving forces. Strategic investors, or partners, are defined as those who can fill gaps left by other members of the team. They create balance where imbalance exists. The role of the strategic investor differs according to the needs of a venture. In 1990 British Telecom started looking for a buyer for their 'investment.' In 1992 Schroeders Ventures stepped in and bought out British Telecom. In 2001 Mitel was split in two. The PBX division and the company name were sold back to Terry Matthews; the semiconductor division was given the name Zarlink.

Mitel emerged (see Exhibit 2.9(d)) larger and stronger in people and resources but faced new challenges. Even the best and brightest of new ventures tend to erode over three or more decades into slow-moving, reactive firms. Could Mitel sustain and reinvent its entrepreneurial roots and organization as the opportunity continued to mushroom and competition for markets, people, and technology were greater than ever? Would it become blindsided and eclipsed by a new disruptive technology? It hoped that its merger with Inter-Tel and partnership with Sun Microsystems would take it in the right direction.

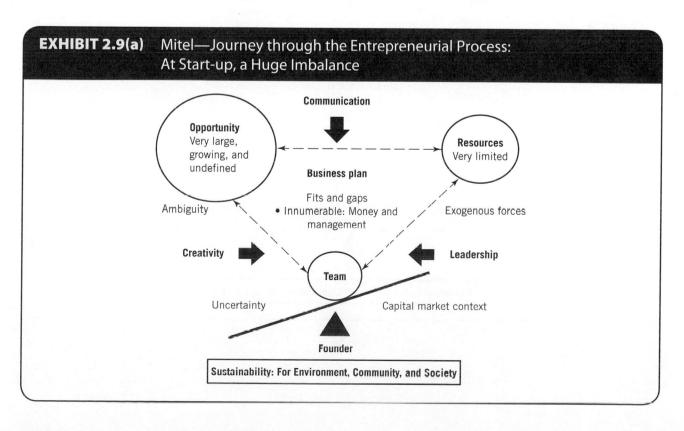

EXHIBIT 2.9(a) Mitel—Journey through the Entrepreneurial Process: At Start-up, a Huge Imbalance

EXHIBIT 2.9(b)   Mitel—Journey through the Entrepreneurial Process:
At IPO, toward a New Balance

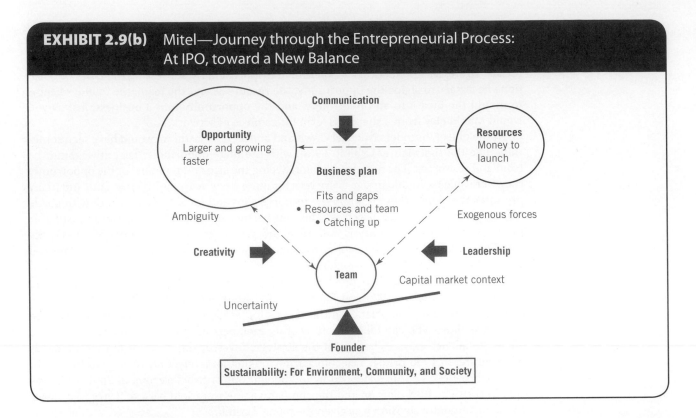

EXHIBIT 2.9(c)   Mitel—Journey through the Entrepreneurial Process:
British Telecom Steps In (and Then Out), a New Balance

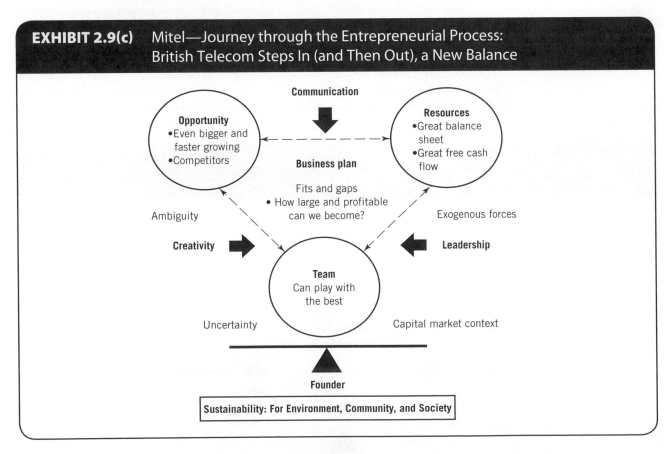

EXHIBIT 2.9(d) Mitel—Journey through the Entrepreneurial Process: Merger with Inter-Tel, a New Imbalance

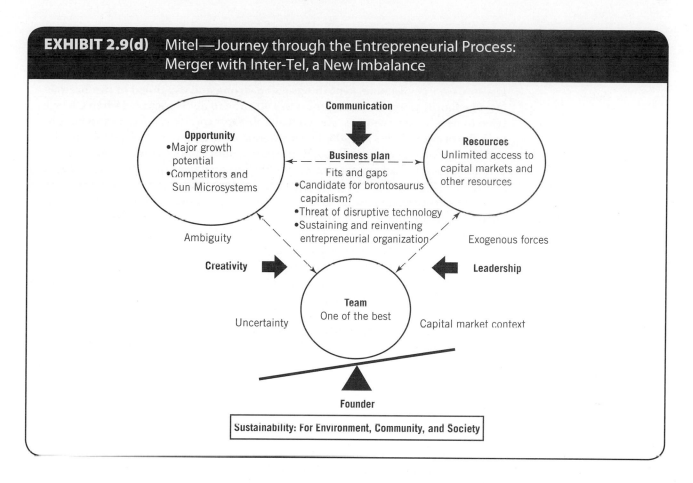

This iterative entrepreneurial process is based on both logic and trial and error. It is both intuitive and consciously planned. It is a process not unlike what the Wright brothers originally engaged in while creating the first self-propelled airplane. They conducted more than 1,000 glider flights before succeeding. These trial-and-error experiments led to the new knowledge, skills, and insights needed to actually fly. Entrepreneurs have similar learning curves.

The fit issue can be appreciated in terms of a question: This is a fabulous opportunity, but for whom? Some of the most successful investments ever were turned down by numerous investors before the founders received financial backing. And even if investors remain elusive, alternatives include licensing and franchising to fuel growth. Time and again, there can be a mismatch between the type of business and investors, the chemistry between founders and backers, or a multitude of other factors that cause a rejection. Thus, how the unique combination of people, opportunity, and resources come together at a particular time may determine a venture's ultimate chance for success.

The potential for attracting outside funding for a proposed venture depends on this overall fit and how the investor believes he or she can add value to this fit and improve the fit, risk–reward ratio, and odds for success. Exhibit 1.11 in the previous chapter shows the possible outcome.

Importance of Timing Equally important is the timing of the entrepreneurial process. Each of these unique combinations occurs in real time, where the hourglass drains continually and may be friend, foe, or both. Decisiveness in recognizing and seizing the opportunity can make all the difference. Don't wait for the perfect time to take advantage of an opportunity; there is no perfect time. Most new businesses run out of money before they can find enough customers and the right team for their great idea. Opportunity is a moving target.

Beer: It Must Be in the Sleeman Family Blood

John H. Sleeman had been brewing beer in Canada since immigrating in 1834. His son, George Sleeman, kept things going strong and expanded to two breweries. The family then lost the business in 1902 due to debts incurred when George tried to develop a streetcar system in Guelph, Ontario. He recovered and bought back the brewery assets in 1906. The temperance movement put a hamper on sales and George Sleeman's sons began delivering product to the United States during prohibition—they got caught and the family business was forced to close in 1933.

John W. Sleeman, great-great grandson of John H. Sleeman, got married in England and returned home to Canada and fought government regulations to become a major importer of British pub beers.[37] He subsequently took a risk and imported inexpensive American beer just as a strike broke out among the Canadian brewers; John W. Sleeman recalled, "We were rewarded with so much cash we needed police escorts to make bank deposits." A few years passed and in 1988, John W. Sleeman, four generations removed from John H. Sleeman brewed his first beer. The company went public in 1996 on the TSX and made its first acquisition—Okanagan Spring Brewery. Sleeman followed by acquiring Upper Canada Brewery in 1998, Maritime Brewing in 2000, and both Shaftsbury Brewing and Unibroue in 2004. In 2006 John W. Sleeman put the enterprise up for sale and Sapporo Breweries of Japan took ownership of his namesake for $400 million and promised to keep him on as CEO for at least a handful of years.

Recent Research Supports the Model

The Timmons Model evolved from Jeffry Timmons' doctoral dissertation research at the Harvard Business School, about new and growing ventures. Over nearly four decades, the model has evolved and been enhanced by ongoing research, case development, teaching, and experience in high potential ventures and venture capital funds. The fundamental components of the model have not changed, but their richness and relationships of each to the whole have been steadily enhanced as they have become better understood. Numerous other researchers have examined a wide range of topics in entrepreneurship and new venture creation. The bottom line is that the model, in its simple elegance and dynamic richness, harnesses what you need to know about the entrepreneurial process in order to get the odds in your favour. As each of the chapters and accompanying cases, exercises, and issues expand on the process, addressing individual dimensions, a detailed framework with explicit criteria will emerge. If you engage this material fully, you cannot help but improve your chances of success.

A research effort focused on 906 high growth companies provides important benchmarks of the practices in a diverse group of industries.[38]

Most significantly, these results reconfirm the importance of the model and its principles: the team, the market opportunity, the resource strategies, most of the individual criteria, the concept of fit and balance, and the holistic approach to entrepreneurship.

Exhibit 2.10 summarizes the 26 leading practices identified in four key areas: marketing, finance, management, and planning.

EXHIBIT 2.10   Leading Practices

Leading marketing practices of fast growth firms

- Deliver products and services that are perceived as highest quality to expanding segments.

- Cultivate pacesetting new products and services that stand out in the market as best of the breed.

- Deliver product and service benefits that demand average or higher market pricing.

- Generate revenue flows from existing products and services that typically sustain approximately 90 percent of the present revenue base, while achieving flows from new products and services that typically expand revenue approximately 20 percent annually.

- Generate revenue flows from existing customers that typically sustain approximately 80 percent of the ongoing revenue base, while achieving flows from new customers that typically expand revenue flows by about 30 percent annually.

- Create high impact, new product and service improvements with development expenditures that typically account for no more than approximately 6 percent of revenues.

- Utilize a high yield sales force that typically accounts for approximately 60 percent of marketing expenditures.

- Rapidly develop broad product and service platforms with complementary channels to help expand a firm's geographic marketing area.

Leading financial practices of fast growth firms

- Anticipate multiple rounds of financing (on average every 2.5 years).

- Secure funding sources capable of significantly expanding their participation amounts.

- Utilize financing vehicles that retain the entrepreneur's voting control.

- Maintain control of the firm by selectively granting employee stock ownership.

- Link the entrepreneur's long-term objectives to a defined exit strategy in the business plan.

Leading management practices of fast growth firms

- Use a collaborative decision-making style with the top management team.

- Accelerate organizational development by assembling a balanced top management team with or without prior experience of working together.

- Develop a top management team of three to six individuals with the capacity to become the entrepreneur's entrepreneurs. Align the number of management levels with the number of individuals in top management.

- Establish entrepreneurial competency first in the functional areas of finance, marketing, and operations. Assemble a balanced board of directors comprised of both internal and external directors.

- Repeatedly calibrate strategies with regular board of directors meetings.

- Involve the board of directors heavily at strategic inflection points.

Leading planning practices of fast growth firms

- Prepare detailed written monthly plans for each of the next 12 to 24 months and annual plans for three or more years.

- Establish functional planning and control systems that tie planned achievements to actual performance and adjust management compensation accordingly.

- Periodically share with employees the planned versus actual performance data directly linked to the business plan.

- Link job performance standards that have been jointly set by management and employees to the business plan.

- Prospectively model the firm based on benchmarks that exceed industry norms, competitors, and the industry leader.

Chapter Summary

1. We began to demystify entrepreneurship by examining its classic start-up definition and a broader, holistic way of thinking, reasoning, and acting that is opportunity obsessed and leadership balanced.

2. Entrepreneurship has many metaphors and poses many paradoxes.

3. Getting the odds in your favour is the entrepreneur's perpetual challenge.

4. Thinking big enough can improve the odds significantly. Higher potential ventures are sought by successful entrepreneurs, venture capitalists, and private investors.

5. The Timmons Model is at the heart of spotting and building the higher potential venture and understanding its three driving forces: the team, opportunity, and resources. The concept of fit and balance is crucial.

6. Research on entrepreneurs and their fast-growth ventures adds validity to the model.

Study Questions

1. Can you define what is meant by classic entrepreneurship and the high potential venture? Why and how are threshold concepts, cover your equity, bootstrapping of resources, fit, and balance important?

2. "People don't want to be managed, they want to be led." Explain what this means and its importance and implications for developing your own style and leadership philosophy.

3. What are the most important determinants of success and failure in new businesses? Who has the best and worst chances for success, and why?

4. What are the most important things you can do to get the odds in your favour?

5. What criteria and characteristics do high growth entrepreneurs, venture capitalists, and private investors seek in evaluating business opportunities? How can these make a difference?

6. Define and explain the Timmons Model. Apply it and graphically depict, as in the Mitel example, the first five years or so of a new company with which you are familiar.

7. What are the most important skills, values, talents, abilities, and mind-sets one needs to cultivate as an entrepreneur?

Mind Stretchers   *Have you considered?*

1. Who can be an entrepreneur? When?

2. More than 80 percent of entrepreneurs learn the critical skills they need after age 21. What does this mean for you?

3. In your lifetime, the odds are that leading firms today such as Sony, Research In Motion, Apple, Air Canada, McDonald's, and the Gap will be knocked off by upstarts. How can this happen? Why does it present an opportunity, and for whom?

4. What do you need to be doing now, and in the next 12 months, to get the odds in your favour?

5. List 20 ideas and then pick out the best two that might be an opportunity. How can these become opportunities? Who can make them opportunities?

6. How many different ways can a new venture go off the tracks?

EXERCISE   Visit with an Entrepreneur and Create a Lifelong Learning Log

Through an interview with entrepreneurs who have, within the past 5 to 10 years, started firms with significant growth and are profitable, you can gain insight into an entrepreneur's reasons, strategies, approaches, and motivations for starting and owning a business. Gathering information through interviewing is a valuable skill to practise. You can learn a great deal in a short time through interviewing if you prepare thoughtfully and thoroughly.

The Visit with an Entrepreneur Exercise has helped students interview successful entrepreneurs. While there is no right way to structure an interview, the format in this exercise has been tested successfully on many occasions. A breakfast, lunch, or dinner meeting is often an excellent vehicle.

Select two entrepreneurs and businesses about which you would like to learn. This could be someone you see as an example or role model to which you aspire, or which you know the least about but are eager to learn. Interview at least two entrepreneurs with differing experiences, such as a high potential (e.g., $5 million revenue plus) and a lifestyle business (usually much smaller, but not necessarily).

Create a Lifelong Learning Log

Create a computer file or acquire a notebook or binder in which you record your goals, triumphs and disappointments, and lessons learned. This can be done as key events happen or on some other frequent basis. You might make entries during times of crisis and at year's end to sum up what you accomplished and your new goals. The record of personal insights, observations, and lessons learned can provide valuable anchors during times of difficult decisions as well as interesting reading—for you at least.

A Visit with an Entrepreneur

Step 1   Contact the person you have selected and make an appointment.

Be sure to explain why you want the appointment and to give a realistic estimate of how much time you will need.

Step 2   Identify specific questions you would like to have answered and the general areas about which you would like information. (See The Interview in STEP 3.)

Using a combination of open-end questions, such as general questions about how the entrepreneur got started, what happened next, and so forth, and closed-end questions, such as specific questions about what his or her goals were, if he or she had to find partners, and so forth, will help keep the interview focused and yet allow for unexpected comments and insights.

Step 3   Conduct the interview.

Recording this interview on audiotape can be helpful and is recommended unless you or the person being interviewed objects. Remember, too, that you most likely will learn more if you are an interested listener.

The Interview

Questions for Gathering Information

- Would you tell me about yourself before you started your first venture?

  Who else did you know while you were growing up who had started or owned a business, and how did they influence you? Anyone later, after you were 21 years old?

  Were your parents, relatives, or close friends entrepreneurial? How so?

  Did you have role models?

  What was your education/military experience? In hindsight, was it helpful? In what specific ways?

  Did you have a business or self-employment during your youth?

  In particular, did you have any sales or marketing experience? How important was it, or a lack of it, to starting your company?

  When, under what circumstances, and from whom did you become interested in entrepreneurship and learn some of the critical lessons?

- Describe how you decided to create a job by starting your venture instead of taking a job with someone else.

  How did you spot the opportunity? How did it surface?

  What were your goals? What were your lifestyle needs or other personal requirements? How did you fit these together?

  How did you evaluate the opportunity in terms of the critical elements for success? The competition? The market? Did you have specific criteria you wanted to meet?

  Did you find or have partners? What kind of planning did you do? What kind of financing did you have?

  Did you have a start-up business plan of any kind? Please tell me about it.

  How much time did it take from conception to the first day of business? How many hours a day did you spend working on it?

  How much capital did it take? How long did it take to reach a positive cash flow and break-even sales volume? If you did not have enough money at the time, what were some ways in which you bootstrapped the venture (bartering, borrowing, and the like)? Tell me about the pressures and crises during that early survival period.

  What outside help did you get? Did you have experienced advisors? lawyers? accountants? tax experts? patent experts? How did you develop these networks and how long did it take?

How did any outside advisors make a difference in your company?

What was your family situation at the time?

What did you perceive to be the strengths of your venture? Weaknesses?

What was your most triumphant moment? Your worst moment?

Did you want to have partners or do it solo? Why?

- Once you got going:

  What were the most difficult gaps to fill and problems to solve as you began to grow rapidly?

  When you looked for key people as partners, advisors, or managers, were there any personal attributes or attitudes you were particularly seeking because you knew they would fit with you and were important to success? How did you find them?

  Are there any attributes among partners and advisors that you would definitely try to avoid?

  Have things become more predictable? Or less?

  Do you spend more time, the same amount of time, or less time with your business now than in the early years?

  Do you feel more managerial and less entrepreneurial now?

  In terms of the future, do you plan to harvest? To maintain? To expand?

  In your ideal world, how many days a year would you want to work? Please explain.

  Do you plan ever to retire? Would you explain?

  Have your goals changed? Have you met them?

  Has your family situation changed?

  What do you learn from both success and failure?

  What were/are the most demanding conflicts or trade-offs you face (e.g., the business versus personal hobbies or a relationship, children, etc.)?

  Describe a time you ran out of cash, what pressures this created for you, the business, your family, and what you did about it. What lessons were learned?

  Can you describe a venture that did not work out for you and how this prepared you for your next venture?

Questions for Concluding

- What do you consider your most valuable asset, the thing that enabled you to make it?

- If you had it to do over again, would you do it again, in the same way?

- As you look back, what do you believe are the most critical concepts, skills, attitudes, and know-how you needed to get your company started and grown to where it is today? What will be needed for the next five years? To what extent can any of these be learned?

- Some people say there is a lot of stress being an entrepreneur. What have you experienced? How would you say it compares with other "hot seat" jobs, such as the head of a big company, or a partner in a large law or accounting firm?

- What things do you find personally rewarding and satisfying as an entrepreneur? What have been the rewards, risks, and trade-offs?

- Who should try to be an entrepreneur? And who should not?

- What advice would you give an aspiring entrepreneur? Could you suggest the three most important lessons you have learned? How can I learn them while minimizing the tuition?

- Would you suggest any other entrepreneur I should talk to?

- Are there any other questions you wished I had asked, from which you think I could learn valuable lessons?

Step 4   Evaluate what you have learned.

Summarize the most important observations and insights you have gathered from these interviews. Contrast especially what patterns, differences, and similarities exist between lifestyle and high potential entrepreneurs. Who can be an entrepreneur? What surprised you the most? What was confirmed about entrepreneurship? What new insights emerged? What are the implications for you personally, your goals, career aspirations?

Step 5   Write a thank you note.

This is more than a courtesy; it will also help the entrepreneur remember you favourably should you want to follow up on the interview.

CASE   SHOEGURU.CA

Preparation Questions

1. What items or options can ShoeGuru provide in the proposal to attract the distributor?
2. How can ShoeGuru convince the distributor that it has the ability to be an effective partner?
3. Does ShoeGuru and its model provide any sustainable competitive advantage that would be hard to recreate by competitors? Does ShoeGuru have any competitive disadvantages with its model?

Introduction

It was a regular afternoon at the college. Tom Jablonski set up his PowerPoint presentation quietly in a computer lab. Tom had a new business proposal for his company and wanted to gain some insight from professors at the college before pursuing it. He found that the growth of his company was slowing and was essentially limited by his current situation. Business could not continue this way and something needed to change. A solution Tom thought up was that rather than having his company, ShoeGuru, responsible for shipping to customers, he would ask the distributor to take care of shipping for him. This would allow Tom to focus on the global market and pursue the desired growth opportunities for his company. He felt that this proposal would be advantageous for both parties; ShoeGuru could increase its revenue due to the removal of inventory constraints and his distributor would benefit by selling more shoes. Was there enough trust for Tom to convince his distributor to accept this proposal? Could Tom, a college student, really offer that much benefit to a large distributor?

Tom and ShoeGuru

Tom was in his second year of commerce at an Edmonton college. Tom was also an avid entrepreneur, and current owner and operator of ShoeGuru.ca. He entered the world of online sales with visions of opportunities. He found a distributor in the United States that had fashionable English sporting shoes and decided to start up his company, ShoeGuru, selling these shoes online. He had never actually met in person with his current distributor. His distributor was unaware of his age and the fact that he was still a student in college. All contact between the two parties had been made over the phone and the Internet. Tom viewed this as an advantage because it gave him the opportunity to establish himself as a serious businessperson and to be taken seriously—rather than as just a student.

Tom started ShoeGuru during his first year at the college. With a bit of financial support from his dad and some Web site design help from his friends, he opened a business selling shoes targeting men on the Internet. Tom was not your average student at the college; while other students focused on studying and living the college life, Tom devoted his time to an entrepreneurial aspiration to make money. Most students chose to finish their education before pursuing such endeavours, but not Tom. He is greatly enticed by the many different opportunities that exist in the world of business and feels it would be a waste not to get a head start. A close friend

of Tom's is involved in the online car import business. Tom actively observed many of his friend's successes and saw a clear opportunity that existed in the area of online shopping.

ShoeGuru and the Online Market

ShoeGuru was a self-managed online company specializing in the sale of fashionable men's footwear. Since launching his Web site ShoeGuru.ca, in July 2007, Tom had already been nominated in the category of "top 20 e-commerce Web site designs" by www.tutorialblog.org. With the help of a local Web designer Tom was able to develop an interactive Web site where the shoes featured were positioned and displayed in different environments rather than the common white, one dimensional background. Online shoppers could not only see the shoe, but could flip it around and look at it from different angles and views giving them a better idea of the styles and specific features of each individual shoe. Tom's success had been built on ShoeGuru's customer service, quality of products, free shipping within Canada, and low competitive pricing worldwide.

It has been predicted by many that sales in online shopping would more than double in the next five years. Tom recollected reading a global Internet survey that concluded that online consumers spend 15 percent of their total shopping dollars on the online market, and that this number would jump to 36 percent in the next three years. People were becoming more amenable to purchasing products and services online. In addition, the Internet market's growth had been attributed to increased security measures. Payment methods such as PayPal had added very secure means for online payments. This payment system was readily available for use by many different online vendors. ShoeGuru was one of the many Web sites that chose to use PayPal for secure payment transactions. As the online shopping market grew, so had methods of online marketing and advertising. In recent years online advertising had developed rapidly, helping to target consumers with interests in certain products. With essentially free methods of storage and data transferring, online companies found fewer constraints to enter the market.

Some of the major companies that existed on the Internet took full advantage of the online market. By eliminating the physical store from the shopping equation they were able to offer lower prices. The main concept held by them was that if they could offer products for cheaper prices on the Internet, people would be more attracted to buy online. The customers they were trying to attract were the people who wanted to save money. These store Web sites often consisted of a crowded

This case was written by Gordon Lucyk and Daniel Mireault (both of Grant MacEwan University) for purposes of classroom discussion.

layout. They were "busy," containing many smaller images that they hoped would catch the average Internet user's eyes. Most Web sites had a relatively standard design and Tom believed that there was not one shoe site that really stood out from the rest. This standard design divided the site into a men's section, women's section, and sometimes a children's section. Most of these companies had large inventories and tried to position themselves in Google's search engines to receive high amounts of traffic. Tom thought that one of the main customers these companies were not supplying was the person who sought the shopping experience; going to the store, holding the shoe and seeing how it may look on them. Could this type of shopper be attracted to online shopping? One of the biggest fears with buying clothing and accessories online was that they wouldn't fit. The aforementioned survey also suggested that another reason consumers worry most about online shopping was high shipping costs. Could there be a supplier in the market that could overcome these worries and convince more shoppers into buying wearable merchandise? Tom felt there was and wanted to develop his business around these ideas. ShoeGuru made it very clear on their Web site that customers should feel free to contact Tom about any concerns relating to fit or other specific details.

SHOEGURU.CA WEB SITE

We here at ShoeGuru believe that shoes should be both comfortable and fashionable. That is why we shop the world for the most modern and conventional fashions to make your feet both look and feel good. Unlike other stores we offer a variety of services to help our customers find what they're looking for through more interactive methods. With our Fashion Weekly section, customers can see and get a feel for the products before they buy, through photos, reviews and much more.

ShoeGuru thrives on customer satisfaction and if you have any questions concerns or even want some advice, please feel free to contact our shoe experts. We stand behind every item we sell and inspect everything to make sure that it is of the highest quality. We are very confident that we can cater to your fashion footwear needs and hope to do business with you very soon.

Was online shopping really that different from shopping at the mall? Tom believed that most malls had two common types of stores; the discount store where you go to save money, and the store where you go to find the latest trends. The stores where you go to save money were usually larger, dull, and had lots of products. The customer service you received at a store like this was usually minimal. The trendy stores offered an upscale atmosphere, mannequins, and tried to offer a better customer experience. The customer service was usually much greater at these stores and sometimes the sales associates would even offer an opinion on how the products look. One of the main focuses of ShoeGuru's Web site was to recreate the same atmosphere that you got from going to a trendy store into an online format.

In Tom's opinion, ShoeGuru offered a superior Web layout than its competitors. They not only wanted to sell shoes, they also wanted to offer a shopping experience. They followed the concept of what a customer would experience in going to the mall. Tom felt that the trendier the store looked, the more likely you were to check it out. Currently ShoeGuru did minimal advertising, as their Web layout alone attracted enough

potential buyers. ShoeGuru hoped to use advertising such as AdWords by Google in the future. This would offer the potential for millions of online consumers to be directed to their Web site whenever searches relating to shoes were placed on Google. It would allow them to narrow in on their target market and select search terms they wanted to be associated with, such as "men's shoes" or "fashionable footwear." ShoeGuru was currently being published in a book on "1,000 best Web designs of the year," and had a feature article in an issue of the online magazine ImportOnly. Tom was striving to take the Internet shopping experience to the next level by treating customers as individuals with specific needs. He wanted to develop real-life advertising that provided the shopper with the ability to get an accurate perspective of the product. He wanted to attract more than just the customer who thinks prices are cheaper on the Internet. He wanted to attract the customer looking for the latest trends.

In pursuing these fashionable markets Tom also saw great potential in the global market. A main benefit from being an online company was that the seller was essentially connected to the world market. ShoeGuru had staff that spoke three languages fluently, and many of ShoeGuru's sales were currently to customers in European countries. The fashionable men's footwear sector showed potential for strong European market growth. Tom thought that with proper research on the global market, expansion could truly be remarkable for a company that possessed the ability to supply it. ShoeGuru hoped to gain the ability to access these markets as well as local markets more effectively and efficiently.

ShoeGuru and Basement Inventory

ShoeGuru's business idea of where it wanted to be was pretty much established; the uncertainty lay in how it would get there. Tom currently found himself operating his business from his basement. The shoe inventory in his basement was something he was tired of being surrounded by. Inventory was also a huge limiting factor for Tom right now. Tom currently had to carefully select what he was going to order from the distributor to make sure it sold well. If the shoes he selected did not have a fast turnover rate, inventory accumulation became excessive, and his working capital became a concern. This prevented him from ordering new products and staying up to date with current trends.

As inventory has accumulated, Tom has reduced his selection of items and has removed product descriptions from his Web site, leaving blank spaces. These spaces have in part developed as a result of Tom struggle with inventory. The benefits gained by having his basement full of shoes are no longer worth it for him. Tom is tired of being constrained by the lack of new inventory. Many growth opportunities exist in markets all over the world if he could just overcome the problems of inventory.

Tom felt the need to change his supply model in order to move forward. He has considered many different alternatives in expanding his company in order to make it more profitable. One idea considered was finding inventory space in which he could store the shoes. He could rent or buy a large space and keep all his shipments of shoes in it until he shipped them to the customer. This idea would work but the costs of implementing it would be quite high. Organizing and maintaining the warehouse, as well as tracking shoe inventory would provide a new level of complexity, as well as a new level of cost. Another idea considered was to find a warehouse on the U.S. side of the border that could simplify the process. Instead of shipping the shoes from the U.S. into Canada, Tom could have the shoes shipped to a central location. Shipping across the border results in an extra expense; if Tom could reduce the amount of times his shoes had to cross borders he would be lowering his costs. The central location that would warehouse the shoes would result in an extra employee and also the costs of having a warehouse. Tom would have lowered expenses by eliminating double shipping, while increasing warehousing costs. This solution, like the previous ideas contemplated by Tom, was not all that attractive after he performed some analysis.

The next idea Tom came up with was to create a "drop-shipping" strategy in which the distributor took care of all the shipping. ShoeGuru simply would take the orders and relay them to the distributor to ship. This made a lot of sense because it allowed ShoeGuru to focus on the aspects of the business they were best at. They could focus on establishing their Web site, increasing their ad campaigns, and concentrate on taking care of their customers. By doing these three things Tom could establish a solid base and create the company he wanted ShoeGuru to be.

The first benefit Tom would gain would be to avoid the hassles of shipping. Every time Tom shipped a pair of shoes he had to receive the package from the distributor, open the package, check the package, re-seal the package, and then ship the package to the customer. By avoiding double shipping he could put more effort into other areas and simplify his business process. Double shipping held huge disadvantages for Tom. Crossing up to three borders every time a customer purchased a pair shoes was becoming expensive. Another benefit was that Tom could offer his customers a larger selection of products. He could do this without having to store a single pair of shoes in his basement. This thought alone made him very happy. Tom then began to realize the opportunities that existed in cost savings. He began to calculate that the price of shoes could be decreased by $30 to $40 per pair, which is a savings of nearly 20 to 30 percent for the consumer. The cost savings were huge. This gave ShoeGuru great leverage in setting their prices online. Tom believed the opportunities were endless; he could even add a section onto the Web site for women's shoes if he wanted. The selection of shoes Tom could offer would increase greatly, giving shoppers a variety of styles to choose from. Tom would also be able to stay up to date with all the current trends. The opportunities Tom would gain from a drop-shipping proposal would be tremendously advantageous.

The First Phone Call

Tom thought over his ideas about the drop-shipping possibility. He came to the conclusion that it was a great idea and he should pursue it. That same day he made a phone call to his distributor. He had become familiar with most of the people in the office of the distributor and thought that introducing the idea to them would be a good place to start. He called and talked to one of the representatives from the distributor. He explained the business idea to them and stated how much it could increase sales. The response they gave was neutral and the main concern they conveyed regarded return policy. The distributor stated that their biggest fear was having to deal with potential returns and phone calls from customers.

In the past, ShoeGuru had a very low rate of returns from their customers. In fact there was only one incident to date; Tom mixed up two pairs of shoes prior to mailing them. The incident actually had nothing to do with the customer being unsatisfied with the product. ShoeGuru currently offered a return policy in which they accepted shoes as long as the customer paid for return shipping. Tom felt this return policy was important in order to adhere to their customer-oriented service policy.

SHOEGURU.CA WEB SITE

Returns and Exchanges

Unworn merchandise may be returned for store credit or exchange. Merchandise must be returned within 30 days of purchase, in original packaging and in the same condition that it was received in. *Customer is responsible for all shipping costs.*

With this in mind, Tom felt confident he could take care of any returns that might occur. The proposed idea of the distributor shipping the shoes to customers still seemed good.

The Proposal

Tom now had to decide what he was going to do next. He decided that he should prepare a proposal that he would formally submit to the distributor. Tom started to prepare his proposal and was overcome by the many different questions that began to emerge. What items should the proposal include? How am I going to submit the proposal? When should I finish the proposal by?

The questions continued piling up. There were many different directions Tom could go with his proposal. He could offer the distributor a little more money to ship the shoes. The distributor would gain by selling more shoes and making more money. Was this enough though? Even if the distributor agreed would Tom be able to trust them to ship the shoes to his customers? Tom then thought he could create a shipping contract that was inversely related to volume. If Tom sold a small quantity of shoes from his Web site the distributor would collect a larger percentage of profit from Tom. If Tom sold large quantities of shoes the percentage collected would gradually go down. This would signal to the distributor that Tom was confident in his ability to sell large quantities of shoes and persuade the distributor to do business with him. Tom began to consider their relationship and realized both parties would have to work together to make the proposal a success. In exploring all this new information he decided to create a PowerPoint presentation and turn to a valuable resource he had for guidance; his instructors. Tom scheduled a meeting with instructors from the school's Negotiation, Supply Chain, Finance, and Accounting courses to deliver his primary pitch.

The October 10 Meeting

Tom set up his PowerPoint presentation quietly in a computer lab. Tom hoped to gain some valid insight, as the instructors possessed a great deal of experience and knowledge.

Tom presented his presentation to the instructors and explained his situation as in-depth as he could. He made sure everyone in the meeting had a clear understanding of his business process and continued by asking for some feedback. The first response he got was that the proposal seemed very good for ShoeGuru but lacked any incentive for a large distributor. Another response focused on the Internet side of things; was Tom aware of the threats that could result from having a Canadian Internet domain (www.ShoeGuru.ca)? If ShoeGuru was to expand into a larger Internet retailer, customers may expect a dot-com domain (www.ShoeGuru.com). If ShoeGuru did not have rights to this domain anybody could operate the domain. Anything from ladies fashion reports to foot-fetish pornography could come up with the click of a button. This dot-com domain could be important in the long run. Tom would have to look into purchasing the domain, which could be very costly. An example of the ShoeGuru.ca Web site has been included in Exhibit 1.

The next instructor asked how Tom was going to present his proposal. Would he present it in person or was email good enough? Also, when was his deadline? Tom was not sure if he really had a deadline.

The next idea that came up was the concept of trust. Could Tom trust the distributor to represent the ShoeGuru name? The ShoeGuru Web site contained a 5–10 day shipping policy that Tom felt was important in satisfying customers. Would the distributor adhere to some of the main values of Shoe-Guru, and if not was it still worthwhile to implement the drop-shipping policy? As complications continued to surface he realized there was still a lot to prepare for. The answers were certainly not coming as easily as he would have liked.

After the meeting he realized that he needed to review some fundamental issues. He questioned the relationship he had with the large distributor. Was the large distributor going to take him

seriously and take full responsibility for ShoeGuru's shipping? Could Tom maybe find another distributor that would be a better fit for him? Many distributors existed and maybe Tom was being unwise in only considering the first one he did business with.

Tom eventually concluded that business is about taking risks and decided to continue with his current distributor. Tom had many other things to review before making his next move on his proposed business solution, which was to call the main manager of the distributor and gain some more insight on the form his proposal should take.

The Second Phone Call and the Deadline

Tom sat at his kitchen table preparing what he was going to say in his next phone call. He reluctantly dialed the number of the distributor. The main manager of the distributor answered the phone. He and the manager began to talk about the proposal. The distributor said a written proposal would be fine as long as it included all the necessary details. A relative deadline was established, giving Tom a couple weeks to prepare. He was still left with a limited idea of what to include in the proposal.

Three days later Tom's cellphone rang; it was the manager from the distributor. The manager said he was going on a vacation and needed the proposal by the end of the week. This gave Tom less than three days to complete and submit the proposal. He struggled to balance some studying for a midterm he had

---

EXHIBIT 1   Browser shot of ShoeGuru.ca Web site

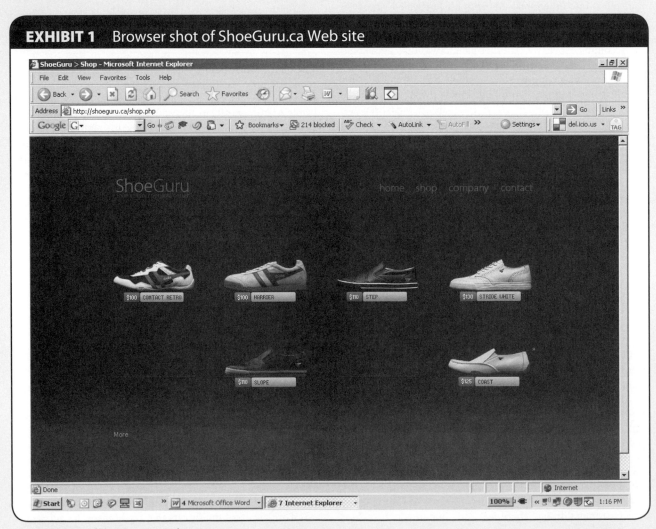

Source: Courtesy of ShoeGuru, www.shoeguru.ca.

the next day and began to compile a rough draft. After his class he went to get some last minute advice from a professor at the college. The professor gave Tom some guidelines to portray his proposal as mutually beneficial. He suggested a win–win approach would have to be present in order to be successful. In the previous meeting he mentioned that Tom made it sound like the distributor was doing him a favour. Tom needed to move away from that perception so that both parties would feel they were deriving benefit from the relationship.

Tom sat down and began to look at the advantages and disadvantages for ShoeGuru and his distributor. How could he construct this proposal to portray the mutual benefits each party would receive? ShoeGuru had a great chance to establish itself successfully in the online market. Tom didn't want to miss out on this opportunity. He was not sure if all the pieces were fitting together though. There were many things he might have been overlooking. He had never done anything like this before and was worried that he was rushing in too quickly. At the same time he was worried that he would miss his opportunity. Tom began typing his proposal.

What conditions did Tom need to include in making the proposal a success? Tom was not sure if he should emphasize the benefits to the distributor and just mention the benefits of ShoeGuru, or if he should emphasize all the benefits of the proposal. How was Tom going to achieve this win–win mentality? What was the distributor expecting from him? As Tom began to write his proposal he began to feel like an average college student. The reality was Tom actually was a college student. What could the large distributor really gain from doing business with a college student? The world of business was a large sea of competition and Tom felt like a small fish with a good idea.

Find more great exercises and additional study tools on the Online Learning Centre at
www.mcgrawhill.ca/olc/timmons

3

THE OPPORTUNITY: CREATING, SHAPING, RECOGNIZING, SEIZING

You miss 100 percent of the shots you don't take.

Wayne Gretzky

Upon completion of this chapter, you will be able to:

1. Appreciate the importance of thinking big enough.

2. Assess opportunity via a zoom lens on the criteria used by successful entrepreneurs, angels, and venture capital investors in evaluating potential ventures.

3. Describe how the most successful ventures track a "circle of ecstasy" and match investors' appetites in "the food chain" for ventures.

4. Differentiate between an idea and an opportunity.

5. Explain the role of ideas, pattern recognition, and the creative process in entrepreneurship.

6. Identify sources of information for finding and screening venture opportunities.

THINK BIG ENOUGH

Since its inception, *New Venture Creation* has attempted to inspire aspiring entrepreneurs to "think big enough." Time and again the authors have observed the classic small business owner who, almost like a dairy farmer, is enslaved by and wedded to the business. Extremely long hours of 70, 80, or even 100 hours a week, and rare vacations, are often the rule rather than the exception. And these hardworking owners rarely build equity, other than in the real estate they may own for the business. One of the big differences between the growth- and equity-minded entrepreneur and the traditional small business owners is that the entrepreneur thinks *bigger*. Patricia Cloherty puts it this way: "It is critical to think big enough. If you want to start and build a company, you are going to end up exhausted. So you might as well think about creating a BIG company. At least you will end up exhausted and *rich*, not just exhausted!"

Her theme of thinking bigger is embedded throughout this book. How can you engage in a "think big" process that takes you on a journey treading the fine line between high ambitions and being totally out of your mind? How do you know whether the idea you are chasing is a worthy endeavour or a waste of time and energy? You can never know which side of the line you are on—and can stay on—until you try and until you undertake the journey. This is not to say that being big is all that matters. A small business owner may judge their effort to be a success even if the business does not pass a certain size threshold. There are examples of firms that remained small by staying within their objectives and remaining true to their strengths, resources, and capabilities or were limited by the scope of the opportunity. Further, a lifestyle or hobby enterprise may satisfy the proprietor for many years despite low margins or revenues. But for those of you wanting more, the content in this book should provide a solid basis for reaching those goals!

OPPORTUNITY THROUGH A ZOOM LENS

Many many proposals to launch new companies are turned down by venture capital investors each year. The opportunity recognition process is complex, subtle, and situational (at the time, in the market space, in relation to the investor's other alternatives, etc.). If the brightest, most knowledgeable, and most sophisticated investors in the world miss good opportunities and occasionally hop on board with the losers, we can conclude that the journey from idea to high potential opportunity is illusive, contradictory, and perilous. Think of this journey as a race through varied terrain and weather conditions. At times, the journey consists of full sunshine and straight, smooth highways, as well as twisting, turning, narrow one-lane passages that can lead to breathtaking views. Along the way you also will unexpectedly encounter fog, hail storms, white-out conditions, and freezing rain. All too often you seem to run out of gas and obstacles and hold-ups come when you least expect them. This is the entrepreneur's journey. As Aydin Mirzaee put it, "You have to make every decision right every step of the way." One wrong move and you're done. If too much equity is doled out too quickly, later round investors won't hop on board.

Transforming Caterpillars into Butterflies

This chapter is dedicated to making that journey friendlier by focusing a zoom lens on the opportunity. It shares the road maps and benchmarks used by successful (and unsuccessful) entrepreneurs, venture capitalists, angels, and other private equity investors in their quest to transform the often amorphous, fuzzy idea into a spectacularly prosperous venture. These criteria comprise the core of their due diligence to ascertain the viability and profit potential of the proposed business, and therefore, the balance of risk and reward. It will examine the role of ideas and pattern recognition in the creative process of entrepreneurship.

You will come to see the criteria used to identify higher potential ventures as jumping-off points at this rarefied end of the opportunity continuum, rather than mere endpoints. One to 10 out of 100 entrepreneurs create ventures that separate themselves from the pack. Scrutinized through our lens, these ventures reveal a highly dynamic, constantly moulding, shaping, and changing work of art, rather than a product of a formula or a meeting of certain items on a checklist. This highly organic and situational character of the entrepreneurial process underscores the criticality of determining *fit* and balancing *risk and reward*. As the authors have argued for decades: The business plan is obsolete as soon as it comes off the printer! It is in this shaping process that the best entrepreneurial leaders and investors add the greatest value to the enterprise and creatively transform an idea into a venture.

New Venture Realities

It is useful to put the realities faced by countless entrepreneurs into perspective. Consider the following fundamental realities as normal as you seek to convert your amorphous idea into a successfully realized outcome:

New Ventures: Fundamental Realities

✓ Most new ventures are works in process and not works of art. What you start out to do is not what you end up doing.

✓ Most business plans are obsolete at the printer.

✓ Onset Venture Partners[1] found that 91 percent of portfolio companies that followed their business plans failed!

✓ Speed, adroitness of reflex, and adaptability are crucial. Keep your knees bent!

✓ The key to succeeding is failing quickly and recouping quickly, and keeping the tuition low.

✓ Success is highly situational, depending on time, space, context, and stakeholders.

✓ The best entrepreneurs specialize in making "new mistakes" only.

✓ Starting a company is a lot harder than it looks, or you think it will be; but you can last a lot longer and do more than you think if you do not try to do it solo, and you don't give up prematurely.

These realities are intended to convey the highly transient, at times chaotic, nature of this beast, and the dynamic context within which most new ventures evolve. Such realities present so much room for the unexpected and the contradictory that it places a premium on thinking bold enough and doing everything you can to make sure your idea becomes an opportunity. Therefore, how can the aspiring entrepreneur think about this complex, even daunting challenge?

The Circle of Ecstasy and the Food Chain for Ventures

What most small businesses do not know, but what is a way of life in the world of high potential ventures, is what we will call the "circle of venture capital ecstasy" (Exhibit 3.1) and "the food chain for entrepreneurial ventures" (Exhibit 3.2). These concepts enable the

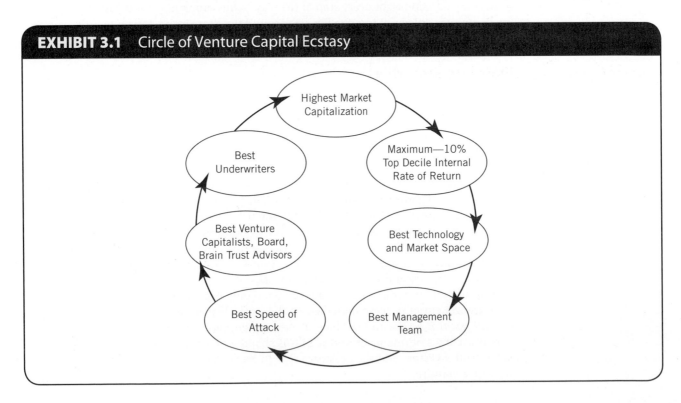

EXHIBIT 3.1   Circle of Venture Capital Ecstasy

- Highest Market Capitalization
- Maximum—10% Top Decile Internal Rate of Return
- Best Technology and Market Space
- Best Management Team
- Best Speed of Attack
- Best Venture Capitalists, Board, Brain Trust Advisors
- Best Underwriters

EXHIBIT 3.2   The Capital Markets Food Chain for Entrepreneurial Ventures

Stage of Venture	R&D	Seed	Launch	High Growth
Company Enterprise Value at Stage	Less than $1 million	$1–$5 million	>$1–$50 million-plus	More than $100 million
Sources	Founders High net worth individuals FFF* SR&ED,	FFF* Angel funds Seed funds SR&ED**	Venture capital series A, B, C . . .† Strategic partners Very high net worth individuals Private equity	IPOs Strategic acquirers Private equity
Amount of Capital Invested	Up to $200,000	$10,000–$500,000	$500,000–$20 million	$10–$50 million-plus
% Company Owned at IPO	10–25%	5–15%	40–60% by prior investors	15–25% by public
Share Price and Number‡	$.01–$.50 1–5 million	$.50–$1.00 1–3 million	$1.00–$8.00+/− 5–10 million	$12–$18+ 3–5 million

* Friends, Families, and Fools

† Venture Capital Series A, B, C . . . (Average Size of Round)

	A	@ $5.1 million—start-up
Round	B	@ $8.1 million—product development
	C+	@ $11.3 million—shipping product

Valuations vary markedly by industry (e.g., $2x^s$)

Valuations vary by region and VC cycle

‡ At Post–IPO

** Scientific Research and Experimental Development tax incentive program.

entrepreneur to visualize how the company building-investing-harvesting cycle works. Understanding this cycle and the appetites of different suppliers in the capital markets food chain enables you to answer the questions for *what* reason does this venture exist and for *whom*? Knowing the answers to these questions has profound implications for fundraising, team building, and growing and harvesting the company—or coming up short in any of these critical entrepreneurial tasks.

Exhibit 3.1 shows that the key to creating a company with the highest value (e.g., market capitalization) begins with identifying an opportunity in the "best technology and market space," which creates the attraction for the "best management team." Speed and agility to move quickly attracts the "best venture capitalists, board members, and other mentors and advisors" who can add value to the venture.

Exhibit 3.2 captures the food chain concept, which will be discussed again in greater detail in Chapter 9 "Financing the Venture." Different players in the food chain have very different capacities and preferences for the kind of venture in which they want to invest. The vast majority of start-up entrepreneurs spend inordinate amounts of time chasing the wrong sources with the wrong venture. One goal in this chapter, and again in Chapter 9, is to provide a clear picture of what those criteria are and to grasp what "think big enough" means to the players in the food chain. This is a critical early step to avoid wasting time chasing venture capitalists, angels, and others when there is a misfit from the outset. As one CEO put it, "There are so many investors out there that you could spend the rest of your career meeting with them and still not get to all of them." In fact, the problem is compounded when seeking angel or informal investors since there are a hundred times more of them than there are venture capitalists.

Why waste time thinking too small and on ventures for which there is no appetite in the financial marketplace? Knowing how capital suppliers and entrepreneurs think about the opportunity creation and recognition process, their search and evaluation strategies, and what they look for is a key frame of reference.

When Is an Idea an Opportunity?

The Essence: Four Anchors   If an idea is not an opportunity, what is an opportunity? Superior business opportunities have the following four fundamental anchors:

1. They create or add significant value to a customer or end-user.
2. They do so by solving a significant problem, removing a serious pain-point, or meeting a significant want or need—for which someone is willing to pay a premium.
3. They have robust market, margin, and moneymaking characteristics that will allow the entrepreneur to estimate and communicate sustainable value to potential stakeholders.
4. They are a good *fit* with the founder(s) and management team at the time and market-place—along with an attractive *risk-reward* balance.

For an opportunity to have these qualities, the "window of opportunity" is opening and will remain open long enough. Further, entry into a market with the right characteristics is feasible, and the management team is able to achieve it. The venture has or is able to gain a competitive advantage (i.e., to achieve leverage). Finally, the economics of the venture are rewarding and forgiving enough to allow for significant profit and growth potential.

To summarize: *A superior opportunity has the qualities of being attractive, durable, and timely and is anchored in a product or service which creates or adds value for its buyer or end-user—usually by solving a very painful, serious problem.*[2] The most successful entrepreneurs, venture capitalists, and private investors are opportunity-focused; that is, they start with what customers and the marketplace want, and do not lose sight of this.

The Real World

Opportunities are created, or built, using ideas and entrepreneurial creativity. Yet, while the image of a carpenter or mason at work is useful, in reality the process is more like the collision of particles in a nuclear reaction or like the spawning of hurricanes over the ocean. Ideas interact with real-world conditions and entrepreneurial creativity at a point in time. The product of this interaction is an opportunity around which a new venture can be created.

The business environment in which an entrepreneur launches his or her venture cannot be altered significantly. Despite assumptions often made concerning social and non-profit organizations, they also are subject to market forces and economic constraints. Consider, for instance, what would happen to donations if it were perceived that a non-profit organization was not reinvesting its surplus returns, but instead was paying management excessive salaries. Or what if a socially oriented organization concentrated all its efforts on the social mission, while neglecting revenues? Clearly, dealing with suppliers, production costs, labour, and distribution is critical to the health of these social corporations. Thus, social and non-profit organizations are just as concerned with positive cash flow and generating sufficient cash flows, even though they operate in a different type of market than for-profit organizations. For-profit businesses operate in a free enterprise system characterized by private ownership and profits.

Spawners and Drivers of Opportunities

In a free enterprise system, changing circumstances, chaos, confusion, inconsistencies, lags or leads, knowledge and information gaps, and a variety of other vacuums in an industry or market spawn opportunities.

Changes in the business environment and the ability to anticipate these changes are so critical in entrepreneurship that constant vigilance for changes is a valuable habit. An entrepreneur with credibility, creativity, and decisiveness can seize an opportunity while others study it.

Opportunities are situational. Some conditions under which opportunities are spawned are idiosyncratic, while at other times they are generalizable and can be applied to other industries, products, or services. In this way, cross-association can trigger in the entrepreneurial mind the crude recognition of existing or impending opportunities. It is often assumed that a marketplace dominated by large, multi-billion-dollar players is impenetrable by smaller, entrepreneurial companies. You can't possibly compete with entrenched, resource-rich, established companies. The opposite can be true for several seasons. It can take three to five years or more for a large company to change its strategy and even longer to implement the new strategy, since it can take 10 years or more to change the culture enough to operate differently. For a new or small company, 10 or more years can be forever.[3] It may even be easier for a large company to try something new by adopting a new name or spinning off a new division. General Motors created Saturn in 1985 to try something different and more recently distanced itself from Hummer. Air Canada Jazz is separate from Air Canada. In 2001 Air Canada launched Tango, the same year that Canada 3000 went bankrupt. In 2002 Air Canada launched Zip. Though Zip operated as a totally separate airline it was dissolved in 2004. Tango—short for "Tan and Go"—competed against the likes of Air Transat in the lucrative southern winter destination markets and like Zip the plug was pulled on Tango in 2004.

Some of the most exciting opportunities have come from fields the conventional wisdom said are the domain of big business: technological innovation. The performance of smaller firms in technological innovation is remarkable—95 percent of the radical innovations since World War II have come from new and small firms, not the giants. According to Tom Brzustowski, president of the Natural Sciences and Engineering Research Council from 1995 to 2005:

> As far as innovations are concerned, with the exception of Nortel, I believe that all radical innovations in Canada have come from companies with fewer than 10,000 employees. Take Magna, though a large company by Canadian standards, its radical innovation—pressure forming—emerged from one of their small constituent companies.
>
> Commercialization of radical innovations is not the same as being the source of the IP behind the innovation. The companies that produced the radical innovations may have acquired somebody else's intellectual property to do it.

In his book, *The Way Ahead*, Tom Brzustowski calls "for entrepreneurial managers in companies of all sizes in all sectors to be on the prowl for opportunities to add new value in what they do and make, and thus to produce innovations that will let them operate in a price-setting mode."[4]

There can be exciting opportunities in ordinary businesses that might never get the attention of venture capital investors. The revolution in microcomputers, management information systems (MIS), and computer networking had a profound impact on a number of businesses that had changed little in decades. The used-auto-parts business had been stagnant for generations. Yet, the team at Pintendre Auto Inc., saw a new opportunity in this field by applying the latest computer and information technology to a traditional business that relied on crude, manual methods to track inventory and find parts for customers.[5] In just three years, Pintendre Auto grew to $16 million in sales. Today this Québec-based enterprise owns and operates over 100 facilities in the U.S. and Canada.

Technology and regulatory changes have profoundly altered and will continue to alter the way we conceive of opportunities. Cable television with its hundreds of channels came of age in the 1990s and brought with it new opportunities in the sale and distribution of goods from infomercials to shopping networks to pay-per-view. The Internet has created an even more diverse set of opportunities in sales and distribution, most notably Amazon. com, iTunes, Craigslist, Priceline, YouTube, and eBay.

Consider the following example that illustrates the phenomenon of vacuums in which opportunities are spawned:

Bulldog Fitness for Kids

Bulldog Interactive Fitness was opened by Holly Bond as a gym for youth in Dartmouth, Nova Scotia. This innovative kids-only fitness centre was developed to fill a market need. With so many overweight children, largely the result of a sedentary lifestyle (TV, computer, videogames), she asked why not combine gaming with exercise? "She went looking for a high-tech solution, but found no specialized equipment on the market... Bond sensed a gap and decided to capitalize on the opportunity."[6]

The gym, targeted at getting the "Xbox generation" off the couch, opened in 2005 after nearly a year of hard work and research. Holly became a certified personal trainer and with her husband drew up a business plan and secured financing, all in secrecy. "We didn't even tell our best friends what we were doing," said Bond. "We were so afraid that someone else was going to do it first." Niche fitness chains like women-only Curves and Sisters Pace Fitness proved that demographic-specific gyms could access a market that others missed.

About a year and half into operations, Bond decided to franchise. "It was always our intention to franchise," says Bond, "but we thought we'd be doing that later, maybe in three or four years, once we had a few of our own open." With a steady stream of enquiries and $200,000 from angel investors in Halifax the franchising began. The interactive equipment was a hit, exercise bikes provided input to PlayStation games on big wall mounted screens, rowing machines hooked up to display the user competing with others and escaping from sea monsters, Dance Dance Revolution, a rock climbing treadmill, Wii stations, and many others—including some old fashioned dodge-ball type activities—kept the business and business model thriving.[7]

With a handful of Canadian franchises and some U.S. ones in the works, Holly Bond expected the brand to explode. She publicly shared her ambitious goal of 400 franchises worldwide by 2011. She picked up a 2007 Export Achievement Award and admitted, "We're all exhausted, but it's an exciting exhausted." With her sights set on launching a DVD, writing a book, developing a line of kid-size workout equipment, and creating a TV show, she caught the attention of DHX Media Ltd., an independent producer and distributor of TV programming and interactive content. David Regan, executive VP at DHX Media said, "We've been tracking these guys for awhile as they've been refining their model and think they've come a long way from where they started out." DHX Media acquired Bulldog Interactive Fitness Inc. for $625,000 and 99,333 shares in DHX (locked for one year). Bond stayed on at the helm and additional compensation was tied to meeting financial performance benchmarks. Holly indicated, "There is a huge amount of synergy between the two companies and this allows us to operate at an entirely new level."[8] A Bulldog Interactive Fitness franchise started with a fee of $34,900, capital costs of between $250,000 and $400,000, and royalty fees of 7 percent gross sales and 2 percent for national advertising.

Exhibit 3.3 summarizes the major types of discontinuities, asymmetries, and changes that can result in high potential opportunities. Creating such changes through technical innovation (PCs, wireless telecommunications, Internet servers, software), influencing and creating the new rules of the game (airlines, telecommunications, financial services and banking, medical products), and anticipating the various impacts of such changes is central to recognizing opportunities.

Search for Sea-Changes

A simple criterion for the highest potential ventures comes from Vancouver's Ventures West, "We target companies that are addressing worldwide markets which are large enough to allow the portfolio company to grow to a significant size." Garage Technology Ventures states: "We're looking to invest in entrepreneurial teams with big ideas and a need for seed capital to turn their ideas into great companies. We are willing to invest in unproved teams attacking unproven markets with unproven solutions." The best place to start in seeking to identify such ideas in a macro sense is to identify significant sea-changes that are occurring or will occur. Think of the profound impact that personal computing, biotechnology, and the Internet have had on the past generation. The great new ventures of the next generation will come about by the same process and will define these next great sea-changes. Exhibit 3.4 summarizes some categories for thinking about such changes. These include

EXHIBIT 3.3 Summary of Opportunity Spawners and Drivers

Root of Change/Chaos/Disontinuity	Opportunity Creation
Regulatory changes	Airlines, insurance, telecommunications, medical, pension fund management, financial services, banking, tax laws and securities regulations.
10-fold change in 10 years or less	Moore's Law—computer chips double productivity every 18 months: financial services, private equity, consulting, Internet, biotech, information age, publishing
Reconstruction of value chain and channels of distribution	Superstores—Loblaws, Wal-Mart; publishing; automobiles; Internet sales and distribution of all services
Proprietary or contractual advantage	Technological innovation: patent, licence, contract, franchise, copyrights, distributorship
Existing management/investors burned out/undermanaged	Turnaround, new capital structure, new breakeven, new free cash flow, new team, new strategy; owners' desires for liquidity, exit; telecom, waste management service, retail businesses
Entrepreneurial leadership	New vision and strategy, new team equals secret weapon; organization thinks, acts like owners
Market leaders are customer obsessed or customer blind	New, small customers are low priority or ignored: hard disk drives, paper, chemicals, mainframe computers, centralized data processing, desktop computers, corporate venturing, office superstores, automobiles, software, most services

EXHIBIT 3.4 Ideas versus Opportunities: Search for Sea-Changes

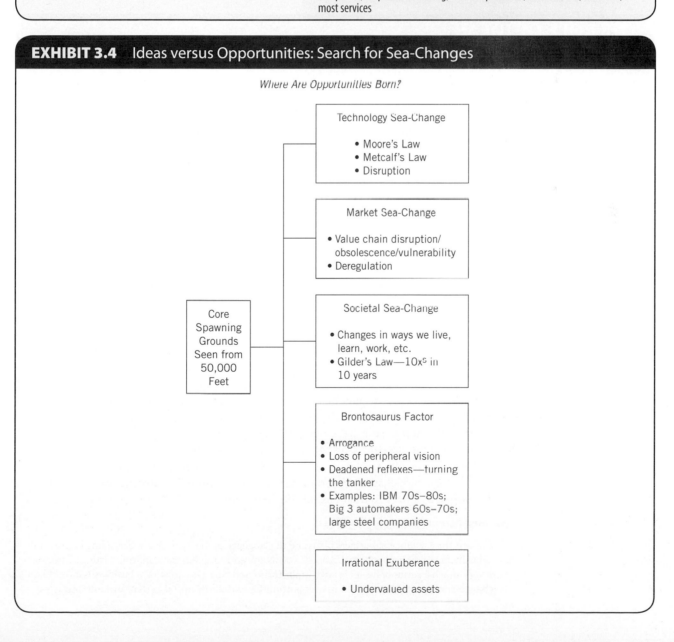

Where Are Opportunities Born?

Core Spawning Grounds Seen from 50,000 Feet

Technology Sea-Change
- Moore's Law
- Metcalf's Law
- Disruption

Market Sea-Change
- Value chain disruption/ obsolescence/vulnerability
- Deregulation

Societal Sea-Change
- Changes in ways we live, learn, work, etc.
- Gilder's Law—10xs in 10 years

Brontosaurus Factor
- Arrogance
- Loss of peripheral vision
- Deadened reflexes—turning the tanker
- Examples: IBM 70s–80s; Big 3 automakers 60s–70s; large steel companies

Irrational Exuberance
- Undervalued assets

technology, market and societal shifts, and even opportunities spawned from the excesses produced by the Internet boom. Moore's Law (the computing power of a chip doubles every 18 months) has been a gigantic driver of much of our technological revolution over the past 30 years. Breakthroughs in gene mapping and cloning, biotechnology, and nano-technology and changes brought about by the Internet will continue to create huge opportunities for the next generation. Beyond the macro view of sea-changes, how can one think about opportunities in a more practical, less abstract sense? What are some parameters of business/revenue models that increase the odds of thinking big enough and therefore appeal to the food chain? To go with this chapter is the online Sea-Change Exercise, which will challenge you to think creatively and expansively about how new technology discoveries will drive the next new industries. This pattern continues to this day.

Desirable Business/Revenue Model Metrics

We will emphasize time and again in *New Venture Creation* that *happiness is a positive cash flow!—but think cash last.* You don't have an entry strategy until you have said no to lots of ideas; ideas that just come to you aren't usually opportunities; and the numbers don't matter but the economics really do matter.

THE ROLE OF IDEAS

Ideas as Tools

A good idea is nothing more than a tool in the hands of an entrepreneur. Finding a good idea is the first step in the process of converting an entrepreneur's creativity into an opportunity.

The importance of the idea is often overrated at the expense of underemphasizing the need for products or services, or both, that can be sold in enough quantity to real customers.

Further, the new business that simply bursts from a flash of brilliance is rare. Usually a series of trial-and-error iterations, or repetitions, is necessary before a crude and promising product or service fits with what the customer is willing to pay. Howard Head made 40 different metal skis before he finally made the model that worked consistently. With surprising frequency, major businesses are built around totally different products than those originally envisioned. Consider these examples:

✓ Swedish born Canadian Gideon Sundback patented a "separable fastener" in 1917. It took 20 years for this device—later dubbed "zipper"—to be adopted by the fashion industry.

✓ Polaroid Corporation was founded with a product based on the principle of polarized light. It was thought that polarized lamps would prevent head-on collisions between cars by preventing the "blinding" glare of oncoming headlights. But the company grew to its present size based on another application of the same technology: instant photography. Polaroid excelled until a disruptive technology (digital imaging) pushed them into bankruptcy.

✓ Medical doctor Wilbur Franks led a team of Canadians that developed an anti-gravity suit in 1941 to prevent pilot blackout from acceleration (G-force). G-suits had been around since 1906 for clinical surgery. George Crile, a founder of the Cleveland Clinic, developed a rubber suit that could be inflated by bicycle pump to apply force and maintain blood pressure preventing loss of consciousness.

✓ William Steere, CEO of Pfizer, described the discovery of Viagra, the fastest-selling drug in history, as having "a certain serendipity" behind it. The drug was originally developed by Pfizer to treat angina—its real "potency" was discovered as a side effect.[9]

As one entrepreneur expressed it:

> Perhaps the existence of business plans and the language of business give a misleading impression of business building as a rational process. But, as any entrepreneur can confirm, starting a business is very much a series of fits and starts, brainstorms and barriers. Creating a business is a round of chance encounters that leads to new opportunities and ideas, mistakes that turn into miracles.[10]

The Great Mousetrap Fallacy

Perhaps no one did a greater disservice to generations of would-be entrepreneurs than Ralph Waldo Emerson in his oft-quoted line: "If a man can make a better mousetrap than his neighbour, though he builds his house in the woods the world will make a beaten path to his door."

What can be called the great mousetrap fallacy was thus spawned. It is often assumed that success is possible if an entrepreneur can just come up with a new idea. In today's changing world, if the idea has anything to do with technology, success is certain—or so it would seem.

But the truth is that ideas are inert and, for all practical purposes, worthless. Ideas are infinite but resources simply are not. Further, the flow of ideas is phenomenal. Venture capital investors, for instance, during the investing boom of the late 1990s, received as many as 100 to 200 proposals and business plans each month. Only 1 to 3 percent of these actually received financing, however.

Yet the fallacy persists despite the lessons of practical experience noted long ago in the insightful reply to Emerson by Owen B. Winters: "The manufacturer who waits for the world to beat a path to his door is a great optimist. But the manufacturer who shows this 'mousetrap' to the world keeps the smoke coming out his chimney."

Contributors to the Fallacy

One cannot blame it all on Ralph Waldo Emerson. There are several reasons for the perpetuation of the fallacy. One is the portrayal in oversimplified accounts of the ease and genius with which such ventures as Xerox, Seagram's, and Polaroid made their founders wealthy. Unfortunately, these exceptions do not provide a useful rule to guide aspiring entrepreneurs.

Another is that inventors seem particularly prone to mousetrap myopia. Perhaps, like Emerson, they are substantially sheltered in viewpoint and experience from the tough, competitive realities of the business world. Consequently, they may underestimate, if not seriously discount, the importance of what it takes to make a business succeed. Frankly, inventing and brainstorming may be a lot more fun than the diligent observation, investigation, and nurturing of customers that are often required to sell a product or service. Canadian James Gosling created the Java programming language at Sun Microsystems. It quickly gained notoriety and became ubiquitous; it also quickly became open source free software.

Contributing also to the great mousetrap fallacy is the tremendous psychological ownership attached to an invention or to a new product. This attachment is different from attachment to a business. While an intense level of psychological ownership and involvement is certainly a prerequisite for creating a new business, the fatal flaw in attachment to an invention or product is the narrowness of its focus. The focal point needs to be the building of the business, rather than just one aspect of the idea.

Another source of mousetrap fallacy myopia lies in a technical and scientific orientation, that is, a desire to do it better. A good illustration of this is the experience of a Canadian entrepreneur who with his brother founded a company to manufacture truck seats. The entrepreneur's brother had developed a new seat for trucks that was a definite improvement over other seats. The entrepreneur knew he could profitably sell the seat his brother had designed, and they did so. When they needed more manufacturing capacity, one brother had several ideas on how to improve the seat. The first brother stated: "If I had listened to him, we probably would be a small custom shop today, or out of business. Instead, we concentrated on making seats that would sell at a profit, rather than just making a better and better seat. Our company has several million dollars of sales today and is profitable."

Related to "doing it better" is the idea of doing it first. Having the best idea first is by no means a guarantee of success. There can be a liability—a painful downside—to being first. Sometimes the first ones merely prove to the competition that a market exists to be snared. Therefore, unless having the best idea also includes the capacity to pre-empt other competitors by capturing a significant share of the market or by erecting insurmountable barriers to entry, first does not necessarily mean most viable. And sometimes the quick follower sees things more clearly than the first-mover, capturing benefits of vicarious learning.

Spotting an opportunity within an existing market was a key aspect in the development of a mass-produced rotary electric toothbrush. The founding entrepreneur had noted a large pricing spread among retail products. At the low end were devices in the range of $5. There was then a jump to the $60 to $80 range, and then another jump to products that were selling for well over $100. His research showed that new battery technology, plus outsourcing and a new rotary design, could result in a disposable product that would fill the gaps, steal market share, and yield substantial profits. His $1.75-million business turned into $475 million when his company was sold to Procter & Gamble. This is an excellent example of a clear pricing pattern that can be applied elsewhere.

PATTERN RECOGNITION

The Experience Factor

One cannot build a successful business without ideas. In this regard, experience is vital in looking at new venture ideas.

Time after time, experienced entrepreneurs exhibit an ability to recognize quickly a pattern—and an opportunity—while it is still taking shape. Nobel laureate Herbert Simon wrote extensively about pattern recognition. He described the recognition of patterns as a creative process that is not simply logical, linear, and additive but intuitive and inductive as well. It involves, he said, the creative linking, or cross-association, of two or more in-depth "chunks" of experience, know-how, and contacts.[11] Simon contended that it takes 10 years or more for people to accumulate what he called the "50,000 chunks" of experience that enable them to be highly creative and recognize patterns—familiar circumstances that can be translated from one place to another.

Thus, the process of sorting through ideas and recognizing a pattern can also be compared to the process of fitting pieces into a three-dimensional jigsaw puzzle. It is impossible to assemble such a puzzle by looking at it as a whole unit. Rather, one needs to see the relationships between the pieces and be able to fit together some that are seemingly unrelated before the whole is visible.

Recognizing ideas that can become entrepreneurial opportunities stems from a capacity to see what others do not—that one plus one equals three. Consider the following examples of the common thread of pattern recognition and new business creation by linking knowledge in one field or marketplace with quite different technical, business, or market know-how:

✓ Jim Treliving quit the RCMP to open a franchise restaurant—Boston Pizza. The leap was made after Jim ate at the original restaurant in Edmonton; Jim recounts, "It was love at first bite." Jim partnered with George Melville and over 10 years built up a chain of 16 franchised restaurants. They then turned the tables and took over the 44-restaurant chain for $3.8 million to become the franchisor. They divested 15 of the restaurants keeping one as a corporate training restaurant.

✓ During travel throughout Europe, the eventual founders of Crate & Barrel frequently saw stylish and innovative products for the kitchen and home that were not yet available in North America. When they returned home, the founders created Crate & Barrel to offer these products for which market research had, in a sense, already been done. In Crate & Barrel, the knowledge of consumer buying habits in one geographical region, Europe, was transferred successfully to another, the U.S. and Canada.

✓ Laurence Lewin, worked in a variety of jobs before settling on the fashion industry in the mid-1970s. Lewin failed to complete medical school; joined the military where he lost his rifle; barely passed England's lowest level accounting qualification; and then worked in the computer industry. He went to work for Suzy Shier in 1987 and in 1990 co-founded La Senza. A few years later Suzy Shier was cast off for cash to fuel growth of La Senza. Today Lewin heads an empire of 700 stores, about half of which are in Canada and the remainder in 40 other countries.

Enhancing Creative Thinking

The creative thinking described above is of great value in recognizing opportunities, as well as other aspects of entrepreneurship. The notion that creativity can be learned or enhanced holds important implications for entrepreneurs who need to unlock imaginative solutions. Most people can certainly spot creative flair. Children seem to have it, and many seem to lose it. Several studies suggest that creativity actually peaks around the first grade because a person's life tends to become increasingly structured and defined by others and by institutions. Further, the development of intellectual discipline and rigour in thinking takes on greater importance in school than during the formative years, and most of our education beyond grade school stresses a logical, rational mode of orderly reasoning and thinking. Finally, social pressures may tend to be a taming influence on creativity.

Evidence suggests that one can enhance creative thinking in later years. The Eureka! Ranch (www. eurekaranch.com) was founded on the principle that creativity is inherent in most people and can be unleashed by freeing them from convention. Often, executives will be doused with water as they step out of their vehicles onto the ranch.

Approaches to Unleashing Creativity

Since the 1950s, much has been learned about the workings of the human brain. Today, there is general agreement that the two sides of the brain process information in different ways. The left side performs rational, logical functions, while the right side operates the intuitive and nonrational modes of thought. A person uses both sides, actually shifting from one mode to the other (see Exhibit 3.5). Approaching ideas creatively and maximizing the control of these modes of thought can be of value to the entrepreneur.

More recently, attention has focused on the creativity process. For instance, evidence is mounting that administrative tasks crowd out more contemplative but non-urgent tasks:

> Entrepreneurs are creative people who follow passions and may toy with 101 ideas for a business before starting one. Then come the endless Things That Must be Done: raising capital, closing sales, hiring staff, securing suppliers. Activities that don't have deadlines, such as inventing, designing, and concocting new products, can get pushed to the bottom of to-do lists. As more time-sensitive and urgent tasks accumulate at the top of those lists, the creative stuff simply falls off.[12]

To keep the creative visualization process alive, entrepreneurs need to carve out some time to think freely. A walk in the woods is often pointed to as a prime setting for the activity.

Team Creativity

Teams of people can generate creativity that may not exist in a single individual. The creativity of a team of people is impressive, and comparable or better creative solutions to problems evolving from the collective interaction of a small group of people have been observed.

A good example of the creativity generated by using more than one head is that of Spin Master. It was founded when three friends who had just graduated from the University of Western Ontario, armed with $10,000 set out to build a business. Earth Buddy, a small, pantyhose-covered head filled with grass seeds that sprouted hair when watered was their first product. It was a huge hit—a Pet Rock-like phenomenon—providing the team a foundation to sprout their next idea. The venture boasts a willingness to take risks, creativity, playfulness, and constant scanning for great new innovative toys.

Students interested in exploring this further may want to do the Creative Squares exercise online after completing this chapter. To access the exercise and many other useful tools, visit the Online Learning Centre at www.mcgrawhill.ca/olc/timmons.

EXHIBIT 3.5   Comparison of Left-Mode and Right-Mode Brain Characteristics

L-Mode	R-Mode
Verbal: Using words to name, describe, and define.	Nonverbal: Awareness of things, but minimal connection with words.
Analytic: Figuring things out step-by-step and part-by-part.	Synthetic: Putting things together to form wholes.
Symbolic: Using a symbol to stand for something. For example, the sign + stands for the process of addition.	Concrete: Relating to things as they are at the present moment.
Abstract: Taking out a small bit of information and using it to represent the whole thing.	Analogic: Seeing likenesses between things; understanding metaphoric relationships!
Temporal: Keeping track of time, sequencing one thing after another, doing first things first, second things second, etc.	Nontemporal: Without a sense of time.
Rational: Drawing conclusions based on reason and facts.	Nonrational: Not requiring a basis of reason or facts; willingness to suspend judgment.
Digital: Using numbers as in counting.	Spatial: Seeing where things are in relation to other things, and how parts go together to form a whole.
Logical: Drawing conclusions based on logic; one thing following another in logical order—for example, a mathematical theorem or a well-stated argument.	Intuitive: Making leaps of insight, often based on incomplete patterns, hunches, feelings, or visual images.
Linear: Thinking in terms of linked ideas, one thought directly following another, often leading to a convergent conclusion.	Holistic: Seeing whole things all at once; perceiving the overall patterns and structures, often leading to divergent conclusions.

Source: "A Comparison of Left-Mode and Right-Mode Characteristics," from *Drawing on the Right Side of the Brain* by Betty Edwards (New York, NY: Putnam Books, 1999).

Big Opportunities with Little Capital

Within the dynamic free enterprise system, opportunities are apparent to a limited number of individuals—and not just to the individuals with financial resources. Ironically, successful entrepreneurs such as Howard Head attribute their success to the discipline of limited capital resources. Many entrepreneurs have learned the key to success is in the art of bootstrapping, which "in a start-up is like zero inventory in a just-in-time system: it reveals hidden problems and forces the company to solve them."[13] And Canadians take pride in their conservative nature—often avoiding risks associated with becoming highly leveraged (see Chapter 11 "Obtaining Debt Capital")—growing through retained earnings. Consider the following:

- Approximately three-quarters of start-ups launch with $50,000 or less; half begin with $10,000 or less as seed capital. Further, the primary source of capital was, overwhelmingly, personal savings (77 percent), rather than outside investors with deep pockets.[14]

- In the 1930s, Josephine Esther Mentzer assisted her uncle by selling skin care balm and quickly created her own products with an initial investment of $100. After convincing the department stores rather than the drugstores to carry her products, Estee Lauder was on its way to becoming a corporation with 2008 sales of US$8 billion.[15]

- Putting their talents (cartooning and finance) together, Roy and Walt Disney moved to California and started their own film studio—with $290 in 1923. By 2009, the Walt Disney Co. had a market capitalization exceeding $50 billion.

- While working in real estate, Montréal immigrant Assaad Abdelnour's vision for CLIC Foods began. He later bought and operated a supermarket and the full concept took shape. CLIC (Canadian Lebanese Investment Corporation) became a pioneer in ethnic foods and today is a leader in the production and distribution of international food products with annual sales of nearly $40 million. CLIC boasts 200 employees at six locations across Canada, derives 25 percent of revenues from exports, and in 2007 opened a facility in New Jersey.

- With $100 Calgary-native Nicholas Graham, age 24, went to a local fabric store, picked out some fabrics, and made $100 worth of ties. Having sold the ties to specialty shops, Graham was approached by Macy's to place his patterns on men's underwear. So Joe

Boxer Corporation was born and "six months into Joe Boxer's second year, sales had already topped $1 million."[16] Graham, CUO (Chief Underpants Officer) successfully harvested the business a few years later when annual sales reached US$20 million.

Real Time

Opportunities exist or are created in real time and have what we call a window of opportunity. For an entrepreneur to seize an opportunity, the window must be open and remain open long enough to achieve market-required returns.

Exhibit 3.6 illustrates a window of opportunity for a generalized market. Markets grow at different rates over time and as a market quickly becomes larger, more and more opportunities are possible. As the market becomes established, conditions are not as favourable. Thus, at the point where a market starts to become sufficiently large and structured (e.g., at five years in Exhibit 3.6), the window opens; the window begins to close as the market matures (e.g., at 12 to 13 years in the exhibit).

The curve shown describes the rapid growth pattern typical of such new industries as microcomputers and software, cellphones, quick oil changes, and nanotechnology. For example, in the cellular phone industry, most major cities began service between 1984 and 1985. In 1996, U.S. and Canadian cellphone use was comparable, 13 in 100 U.S. residents and 9 in 100 Canadian residents had one, but by 2007, U.S. penetration reached 76 percent while Canada was at 60 percent.[17] In other industries where growth is not so rapid, the slope of a curve would be less steep and the possibilities for opportunities fewer.

In considering the window of opportunity, the length of time the window will be open is important. It takes a considerable length of time to determine whether a new venture is a success or a failure. And, if it is to be a success, the benefits of that success need to be realized.

Evidence shows that for venture-capital-backed firms, the lemons (i.e., the losers) ripen in about two and a half years, while the pearls (i.e., the winners) take seven or eight years to mature. An extreme example of the length of time it can take for a pearl to be harvested is the experience of one Silicon Valley venture capital firm that invested in a new firm in 1966 and was finally able to realize a capital gain in early 1984. Another way to think of the process of creating and seizing an opportunity in real time is to think of it as a process of selecting objects (opportunities) from a conveyor belt moving through an open window,

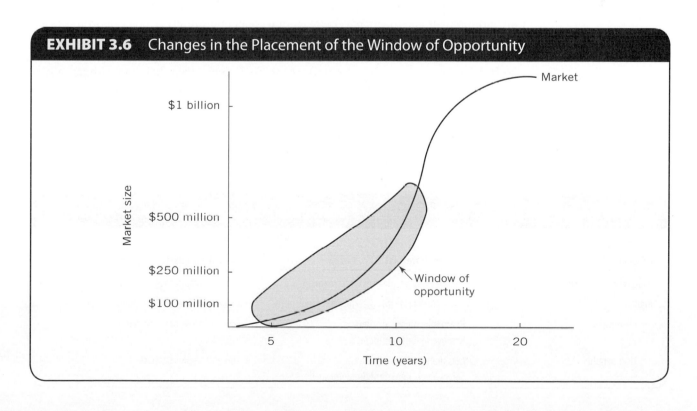

EXHIBIT 3.6   Changes in the Placement of the Window of Opportunity

the window of opportunity. The speed of the conveyor belt changes, and the window through which it moves is constantly opening and closing. The continually opening and closing window and the constantly changing speed of the conveyor belt represent the volatile nature of the marketplace and the importance of timing. For an opportunity to be created and seized, it needs to be selected from the conveyor belt before the window closes.

The ability to recognize a potential opportunity when it appears and the sense of timing to seize that opportunity, as the window is opening, rather than slamming shut, are critical. That opportunities are a function of real time is illustrated in a statement made by Ken Olsen, then president and co-founder of Digital Equipment Corporation, in 1977, "There is no reason for any individual to have a computer in their home." Though taken out of context, Ken Olsen did take the fall in 1992 and within the decade the struggling company's assets were sold off.[18] It is not easy for even the world's leading experts to predict just which innovative ideas and concepts for new business will evolve into the major industries of tomorrow. This is vividly illustrated by several quotations from famous innovators. In 1901, two years before the famous flight, Wilbert Wright said, "Man will not fly for 50 years." In 1910, Thomas Edison said, "The nickel-iron battery will put the gasoline buggy . . . out of existence in no time." Albert Einstein in 1932 made it clear, "[There] is not the slightest indication that nuclear energy will ever be obtainable. It would mean that the atom would have to be shattered at will." Thomas Watson, IBM Chairman in 1943 predicted, "I think there is a world market for maybe five computers." And in 1981 Bill Gates, Microsoft Chairman stated, "640K ought to be enough for anybody."

Clearly predicting opportunity is tricky business. Charles Duell, commissioner at the U.S. Office of Patents in 1899 stated, "Everything that can be invented has been invented." While today just about every appliance on the kitchen counter has a computer, some are foretelling that the desktop/home computer may fade as more "Net" devices and individuals tap into a CPU remotely. Sun Microsystems' business model and mantra has been: "The network is the computer." Presently, Edison's belief that a battery-powered vehicle would replace gasoline-powered ones is looking ever more likely.

Relation to the Framework of Analysis

Successful opportunities, once recognized, fit with the other forces of new venture creation. This iterative process of assessing and reassessing the fit among the central driving forces in the creation of a new venture were shown in Chapter 2. Of utmost importance is the fit of the lead entrepreneur and the management team with an opportunity. Good opportunities are both desirable to and attainable by those on the team using the resources that are available.

To understand how the entrepreneurial vision relates to the analytical framework, it may be useful to look at an opportunity as a three-dimensional relief map with its valleys, mountains, and so on, all represented. Each opportunity has three or four critical factors (e.g., proprietary licence, patented innovation, sole distribution rights, an all-star management team, breakthrough technology). These elements pop out at the observer; they indicate huge possibilities where others might see obstacles. Thus, it is easy to see why there are thousands of exceptional opportunities that will fit with a wide variety of entrepreneurs but that might not fit neatly into the framework outlined in Exhibit 3.7.

EXHIBIT 3.7   Criteria for Evaluating Venture Opportunities

Criteria	Attractiveness	
	Highest Potential	**Lowest Potential**
Industry and Market	Changes way people live, work, learn, etc.	Incremental improvement only
Market:	Market driven; identified; recurring revenue niche	Unfocused; onetime revenue
Customers	Reachable; purchase orders Remove serious pain-point	Loyal to others or unreachable
User benefits	Less than one-year payback Solves a very important problem/need	Three years plus payback

EXHIBIT 3.7   Criteria for Evaluating Venture Opportunities *(continued)*

	Attractiveness	
Criteria	**Highest Potential**	**Lowest Potential**
Value added	High; advance payments	Low; minimal impact on market
Product life	Durable	Perishable
Market structure	Imperfect, fragmented competition or emerging industry	Highly concentrated or mature or declining industry
Market size	$100 million to $1 billion sales potential	Unknown, less than $20 million or multibillion sales
Growth rate	Growth at 30–50% or more	Contracting or less than 10%
Market capacity	At or near full capacity	Undercapacity
Market share attainable (Year 5)	20% or more; leader	Less than 5%
Cost structure	Low-cost provider; cost advantages	Declining cost
Economics		
Time to break even/positive cash flow	Under $1\frac{1}{2}$–2 years	More than 4 years
ROI potential	25% or more; high value	Less than 15–20%; low value
Capital requirements	Low to moderate; fundable/bankable	Very high; unfundable or unbankable
Internal rate of return potential	25% or more per year	Less than 15% per year
Free cash flow characteristics:	Favourable; sustainable; 20–30% or more of sales	Less than 10% of sales
Sales growth	Moderate to high (15–20%)	Less than 10%
Asset intensity	Low/sales $	High
Spontaneous working capital	Low, incremental requirements	High requirements
R&D/capital expenditures	Low requirements	High requirements
Gross margins	Exceeding 40% and durable	Under 20%
After-tax profits	High; greater than 10%; durable	Low
Time to break-even profit and loss	Less than two years; breakeven not creeping or leaping	Greater than four years; breakeven creeping or leaping up
Harvest Issues		
Value-added potential	High strategic value	Low strategic value
Valuation multiples and comparables	Price/earning = 20x; 8 – 10x EBIT; 1.5 – 2x revenue: Free cash flow 8 – 10x	Price/earnings ≤ 5x, EBIT ≤ 3 – 4x; revenue ≤ .4
Exit mechanism and strategy	Present or envisioned options	Undefined; illiquid investment
Capital market context	Favourable valuations, timing, capital available; realizable liquidity	Unfavourable; credit crunch
Competitive Advantage Issues		
Fixed and variable costs	Lowest; high operating leverage	Highest
Control over costs, prices, and distribution	Moderate to strong	Weak
Barriers to entry:	Knowledge to overcome	
Proprietary protection	Have or can gain	None
Response/lead time	Competition slow; napping	Unable to gain edge
Legal, contractual advantage	Proprietary or exclusivity	None
Contracts and networks	Well-developed; accessible	Crude; limited
Key people	Top talent; an A team	B or C team

(continued)

EXHIBIT 3.7   Criteria for Evaluating Venture Opportunities *(continued)*

Criteria	Attractiveness	
	Highest Potential	**Lowest Potential**
Management Team		
Entrepreneurial team	All-star combination; free agents	Weak or solo entrepreneur; not free agents
Industry and technical experience	Top of the field; super track record	Underdeveloped
Integrity	Highest standards	Questionable
Intellectual honesty	Know what they do not know	Do not want to know what they do not know
Fatal-Flaw Issue	Nonexistent	One or more
Personal Criteria		
Goals and fit	Getting what you want; but wanting what you get	Surprises; only making money
Upside/downside issues	Attainable success/limited risks	Linear; on same continuum
Opportunity costs	Acceptable cuts in salary, etc.	Comfortable with status quo
Desirability	Fits with lifestyle	Simply pursuing big money
Risk/reward tolerance	Calculated risk; low risk/reward ratio	Risk averse or gambler
Stress tolerance	Thrives under pressure	Cracks under pressure
Strategic Differentiation		
Degree of fit	High	Low
Team	Best in class; excellent free agents	B team; no free agents
Service management	Superior service concept	Perceived as unimportant
Timing	Rowing with the tide	Rowing against the tide
Technology	Groundbreaking; one of a kind	Many substitutes or competitors
Flexibility	Able to adapt; commit and decommit quickly	Slow; stubborn
Opportunity orientation	Always searching for opportunities	Operating in a vacuum; napping
Pricing	At or near leader	Undercut competitor; low prices
Distribution channels	Accessible; networks in place	Unknown; inaccessible
Room for error	Forgiving and resilient strategy	Unforgiving, rigid strategy

SCREENING OPPORTUNITIES

Opportunity Focus

Opportunity focus is the most fruitful point of departure for screening opportunities. The screening process should not begin with strategy (which derives from the nature of the opportunity), nor with financial and spreadsheet analysis, nor with estimations of how much the company is worth and who will own what shares.

These starting points, and others, usually place the cart before the horse. Also, many entrepreneurs who start businesses—particularly those for whom the ventures are their first—run out of cash at a faster rate than they bring in customers and profitable sales. There are lots of reasons why this happens, but one thing is certain: These entrepreneurs have not focused on the right opportunity.

Over the years, those with experience in business and in specific market areas have developed rules to guide them in screening opportunities. For example, during the initial stages of the irrational exuberance about the dot-com phenomenon, number of "clicks" changed to attracting "eyeballs," which changed to pages viewed. Many investors got caught up in false metrics. Those who survived the stock market crash of 2000–2001 understood that dot-com survivors would be the ones who executed transactions. Number of customers, amount of the transaction, and repeat transactions became the recognized standards.[19] And in the aftermath of the 2009 financial downturn the winners and losers were revealed. A stout recession provided threats to established enterprises and opportunities for new ventures. During such transformation periods the status quo is repeatedly proved to be no longer viable and business models are quickly evaluated and refined as consumers shift priorities dramatically.

Screening Criteria: The Characteristics of High Potential Ventures

Venture capitalists, savvy entrepreneurs, and investors also use this concept of boundaries in screening ventures. Exhibit 3.7 summarizes criteria used by venture capitalists to evaluate opportunities: opportunities, many of which tend to have a high-technology bias. As will be seen later, venture capital investors reject 60 to 70 percent of the new ventures presented to them very early in the review process, based on how the entrepreneurs satisfy these criteria.

However, these criteria are not the exclusive domain of venture capitalists. The criteria are based on good business sense that is used by successful entrepreneurs, angels, private investors, and venture capitalists. Consider the following examples of great small companies built without a dime of professional venture capital.

Herb and Rhoda Singer established Discount Car & Truck Rentals in 1980. Discount has grown from the first location in Hamilton, Ontario, to 300 locations, most of which are franchises. It has a few locations in Australia and has expansion plans for the United States. Discount included hybrids in its fleet in 2004, and in 2008 during a looming Toronto Transit Authority strike, offered discounts to stranded public transportation riders.

Wester's Garage, located in Tilley, Alberta (pop. 397), "in the heart of truck country, surrounded by oil fields and wide open space" provides custom performance tuning for trucks and cars. Owner, Lyndon Wester offers reprogramming of the computer chip that controls the engine. It all started in late 1998 with some simple electronics work, but by 2000 they had developed custom performance profiles for the Pontiac Fiero and GM diesel trucks. Their first big break was an order in July 2002 for converting UPS vans across North America. In 2003 Lyndon Wester secured a U.S. military contract for 50 Chevy Suburbans and two local contracts for oil service company fleet vehicles to modify GM trucks to improve fuel economy, limit speed, and alter powertrain parameters. These contracts secured the future for Wester's Garage. While maintaining customers in Alberta's oil fields they thrived with performance tuning for car and truck enthusiasts—even the occasional boat engine. As one online bulletin board posting noted, "Seems amazing that someone living 13 miles from nowhere is getting computers shipped to him from all over North America."

In 1986 Pleasant Rowland founded the Pleasant Company as a mail order catalogue company selling the American Girls Collection of historical dolls. She had begun the company with the modest royalties she received from writing children's books and did not have enough capital to compete in stores with the likes of Mattel's Barbie.[20] By 1992 she had grown the company to US$65 million in sales.[21] Mattel acquired it in 1998 for US$770 million, and under Rowland's continued management, the company had sales of US$350 million in 2001.

Edgy musician Ashley MacIsaac offered half of his future revenues on eBay in the summer of 2008 with a minimum bid of $1.5 million. Seeking a patron of the arts, MacIsaac said, "I see this as no different than what they did in Mozart's day." David Bowie issued bonds in the late 1990s using future royalties as guarantee; Bowie collected tens of millions of dollars on the spot.[22] In 2007, Madonna came to a similar arrangement with concert promoter Live Nation Inc. for over $100 million. The point of departure here is opportunity and, implicitly, the customer, the marketplace, and the industry. Exhibit 3.7 shows how higher and lower potential opportunities can be placed along an attractiveness scale. The criteria provide some quantitative ways in which an entrepreneur can make judgments about industry and market issues, competitive advantage issues, economic and harvest issues, management team issues, and fatal flaw issues and whether these add up to a compelling opportunity. For example, *dominant* strength in any one of these criteria can readily translate into a winning entry, whereas a flaw in any one can be fatal.

Entrepreneurs contemplating opportunities that will yield attractive companies, not high potential ventures, can also benefit from paying attention to these criteria. These entrepreneurs will then be in a better position to decide how these criteria can be compromised. As outlined in Exhibit 3.7, business opportunities with the greatest potential will possess many of the following, or they will dominate in one or a few for which the competition cannot come close.

Industry and Market Issues

Market. *Higher potential* businesses can identify a market niche for a product or service that meets an important customer need and provides high value-added or value-created benefits to customers. This invariably means the product or service eliminates or drastically reduces a major pain-point for a customer or end-user, or solves a major problem/bottleneck for which the customer is willing to pay a premium. Customers are reachable and receptive to the product or service, with no brand or other loyalties. The potential payback to the user or customer of a given product or service through cost savings or other value-added or value-created properties is one year or less and is identifiable, repeatable, and verifiable. Further, the life of the product or service exists beyond the time needed to recover the investment, plus a profit. And so much the better if the company is able to expand beyond a single product. If benefits to customers can be calculated in dollar terms, then the market potential is far less difficult and risky to ascertain.

Lower potential opportunities are unfocused regarding customer need, and customers are unreachable and/or have brand or other loyalties to others. A payback to the user of more than three years and low value-added or value-created properties also makes an opportunity unattractive. Being unable to expand beyond a one-product company can make for a lower potential opportunity. The failure of one of the first portable computer companies, Osborne Computer, is a prime example of this. Adam Osborne's business plan called for sales of 10,000 of his Osborn 1 computer over the product's lifespan; sales peaked at 10,000 units per month. Despite market appeal, quality control fell during rushed production. Osborne's boasts of a second-generation model that was months away from release did not boost confidence. Customers poised to buy the current model held off and dealers cancelled orders for the Osborne 1. The young venture never recovered and his blunder came to be known as "Osborneing." Med-Eng CEO Richard L'Abbe recounts a similar—though non-fatal—scenario. It occurred several iterations into the product line. An update to their bomb disposal suit and helmet combo was introduced half-way through the usual cycle. The word got out and customers held-off buying. Med-Eng quickly took note and went back to their normal update cycle.

Market Structure. Market structure, such as evidenced by the number of sellers, size distribution of sellers, whether products are differentiated, conditions of entry and exit, number of buyers, cost conditions, and sensitivity of demand to changes in price, is significant.

A fragmented, imperfect market or emerging industry often contains vacuums and asymmetries that create unfilled market niches—for example, markets where resource ownership, cost advantages, and the like can be achieved. In addition, those where information or knowledge gaps exist and where competition is profitable, but not so strong as to be overwhelming, are attractive. An example of a market with an information gap is that experienced by an entrepreneur who encountered a large out-of-town company that wanted to dispose of a small, old downtown office building. This office building, because its book value was about $200,000, was viewed by the financially oriented firm as a low-value asset, and the company wanted to dispose of it so the resulting cash could be put to work for a higher return. The buyer, who had done more homework than the out-of-town sellers, bought the building for $200,000 and resold it in less than six months for more than $8 million.

Industries that are highly concentrated, that are perfectly competitive, or that are mature or declining are typically unattractive. The capital requirements and costs to achieve distribution and marketing presence can be prohibitive, and price-cutting and other competitive strategies in highly concentrated markets can be a significant barrier to entry. (The most blatant example is organized crime and its life-threatening actions when territories are invaded.) Revenge by normal competitors who are well positioned through product strategy, legal tactics, and the like, also can be punishing to the newcomer.

The unattractiveness of perfectly competitive industries is captured by the comment of prominent venture capitalist William Egan, who put it this way: "I want to be in a nonauction market."

Market Size. An attractive new venture sells to a market that is large and growing (i.e., one where capturing a small market share can represent significant and increasing sales volume). A minimum market size of more than $100 million in sales is attractive. In the medical and life sciences today, this target boundary is more like $500 million or $1 billion. Such a market size means it is possible to achieve significant sales by capturing roughly 5 percent or less and thus not threatening competitors. For example, to achieve a sales level of $1 million in a $100-million market requires only 1 percent of the market. Thus, a recreational equipment manufacturer entered a $60-million market that was expected to grow at 20 percent per year to over $100 million by the third year. The founders were able to create a substantial, but smaller company without obtaining a major share of the market and possibly incurring the wrath of existing companies.

However, a market can be too large. A multi-billion-dollar market may be too mature and stable, and such a level of certainty can translate into competition from Fortune 500 firms and, if highly competitive, into lower margins and profitability. Further, an unknown market or one that is less than $10 million in sales also is unattractive. To understand the disadvantages of a large, more mature market consider the entry of a firm into the microcomputer industry today versus the entry of Apple into that market in 1975.

Growth Rate. An attractive market is large and growing (i.e., one where capturing a good share of the increase is less threatening to competitors and where a small market share can represent significant and increasing sales volume). An annual growth rate of 30 to 50 percent creates niches for new entrants, and such a market is a thriving and expansive one, rather than a stable or contracting one, where competitors are scrambling for the same niches. Thus, for example, a $100-million market growing at 50 percent per year has the potential to become a $1-billion industry in a few years, and if a new venture can capture just 2 percent of sales in the first year, it can attain sales in the first year of $1 million. If it just maintains its market share over the next few years, sales will grow significantly.

Market Capacity.   Another signal of the existence of an opportunity in a market is a market at full capacity in a growth situation—in other words, a demand that the existing suppliers cannot meet. Timing is of vital concern in such a situation, which means the entrepreneur should be asking: Can a new entrant fill that demand before the other players can decide to and then actually increase capacity?

Market Share Attainable.   The potential to be a leader in the market and capture at least a 20-percent share can create a very high value for a company that might otherwise be worth not much more than book value. For example, one such firm, with less than $15 million in sales, became dominant in its small market niche with a 70-percent market share. The company was acquired for $23 million in cash.

A firm that will be able to capture less than 5 percent of a market is unattractive in the eyes of most investors seeking a higher potential company.

Cost Structure. A firm that can become the low-cost provider is attractive, but a firm that continually faces declining cost conditions is less so. Attractive opportunities exist in industries where economies of scale are insignificant (or work to the advantage of the new venture). Attractive opportunities boast of low costs of learning by doing. Where costs per unit are high when small amounts of the product are sold, existing firms that have low promotion costs can face attractive market opportunities.

For instance, consider the operating leverage of Johnsonville Sausage. Its variable costs were 6 percent labour and 94 percent materials. What aggressive incentives could management put in place for the 6 percent to manage and to control the 94 percent? Imagine the disasters that would occur if the scenario were reversed!

A word of caution from Scott Kunkel and Charles Hofer, who observed:

> Overall, industry structure ... had a much smaller impact on new venture performance than has previously been suggested in the literature. This finding could be the result of one of several possibilities:
>
> 1. Industry structure impacts the performance of established firms, but does NOT have a significant impact on new venture performance.
> 2. The most important industry structural variables influencing new ventures are different from those which impact established firms and thus research has yet to identify the industry structural variables that are most important in the new venture environment.
> 3. Industry structure does NOT have a significant DIRECT impact on firm performance, as expected. Instead, the impact of industry structure is strongly mitigated by other factors, including the strategy selected for entry.[23]

Economics

Profits After Tax. High and durable gross margins usually translate into strong and durable after-tax profits. Attractive opportunities have potential for durable profits of at least 10 to 15 percent and often 20 percent or more. Those generating after-tax profits of less than 5 percent are quite fragile.

Time to Breakeven and Positive Cash Flow. As mentioned above, breakeven and positive cash flow for attractive companies are possible within two years. Once the time to breakeven and positive cash flow is greater than three years, the attractiveness of the opportunity diminishes accordingly.

Return on Investment Potential. An important corollary to forgiving economics is reward. Very attractive opportunities have the potential to yield a return on investment of 25 percent or more per year. During the 1980s, many venture capital funds achieved only single-digit returns on investment. High and durable gross margins and high and durable after-tax profits usually yield high earnings per share and high return on shareholders' equity, thus generating a satisfactory "harvest" price for a company. This is most likely true whether the company is sold through an initial public offering or privately, or whether it is acquired. Given the risk typically involved, a return on investment potential of less than 15 to 20 percent per year is unattractive.

Capital Requirements. Ventures that can be funded and have capital requirements that are low to moderate are attractive. Realistically, most higher-potential businesses need significant amounts of cash—several hundred thousand dollars and up—to get started. Businesses that can be started with little or no capital are rare, but they do exist. In today's venture capital market, the first round of financing is typically $1 to $2 million or more for a start-up.[24] Some higher potential ventures, such as those in the service sector or "cash sales" businesses, have lower capital requirements than do technology-intensive firms with large research and development expenditures.

If the venture needs too much money or cannot be funded, it is unattractive. An extreme example is a venture that a team of students proposed to repair satellites. The students believed that the required start-up capital was in the $50 to $200 million range. Projects of this magnitude are in the domain of the government and the very large multinational corporation, rather than that of the entrepreneur and the venture capitalist. Think Richard Branson of Virgin Galactic launching commercial space flights!

Internal Rate of Return Potential. Is the risk–reward relationship attractive enough? The response to this question can be quite personal, but the most attractive opportunities often have the promise of—and deliver on—a very substantial upside of 5 to 10 times the original investment in 5 to 10 years. Of course, the extraordinary successes can yield 50 to 100 times or more, but these are exceptions. A 25 percent or more annual compound rate of return is considered very healthy. In economically stable times, those investments considered basically risk free have yields of 3 to 8 percent.

Free Cash Flow Characteristics. Free cash flow is a way of understanding a number of crucial financial dimensions of any business: the robustness of its economics; its capital requirements, both working and fixed assets; its capacity to service external debt and equity claims; and its capacity to sustain growth.[25] We define unleveraged free cash flow (FCF) as earnings before interest but after taxes (EBIAT) *plus* amortization (A) and depreciation (D) *less* spontaneous working capital requirements (WC) *less* capital expenditures (CAPex), or FCF = EBIAT + [A+D] − [+ or − WC] − CAPex. EBIAT is driven by sales, profitability, and asset intensity. Low-asset-intensive, high-margin businesses generate the highest profits and sustainable growth.[26] We will explore this in detail in Chapter 9 "Financing the Venture."

Gross Margins. The potential for high and durable gross margins (i.e., the unit selling price less all direct and variable costs) is important. Gross margins exceeding 40 to 50 percent provide a tremendous built-in cushion that allows for more error and more flexibility to learn from mistakes than do gross margins of 20 percent or less. High and durable gross margins, in turn, mean that a venture can reach breakeven earlier, preferably within the first two years. Thus, for example, if gross margins are just 20 percent, for every $1 increase in fixed costs (e.g., insurance, salaries, rent, and utilities), sales need to increase $5 just to stay even. If gross margins are 75 percent, however, a $1 increase in fixed costs requires a sales increase of just $1.33. One entrepreneur, who built the international division of an emerging software company to $17 million in highly profitable sales in just five years (when he was 25 years old), offers an example of the cushion provided by high and durable gross margins. He stresses there is simply no substitute for outrageous gross margins by saying, "It allows you to make all kinds of mistakes that would kill a normal company. And we made them all. But our high gross margins covered all the learning tuition and still left a good profit."[27] Gross margins of less than 20 percent, particularly if they are fragile, are unattractive.

Time to Breakeven—Cash Flow and Profit and Loss (P&L). New businesses that can quickly achieve a positive cash flow and become self-sustaining are highly desirable. It is often the second year before this is possible, but the sooner the better. Obviously, simply having a longer window does not mean the business will be lousy. Two great companies illustrate that a higher potential business can have a longer window. Pilkington Brothers, an English firm that developed plate glass technology, ran huge losses for over two and a half years before it was regarded as a great company. Similarly, Federal Express went through an early period of enormous negative cash flows of $1 million a month. More recently, auto giant General Motors managed $3.6 billion in negative cash flow for the second quarter of 2008.

Harvest Issues

Value-Added Potential. New ventures that are based on strategic value in an industry, such as valuable technology, are attractive, while those with low or no strategic value are less attractive. For example, most observers contend that technology services capacity of compelling strategic value to HP was acquired when it purchased EDS for $13.9 billion in 2008, whereas the merger with Compaq was less so. "In Compaq, HP grabbed more of what it already had;" with EDS, HP is getting something new.[28] Opportunities with extremely large capital commitments, whose value on exit can be severely eroded by unanticipated circumstances, are less attractive.

Thus, one characteristic of businesses that command a premium price is that they have high value-added strategic importance to their acquirer, such as distribution, customer base, geographic coverage, proprietary technology, contractual rights, and the like. Such companies might be valued at four, five, or even six times (or more) last year's sales, whereas perhaps 60 to 80 percent of companies might be purchased at .75 to 1.25 times sales.

Valuation Multiples and Comparables. Consistent with the above point, there is a large spread in the value the capital markets place on private and public companies. Part of your analysis is to identify some historical boundaries for valuations placed on companies in the market/industry/technology area you intend to pursue. The rules outlined in Exhibit 3.7 are variable and should be thought of as a boundary and a point of departure.

Exit Mechanism and Strategy. Businesses that are eventually sold—privately or to the public—or acquired, usually are started and grown with a harvest objective in mind. Attractive companies that realize capital gains from the sale of their businesses have, or envision, a harvest or exit mechanism. Unattractive opportunities do not have an exit mechanism in mind. Planning is critical because, as is often said, it is much harder to get out of a business than to get into it. Giving some serious thought to the options and likelihood that the company can eventually be harvested is an important initial and ongoing aspect of the entrepreneurial process.

Capital Market Context. The context in which the sale or acquisition of the company occurs is largely driven by the capital markets at that particular time. Timing can be a critical component of the exit mechanism because, as one study indicated, since World War II, the average bull market on Bay Street has lasted five and a half years, adding from 82 to 266 percent to the market's value and the average bull/bear cycle has been just over six years.[29] "Over the last half century, the average bear market has lasted 12 months. The shortest—four months between August and November 1987—included the Toronto market's biggest one-day crash. Bay Street stocks lost 22 percent of their value on Monday, October 19. But that bear market ushered in the longest bull market in the exchange's history. The bulls ran for almost 10½ years, resulting in an overall return of 247 per cent." For a keener appreciation of the critical difference the capital markets can make, one only has to recall such stock market events or even a bank credit crunch. Initial public offerings are especially vulnerable to the vicissitudes of the capital markets; here the timing is vital. Some of the most successful companies seem to have been launched when debt and equity capital were most available and relatively cheap.

Competitive Advantages Issues

Variable and Fixed Costs. An attractive opportunity has the potential for being the lowest-cost producer and for having the lowest marketing and distribution costs. For example, Bowmar was unable to remain competitive in the market for electronic calculators after the producers of large-scale integrated circuits, such as Hewlett-Packard, entered the business. Being unable to achieve and sustain a position as a low-cost producer shortens the life expectancy of a new venture.

Degree of Control. Attractive opportunities have potential for moderate-to-strong degree of control over prices, costs, and channels of distribution. Fragmented markets where there is no dominant competitor—no Rogers, Shaw, or Vidéotron—have this potential. These markets usually have a market leader with a 20-percent market share *or less.* For example, sole control of the source of supply of a critical component for a product or of channels of distribution can give a new venture market dominance even if other areas are weak.

Lack of control over such factors as product development and component prices can make an opportunity unattractive. For example, if a young enterprise's supplier is unable to produce inputs needed at low enough prices or high enough quantities that young enterprise is vulnerable. Maintaining control is a key factor in determining a venture's fate.

A market where a major competitor has a market share of 40 percent or more usually implies a market where power and influence over suppliers, customers, and pricing create a serious barrier and risk for a new firm. Such a firm will have few degrees of freedom. However, if a dominant competitor is at full capacity, is slow to innovate or to add capacity in a large and growing market, or routinely ignores or abuses the customer (Bell Canada is a frequent example), there may be an entry opportunity. However, entrepreneurs usually do not find such sleepy competition in dynamic, emerging industries dense with opportunity.

Entry Barriers. Having a favourable window of opportunity is important. Having or being able to gain proprietary protection, regulatory advantage, or other legal or contractual advantage, such as exclusive rights to a market or with a distributor, is attractive. Having or being able to gain an advantage in response/lead times is important because these can create barriers to entry or expansion by others. For example, advantages in response/lead times in technology, product innovation, market innovation, people, location, resources, or capacity make an opportunity attractive. Possession of well-developed, high-quality, accessible contacts that are the product of years of building a top-notch reputation and that cannot be acquired quickly is also advantageous. Sometimes this competitive advantage may be so strong as to provide dominance in the marketplace, even though many of the other factors are weak or average. An example of how quickly the joys of start-up may fade if others cannot be kept out is the experience of firms in the hard disk industry that were unable to erect entry barriers into the market in the early to mid-1980s. During this period nearly 100 hard disk drive companies were launched and severe price competition led to a major industry shakeout.

If a firm cannot keep others out or if it faces already existing entry barriers, it is unattractive. An easily overlooked issue is a firm's capacity to gain distribution of its product. As simple as it may sound, even venture-capital-backed companies fall victim to this market issue. Air Florida apparently assembled all the right ingredients, including substantial financing, yet was unable to secure sufficient gate space for its airplanes. Even though it sold passenger seats, it had no place to pick the passengers up or drop them off!

Management Team Issues

Entrepreneurial Team. Attractive opportunities have existing teams that are strong and contain industry superstars. The team has proven profit and loss experience in the same technology, market, and service area, and members have complementary and compatible skills. An unattractive opportunity does not have such a team in place or has no team.

Industry and Technical Experience. A management track record of significant accomplishment in the industry, with the technology, and in the market area, with a proven profit and lots of achievements where the venture will compete is highly desirable. A top-notch management team can become the most important strategic competitive advantage in an industry. Imagine relocating the Chicago Bulls or the Phoenix Suns to Halifax, Nova Scotia. Do you think you would have a winning competitor in the National Basketball Association?

Integrity. Trust and integrity are the oil and glue that make economic interdependence possible. Having an unquestioned reputation in this regard is a major long-term advantage for entrepreneurs and should be sought in all personnel and backers. A shady past or record of questionable integrity is for B team players only.

Intellectual Honesty. There is a fundamental issue of whether the founders know what they do and do not know, as well as whether they know what to do about shortcomings or gaps in the team and the enterprise.

Fatal-Flaw Issues. Basically, attractive ventures have no fatal flaws; an opportunity is rendered unattractive if it suffers from one or more fatal flaws. Usually, these relate to one of the above criteria, and examples abound of markets that are too small, that have overpowering competition, where the cost of entry is too high, where an entrant is unable to produce at a competitive price, and so on. An example of a fatal-flaw entry barrier is experience. Linda Collier, former Canadian Woman Entrepreneur of the Year, president and CEO of Tri-ad International Freight Forwarding (i.e., air, sea, land) was doing "brisk business" and wanted to expand. She "hired a vice-president to assist with that task. Eight months later, he launched a rival company, taking five Tri-ad employees with him." Fortunately for Collier, the VP had a fatal flaw: inexperience. "This industry is easy to get into. To stay and grow in it is completely different." Within six months his business was bankrupt. This incident with her VP was the second of four tries her employees have made to come after her business. "I must make it look easy," Collier jokes. She has since put multiple measures in place to protect databases, customer profiles, service rates, and non-compete agreements to stymie staff from becoming competitors.[30]

Personal Criteria

Goals and Fit. Is there a good match between the requirements of business and what the founders want out of it? The crux of this is contained in the adage: "Success is *getting* what you want. Happiness is wanting what you get."

Upside/Downside Issues. An attractive opportunity does not have excessive downside risk. The upside and the downside of pursuing an opportunity are not linear, nor are they on the same continuum. The upside is easy, and it has been said that success has a thousand sires. The downside is another matter; it has also been said that failure is an orphan. An entrepreneur needs to be able to absorb the financial downside in such a way that he or she can rebound without becoming indentured to debt obligations. If an entrepreneur's financial exposure in launching the venture is greater than his or her net worth—the resources he or she can reasonably draw upon, and his or her alternative disposable earnings stream if it does not work out—the deal may be too big. While today's bankruptcy laws are generous, the psychological burdens of living through such an ordeal are infinitely more painful than the financial consequences. An existing business needs to consider if a failure will be too demeaning to the firm's reputation and future credibility, aside from the obvious financial consequences.[31]

Opportunity Cost. In pursuing any venture opportunity, there are also opportunity costs. An entrepreneur who is skilled enough to grow a successful, multi-million-dollar venture has talents that are highly valued by medium- to large-size firms as well. While assessing benefits that may accrue in pursuing an opportunity, an entrepreneur needs to heed other alternatives, including potential "golden handcuffs," and account honestly for any cut in salary that may be involved in pursuing a certain opportunity.

Further, pursuing an opportunity can shape an entrepreneur in ways that are hard to imagine. An entrepreneur will probably have time to execute between two and four multi-million-dollar ventures between the ages of 25 and 50. Each of these experiences will position him or her, *for better or for worse*, for the next opportunity. Since an entrepreneur in the early years needs to gain relevant management experience and since building a venture (either one that works or one that does not) takes more time than is commonly believed, it is important to consider alternatives while assessing an opportunity.

Desirability. A good opportunity is not only attractive but also desirable (i.e., good opportunity fits). An intensely personal criterion would be the desire for a certain lifestyle. This desire may preclude pursuing certain opportunities that may be excellent for someone else. The founders of new start-ups are taking time to consider the location of their work. Basing that decision on a telephone area code, favourite mountain bike trail, or a host of other social, cultural, and demographic characteristics of a city or region. Richard Florida of the University of Toronto delivered a keynote address in Saint John, New Brunswick.[32] Florida, drawing on his latest book *Who's Your City?* highlights that the creative economy is making the place where you live the most important decision of your life. Place is not only important, it's more important than ever. Place is becoming more relevant to our individual lives. Where to live is not an arbitrary choice.

Risk/Reward Tolerance. Successful entrepreneurs take calculated risks or avoid risks they do not need to take. This is not to suggest that all entrepreneurs are gamblers or have the same risk tolerance; some are quite conservative while others actually seem to get a kick out of the inherent danger and thrill in higher risk and higher stake games. The real issue is fit—recognizing that gamblers and overly risk-averse entrepreneurs are unlikely to sustain any long-term successes.

Stress Tolerance. Another important dimension of the fit concept is the stressful requirements of a fast-growth high-stakes venture. But having to keep up may not be the sole reason for stress. One investigation of the 62 serial entrepreneurs in the 2007 Profit 100 found that the initial start-up stage was the most stressful time.[33] Brik Eksten of Markham, Ontario-based Digital Rapids Corp., which helps TV and film producers place content on the Internet, notes that things get easier the more ventures you have under your belt: Eksten went from "only the worried survive" to "there will always be setbacks. Eventually, you become accustomed to a certain level of bombardment." A 2008 study published in the *Journal of Business Venturing* revealed that thinking and planning for the future may reduce the stress an entrepreneur faces.[34]

Strategic Differentiation

Degree of Fit. To what extent is there a good fit among the driving forces (founders and team, opportunity, and resource requirements) and the timing given the external environment?

Team. There is no substitute for an absolutely top quality team. The execution of and the ability to adapt and to devise constantly new strategies is vital to survival and success. A team is nearly unstoppable if it can inculcate into the venture a philosophy and culture of superior learning, as well as teaching skills, an ethic of high standards, delivery of results, and constant improvement. Are they free agents—clear of employment, noncompete, proprietary rights, and trade secret agreements—who are able to pursue the opportunity?

Service Management. Research was conducted across a wide range of industries with several hundred companies to determine why customers stopped buying these companies' products. The results were surprising: 15 percent of the customers defected because of quality and 70 percent stopped using a product or service because of bad customer service. Having a "turbo-service" concept that can be delivered consistently can be a major competitive weapon against small and large competitors alike. Home Depot, in the home supply business, and Lexus, in the auto industry, have set an entirely new standard of service for their respective industries. Studies have also shown that service recovery is an important ingredient. When things do go wrong, what transpires to "recover" can be crucial: We're sorry your meal is late, how can we make it up to you? We apologize for overbooking, how can we make this right? A loyal customer is worth a lot. Customer relations can be managed and the best individuals and organizations have learned how to keep customers loyal.

Timing. From business to historic military battles to political campaigns, timing is often the one element that can make a significant difference. Time can be an enemy or a friend; being too early or too late can be fatal. The key is to row with the tide, not against it. Strategically, ignoring this principle is perilous.

Technology. A breakthrough, proprietary product is no guarantee of success, but it creates a formidable competitive advantage (see Exhibit 3.8).

Flexibility. Maintaining the capacity to commit and uncommit quickly, to adapt, and to abandon if necessary is a major strategic weapon, particularly when competing with larger organizations. Larger firms can typically take six years or more to change basic strategy and 10 to 20 years or more to change the culture.

Opportunity Orientation. To what extent is there a constant alertness to the marketplace? A continual search for opportunities? As one insightful entrepreneur put it, "Any opportunity that just comes in the door to us, we do not consider an opportunity. And we do not have a strategy until we are saying no to lots of opportunities."

Pricing. One common mistake of new companies, with high-value-added products or services in a growing market, is to underprice. A price slightly below to as much as 20 percent below competitors is rationalized as necessary to gain market entry. In a 30-percent gross margin business, a 10-percent price increase results in a 20 to 36-percent increase in gross margin and will lower the breakeven sales level for a company with $900,000 in fixed costs to $2.5 million from $3 million. At the $3-million sales level, the company would realize an extra $180,000 in pre-tax profits.

Distribution Channels. Having access to the distribution channels is sometimes overlooked or taken for granted. New channels of distribution can leapfrog and demolish traditional channels;[35] for example, direct mail, home shopping networks, infomercials, the World Wide Web, and the coming revolution in interactive television in your own home.

Room for Error. How forgiving is the business and the financial strategy? How wrong can the team be in estimates of revenue costs, cash flow, timing, and capital requirements? How bad can things get, yet be able to survive? If some single-engine planes are more prone to accidents, by 10 or more times, which plane do you want to fly in? High leverage, lower gross margins, and lower operating margins are the signals in a small company of flights destined for fatality.

EXHIBIT 3.8   Canadian Inventions in the 20th Century

Hydrofoil boat	Alexander Bell and Casey Baldwin (1908)
Jolly Jumper	Olivia Pool (1910)
Variable pitch propeller	Wallace Turnbull (1918)
Ski-Doo	Armand Bombardier (1922)
Snowblower	Arthur Sicard (1925)
Quartz clock	Warren Marrison (1927)
Pablum	Alan Brown, Theodore Drake, and Frederick Tisdall (1930)
Plexiglass	Wiliam Chalmers (1931)
Scanning electron microscope	James Hillier and Albert Prebus (1939)
Paintroller	Norman Breakey (1940)
Walkie-talkie	Donald L. Hings (1942)
Garbage bag	Harry Wasylyk and Larry Hansen (1950)
Electric wheelchair	George Klein (1952)
Instant replay	CBC's Hockey Night in Canada (1955)
Alkaline battery	Lewis Urry (1959)
Wonderbra	Louise Poirier (1964)
IMAX	Grahame Ferguson , Roman Kroitor, and Robert Kerr (1968)
UV degradable plastics	James Guillet (1971)
Computerized Braille	Roland Galarneau (1972)
Digital film colourization	Wilson Markle and Brian Hunt (1983)
Abdominizer	Dennis Colonello (1984)
Newt suit	Phil Nuytten (1987)
CPR mannequin	Diane Croteau and Richard Brault (1989)
Infant stretcher	Wendy Murphy (1990)

GATHERING INFORMATION

Finding Ideas

Finding a potential opportunity is most often a matter of being the right person, in the right place, at the right time. Certainly past experience and industry exposure can help, but one also has to be tuned in and astutely listening. Creativity again plays a role in sense-making and generating connections to make mental leaps. How can you increase your chances of being the next Anita Roddick of The Body Shop or Ablan Leon of Leon's Furniture? Numerous sources of information can help generate ideas.

Existing Businesses   Purchasing an ongoing business is an excellent way to find a new business idea. Such a route to a new venture can save time and money and can reduce risk as well. Investment bankers and business brokers are knowledgeable about businesses for sale, as are trust officers. However, brokers do not advertise the very best private businesses for sale, and the real gems are usually bought by the individuals or firms closest to them, such as management, directors, customers, suppliers, or financial backers. Bankruptcy judges have a continual flow of ventures in serious trouble. Excellent opportunities may be buried beneath all the financial debris of a bankrupt firm.

Franchises   Franchising is another way to enter an industry, by either starting a franchise operation or becoming a franchisee. This is a fertile area. The number of franchisors nationally stands at more than 400, according to the Canadian Franchise Association and franchisors account for well over $100 billion in sales annually and approximately one-fifth of all retail sales. See Chapter 13 "Franchising" for a more complete discussion of franchises, including resource information.

Patents   Patent brokers specialize in marketing patents that are owned by individual inventors, corporations, universities, or other research organizations to those seeking new commercially viable products. Some brokers specialize in international product licensing, and occasionally a patent broker will purchase an invention and then resell it. Although, over the years, a few unscrupulous brokers have tarnished the patent broker's image, acquisitions effected by reputable brokers have resulted in significant new products. For example, Bausch & Lomb acquired, through National Patent Development Corporation, the rights to hydron, a material used in contact lenses. Some patent brokers are:

- Inventarium, Montréal, Québec
- Furman & Kallio, Regina, Saskatchewan
- Battison Williams Dupuis, Winnipeg, Manitoba
- Mario Theriault & Co., Fredericton, New Brunswick
- Stewart McKelvey, Halifax, Nova Scotia and the rest of Atlantic Canada
- Adams Patent & Trademark Agency, Kanata, Ontario
- Semiconductor Insights, Kanata, Ontario
- Borden Ladner Gervais, nationwide, Canada
- Smart & Biggar/Fetherstonaugh, nationwide, Canada
- McCarthy Tétrault, nationwide, Canada

Product Licensing   A good way to obtain exposure to many product ideas available from universities, corporations, and independent investors is to subscribe to information services such as the *American Bulletin of International Technology*, *Selected Business Ventures* (published by General Electric), *Technology Mart*, *Patent Licensing Gazette*, and the National Technical Information Service. In addition, corporations, not-for-profit research institutions, and universities are sources of ideas.

Corporations. Corporations engaged in R&D often develop inventions or services that they do not exploit commercially. These inventions either do not fit existing product lines or marketing programs or do not represent sufficiently large markets to be interesting to major corporations. A good number of such corporations license these kinds of inventions, either through patent brokers, product-licensing information services, or their own patent-marketing efforts. Directly contacting a corporation with a licensing program may prove fruitful. Among the major corporations known to have active internal patent-marketing efforts are the following:

- Mosaid[36]
- Texas Instruments
- Nortel Networks
- Intel
- Dow Chemical
- Volkswagen
- Juniper Networks

Not-for-Profit Research Institutes. These non-profit organizations do R&D under contract to the government and private industry as well as some internally sponsored investigation of new products and processes that can be licensed to private corporations for further development, manufacturing, and marketing. One example of how this works is

Battelle Memorial Institute's participation in the development of xerography and the subsequent license of the technology to the Haloid Corporation, now Xerox Corporation. Canada's National Research Council (NRC) is composed of over 20 institutes with active licensing programs.

Universities. A number of universities are active in research in the physical sciences and seek to license inventions that result from this research either directly or through an associated research foundation that administers its patent program. Massachusetts Institute of Technology and the California Institute of Technology publish periodic reports containing abstracts of inventions they own that are available for licensing. In addition, since a number of very good ideas developed in universities never reach formal licensing outlets, another way to find these ideas is to become familiar with the work of researchers in your area of interest. Among the universities that have active licensing programs are:

- University of Alberta
- University of British Columbia
- University of Waterloo
- McMaster University
- Carleton University
- University of Montréal
- Memorial University of Newfoundland

Industry and Trade Contacts

Trade Shows and Association Meetings. Trade shows and association meetings in a number of industries can be an excellent way to examine the products of many potential competitors, meet distributors and sales representatives, learn of product and market trends, and identify potential products. The Canadian Photonics Consortium is a good example of an association that holds such seminars and meetings.

Customers. Contacting potential customers of a certain type of product can identify a need and where existing products might be deficient or inadequate. Discussions with doctors who head medical services at hospitals might lead to product ideas in the biomedical equipment business.

Distributors and Wholesalers. Contacting people who distribute a certain type of product can yield extensive information about the strengths and weaknesses of existing products and the kinds of product improvements and new products that are needed by customers.

Competitors. Examining products offered by companies competing in an industry can show whether an existing design is protected by patent and whether it can be improved or imitated.

Former Employers. A number of businesses are started with products or services, or both, based on technology and ideas developed by entrepreneurs while others employed them. In some cases, research laboratories were not interested in commercial exploitation of technology, or the previous employer was not interested in the ideas for new products, and the rights were given up or sold. In others, the ideas were developed under government contract and were in the public domain. In addition, some companies will help entrepreneurs set up companies in return for equity. Nortel Networks has done this repeatedly.

Professional Contact. Ideas can also be found by contacting such professionals as patent agents, accountants, commercial bankers, and venture capitalists who come into contact with those seeking to license patents or to start a business using patented products or processes.

Consulting. A method for obtaining ideas that has been successful for technically trained entrepreneurs is to provide consulting and one-of-a-kind engineering designs for people in fields of interest. For example, an entrepreneur wanting to establish a medical equipment company can do consulting or can design experimental equipment for medical researchers.

These kinds of activities often lead to prototypes that can be turned into products needed by a number of researchers. For example, this approach was used in establishing a company to produce psychological testing equipment that evolved from consulting done at a hospital. In another instance the design and manufacture of oceanographic instruments came out of what was developed from consulting done for an oceanographic institute.

Networking. Social networks can be a stimulant and source of new ideas, as well as a source of valuable contacts with people. Much of this requires personal initiative on an informal basis, but around the country, organized networks can facilitate and accelerate the process of making contacts and finding new business ideas. The Digital Moose Lounge is a network for Canadian expatriates living in Silicon Valley and greater San Francisco Bay area. TiE (The Indus Entrepreneurs) is another such organization; with its genesis in Silicon Valley it has grown to over 50 chapters in a dozen countries. Outside of Canada, most Canadian embassies and consulates organize Terry Fox Runs—a great chance to meet up with fellow Canadians.

Shaping Your Opportunity

You will need to invest in thorough research to shape your idea into an opportunity. *Data available about market characteristics, competitors, and so on, are frequently inversely related to the real potential of an opportunity*; that is, if market data are readily available and if the data clearly show significant potential, then a large number of competitors will enter the market and the opportunity will diminish.

The good news: Most data will be incomplete, inaccurate, and contradictory, and their meaning will be ambiguous. For entrepreneurs, gathering the necessary information and seeing possibilities and making linkages where others see only chaos are essential.

Jonathan Calof, director of the Canadian Institute of Competitive Intelligence, defined competitor intelligence as specific and timely information about a business adversary. Finding out about competitors' sales plans, key elements of their corporate strategies, the capacity of their plants and the technology used in them, who their principal suppliers and customers are, and what new products rivals have under development is difficult, but not impossible, even in emerging industries, when talking to intelligence sources.[37]

Using published resources is one source of such information. Interviewing people and analyzing data are also critical. Leonard Fuld believes that because business transactions generate information, which flows into the pubic domain, one can locate intelligence sources by understanding the transaction and how intelligence behaves and flows.[38]

This can be done legally and ethically. There are, of course, less-than-ethical (not to mention illegal) tactics, which include conducting phony job interviews, getting customers to put out phony bid requests, and lying, cheating, and stealing. Entrepreneurs need to be very careful to avoid such practices and are advised to consult legal counsel when in doubt.

The information sources provided on the next page are just a small start. Much creativity, work, and analysis will be involved to find intelligence and to extend the information obtained into useful form. For example, a competitor's income statement and balance sheet will rarely be handed out. Rather, this information must be derived from information in public filings or news articles or from credit reports, financial ratios, and interviews many of which are available on the Internet.[39]

PUBLISHED SOURCES

The first step is a complete search of materials in libraries and on the Internet. You can find a huge amount of published information, databases, and other sources about industries, markets, competitors, and personnel. Some of this information will have been uncovered when you search for ideas. Listed below are additional sources that should help get you started.

Guides and Company Information

Valuable information is available in special issues and the Web sites of *Business 2.0*, *Canadian Business*, *INC.*, *Fast Company*, *Mercury News*, and *Fortune*.

Additional Sources of Intelligence

Everything entrepreneurs need to know will not be found in libraries because this information needs to be highly specific and current. This information is most likely available from people—industry experts, suppliers, and the like. Summarized below are some useful sources of intelligence.

Trade Associations   Trade associations, especially the editors of their publications and information officers, are good sources of information. Trade shows and conferences are prime places to discover the latest activities of competitors.[40]

Employees   Employees who have left a competitor's company often can provide information about the competitor, especially if the employee departed on bad terms. Also, a firm can hire people away from a competitor. While consideration of ethics in this situation is very important, the number of experienced people in any industry is limited, and competitors must prove that a company hired a person intentionally to get specific trade secrets in order to challenge any hiring legally. Students who have worked for competitors are another source of information.

Consulting Firms   Consulting firms frequently conduct industry studies and then make this information available. Frequently, in such fields as computers or software, competitors use the same design consultants, and these consultants can be sources of information.

Market Research Firms   Firms doing market studies, such as those listed under published sources above, can be sources of intelligence.

Key Customers, Manufacturers, Suppliers, Distributors, and Buyers   These groups are often a prime source of information.

Public Filings   Federal, provincial, and local filings, such as with the Canadian Securities Administrators, Canadian Intellectual Property Office, or Access to Information Act, can reveal a surprising amount of information. There are companies that process inquiries of this type.

Reverse Engineering   Reverse engineering can be used to determine costs of production and sometimes even manufacturing methods. An example of this practice is the experience of Advanced Energy Technology, which learned firsthand about such tactics. No sooner had it announced a new product, which was patented, when it received 50 orders, half of which were from competitors asking for only one or two of the items.

Networks   The networks mentioned in Chapter 2 as sources of new venture ideas also can be sources of competitor intelligence.

Other   Classified ads, buyers guides, labour unions, real estate agents, courts, local reporters, and so on, can all provide clues.[41]

INTERNET IMPACT: RESEARCH AND LEARNING

The Internet has become the resource for entrepreneurial research and opportunity exploration. The rapid growth of data sources, Web sites, sophisticated search engines, and consumer response forums allows for up-to-date investigations of business ideas, competitive environments, and value chain resources.

Google is currently the top search engine in the world. One of the reasons for Google's success is its increasingly deep and wide platform of tools. Google offers the means to view, for example, the text of patents and scholarly publications, archives of news stories, and blogs on hundreds of subjects.

As virtual communities of people who share a common interest or passion, blogs can be a tremendously valuable resource of insights and perspectives on potential opportunities. Proactive, low- or no-cost research can also be conducted with emailed questionnaires or by directing potential subjects to a basic Web site set up to collect responses. In addition, the Internet provides entrepreneurs and other proactive searchers with the extraordinary capability to tap wisdom and advice from experts on virtually anything—anywhere in the world.

SCREENING VENTURE OPPORTUNITIES

Time is the ultimate ally and enemy of the entrepreneur. The harsh reality is that you will not have enough time in a quarter, a year, or a decade to pursue all the ideas for businesses you and your team can think of. Perhaps the cruelest part of the paradox is that you have to find and make the time for the good ones. To complicate the paradox, you do not have a strategy until you are saying no to lots of opportunities! This demand is part of the both punishing and rewarding Darwinian aspect of entrepreneurship: Many will try, many will fail, some will succeed, and a few will excel. While the number of new enterprises launched in Canada can vary widely from year to year, only a small percentage of those will ever prove to be opportunities that achieve sales of $1 million or more. Many live by the creed: "Go big or go home!" and feel being bold is critical to getting noticed. Studies show that those who are outspoken are rewarded more.

QuickScreen

If most sophisticated private equity investors and venture capitalists invest in only 2 to 3 out of 100 ideas, then one can see how important it is to focus on a few superior ideas. The ability to quickly and efficiently reject ideas is a very important entrepreneurial mind-set. To make the struggle more manageable, two methodologies are provided on the Online Learning Centre at www.mcgrawhill.ca/olc/timmons. The first, QuickScreen, should enable you to conduct a preliminary review and evaluation of an idea in an hour. Unless the idea has been, or you are confident it can be, moulded and shaped so that it has the four anchors, you will waste a lot of time on a lower potential idea.

Venture Opportunity Screening Exercises (VOSE)

The second methodology, the Venture Opportunity Screening Exercises, is also located on the Online Learning Centre at www.mcgrawhill.ca/olc/timmons. These exercises are designed to segment the screening of ideas into manageable pieces. The QuickScreen provides a broad overview of an idea's potential. In a team effort, each member of the team should complete the exercise separately and then meet as a team to merge the results. After each VOSE, you should revisit the QuickScreen and reevaluate your scoring.

Chapter Summary

1. Ideas are a dime a dozen. Perhaps 1 out of 100 becomes a truly great business, and 1 in 10 to 15 becomes a higher potential business. The complex transformation of an idea into a true opportunity is akin to a caterpillar becoming a butterfly.

2. High potential opportunities invariably solve an important problem, want, or need that someone is willing to pay for now. In renowned venture capitalist Arthur Rock's words: "I look for ideas that will change the way people live and work."

3. There are decided patterns in superior opportunities, and recognizing these patterns is an entrepreneurial skill aspiring entrepreneurs need to develop.

4. Rapid changes and disruptions in technology, regulation, information flows, and the like cause opportunity creation. The journey from idea to high potential opportunity requires navigating an undulating, constantly changing, three-dimensional relief map while inventing the vehicle and road map along the way.

5. Some of the best opportunities actually require some of the least amount of capital, especially via the Internet.

6. The best opportunities often don't start out that way. They are crafted, shaped, moulded, and reinvented in real time and market space. Fit with the entrepreneur and resources, the timing, and the balance of risk and reward govern the ultimate potential.

7. The highest potential ventures are found in high growth markets, with high gross margins, and robust free cash flow characteristics, because their underlying products or services add significantly greater value to the customer, compared with the next best alternatives.

8. Trial and error. Learning-by-doing alone is not enough for developing breakthrough ventures, which require experience, creativity, and conceptualizing.

Study Questions

1. What is the difference between an idea and a good opportunity?

2. Why is it said that ideas are a dime a dozen?

3. What role does experience play in the opportunity creation process, and where do most good opportunities come from? Why is trial-and-error learning not good enough?

4. List the sources of ideas that are most relevant to your personal interests, and conduct a search using the Internet.

5. What conditions and changes that may occur in society and the economy spawn and drive future opportunities? List as many as you can think of as you consider the next 10 years.

6. Evaluate your best idea against the summary criteria in Exhibit 3.7. What appears to be its potential? What has to happen to convert it into a high potential business?

Mind Stretchers   *Have you considered?*

1. Steve Jobs and Steve Wozniak, co-founders of Apple, were kids when they built their first computers. Colonel Sanders was 65 years old when he started to expand Kentucky Fried Chicken. What is an opportunity for whom?

2. Most successful existing businesses are totally preoccupied with their most important, existing customers and therefore lack the peripheral opportunity vision to spot new products and services. Is this happening where you work? Is this an opportunity for you?

3. The most successful ventures have leadership and people as important competitive advantages. How does this change the way you think about opportunities?

4. Who can you work with during the next few years to learn a business and have the chance to spot new opportunities outside the weak peripheral vision of an established business?

5. Barriers to entry can create opportunities for those with the right knowledge and experience. Why is this so? Can you find some examples?

EXERCISE   Idea Generation Guide

Before beginning the process of generating ideas for new ventures, it is useful to reflect on an old German proverb that says, "Every beginning is hard." If you allow yourself to think creatively, you will be surprised at the number of interesting ideas you can generate once you begin.

The Idea Generation Guide is an exercise in generating ideas. The aim is for you to generate as many interesting ideas as possible. *While generating your ideas, do not evaluate them or worry about their implementation.* Discussion and exercises in the rest of the book will allow you to evaluate these ideas to see if they are opportunities and to consider your own personal entrepreneurial strategy.

And remember—in any creative endeavour there are no right answers.

Name: _____

Date: _____

Step 1

Generate a list of as many new venture ideas as possible. As a consumer or paid user, think of the biggest, most frustrating, and painful task or situation you continually must take, and one which would be worth a lot to eliminate or minimize. These are often the seeds of real opportunities. Thinking about any unmet or poorly filled customer needs you know of that have resulted from regulatory changes, technological changes, knowledge and information gaps, lags, asymmetries, inconsistencies, and so forth, will help you generate such a list. Also, think about various products and services (and their substitutes) and the providers of these products or services. If you know of any weaknesses or vulnerabilities, you may discover new venture ideas.

Step 2

Expand your list if possible. Think about your personal interests, your desired lifestyle, your values, what you feel you are likely to do very well, and contributions you would like to make.

Step 3

Ask at least three people who know you well to look at your list, and revise your list to reflect any new ideas emerging from this exchange. See the discussion about getting feedback in Chapter 1.

Step 4

Jot down insights, observations, and conclusions that have emerged about your business ideas or your personal preferences. Which ones solve the greatest pain-point/aggravation/frustration for which you (and others you have spoken with) would pay a significant premium to eliminate?

CASE   WE BUILT IT, NOW WILL THEY COME? bOK SYSTEMS CORP.

Preparation Questions

1. If you were the CEO of bOK Systems which option or combination of options would you choose?

2. How would you go about implementing those choices?

The Problem

Aydin Mirzaee was about to graduate with a degree in Electrical and Computer Engineering and a minor in Entrepreneurship and Management. While in school, Aydin found it almost impossible to effectively use his cellphone. Cellphones were obviously very convenient as they were portable. Unfortunately, in Canada, cellphone use was not practical from a price perspective.

Aydin had a cellphone plan that included 100 daytime outgoing minutes. If he ever used more than his allotted minutes, his phone company would charge him approximately 35 cents a minute. This meant that an hour-long conversation would cost over $20. Long distance calls to cities within Canada or to the U.S. were equally expensive (e.g., calling another city such as Montreal, Toronto, or Calgary cost him about 35 cents a minute).

Having grown up in New York, Aydin found it very expensive to call his family and friends to keep in touch. Calling cards were an option, but they were definitely not hassle free. With calling cards, one had to dial a 1-800 number and then enter an access code. Every time the calling card ran out of funds, a trip to the convenience store was necessary to purchase another one. With a busy schedule, this was not convenient. As a student, having a $100/month cellphone bill was not easy to justify. This was not just a problem for Aydin but one that was shared

This case was written by Aydin Y. Mirzaee and Prescott C. Ensign, for purposes of classroom discussion.

by many. A better alternative was needed. This realization was what led Aydin to start bOK Systems (www.bOKnow.com).

bOK Systems was Aydin's first major start-up and was proving to be a great learning experience. It was now October 2007, nearly 18 months after graduation, Aydin worked full-time for a large multinational telecommunications equipment manufacturer and was discovering that living the life of an entrepreneur had its glamour and fun times but it also had its share of challenges, stressful decisions, and sleepless nights.

The Solution

The structure of cellphone plans in Canada led Aydin to wonder if there was a way to transform all outgoing calls into incoming ones. If such a method could be discovered, then this would potentially give him the opportunity to make as many calls as he wanted to without using up his daytime minutes. The idea was simply this:

Instead of just calling someone directly, one could...

1. Compose a text message that contained the destination number.
2. Send this text message to the bOK number.
3. Receive an incoming call. Pick up and talk.

For example, assume that Amanda lives in Ottawa and would like to call her friend Jill in New York. Amanda creates a text message that contains nothing but Jill's phone number in New York, which is: 7185207734. She sends this text message to the bOK Ottawa number, which is: 6132552437. After about 5–10 seconds, both Amanda and Jill receive a local incoming call on their phones. When they pick up, they can start talking. In the process, Jill will not notice a difference in the way she receives the call. Amanda saves money and the friends can talk for as long as they want.

The advantage here was that one could initiate a call as an incoming one rather than an outgoing one and anyone with an unlimited incoming call plan, would not use up their minutes. The destination party would not notice a difference between a call initiated through bOK and one initiated through conventional means.

This all sounded very nice. However, there was a long way to go. Aydin spoke to his brother Amin at McGill about the idea and together they set forth the plan to complete the project. The process was long and arduous. Aydin and Amin decided to bring two other engineers on board, an accomplished mathematician from Chicago also studying at McGill and a cousin in Toronto to help create the final product. After about three to four months of work, the first version of bOK was ready. The first version was really more a test than anything else.

The founders started using bOK on their own. They told a few friends but made sure to tell them not to spread the word. Almost overnight, about 150 people started using the system to make their phone calls. The traffic was too high for the platform in place at the time to handle. It was for this reason that the founders had to shut down the system and go back to the drawing board. Except, what they realized was that there was a lot of interest in the product that they had put together. This was very exciting and it was the beginning of their business endeavour. The founders realized that this could be turned into a very viable operation if a good business model were put together.

The business model originally conceived would allow users to call any location in North America or internationally for prices lower than what phone cards offered. bOK would be able to undercut phone card prices as they would be dealing directly with end consumers whereas phone card companies had to deal with many intermediaries before their product reached their target customers. This was a unique business model and everyone was quite excited about the possibilities.

Alternatives

The bOK founding team had to make a decision on what to do and it needed to act fast as things were changing rapidly around them. The truth was that bOK was late to market and this made things difficult. At the time, a few options came to mind:

1. Quit and try a new idea.
2. Tweak the idea to make bOK ahead of the game.
3. Obtain venture capital/angel funding.
4. Attempt to sell the product/firm.
5. Bring in a new CEO.
6. Quit all other engagements and focus on bOK full time.

The options were many and each required further analysis. Aydin wondered as CEO, which option he should choose? There may be no "right answer" in business, but some paths were better than others. And how would he go about implementing his decisions?

4

THE BUSINESS PLAN

Madame, enclosed please find the novel you commissioned. It is in two volumes. If I had had more time I could have written it in one.

Voltaire

Upon completion of this chapter, you will be able to:

1. Utilize a business plan model proven and refined through years of use.

2. Determine what needs to be included in the plan, why, and for whom. Remember, the business plan (which is not the business!) is written for an intended audience.

3. Identify some of the pitfalls in the business plan preparation process and how to avoid these.

4. Appreciate what has to be done to develop and complete a business plan for your proposed venture.

5. See that a well-articulated business plan is an important part of the entrepreneurial process, not an end in itself.

6. Critically examine a business plan developed by a young entrepreneur to raise capital for Chide.it—a new crowdsourcing Internet venture.

DEVELOPING THE BUSINESS PLAN

The business plan itself is the culmination of a usually lengthy, arduous, creative, and iterative process that, as we explored in Chapter 3 and the accompanying exercises, can transform a raw idea into a magnificent opportunity. The plan will carefully articulate the merits, requirements, risks, and potential rewards of the opportunity and how it will be seized. It will demonstrate how the *Four Anchors* noted below (and in the online exercises for Chapter 3) reveal themselves to the founders and investors by converting all the research, careful thought, and creative problem solving from the online Venture Opportunity Screening Exercises into a thorough plan. The business plan for a high potential venture reveals the business's ability to:

- *Create* or add significant value to a customer or end-user.

- *Solve* a significant problem, or meet a significant want or need for which someone will pay a premium.

- *Have* robust market, margin, and moneymaking characteristics: large enough ($50-plus million), high growth (20-plus percent), high margins (40-plus percent), strong and early free cash flow (recurring revenue, low assets, and working capital), high profit potential (10 to 15 percent after tax), and attractive realizable returns for investors (25 to 30 percent IRR).
- *Fit* well with the founder(s) and management team at the time, in the marketspace, and with the risk-reward balance.

The plan becomes the point of departure for prospective investors to begin their due diligence to ascertain potential and various risks of the venture: technology risks, market risks, management risks, competitive and strategic risks, and financial risks. Even if you do not intend to raise outside capital, this homework is vital. The collisions between founders and investors that occur during meetings, discussions, and investigations reveal a great deal to all parties and begin to set the code for their relationship and negotiations. Getting to know each other much more closely is a crucial part of the evaluation process. Everyone will be thinking: Are these intelligent people; can we work well with them during thick but especially thin times; are they creative; do they listen; can they add value to the venture; is this the right management; do I want them as business partners; are they honest; are we having fun yet? Recent research points to the important role that "storytelling" plays in securing funding.[1] Martin Martens of Concordia University, Jennifer Jennings, and Dev Jennings both of the University of Alberta discovered that effective narratives convey credible information to those that are in a position to invest.

The investors who can bring the most insight, know-how, and contacts to the venture, and thus add the greatest value, will reveal themselves as well. The most valuable investors will see weaknesses, even flaws, in how the market is viewed, the technology or service, the strategies, the proposed size and structure of the financing, and the team, and will propose strategies and people to correct these. If it is the right investor, it can make the difference between an average and a good or great venture.

The Plan Is Obsolete at the Printer

The authors have argued for four decades that the plan is obsolete the instant it emerges from the printer. In today's fast-paced climate, it is obsolete before it goes into the printer! The pace of technological and information-age change, and the dynamism of the global marketplace, shorten the already brief life expectancy of any business plan. It is nearly impossible to find a year-old venture today that is identical in strategy, market focus, products or services, and team as the original business plan described.

Work in Progress—Bent Knees Required

In such a rapidly changing environment, flexibility and responsiveness become critical survival skills. Developing an idea into a business, and articulating how this will be done via a business plan, requires an open mind and "bent knees," along with clear focus, commitment, and determination.

The business plan should be thought of as a work in progress. Though it must be completed if you are trying to raise outside capital, attract key advisors, directors, team members, or the like, it can never be considered finished. And as Yuval Deutsch of York University and Thomas Ross of the University of British Columbia point out, having good reputable directors onboard allows a young firm to send a positive signal of high quality.[2] Like a cross-country flight plan, many unexpected changes can occur along the way: a thunderstorm, smoke-impaired visibility, fog, or powerful winds can develop. One has to be prepared to continually adjust course to minimize risk and ensure successful completion of the journey. Such risk-reward management is inherent in the business planning process.

The Plan Is Not the Business

Developing the business plan is one of the best ways to define the blueprint, strategy, resources, and people requirements for a new venture. It is this document that focuses and communicates the founder's vision. The vast majority of INC.'s 500 fastest growing companies had business plans at the outset. Without a business plan, it is exceedingly difficult to raise capital from informal or formal investors.

Too often first-time entrepreneurs jump to a simplistic conclusion: All that is needed is a fat, polished, and enticing business plan and the business will automatically be successful. They confuse the plan with building the business. Some of the most impressive business plans never become great businesses. And some of the weakest plans lead to extraordinary businesses. Mitch Kapor's original business plan for Lotus Development Corporation, creator of the 1-2-3 spreadsheet, was a brief letter, some descriptions of the personal computer market, a description of nearly 10 separate products, a one-year monthly start-up budget, and a five-year goal of $30 million in revenue, which would require about $200,000 to $300,000 in capital. Venture capital backers Sevin-Rosen basically discarded the plan, the strategy, the product mix, the capital requirements, the launch plan, and the vision for the venture's first five years. These venture capitalists concluded the opportunity was much bigger, that $1 million of start-up capital was required, that the company would either be several hundred million dollars in revenue in five years, or would not be in business, even at $30 million in sales. The first-mover advantage of a warp-speed launch strategy was vital, and the rocket needed to be lit. The rest is history. Lotus Development reached $500 million in revenue in the first five years. Though the business plan called for sales of $1 million the first year, actual sales were $53 million. The following year, sales reached $156 million. The company was later purchased by IBM for $3.5 billion. But on the whole, evidence suggests that good business plans lead to prosperous businesses. According to Kevin Hindle of the Australian Graduate School of Entrepreneurship and Brent Mainprize of Royal Roads University: "With a good plan in hand, an entrepreneur should not let a lack of resources inhibit his or her pursuit of opportunity."[3]

The message here is two-edged. The odds can be shaped in your favour through the development of a business plan. But just because you have a plan does not mean the business will be an automatic success. Unless the fundamental opportunity is there, along with the requisite resources and team needed to pursue it, the best plan in the world won't make much difference. Some helpful tips in preparing a business plan are summarized in Exhibit 4.1.

Some Tips from the Trenches

The most valuable lessons about preparing a business plan and raising venture capital come from entrepreneurs who have succeeded in these endeavours. Thomas Huseby, founder and head of SeaPoint Ventures, is a remarkable entrepreneur who has raised more than $80 million of venture capital as CEO of two telecommunications start-up companies that subsequently became publicly traded. Consider the following wisdom gleaned from his own experience on both sides of the negotiating table: entrepreneur/CEO and venture capitalist.

RE: Venture Capitalists
- There are a lot of venture capitalists. Once you meet one you could end up meeting all 700-plus of them.
- Getting a "no" from venture capitalists is as hard as getting a "yes;" qualify your targets and force others to say "no."
- Be vague about what other venture capitalists you are talking to.
- Don't ever meet with an associate or junior member twice without also meeting with a partner in that venture capital firm.

RE: The Plan
- Stress your business concept in the executive summary.
- The numbers don't matter; but the economics (e.g., value proposition and business model) really matter.
- Make the business plan look and feel good.

EXHIBIT 4.1   Do's and Don'ts for Preparing a Business Plan

Do
Involve all of the management team in the preparation of the business plan.
Make the plan logical, comprehensive, readable, and as short as possible.
Demonstrate commitment to the venture by investing a significant amount of time and some money in preparing the plan.
Articulate what the critical risks and assumptions are and how and why these are tolerable.
Disclose and discuss any current or potential problems in the venture.
Identify several alternative sources of financing.
Spell out the proposed deal—how much for what ownership share—and how investors will win.
Be creative in gaining the attention and interest of potential investors.
Remember that the plan is not the business and that an ounce of can-do implementation is worth two pounds of planning.
Accept orders and customers that will generate a positive cash flow, even if it means you have to postpone writing the plan.
Know your targeted investor group (e.g., venture capitalist, angel investor, bank, or leasing company) and what they really want and what they dislike, and tailor your plan accordingly.
Let realistic market and sales projections drive the assumptions underlying the financial spreadsheets, rather than the reverse.

Don't
Have unnamed, mysterious people on the management team (e.g., a "Mr. G" who is currently a financial vice president with another firm and who will join you later).
Make ambiguous, vague, or unsubstantiated statements, such as estimating sales on the basis of what the team would like to produce.
Describe technical products or manufacturing processes using jargon or in a way that only an expert can understand, because this limits the usefulness of the plan.
Spend money on developing fancy brochures, elaborate PowerPoint and Flash presentations, and other "sizzle"; instead, show the "steak."
Waste time writing a plan when you could be closing sales and collecting cash.
Assume you have a done deal when you have a handshake or verbal commitment but no money in the bank. (The deal is done when the cheque clears!)

- Prepare lots of copies of published articles, contracts, market studies, purchase orders, and the like.
- Prepare very detailed résumés and reference lists of key players in the venture.
- If you can't do the details, make sure you hire someone who can.

RE: The Deal
- Make sure your current investors are as desperate as you are.
- Create a market for your venture.
- Never say "no" to an offer price.
- Use a lawyer who is experienced at closing venture deals.
- Don't stop selling until the money is in the bank.
- Make it a challenge.
- Never lie.

RE: The Fund-Raising Process
- It is much harder than you ever thought it could be.
- You can last much longer than you ever thought you could.
- The venture capitalists have done this before and have to do this for the rest of their lives!

This is particularly valuable advice for any entrepreneur seeking outside capital and anticipating dealing with investors.[4]

What about the possible loss of critical members of your new ventures team? The Chide.it sample business plan (found at the end of this chapter) value proposition is based heavily on the knowledge and skill found within key individuals. Shelley MacDougall of Acadia University and Deborah Hurst of Athabasca University point out that "knowledge-intensive businesses in the fast-moving high technology sector are dependent upon the creation and transfer of knowledge among skilled employees. Ironically, this critical feature of organizational success resides with employees who tend to be somewhat transient." MacDougall and Hurst identify how entrepreneurs can work to become adept at coping with these challenges by: (1) maintaining an environment that fosters creativity, thus encouraging employees to stay and (2) managing the departure of those that leave.[5]

Reaching that receptive audience is key; particularly, if the venture is pushing a product or service in a new realm. A certain amount of specific knowledge would be required to assess Chide.it's business model. Knowledge-based businesses in general may not be readily appreciated. Research by Gary Gorman of Memorial University of Newfoundland, Peter Rosa of the University of Edinburgh, and Alex Faseruk of Memorial University of Newfoundland examines how new knowledge-based ventures fare compared to ventures in traditional industries when it comes to external financing. The risk assessment practices of chartered banks and government agencies have modified traditional lending approaches to meet the needs of knowledge-based firms. Their findings show that specialized processes are only partially developed and still evolving to handle these new types of ventures. Those providing external financing very much learn during the course of the due diligence and the conclusion is that such lenders must be purposefully sought out![6]

How to Determine If Investors Can Add Value

One of the most frequently missed opportunities in the entire process of developing a business plan and trying to convince outside investors to part with their cash is a consequence of sell-sell-sell! myopia by the founders. Selling ability is one of the most common denominators among successful entrepreneurs.

Too often, however, entrepreneurs—typically out of cash, or nearly so—become so obsessed with selling to prospective investors that they fail to ask great questions and do little serious listening. As a result, these founders learn very little from these prospects, even though they probably know a great deal about the technology, market, and competitors. After all, that is the investor's business.

Entrepreneurs who not only succeed at developing a great business concept but also attract the right investors who can add a great deal of value to the venture through their experience, wisdom, and networks are usually very savvy listeners. They use the opportunity, beyond presenting their plan and selling themselves, to carefully query prospective investors: You've seen our concept, our story, and our strategies, what have we missed? Where are we vulnerable? How would you knock us off? Who will knock us off? How would you modify our strategy? What would you do differently? Who do we need with us to make this succeed? What do you believe has to happen to make this highly successful? Be as blunt as you wish.

Two powerful forces are unleashed in this process. First, as a founder, you will begin to discern just how smart, knowledgeable, and, most important, creative the investors are about the proposed business. Do they have creative ideas, insights, and alternative ways of thinking about the opportunity and strategy that you and your team may not have thought of? This enables you, the founder, to ascertain just what value the investors might add to the venture and whether their approach to telling you and your team that you are "all wet" on certain things is acceptable. Would the relationship be likely to wear you out over time and demoralize you? In the process you will learn a great deal about your plan and the investors.

The second powerful force is the message implicitly sent to the investors when you make such genuine queries and listen, rather than become argumentative and defensive (which they may try to get you to do): We have given this our best shot. We are highly committed to our concept and believe we have the right strategy, but our minds are open. We listen; we learn; we have bent knees; we adapt and change when the evidence and ideas are compelling; we are not granite heads. Investors are much more likely to conclude that you are a founder and a team with which they can work.

The Dehydrated Business Plan

A dehydrated business plan usually runs from four to 10 pages, but rarely more. It covers key points, such as those suggested for the executive summary in the business planning guide that follows. Essentially, such a plan documents the analysis of and information about the heart of the business opportunity, competitive advantages the company will enjoy, and creative insights that an entrepreneur often has.

Since it can usually be prepared in a few hours, it is preferred by entrepreneurs who find it difficult to find enough slack time while operating a business to write a complete plan. In many instances, investors prefer a dehydrated plan in the initial screening phase.

A dehydrated plan is not intended to be used exclusively in the process of raising or borrowing money; it can be a valuable compass to keep you on track. Consider it a map of the main battleground ahead, but remember that it will not provide the necessary details and tactics necessary to conduct the battle.

Who Develops the Business Plan?

Consideration often is given to hiring an outside professional to prepare the business plan, so the management team can use its time to obtain financing and start the business.

There are compelling reasons why it is not a good idea to hire outside professionals. In the process of planning and of writing the business plan, the consequences of different strategies and tactics and the human and financial requirements for launching and building the venture can be examined, before it is too late. For example, one entrepreneur discovered, while preparing his business plan, that the major market for his biomedical product was in nursing homes, rather than in hospital emergency rooms, as he and his physician partner had previously assumed. This realization changed the focus of the marketing effort. Had he left the preparation to an outsider, this might not have been discovered or, at the very least, it is unlikely he would have had the same sense of confidence and commitment to the new strategy.

Who is the Business Plan For?

Identifying and understanding the audience is important. Allan Riding, Deloitte Chair in the Management of Growth Enterprises at the University of Ottawa, notes, "I usually recommend multiple plans, varying according to the purpose. One business plan for VCs might stress the upside potential while a business plan for getting a loan might stress the value of the assets and the track record of the owner(s). Likewise, I would use an entirely different plan for managing day-to-day operations. So, my question back to the entrepreneur is always 'what is the purpose of this particular plan?' In my view the purpose should be stated right up front... along with a demonstration that the team and product have the vision and talent to make it all work!"

The sample business plan provided in this chapter, Chide.it, is intended for a venture capital audience that might provide an A round of risk capital. This business plan from the real world is not perfect and some confidential information has been omitted. The goal for this business plan was to open doors and get a dialogue started. The plan contains greater justification for projected revenue generation but far less detail on the expense side. Is this enough to scare off readers? Does the reader need greater explanation for payroll expenditures? Do the increases in rent seem justifiable? What about salary and server costs?[7]

A CLOSER LOOK AT THE WHAT

The Relationship between Goals and Actions

Consider a team that is enthusiastic about an idea for a new business and has done a considerable amount of thinking and initial work evaluating the opportunity (such as thoroughly working through the Venture Opportunity Screening Exercises, found online at www.mcgrawhill.ca/olc/timmons). Team members believe the business they are considering has excellent market prospects and fits well with the skills, experience, personal goals, values, and aspirations of its lead entrepreneur and the management team. They now need to ask about the most significant risks and problems involved in launching the enterprise, the long-term profit prospects, and the future financing and cash flow requirements. The team must determine the demands of operating lead times, seasonality, facility location, marketing and pricing strategy needs, and so forth, so they can take action.

These questions now need to be answered convincingly with the evidence for them shown *in writing*. The planning and the development of such a business plan is neither quick nor easy. In fact, effective planning is a difficult process that demands time, discipline, commitment, dedication, and practice. However, it also can be stimulating and fun as innovative solutions and strategies to solve nagging problems are found.

The skills to write a business plan are not necessarily the ones needed to make a venture successful (although some of these skills are certainly useful). The best single point of departure for, and an anchor during, the planning process is the motto "Can Do," and is an apt one for planning and for making sure that a plan serves the very practical purpose for which it is intended.

Further, if a venture intends to use the business plan to raise capital, it is important for the team to do the planning and write the plan itself. Investors attach great importance to the quality of the management team *and* to their complete understanding of the business they are preparing to enter. Thus, investors want to be sure that what they see is what they get—that is, the team's analysis and understanding of the venture opportunity and its commitment to it. Investors usually correlate a team's ability to communicate the vision with their ability to make it a reality. They are going to invest in a team and a leader, not in a consultant. Nothing less will do, and anything less is usually obvious.

Segmenting and Integrating Information

When planning and writing a business plan, it is necessary to organize information in a way that it can be managed and that is useful.

An effective way to organize information with the idea of developing a business plan is to segment the information into sections, such as the target market, the industry, the competition, the financial plan, and so on, and then integrate the information into a business plan.

This process works best if sections are discrete and the information within them digestible. Then the order in which sections are developed can vary, and different sections can be developed simultaneously. For example, since the heart and soul of a plan lies in the analysis of the market opportunity, of the competition, and of a resultant competitive strategy that can win, it is a good idea to start with these sections and integrate information along the way. Because the financial and operations aspects of the venture will be driven by the rate of growth and the magnitude and the specific substance of the market revenue plans, these can be developed later.

The information is then further integrated into the business plan. The executive summary is prepared last.

Establishing Action Steps

The following steps, centred around actions to be taken, outline the process by which a business plan is written. These action steps are presented in the exercise found at the end of the chapter, "The Business Plan Guide."

- *Segmenting information.* An overall plan for the project, by section, needs to be devised and needs to include priorities—who is responsible for each section, the due date of a first draft, and the due date of a final draft.
- *Creating an overall schedule.* Next, create a more specific list of tasks, identify priorities and who is responsible for them. Determine when they will be started, and when they will be completed. This list needs to be as specific and detailed as possible. Tasks need to be broken down into the smallest possible component (e.g., a series of phone calls may be necessary before a trip). The list then needs to be examined for conflicts and lack of reality in time estimates. Peers and business associates can be asked to review the list for realism, timing, and priorities.
- *Creating an action calendar.* Tasks on the do list then need to be placed on a calendar. When the calendar is complete, the calendar needs to be re-examined for conflicts or lack of realism.
- *Doing the work and writing the plan.* The necessary work needs to be done and the plan written. Adjustments need to be made to the do list and the calendar, as necessary. As part of this process, it is important to have a plan reviewed by a lawyer to make sure it contains no misleading statements, unnecessary information, and caveats. The plan also needs to be reviewed by an objective outsider, such as an entrepreneurially minded executive who has significant profit and loss responsibility, or a venture capitalist who would not be a potential investor. No matter how good the lead entrepreneur and his or her team are in planning, there will be issues that they will overlook and certain aspects of the presentation that are inadequate or less than clear. A good reviewer also can act as a sounding board in the process of developing alternative solutions to problems and answers to questions investors are likely to ask.

PREPARING A BUSINESS PLAN

A Complete Business Plan

It may seem to an entrepreneur who has completed the online exercises for Chapter 3 and who has spent hours informally thinking and planning that jotting down a few things is all that needs to be done. *However, there is a great difference between screening an opportunity and developing a business plan.*

There are two important differences in the way these issues need to be addressed. First, a business plan can have two uses: (1) inducing someone to part with $250,000 to $2 million or more, and (2) guiding the policies and actions of the firm over a number of years. Therefore, strategies and statements need to be well thought out, unambiguous, and capable of being supported.

Another difference is that more detail is needed. (The exception to this is the dehydrated business plan discussed earlier in this chapter.) This means the team needs to spend more time gathering detailed data, interpreting it, and presenting it clearly. "Exploitation should begin based primarily on when an entrepreneur's ignorance has been sufficiently reduced through knowledge accumulation."[8] For example, for the purpose of screening an opportunity, it may be all right to note (if one cannot do any better) that the target market for a product is in the $30 to $60 million range and the market is growing over 10 percent per year. For planning an actual launch, this level of detail is not sufficient. The size range would need to be narrowed considerably; if it were not narrowed, those reading or using the plan would have little confidence in this critical number. And saying the target market is growing at over 10 percent is too vague. Does that mean the market grew at the stated rate between last year and the year before, or does it mean that the market grew on average by this amount over the past three years? Also, a statement phrased in terms of "over 10 percent" smacks of imprecision. The actual growth rate needs to be known and needs to be stated. Whether the rate will or will not remain the same, and why, needs to also be explained.

Preparing an effective business plan for a start-up can easily take 200 to 300 hours. Squeezing that amount of time into evenings and weekends can make the process stretch over three to 12 months.

A plan for a business expansion or for a situation such as a leveraged buyout typically takes half this effort because more is known about the business, including the market, its competition, financial and accounting information, and so on.

Exhibit 4.2 is a sample table of contents for a business plan. The information shown is included in most effective business plans and is a good framework to follow. Organizing the material into sections makes dealing with the information more manageable. Also, while the amount of detail and the order of presentation may vary for a particular venture

EXHIBIT 4.2   Business Plan Table of Contents

I. EXECUTIVE SUMMARY
Description of the Business Concept and the Business Opportunity and Strategy.
Target Market and Projections.
Competitive Advantages.
Costs.
Sustainability.
The Team.
The Offering.

II. THE INDUSTRY AND THE COMPANY AND ITS PRODUCT(S) OR SERVICE(S)
The Industry.
The Company and the Concept.
The Product(s) or Service(s).

III. MARKET RESEARCH AND ANALYSIS
Customers.
Market Size and Trends.
Competition and Competitive Edges.
Estimated Market Share and Sales.
Ongoing Market Evaluation.

IV. THE ECONOMICS OF THE BUSINESS
Gross and Operating Margins.
Profit Potential and Durability.
Fixed, Variable, and Semi-variable Costs.
Months to Breakeven.
Months to Reach Positive Cash Flow.

V. MARKETING PLAN
Overall Marketing Strategy.
Pricing.
Sales Tactics.
Service and Warranty Policies.
Advertising and Promotion.
Distribution.

VI. DESIGN AND DEVELOPMENT PLANS
Development Status and Tasks.
Difficulties and Risks.
Product Improvement and New Products.
Costs.
Proprietary Issues.

VII. MANUFACTURING AND OPERATIONS PLAN
Operating Cycle.
Geographical Location.
Facilities and Improvements.
Strategy and Plans.
Regulatory and Legal Issues.

VIII. MANAGEMENT TEAM
Organization.
Key Management Personnel.
Management Compensation and Ownership.
Other Investors.
Employment and Other Agreements and Stock Option and Bonus Plans.
Board of Directors.
Other Shareholders, Rights, and Restrictions.
Supporting Professional Advisors and Services.

IX. OVERALL SCHEDULE

X. CRITICAL RISKS, PROBLEMS, AND ASSUMPTIONS

XI. THE FINANCIAL PLAN
Actual Income Statements and Balance Sheets.
Pro Forma Income Statements.
Pro Forma Balance Sheets.
Pro Forma Cash Flow Analysis.
Breakeven Chart and Calculation.
Cost Control.
Highlights.

XII. PROPOSED COMPANY OFFERING
Desired Financing.
Offering.
Capitalization.
Use of Funds.
Investor's Return.

XIII. APPENDICES

according to its circumstances, most effective business plans contain this information in some form. (The amount of detail and the order in which information is presented is important. These can vary for each particular situation and will depend upon the purpose of the plan and the age and stage of the venture, among other factors.)

A Final Checklist*

This list will help you allocate your time and maintain your focus!
These points will also be important as you prepare for an
oral presentation of your business plan.

Make Your Point Quickly and Give Hierarchy to Your Data—The Details Matter!

✓ Hook the readers, especially in the executive summary, by having a compelling opportunity where you can:
  • Identify a need or opportunity in a large and growing market.
  • Conceptualize a business that will fill that need, or take advantage of that opportunity.
  • Demonstrate that you have the know-how and the team to effectively build a profitable and sustainable business (or identify how you will create such a team).

✓ Prioritize the points you are making into three categories:
  • Essential—without this the plan makes no sense.
  • Good to know—directly supports and gives context to your essential points.
  • Interesting—provides a higher level of understanding of market dynamics, industry, etc., but may not relate directly to the nuts and bolts of your business plan. Interesting information should be relegated to the appendix so it doesn't get in the way of the reader.

✓ Articulate the size of your market: who are your customers, why they will purchase your product or service, how much they will buy at what price.

✓ Include evidence of customers—this will increase your credibility.

✓ Discuss the competition, and why the customer will buy your product or service versus the alternatives.

✓ Articulate your marketing strategy. How will customers become aware of your product and service, and how will you communicate the benefits?

✓ Be specific when discussing your team. Articulate what relevant experience each brings to the business. If you can't identify key managers, you should outline the type of experience you want and a plan for recruiting that person.

✓ Edit for the details—clarity and typos—a sloppy presentation says a lot!

* The authors are grateful to Greg White of Chicago Venture Partners who developed this list and to longtime friend and entrepreneur Frederic Alper for sharing this with us.

INTERNET IMPACT: OPPORTUNITY

Small Business Commerce

An eBay-commissioned telephone survey of companies with less than 100 full-time employees consisted of two sampling components: a random sample of 200 businesses that fit the target criteria, and a random sample of 200 similar businesses that had, in addition, used eBay for purchasing in the past 12 months.

Fifty-one percent of the respondents indicated that the Internet had improved their profitability, and 58 percent said the medium had helped their businesses to grow or expand.

Fully one-third of the participants in the survey sold goods and services online, and 15 percent said the Internet was essential to their survival.

Not surprisingly, survey participants themselves were e-commerce consumers: 54 percent said that they've purchased computers and office technology online, 48 percent have acquired capital equipment and supplies, and 21 percent bought office furnishings. One-third purchased inventory to resell online and 59 percent used the Internet to purchase other business-related goods.

Chapter Summary

1. The business plan is more of a process and work in progress than an end in itself.
2. Given today's pace of change in all areas affecting an enterprise, the plan is obsolete the moment it emerges from the printer.
3. The business plan is a blueprint and flight plan for a journey that converts ideas into opportunities, articulates and manages risks and rewards, and articulates the likely flight path and timing for a venture.
4. The numbers in a business plan don't matter, but the economics of the business model and value proposition matter enormously.
5. The plan is not the business; some of the most successful ventures were launched without a formal business plan or with one that would be considered weak or flawed.
6. Preparing and presenting the plan to prospective investors is one of the best ways for the team to have a trial marriage, to learn about the venture strategy, and to determine who can add the greatest value.
7. The dehydrated business plan can be a valuable shortcut in the process of creating, shaping, and moulding an idea into a business.

Study Questions

1. What is a business plan, for whom is it prepared, and why?
2. Why not hire someone else to write your business plan?
3. How is the plan used by potential investors, and what are the four anchors they are attempting to validate?
4. Please explain the expression: The numbers in the plan don't matter.
5. How can entrepreneurs use the business plan process to identify the best team members, directors, and value-added investors?

Mind Stretchers   *Have you considered?*

1. Under what conditions and circumstances is it not to your advantage to prepare a business plan?
2. Some of the most valuable critiques and inputs on your venture will come from outside your team. Who else should review your plan; who knows the industry/market/technology/competitors?
3. A good friend offers you a look at a business plan. You are a director of a company that is a potential competitor of the venture proposed in the plan. What would you do?

www.mcgrawhill.ca/olc/timmons

EXERCISE   The Business Plan Guide

An Exercise and Framework

This Business Plan Guide follows the order of presentation outlined in Exhibit 4.2. Originally developed by Leonard Smollen and Brian Haslett, based on more than 30 years of observing and working with entrepreneurs and actually preparing and evaluating hundreds of plans, it is intended to make this challenging task easier.

There is no single best way to write a business plan; the task will evolve in a way that suits you and your situation. While there are many ways to approach the preparation for and writing of a business plan, it is recommended that you begin with the market research and analysis sections. In writing your plan, you should remember that although one of the important functions of a business plan is to influence investors, rather than preparing a fancy presentation, you and your team need to prove to yourselves and others that your opportunity is worth pursuing, and to construct the means by which you will do it. Gathering information, making hard decisions, and developing plans comes first.

The Business Plan Guide shows how to present information succinctly and in a format acceptable to investors. While it is useful to keep in mind who your audience is and that information not clearly presented will most likely not be used, it also is important not to be concerned just with format. The Business Plan Guide indicates specific issues and shows you what needs to be included in a business plan and why.

You may feel as though you have seen much of this before. You should. The guide is based on the analytical framework described in the book and builds upon the online Venture Opportunity Screening Exercises. If you have not completed these exercises, it is helpful to do so before proceeding. The Business Plan Guide will allow you to draw on data and analysis developed in the Venture Opportunity Screening Exercises as you prepare your business plan.

As you proceed through the Business Plan Guide, remember that statements need to be supported with data whenever possible. Note also that it is sometimes easier to present data in graphic, visual form. Include the source of all data, the methods and/or assumptions used, and the credentials of people doing research. If data on which a statement is based are available elsewhere in the plan, be sure to reference where.

Remember that the Business Plan Guide is just that—a guide. It is intended to be applicable to a wide range of product and service businesses. For any particular industry or market, certain critical issues are unique to that industry or market. In the chemical industry, for example, some special issues of significance currently exist, such as increasingly strict regulations at all levels of government concerning the use of chemical products and the operation of processes, diminishing viability of the high capital cost, special-purpose chemical processing plants serving a narrow market, and long delivery times of processing equipment. In the electronics industry, the special issues may be the future availability and price of new kinds of large-scale integrated circuits. Common sense should rule in applying the guide to your specific venture.

The Guide

Name: _____

Venture: _____

Date: _____

Step 1   Segment Information into Key Sections

Establish priorities for each section, including individual responsibilities, due dates for drafts and the final version. When you segment your information, it is vital to keep in mind that the plan needs to be logically integrated and that information should be consistent. Because the market opportunity section is the heart and soul of the plan, it may be the most difficult section to write; but it is best to assign it a high priority and to begin working there first. Remember to include such tasks as printing in the list.

Section or Task	Priority	Person(s) Responsible	Date to Begin	First Draft Due Date	Date Completed or Final Version Due Date

Step 2   List Tasks That Need to Be Completed

Devise an overall schedule for preparing the plan by assigning priority, persons responsible, and due dates to each task necessary to complete the plan. It is helpful to break larger items (fieldwork to gather customer and competitor intelligence, trade show visits, etc.) into small, more manageable components (such as phone calls required before a trip can be taken) and to include the components as a task. *Be as specific as possible.*

Task	Priority	Person Responsible	Date to Begin	Date of Completion

Step 3   Combine the List of Segments and the List of Tasks to Create a Calendar

In combining your lists, consider if anything has been omitted and whether you have been realistic in what people can do, when they can do it, what needs to be done, and so forth. To create your calendar, place an X in the week when the task is to be started and an X in the week it is to be completed and then connect the Xs. When you have placed all tasks on the calendar, look carefully again for conflicts or lack of realism. In particular, evaluate if team members are overscheduled.

Task	Week														
	1	2	3	4	5	6	7	8	9	10	11	12	13	14	15

Step 4 A Framework to Develop and Write a Business Plan

As has been discussed, the framework below follows the order of presentation of the table of contents shown in Exhibit 4.2. While preparing your own plan, you will most likely want to consider sections in a different order from the one presented in this exhibit. (Also, when you integrate your sections into your final plan, you may choose to present material somewhat differently.)

Cover

The cover page includes the name of the company, its address, its telephone number, the date, and the securities offered. Usually, the name, address, telephone number, and the date are centred at the top of the page and the securities offered are listed at the bottom. Also suggested on the cover page at the bottom is the following text:

> This business plan has been submitted on a confidential basis solely for the benefit of selected, highly qualified investors in connection with the private placement of the above securities and is not for use by any other persons. Neither may it be reproduced, stored, or copied in any form. By accepting delivery of this plan, the recipient agrees to return this copy to the corporation at the address listed above if the recipient does not undertake to subscribe to the offering. Do not copy, fax, reproduce, or distribute without permission.

Table of Contents

Included in the table of contents is a list of the sections, subsections, and any appendices, and the pages on which they can be found. (See Exhibit 4.2.)

I. Executive Summary   The first section in the body of the business plan is usually an executive summary. The summary is usually short and concise (one or two pages). The summary articulates what the opportunity conditions are and why they exist, who will execute the opportunity and why they are capable of doing so, how the firm will gain entry and market penetration—it answers the questions we asked in Chapter 3: "For *what* reason does this venture exist and for *whom*?"

Essentially, the summary for your venture needs to mirror the criteria shown in Exhibit 3.7 and the Venture Opportunity Screening Exercises available at www.mcgrawhill.ca/olc/timmons. This is your chance to clearly articulate how your business is durable and timely, and how it will create or add value to the buyer or end-user.

The summary is usually prepared after the other sections of the business plan are completed. As the other sections are drafted, it is helpful to note one or two key sentences, and some key facts and numbers from each.

The summary is important for those ventures trying to raise or borrow money. Many investors, bankers, managers, and other readers use the summary to determine quickly whether they find the venture of interest. Therefore, unless the summary is appealing and compelling, it may be the only section read, and you may never get the chance to make a presentation or discuss your business in person.

Leave plenty of time to prepare the summary. (Successful public speakers have been known to spend an hour of preparation for each minute of their speech.)

The executive summary usually contains a paragraph or two covering each of the following:

A. *Description of the business concept and the business.* Describe the business concept for the business you are or will be in. Be sure the description of your concept explains how your product or service will fundamentally change the way customers currently do certain things. For example, Arthur Rock, the lead investor in Apple and Intel, has stated that he focuses on concepts that will change the way people live and/or work. You need to identify when the company was formed, what it will do, what is special or proprietary about its product, service, or technology, and so forth. Include summary information about any proprietary technology, trade secrets, or unique capabilities that give you an edge in the marketplace. If the company has existed for a few years, a brief summary of its size and progress is in order. Try to make your description 25 words or less, and briefly describe the specific product or service.

B. *The opportunity and strategy.* Summarize what the opportunity is, why it is compelling, and the entry strategy planned to exploit it. Clearly state the main point or benefit you are addressing. This information may be presented as an outline of the key facts, conditions, competitors' vulnerabilities ("sleepiness," sluggishness, poor service, etc.), industry trends (is it fragmented or emerging?), and other evidence and logic that define the opportunity. Note plans for growth and expansion beyond the entry products or services and into other market segments (such as international markets) as appropriate.

C. *The target market and projections.* Identify and briefly explain the industry and market, who the primary customer groups are, how the product(s) or service(s) will be positioned, and how you plan to reach and service these groups. Include information about the structure of the market, the size and growth rate for the market segments or niches you are seeking, your unit and dollar sales estimates, your anticipated market share, the payback period for your customers, and your pricing strategy (including price versus performance/value/ benefits considerations).

D. *The competitive advantages.* Indicate the significant competitive edges you enjoy or can create as a result of your innovative product, service, and strategy; advantages in lead time or barriers to entry; competitors' weaknesses and vulnerabilities; and other industry conditions.

E. *Sustainability.* Discuss the social, economic, and environmental sustainability of your business model. Summarize the employment opportunities that your business is likely to create, and describe any plans for outsourcing or using offshore labour and how that might impact the community and your labour pool. Briefly describe any environmental issues related to your business with regard to resources, waste generation, and legislative compliance.

F. *The team.* Summarize the relevant knowledge, experience, know-how, and skills of the lead entrepreneur and any team members, noting previous accomplishments, especially those involving profit and loss responsibility and general management and people management experience. Include significant information, such as the size of a division, project, or prior business with which the lead entrepreneur or a team member was the driving force.

G. *The offering.* Briefly indicate the dollar amount of equity and/or debt financing needed, how much of the company you are prepared to offer for that financing, what principal use will be made of the capital, and how the investor, lender, or strategic partner will achieve its desired rate of return. Remember, your targeting resource provider has a well-defined appetite and you must understand the "Circle of Venture Capital Ecstasy" (Exhibit 3.1).

II. The Industry and the Company and Its Product(s) or Service(s)   A major area of consideration is the company, its concept for its product(s) and service(s), and its interface with the industry in which it will be competing. This is the context into which the marketing information, for example, fits. Information needs to include a description of the industry, a description of the concept, a description of your company, and a description of the product(s) or service(s) you will offer, the proprietary position of these product(s) or service(s), their potential advantages, and entry and growth strategy for the product(s) or service(s).

A. *The industry.*
   - Present the current status and prospects for the industry in which the proposed business will operate. Be sure to consider industry structure.
   - Discuss briefly market size, growth trends, and competitors.
   - Discuss any new products or developments, new markets and customers, new requirements, new entrants and exits, and any other national or economic trends and factors that could affect the venture's business positively or negatively.
   - Discuss the environmental profile of the industry. Consider energy requirements, supply chain factors, waste generation, and recycling capabilities. Outline any new green technologies or trends that may have an impact on this opportunity.

B. *The company and the concept.*
   - Describe generally the concept of the business, what business your company is in or intends to enter, what product(s) or service(s) it will offer, and who are or will be its principal customers.
   - By way of background, give the date your venture was incorporated and describe the identification and development of its products and the involvement of the company's principals in that development.
   - If your company has been in business for several years and is seeking expansion financing, review its history and cite its prior sales and profit performance, and if your company has had setbacks or losses in prior years, discuss these and emphasize current and future efforts to prevent a recurrence of these difficulties and to improve your company's performance.

C. *The product(s) or service(s).*
   - Describe in some detail each product or service to be sold.
   - Discuss the application of the product or service and describe the primary end use as well as any significant secondary applications. Articulate how you will solve a problem, relieve pain, or provide a benefit or needed service.
   - Describe the service or product delivery system.

   - Emphasize any unique features of the product or service and how these will create or add significant value; also, highlight any differences between what is currently on the market and what you will offer that will account for your market penetration. Be sure to describe how value will be added and the payback period to the customer—that is, discuss how many months it will take for the customer to cover the initial purchase price of the product or service as a result of its time, cost, or productivity improvements.
   - Include a description of any possible drawbacks (including problems with obsolescence) of the product or service.
   - Define the present state of development of the product or service and how much time and money will be required to fully develop, test, and introduce the product or service. Provide a summary of the functional specifications and photographs, if available, of the product.
   - Discuss any head start you might have that would enable you to achieve a favoured or entrenched position in the industry.
   - Describe any features of the product or service that give it an "unfair" advantage over the competition. Describe any patents, trade secrets, or other proprietary features of the product or service.
   - Discuss any opportunities for the expansion of the product line or the development of related products or services. (Emphasize opportunities and explain how you will take advantage of them.)

D. *Entry and growth strategy.*
   - Indicate key success variables in your marketing plan (e.g., an innovative product, timing advantage, or marketing approach) and your pricing, channel(s) of distribution, advertising, and promotion plans.
   - Summarize how fast you intend to grow and to what size during the first five years and your plans for growth beyond your initial product or service.
   - Show how the entry and growth strategy is derived from the opportunity and value-added or other competitive advantages, such as the weakness of competitors.
   - Discuss the overall environmental and social sustainability of your growth plan. Consider the effect on the community if the growth strategy involves offshore manufacturing or outsourced labour. Examine the potential environmental impact of your business as it grows.

III. Market Research and Analysis   Information in this section needs to support the assertion that the venture can capture a substantial market in a growing industry and stand up to competition. Because of the importance of market analysis and the critical dependence of other parts of the plan on this information, you are advised to prepare this section of the business plan before any other. Take enough time to do this section very well and to check alternative sources of market data.

This section of the business plan is one of the most difficult to prepare, yet it is one of the most important. Other sections of the business plan depend on the market research and analysis presented here. For example, the predicted sales levels directly influence such factors as the size of the manufacturing operation, the marketing plan, and the amount of debt and equity capital you will require. Most entrepreneurs seem to have great difficulty preparing and presenting market research and analyses that show that their ventures' sales estimates are sound and attainable.

A. *Customers.*

- Discuss who the customers for the product(s) or service(s) are or will be. Note that potential customers need to be classified by relatively homogeneous groups having common, identifiable characteristics (e.g., by major market segment). For example, an automotive part might be sold to manufacturers and to parts distributors supplying the replacement market, so the discussion needs to reflect two market segments.
- Show who and where the major purchasers for the product(s) or service(s) are in each market segment. Include national regions and foreign countries, as appropriate.
- Indicate whether customers are easily reached and receptive, how customers buy (wholesale, through manufacturers' representatives, etc.), where in their organizations buying decisions are made, and how long decisions take. Describe customers' purchasing processes, including the bases on which they make purchase decisions (e.g., price, quality, timing, delivery, training, service, personal contacts, or political pressures) and why they might change current purchasing decisions.
- List any orders, contracts, or letters of commitment that you have in hand. These are *the most powerful data* you can provide. List also any potential customers who have expressed an interest in the product(s) or service(s) and indicate why; also list any potential customers who have shown no interest in the proposed product or service and explain why they are not interested and explain what you will do to overcome negative customer reaction. Indicate how fast you believe your product or service will be accepted in the market.
- If you have an existing business, list your principal current customers and discuss the trends in your sales to them.

B. *Market size and trends.*

- Show for five years the size of the current total market and the share you will have, by market segment, and/or region, and/or country, for the product or service you will offer, in units, dollars, and potential profitability.
- Describe also the potential annual growth for at least three years of the total market for your product(s) or service(s) for each major customer group, region, or country, as appropriate.
- Discuss the major factors affecting market growth (e.g., industry trends, socioeconomic trends, government policy, environmental impacts, and population shifts) and review previous trends in the market. Any differences between past and projected annual growth rates need to be explained.

C. *Competition and competitive edges.*

- Make a realistic assessment of the strengths and weaknesses of competitors. Assess the substitute and/or alternative products and services and list the companies that supply them, both domestic and foreign, as appropriate.
- Compare competing and substitute products or services on the basis of market share, quality, price, performance, delivery, timing, service, warranties, and other pertinent features.
- Compare the fundamental value that is added or created by your product or service, in terms of economic benefits to the customer and to your competitors.
- Discuss the current advantages and disadvantages of these products and services and say why they are not meeting customer needs.
- Indicate any knowledge of competitors' actions that could lead you to new or improved products and an advantageous position. For example, discuss whether competitors are simply sluggish or nonresponsive or are asleep at the switch.
- Identify the strengths and weaknesses of the competing companies and determine and discuss each competitor's market share, sales, distribution methods, and production capabilities.
- Review the financial position, resources, costs, and profitability of the competition and their profit trend. Note that you can utilize Risk Management Association data for comparison.
- Indicate who are the service, pricing, performance, cost, and quality leaders. Discuss why any companies have entered or dropped out of the market in recent years.
- Discuss the three or four key competitors and why customers buy from them, and determine and discuss why customers leave them. Relate this to the basis for the purchase decision examined in Part IIIA.
- From what you know about the competitors' operations, explain why you think they are vulnerable and you can capture a share of their business. Discuss what makes you think it will be easy or difficult to compete with them. Discuss, in particular, your competitive advantages gained through such "unfair" advantage as patents.

D. *Estimated market share and sales.*

- Summarize what it is about your product(s) or service(s) that will make it saleable in the face of current and potential competition. Mention, especially, the fundamental value added or created by the product(s) or service(s).
- Identify any major customers (including international customers) who are willing to make, or who have already made, purchase commitments. Indicate the extent of those commitments, and why they were made. Discuss which customers could be major purchasers in future years and why.
- Based on your assessment of the advantages of your product or service, the market size and trends, customers, competition and their products, and the trends of sales in prior years, estimate the share of the market and the sales in units and dollars that you will acquire in each of the next three years. Remember to show assumptions used.
- Show how the growth of the company sales in units and its estimated market share are related to the growth of the industry, the customers, and the strengths and weaknesses of competitors. Remember, the assumptions used to estimate market share and sales need to be clearly stated.

- If yours is an existing business, also indicate the total market, your market share, and sales for two prior years.

E. *Ongoing market evaluation.*

- Explain how you will continue to evaluate your target markets; assess customer needs and service; guide product improvement, pricing, and new product programs; plan for expansions of your production facility; and guide product/service pricing.

IV. The Economics of the Business
The economic and financial characteristics, including the apparent magnitude and durability of margins and profits generated, need to support the fundamental attractiveness of the opportunity. The underlying operating and cash conversion cycle of the business, the value chain, and so forth need to make sense in terms of the opportunity and strategies planned.

A. *Gross and operating margins.*

- Describe the magnitude of the gross margins (i.e., selling price less variable costs) and the operating margins for each of the product(s) and/or service(s) you are selling in the market niche(s) you plan to attack. Include results of your contribution analysis.

B. *Profit potential and durability.*

- Describe the magnitude and expected durability of the profit stream the business will generate—before and after taxes—and reference appropriate industry benchmarks, other competitive intelligence, or your own relevant experience.
- Address the issue of how perishable or durable the profit stream appears to be. Provide reasons why your profit stream is perishable or durable, such as barriers to entry you can create, your technological and market lead-time, and environmental sustainability, which in some cases can be a driver for cost reduction.

C. *Fixed, variable, and semivariable costs.*

- Provide a detailed summary of fixed, variable, and semivariable costs, in dollars and as percentages of total cost as appropriate, for the product or service you offer and the volume of purchases and sales upon which these are based.
- Show relevant industry benchmarks.

D. *Months to breakeven.*

- Given your entry strategy, marketing plan, and proposed financing, show how long it will take to reach a unit breakeven sales level.
- Note any significant stepwise changes in your breakeven that will occur as you grow and add substantial capacity.

E. *Months to reach positive cash flow.*

- Given the above strategy and assumptions, show when the venture will attain a positive cash flow.
- Show if and when you will run out of cash. Note where the detailed assumptions can be found.
- Note any significant stepwise changes in cash flow that will occur as you grow and add capacity.

V. Marketing Plan
The marketing plan describes how the sales projections will be attained. The marketing plan needs to detail the overall marketing strategy that will exploit the opportunity and your competitive advantages. Include a discussion of sales and service policies; pricing, distribution, promotion, and advertising strategies; and sales projections. The marketing plan needs to describe *what* is to be done, *how* it will be done, *when* it will be done, and *who* will do it.

A. *Overall marketing strategy.*

- Describe the specific marketing philosophy and strategy of the company, given the value chain and channels of distribution in the market niche(s) you are pursuing. Include, for example, a discussion of the kinds of customer groups that you already have orders from or that will be targeted for initial intensive selling effort and those targeted for later selling efforts; how specific potential customers in these groups will be identified and how they will be contacted; what features of the product or service, such as service, quality, price, delivery, warranty, or training, will be emphasized to generate sales; if any innovative or unusual marketing techniques will enhance customer acceptance, such as leasing where only sales were previously attempted; and so forth.
- Indicate whether the product(s) or service(s) will initially be introduced internationally, nationally, or regionally; explain why; and if appropriate, indicate any plans for extending sales at a later date.
- Discuss any seasonal trends that underlie the cash conversion cycle in the industry and what can be done to promote sales out of season.
- Describe any plans to obtain government contracts as a means of supporting product development costs and overhead.
- Describe any sustainability advantages you have or can develop, and how these aspects relate to building customer loyalty and community support for your product(s) or service(s).

B. *Pricing.*

- Discuss pricing strategy, including the prices to be charged for your product and service, and compare your pricing policy with those of your major competitors, including a brief discussion of payback (in months) to the customer.
- Discuss the gross profit margin between manufacturing and ultimate sales costs and indicate whether this margin is large enough to allow for distribution and sales, warranty, training, service, amortization of development and equipment costs, price competition, and so forth, and still allow a profit.
- Explain how the price you set will enable you (1) to get the product or service accepted, (2) to maintain and increase your market share in the face of competition, and (3) to produce profits.
- Justify your pricing strategy and differences between your prices and those for competitive or substitute products or services in terms of economic payback to the customer and value added through newness, quality, warranty, timing, performance, service, cost savings, efficiency, and the like.

- If your product is to be priced lower than those of the competition, explain how you will do this and maintain profitability (e.g., through greater value added via effectiveness in manufacturing and distribution, lower labour costs, lower material costs, lower overhead, or other cost component).

- Discuss your pricing policy, including a discussion of the relationship of price, market share, and profits.

C. *Sales tactics.*

- Describe the methods (e.g., own sales force, sales representatives, ready-made manufacturers' sales organizations, direct mail, or distributors) that will be used to make sales and distribute the product or service and both the initial plans and longer-range plans for a sales force. Include a discussion of any special requirements (e.g., refrigeration).

- Discuss the value chain and the resulting margins to be given to retailers, distributors, wholesalers, and salespeople and any special policies regarding discounts, exclusive distribution rights, and so on, given to distributors or sales representatives and compare these to those given by your competition. (See the online Venture Opportunity Screening Exercises.)

- Describe how distributors or sales representatives, if they are used, will be selected, when they will start to represent you, the areas they will cover and the head count of dealers and representatives by month, and the expected sales to be made by each.

- If a direct sales force is to be used, indicate how it will be structured and at what rate (a head count) it will be built up; indicate if it is to replace a dealer or representative organization and, if so, when and how.

- If direct mail, magazine, newspaper, or other media, telemarketing, or catalogue sales are to be used, indicate the specific channels or vehicles, costs (per 1,000), expected response rates, and so on. Discuss how these will be built up.

- Show the sales expected per salesperson per year and what commission, incentive, and/or salary they are slated to receive, and compare these figures to the average for your industry.

- Present a selling schedule and a sales budget that includes all marketing promotion and service costs.

D. *Service and warranty policies.*

- If your company will offer a product that will require service, warranties, or training, indicate the importance of these to the customers' purchasing decisions and discuss your method of handling service problems.

- Describe the kind and term of any warranties to be offered, whether service will be handled by company service people, agencies, dealers and distributors, or returns to the factory.

- Indicate the proposed charge for service calls and whether service will be a profitable or breakeven operation.

- Compare your service, warranty, and customer training policies and practices to those of your principal competitors.

E. *Advertising and promotion.*

- Describe the approaches the company will use to bring its product or service to the attention of prospective purchasers.

- For original equipment manufacturers and for manufacturers of industrial products, indicate the plans for trade show participation, trade magazine advertisements, direct mailings, the preparation of product sheets and promotional literature, and use of advertising agencies.

- For consumer products, indicate what kind of advertising and promotional campaign will introduce the product, including sales aids to dealers, trade shows, and so forth.

- Present a schedule and approximate costs of promotion and advertising (direct mail, telemarketing, catalogues, etc.), and discuss how these costs will be incurred.

F. *Distribution.*

- Describe the methods and channels of distribution you will employ. Discuss the availability and capacity of these channels.

- Indicate the sensitivity of shipping cost as a percent of the selling price.

- Note any special issues or problems that need to be resolved or present potential vulnerabilities.

- If international sales are involved, note how these sales will be handled, including distribution, shipping, insurance, credit, and collections.

VI. Design and Development Plans   The nature and extent of any design and development work and the time and money required before a product or service is marketable need to be considered in detail. (Note that design and development costs are often underestimated.) Design and development might be the engineering work necessary to convert a laboratory prototype to a finished product; the design of special tooling; the work of an industrial designer to make a product more attractive and saleable; or the identification and organization of employees, equipment, and special techniques, such as equipment, new computer software, and skills required for computerized credit checking, to implement a service business.

A. *Development status and tasks.*

- Describe the current status of each product or service and explain what remains to be done to make it marketable.

- Describe briefly the competence or expertise that your company has or will require to complete this development.

- List any customers or end-users that are participating in the development, design, and/or testing of the product or service. Indicate results to date or when results are expected.

B. *Difficulties and risks.*

- Identify any major anticipated design and development problems and define approaches to their solution.

- Discuss the possible effect on the cost of design and development, on the time to market introduction, and so forth, of such problems.

C. *Product improvement and new products.*

- In addition to describing the development of the initial products, discuss any ongoing design and development work that is planned to keep the product(s) or service(s) that can be sold to the same group of customers. Discuss customers who have participated in these efforts and their reactions, and include any evidence that you may have.

- With regard to ongoing product development, outline any compliance issues relating to new, pending, or potential environmental legislation. Discuss any green technologies or production capabilities that could enhance sustainability.

D. *Costs.*

- Present and discuss the design and development budget, including costs of labour, materials, consulting fees, and so on.

- Discuss the impact on cash flow projections of underestimating this budget, including the impact of a 15 to 30 percent contingency.

E. *Proprietary issues.*

- Describe any patent, trademark, copyright, or intellectual property rights you own or are seeking.

- Describe any contractual rights or agreements that give you exclusivity or proprietary rights.

- Discuss the impact of any unresolved issues or existing or possible actions pending, such as disputed rights of ownership, relating to proprietary rights on timing and on any competitive edge you have assumed.

VII. Manufacturing and Operations Plan   The manufacturing and operations plan needs to include such factors as plant location, the type of facilities needed, space requirements, capital equipment requirements, and labour force (both full- and part-time) requirements. For a manufacturing business, the manufacturing and operations plan needs to include policies on inventory control, purchasing, production control, and which parts of the product will be purchased and which operations will be performed by your workforce (called make-or-buy decisions). A service business may require particular attention to location (proximity to customers is generally a must), minimizing overhead, and obtaining competitive productivity from a labour force.

A. *Operating cycle.*

- Describe the lead/lag times that characterize the fundamental operating cycle in your business. (Include a graph similar to the one found in the online Venture Opportunity Screening Exercises.)

- Explain how any seasonal production loads will be handled without severe dislocation (e.g., by building to inventory or using part-time help in peak periods).

B. *Geographical location.*

- Describe the planned geographical location of the business. Include any location analysis, and so on, that you have done.

- Discuss any advantages or disadvantages of the site location in terms of labour (including labour availability,

whether workers are unionized, wage rates, and outsourcing), closeness to customers and/or suppliers, access to transportation, provincial and local taxes and laws (including zoning and environmental impact regulations), access to utilities (energy use and sustainability), and so forth.

C. *Facilities and improvements.*

- For an existing business, describe the facilities, including plant and office space, storage and land areas, special tooling, machinery, and other capital equipment currently used to conduct the company's business, and discuss whether these facilities are adequate and in compliance with health, safety, and environmental regulations. Discuss any economies of scale.

- For a start-up, describe how and when the necessary facilities to start production will be acquired.

- Discuss whether equipment and space will be leased or acquired (new or used) and indicate the costs and timing of such actions and how much of the proposed financing will be devoted to plant and equipment.

- Explain future equipment needs in the next three years.

- For start-ups expecting to outsource manufacturing, indicate the location and size of the firm, and discuss the advantages, risks, and monitoring regime.

- Discuss how and when, in the next three years, plant space and equipment will be expanded and capacities required by future sales projections and any plans to improve or add existing plant space. Discuss any environmental impacts related to those expansion requirements. If there are any plans to move the facility, outsource labour, or move production overseas, discuss the impact on the local community. Indicate the timing and cost of such acquisitions.

D. *Strategy and plans.*

- Describe the manufacturing processes involved in production of your product(s) and any decisions with respect to subcontracting of component parts, rather than complete in-house manufacture.

- Justify your proposed make-or-buy policy in terms of inventory financing, available labour skills, and other nontechnical questions, as well as production, cost, and capability issues.

- Discuss who potential subcontractors and/or suppliers are likely to be and any information about, or any surveys that have been made of, these subcontractors and suppliers.

- Present a production plan that shows cost/volume/inventory level information at various sales levels of operation with breakdowns of applicable material, labour, purchased components, and factory overhead.

- Describe your approach to quality control, production control, and inventory control; explain what quality control and inspection procedures the company will use to minimize service problems and associated customer dissatisfaction.

- Describe the environmental sustainability of your operations, including the activities of your subcontractors and suppliers.

E. *Regulatory and legal issues.*

- Discuss any relevant provincial, federal, or foreign regulatory requirements unique to your product, process, or service such as licences, zoning permits, health permits, and environmental approvals necessary to begin operation.
- Note any pending regulatory changes that can affect the nature of your opportunity and its timing.
- Discuss any legal or contractual obligations that are pertinent as well.

VIII. Management Team   This section of the business plan includes a description of the functions that will need to be filled, a description of the key management personnel and their primary duties, an outline of the organizational structure for the venture, a description of the board of directors, a description of the ownership position of any other investors, and so forth. You need to present indications of commitment, such as the willingness of team members to initially accept modest salaries, and of the existence of the proper balance of technical, managerial, and business skills and experience in doing what is proposed.

A. *Organization.*

- Present the key management roles in the company and the individuals who will fill each position. (If the company is established and of sufficient size, an organization chart needs to be appended.)
- If it is not possible to fill each executive role with a full-time person without adding excessive overhead, indicate how these functions will be performed (e.g., using part-time specialists or consultants to perform some functions), who will perform them, and when they will be replaced by a full-time staff member.
- If any key individuals will not be on board at the start of the venture, indicate when they will join the company.
- Discuss any current or past situations where key management people have worked together that could indicate how their skills complement each other and result in an effective management team.

B. *Key management personnel.*

- For each key person, describe in detail career highlights, particularly relevant know-how, skills, and track record of accomplishments that demonstrate his or her ability to perform the assigned role. Include in your description sales and profitability achievements (budget size, number of subordinates, new product introductions, etc.) and other prior entrepreneurial or general management results.
- Describe the exact duties and responsibilities of each of the key members of the management team.
- Complete résumés for each key management member need to be included here or as an exhibit and need to stress relevant training, experience, and concrete accomplishments, such as profit and sales improvement, labour management success, manufacturing or technical achievements, and meeting budgets and schedules.

C. *Management compensation and ownership.*

- State the salary to be paid, the stock ownership planned, and the amount of equity investment (if any) of each key member of the management team.

- Compare the compensation of each key member to the salary he or she received at his or her last independent job.

D. *Other investors.*

- Describe here any other investors in your venture, the number and percentage of outstanding shares they own, when they were acquired, and at what price.

E. *Employment and other agreements and stock option and bonus plans.*

- Describe any existing or contemplated employment or other agreements with key members.
- Indicate any restrictions on stock and investing that affect ownership and disposition of stock.
- Describe any performance-dependent stock option or bonus plans.
- Summarize any incentive stock option or other stock ownership plans planned or in effect for key people and employees.

F. *Board of directors.*

- Discuss the company's philosophy about the size and composition of the board.
- Identify any proposed board members and include a one- or two-sentence statement of each member's background that shows what he or she can bring to the company.

G. *Other shareholders, rights, and restrictions.*

- Indicate any other shareholders in your company and any rights, restrictions, or obligations, such as notes or guarantees, associated with these. (If they have all been accounted for above, simply note that there are no others.)

H. *Supporting professional advisors and services.*

- Indicate the supporting services that will be required.
- Indicate the names and affiliations of the legal, accounting, advertising, consulting, and banking advisors selected for your venture and the services each will provide.

IX. Overall Schedule   A schedule that shows the timing and interrelationship of the major events necessary to launch the venture and realize its objectives is an essential part of a business plan. The underlying cash conversion and operating cycle of the business will provide key inputs for the schedule. In addition to being a planning aid, by showing deadlines critical to a venture's success, a well-presented schedule can be extremely valuable in convincing potential investors that the management team is able to plan for venture growth in a way that recognizes obstacles and minimizes investor risk. Since the time to do things tends to be underestimated in most business plans, it is important to demonstrate that you have correctly estimated these amounts in determining the schedule. Create your schedule as follows:

1. Lay out (use a bar chart) the cash conversion cycle of the business for each product or service expected, the lead and elapsed times from an order to the purchase of raw materials, or inventory to shipping and collection.

2. Prepare a month-by-month schedule that shows the timing of product development, market planning, sales programs, production, and operations, and that includes sufficient detail to show the timing of the primary tasks required to accomplish an activity.

3. Show on the schedule the deadlines or milestones critical to the venture's success, such as:

   - Incorporation of the venture.
   - Completion of design and development.
   - Completion of prototypes.
   - Obtaining sales representatives.
   - Obtaining product display at trade shows.
   - Signing of distributors and dealers.
   - Ordering of materials in production quantities.
   - Starting of production or operation.
   - Receipt of first orders.
   - Delivery on first sale.
   - Receiving the first payment on accounts receivable.

4. Show on the schedule the "ramp up" of the number of management personnel, the number of production and operations personnel, and plant or equipment and their relation to the development of the business.

5. Discuss in a general way the activities most likely to cause a schedule slippage, what steps will be taken to correct such slippages, and the impact of schedule slippages on the venture's operation, especially its potential viability and capital needs.

X. Critical Risks, Problems, and Assumptions   The development of a business has risks and problems, and the business plan invariably contains some implicit assumptions about them. You need to include a description of the risks and the consequences of adverse outcomes relating to your industry, your company and its personnel, your product's market appeal, and the timing and financing of your start-up. Be sure to discuss assumptions concerning sales projections, customer orders, and so forth. If the venture has anything that could be considered a fatal flaw, discuss why it is not. The discovery of any unstated negative factors by potential investors can undermine the credibility of the venture and endanger its financing. Be aware that most investors will read the section describing the management team first and then this section.

Do not omit this section. If you do, the reader will most likely come to one or more of the following conclusions:

1. You think he or she is incredibly naive or stupid, or both.

2. You hope to pull the wool over his or her eyes.

3. You do not have enough objectivity to recognize and deal with assumptions and problems.

Identifying and discussing the risks in your venture demonstrate your skills as a manager and increase the credibility of you and your venture with a venture capital investor or a private investor. Taking the initiative on the identification and discussion of risks helps you to demonstrate to the investor that you have thought about them and can handle them. Risks then tend not to loom as large black clouds in the investor's thinking about your venture.

1. Discuss assumptions and risks implicit in your plan.

2. Identify and discuss any major problems and other risks, such as:

   - Running out of cash *before* orders are secured.
   - Potential price cutting by competitors.
   - Any potentially unfavourable industry trends.
   - Design or manufacturing costs in excess of estimates.
   - Sales projections not achieved.
   - An unmet product development schedule.
   - Difficulties or long lead times encountered in the procurement of parts or raw materials.
   - Difficulties encountered in obtaining needed bank credit.
   - Larger-than-expected innovation and development costs.
   - Running out of cash *after* orders pour in.

3. Indicate what assumptions or potential problems and risks are most critical to the success of the venture, and describe your plans for minimizing the impact of unfavourable developments in each case.

XI. The Financial Plan   The financial plan is basic to the evaluation of an investment opportunity and needs to represent your best estimates of financial requirements. The purpose of the financial plan is to indicate the venture's potential and to present a timetable for financial viability. It also can serve as an operating plan for financial management using financial benchmarks. In preparing the financial plan, you need to look creatively at your venture and consider alternative ways of launching or financing it.

As part of the financial plan, financial exhibits need to be prepared. To estimate *cash flow needs*, use cash-based, rather than an accrual-based, accounting (i.e., use a real-time cash flow analysis of expected receipts and disbursements). This analysis needs to cover three years, including current- and prior-year income statements and balance sheets, if applicable; profit and loss forecasts for three years; pro forma income statements and balance sheets; and a breakeven chart. On the appropriate exhibits, or in an attachment, assumptions behind such items as sales levels and growth, collections and payables periods, inventory requirements, cash balances, and cost of goods need to be specified. Your analysis of the operating and cash conversion cycle in the business will enable you to identify these critical assumptions.

Pro forma income statements are the plan-for-profit part of financial management and can indicate the potential financial feasibility of a new venture. Because usually the level of profits, particularly during the start-up years of a venture, will not be sufficient to finance operating asset needs, and because actual cash inflows do not always match the actual cash outflows on a short-term basis, a cash flow forecast indicating these conditions and enabling management to plan cash needs is recommended. Further, pro forma balance sheets are used to detail the assets required to support the projected level of operations and, through liabilities, to show how these assets are to be financed. The projected balance sheets can indicate if debt-to-equity ratios, working capital, current ratios, inventory turnover, and the like are within the acceptable limits required to justify future financings that are projected for the venture. Finally, a breakeven chart showing the level of sales and production that will cover all costs, including those costs that vary with production level and those that do not, is very useful.

A. *Actual income statements and balance sheets.* For an existing business, prepare income statements and balance sheets for the current year and for the prior two years.

B. *Pro forma income statements.*

- Using sales forecasts and the accompanying production or operations costs, prepare pro forma income statements for at least the first three years.

- Fully discuss assumptions (e.g., the amount allowed for bad debts and discounts, or any assumptions made with respect to sales expenses or general and administrative costs being a fixed percentage of costs or sales) made in preparing the pro forma income statement and document them.

- Draw on Section X of the business plan and highlight any major risks, such as the effect of a 20 percent reduction in sales from those projected or the adverse impact of having to climb a learning curve on the level of productivity over time, that could prevent the venture's sales and profit goals from being attained, plus the sensitivity of profits to these risks.

C. *Pro forma balance sheets.* Prepare pro forma balance sheets semi-annually in the first year and at the end of each of the first three years of operation.

D. *Pro forma cash flow analysis.*

- Project cash flows monthly for the first year of operation and quarterly for at least the next two years. Detail the amount and timing of expected cash inflows and outflows. Determine the need for and timing of additional financing and indicate peak requirements for working capital. Indicate how necessary additional financing is to be obtained, such as through equity financing, bank loans, or short-term lines of credit from banks, on what terms, and how it is to be repaid. Remember they are based on cash, not accrual, accounting.

- Discuss assumptions, such as those made on the timing of collection of receivables, trade discounts given, terms of payments to vendors, planned salary and wage increases, anticipated increases in any operating expenses, seasonality characteristics of the business as they affect inventory requirements, inventory turnovers per year, capital equipment purchases, and so forth. Again, these are real time (i.e., cash), not accruals.

- Discuss cash flow sensitivity to a variety of assumptions about business factors (e.g., possible changes in such crucial assumptions as an increase in the receivable collection period or a sales level lower than that forecasted).

E. *Breakeven chart.*

- Calculate breakeven and prepare a chart that shows when breakeven will be reached and any stepwise changes in breakeven that may occur.

- Discuss the breakeven shown for your venture and whether it will be easy or difficult to attain, including a discussion of the size of breakeven sales volume relative to projected total sales, the size of gross margins and price sensitivity, and how the breakeven point might be lowered in case the venture falls short of sales projections.

F. *Cost control.* Describe how you will obtain information about report costs and how often, who will be responsible for the control of various cost elements, and how you will take action on budget overruns.

G. *Highlights.* Highlight the important conclusions, including the maximum amount and timing of cash required, the amount of debt and equity needed, how fast any debts can be repaid, etc.

XII. Proposed Company Offering The purpose of this section of the plan is to indicate the amount of money that is being sought, the nature and amount of the securities offered to investors, a brief description of the uses that will be made of the capital raised, and a summary of how the investor is expected to achieve its targeted rate of return. It is recommended that you read the discussion about financing in Part IV of this book.

The terms for financing your company that you propose here are the first steps in the negotiation process with those interested in investing, and it is very possible that your financing will involve different kinds of securities than originally proposed.

A. *Desired financing.* Based on your real-time cash flow projections and your estimate of how much money is required over the next three years to carry out the development and/or expansion of your business as described, indicate how much of this capital requirement will be obtained by this offering and how much will be obtained via term loans and lines of credit.

B. *Offering.*

- Describe the type (e.g., common stock, convertible debentures, debt with warrants, debt plus stock), unit price, and total amount of securities to be sold in this offering. If securities are not just common stock, indicate by type, interest, maturity, and conversion conditions.

- Show the percentage of the company that the investors of this offering will hold after it is completed or after exercise of any stock conversion or purchase rights in the case of convertible debentures or warrants.

- Securities sold through a private placement and that therefore are exempt from SEC registration should include the following statement in this part of the plan:

- The shares being sold pursuant to this offering are restricted securities and may not be resold readily. The prospective investor should recognize that such securities might be restricted as to resale for an indefinite period of time. Each purchaser will be required to execute a Non-Distribution Agreement satisfactory in form to corporate counsel.

C. *Capitalization.*

- Present in tabular form the current and proposed (post-offering) number of outstanding shares of common stock. Indicate any shares offered by key management people and show the number of shares that they will hold after completion of the proposed financing.

- Indicate how many shares of your company's common stock will remain authorized but unissued after the offering and how many of these will be reserved for stock options for future key employees.

D. *Use of funds.* Investors like to know how their money is going to be spent. Provide a brief description of how the capital raised will be used. Summarize as specifically as possible what amount will be used for such things as product design and development, capital equipment, marketing, and general working capital needs.

E. *Investors' return.* Indicate how your valuation and proposed ownership shares will result in the desired rate of return for the investors you have targeted and what the likely harvest or exit mechanism (IPO, outright sale, merger, management buyout, etc.) will be.

XIII. Appendices   Include pertinent information here that is too extensive for the body of the business plan but that is necessary (product specs or photos; lists of references, suppliers of critical components; special location factors, facilities, or technical analyses; reports from consultants or technical experts; and copies of any critical regulatory approval, licences, etc).

Step 5   Integrate Sections

Integrate the discrete sections you have created into a coherent business plan that can be used for the purpose for which it was created.

Step 6   Get Feedback

Once written, it is recommended that you get the plan reviewed. No matter how good you and your team are, you will most likely overlook issues and treat aspects of your venture in a manner that is less than clear. A good reviewer can give you the benefit of an outside objective evaluation. Your lawyer can make sure that there are no misleading statements in your plan and that it contains all the caveats and the like.

CASE   SCAVENGER ENERGY: FROM THE GROUND UP

Preparation Questions

1. With no significant assets and no track record as a CEO, can Raza Hasanie make it?

2. What financing structure will satisfy investors?

3. How much will Raza Hasanie have to give up?

On the kitchen counter of Raza Hasanie's Calgary home, there were a dozen neatly bound copies of a business plan, ready for distribution to prospective investors. Hasanie, a geologist, had developed the business concept while studying for his MBA.

The plan outlined an oil-and-gas opportunity that could exploit suspended wells to yield a 5 to 15 times return on investment, and called for roughly $1 million in seed-capital funding. The business model was a common one for hundreds of small-scale companies and independent operators: Scavenger would bid on mineral rights for sites with intact wells, equipment, and infrastructure left over from previous drilling activities, and extract smaller deposits left behind by large-scale exploration and extraction operations. These bypassed opportunities weren't individually big enough to meet the investment hurdle rates set by large energy firms, but could offer excellent returns for a company ready to pursue many bypassed wells in parallel — precisely Scavenger's business model.

But there was a hitch: The company existed only in the pages of Hasanie's business plan. Scavenger Energy had no employees, no operations, and no customers. Its CEO, freshly graduated from business school, had no resources of his own to invest in the firm. In fact, Hasanie was still working a day job at IBM's geological software group. And while he was a skilled earth scientist, he had no experience leading a start-up company.

Hasanie needed to work his personal networks to get in front of investors. But even if he could find angels to pitch to, it would be a tough sell: The young entrepreneur would be asking investors to take a million-dollar gamble on an unproven founder with little to offer but some technical know-how and an idea.

First Pitch

Hasanie's first calls were to a handful of well-connected supporters. While completing his MBA in Ontario, he pitched the Scavenger concept in a pair of business-plan competitions, netting him some $15,000 in prize money and providing an introduction to two seasoned angel investors and an Ottawa venture capitalist. The VC provided Hasanie with introductions into a small circle of Ottawa investors, to whom Hasanie made his first pitch.

That pitch took place in the national capital during the summer of 2004. Not one potential investor could boast of any experience in the energy industry, but everyone's ears perked up when a particular phrase rose above the technical lingo: "5x to 15x returns."

The story they were being told was about overlooked opportunities. There were millions of barrels of oil left behind in the Alberta oilfields, Hasanie explained to his audience, ignored and all but forgotten by Canadian energy companies. Hasanie himself had exploited one of these wells while with a small Calgary firm, and turned the company's $30,000 investment into $300,000 in natural gas production.

It wasn't just dumb luck: With the right software and technical expertise, public-domain information could be used to zero in on only those wells with a high chance for hydrocarbon recovery. Hasanie did enjoy some good fortune too, however— because the oil and gas industry is built on high risks and stratospheric rewards, few energy-industry titans were eager to pick through the modest remains of shut-in wells when they had larger, more attractive opportunities to pursue.

This case was written by Lukas Neville, Ph.D. student, Queen's School of Business, and Professor Elspeth J. Murray, CIBC Teaching Fellow in Entrepreneurship, Queen's School of Business, Queen's University. This case was developed with the support of the CIBC Curriculum Development Fund at the Queen's Centre for Business Venturing, for purposes of classroom discussion.

The only people interested in these overlooked opportunities were independent operators and very small-scale companies, which would pursue wells individually and within certain geographical boundaries—the oilpatch version of a lifestyle business. Each individual well would ultimately yield under half a million dollars—enough to keep slow-growth individual operators comfortable, but far less than needed to attract the interest of the energy giants. By pursuing large numbers of these small opportunities, Hasanie hoped to develop a low-risk, high-margin business—profitable after the first operation, and reaching after-tax net annual income exceeding $3.5 million by the third year.

The Ottawa investors followed up Hasanie's pitch with several rounds of meetings and due diligence. Their interest had been piqued, and by the end of the summer, they had informally committed $500,000 in financing to launch Scavenger.

Feedback

That half-million wouldn't be enough. The same summer, in parallel with his Ottawa meetings, Hasanie met with a number of Calgary oil-and-gas investors and consultants, hoping they'd validate his concept and maybe lead him to some industry "grey-hair" who would join his advisory board. Following a meeting with one energy-sector private equity lender, Hasanie dashed off an email to a former professor, a trusted advisor. "He's concerned that I'm only looking for $500K," he typed. "He was thinking upwards of $5 million would be needed. I'm not sure we need that much, but he did make some good points about the cost of delays or problems in the field. The first shut-in well I did with my previous company went flawlessly, so I hoped Scavenger would have similar luck. That might be a bit naive."

Scavenger's approach was incredibly economical, avoiding the immense costs of drilling, testing, and surface-rights negotiation usually borne by traditional exploration companies. "We're not even going after low-hanging fruit," Hasanie joked in his presentation. "This is picking up the berries off the ground." But Hasanie quickly discovered that everyone felt he needed more—whether it was oilpatch veterans saying $5 million or his conservative advisors in Toronto, who suggested a minimum of $2 million. Scavenger's expenses would come from its analysis process, land purchases, facility-use negotiations, and the cost of extraction. Using publicly available data, Scavenger would identify sites with the right mineral rights and infrastructure available, and then select those with a reasonably high recoverable amount of natural gas. With sites identified, they would bid on the land in an auction, negotiate usage rights for the facilities, and hire independent contractors to reopen the well. Commodity price increases could lead to volatility in labour markets and in auction prices for mineral rights. Moreover, it was entirely possible that problems with decades-old well equipment could push up costs. "I do need to take into consideration that field problems will ultimately occur," Hasanie wrote to his advisor, "and I should be pre-pared to 'spend' my way out of trouble when needed." Hasanie worked in consultation with his advisors and experts to arrive at a more realistic target for his fundraising. After three rounds of revised financials, it was clear he would need to expand his financing round beyond his early supporters in Ottawa—and would need to be seeking some $2 million in financing, with at least $750,000 in the immediate term.

Hasani returned, hat in hand, to his alma mater. He met with prominent alumni over drinks at the storied National Club in Toronto and was reunited with one of the judges from his business-plan competition. That judge, a serial entrepreneur and angel investor himself, wanted to help: "What I wanted to do is to give the business a chance to succeed," he explains. "So I helped him get the right supporters with the right resources." With Hasanie ready to seek a larger and more complicated financing deal, he'd need top-notch legals. The B-plan judge introduced Hasanie to a senior partner and the chair of Stikeman Elliott, a white-shoe Toronto law firm. The partner agreed to help Hasanie with complimentary legal work.

Hasanie's new evangelist also helped introduce him to potential investors. Meeting at his alma mater's satellite office in downtown Toronto, Hasanie pitched to a host of high-profile business leaders, venture capitalists, and angel investors. They, too, were attracted by Scavenger's risk-and-reward profile. But they also had a range of serious concerns.

First, Hasanie had no "skin in the game"—he had sunk a few thousand dollars of B-plan prize money into registering his business and doing preliminary research, but the investors wanted to see more on the line for the young CEO. Hasanie noted to the investors that his family and close friends were all willing to invest, but the angels were not necessarily keen on that idea: It would secure founder commitment, but it would also add complexity and risk to the capitalization structure. The investors were concerned that a cluttered list of investors would make governance and the structure of an eventual exit more difficult.

Secondly, the investors were nervous about the lack of operational experience—Hasanie had never run a company, they noted. Lacking oil-and-gas experience themselves, they wanted a director from the energy industry, something Hasanie hadn't been able to secure.

Finally, there was a considerable challenge in terms of ownership and founder incentives. While there was interest on all sides to keep the founder happy and focused on growing the business, the angels couldn't justify giving the founder a fifth of the business simply for having the idea. They needed Hasanie to invest upfront—or find a way for him to earn his equity stake.

Hasanie, grappling with the feedback from investors, wrote again to his former professor to convey his concerns. "It looks like my ownership of the company is going to be significantly reduced from what I had expected," he confessed. "Once the investors and lawyers get their hands into the agreement, my stake is going to be pretty diluted."

SAMPLE BUSINESS PLAN

I. EXECUTIVE SUMMARY

The Premise

Criticism is something that everyone loves to provide. The trouble is that sometimes criticism can be *constructive* (good) and other times it can be *baseless* (bad). Criticism, *if done correctly*, and most importantly, **constructively**, can prove to be tremendously beneficial in improving ideas, businesses, studies, philosophies, fashions, and an endless list of other areas.

The Problem

The problem is that in the real world, criticism and the process of providing constructive feedback is an *inefficient* and mostly *unproductive* phenomenon:

- **There is no way** to differentiate between constructive and baseless criticism.
- **There is no way** to tell if a criticism is good, proper, and popular.
- **There is no way** to freely and anonymously express one's own constructive feedback.
- **There is no way** to solicit "constructive feedback" from the community and organize that information.

The Pitch

IF there were a way to:

- Tell the difference between a constructive criticism and a baseless one.
- Provide constructive feedback on a topic anonymously.
- Gather all constructive feedback on a topic in one location and sort it.
- Find out what the most popular and agreed upon constructive feedback is amongst experts in the community.

THEN this would have a tremendously positive impact on all topics being analyzed and constructively criticized. It would bring the power of the community together to improve ideas, philosophies, products, services, etc. from around the world.

This Sample Business Plan is published with the permission of Aydin Mirzaee, Co-CEO of chide.it Inc.

The Solution

Chide.it is a comprehensive Web crowdsourcing tool that harnesses the power of the Internet community to gather, sort, and rank constructive criticism from people around the world. It is a community based on constructive feedback. It is a place where anyone can be a critic and where only the best critics rise in popularity. It is a community that is focused on "constructive feedback" and rewards those who provide it.

Target Market

Chide.it is initially targeting tech savvy and analytical people that have strong opinions and make it a point to express these opinions. Bloggers are a major part of this category. Chide.it is also targeting tech savvy individuals/organizations that want to receive constructive feedback from the community.

Current Status

Chide.it is currently a federally incorporated company with an office in Ottawa, Canada. Chide.it has a strong management team with a track record of building successful companies. The company has a strong development team of four and is committed to agile development.

The company has launched an alpha version of its product and is actively testing the product to prepare for the beta release. A current version of the product can be viewed at www.chide.it/.

What is the Business Model?

The Internet is becoming more and more cluttered every day. In order to get exposure, one must obtain prime real estate on popular Web sites. If one uploads a video onto YouTube today, chances are that the video will not get much attention since over 10,000 videos are uploaded onto YouTube daily. If a video, however, were listed on the front page of YouTube, it would indeed get attention from the community.

Chide.it intends to apply the YouTube analogy to its business model. If one wants to have his posting appear on the front page of chide.it, he has to bid for space on the front page. The highest bidder will have the most prominent placement on the front page of chide.it. With prominent placement, more people will view the topic that is posted, and more people will provide constructive feedback.

Chide.it intends to revenue share with the critics who provide the best constructive feedback, as determined by the community through voting and ranking. Through revenue sharing, chide.it will entice its group of expert critics to provide high quality constructive feedback.

Through ranking and voting by the community, a true crowdsourcing approach, chide.it will identify the top experts in a broad range of topics and categories. This community of expert critics will be a very valuable and differentiating asset for chide.it.

Scalability/R&D/Open Source

Chide.it is currently using a new python-based Web platform called "Django." Django is an open source platform that allows for rapid and agile development while keeping in mind scalability at all times. Chide.it is a big supporter of open source. Open source has allowed chide.it to build faster and focus most of its efforts on its differentiating intellectual property (i.e., ranking algorithms and branding) and not on commodity technology.

Financial Projections

Chide.it will have revenues of approximately $200,000 in year 1, $1.5 million in year 2, and $6.25 million in year 3. The revenues will come primarily from organizations using the Web site as a crowdsourcing tool. Chide.it will also serve targeted advertisements on its Web site in order to add to its revenue streams.

Competition

Because chide.it begins its life as a tool to facilitate the process of gaining constructive feedback with the help of the Internet community, it can be considered a crowdsourcing application. Crowdsourcing refers to the process of using the community to get a task done for free or by only paying for results. Crowdsourcing is a fairly new phenomenon that is gaining ground fast. Some of the most interesting and relevant crowdsourcing organizations in existence today are:

- Amazon Mechanical Turk
- InnoCentive

By specializing in constructive criticisms and providing tools to further the process, chide. it will establish itself in this niche.

Management Team

Aydin Mirzaee, Co-founder, CEO
- Founder and CEO of bOK Systems Corp.
- Design team leader at Nortel Networks in the Platform Network Management division of the company.
- Assistant to the executive director of the Student World Assembly.
- Graduated from the Electrical Engineering/Management program at the University of Ottawa with a near perfect GPA.

Eli Fathi, Co-founder, Chief Strategist
- Founder and CEO of OrbitIQ, a business accelerator company with globally deployed channels to market.
- Founder of Telexis—acquired in May 2000, and became March Networks.
- Serves on a number of boards including, Ottawa Centre for Research and Innovation from 1999 to 2007, Ottawa Chamber of Commerce, and the Canadian Advanced Technology Association. Serves on the board of C-Com, a publicly traded company on the TSX-V.

Peter Okulich, VP Operations
- Co-founder and vice president Global Operations (Administration, Finance, and Legal) of OrbitIQ.
- Over 30 years with both start-up and international companies: Peleton Photonic Systems, Telexis (March Networks), Mitel Corporation, Digital Equipment Canada, Leigh Instruments, and Consolidated Computer Inc.

Advisors

Peter Craig, Sales Advisor
- Has over 20 years of experience in leading teams in sales.
- Served as founder and managing director of Maxima Consulting Group and as president of Telax Systems Inc.

- Member of a 3,000 person sales force at Nortel, he regularly placed in the top 1 percent of sales leaders.
- Held senior sales and marketing positions, up to the vice president level, with firms such as AT&T, Scientific Atlanta, Paradyne, and Computer Task Group.

Dr. Alan Aitkin, Marketing Advisor

- From the University of Strathclyde, Scotland he holds a Ph.D. in applied physics.
- Held senior positions at Nortel and Mitel.
- In 1994, he received 1 of 10 IEEE Ottawa, 50th Anniversary "Pioneers in Technology" awards.
- Recently served as vice president in March Networks, a broadband applications company headed by Terry Matthews in Kanata, Ontario.

Dr. Sorin Cohn, Marketing Advisor

- Has over 30 years of global management experience.
- Co-founder and president of OrbitIQ.
- Co-founder and CTO of Wireless Multimedia Solutions.
- Held senior management positions with Nortel Networks and Bell Northern Research.
- Has several patents and has published over 50 journal articles.
- Holds a Ph.D. in electrical engineering from McMaster University, an M.Sc. in physics from the University of Calgary, and an M.Eng. from the Polytechnic Institute of Bucharest.

Peter Griffiths, Technology Advisor

- Has worked in the communications industry for over 30 years for Morganite Research, Tandata, Newbridge Networks, and March Networks.
- Holds qualifications in chemistry, electronics, electrical engineering, computing, and data processing; he is also a member of the Royal Society of Chemistry.

Development Team

- Amin Mirzaee
- Samuel Cormier-Iijima
- Marc-Andre Plouffe
- Andrew Pitt

The Ask

Chide.it is looking to raise $1 million Series A round of financing, 6 to 12 months from now.

II. WHAT IS CHIDE.IT?

Chide.it begins its life as a tool to facilitate the process of gathering, sorting, and understanding constructive feedback. Chide.it is a tool that anyone can use to gain constructive feedback from a given audience. The vision for chide.it is to develop a tool that people can easily use. As the content on the Web site increases, community features will be built around it. Eventually, chide.it will become a portal with many different verticals (business, health, science, philosophy, products, services, etc.). Each of the verticals will contain a wealth of information making chide.it a Wikipedia (user generated encyclopedia) of constructive feedback from topics around the world.

At the same time, through ranking and voting, chide.it will be able to identify experts in each of the verticals on the Web site. These experts will be a tremendous asset to chide.it.

TABLE 1   Chide.it Homepage

The opinions and feedback of these critics is what will drive marketers to use the Web site and the community surrounding it to conduct focus groups and gain market feedback.

As chide.it develops as a community, the top ranking critics will establish a place for themselves on the Web site and gain celebrity status. Other users can become fans of the celebrity critics and follow the content that they produce. These VIP users will have the ability to develop reputations on chide.it that will make them first in line for private focus groups conducted on the Web site (as described in the "business model" section of this document) for which they will be paid—a true example of crowdsourcing.

What Makes Chide.it Different from Other Web sites?

It is true indeed that there are many Web sites on the Internet that give users the option to comment and even vote on the best comments. Chide.it is building a tool that will do much more than this and will focus on building a niche instrument with features that will facilitate the process of providing "constructive" feedback. Most Web sites out there will give users a "blank textbox" to provide comments/suggestions. The trouble with this approach is that it is very difficult to separate and categorize content that is generated by the users.

The analogy to this is the concept of a focus group with a moderator. In focus groups, the purpose of the moderator is to guide the participants by asking specific questions and preventing them from sidetracking. Chide.it as a tool acts like the moderator in a focus group and asks the right questions to get the right type of feedback.

Chide.it's main focus is not on what is good and what is bad. Chide.it takes things one step further by asking users the correct questions to determine how to improve things. Further to this, depending on how people answer questions, chide.it will sort the incoming feedback so that the person who is seeking the feedback can properly parse through all the incoming information.

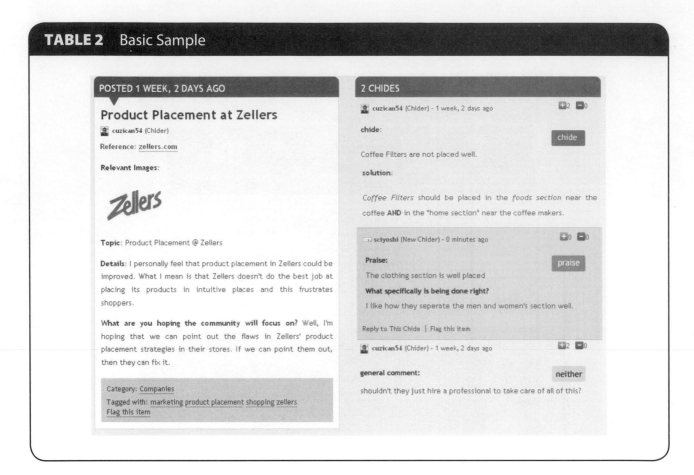

TABLE 2   Basic Sample

How Does it Work?

There are basically three simple steps involved in using chide.it as a tool:

1. *Post a Topic:* Users can post a fairly comprehensive topic on the Web site, which can include formatting, videos and images. In this post they can describe all the issues that they'd like to address.

2. *Invite Relevant Parties:* Once a topic has been created, users can invite a list of people that they believe may be interested in critiquing the topic that was posted.

3. *Start Chiding:* When the originator of the post, the parties that were invited to the post, or even the general community comes to the Web site, they will have the chance to use chide.it to provide constructive feedback.

What is the Development Approach?

Chide.it believes in iteration through customer feedback. The team will continue to build new features and tweak what is currently on the Web site based on feedback that it gets from its userbase. Chide.it has a very short micro release cycle (three weeks) and also has a major goal four times a year.

III. MARKETING TACTICS AND PRODUCT FEATURES

How to Gain Critical Mass

This section focuses on some of the features that will be developed and some of the tactics that will be used in order to build critical mass for chide.it. Before going through the details, it is important to note that the chide.it strategy is to begin to offer itself as a useful tool for soliciting, gathering, and sorting constructive feedback. If this is accomplished well, more people will use the site as a tool and as a result build up the content available on the site. Once the site has enough content, more community features shall be built into the Web site allowing for a more enjoyable and fulfilling experience for users.

Further to this, the more content there is on the Web site, the more search engine leads the Web site can attain. For example, if there are multiple pages on the Web site providing constructive feedback for a product like the iPhone, these pages will appear in search engine results. This in turn will bring in more search engine traffic. As more visitors come to the Web site, a percentage of those visitors will also contribute to the Web site and the cycle continues to repeat.

In summary, the strategy is to build the site as a useful tool so that people use it to provide constructive feedback. As the site builds up in content, through search engines and other links throughout the Web, more people will visit chide.it and produce more content. As the Web site becomes larger, more community features will be provided to keep the user's experience enjoyable and entice visitors to return.

Is This a Proven and Tested Concept?   Absolutely. Successful Web sites such as Meemix.com (a network based on music) and Shopify.com (a shopping network) both began as niche tools and then built a community around those tools. The approach has been very successful for both companies. Aydin Mirzaee (co-founder of chide.it) is good friends with the CEOs of both companies and with their advice and help will lead the same strategy at chide.it.

The following are some of the features that will be built into the Web site to encourage the initial users to visit and use chide.it as a tool.

Blog Post-Back

As mentioned previously, bloggers represent a good market to be introduced to chide.it. Bloggers not only are a part of the target market that the company is trying to reach, but they also have an audience that follows them. If chide.it is able to woo the bloggers, others will follow. Bloggers will help create the initial content on the Web site and this in itself will lead to a better experience for all visitors. Further to this, if bloggers like chide.it as a tool, they will write about it and their visitors will read what they wrote, which will lead a percentage of those visitors to come to the Web site.

If blogs are analyzed closely, one will realize that one of the common things that all bloggers do is review products, events, services, etc. and write about them. Since chide.it is a tool to review and criticize, it is something that bloggers can utilize in order to create their reviews, point out flaws, and supply constructive feedback assuming two things:

1. Chide.it really is a great tool that makes the process of writing a review and providing constructive feedback easier and more efficient than writing something without any aids.
2. The blogger can take credit for the work that he has done and drive traffic to his own blog by using chide.it.

So, How is This Accomplished?   Chide.it uses agile development and frequent release cycles in order put out a product and tweak it until it fulfills the needs of the customer. Aydin Mirzaee (co-founder and CEO) of chide.it is a blogger and also keeps close ties with other bloggers in the tech community. This will ensure that feedback from the blogging community drives the features that are built into chide.it.

When a blogger uses chide.it to create a review, he will have the option to automatically post the review to his blog. Therefore, not only does he get the benefit of using chide.it as a tool to create his review, but also he is able to post this review back to his blog automatically. This process is actually mutually beneficial for chide.it and the bloggers.

Chide.it benefits by having the community create content on its Web site. Furthermore, because the chide.it reviews that are created also get posted to the bloggers' own Web sites, this leaves a trail back to chide.it. Increasing traffic to chide.it is highly dependent on the number of external links to the Web site.

When a chide.it review is automatically posted on someone's blog, there will be a "created by chide.it" logo on the bottom of the post that will link back to chide.it. Not only does this serve as a cookie crumb back to the chide.it Web site, but it also helps increase chide.it's search engine ranking.

How will Chide.it Market to Bloggers?   Aydin Mirzaee (co-founder), Marc-Andre Plouffe (designer), and Samuel Cormier-Iijima (developer) are all members of the chide.it team that currently blog and have an active blogging network. All three members will use the chide.it widget on their blogs and ask that their close blogger friends also put the widget on a trial basis on their blogs. These initial trials will serve the purpose of testing the widget so that it can be improved, and most importantly, set precedence for its use. With precedence, other bloggers will be contacted through email and other social networking means to begin to use the tool. Every time a blogger uses chide.it in this way, more of the readers of that blog (and other bloggers) will become aware of chide.it.

Chide.it Widgets

Many Web sites or companies may want to get feedback from their users and visitors. They can use chide.it to create a special page (a "chide.it lounge") where they can gather all of this feedback.

Once they have created this page, they can put a chide.it widget on their Web site where they can solicit feedback from those that visit the Web site. This again is extremely advantageous to chide.it since anyone that ends up providing feedback through the widget will sign up for chide.it and try out the service. Further to this, the number of linkbacks that are attained through the process is also very useful in terms of search engine ranking and optimization for chide.it.

In summary, chide.it will allow people/organizations to create a "lounge" to obtain constructive feedback from the community. Links to these "lounges" can be placed in the form of a widget on external Web sites in order to solicit feedback in one place, on specified topics, while sorting and ranking the feedback at the same time.

How will Chide.it Market its Widgets?   Chide.it will initially use the network of friends and colleagues of its founding team to try out the widget on their Web site. The feedback from this group will be used to improve the widget and process. Chide.it will then use this precedence to convince other Web site owners and organizations to also use this widget. Chide.it will contact these publishers directly via email/telephone and most importantly, utilize current social networks such as LinkedIn, Facebook, Twitter, and Bebo to contact this group of people.

Chide.it @ Events

It is very common that at the end of an event/gathering, the host will provide the attendants with a way to provide feedback. Sometimes the host will mention an email address that the attendants can use to send their feedback. Other times, the host may provide a physical paper form that the attendant can use to provide their commentary.

There are problems with both of these methods of feedback. One must keep in mind that email is not anonymous and so it will not really give users full freedom of expression. Furthermore, email is not a guided means of providing feedback. Email is essentially a blank text box that does not guide users in providing their constructive feedback and does not provide those who receive the feedback with a standard way of organizing and dealing with the feedback coming in.

Physical paper forms also present some of the same issues. Users may want to give their feedback at a time of their own convenience and not right after the event (they may have to leave immediately or simply may not be in the mood to provide feedback at that time). Furthermore, anonymity may not be achieved for those who are providing their feedback through this means as they may end up filling out the forms in front of the host who is requesting the feedback.

The advantage of using chide.it at events in terms of marketing is that it is a very viral and "offline" approach, as opposed to an "online" or Internet based approach, for chide.it to amass users. Chide.it will market itself to event hosts so that they can create chide.it lounges for their events. These chide.it "lounges" are simply pages that contain a variety of topics that the event host believes he could use feedback on. Once this page is created, the host would communicate the URL of this chide.it lounge to attendants whom he would like to solicit feedback from. These users, in turn, will visit the Web site in order to provide feedback. In the process, they will sign up for chide.it and learn about the services that it offers.

How will Chide.it Market itself as an Events Tool?   DemoCampOttawa8, which is an event that will be held at the end of March 2008, is the first event that will try out chide.it for this purpose. Feedback from this event will be used to improve the tool, and most importantly, set precedence for its use. Chide.it will continue to present at various Demo-Camp, BarCamp, and Startup Camps across Canada to present itself as a tool for events and encourage its spread throughout these events held around the world. The chide.it team is also in contact with David Crow who is the person who brought DemoCamp/Bar-Camp/Startup Camp events to Canada in the first place. David has agreed to help chide.it in its endeavour to make chide.it a default tool for this category of events.

Further to this, Marc-Andre-Plouffe (designer), who is a member of the chide.it team also is close friends with some of the organizers of these events in Sweden who have also agreed to help chide.it in its endeavours. This will help promote chide.it's adoption in Europe.

Aydin Mirzaee is also meeting with Jeff Pulver (founder of VON—one of the world's most publicized Telecom Events) at the end of March 2008 to solicit his feedback and understand what features will need to be implemented in chide.it for it to be used as a tool at Jeff's Social Media Breakfasts around the world (which have been publicized broadly in the media—including *Fortune Magazine*) in addition to VON itself.

By targeting one event at a time in the beginning, the chide.it team believes that it can gain enough feedback to build its tool to be fitted and very useful for events. Every event that the tool is used for will lead to a domino effect in that more people will become aware of chide.it as a tool for events. This is chide.it's "offline" viral marketing tactic.

Chide.it Toolbar

The chide.it toolbar is a plugin for Internet browsers. Prolific chide.it users can install this plugin and use it to make the process of posting something to chide.it a lot easier and faster. This way, when users visit a Web site and spot something that is of interest to them, they can use the toolbar to make the process of posting that topic onto chide.it, inviting friends to also check it out, and providing constructive feedback a lot easier. Because chide.it is being pitched as a tool, it is important for different options to be available for those that want to use it.

The chide.it team recognizes that a very small percentage of its userbase will use the toolbar. However, the most important thing to note is that small percentage will also be chide.it's most active users. It is of extreme importance that these users are valued and provided for, as they will lead the spread of chide.it.

How will Chide.it Market its Toolbar?   Chide.it will make its toolbar available on its own Web site and other popular download Web sites such as download.com. The goal isn't to push the toolbar on everyone (that is unnecessary and can be considered spamming). Chide.it will instead directly inform only its most active users of the availability of the toolbar.

Feeds Page/Email Updates

Another very useful marketing tactic for chide.it to boost its traffic involves sending users email summaries of their activity on chide.it and updates to threads that they have participated in. For example, if someone posts a topic on the Web site and another person provides some constructive criticism on the topic, the originator of the topic will get an email informing him of this constructive feedback. The originator can then visit the Web site again and make use of the feedback but also respond to it if he doesn't agree with it or has a different viewpoint.

The key point in emailing users is to respect the privacy and wishes of the userbase. Facebook (www.facebook.com) and Plaxo (www.plaxo.com) are two of the more successful Web sites out there that learned this lesson the hard way. Chide.it will, only send updates to users in the form of a summary once a week (if there is an update worthy of sending) and also will give users the option to vary how often they should be sent a summary and to opt out if they wish to do so.

Another attractive option for chide.it users is that their accounts page will have a very nice feed of information that is relevant to them (very similar to Facebook Friend's Feed and Plaxo's Feed). Users will also be enticed to visit the Web site so that they can view the latest discussions relevant to them through their accounts page.

Facebook, OpenSocial, Mobile Applications

Chide.it must make itself available in as many channels as possible to have the most penetration. It is for this reason that the team must build Facebook and OpenSocial applications in order to publicize its services and make itself available to users through social networks as well.

In addition to this, with the advent of the iPhone and unlimited data plans, more people are using their phones to surf the Internet. It is important that chide.it be very accessible to mobile users who may want to use chide.it as a tool on the go.

IV. MARKET RESEARCH AND ANALYSIS

Market Background & Information

The success of social networks has highlighted the acceptance of Web 2.0 online interactive communications and the opportunities this class of services provides to expand the use of the Internet. The success of the original social networks was based on the latent desire of people to form a community for free interaction. In North America in 2007, 37 percent of adults and 70 percent of teens were using social networks. The emphasis now is to provide a forum to connect people through common interest not just networks of people connecting with one another for the sake of connecting.

Bradley Horowitz of Yahoo has stated that 1 percent of the Web users are creators, 10 percent are active participants in what others have initiated, and the balance are users of what others contribute. A challenge is to fully expand the 11 percent who are fully engaged by increasing the interest level of content and discussion forums on the social network. The most important market challenge for social networks is developing a business model that creates positive cash flow. Various models are suggested for generating revenue; however, a number of common factors are critical to creating a valuable investment:

* A large audience
* Content that encourages the users to return regularly
* Active participation
* Recognized value to consumers and business
* The marketing plan has to focus on satisfying these criteria.

Content

The most important factor in attracting an audience is content and in the case of chide. it also controversial topics to encourage involvement in the interactive forums. Chide.it will contribute both; however, as the site grows external contributors will be the primary source. Chide.it will have the resources to implement forums on current hot topics whether entertainment, politics, special or international events. Many of these topics will run for a short time, reflecting public interest. As the interest in chide.it grows, it will increasingly not just be a forum to critique issues or content but a forum where interaction leads to improvement through help from others.

Audience Growth

Social networks have largely grown through referrals and invitations to join groups. Repeat visits come because the network content sparks interest and enthusiasm. Proactive action is required to grow the audience, particularly growing an audience with common interests or demographics to interest sponsors. While some organizations have the capability to establish their own blogs or online focus groups, many do not. Chide.it will provide them with a forum to do this with minimal investment. They will bring topics of interest to their community and provide moderators who will be coached on making the site controversial to stimulate interaction. Partnerships will be established with organizations such as educational institutions, not for profit and business organizations. Chide.it will create links with other sites to expand the audience reach.

Active Participation

Everyone likes to voice opinions and criticize. There is often a reticence to speak openly. The anonymity enables everyone to participate without being identified, if that is preferred. Moderators will receive instruction on how to encourage the audience to participate in discussions and to originate topical forums. As an incentive, the top five contributions to selected forums will receive prizes.

Recognized Value to Consumers and Business

For consumers, the content on chide.it must be compelling to retain interest. It is initially expected that criticism will dominate the discussions. This in itself has value by exposing readers to many different viewpoints. A more positive value will emerge over time as contributors start providing suggestions on how contributors can improve their content, creative work, or even improve their arguments to be presented in other forums.

Business is often reluctant to expose their actions or products to criticism. For many, chide.it will provide an opportunity to field test their new products or marketing programs. Refinements can be made before a full expensive launch, exposing the company to negative publicity for uncorrected errors or shortcomings in the marketing pitch. This can be done to the broad audience or through an online forum, restricted to an invited audience such as existing clients, staff, or other targeted group. Chide.it, through partnerships, will build a user base from targeted demographic groups.

Revenue Opportunities

Initially chide.it will be offering free services until the client base grows and the site's brand name obtains broader recognition. The following opportunities will be targeted when these conditions are met:

- Sponsored topics by enterprises that wish to promote their activities, products, or brand.

- Pay per click is a standard advertising target. Online advertising is growing although social networks have not been as successful in attracting advertising revenue as many other Internet sites. Chide.it will attract advertising related to the content and user interests that attract the largest audience.
- Licensing of the technology to business for online focus groups. These forums can be moderated by chide.it (for an extra fee) or moderated by the client. Potential clients include the enterprises and companies that organize focus groups.

Competition

The first competition that must be addressed is the popular social networks that dominate the audience base at this time. The attraction of chide.it to that existing audience will be the participation in an active issues-driven network and not a people linkage network. The attraction will be participant's ability to voice opinions and receive feedback on their own contributions.

Social networks that have a targeted audience will be either competition or potential partners with chide.it; where chide.it is a linked forum to stimulate discussions on issues of interest to that network's active audience. Chide.it's strategy will be to create topical forums reflecting issues of the day.

Chide.it's advantage for online focus group activities will lie in its large established user base that will provide candidates for focus groups. As is often the case, the sponsoring organization will provide incentives for participation by chide.it's audience to participate. Chide.it's technology will make it simple for clients to establish an online focus group.

Competitors

Because chide.it begins its life as a tool to facilitate the process of gaining constructive feedback with the help of the community, it can be considered a crowdsourcing application. Crowdsourcing refers to the process of using the community to get a task done for free or by only paying for results. Crowdsourcing is a fairly new phenomenon that is gaining ground fast. Some of the most interesting and relevant crowdsourcing organizations in existence today are: **Amazon Mechanical Turk** (www.mturk.com/) and **InnoCentive** (www.innocentive.com/).

Some crowdsourcing applications are even more specific such as **Cambrian House** (www.cambrianhouse.com/) that focuses on using the community to build Web projects and **Threadless** (www.threadless.com/) that uses the community to design t-shirts.

Chide.it can be considered a specialized crowdsourcing application with a twist. Chide.it focuses on finding flaws in a variety of areas and proposing solutions to these problems. By specializing in constructive criticisms and providing tools to further the process, chide.it will establish itself in this niche.

Chide.it in general also has competitive features in comparison to companies like **Opinion Labs**.com that specialize in helping Web sites get basic feedback from their visitors. Chide.it is different from OpinionLabs in that it allows more control to the Web sites in what they ask users and the detail of the information that they glean. Further to this, chide.it takes more of a community approach to gathering information while companies like OpinionLabs really take a one-on-one approach.

As mentioned previously, once there is enough content on the Web site, chide.it will be able to attract marketers to the Web site in order to research the opinions of experts in the community. There are companies such as **Sysomos** (www.sysomos.com/) that help marketers browse through user generated content on the Internet today in order to determine what is relevant to them. Chide.it takes a bit of a different approach in that it allows marketers to conduct crowdsourced focus groups in order to assemble relevant information.

Market Development Plan

Brand Recognition   The initial focus is on increasing the audience base. Selected topics identified of interest will provide the initial forums. To make them interesting the following actions will be taken:

- Use moderators with strong interest in the topic and experience in stimulating focused and controversial discussions.
- Ensure that the topics are current.
- Use key words that will obtain a high rating on search engines.
- Provide links to relevant sites to direct audience to chide.it.
- Provide incentives for users to submit content, contributions etc.

Targeted Audience   Analysis of initial audience performance:

- Statistics will be gathered on the activity in each forum to identify most popular issues, geographic location, number of participants, etc. to optimize the introduction of the most interesting forums.
- Target demographic groups through promotions, advertising, search engines, links to social networks.
- Expand the content on the site through chide.it and audience contributions. This can include news, videos, and today's international or local issues as examples.

Mobile Clients   Mobile phones and the use of them is increasingly oriented towards data services. We will ensure the site is compatible with mobile services:

- Increased data transfer rates will enable an ongoing broader range of mobile activities.
- Explore opportunities for forums specifically targeting mobile users.

Sponsored Forums   Introduce topics relevant to the activities or business interest of the sponsoring organizations. Provide links, banners, etc. related to the organization. We will gather data requested by the organization; provide a qualified moderator for the forum; provide links to related sites, and use key words in contributions to obtain high search engine recognition.

Licensing to Enterprises   Organize data to demonstrate activity on the Web site; categorize users according to demographics, interests, participation, etc., and implement a platform that facilitates the enterprises to establish an intuitive private or public forum.

V. BUSINESS MODEL

Premium Placement

YouTube.com Model   As the Web becomes more and more cluttered daily, it becomes more difficult to get noticed. Over 10,000 videos are uploaded onto YouTube daily. No matter how good a video is, it will not get noticed unless a lot of hacks are put into place. For example, a number of large companies (such as Nortel) have put on YouTube very professionally made videos that have only succeeded in attaining roughly 2,000 views, whereas, truly successful videos have been viewed over 5 million times. However, if a video that Nortel produced was put on the first page of the Web site (a sponsored video), it would get a lot of attention and views. Videos placed on the front page easily get watched over a million times.

Google Sponsored Search Model   Google Search has a similar model. Assume that a plumber in Toronto wants his Web site to appear as the first result when someone searches "Toronto Plumber." He would have a few options open to him. The easiest and fastest approach for him to get his Web site listed as the first search result would be to pay for a sponsored listing. Google bases its sponsored search model on a bidding system. In other words, the more one pays, the higher the chance of his Web site appearing in the search results for the keywords "Toronto Plumber."

Chide.it will use a similar model as that of YouTube and Google. Chide.it will have a bidding system. The highest bidders will be able to get their topic to have the best placement on the Web site. The idea is that the better placement a topic has, the more views it will get and the more constructive feedback it can get from the community.

Premium Membership

By default, when someone posts something on chide.it, the community can have access to the posting. Sometimes, a company or organization may want to invite a private group to critique the post. The originator of the topic may also want all the critique to remain private. In order to accomplish this, the members must sign up for a premium membership ($10/month). As chide.it develops as a product, most of the features on the Web site will be free but some of them will only be available to premium members. This is a model that is also implemented in a number of other successful Web businesses such as Basecamp. com and Shopify.com.

Enterprise Membership

As is the case with some other successful companies such as Basecamp and Ning, larger enterprises generally may want to use chide.it's Web site and its services as a white label solution. They may want to use it internally as a tool to conduct surveys or focus groups with their employees or even customers. As part of their requirements, it may be necessary to have the companies branding and logo appear everywhere such that the tool itself appears as something that was developed within the company.

If a company purchases enterprise membership with chide.it, they will be able to use the services that the Web site offers as a white label, hosted, or off box service. The exact pricing for this is still to be determined; however, a current base price of $250/month is what is being advertised presently.

Targeted Advertising

Advertising using Google, Yahoo!, Microsoft, and a whole slew of other companies has recently been a very good model for highly trafficked Web sites to use in order to earn revenue. Plentyoffish.com (a one-man company), which is Canada's largest free dating Web site, is earning upwards of $10 million a year in revenue from Google Adsense (Google's offsite advertising program) alone.

Chide.it will display advertising on its Web site from the very beginning. As ad-serving technology improves in the coming years, chide.it will be able to earn more on a CPM basis (i.e., money one can earn for every 1,000 page-views). Further to this, because chide.it will have a lot of very specific and targeted pages, the advertisements displayed will also be quite targeted. The more targeted the advertising on the Web site, the higher the CPM that chide.it can earn. As an example, assume a lounge on chide.it that specifically talks about the iPhone. This page would obviously then have related cellphone advertisements.

VI. EXECUTION AND RISKS

The execution roadmap for chide.it begins by developing the chide.it tool and popularizing its use. Once this has taken place, then community features shall be built into the Web site and chide.it's products shall be directly advertised to enterprises.

The following is a high level focus Road Map for the first two years:

1–3 months

- Refine chide.it as a tool through iterative design and feedback from community so that it is a very useful tool for soliciting constructive feedback.
- Focus on chide.it as a tool for events. Refine the technology for this purpose and market it heavily for use at public gatherings.

3–6 months

- Build the chide.it widgets technology that will allow Web sites to solicit feedback from their users and focus on gaining adoption for this feature.

6–9 months

- Build the blog post-back feature and market to bloggers for adoption.
- Build a Facebook/OpenSocial application to publicize chide.it's features.

9–12 months

- Build the chide.it toolbar and publicize to most active users on the Web site.
- Build the activity feeds (community feature) on the Web site so that users can more accurately follow their activities on the Web site.

12–18 months

- Start premium membership plans on the Web site and create more features for premium members.

18–24 months

- Focus on enterprise memberships and white-labelling the service for larger companies.

In terms of risks involved in building chide.it, there are a few. The first point that comes to mind is the state of online advertising going forward. Many have predicted that the online advertising industry is currently inflated and that spending on the Internet will not grow as fast as the industry hopes. This in turn can affect the profit margins of companies that heavily rely on advertising. Fortunately, advertising is not the only revenue stream for chide.it and so it does have a backup plan for revenue in the event of an industry downturn.

Further to this, the risk for any online Web site with initial success is that copycats will come along and copy the model. The same has happened for the likes of Facebook and Digg. It is for this reason that chide.it has to focus on building its brand so that its users come to the Web site for more than just the feature set. Additionally, chide.it should fairly quickly provide language support for a variety of different countries so that international clones of the Web site have a lower chance of success by playing only the language card. Finally, chide.it must attempt to get as many users as fast as possible to stay ahead of the game.

A final potential risk as with any other UGC (user generated content) Web site is that there may be inappropriate, slanderous, inaccurate material placed on the Web site which may lead to legal risks. Chide.it intends to deal with this risk by having everyone sign terms of use on the Web site and by also implementing a flagging system that allows the community to flag such material for removal. With the use of the flagging system and human moderation, this risk will be mitigated.

VII. FINANCES

The following is a summary of chide.it's revenue projections over the next five years. As the table shows, chide.it will earn its revenue from serving targeted ads, sponsored topics on the Web site, basic membership, and enterprise membership.

	Year 1	Year 2	Year 3	Year 4	Year 5
Effective CPM	$0.50	$0.75	$1.00	$1.25	$1.50
Visitors/Month	1,081,080	3,392,892	6,093,147	9,755,324	13,908,760
Ad Revenue	$111,962	$953,623	$3,655,888	$7,316,493	$12,517,884
Sponsored Topics	$89,508	$508,599	$2,010,738	$3,511,917	$5,424,416
Basic Membership	$	$50,860	$175,483	$327,779	$534,096
Enterprise Membership	$	$50,860	$438,707	$936,511	$1,669,051
Total Income	$201,470	$1,563,941	$6,280,816	$12,092,700	$20,145,448

Advertising   The amount of money earned from advertising depends on the number of page views that users of the Web site view per month. The assumption is that every active user on chide.it will view about 50 pages per month. This is a reasonable number considering the fact that on some popular social networks such as Facebook/Bebo, users will view over 50 pages each time they log in whereas chide.it is assuming this number for the entire month. Chide.it also assumes an effective CPM of 50 cents for year one, 75 cents, $1, $1.25, $1.50 respectively for the years after that. These are reasonable figures when compared to other successful Web sites on the Internet. Facebook estimates that it will be able to earn about $8 CPM by the year 2015. In terms of the visitor count, chide.it expects to have about 14 million visitors a month in five years. This is also a reasonable number when compared to plentyoffish.com (largest dating site in Canada) that has over 30 million visitors a month.

Sponsored Topics   Chide.it will earn about $20/CPM for sponsored topics in the first year and this amount will increase every year as the effective CPM for advertising also increases.

Basic Membership and Enterprise Membership   The assumptions being made here are that approximately 1 in 5,000 active users will subscribe to a premium membership and that for every 50,000 people that sign up, one more enterprise client can be signed up by the chide.it sales team. Basic memberships will start at $10/month while enterprise memberships will start at $250/month. The following table shows the profit/loss summary for chide.it for the first year:

The expenses in the first year are quite low because chide.it is currently in bootstrapping mode and is not paying any of the members of the team. The expenses jump dramatically in year 2 as shown in the table below.

	Year 1	Year 2	Year 3	Year 4	Year 5
Total Revenue	$201,470	$1,563,941	$6,280,816	$12,092,700	$20,145,448
Total Expenses	$42,520	$1,061,940	$2,064,411	$3,269,916	$4,915,291
Net Profit	$158,950	$502,001	$4,216,405	$8,822,784	$15,230,157

The detailed profit/loss statements for the first five years of operation can be found in the Financial Appendix at the end of this report. The following is a brief table that summarizes the cash flow position of the company for the first two years:

	Monthy Cash Flow	Cumulative Cash Flow
March 2008	$(3,239)	$(3,239)
April 2008	$(3,229)	$(6,468)
May 2008	$(3,179)	$(9,648)
June 2008	$(2,679)	$(12,327)
July 2008	$(992)	$(13,318)
Aug 2008	$3,508	$(9,810)
Sept 2008	$10,198	$388
Oct 2008	$16,798	$17,187
Nov 2008	$24,638	$41,825
Dec 2008	$33,143	$74,968
Jan 2009	$40,304	$115,273
Feb 2009	$43,677	$158,950
March 2009	$(20,937)	$138,013
April 2009	$(13,833)	$124,180
May 2009	$(5,788)	$118,392
June 2009	$2,801	$121,193
July 2009	$12,535	$133,728
Aug 2009	$23,033	$156,761
Sept 2009	$33,552	$190,313
Oct 2009	$46,508	$236,821
Nov 2009	$60,500	$297,320
Dec 2009	$75,967	$373,287
Jan 2010	$91,952	$465,239
Feb 2010	$110,711	$575,951

Cost Per User/Value of Chide.it   For the purposes of future projections, based on the $5.6 million that will be spent on sales and marketing over the next five years and the approximately 14 million projected unique visitors, the approximate visitor acquisition cost for chide.it is $2.50. To put this into perspective, Bebo was recently purchased by AOL for approximately $20/user.

Investors   Chide.it is looking to raise $1 million from investors in the next 6–12 months. The current financial model assumes organic growth for the company. The investment will allow for faster development early on in the cycle of the company, a faster go to market timeline, and more money for the purposes of marketing the product.

VIII. CHIDE.IT TEAM

Management Team

Aydin Mirzaee (Co-founder, CEO)   Aydin leads the day-to-day operation of the company, product development, and team.

Background: Aydin was the founder and CEO of bOK Systems Corp. (www.bOKnow. com/). bOK is currently in the business of helping thousands of people save money on their cellphone bills using VoIP technology. Before that, Aydin served as a design team leader at Nortel Networks in the Platform Network Management division of the company. Prior to that, Aydin served as the assistant to the executive director of the Student World Assembly, an organization that started with about 10 members and now has over 12,000 people from all over the world. Aydin graduated from the Electrical Engineering/Management program at the University of Ottawa with a near perfect GPA.

Eli Fathi (Co-founder, Chief Strategist)   Eli works with Aydin on a daily basis to manage the company, refine its roadmap, and formulize its business model. Eli, with his vast network of colleagues around the world is also instrumental in the process of forming strategic partnerships with various organizations. Further to this, Eli has had a great deal of experience in fund-raising (having raised over $75 million for his last company) and his experience in this area has shaped the roadmap that chide.it currently has.

Background: Eli Fathi is the CEO and founder of OrbitIQ, a business accelerator company with globally deployed channels to market. Eli has been a technology entrepreneur for the past 25 years. In 1986, Eli founded Applied Silicon Inc. Canada to provide engineering consulting services to the private and public sectors. Following an investment from Newbridge Networks in 1996, the company (Telexis) shifted its focus to video over IP solutions, growing to 180 employees. Telexis was acquired in May 2000, and became March Networks.

Eli has been involved in the high-tech community by serving on a number of boards including, Ottawa Centre for Research and Innovation (OCRI), Ottawa Chamber of Commerce, and Canadian Advanced Technology Association (CATA). He has been involved in a number of task forces including chairing the Ottawa-Gatineau Commercialization Task Force, participated on the CATA outsourcing and commercialization committees, a member of the Conference Board of Canada Leader's Roundtable on Commercialization from 2004 to 2006, and is a member of the Ottawa Innovation Hub committee. He chairs the Advisory Board for the Electronics Department at Algonquin College and at the University of Ottawa organized advisory forums for the Dean of the Telfer School of Management and serves on the Dean of Engineering's Advisory Board. He joined the board of the Ottawa Community Loan Fund. Eli also serves on the board of C-Com, a publicly traded company on the TSX-V.

Eli Fathi earned an Electrical Engineering degree in 1978 and a Master of Science degree in 1982 from the University of Ottawa. He received the University of Ottawa Faculty of Engineering Alumni Award of excellence for 2002. In 2004 he was the Recipient of the Order of Ottawa for Economic Development, and was the Recipient of OCRI 2004 Civic Entrepreneur of the Year award.

Peter Okulich (VP Operations)   Peter manages the day-to-day legal, accounting, HR, and operational aspects of the company.

Background: Peter Okulich is a co-founder and vice president Global Operations (Administration, Finance, and Legal) of OrbitIQ. He is a seasoned management professional who has been involved in the telecommunications industry for over 30 years with both start-up and international companies. Before joining OrbitIQ, he worked for Peleton Photonic Systems, Telexis (March Networks), Mitel Corporation, Digital Equipment Canada, Leigh Instruments, and Consolidated Computer Inc.

His previous experience includes the successful introduction of several new products from the design stage into volume manufacturing, the start-up of two production facilities, and senior management positions in operations, engineering, manufacturing, and contract administration. Mr. Okulich has successfully guided high-tech organizations through fast growth periods and has started and developed human resources, IT, facilities, and manufacturing departments from concept. As COO at Telexis, he helped transition the company from providing consulting engineering services into a product-oriented corporation.

Mr. Okulich is a member of the Professional Engineers Association of Ontario. He holds a B.Sc. and an M.Eng. in Electrical Engineering from the University of Ottawa.

Development Team

Chide.it currently has four developers working on the team. All the developers on the team work on various aspects of the product. Each, though, specializes in a different area:

Amin Mirzaee is experienced with Javascript and specifically Ajax. He leads the effort in contributing to the Ajax developments on chide.it.

Samuel Cormier-Iijima is the python guru on the team and usually does the initial architecting of new features in Django.

Marc-Andre Plouffe has a great deal of design and aesthetics experience. He leads the branding efforts and the design of the various pages on the Web site.

Andrew Pitt is experienced in building big projects and unit testing. He leads the overall robustness testing and quality assurance of the Web applications and the features that they have.

Advisory Board

Dr. Sorin Cohn is co-founder and president of OrbitIQ Global Portfolio with responsibility for business development and client acquisition. He brings over 30 years of international business and technology management experience. Prior to joining OrbitIQ, he co-founded Wireless Multimedia Solutions and was its CTO. Previously, Dr. Cohn held several senior management positions with Nortel Networks, driving their Satellite Network Solutions Group to key global accounts, initiating and managing Nortel's first wireless data initiatives, and in the late 80s, initiating and managing the Companion portfolio—the world's first and most successful wireless office systems. Prior to Nortel, he was with Bell-Northern Research as director for Exploratory Programs in Integrated Office Systems. In the 80s, Dr. Cohn created the BNR laboratories for Man-Machine Technologies leading to the conception of the world's first touch-sensitive display phone, multimedia teleconferencing, Meridian VMail, echo cancellers, etc. He developed the digital signal processing subsystems in the world's first digital central office exchange—the DMS-100.

Dr. Cohn has several essential patents in Web services, wireless, telecommunications, and digital signal processing. He has published over 50 journal articles and participated as organizer, chairman, and presenter at countless industry conferences and forums.

Dr. Cohn has been a Killam Scholar and the recipient of many corporate and national awards. He is a senior member of IEEE. Dr. Cohn has been an adjunct professor at the University of Ottawa, where he introduced advanced telecommunications courses. He holds a Ph.D. in Electrical Engineering from McMaster University, an M.Sc. in Physics from the University of Calgary, and an M.Eng. from the Polytechnic Institute of Bucharest.

Peter Craig has over 20 years of experience in leading teams in sales, sales management, and marketing of high technology products and services to businesses. During his career he has demonstrated the value of strategic sales management and strategic account management, and has made this a personal area of study and practice. Mr. Craig has been a resident of the greater Toronto area for the past 17 years after moving from Ottawa, where he grew up and attended Carleton University's Engineering Program.

Most recently Mr. Craig has served as founder and managing director of Maxima Consulting Group and as president of Telax Systems Inc. Maxima Consulting is a management consulting firm working with emerging high technology companies in the area of business development. Telax Systems is a leader in providing virtual call centre services. Prior to this, Mr. Craig had developed a reputation as a strong leader and catalyst for change in the firms he worked with. Most recently, as member of a 3,000 person sales force at Nortel, he regularly placed in the top 1 percent of sales leaders and achievers and was responsible for building and leading sales teams responsible for introducing new products to new accounts and existing strategic accounts. During his tenure at Nortel he rose through the ranks rapidly, joining as senior account executive serving multiple positions at the director level.

Mr. Craig has held senior sales and marketing positions, up to the vice president level, with firms such as AT&T, Scientific Atlanta, Paradyne, and Computer Task Group. Responsibilities typically included building and mentoring sales teams and closing new business. Mr. Craig has been regularly acknowledged as a mentor to subordinates and to peers.

Dr. Alan Aitken graduated from the University of Edinburgh in 1964 with a B.Sc. degree in Physics and from the University of Strathclyde, Scotland with a Ph.D. degree in Applied Physics in 1969. In 1969 he joined Northern Telecom Research Labs. (now Nortel Technologies) where he was a manager responsible for development of new technologies required for the manufacture of proprietary integrated circuits used in Nortel's communications equipment. In 1976, he joined Mitel Corporation with responsibility for the operations and technology R&D in a new semiconductor operation. In 1984, he left Mitel to act as a consultant to the electronics industry. He co-founded the Canadian Semiconductor Design Association and acted as president from 1985 until 1996. He has been instrumental in establishing a number of partnerships between companies and in launching new initiatives, which have enhanced the electronic infrastructure in Canada. He was the founding executive director of OCRInet Inc., the high speed ATM network connecting major research centres in the Ottawa-Carleton region that provided connection to the national CANARIE network. He was an original member of the CANARIE Technical Network Operating Committee.

In 1994, he received 1 of 10 IEEE Ottawa, 50th Anniversary "Pioneers in Technology" awards for his contribution to new technology development in the Ottawa region.

Alan Aitken was a member of the federal government Blue Ribbon panel (1998), advising the federal Minister of Industry on the terms of reference for the Smart Communities Initiative. Alan Aitken served on the board of directors of a U.K./Canadian networking company, the board of Actua, the Canadian engineering student run summer camp program, and on the board of the Ottawa Life Sciences Council from 2001 to 2003. He was a member of a CIDA/Philippine study, which identified and proposed strategic initiatives in information technology to accelerate the deployment of telecommunications in the Philippines. He prepared a business plan for the implementation of the BADLAB at the Communications Research Centre that has become the primary Canadian centre for development of expertise and international links over broadband networks. He has served on a number of Ontario government committees for microelectronics and high speed networking in the province.

Recently he served as vice president at March Networks, a broadband applications company headed by Terry Matthews in Kanata, Ontario. He was a consultant to Connect North/Connect Nord on network operations and to the Ontario government Connect Ontario program. Alan presently serves as vice president of Marketing and Competitiveness for OrbitIQ.

Peter Griffiths has worked in the communications industry for over 30 years for companies both large and small, holding many diverse roles, which include overseeing large communication projects and running competitive intelligence laboratories. Peter started his career as a chemist for Morganite Research and Development before moving into the high-tech field. In high-tech, he has worked as both a technical support engineer and an applications engineer for companies such as Tandata and Newbridge in the U.K., and Newbridge and March Networks in Canada.

Peter is familiar with many forms of microprocessor controlled electronic communication involving computers and terminals, including their use with radio, PABX equipment, Multiplexers, LANs, Frame Relay, ATM Switches, and modems.

Peter has first-hand experience of MS/DOS, Windows, CP/M, BASIC, Visual Basic, Front Page, and Assembler (Mainly 6502 and 8086 some Z80) and has produced sophisticated terminal programs for the BBC microcomputer and print redirection programs for the IBM PC in Assembler. He has also supervised the writing of programs for MS/DOS, CP/M, CP/M-86, and Q/DOS applications, using synchronous, asynchronous modems, and data controllers with minis, micros, and terminals.

Peter first started to work with OrbitIQ in 2003 and brings an unprecedented range of technical skills and experience. Part of his responsibilities involves the training of staff in the installation and use of equipment and applications and supporting customers and staff.

Peter also acts as the technical interface between the customer and the OrbitIQ clients, and often recommends improvements, new features and modification of existing product.

In addition Peter is quite familiar with the server side programming languages such as PHP, PERL, HTML, and databases as required for enhanced functionality of today's Web sites.

Peter Griffiths holds qualifications in chemistry, electronics, electrical engineering, computing and data processing; he is also a member of the Royal Society of Chemistry.

IX. APPENDIX

INCOME STATEMENT

		Year 1
Sales		
Net Sales		$201,469.60
Cost of Goods Sold		$–
Gross Margin on Sales		$201,469.60
R&D Costs		
Payroll		
Salaries/Benefits/Commissions		$–
	Subtotal	$–
Outsourced Dev/Support		
Salaries/Benefits/Commissions		$–
	Subtotal	$–
R&D		
Server Rental		$3,450.00
Amazon Web Services		$720.00
Server/Security Software		$250.00
Other Software/Services/Certificates		$1,000.00
	Subtotal	$5,420.00
	R&D Subtotal	$5,420.00
	% of sales	$0.027
Sales & Marketing		
Payroll		
Salaries/Benefits/Commissions		$–
	Subtotal	$–
Internet Advertising		
Facebook Ads		$6,000.00
Google Ads		$3,000.00
Other Internet Spending		$3,000.00
	Subtotal	$12,000.00
Travel		
Air Travel		$3,500.00
Meals and Entertainment		$500.00
Accommodation		$1,000.00
Other Travel (Car/Rental)		$5,000.00
	Subtotal	$10,000.00
Company Promotions		
Conferences & Tradeshows		$2,000.00
PR Agency Fee		$–
Corporate Memberships/Sponsorships		$–
Promotional Publications		$1,000.00
Other Marketing		$500.00
	Subtotal	$3,500.00
	Sales/Marketing Subtotal	$25,500.00
	% of sales	$0.127

INCOME STATEMENT (continued)

		Year 1
Operating Expenses		
Accounting/Legal		
Accounting		$6,000.00
Legal		$5,000.00
Administrative		$—
Payroll		
Salaries/Benefits/Commissions		$—
	Subtotal	$—
Facilities		
Office Rent		$—
Facilities Rent (Special Events)		$—
One-Time Office Supplies		$—
	Subtotal	$—
Communications		
Office Phone (Skype Accounts)		$100.00
Cell Phones		$—
Internet Access		$—
	Subtotal	$100.00
Consumable Expenses		
Non-Capitalized Equipment		$—
Office Supplies		$250.00
Courier/Shipping/Fax		$250.00
	Subtotal	$500.00
Human Resources		
Recruiting & Training		$—
	Subtotal	$—
Insurance		
Office Insurance		$—
D&O Liability Insurance		$—
E&O Liability Insurance		$—
	Subtotal	$—
	Operating Expenses	$11,600.00
	% of sales	$0.058
Total Revenue		$201,470.00
Total Expenses		$42,520.00
Net Profit		$158,950.00

INCOME STATEMENT

		Year 2
Sales		
Net Sales		$1,563,940.92
Cost of Goods Sold		$–
Gross Margin on Sales		$1,563,940.92
R&D Costs		
Payroll		
Salaries/Benefits/Commissions		$224,000.00
	Subtotal	$224,000.00
Outsourced Dev/Support		
Salaries/Benefits/Commissions		$–
	Subtotal	$–
R&D		
Server Rental		$13,650.00
Amazon Web Services		$4,740.00
Server/Security Software		$2,250.00
Other Software/Services/Certificates		$20,000.00
	Subtotal	$40,640.00
	R&D Subtotal	$264,640.00
	% of sales	$0.169
Sales & Marketing		
Payroll		
	Subtotal	$95,200.00
Internet Advertising		
Facebook Ads		$20,000.00
Google Ads		$20,000.00
	Subtotal	$90,000.00
Travel		
Air Travel		$24,000.00
Accommodation		$24,000.00
Other Travel (Car/Rental)		$12,000.00
	Subtotal	$66,000.00
Company Promotions		
Conferences & Tradeshows		$50,000.00
PR Agency Fee		$25,000.00
Corporate Memberships/Sponsorships		$10,000.00
Promotional Publications		$5,000.00
Other Marketing		$25,000.00
	Subtotal	$115,000.00
	Sales/Marketing Subtotal	$366,200.00
	% of sales	$0.234
Operating Expenses		
Accounting/Legal		
Accounting		$25,000.00
Legal		$25,000.00
Administrative		$28,000.00
	Subtotal	$78,000.00
Payroll		
Salaries/Benefits/Commissions		$190,400.00
	Subtotal	$190,400.00

INCOME STATEMENT (continued)

		Year 2
Facilities		
Office Rent		$38,400.00
Facilities Rent (Special Events)		$10,000.00
One-Time Office Supplies		$48,000.00
	Subtotal	$96,400.00
Communications		
Office Phone (Skype Accounts)		$600.00
Cell Phones		$2,400.00
Internet Access		$2,500.00
	Subtotal	$5,500.00
Consumable Expenses		
Non-Capitalized Equipment		$1,200.00
Office Supplies		$2,000.00
Courier/Shipping/Fax		$2,000.00
	Subtotal	$5,200.00
Human Resources		
Recruiting & Training		$24,000.00
	Subtotal	$24,000.00
Insurance		
Office Insurance		$1,600.00
D&O Liability Insurance		$10,000.00
E&O Liability Insurance		$20,000.00
	Subtotal	$31,600.00
	Operating Expenses	$431,100.00
	% of sales	$0.276
Total Revenue		$1,563,941.00
Total Expenses		$1,061,940.00
Net Profit		$502,001.00

INCOME STATEMENT

	Year 3
Sales	
Net Sales	$6,280,815.75
Cost of Goods Sold	$-
Gross Margin on Sales	$6,280,815.75
R&D Costs	
Payroll	
Salaries/Benefits/Commissions	$380,800.00
Subtotal	$380,800.00
Outsourced Dev/Support	
Salaries/Benefits/Commissions	$25,000.00
Subtotal	$25,000.00
R&D	
Server Rental	$29,247.00
Amazon Web Services	$18,279.00
Server/Security Software	$3,656.00
Other Software/Services/Certificates	$6,093.00
Subtotal	$57,276.00
R&D Subtotal	$463,076.00
% of sales	$0.074
Sales &Marketing	
Payroll	
Salaries/Benefits/Commissions	$345,520.00
Subtotal	$345,520.00
Internet Advertising	
Facebook Ads	$40,000.00
Google Ads	$40,000.00
Other Internet Spending	$100,000.00
Subtotal	$180,000.00
Travel	
Air Travel	$49,500.00
Meals and Entertainment	$18,000.00
Accommodation	$45,000.00
Other Travel (Car/Rental)	$22,500.00
Subtotal	$135,000.00
Company Promotions	
Conferences Tradeshows	$150,000.00
PR Agency Fee	$50,000.00
Corporate Memberships/Sponsorships	$25,000.00
Promotional Publications	$10,000.00
Other Marketing	$50,000.00
Subtotal	$285,000.00
Sales/Marketing Subtotal	$945,520.00
% of sales	$0.151
Operating Expenses	
Accounting/Legal	
Accounting	$30,000.00
Legal	$30,000.00
Administrative	$30,800.00
Subtotal	$90,800.00

INCOME STATEMENT (continued)

	Year 3
Payroll	
Salaries/Benefits/Commissions	$304,640.00
Subtotal	$304,640.00
Facilities	
Office Rent	$72,000.00
Facilities Rent (Special Events)	$20,000.00
One Time Office Supplies	$42,000.00
Subtotal	$134,000.00
Communications	
Office Phone (Skype Accounts)	$1,125.00
Cell Phones	$4,500.00
Internet Access	$3,000.00
Subtotal	$8,625.00
Consumable Expenses	
Non Capitalized Equipment	$2,250.00
Office Supplies	$3,750.00
Courier/Shipping/Fax	$3,750.00
Subtotal	$9,750.00
Human Resources	
Recruiting Training	$75,000.00
Subtotal	$75,000.00
Insurance	
Office Insurance	$3,000.00
D&O Liability Insurance	$10,000.00
E&O Liability Insurance	$20,000.00
Subtotal	$33,000.00
Operating Expenses	$655,815.00
% of sales	$0.104
Total Revenue	$6,280,816
Total Expenses	$2,064,411
Net Profit	$4,216,405

INCOME STATEMENT

		Year 4
Sales		
Net Sales		$12,092,700.11
Cost of Goods Sold		$–
Gross Margin on Sales		$12,092,700.11
R&D Costs		
Payroll		
Salaries/Benefits/Commissions		$630,560.00
	Subtotal	$630,560.00
Outsourced Dev/Support		
Salaries/Benefits/Commissions		$82,500.00
	Subtotal	$82,500.00
R&D		
Server Rental		$46,826.00
Amazon Web Services		$29,266.00
Server/Security Software		$5,853.00
Other Software/Services/Certificates		$9,755.00
	Subtotal	$91,700.00
	R&D Subtotal	$804,760.00
	% of sales	$0.067
Sales & Marketing		
Payroll		
Salaries/Benefits/Commissions		$598,472.00
	Subtotal	$598,472.00
Internet Advertising		
Facebook Ads		$80,000.00
Google Ads		$80,000.00
Other Internet Spending		$200,000.00
	Subtotal	$360,000.00
Travel		
Air Travel		$90,000.00
Meals and Entertainment		$39,600.00
Accommodation		$72,000.00
Other Travel (Car/Rental)		$36,000.00
	Subtotal	$237,600.00
Company Promotions		
Conferences & Tradeshows		$175,000.00
PR Agency Fee		$75,000.00
Corporate Memberships/Sponsorships		$50,000.00
Promotional Publications		$15,000.00
Other Marketing		$100,000.00
	Subtotal	$415,000.00
	Sales/Marketing Subtotal	$1,611,072.00
	% of sales	$0.133
Operating Expenses		
Accounting/Legal		
Accounting		$40,000.00
Legal		$35,000.00
Administrative		$61,880.00
	Subtotal	$136,880.00

INCOME STATEMENT (continued)

		Year 4
Payroll		
Salaries/Benefits/Commissions		$335,104.00
	Subtotal	$335,104.00
Facilities		
Office Rent		$115,200.00
Facilities Rent (Special Events)		$30,000.00
One Time Office Supplies		$54,000.00
	Subtotal	$199,200.00
Communications		
Office Phone (Skype Accounts)		$1,800.00
Cell Phones		$7,200.00
Internet Access		$3,500.00
	Subtotal	$12,500.00
Consumable Expenses		
Non Capitalized Equipment		$3,600.00
Office Supplies		$6,000.00
Courier/Shipping/Fax		$6,000.00
	Subtotal	$15,600.00
Human Resources		
Recruiting & Training		$120,000.00
	Subtotal	$120,000.00
Insurance		
Office Insurance		$4,800.00
D&O Liability Insurance		$10,000.00
E&O Liability Insurance		$20,000.00
	Subtotal	$34,800.00
	Operating Expenses	$854,084.00
	% of sales	$0.071
Total Revenue		$12,092,700
Total Expenses		$3,269,916
Net Profit		$8,822,784

INCOME STATEMENT

		Year 5
Sales		
Net Sales		$20,145,447.91
Cost of Goods Sold		$–
Gross Margin on Sales		$20,145,447.91
R&D Costs		
Payroll		
Salaries/Benefits/Commissions		$925,372.00
	Subtotal	$925,372.00
Outsourced Dev/Support		
Salaries/Benefits/Commissions		$151,250.00
	Subtotal	$151,250.00
R&D		
Server Rental		$66,762.00
Amazon Web Services		$41,726.00
Server/Security Software		$8,345.00
Other Software/Services/Certificates		$13,909.00
	Subtotal	$130,742.00
	R&D Subtotal	$1,207,364.00
	% of sales	$0.060
Sales & Marketing		
Payroll		
Salaries/Benefits/Commissions		$949,519.20
	Subtotal	$949,519.20
Internet Advertising		
Facebook Ads		$150,000.00
Google Ads		$150,000.00
Other Internet Spending		$500,000.00
	Subtotal	$800,000.00
Travel		
Air Travel		$148,500.00
Meals and Entertainment		$69,300.00
Accommodation		$99,000.00
Other Travel (Car/Rental)		$49,500.00
	Subtotal	$366,300.00
Company Promotions		
Conferences & Tradeshows		$200,000.00
PR Agency Fee		$10,000.00
Corporate Memberships/Sponsorships		$100,000.00
Promotional Publications		$20,000.00
Other Marketing		$250,000.00
	Subtotal	$580,000.00
	Sales/Marketing Subtotal	$2,695,819.20
	% of sales	$0.134
Operating Expenses		
Accounting/Legal		
Accounting		$44,000.00
Legal		$40,000.00
Administrative		$66,668.00
	Subtotal	$150,668.00

INCOME STATEMENT (continued)

		Year 5
Payroll		
Salaries/Benefits/Commissions		$368,614.40
	Subtotal	$368,614.40
Facilities		
Office Rent		$158,400.00
Facilities Rent (Special Events)		$40,000.00
One-Time Office Supplies		$54,000.00
	Subtotal	$252,400.00
Communications		
Office Phone (Skype Accounts)		$2,475.00
Cell Phones		$9,900.00
Internet Access		$5,000.00
	Subtotal	$17,375.00
Consumable Expenses		
Non-Capitalized Equipment		$4,950.00
Office Supplies		$8,250.00
Courier/Shipping/Fax		$8,250.00
	Subtotal	$21,450.00
Human Resources		
Recruiting & Training		$165,000.00
	Subtotal	$165,000.00
Insurance		
Office Insurance		$6,600.00
D&O Liability Insurance		$10,000.00
E&O Liability Insurance		$20,000.00
	Subtotal	$36,600.00
	Operating Expenses	$1,012,107.40
	% of sales	$0.050
Total Revenue		$20,145,448.00
Total Expenses		$4,915,291.00
Net Profit		$15,230,157.00

PART

III

THE FOUNDER AND TEAM

Entrepreneurial founders must take a personal role in attracting, motivating, inspiring, and retaining an effective team of both specialists and generalists. The quality of that team has never been more fundamental and important than it is now. The new millennium ushered in a wave of new opportunities requiring nimble and creative teams. Some pundits have characterized this time as the communication era, characterized by galloping innovation—fuelled by the ability of inventive engineers and creative entrepreneurs to instantly access and share information worldwide. Investors stung by the dot-com fallout and the recession that ensued regained confidence as another boom wave followed. This was interrupted more recently by a global slump that hit harder and deeper than expected; private and venture capital investors emerge with a renewed appreciation for the time-tested wisdom that successful new ventures are often all about the team. Chapter 5 "The Entrepreneurial Leader" looks at the leadership issues inherent in building a company from scratch—and the significant recruiting, sales, and management skills the founder(s) must bring to bear as the enterprise grows through various stages.

Entrepreneurship titles now dominate the business sections at major booksellers like Chapters, and a growing number of students and professionals are seeking career opportunities in the entrepreneurial sector. While this has created a significant pool of talent to support the development of new ventures, one of the most critical aspects of entrepreneuring is in being able to attract the *right* people: team players whose skills and know-how are critical to the success of the enterprise. Ambiguity, risk, and the need to collectively turn on a dime in the face of shifting competitive landscapes require that entrepreneurial teams be greater than the sum of their parts. Like marriage, forming and building that team can be a rather unscientific, occasionally unpredictable, and frequently surprising experience. In Chapter 6 "The New Venture Team" we put a zoom lens on the "people" portion of the Timmons Model.

The solo entrepreneur may make a living, but it is the team builder who develops an organization and a company with sustainable value and attractive harvest options. The vision of what these founders are trying to accomplish provides the unwritten ground rules that become the fabric, character, and purpose behind the venture. Effective lead entrepreneurs are able to build a culture around the business mission and the brand by rewarding success, supporting honest failure, sharing the wealth with those who helped to create it, and setting high ethical standards of conduct. Chapter 7 "Ethical Decision Making and the Entrepreneur" addresses the complex and thorny issues of ethics and integrity for the entrepreneur, and how those decisions and choices can have a significant impact on future success.

C·H·A·P·T·E·R

5

THE ENTREPRENEURIAL LEADER

I have found that great people do have in common an immense belief in themselves and in their mission. They also have great determination as well as an ability to work hard. At the crucial moment of decision, they draw on their accumulated wisdom. Above all they have integrity.

Yousuf Karsh
Turkish born Canadian Photographer

RESULTS EXPECTED

Upon completion of this chapter, you will be able to:

1. Explain the difference between an entrepreneurial leader and a manager, and appreciate why the team is so important.

2. Identify stages of growth that entrepreneurial ventures go through, the venture modes characteristic of the entrepreneurial domain, and the principal forces acting in the domain.

3. Articulate the skills, competencies, and philosophies entrepreneurial-thinking founders apply as they form, build, and lead a new venture team, and discuss the critical issues and hurdles they face.

THE ENTREPRENEURIAL DOMAIN

Converging on the Entrepreneurial Leader

There are convergent pressures on being an entrepreneur and being a manager as a venture accelerates and grows beyond founder-driven and founder-dominated survival. Key to achieving sustained growth, and an eventual harvest, is an entrepreneur's ability to have or develop competencies as an entrepreneurial leader.

In the past, those studying entrepreneurship and others active in starting new ventures, such as venture capitalists, professors, and researchers, have generally believed that the kind of person with the entrepreneurial spirit required to propel a new venture through start-up to a multi-million-dollar annual sales level is different from the kind of person who has the capacity to manage the new firm as it grows from zero to $20 million or more in sales. Further, it has long been thought that the entrepreneur who clings to the lead role too long will limit or impede company growth. However, many VCs will be set on replacing the entrepreneur with "professional management" as the enterprise transitions through stages. But "entrepreneurs should not automatically be forced from their firms early. Several factors decide when the founder should step aside."[1]

Canadian economist John Kenneth Galbraith explained in 1971, "The great entrepreneur must, in fact, be compared in life with the male *apis mellifera*. He accomplishes his act of conception at the price of his own extinction."[2] In short, conventional wisdom stated that a good entrepreneur is usually not a good manager, since he or she lacks the necessary management skill and experience. Likewise, it is assumed that a manager is not an entrepreneur, since he or she lacks some intense personal qualities and the orientation required to launch a business from ground zero.

While results are mixed, some evidence suggests that new ventures that flourish beyond start-up and grow to become substantial, successful enterprises can be headed by entrepreneurs who are also effective leaders. Testing conventional wisdom, two researchers empirically studied the tenure of 54 Fortune 1,000 corporations' founders. They assumed that there are three ways founders have to adapt: (1) shift from creation to exploitation, (2) shift from passionate commitment to dispassionate objectivity, and (3) shift from direct personal control over organizational actions to indirect impersonal control. Taking into account the growth rate, the timing of the initial public offering, the founder's age, education, and other factors, this study found the following:

1. If the firm grows relatively slowly, and the founder is capable of some adaptation, then the firm can become quite large.
2. Founders with scientific or engineering backgrounds remain in control of the companies for shorter periods than do founders whose academic focus was business.
3. The founder's tenure will typically be longer in family-dominated firms.[3]

More recently, researchers "observed that many founders can and do manage growth successfully. The applicability of conventional wisdom regarding the 'leadership crisis' in rapid-growth entrepreneurial firms may no longer be valid, if, in fact, it ever was."[4] Terry Mathews is once again at the helm of the company he built—Mitel. Founder Bill Gates headed Microsoft until mid-2008, Ted Rogers, Jr. continued to lead his namesake—Rogers Communications—until his death in late 2008. Steve Jobs returned to the helm of Apple after stepping aside thinking that was best for the company he co-founded, and 40 years later Andy Grove is now the senior advisor to executive management at Intel. Numerous examples such as these clearly indicate founders can learn and grow faster than their companies do.

These and other data seem to defy the notion that entrepreneurs can start but cannot manage growing companies. While the truth is probably somewhere in between, one thing is apparent: Growing a higher potential venture requires leadership skills.

Clearly, a complex set of factors goes into making someone a successful entrepreneurial leader. Launching a new venture and then managing rapid growth involves skills not found in most mature or stable environments. Further, one of the greatest strengths of successful entrepreneurs is that they know what they do and do not know. They have disciplined intellectual honesty, which prevents their optimism from becoming myopic delusion and their dreams from becoming blind ambition. No individual has all these skills, nor does the presence or absence of any single skill guarantee success or failure. That an entrepreneur knows that he or she needs a certain skill and knows where to get it is as valuable as knowing whether he or she already has it.

Principal Forces and Venture Modes

Companies, whether they are new, growing, or mature, occupy a place in either a managerial or an entrepreneurial domain, an area influenced by certain principal forces and characterized by ways of acting, called venture modes. Exhibits 5.1 and 5.2 illustrate the entrepreneurial and managerial domains and the dynamic of the principal forces acting in the domains and the dominant venture modes that result.

In the exhibits, the four cells are defined by the stage of the venture (upper axis), the extent of change and uncertainty accompanying it (right axis), and the degree to which a venture is managerial (bottom axis) or entrepreneurial (left axis). Clearly, the entrepre-

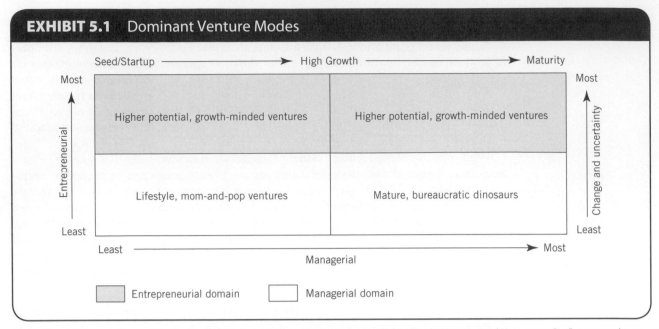

Source: These exhibits are built on work by Timmons and Stevenson: See Howard H. Stevenson, "A New Paradigm for Entrepreneurial Management," in *Entrepreneurship: What It Is and How to Teach It* (Harvard Business School, 1985), 30–51; and Jeffry A. Timmons and Howard H. Stevenson, "Entrepreneurship Education in the 80s: What Entrepreneurs Say," in *Entrepreneurship: What It Is and How to Teach It*, 115–34.

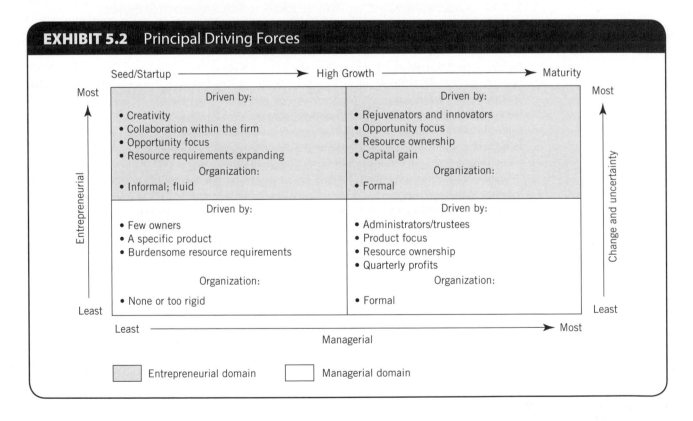

neurial domain is the two upper cells in both exhibits, and the domains are functions of both the change and uncertainty facing a venture and the stage of growth of the venture.

Each venture mode (i.e., way of acting) for firms in each cell is driven by certain principal forces. These forces are shown in Exhibit 5.2. Shown in Exhibit 5.1 are dominant venture modes characteristic of firms in each cell. Organizations at different stages are characterized by differing degrees of change and uncertainty and are therefore more or less entrepreneurial or more or less managerial. Thus, for example, a new venture in the seed/start-up stage, which is characterized by high change and uncertainty, is most entrepreneurial. These firms will be new, innovative, or backbone ventures; will be led by a team; will be driven by their founders' goals, values, commitment, and perceptions of the opportunities; and will minimize the use of resources. At the other extreme is a mature firm, one that is in the maturity stage and characterized by low change and uncertainty, is stable or contracting, is led by a manager, is driven by resource ownership and managerial efficiency, and is reactive. Other firms fall in between.

The managerial skills required of the firms in each cell are more evident upon examination of these principal forces and dominant venture modes. For example, creativity and comprehensive managerial skills are required to lead firms in both cells in the entrepreneurial domain. In the upper-left-hand cell, entrepreneurial leaders need to cope effectively with high levels of change and uncertainty, whether their management skills can be affectionately labelled MBWA (management by wandering around) or management by muddling through. Certainly, as the firm enters the high-growth stage, this changes.

STAGES OF GROWTH

A Theoretical View

Clearly, entrepreneurship is not static. Exhibit 5.3 represents a *theoretical* view of the process of gestation and growth of new ventures and the transitions that occur at different "boundaries" in this process.[5] Ventures are sown, sprout, grown, and harvested. Even those successful ventures that are not grown to harvest (i.e., those that have been defined as "attractive") go through stages of growth.

This smooth, S-shape curve in the exhibit is rarely, if ever, replicated in the real world. If one actually tracked the progress of most emerging companies, the "curve" actually would

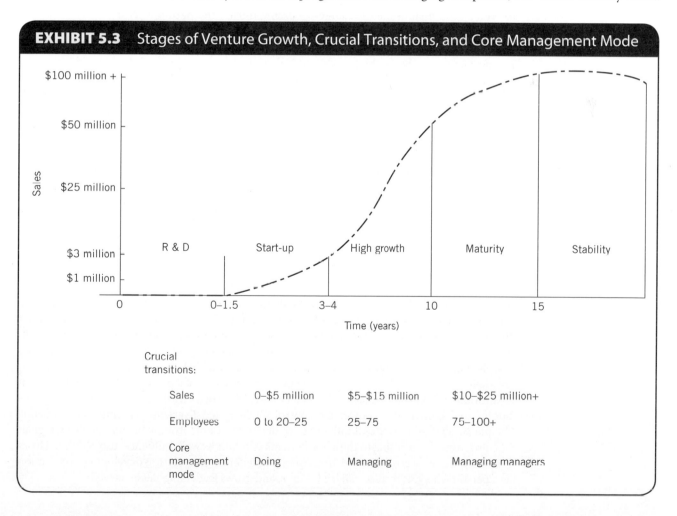

EXHIBIT 5.3   Stages of Venture Growth, Crucial Transitions, and Core Management Mode

Crucial transitions:			
Sales	0–$5 million	$5–$15 million	$10–$25 million+
Employees	0 to 20–25	25–75	75–100+
Core management mode	Doing	Managing	Managing managers

be a ragged and jagged line with many ups and downs; these companies would experience some periods of rapid progress followed by setbacks and accompanying crises.

For the purposes of illustration, Exhibit 5.3 shows venture stages in terms of time, sales, and number of employees. It is at the boundaries between stages that new ventures seem to experience transitions. Several researchers have noted that the new venture invariably goes through transition and will face certain issues.[6] Thus, the exhibit shows the crucial transitions during growth and the key management tasks of the chief executive officer or founders. Most important and most challenging for the founding entrepreneur or a chief executive officer is coping with crucial transitions and the change in management tasks, going from leading to leading leaders, as a firm grows to roughly 30 employees, to 50, to 75, and then up.

The *research and development stage*, sometimes referred to as the nascent stage, is characterized by a single aspiring entrepreneur, or small team, doing the investigation and due diligence for their business idea. The nascent stage can be as short as a few months or can last years. Research indicates that if an idea is not turned into a going concern within 18 months, the chances of a start-up fall dramatically. Nascent entrepreneurs have many fits and starts, and the business model can change often in the process.

The *start-up stage*, a stage that usually covers the first two or three years but perhaps as many as seven, is by far the most perilous stage and is characterized by the direct and exhaustive drive, energy, and entrepreneurial talent of a lead entrepreneur and a key team member or two. Here, the critical mass of people, market and financial results, and competitive resiliency are established, while investor, banker, and customer confidence is earned. The level of sales reached varies widely, but typically ranges from $2 to $20 million. A new company then begins its high growth stage. The exact point at which this occurs can rarely be identified by a date on the calendar until well after the fact. It is in this stage that new ventures exhibit a failure rate exceeding 60 percent; that is, it is in this stage that the lemons ripen.

As with the other stages, the length of time it takes to go through the *high growth stage*, as well as the magnitude of change occurring during the period, varies greatly. Probably the most difficult challenge for the founding entrepreneur occurs during the high growth stage, when he or she finds it is necessary to let go of power and control (through veto) over key decisions that he or she has always had, and when key responsibilities need to be delegated without abdicating ultimate leadership and responsibility for results. But the challenges do not end there. The next batch of up-and-comers, poised for explosive growth include: Overlay.TV, which enables layers and links to be added to streaming video; Idée Inc., which develops image recognition and visual search software; Sempa Power Systems, which offers hybrid heating to reduce energy consumption; Akoha, which created a reality-based social game; GiveMeaning, which hosts a multitude of charities online for free; and LearnHub, a social learning network.

From the high growth stage, a company then moves to what is called the *maturity stage*. In this stage, the key issue for the company is no longer survival; rather, it is one of steady, profitable growth. The *stability stage* usually follows.

Managing for Rapid Growth

Managing for rapid growth involves a leadership orientation not found in mature and stable environments. (This topic will be addressed again in Chapter 12.) For one thing, the tenet that one's responsibility must equal one's authority is often very counterproductive in a rapid-growth venture. Instead, results usually require close collaboration of a manager with other people than his or her subordinates, and managers invariably have responsibilities far exceeding their authority. Politics and personal power can be a way of life in many larger and stagnant institutions, as managers jockey for influence and a piece of a shrinking pie in a zero-sum game; but in rapid-growth firms, power and control are delegated. Everyone is committed to making the pie larger, and power and influence are derived not only from achieving one's own goals but also from contributing to the achievements of others as well. Influence also is derived from keeping the overall goals in mind, from resolving differences, and from developing a reputation as a person who gets results, can lead others, and grows leadership talent as well.

Thus, among successful entrepreneurs and entrepreneurial leaders, there is a well-developed capacity to exert influence *without* formal power. These people are adept at conflict resolution. They know when to use logic and when to persuade, when to make a concession and when to exact one. To run a successful venture, an entrepreneur learns to get along with many different constituencies, often with conflicting aims—the customer, the supplier, the financial backer, and the creditor, as well as the partners and others on the inside. Similarly, an entrepreneurial leader must operate in a world that is increasingly interdependent. Attempting to advise managers on how to exert "influence without authority," Allan Cohen and David Bradford assert, "If you are a manager, you not only need to exercise influence skills with your peers and your own boss, but also to help the people who work for you learn to be effective influencers—even of you—since that will free you to spend more of your time seeking new opportunities and working the organization above and around you."[7]

Whereas successful entrepreneurs are interpersonally supporting and nurturing—not interpersonally competitive—successful entrepreneurial leaders understand their interdependencies and have learned to incorporate mutual respect, openness, trust, and mutual benefit into their management style. Fundamental to this progressive style of management is the awareness and practice of reciprocity for mutual gain.[8] When a strong need to control, influence, and gain power over others characterizes the lead entrepreneur, or when he or she has an insatiable appetite for putting an associate down, more often than not the venture gets into trouble. A dictatorial, adversarial, and dominating management style makes it very difficult to attract and keep people who thirst for achievement, responsibility, and results. Compliant partners and managers are often chosen. Destructive conflicts often erupt over who has the final say, who is right, and whose prerogatives are what.

In the corporate setting, the "hero-making" ability is identified as an essential attribute of successful entrepreneurial leaders.[9] These hero makers try to make the pie bigger and better, rather than jealously clutching and hoarding a tiny pie that is all theirs. They have a capacity for objective interpersonal relationships as well, which enables them to smooth out individual differences of opinion by keeping attention focused on the common goal to be achieved.[10]

Exhibit 5.4 characterizes probable crises that growing ventures will face, including erosion of creativity by founders and team members; confusion or resentment, or both, over ambiguous roles, responsibilities, and goals; failure to clone founders; specialization and eroding of collaboration; desire for autonomy and control; need for operating mechanisms and controls; and conflict and divorce among founders and members of the team. The exhibit further delineates issues that confront entrepreneurial leaders.

EXHIBIT 5.4 Entrepreneurial Transitions

Modes/Stages	Planning	Doing	Leading	Leading Leaders
Sales	$0	$0–$5 million	$5–$15 million	$10 million or more
Employees	0–5	0–30	30–75	75 and up
Transitions	Characteristics:	Characteristics:	Probable crises:	Probable crises:
	Founder-driven	Founder-driven creativity	Erosion of creativity of founders	Failure to clone founders
	Wrenching changes	Constant change, ambiguity, and uncertainty	Confusion over ambiguous roles, responsibilities, and goals	Specialization/eroding of collaboration versus practice of power, information, and influence
	Highly influential informal advisor	Time compression	Desire for delegation versus autonomy and control	Need for operating controls and mechanisms
	Resource desperation	Informal Communications	Need for organization and operating policies	Conflict among founders
	Very quick or very slow decision making	Counterintuitive decision making and structure		
		Relative inexperience		

Compounding of Time and Change   In the high growth stage, change, ambiguity, and uncertainty seem to be the only things that remain constant. Change creates higher levels of uncertainty, ambiguity, and risk, which, in turn, compound to shrink time, an already precious commodity. One result of change is a series of shock waves rolling through a new and growing venture by way of new customers, new technologies, new competitors, new markets, and new people. In industries characterized by galloping technological change, with relatively minuscule lead and lag times in bringing new products to market and in weathering the storms of rapid obsolescence, the effects of change and time are extreme. For example, the president of a rapidly growing, small computer company said, "In our business it takes 6 to 12 months to develop a new computer, ready to bring to the market, and product technology obsolescence is running about 9 to 12 months." This time compression has been seen in such industries as electronics and aerospace in the 1960s; small computers, integrated circuits, and silicon chips in the 1970s; microcomputers in the 1980s; telecommunications, the Internet, and biotechnology in the 1990s; and nano and green/clean technology in the 2000s.

Nonlinear and Nonparametric Events   Entrepreneurial leadership is characterized by nonlinear and nonparametric events. Just as the television did not come about by a succession of improvements in the radio, and the jet plane did not emerge from engineers and scientists attempting to develop a better and better piston engine plane, so too events do not follow straight lines, progress arithmetically, or even appear related within firms. Rather, they occur in bunches and in stepwise leaps. For example, a firm may double its sales force in 15 months, rather than over eight years, while another may triple its manufacturing capacity and adopt a new materials resource planning system immediately, rather than utilizing existing capacity by increasing overtime, then adding a third shift nine months later, and finally adding a new plant three years hence.

Relative Inexperience   In addition, the management team may be relatively inexperienced. The explosive birth and growth of these firms are usually unique events that cannot be replicated, and most of the pieces in the puzzle—technology, applications, customers, people, the firm itself—are usually new. Stewart Butterfield from Victoria, B.C. and his wife Caterina Fake founded Ludicorp in Vancouver and began to work on an online multiplayer game. The tools for this project were re-deployed for Flickr—a far more promising opportunity. The move proved to be a shrewd one; Flickr launched in February 2004 and immediately captured users and industry attention. In March 2005 Yahoo! acquired this phenomenally growing enterprise.

Counterintuitive, Unconventional Decision Making   Yet another characteristic of rapidly growing ventures in the entrepreneurial domain is counterintuitive, unconventional patterns of decision making. For example, a computer firm needed to decide what approach to take in developing and introducing three new products in an uncertain, risky marketplace. Each proposed new product appeared to be aimed at the same end-user market, and the person heading each project was similarly enthusiastic, confident, and determined about succeeding. A traditional approach to such a problem would have been to determine the size and growth rates of each market segment; evaluate the probable estimates of future revenue costs and capital requirements for their accuracy; compare the discounted, present-value cash flow that will emerge from each project; and select the project with the highest yield versus the required internal rate of return. Such an analysis sometimes overlooks the fact that most rapid growth companies have many excellent alternatives and, more commonly, the newness of technology, the immaturity of the marketplace, and the rapid discovery of further applications make it virtually impossible to know which of any product proposals is best. The computer firm decided to support all three new products at once, and a significant new business was built around each one. New market niches were discovered simultaneously and the unconventional approach paid off.

Fluid Structures and Procedures   Most rapid growth ventures also defy conventional organizational patterns and structures. It is common to find a firm that has grown $25 million, $50 million, or even $150 million per year in sales and that still has no formal organizational chart. If an organizational chart does exist, it usually has three distinguishing features: First, it is inevitably out of date. Second, it changes frequently. For example, one firm had eight major reorganizations in its first five years as it grew to $5 million. Third, the organizational structure is usually flat (i.e., it has few management layers), and there is easy accessibility to the top decision makers. But the informality and fluidity of organization structures and procedures do not mean casualness or sloppiness when it comes to goals, standards, or clarity of direction and purpose. Rather, they translate into responsiveness and readiness to absorb and assimilate rapid changes while maintaining financial and operational cohesion.

Entrepreneurial Culture   There exists in growing new ventures a common value system, which is difficult to articulate, is even more elusive to measure, and is evident in behaviour and attitudes. There is a belief in and commitment to growth, achievement, improvement, and success and a sense among members of the team that they are "in this thing together." Goals and the market determine priorities, rather than whose territory or whose prerogatives are being challenged. Managers appear unconcerned about status, power, and personal control. They are more concerned about making sure that tasks, goals, and roles are clear than whether the organizational chart is current or whether their office and rug reflect their current status. Likewise, they are more concerned about the evidence, competence, knowledge, and logic of arguments affecting a decision than the status given by a title or the formal position of the individual doing the arguing. Royston Greenwood and Roy Suddaby, both of the University of Alberta, explore institutional entrepreneurship, which is viewed as an oxymoron by some. How can those embedded within constraining structures, systems, and processes be motivated and able to promote change? Greenwood and Suddaby's research shows that such entrepreneurial actions are more likely at the periphery, among those less connected and who may be disadvantaged by prevailing arrangements and can benefit from change.[11] Japan and Korea are known to be discouraging environments for entrepreneurship whereas Taiwan encourages new business ventures and supports start-ups with the necessary resources to succeed.[12] Culture—be it national or corporate—clearly has a bearing on entrepreneurial activity.

This entrepreneurial climate, or culture, exists in larger firms also. Such a climate attracts and encourages the entrepreneurial achievers, and it helps perpetuate the intensity and pace so characteristic of high growth firms. Exhibit 5.5 shows how five companies studied by Rosabeth Moss Kanter range from most to least entrepreneurial. Kanter, who has been studying "intrapreneurship" since the 1980s, asserted that the global economy was experiencing the postentrepreneurial revolution, which "takes entrepreneurship a step further, applying entrepreneurial principles to the traditional corporation, creating a marriage between entrepreneurial creativity and corporate discipline, cooperation, and teamwork."[13] This revolution has not made managing any easier; in fact, Kanter suggests, "This constitutes the ultimate corporate balancing act. Cut back and grow. Trim down and build. Accomplish more, and do it in new areas, with fewer resources."[14] Clearly, some corporations will embrace these challenges with more success than others; the following section will shed some light on how "giants learn to dance."[15]

What Entrepreneurial Leaders Need to Know

Much of business education traditionally has emphasized and prepared students for life in the managerial domain. There is nothing wrong with that, but education preparing students to start and lead vibrant, growing new ventures cannot afford to emphasize managerial efficiency, maintenance tasks, resource ownership, and institutional formalization. Rather, such a program needs to emphasize skills necessary for life in the entrepreneurial domain. For example, effective entrepreneurial leaders need to be especially skillful at regulating conflict, resolving differences, balancing multiple viewpoints and demands, and building teamwork and consensus. These skills are particularly difficult when working with others outside one's immediate formal chain of command.

In talking of larger firms, Kanter identifies power and persuasion skills, skill in managing problems accompanying team and employee participation, and skill in understanding how change is designed and constructed in an organization as necessary. Kanter notes:

EXHIBIT 5.5   Characteristics of Five Companies, Ranging from Most to Least Entrepreneurial

	Companies Studied				
	Chipco	Radco	Medco	Finco	Utico
Percent of effective managers with entrepreneurial accomplishments	71%	69%	67%	47%	33%
Economic trend	Steadily up	Trend up but now down	Upward trend	Mixed	Downward trend
Change issues	Change normal; constant change in product generation; proliferating staff and units.	Change normal in products, technologies; changeover to second management generation with new focus.	Reorganized 2–3 years ago to install matrix; normal product and technology changes.	Change a shock; new top management group from outside reorganizing and trying to add competitive market posture.	Change a shock; undergoing reorganization to install matrix and add competitive market posture and reducing staff.
Organization structure	Matrix	Matrix in some areas; product lines act as quasi divisions.	Matrix in some areas.	Divisional; unitary hierarchy within division; some central officers.	Functional organization; currently overlaying matrix of regions and markets.
Information flow	Decentralized	Mixed	Mixed	Centralized	Centralized
Communication emphasis	Free Horizontal	Free Horizontal	Moderately free Horizontal	Constricted Vertical	Constricted Vertical
Culture	Clear, consistent; favours individual initiative.	Clear, though in transition from invention emphasis to routinization and systems.	Clear; pride in company; belief that talent will be rewarded.	Idiosyncratic; depends on boss and area.	Clear but undergoing changes; favours security, maintenance, and protection.
Emotional climate	Pride in company, team feeling, some burnout.	Uncertainty regarding changes.	Pride in company; team feeling.	Low trust; high uncertainty.	High uncertainty, confusion.
Rewards	Abundant; visibility, chance to do more challenging work in the future, and get bigger budget projects.	Abundant; visibility, chance to do more challenging work in the future, and get bigger budget projects.	Moderately abundant; conventional.	Scarce; primarily monetary.	Scarce; promotion and salary freeze; recognition by peers grudging.

In short, individuals do not have to be doing "big things" in order to have their cumulative accomplishments eventually result in big performance for the company… They are only rarely the inventors of the "breakthrough" system. They are only rarely doing something that is totally unique or that no one, in any organization, ever thought of before. Instead, they are often applying ideas that have proved themselves elsewhere, or they are rearranging parts to create a better result, or they are noting a potential problem before it turns into a catastrophe and mobilizing the actions to anticipate and solve it.[16]

A study of midsized growth companies having sales or profit growth of more than 15 percent annually over five years confirms the importance of many of these same fundamentals of entrepreneurial management.[17] For one thing, these companies practised opportunity-driven management. According to the study, they achieved their first success with a unique product or distinctive way of doing business and often became leaders in market niches by delivering superior value to customers, rather than through low prices. They are highly committed to serving customers and pay very close attention to them. For another thing, these firms emphasize financial control and managing every element of the business.

In a book that follows up on the implementation issues of how one gets middle managers to pursue and practise entrepreneurial excellence (first made famous in *In Search of Excellence* by Tom Peters and Bob Waterman), two authors note that some of the important fundamentals practised by team-builder entrepreneurs—who are more intent on getting results than just getting their own way—also are emulated by effective middle managers.[18] Or as John Sculley, of Apple, explained:

> The heroic style—the lone cowboy on horseback—is not the figure we worship anymore at Apple. In the new corporation, heroes won't personify any single set of achievements. Instead, they personify the process. They might be thought of as gatekeepers, information carriers, and teams. Originally heroes at Apple were the hackers and engineers who created the products. Now, more teams are heroes.[19]

The ability to shape and guide a cohesive team is particularly critical in high-tech firms where the competitive landscape can shift dramatically in the face of disruptive technologies. In his book *The Innovator's Dilemma*, Clayton Christensen finds that even aggressive, innovative, and customer-driven organizations can be rendered obsolete if they fail to take decisive, and at times radical, actions to stay competitive.[20] The point of greatest peril in the development of a high-tech market, writes Geoffrey Moore in his book *Crossing the Chasm*, lies in making the transition from an early market, dominated by a few visionary customers, to a mainstream market that is dominated by a large block of customers who are predominantly pragmatists in orientation.[21] In Exhibit 5.6, entrepreneur Edward Marram describes this as the "Blunder" stage of growth, perilously positioned between "Wonder" and Thunder."

Lead entrepreneurs whose companies successfully break into the mass market must then find a way to manage the hyper-growth and gigantic revenues that can result from an international surge in demand.[22] Several entrepreneurial leaders who have skillfully negotiated these high-tech waters are as well-known as the companies they founded: think Michael Dell, Robert Herjavec, Michael Cowpland, and Suhayya Abu-Hakima. What sort of skills and personality are required to achieve such high levels of performance in a dynamic and uncertain marketplace? As portrayed in Stephen Covey's classic work, *The 7 Habits of Highly Effective People*, these individuals are curious, proactive team builders who have a passion

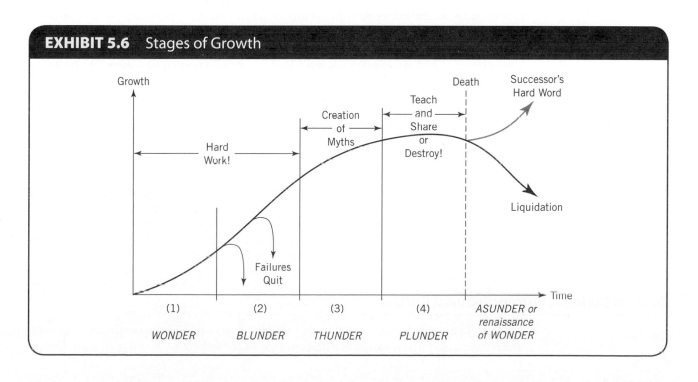

EXHIBIT 5.6   Stages of Growth

for continuous improvement and renewal in their lives and in their ventures. Maybe most important in this context: these leaders have "the ability to envision, to see the potential, to create with their minds what they cannot at present see with their eyes . . . "[23]

Ethical Entrepreneurial Leadership

According to Donald Kuratko, an authority in the field, "No perspective of entrepreneurial leadership would be complete without the acknowledgement of the ethical side of enterprise. ... A leader has the unique opportunity to display honesty, integrity, and ethics in all key decisions." A leader's behaviour serves as a model for others to emulate.[24] Clearly the entrepreneurial leader's value system plays an important role, one that will be more fully explored in Chapter 7 "Ethical Decision Making and the Entrepreneur."

"In entrepreneurial ventures, the ethical influence of the owner is more powerful than in larger corporations because his or her leadership is not diffused through layers of management."[25] A venture founder is readily recognized and under constant scrutiny by the whole team. Entrepreneurial owners have the potential to set high ethical standards in all business decisions.[26] It is worth noting that there is a 'dark side' of entrepreneurial behaviour—a potentially destructive element resides within the energetic drive of successful entrepreneurs."[27] Leaders must monitor their entrepreneurial ego and know that an inflated self-view can have negative repercussions. Beyond the notion that 'power corrupts,' risk, control, trust, and optimism are all forces that entrepreneurs must embrace. Risk, for example, is something both sought after and avoided by entrepreneurs in a manner different from non-entrepreneurs.

COMPETENCIES AND SKILLS

Entrepreneurs who build substantial companies that grow to more than $10 million in sales and 75 to 100 employees are good entrepreneurs and good leaders. Typically, they will have developed a solid base and a wide breadth of leadership skills and know-how over a number of years working in different areas (e.g., sales, marketing, manufacturing, and finance). It would be unusual for any single entrepreneur to be outstanding in all areas. More likely, a single entrepreneur will have strengths in one area, such as strong people management, conceptual and creative problem-solving skills, and marketing know-how, as well as some significant weaknesses. While it is risky to generalize, often entrepreneurs whose background is technical are weak in marketing, finance, and general management. Entrepreneurs who do not have a technical background are, as you might expect, often weakest in the technical or engineering aspects. Honest self-assessment is therefore key. Knowing one's strengths and weaknesses is crucial to starting and growing a venture. Interestingly, Don Moore of Carnegie Mellon University, John Oesch of the University of Toronto, and Charlene Zietsma of the University of Western Ontario examined entrepreneurs, would be entrepreneurs, and conducted an experiment using undergraduate students at a Canadian university. Their results show that "entrepreneurs tend to overweight personal factors and underweight consideration of the competition when making venturing decisions."[28]

Throughout this book, the concept of fit has been stressed. Having a management team whose skills are complementary is important, not the possession by an individual of a single, absolute set of skills or a profile. The art and craft of entrepreneuring involves recognizing the skills and know-how needed to succeed in a venture, knowing what each team member does or does not know, and then compensating for shortcomings, either by getting key people on board to fill voids or by an individual accumulating the additional "chunks" before he or she takes the plunge. After all, the venture and the people are works in progress.

Skills in Building Entrepreneurial Culture

Leaders of entrepreneurial firms need to recognize and cope with innovation, taking risks, and responding quickly, as well as with absorbing major setbacks. The most effective leaders seem to thrive on the hectic, and at times chaotic, pace and find it challenging and stimulating, rather than frustrating or overwhelming. They use a consensus approach to build a motivated and committed team, they balance conflicting demands and priorities, and they manage conflicts adroitly.

These leaders thus need interpersonal/teamwork skills that involve (1) the ability to create, through management, a climate and spirit conducive to high performance, including pressing for performance while rewarding work well done and encouraging innovation, initiative, and calculated risk taking; (2) the ability to understand the relationships among tasks and between the leader and followers; and (3) the ability to lead in those situations where it is appropriate, including a willingness to manage actively, supervise and control activities of others through directions, suggestions, and the like.

Hao Ma of Peking University and Justin Tan of York University see the entrepreneur as a pioneer. Whether building a new venture or via intrapreneurship, pioneers are relentless champions of creativity and innovation.[29] Characteristics of pioneers include: passion, perseverance, purposeful, persuasive, and relentless in pursuit of goals. Bruno Dyck and Frederick Starke both of the University of Manitoba observed a number of instances where individuals either broke away from an existing business to start a new venture as a result of a polarizing event or were assuaged to stay. A leader can learn to handle such situations and recognize causes of conflict and instill harmony.[30]

These interpersonal skills can be called entrepreneurial influence skills, since they have a great deal to do with the way these managers exact influence over others.

Leadership, Vision, Influence   Successful entrepreneurs are skillful in creating clarity out of confusion, ambiguity, and uncertainty. These entrepreneurial leaders are able to define adroitly and gain agreement on who has what responsibility and authority. Further, they do this in a way that builds motivation and commitment to cross-departmental and corporate goals, not just parochial interests. But this is not perceived by other managers as an effort to jealously carve out and guard personal turf and prerogatives. Rather, it is seen as a genuine effort to clarify roles, tasks, and responsibilities, and to make sure there is accountability and appropriate approvals. This does not work unless the leader is seen as willing to relinquish his or her priorities and power in the interest of an overall goal. It also requires skill in making sure the appropriate people are included in setting cross-functional or cross-departmental goals and in making decisions. When things do not go as smoothly as was hoped, the most effective leaders work them through to an agreement. Those who are accustomed to traditional line/staff or functional chains of command are often baffled and frustrated in their new role. While some may be quite effective in dealing with their own subordinates, it is a new task to manage and work with peers, the subordinates of others, and even superiors outside one's chain of command.

Glenn Rowe of Memorial University of Newfoundland examines the paradox of leading and managing. He finds that strategic leadership is a necessary ingredient for wealth-creation in entrepreneurial and established organizations.[31] Rowe notes that visionary leaders are more future-oriented and embrace risk-taking more readily. He provides examples of enterprises that have benefitted by having both a visionary leader as well as a managerially minded leader. The managerially minded leader is concerned with financial controls and formal, traditional mechanisms and maintains rather than creates wealth.

Helping, Coaching, and Conflict Management   The most effective leaders are very creative and skillful in handling conflicts, generating consensus decisions, and sharing their power and information. They are able to get people to open up, instead of clamming up; they get problems out on the table, instead of under the rug; and they do not become defensive when others disagree with their views. They seem to know that high-quality decisions require a rapid flow of information in all directions and that knowledge, competence, logic, and evidence need to prevail over official status or formal rank in the organization. The way they manage and resolve conflicts is intriguing. They can get potential adversaries to be creative and to collaborate by seeking a reconciliation of viewpoints. Rather than emphasizing differences and playing the role of hard-nose negotiator or devil's advocate to force their own solution, they blend ideas. They are more willing to risk personal vulner-

164   PART III   The Founder and Team

ability in this process—often by giving up their own power and resources—than are less-effective leaders. They insist on fairness and integrity in the short and long term, rather than short-term gain. The trade-offs are not easy: At the outset, such an approach involves more managers, takes more time, often appears to yield few immediate results, and seems like a more painful way to lead. Later, however, the gains from the motivation, commitment, and teamwork anchored in consensus are striking. For one thing, there is swiftness and decisiveness in actions and follow-through because the negotiating, compromising, and accepting of priorities is history. For another, new disagreements that emerge do not generally bring progress to a halt, since there is both high clarity and broad acceptance of the overall goals and underlying priorities. Without this consensus, each new problem or disagreement often necessitates a time-consuming and painful confrontation and renegotiation simply because it was not done initially. Apparently, the Japanese understand this quite well.

Teresa Coady and Bunting Coady Architects

Teresa Coady's university thesis on "living breathing buildings" was rejected as not being architecture. Ahead of her time, it envisioned structures that would enhance, not harm, the natural environment—providing healthy and aesthetic surroundings for the buildings' inhabitants. Teresa overcame that obstacle and pushed for greener, cleaner building solutions. Today as CEO of the firm she founded with Tom Bunting, she leads over 50 full-time employees on cutting-edge projects. On the subject of her clients, she says: "They love the way we work and they love our values."[32]

Teresa's Vancouver-based firm has a positive impact on resource use. The work climate is collaborative from start to finish delivering a building. Teresa is credited with pioneering the integrated design process. This defies the traditional view of the architect as a sole creator, accepting no outside input. Both Teresa Coady and her firm contribute to causes of interest, including scholarships and hospital charities. Teresa sits on the boards of directors for both the U.S. and Canadian green building councils.[33]

An employee describes Teresa as an "inspirational leader" indicating that Teresa is very positive and asks others to never criticize. In an interview when she received a 2008 Canadian Woman Entrepreneur Award, Teresa said, "It's so important to find your passion in life. And once you do everything you learn will just go in effortlessly. And when you have a passion other people will recognize it in you and help you achieve your goals."[34]

Teamwork and People Management   Another form of entrepreneurial influence has to do with encouraging creativity and innovation, and with taking calculated risks. Entrepreneurial leaders build confidence by encouraging innovation and calculated risk taking, rather than by punishing or criticizing whatever is less than perfect. They breed independent, entrepreneurial thinking by expecting and encouraging others to find and correct their own errors and to solve their own problems. This does not mean they follow a throw-them-to-the-wolves approach. Rather, they are perceived by their peers and other managers as accessible and willing to help when needed, and they provide the necessary resources to enable others to do the job. When it is appropriate, they go to bat for their peers and subordinates, even when they know they cannot always win. An ability to make heroes out of other team members and contributors and to make sure others are in the limelight, rather than accept these things oneself, is another critical skill.

The capacity to generate trust—the glue that binds an organization or relationship together—is critical. The most effective leaders are perceived as trustworthy; they behave in ways that create trust. They do this by being straightforward. They do what they say they are going to do. They are not the corporate rumour carriers. They are open and spontaneous, rather than guarded and cautious with each word. And they are perceived as being honest and direct. They treat their associates with respect, as they would want to be treated. They share the wealth with those who help create it by their high performance.

Also, it is easy to envision the kind of track record and reputation these entrepreneurial leaders build for themselves. They have a reputation of getting results, because they understand that the task of managing in a rapid growth company usually goes well beyond one's immediate chain of command. They become known as the creative problem solvers who have a knack for blending and balancing multiple views and demands. Their calculated risk-taking works out more often than it fails. And they have a reputation for developing human capital (i.e., they groom other effective and capable individuals to lead growth).

Other Necessary Competencies

Entrepreneurial leaders need a sound foundation in what are considered traditional management skills. Interestingly, in a study of practising entrepreneurs mentioned earlier, no one assigned much importance to capital asset-pricing models, beta coefficients, linear programming, and so forth, the prevailing and highly touted "new management techniques."[35] The list below is divided into six areas.

Marketing
- *Market research and evaluation.* Ability to analyze and interpret market research study results, including knowing how to design and conduct studies and to find and interpret industry and competitor information, and a familiarity with questionnaire design and sampling techniques. One successful entrepreneur stated that what is vital "is knowing where the competitive threats are and where the opportunities are and an ability to see the customers' needs."
- *Marketing planning.* Skill in planning overall sales, advertising, and promotion programs and in deciding on effective distributor or sales representative systems and setting them up.
- *Product pricing.* Ability to determine competitive pricing and margin structures and to position products in terms of price and ability to develop pricing policies that maximize profits.
- *Sales management.* Ability to organize, supervise, and motivate a direct sales force, and the ability to analyze territory and account sales potential and to manage a sales force to obtain maximum share of market.
- *Direct selling.* Skills in identifying, meeting, and developing new customers and in closing sales. Without orders for a product or service, a company does not really have a business.
- *Service management.* Ability to perceive service needs of particular products and to determine service and spare-part requirements, handle customer complaints, and create and manage an effective service organization.
- *Distribution management.* Ability to organize and manage the flow of product from manufacturing through distribution channels to ultimate customer, including familiarity with shipping costs, scheduling techniques, and so on.
- *Product management.* Ability to integrate market information, perceived needs, research and development, and advertising into a rational product plan, and the ability to understand market penetration and breakeven.
- *New product planning.* Skills in introducing new products, including market testing, prototype testing, and development of price/sales/merchandising and distribution plans for new products.

Operations/Production
- *Manufacturing management.* Knowledge of the production process, machines, personnel, and space required to produce a product and the skill in managing production to produce products within time, cost, and quality constraints.
- *Inventory control.* Familiarity with techniques of controlling in-process and finished goods inventories of materials.
- *Cost analysis and control.* Ability to calculate labour and materials costs, develop standard cost systems, conduct variance analyses, calculate overtime labour needs, and manage/control costs.

- *Quality control.* Ability to set up inspection systems and standards for effective control of quality of incoming, in-process, and finished materials. Benchmarking continuous improvement.
- *Production scheduling and flow.* Ability to analyze work flow and to plan and manage production processes, to manage work flow, and to calculate schedules and flows for rising sales levels.
- *Purchasing.* Ability to identify appropriate sources of supply, to negotiate supplier contracts, and to manage the incoming flow of material into inventory, and familiarity with order quantities and discount advantages.
- *Job evaluation.* Ability to analyze worker productivity and needs for additional help, and the ability to calculate cost-saving aspects of temporary versus permanent help.

Finance
- *Raising capital.* Ability to decide how best to acquire funds for start-up and growth; ability to forecast funds needs and to prepare budgets; and familiarity with sources and vehicles of short- and long-term financing, formal and informal.
- *Managing cash flow.* Ability to project cash requirements, set up cash controls, and manage the firm's cash position, and the ability to identify how much capital is needed, when and where you will run out of cash, and breakeven.
- *Credit and collection management.* Ability to develop credit policies and screening criteria, and to age receivables and payables, and an understanding of the use of collection agencies and when to start legal action.
- *Short-term financing alternatives.* Understanding of payables management and the use of interim financing, such as bank loans, factoring of receivables, pledging and selling notes and contracts, bills of lading and bank acceptance; and familiarity with financial statements and budgeting/profit planning.
- *Public and private offerings.* Ability to develop a business plan and an offering memo that can be used to raise capital, a familiarity with the legal requirements of public and private stock offerings, and the ability to manage shareholder relations and to negotiate with financial sources.
- *Bookkeeping, accounting, and control.* Ability to determine appropriate bookkeeping and accounting systems as the company starts and grows, including various ledgers and accounts and possible insurance needs.
- *Other specific skills.* Ability to read and prepare an income statement and balance sheet, and the ability to do cash flow analysis and planning, including breakeven analysis, contribution analysis, profit and loss analysis, and balance sheet management.

Entrepreneurial Management
- *Problem solving.* Ability to anticipate potential problems; ability to gather facts about problems, analyze them for real causes, and plan effective action to solve them; and ability to be very thorough in dealing with details of particular problems and to follow through.
- *Communications.* Ability to communicate effectively and clearly—orally and in writing—to media, public, customers, peers, and subordinates.
- *Planning.* Ability to set realistic and attainable goals, identify obstacles to achieving the goals, and develop detailed action plans to achieve those goals, and the ability to schedule personal time very systematically.
- *Decision making.* Ability to make decisions on the best analysis of incomplete data, when the decisions need to be made.
- *Project management.* Skills in organizing project teams, setting project goals, defining project tasks, and monitoring task completion in the face of problems and cost/quality constraints.
- *Negotiating.* Ability to work effectively in negotiations, and the ability to balance quickly value given and value received. Recognizing onetime versus ongoing relationships.
- *Managing outside professionals.* Ability to identify, manage, and guide appropriate legal, financial, banking, accounting, consulting, and other necessary outside advisors.
- *Personnel administration.* Ability to set up payroll, hiring, compensation, and training functions.

Law and Taxes

- *Corporate and securities law.* Familiarity with the commercial codes, including forms of organization and the rights and obligations of officers, shareholders, and directors; and familiarity with securities regulations, and other provincial and federal laws concerning the commercial activity of your firm, both registered and unregistered, and the advantages and disadvantages of different instruments.
- *Contract law.* Familiarity with contract procedures and requirements of government and commercial contracts, licences, leases, and other agreements, particularly employment agreements and agreements governing the vesting rights of shareholders and founders.
- *Law relating to patent and proprietary rights.* Skills in preparation and revision of patent applications and the ability to recognize a strong patent, trademark, copyright, and privileged information claims, including familiarity with claim requirements, such as intellectual property.
- *Tax law.* Familiarity with provincial and federal reporting requirements, including specific requirements of a particular form of organization, of profit and other pension plans, and the like.
- *Real estate law.* Familiarity with leases, purchase offers, purchase and sale agreements, and so on, necessary for the rental or purchase and sale of property.
- *Bankruptcy law.* Knowledge of bankruptcy law, options, and the forgivable and nonforgivable liabilities of founders, officers, and directors.

Information Technology

- Information and management systems tools from laptop to Internet: sales, supply chain, inventory, payroll, etc.
- Business to business, business to consumer, business to government via the Internet.
- Sales, marketing, manufacturing, and merchandising tools.
- Financial, accounting, and risk analysis and management tools (e.g., Cognos's business intelligence software).
- Telecommunications and wireless solutions for corporate information, data, and process management.

As has been said before, not all entrepreneurs will find they are greatly skilled in the areas listed above, and if they are not, they will most likely need to acquire these skills, either through apprenticeship, through partners, or through the use of advisors. However, while many outstanding advisors, such as lawyers and accountants, are of enormous benefit to entrepreneurs, these people are not always businesspeople and they often cannot make the best business judgments for those they are advising. For example, lawyers' judgments, in many cases, are so contaminated by a desire to provide perfect or fail-safe protection that they are totally risk averse.

Chapter Summary

1. The growing enterprise requires that the founder and team develop competencies as entrepreneurial leaders.
2. Founders who succeed in growing their firms beyond $5 million in sales learn to adapt and grow quickly themselves as leaders, or they do not survive.
3. Founders of rapidly growing firms defy the conventional wisdom that entrepreneurs cannot manage growing beyond the start-up.
4. Ventures go through stages of growth from start-up, through rapid growth, to maturity, to decline and renewal. Leaders are also expected to evolve and go through transitions.
5. The largest single factor that increases the complexity and difficulty of leading a young company is its rate of growth in orders and revenue.
6. The faster the rate of growth, the more difficult and challenging are the issues, and the more flexible, adaptive, and quick learning must be the organization.
7. Entrepreneurs create and invent new and unique approaches to organizing and leading teams.
8. As ventures grow, the core competencies need to be covered by the team.

www.mcgrawhill.ca/olc/timmons

Study Questions

1. What is the difference between an entrepreneurial leader and a manager?

2. What must founders and teams do to grow their ventures? What leadership skills and abilities are necessary?

3. Define the stages that most companies experience as they grow, and explain the leadership issues and requirements anticipated at each stage.

4. What drives the extent of complexity and difficulty of management issues in a growing company?

Mind Stretchers   *Have you considered?*

1. It is often said, "You cannot hire an entrepreneur." What are the implications for large companies today?

2. How would you characterize the attitudes, behaviours, and mind-sets of the most effective leaders and managers you have worked for? The worst? What accounts for the difference?

3. What would be your strategy for changing and creating an entrepreneurial culture in a large, nonentrepreneurial firm? Is it possible? Why, or why not?

EXERCISE   Leadership Skills and Know-How Assessment

Name: _____

Venture: _____

Date: _____

Part I—Competency Inventory

Part I of the exercise involves filling out the Competency Inventory and evaluating how critical certain competencies are either (1) for the venture or (2) personally over the next one to three years. How you rank the importance of competencies, therefore, will depend on the purpose of your assessment.

Step 1   Complete the Competency Inventory on the following pages. For each competency, place a check in the column that best describes your knowledge and experience. Note that a

section is at the end of the inventory for **unique skills** required by your venture; for example, if it is a service or franchise business, there will be some skills and know-how that are unique. Then rank from 1 to 3 particular competencies as follows:

1 = Critical

2 = Very Desirable

3 = Not Necessary

	Competency Inventory				
	Rank	Thorough Knowledge & Experience (Done Well)	Some Knowledge and Experience (So-So)	No Knowledge or Experience (New Ground)	Importance (1–3 Years)
MARKETING					
Market Research and Evaluation Finding and interpreting industry and competitor information; designing and conducting market research studies; analyzing and interpreting market research data; etc.					
Market Planning Planning overall sales, advertising, and promotion programs; planning and setting up effective distributor or sales representative systems; etc.					
Product Pricing Determining competitive pricing and margin structures and breakeven analysis; positioning products in terms of price; etc.					
CUSTOMER RELATIONS MANAGEMENT					
Customer Service Determining customer service needs and spare-part requirements; managing a service organization and warranties; training; technical backup, telecom and Internet systems and tools; etc.					
Sales Management Organizing, recruiting, supervising, compensating, and motivating a direct sales force; analyzing territory and account sales potential; managing sales force; etc.					
Direct Selling Identifying, meeting, and developing new customers, suppliers, investors, brain trust and team; closing sales; etc.					
Direct Mail/Catalogue Selling Identifying and developing appropriate direct mail and catalogue sales and related distribution; etc.					
Electronic and Telemarketing Identifying, planning, implementing appropriate telemarketing programs; Internet-based programs; etc.					
SUPPLY CHAIN MANAGEMENT					
Distribution Management Organizing and managing the flow of product from manufacturing through distribution channels to customers; knowing the margins throughout the value chain; etc.					
Product Management Integrating market information, perceived needs, research and development, and advertising into a rational product plan; etc.					
New Product Planning Planning the introduction of new products, including market testing, prototype testing, and development of price, sales, merchandising, and distribution plans; etc.					

		Competency Inventory			
	Rank	Thorough Knowledge & Experience (Done Well)	Some Knowledge and Experience (So-So)	No Knowledge or Experience (New Ground)	Importance (1–3 Years)
OPERATIONS/PRODUCTION					
Manufacturing Management Managing production to produce products within time, cost, and quality constraints; knowledge of manufacturing resource planning; etc.					
Inventory Control Using techniques of controlling in-process and finished goods inventories; etc.					
Cost Analysis and Control Calculating labour and materials costs; developing standard cost systems; conducting variance analyses; calculating overtime labour needs; managing and controlling costs; etc.					
Quality Control Setting up inspection systems and standards for effective control of quality in incoming, in-process, and finished goods; etc.					
Production Scheduling and Flow Analyzing work flow; planning and managing production processes; managing work flow; calculating schedules and flows for rising sales levels; etc.					
Purchasing Identifying appropriate sources of supply; negotiating supplier contracts; managing the incoming flow of material into inventory; etc.					
Job Evaluation Analyzing worker productivity and needs for additional help; calculating cost-saving aspects of temporary versus permanent help; etc.					
FINANCE					
Accounting Determining appropriate bookkeeping and accounting systems; preparing and using income statements and balance sheets; analyzing cash flow, breakeven, contribution, and profit and loss; etc.					
Capital Budgeting Preparing budgets; deciding how best to acquire funds for start-up and growth; forecasting funds needs; etc.					
Cash Flow Management Managing cash position, including projecting cash requirements; etc.					
Credit and Collection Management Developing credit policies and screening criteria, etc.					
Short-Term Financing Managing payables and receivables; using interim financing alternatives, managing bank and creditor relations; etc.					

	Competency Inventory				
	Rank	Thorough Knowledge & Experience (Done Well)	Some Knowledge and Experience (So-So)	No Knowledge or Experience (New Ground)	Importance (1–3 Years)
Public and Private Offering Skills Developing a business plan and offering memo; managing shareholder relations; negotiating with financial sources deal structuring and valuation; etc.					
ENTREPRENEURIAL LEADERSHIP					
Problem Solving Anticipating problems and planning to avoid them; analyzing and solving problems; etc.					
Culture and Communications Communicating effectively and clearly, both orally and in writing, to customers, peers, subordinates, outsiders, etc. Treating others as you would be treated, sharing the wealth, giving back; etc.					
Planning Ability to set realistic and attainable goals, identify obstacles to achieving the goals, and develop detailed action plans to achieve those goals.					
Decision Making Making decisions based on the analysis of incomplete data; etc.					
Ethical Competency Ability to define and give life to an organization's guiding values; to create an environment that supports ethically sound behaviour; and to instill a sense of shared accountability among employees.					
Project Management Organizing project teams; setting project goals; defining project tasks; monitoring task completion in the face of problems and cost/quality constraints; etc.					
Negotiating Working effectively in negotiations; etc.					
Personnel Management Setting up payroll, hiring, compensation, and training functions; identifying, managing, and guiding appropriate outside advisors; etc.					
Management Information Systems Knowledge of relevant management information systems available and appropriate for growth plans; etc.					
Information Technology and the Internet Using spreadsheet, word processing, and other relevant software; using email, management tools, and other appropriate systems.					
INTERPERSONAL TEAM					
Entrepreneurial Leadership/Vision/ Influence Actively leading, instilling vision and passion in others, and managing activities of others; creating a climate and spirit conducive to high performance; etc.					

www.mcgrawhill.ca/olc/timmons

		Competency Inventory			
	Rank	Thorough Knowledge & Experience (Done Well)	Some Knowledge and Experience (So-So)	No Knowledge or Experience (New Ground)	Importance (1–3 Years)
Helping Determining when assistance is warranted and asking for or providing such assistance.					
Feedback Providing effective feedback or receiving it; etc.					
Conflict Management Confronting differences openly and obtaining resolution; using evidence and logic; etc.					
Teamwork Working with others to achieve common goals; delegating responsibility and coaching subordinates; etc.					
Build a Brain Trust Connecting with experts and seeking advice and value.					
LAW					
Corporations Understanding business law, forms of organization, and the rights and obligations of officers, shareholders, and directors; etc.					
Contracts Understanding the requirements of government and commercial contracts, licences, leases, and other agreements; etc.					
Taxes Understanding provincial and federal reporting requirements; understanding tax shelters, estate planning, fringe benefits, and so forth.					
Securities Understanding regulations of the provincial/territorial securities commission and agencies; etc.					
Patents and Proprietary Rights Understanding the preparation and revision of patent applications; recognizing strong patent, trademark, copyright, and privileged information claims; etc.					
Real Estate Understanding agreements necessary for the lease or purchase and sale of property; etc.					
Bankruptcy Understanding options and the forgivable and nonforgivable liabilities of founders, officers, directors, and so forth.					
Unique Skills List unique competencies required. 1. 2. 3.					

Part II—Competency Assessment

Part II involves assessing strengths and weaknesses, deciding which areas of competence are most critical, and developing a plan to overcome or compensate for any weaknesses and to capitalize on strengths.

Step 1   Assess leadership strengths and weaknesses:

• Which skills are particularly strong?

_____

_____

_____

• Which skills are particularly weak?

_____

_____

_____

• What gaps are evident? When?

_____

_____

_____

Step 2   Circle the areas of competence most critical to the success of the venture, and cross out those that are irrelevant.

Step 3   Consider the implications for you and for developing the venture management team.

• What are the implications of this particular constellation of strengths and weaknesses?

_____

_____

_____

• Who in your team can overcome or compensate for each critical weakness?

_____

_____

_____

• How can you leverage your critical strengths?

_____

_____

_____

• What are the time implications of the above actions? For you? For the team?

_____

_____

_____

• How will you attract and fill the critical gaps in your weaknesses?

_____

_____

_____

_____

Step 4   Obtain feedback. If you are evaluating your competencies as part of the development of a personal entrepreneurial strategy and planning your apprenticeship, refer back to exercise "Crafting a Personal Entrepreneurial Strategy" in Chapter 1.

CASE   MED-ENG SYSTEMS INC.

Preparation Questions

1. What would you do if you were Mr. L'Abbé?
2. How will you satisfy investor demand for growth? Are there new markets on the horizon (e.g., space suits, underwater suits, bear-proof suits)? Are you the best candidate to lead Med-Eng into the future?
3. Where will this industry, this company, and you be in two to three years and in 10-plus years?

A World of Terror

On July 11, 2006 a series of seven explosions within 11 minutes tore through commuter trains in Mumbai, India. The death toll reached 200 with hundreds more injured—four suspects were eventually apprehended. Were these bombings a precursor to the coming G8 summit? Was this '7/11' event tied into others?

9/11, Bali, Madrid, 7/7, Istanbul, Riyadh, and numerous other bombings by fundamentalist organizations increasingly against Westerners caught the attention of the media and changed the mood of the world. In the explosive post-9/11 environment, police forces and militaries had an extraordinary new need to deal with the threat of explosive ordnances. The human tragedy of violent incidents was remarkable and provided impetus for governments throughout the world to take measures necessary to discourage or prevent future occurrences.

Proven Protection for a Dangerous World™

Fortunately, many firms were actively attempting to address the need for better security and had developed products aimed at protecting police and civilians from the growing threat of global terrorism. One such enterprise was Med-Eng Systems Inc. based in Ottawa, Ontario; a leader in the research, design, and manufacture of a plethora of personal protective systems aimed at helping police forces and militaries confront explosive ordnances in a way that ensured the safety of their personnel.

For this privately held venture the key to developing cutting-edge products and staying on top was to "do the right things right every time, through the collaboration of its clients, vendors, and employees."[1] This stakeholder-driven approach to product development and marketing led Med-Eng to be on the receiving end of numerous awards, both for the company's competitive strength and international posture. Superior technologies had also led to superior profit margins. Although at inception the firm manufactured protective helmets solely, Med-Eng went on to garner over 95 percent of the bomb disposal suit market worldwide—a market that the firm was forced to enter in 1991 after Med-Eng fought off a takeover attempt from a U.S.-based competitor.

Even after giving up on testing Med-Eng suits himself—after a noteworthy call from his life insurance agent—L'Abbé's attitude toward the company and its products was steadfast. What had changed, however, was the security environment internationally. Terrorism and escalating conflict in many parts of the world led Med-Eng equipment to markets in over 140 countries worldwide.

Products

Med-Eng Systems did not just produce equipment for the war on terrorism. Med-Eng produced a variety of interrelated wares that were used for other purposes; however, most purchases were for police forces and defence organizations.[2] The firm produced most of its 'gear' with a mix of sourced and in-house components and tried to integrate the ideas and concerns of stakeholders into the process. Med-Eng was reputed for its top-notch research activities (often conducted with the input of customers, suppliers, and users of its equipment). Products sold by Med-Eng were subdivided into six main areas of application:

- Bomb suits and helmets represented the firm's core competency and the firm had upwards of 95 percent of global market share in this area. From the period 2002 to 2005, this segment moved from 80 percent of Med-Eng's overall sales revenue to 20 percent. While sales for this segment had remained steady, efforts to diversify were proving fruitful.
- Remote handling devices known as 'hook and line kits' to move explosive devices.
- Demining visors, helmets, hand protection, and footwear, including the company's trademark Spider boot. With millions of anti-personnel landmines still buried and thousands falling victim each year to landmines left from past wars, Med-Eng made it a priority to manufacture suits to safeguard those removing landmines. This line of business arose from a C$2 million injection of venture capital in 1997, the year that Princess Diana took up the cause and thus influenced the signing, after her death, of the international treaty to ban the use of landmines.
- Force protection outfits were used to equip soldiers facing the threat of being hit by blast, fragmentation, flame, ballistics, and electronic (radio wave) weaponry. These suits were engineered to provide military personnel the best possible protection when faced with serious threat. This segment was pursued as it showed great promise in fulfilling U.S. military need.
- Crowd management solutions included gear for prison riots and public demonstrations where items such as Molotov cocktails, stones, and glass bottles posed a threat to the safety of a security force. Gloves, shin guards, helmets, and

This case was written by Nicholas P. Robinson, Faculty of Law, McGill University, and Prescott C. Ensign, for purposes of classroom discussion.

[1] www.med-eng.com/.

[2] Med-Eng products could be ordered by a government body for official use; no products were available to the public. This was in contrast to companies that 'cashed in' on the public's fear to sell bullet-proof vests, stab-proof clothing, and armour plating for residences and vehicles.

suits were tailored to this purpose. The outfits came in a variety of configurations and colours—depending on application. They could be worn 'armour out' to look tough or could be covered by loose clothing to look less intimidating.

- Personal climate systems such as cooling vests, specialized garments, and chillers were designed and built for use in high temperatures, but recent battlefield reviews from Iraq and Afghanistan were mixed.

Competition and New Entrants

In addition to the public mood shift leading to lower sales, the number of companies offering riot-type protective gear exploded, with many firms offering suits of varying degrees of quality throughout the world. Given the comparably low degree of technological complexity involved in manufacturing and building riot gear, firms from South America, China and other regions of Asia, and Eastern Europe all competed in the market.[3] Whereas the development of a bomb suit required a notable amount of R&D investment and advanced materials engineering,[4] in contrast, designing and building a riot suit was an accomplishable task for a company without the same degree of technological sophistication as Med-Eng.

Med-Eng's problems were further compounded as competitors chose to copy the company's superior product design. This was a sizeable issue in countries where local authorities wanted to buy suits from local companies, and also had little respect for the concept of intellectual property. Resultantly, Med-Eng's designs were replicated and sold throughout the globe— illegally, under different brand names. Roughly seven or eight clones of Med-Eng's product emerged on the world market

and the firm twice successfully challenged and won injunctions against companies that stole Med-Eng's product design.

Ultimately, lagging sales, intense competition, and copycat products led Med-Eng to believe that their entry into this market would prove to be relatively unprofitable. The firm's attempts to diversify its product line by entering the body temperature control market yielded similar lessons. After buying Delta Temax Inc.—a Pembroke, Ontario, body cooling system maker—in January 2001, Med-Eng focused on marketing its new acquisition's line of refrigerated vests to industrial workers by presenting the idea to unions, management, and workers themselves. Med-Eng believed that this approach would open up considerable opportunity and lead to new orders from an entirely new market— thereby diversifying the company and steadying sales.

Closing One Door, Opening Another

The firm's sales in the industrial sector flopped and by summer 2004, Richard L'Abbé decided to "pull the plug" on selling cooling apparel to the industrial market. Coinciding with this let down was a spark—the U.S. Army began to face a dilemma in Iraq: troops located there were having difficulty tolerating the extreme heat of the Middle Eastern climate while driving often un-air conditioned vehicles and wearing several pounds of thick personal body armour and other heavy gear that acted as insulators trapping body heat.

"This was expected to be a very profitable new market for Med-Eng," remarked L'Abbé, "we hoped to see sales of our cooling devices to the U.S. Armed Forces go into the stratosphere." Med-Eng put to use some of Delta Temax's sewing facilities to start manufacturing different items such as the bomb disposal

---

[3] V-Top's guards for ankles, shins, knees, hips, and thighs had even been marketed to crash-prone downhill mountainbikers prior to Med-Eng's acquisition of the company.

[4] Certainly Med-Eng's R&D efforts had put the company sufficiently ahead that competitors were barely recognizable for much of the company's product offerings. And Med-Eng did not rest on its laurels, more and more money was ploughed into product development every year. On several occasions Med-Eng has availed itself of help from the National Research Council's Industrial Research Assistance Program.

suits. On the redeployment of resources L'Abbé commented: "So, despite an unsuccessful bid at selling cooling systems in the industrial market, we managed to acquire a new skill set that could be used more generally in the manufacture of other products."

Selling "Made In Canada" in the USA

Med-Eng's Canadian identity had several interesting impacts on the firm's ability to sell its products in the U.S. and elsewhere internationally. The fact that Canada, under the leadership of Prime Minister Jean Chrétien, had decided in 2002 not to join the U.S.-led 'Coalition of the Willing' to invade Iraq made the company an obvious target for criticism that it was not playing on the right team to do business with the U.S. In the past, the Canadian aura had generally served Med-Eng well; Med-Eng benefited from the popular conception worldwide that Canadians were peacekeepers, polite, friendly, and a good dependable neighbour.

After contemplating several bids for substantial contracts, Med-Eng discovered that, for the most part, lucrative U.S. Government contracts were awarded to large U.S. companies with good connections and a strong presence in the U.S. This meant that, as a medium-sized Canadian company with revenues below the US$100-million mark, chances of single-handedly succeeding in a bid for a sizeable U.S. contract were slim. For this reason, the company pursued partnering with large U.S. firms for larger contracts (over US$20 million). These contracts for military equipment for the U.S. foray into Iraq were often widely publicized and criticized by political pundits; fearful of this, few elected officials wanted to hand out a contract of this nature to a foreign company. Avoiding this dilemma through partnerships while securing big contracts with U.S. defence contractors in need of equipment was a promising avenue for Med-Eng. Furthermore, according to CEO Richard L'Abbé, "getting with the right partner could mean receiving additional support in other areas—it could be a new source of knowledge and skills."

IPO Potential

As Med-Eng grew, those on both the outside and inside began to ask whether a company with revenues in excess of C$50 million would be better served as a publicly held firm. L'Abbé and many others in the firm were convinced that the volatility of the company's revenues would disappoint analysts and create an element of instability. L'Abbé knew that because of their client base and trends in police and defence spending, revenues could not be steadied to the extent that investors would tolerate and that fickle investors would not appreciate the company's business structure. According to L'Abbé, "sometimes, you have to have a bad year before you can have a great year." Besides, L'Abbé felt Med-Eng would not want to have to "drop its pants in front of analysts every quarter just to make them happy." The firm's CEO was convinced that being privately held meant that the company could operate free of the rhetoric and pressures of investors looking for a steady return.

The nature of the company's product also meant that publicly announcing new innovations and strategies would be infeasible. Altogether, despite the firm's size, being privately held meant freedom from undue scrutiny coupled with better control over the company's direction and secrets.[5] In some instances, Med-Eng had to conceal certain information from employees so disclosing these secrets to the public would never be an option.[6]

On top of that, thus far Med-Eng had been successful in getting enough private venture capital to grow. The firm received one round of financing in 1997 of C$2 million, and received a second round in 2000 when upper management had a run-in with the board of directors. Management's vision for Med-Eng conflicted with that of the board, so in early 2000, Schroders & Associates Canada Inc. (www.schroders.ca/), a buyout group from Montreal was approached by Med-Eng management "to buy out the equity participation of a group of four inactive private investors who sought to realize their investment." Med-Eng received approximately C$12 million in venture capital needed to rid itself of directors who were critical of CEO Richard L'Abbé. Less than four years later, Mr. L'Abbé was named 'CEO of the Year' by the *Ottawa Business Journal* as revenues skyrocketed.

Afghanistan, Iraq, and Beyond

Leaning back at his desk in his Ottawa office, Richard L'Abbé, CEO and co-founder of Med-Eng Systems, looked out the window as employees streamed into the parking lot on a cold autumn morning. It was October 2006 and maple leaves were changing colour from green to yellows, oranges, and reds. The U.S. Department of Homeland Security threat advisory colour schema was currently at the midpoint of the scale: Yellow "Elevated: Significant risk of terrorist attacks." The next higher level of terrorist threat was Orange, which was divided into two degrees of severity and had been activated eight times in the four years since the scale was introduced. The first Red alert—the highest likelihood of terrorist attack—occurred in mid-August 2006. Military operations in Afghanistan and Iraq seemed likely to continue. Med-Eng products were increasingly playing a protective role in active combat.

A number of defence contractors were working on personal microclimate cooling systems. There were those worn by the dismounted warfighter—as such, the cooling vest was typically a heat activated cold pack that would absorb the wearer's heat; alternatively there might be a source of power circulating air around the torso to provide cooling. For the mounted warfighter—weight and power were less of a concern. The soldier could be hooked up to a system that cycled refrigerated fluid through a vest. According to one soldier returning from Iraq "You kind of get used to being shot at but you never get used to being hot."[7]

Med-Eng's cupola protective ensemble (CPE) was an integrated system combining both personal safety and cooling. The CPE was worn by the gunner exposed on top of an armoured HUMVEE. The CPE's cooling system might also serve in other

www.mcgrawhill.ca/olc/timmons

---

[5] This is not to say the company received little critical feedback. On the contrary, a board of advisors was often scathing, asked serious questions, and kept L'Abbé and the entire organization in check. L'Abbé was quick to give credit to the advisors for their positive influence, "this was certainly not a group of 'yes men'."

[6] Many business directories listed Med-Eng as a manufacturer of "surgical appliances and supplies," "clothes," or "safety helmets." Little effort was made to correct these inaccuracies, even the company Web site listed the names of no employees, only job titles; email addresses contained neither first names nor last names merely job descriptions (e.g., sales, R&D, recruiting, etc.).

[7] Scott R. Gourley, "Chill Out," www.special-operations-technology.com/.

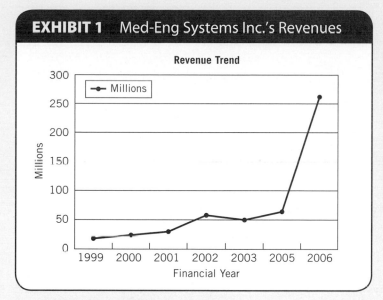

EXHIBIT 1   Med-Eng Systems Inc.'s Revenues

Revenue Trend

Note: These figures are approximations from public sources.

What Next?

Med-Eng needed to increase its markets and find new ways of ensuring sustained revenue growth. The simple fact was that the world had a finite number of police departments and new growth would have to emerge from somewhere. War was becoming a foreseeable constant. There would likely always be a need for manned weapons and the CPE could play a role in protecting gunners in Stryker interim armoured vehicles and up-armoured trucks. Because the CPE was derived from the EOD suits, the product met U.S. Department of Defense approval in just 10 weeks in 2005, including blast tests at Aberdeen Proving Ground. Med-Eng's CPE had been in service with U.S. troops in Iraq since January 2006. With much on his mind, L'Abbé reclined in his chair and pondered the future—both his and MedEng's.

The company had been through 'growing pains.' A decent cadre of middle managers was in place and L'Abbé was confident that his marketing and sales teams were taking initiative. It took some time for them and him to get used to changing roles and responsibilities—things now ran smoothly; freedom, independence, experimentation, and exploration were the norm. While these had always been strengths of engineering and design within Med-Eng Systems, moving these characteristics from the lab to the market had taken effort. Cutting-edge science was not enough; there needed to be similar thinking in approaching the marketplace. Getting entrepreneurial traits to migrate was not easy; sometimes the solution had been to replace rather than remould an employee. L'Abbé recognized that he could no longer hold onto everything, but he still knew about—even if not first hand—everything that was going on. If he had to go on vacation, the place could run without him. He had given his teams room to fail—and they had—but they got it right most of the time. The 'Midas touch' had spoiled them in the past, but at this point only hard work and logic were responsible for their ongoing success.

settings. Dave Hatcher, manager of strategic business development at Med-Eng commented, "we're looking at numerous other applications. If you look at the Abrams, the Stryker, or the Bradley, any one of the vehicles could take that type of cooling system to cool the individuals inside of the vehicle."[8] While the cooling system portion of the ensemble had multiple applications and competitors; the defence portion of the CPE seemed to have at least one more competitor than it did applications. A CROW (common remotely operated weapons station) could replace the exposed gunner. A turret with camera and weapons permitted the soldier to remain inside a vehicle to view a computer screen with one hand on a joystick. At between US$200,000 to US$250,000 per fitting, they were an expensive alternative.

---

[8] Scott R. Gourley, "Chill Out," www.special-operations-technology.com/.

6

THE NEW VENTURE TEAM

In the world today, there's plenty of technology, plenty of entrepreneurs, plenty of venture capital. What's in short supply is great teams. Your biggest challenge will be building a great team.

John Doerr,
Partner, Kleiner, Perkins, Caufield & Byers

RESULTS EXPECTED

Upon completion of this chapter, you will be able to:

1. Articulate the role and significance of teams in building successful new ventures.

2. Recognize successful entrepreneurial philosophies and attitudes that can anchor vision in forming and developing effective new venture teams.

3. Identify the critical issues and hurdles, including common pitfalls, faced by entrepreneurs in forming and building new venture teams.

4. Understand issues of reward that new teams face in slicing the equity pie.

5. Develop a reward system for your own venture.

RESULTS EXPECTED

THE IMPORTANCE OF THE TEAM

The Connection to Success

Evidence suggests that a management team can make all the difference in venture success. There is a strong connection between the growth potential of a new venture (and its ability to attract capital beyond the founder's resources from private and venture capital backers) and the quality of its management team.

The existence of a quality management team is one of the major differences between a firm that provides its founder simply a job substitute, and the ability to employ perhaps a few family members and others, and a higher potential venture. The lone-wolf entrepreneur may make a living, but the team builder creates an organization and a company—a company where substantial value and harvest options are created.

Ventures that do not have teams are not necessarily predestined for the new venture graveyard. Yet, building a higher potential venture without a team is extremely difficult. Some entrepreneurs have acquired a distaste for partners, and some lead entrepreneurs can be happy only if they are in complete control; that is, they want employees, not partners, either internally or as outside investors. Take, for instance, an entrepreneur who founded a high-technology firm that grew steadily, but slowly, over 10 years to nearly $2 million in sales. As new patterns and technological advances in fibre optics drew much interest from venture capitalists, he had more than one offer of up to $5 million of funding, which he turned down because the investors wanted to own 51 percent or more of his venture. Plainly and simply, he said, "I do not want to give up control of what I have worked so long and hard to create." While clearly the exception to the rule, this entrepreneur has managed to grow his business to more than $20 million in sales.

Mahshad Koohgoli, is the founder of Spacebridge Networks, Lantern Communications Canada, and Protecode. On the subject of his start-up Nimcat Networks, he revealed that when the money ran out he called his team together to deliver a difficult message. Koohgoli: "I have enough money to keep the heating on and the lights on; if you leave, I understand. But I'm not going to leave, and I suggest you don't either." Nobody left. Koohgoli explained: "There's no way I can get anything done unless these people succeed so my job is to take away any impediments that might be in their way to success. If they fail it's because I haven't taken care of them." Stephen Daze, executive director of the Entrepreneurship Centre (www.entrepreneurship.com) added, "Koohgoli's faith in his team at Nimcat and their reciprocal faith in him turned out to be well-placed. One month after that tough meeting, the first round of financing came through and within 18 months Nimcat was sold for $50 million, representing over eight times return on investment."[1]

For decades, studies have pointed to the importance of a team approach to new venture creation. Solid teams are far more likely to attract venture capital, team-led start-ups have a greater chance of survival, and those enterprises often realize higher overall returns than ventures run by solo entrepreneurs.

Not only is the existence of a team important, but so too is the quality of that team. Because of this, venture capital investors are often very active in helping to shape—and reshape—management teams. One study demonstrated the increasing importance of team formation, teamwork history, and cooperation between new venture teams and venture capitalists.[2] This is especially true today with highly technical ventures in areas such as biotechnology, nanotechnology, and photonics. Elicia Maine of Simon Fraser University and Elizabeth Garnsey of the University of Cambridge observe "smaller and newer firms are playing an increasing role in the advanced materials sector."[3]

There is, then, a valuable role that the right partner(s) can play in a venture. In addition, mounting evidence suggests that entrepreneurs face loneliness, stress, and other pressures. At the very least, finding the right partner can mitigate these pressures.[4] The key is identifying and working with the right partner or partners. Getting the right partners and working with them successfully usually involves anticipating and dealing with some very critical issues and hurdles, when it is neither too early nor too late.

FORMING AND BUILDING TEAMS

Anchoring Vision in Team Philosophy and Attitudes

The most successful entrepreneurs seem to anchor their vision of the future in certain entrepreneurial philosophies and attitudes (i.e., attitudes about what a team is, what its mission is, and how it will be rewarded). The soul of this vision concerns what the founder or founders are trying to accomplish and the unwritten ground rules that become the fabric, character, and purpose guiding how a team will work together, succeed and make mistakes together, and realize a harvest together. The rewards, compensation, and incentive structures rest on this philosophy and attitudes.

This fundamental mind-set is often evident in later success. The anchoring of this vision goes beyond all the critical nuts-and-bolts issues covered in the chapters and cases on the opportunity, the business plan, financing, and so forth. Each of these issues is vital, but each by itself may not lead to success. A single factor rarely, if ever, does.

The capacity of the lead entrepreneur to craft a vision and then to lead, inspire, persuade, and cajole key people to sign up for and deliver the dream makes an enormous difference between success and failure, between loss and profit, and between substantial harvest and "turning over the keys" to get out from under large personal guarantees of debt. Henry Mitzberg reminds us: "the vision can develop in an emergent fashion, within the new organization, as the founding leader learns from his or her experience."[5]

Marnie Walker grew Student Express, a special needs bussing company, to over $10 million in revenue, 300 employees, and a fleet of 250 vehicles before being offered more money for her start-up than she could say "no" to. Perhaps the words of others best capture Marnie Walker's ability to assemble and rally a cohesive group. According to one member of her team, Sheila Gallagher, operations manager at Student Express: "I was given the opportunity to learn and grow under her leadership. Marnie allows everyone to develop their own style through excellent team leadership and project management skills." A colleague and leadership consultant, Elaine Todres, indicates: "Marnie is straightforward, honest, incisive, focused, driven by the needs of the others, results-oriented, compassionate and devoted to her people." And even a customer from the York District School Board remarked: "She showed she really cared about our community, students, their parents and staff by helping out on committees and giving advice. She became part of our team."

Instilling a vision, and the passion to win, occurs very early, often during informal discussions, and seems to trigger a series of self-fulfilling prophecies that lead to success, rather than to "almosts" or to failure. In a study to determine the actual existence of lead entrepreneurs in INC. 500 firms, it was found that among macro-entrepreneurial teams, lead entrepreneurs do exist and they have stronger entrepreneurial vision and greater self-efficacy or self-confidence to act on their vision and make it real.[6]

Thus, lead entrepreneurs and team members who understand team building and teamwork have a secret weapon. Many with outstanding technical or other relevant skills, educational credentials, and so on, will be at once prisoners and victims of the highly individualistic competitiveness that got them to where they are. They may be fantastic lone achievers, and some may even "talk a good team game." But when it comes to how they behave and perform, their egos can rarely fit inside an airplane hangar. They simply do not have the team mentality.

What are these team philosophies and attitudes that the best entrepreneurs have and are able to identify or instill in prospective partners and team members? These can be traced to the entrepreneurial mind-set discussed in Chapter 1—a mind-set that can be seen actively at work around the team-building challenge. While there are innumerable blends and variations, most likely the teams of those firms that succeed in growing up big will share many of the following:

- *Cohesion.* Members of a team believe they are all in this together, and if the company wins, everyone wins. Members believe that no one can win unless everyone wins and, conversely, if anyone loses, everyone loses. Rewards, compensation, and incentive structures rest on building company value and return on capital invested, no matter how small or sizeable. Mahshad Koohgoli sums it up thus, "It's not about the path of least resistance. If it's easy, everybody else will be doing it…we are doing something that people said couldn't be done. Starting a company is not easy. But it's fun; I wouldn't change it for anything else."[7]

- *Teamwork.* A team that works as a team, rather than one where individual heroes are created, may be the single most distinguishing feature of the higher-potential venture. Thus, on these teams, efforts are made to make others' jobs easier, to make heroes out of partners and key people, and to motivate people by celebrating their successes. As Harold Seigle, the highly successful, now retired, president and chief executive officer of the Sunmark Companies, likes to put it, "High performance breeds strong friendships!"

- *Integrity.* Hard choices and trade-offs are made regarding what is good for the customer, the company, and value creation, rather than being based on purely utilitarian or Machiavellian ethics or narrow personal or departmental needs and concerns. There is a belief in and commitment to the notion of getting the job done without sacrificing quality, health, or personal standards. Of Marnie Walker introduced earlier, Elaine

Todres added: "She is ethical and hardworking. And most enduring of all, Marnie is modest and seeks to learn continuously." Marnie herself revealed that her aim is always to develop a culture of respect and accountability and to focus on long-term relationships.

- *Commitment to the long haul.* Like most organizations, new ventures thrive or wither according to the level of commitment of their teams. Members of a committed team believe they are playing for the long haul and that the venture is not a get-rich-quick drill. Rather, the venture is viewed as a delayed-gratification game in which it can take 5, 7, or even 10 or more years to realize a harvest. *No one gets a windfall profit by signing up now but bailing out early or when the going gets tough.* Stock-vesting agreements reflect this commitment. For example, stock will usually be so vested over five or seven years that anyone who leaves early, for whatever reasons, can keep stock earned to date, but he or she is required to sell the remaining shares back to the company at the price originally paid. Of course, such a vesting agreement usually provides that if the company is unexpectedly sold or if a public offering is made long before the five-or-seven-year vesting period is up, then stock is 100 percent vested automatically with that event. Pat Quinn, former NHL player and coach sums up teamwork: "The big thing is commitment as a group. You have to develop trust amongst each other that revolves around that commitment, that onus on each other to be honest and have that common direction that the team all want to go to."

- *Harvest mind-set.* A successful harvest is the name of the game. This means that eventual capital gain is viewed as the scorecard, rather than the size of a monthly paycheque, the location and size of an office, a certain car, or the like. Dan Martell founded Spheric Technologies in Moncton, New Brunswick, in 2004. Spheric Technologies creates social network applications for corporations, essentially "Myspace for big business without the music." His venture grew to 28 full-time employees and revenues of more than $2.2 million in 2008. Mid-way through that year Dan Martell sold the venture and moved to other things—he co-founded Flowtown. He remains a senior advisor to Spheric Technologies, but in 2009 Spheric Technologies was forced to lay off another round of workers taking them down to 11 full-time employees.[8]

- *Commitment to value creation.* Team members are committed to value creation—making the pie bigger for everyone, including adding value for customers, enabling suppliers to win as the team succeeds, and making money for the team's constituencies and various stakeholders. Harry Chemko and Jason Billingsley graduated from university in 2000 and launched a consulting business for companies wanting an Internet presence. Soon they noticed a demand for online shopping software and jumped at it. They changed the venture's name and mission. Elastic Path's e-commerce platform is used by Aeroplan, Time Inc., Avis, Samsonite, and the Vancouver 2010 Olympic and Paralympic Winter Games. With approximately 200 customers worldwide, a staff of over 100, and $10 million in revenue they were identified by the *Financial Post* as a firm that would grow despite the economic slump of 2009–2010.[9] Vancouver-based Elastic Path has remained privately held and has grown organically without outside capital, but it has partnered extensively in order to expand internationally.

- *Equal inequality.* In successful emerging companies, democracy and blind equality generally do not work very well, and diligent efforts are made to determine who has what responsibility for the key tasks. The president is the one to set the ground rules and to shape the climate and culture of the venture. Bill Foster, founder of Stratus Computer, was asked if he and his partners were all equal. He quipped, "Yes, we are, except I get paid the most and I own the most stock." Stock is usually not divided equally among the founders and key managers. In one company of four key people, stock was split as follows: 34 percent for the president, 23 percent each for the marketing and technical vice presidents, and 6 percent for the controller. The remainder went to outside directors and advisors. In another company, seven founders split the company as follows: 22 percent for the president, 15 percent for each of the four vice presidents, and 9 percent for each of the two other contributors. An example of how failure to differentiate in terms of ownership impacts a business is seen in a third firm, where four owners each had equal share. Yet, two of the owners contributed virtually everything, while the other two actually detracted from the business. Because of this unresolved problem, the company could not attract venture capital and was never able to grow significantly.

- *Fairness.* Rewards for key employees and stock ownership are based on contribution, performance, and results over time. Since these can only be roughly estimated in advance, and since there will invariably be surprises and inequities, both positive and negative, as time goes on, adjustments are made. One good example is a company that achieved spectacular results in just two years in the cellular phone business. When the company was sold, it was evident that two of the six team members had contributed more than was reflected in their stock ownership position. To remedy this, another team member gave one of the two team members stock worth several hundred thousand dollars. Since the team was involved in another venture, the president made adjustments in the various ownership positions in the new venture, with each member's concurrence, to adjust for past inequities. In addition, it was decided to set aside 10 percent of the next venture to provide some discretion in making future adjustments for unanticipated contributions to ultimate success.

- *Sharing of the harvest.* This sense of fairness and justness seems to be extended by the more successful entrepreneurs to the harvest of a company, even when there is no legal or ethical obligation to do so. For example, as much as 10 to 20 percent of the "winnings" is frequently set aside to distribute to key employees. In one such recent harvest, employees were startled and awash with glee when informed they would each receive a year's salary after the company was sold. However, this is not always the case. In another firm, 90 percent of which was owned by an entrepreneur and his family, the president, who was the single person most responsible for the firm's success and spectacular valuation, needed to expend considerable effort to get the owners to agree to give bonuses to other key employees of around $3 million, an amount just over 1 percent of the $250-million sale price. (It is worth considering how this sense of fairness, or lack of it, affects future flows of quality people and opportunities from which these entrepreneurs can choose new ventures.)

A Process of Evolution

An entrepreneur considering issues of team formation will rarely discover black-and-white, bullet-proof answers that hold up over time. Nor is it being suggested that an entrepreneur needs answers to all questions concerning what the opportunity requires, and when, before moving ahead. Emphasis on the importance of new venture teams also does not mean every new venture must start with a full team that plunges into the business. It may take some time for the team to come together as a firm grows, and there will also always be some doubt, a hope for more than a prospective partner can deliver, and a constant recalibration. Again, creative acts, such as running a marathon or entrepreneuring, will be full of unknowns, new ground, and surprises. Preparation is an insurance policy, and thinking through these team issues and team-building concepts in advance is very inexpensive insurance.

The combination of the right team of people and a right venture opportunity can be very powerful. The whole is, in such instances, greater than the sum of the parts. However, the odds for highly successful venture teams are rather thin. Even if a venture survives, the turnover among team members during the early years probably exceeds the national divorce rate. Studies of new venture teams seeking venture capital show many never get off the ground. These usually exhaust their own resources and commitment before raising the venture capital necessary to launch their ventures. Of those that are funded, about 1 in 20 becomes very successful in three to five years, in that it will return in excess of five times the original investment in realizable capital gains.

The formation and development of new venture teams seems to be idiosyncratic, and there seems to be a multitude of ways in which venture partners come together. Some teams form by accidents of geography, common interest, or working together (see Angstrom's Team on the next page). Perhaps the common interest is simply that the team members want to start a business, while in other instances the interest is an idea that members believe responds to a market need. Others form teams by virtue of past friendships. For example, roommates or close friendships in college or graduate school frequently lead to business partnerships. This was the case with two of Jeffry Timmons's MBA classmates who concluded that they would go into business together after rooming together for a week. Leslie Charm and Carl Youngman have been partners for over 35 years as owners of three national franchise companies, an entrepreneurial advisory and troubled-business-management company, and a venture capital company. Jiffy Lube was founded by college football coach Jim Hindman and some of his coaches and players—including Stephen Spinelli.

In the evolution of venture teams, two distinct patterns are identifiable. In the first, one person has an idea (or simply wants to start a business), and then three or four associates join the team over the next one to three years as the venture takes form. Alternatively, an entire team forms at the outset based on such factors as a shared idea, a friendship, an experience, and so forth.

Angstrom's Team

Angstrom Power Inc., located in North Vancouver, British Columbia, is a privately held enterprise "funded by venture partners with experience in advancing new energy technology" (www.angstrompower.com). Angstrom's aim was to bring to market an integrated hydrogen fuel cell, with energy storage and microfluid components for hand-held portable electronics (e.g., smart phone). Take a look at the following individuals and their backgrounds. There are commonalities and differences in their areas of expertise and many have overlapped in working at various organizations.

Paul Zimmerman, CEO, had built and run global businesses for the past 20 years. Paul brings to Angstrom contacts in the technology community (president of Oregon Scientific, senior executive at Cisco Systems, general manager at Samsung Electronics) as well as venture capital arena—including being a founding director of a $2-billion equity fund. His schooling included the University of Toronto (electrical engineering and computer science) and an executive MBA from the International Institute of Management Development in Switzerland.

Dr. Ged McLean, founder, president, and CTO, was director of the Institute for Integrated Energy Systems at the University of Victoria, holds 40 patents and applications. He has past experience in start-up ventures.

Godfrey Forssman, director of Finance, is a Chartered Accountant with 12 years experience in growing entrepreneurial ventures.

Dr. Jeremy Schrooten, director of Fuel Cell Systems, B.Sc. degrees in chemistry and ceramic engineering and a Ph.D. in materials science. He previously worked at UTC Fuel Cells. He is credited with four patents before Angstrom and two while at Angstrom.

Olen Vanderleeden, director of Business Development, B.Eng. from the University of Victoria and an M.B.A. from Simon Fraser University. He worked at Ballard Power for eight years. He holds 11 patents and applications while at Ballard and seven while with Angstrom.

André van Vuuren, director of Engineering, has a background in new product development from prototype through volume production.

Bruce Townson, director of Strategy and Infrastructure, previously worked in partnership development in the hydrogen and fuel cell industries.

Joerg Zimmermann, director of Fueling R&D, worked in the R&D department of Ballard Power Systems for six years before joining Angstrom. He is a named inventor on 25 patents and patents pending.

To the above lineup listed on the venture's Web site in 2008, the following individuals were added in 2009 and Bruce Townson was removed!

John Lee, COO, 25 years of management experience at electrical and power technology companies—including alternative energy.

Jim McBeth, director of Manufacturing Engineering, worked in a variety of industry positions including as a director general with the National Research Council of Canada.

Steven Pratt, director of Engineering, has 15 years of experience in maturing and commercializing emerging technologies and holds more than 40 patents.

Angstrom's Board of Directors:

Chairman: Ake Almgren, Ph.D., serves on other boards, 26-year career at ABB, a worldwide power solutions company. President and CEO of Capstone Turbine 1998–2003.

David Oxtoby, CFA, worked for Ontario Power Generation Ventures, Inc. from 2001–2005. He is currently CEO of CarbonFree Technology Inc.

David Berkowitz has been with Ventures West since 1996 and leads the firm's cleantech practice.

Wal van Lierop, Ph.D., is co-founder, president, and CEO of Chrysalix Energy Venture Capital.

Mark Steinley, was originally Angstrom's president and CEO, while Ged McLean served as CTO, and helped secure the venture's first round of financing ($2.85 million in 2002).

Eric Schwitzer, managing partner at Enterprise Capital Management Inc.

Daniel Muzyka, Ph.D., dean Sauder School of Business, University of British Columbia.

Sources: Angstrom Power's Web site, www.angstrom.com/, LinkedIn public listing for Angstrom Power, BusinessWeek Private Company listing for Angstrom Power Inc.

Filling the Gaps

There is no simple cookbook solution to team formation; rather, there are as many approaches to forming teams as there are ventures with multiple founders.

Successful entrepreneurs search out people and form and build a team based on what the opportunity requires, and when.[10] Team members will contribute high value to a venture if they complement and balance the lead entrepreneur—and each other. Yet, ironically, while a substantial amount of thought usually accompanies the decision of people to go into business together, an overabundance of the thinking, particularly among the less experienced, can focus on less critical issues, such as titles, corporate name, letterhead, or what kind of lawyer or accountant is needed. Thus, teams are often ill-conceived from the outset and can easily plunge headlong into unanticipated and unplanned responses to crises, conflicts, and changes. Just as it is possible to recruit additions to the team from competitors or former employers, it should be noted that it is easy to lose team members that way too. Employees will leave to pursue their own best opportunities.[11]

A team starts with a lead entrepreneur (Ged McLean in the case of Angstrom Power Inc.). In a start-up situation, the lead entrepreneur usually wears many hats. Beyond that, comparison of the nature and demands of the venture and the capabilities, motivations, and interests of the lead entrepreneur will signal gaps that exist and that need to be filled by other team members or by accessing other outside resources, such as a board of directors (see Angstrom's board of directors), consultants, lawyers, accountants, and so on.[12] Elicia Maine, Daniel Shapiro, and Aidan Vining all of Simon Fraser University examined the relationship between clusters and the growth performance of firms. New ventures benefit by having access through proximity to a pool of valuable resources.[13] Tod Rutherford of Syracuse University and John Holmes of Queen's University observe "entrepreneurs are active creators of institutional cluster development," but established firms erect barriers to protect their intellectual property, in an attempt to reduce tacit knowledge flows within the cluster.[14]

Serial entrepreneur, Mahshad Koohgoli, CEO of Protecode, has a product that examines a software developer's project and inspects the content to determine the underlying intellectual property and licensing attributes. With so much opensource software it is important to trace the content for ownership. Lawsuits were filed against Cisco for including some software that was in the public domain.[15]

Mark Dowds, launched BrainPark to make the workplace more collaborative, transparent, and efficient; the goal is to reduce information overload and keep things simple. But collaboration was not only part of the end product, Dowds has used crowdsourcing through blogs and other venues for assistance in designing and promoting his venture. He has also created IndoorPlayground, a physical space for the entrepreneur in need of office space (perhaps to hold a meeting) or the camaraderie and support of others working on start-ups.

Thus, for example, if the strengths of the lead entrepreneur or a team member are technical in nature, other team members, or outside resources, need to fill voids in marketing, finance, and such (see Angstrom's Team). Realistically, there will be an overlapping and sharing of responsibilities, but team members need to complement, not duplicate, the lead entrepreneur's capabilities and those of other team members.

Note that a by-product of forming a team may be alteration of an entry strategy if a critical gap cannot be filled. For example, a firm may find that it simply cannot assault a certain market because it cannot hire the right marketing person. But it may find it could attract a top-notch person to exploit another niche with a modified product or service.

Most important, the process of evaluating and deciding who is needed, and when, is dynamic and not a onetime event. What know-how, skills, and expertise are required? What key tasks and action steps need to be taken? What are the requisites for success? What is the firm's distinctive competence? What external contacts are required? How extensive and how critical are the gaps? How much can the venture afford to pay? Will the venture gain access to the expertise it needs through additions to its board of directors (see Angstrom's board of directors) or outside consultants? Questions such as these determine when and how these needs could be filled. And answers to such questions will change over time.

The following, organized around the analytical framework introduced in Chapter 2, can guide the formation of new venture teams.

The Founder   What kind of team is needed depends upon the nature of the opportunity and what the lead entrepreneur brings to the game. One key step in forming a team is for the lead entrepreneur to assess his or her entrepreneurial strategy. (The personal entrepreneurial strategy exercise for Chapter 1—found online at www.mcgrawhill.ca/olc/timmons—is a valuable input in approaching these issues.) Thus, the lead entrepreneur needs to first consider whether the team is desirable or necessary and whether he or she wants to grow a higher potential company. He or she then needs to assess what talents, know-how, skills, track record, contacts, and resources are being brought to the table; that is, what "chunks" have been acquired. (See the leadership skills and know-how assessment exercise for Chapter 5.) Once this is determined, the lead entrepreneur needs to consider what the venture has to have to succeed, who is needed to complement him or her, and when. The best entrepreneurs are optimistic realists and have a desire to improve their performance. They work at knowing what they do and do not know and are honest with themselves. The lead entrepreneur needs to consider issues such as:

- What relevant industry, market, and technological know-how and experience are needed to win, and do I bring these to the venture? Do I know the revenue and cost model better than anyone?

- Are my personal and business strengths in those specific areas critical to success in the proposed business?
- Do I have the contacts and networks needed (and will the ones I have make a competitive difference), or do I look to partners in this area?
- Can I attract a "first team" of all-star partners inside and externally, and can I lead these people and other team members effectively?
- Why did I decide to pursue this particular opportunity now, and what do I want out of the business (i.e., what are my goals and my income and harvest aspirations)?
- Do I know what the sacrifices and commitment will be, and am I prepared to make these?
- What are the risks and rewards involved, am I comfortable with them, and do I look for someone with a different risk-taking orientation?

Often a student going through this process will conclude that a more experienced person will be needed to lead the venture.

The Opportunity   The need for team members is something an entrepreneur constantly thinks about, especially in the idea stage before start-up. What is needed in the way of a team depends on the matchup between the lead entrepreneur and the opportunity, and how fast and aggressively he or she plans to proceed. (See the online Venture Opportunity Screening Exercises for Chapter 3.) While most new ventures plan to bootstrap it and bring on additional team members only as the company can afford them, the Catch-22 is that if a venture is looking for venture capital or serious private investors, having an established team will yield higher valuation and a smaller ownership share that will have to be parted with. Some questions that need to be considered are:

- Have I clearly defined the value added and the economics of the business? Have I considered how (and with whom) the venture can make money in this business? For instance, whether a company is selling razors or razor blades makes a difference in the need for different team members.
- What are the critical success variables in the business I want to start, and what (or who) is needed to influence these variables positively?
- Do I have, or have access to, the critical external relationships with investors, lawyers, bankers, customers, suppliers, regulatory agencies, and so forth, that are necessary to pursue my opportunity? Do I need help in this area?
- What competitive advantage and strategy should I focus on? What people are necessary to pursue this strategy or advantage?

Outside Resources   In reaction to corporate scandals (e.g., Bre-X, Hollinger, Nortel), governance issues have become more important in recent years, including for start-up enterprises.[16] Gaps can be filled by accessing outside resources, such as boards of directors, accountants, lawyers, consultants, and so forth.[17] Usually, tax and legal expertise can best be obtained initially on a part-time basis. Other expertise (e.g., to design an inventory control system) is specialized and needed only once. Generally, if the resource is a onetime or periodic effort, or if the need is peripheral to the key tasks, goals, and activities required by the business, then an alternative such as using consultants makes sense. However, if the expertise is a must for the venture at the outset and the lead entrepreneur cannot provide it or learn it quickly, then one or more people will have to be acquired. Some questions to consider are:

- Is the need for specialized, one-time, or part-time expertise peripheral or on the critical path?
- Will trade secrets be compromised if I obtain this expertise externally?

Additional Considerations

Forming and building a team is, like marriage, a rather unscientific, occasionally unpredictable, and frequently surprising exercise—no matter how hard one may try to make it otherwise! The analogy of marriage and family, with all the accompanying complexities and consequences, is a particularly useful one. Forming a team has many of the characteristics of the courtship and marriage ritual, involving decisions based in part on emotion. There may well be a certain infatuation among team members and an aura of admiration, respect, and often fierce loyalty. Similarly, the complex psychological joys, frustrations, and uncertainties that accompany the birth and raising of children (here, the product or service) are experienced in entrepreneurial teams as well. Thus, the following additional issues need to be considered:

- *Values, goals, and commitment.* It is critical that a team be well anchored in terms of values and goals. In any new venture, the participants establish psychological contracts and climates. While these are most often set when the lead entrepreneur encourages standards of excellence and respect for team members' contributions, selection of team members whose goals and values are in agreement can greatly facilitate establishment of a psychological contract and an entrepreneurial climate. In successful companies, the personal goals and values of team members align well, and the goals of the company are championed by team members as well. While this alignment may be less exact in large publicly owned corporations and greatest in small closely held firms, significant overlapping of a team member's goals with those of other team members and the overlap of corporate goals and team members' goals is desirable. Practically speaking, these evaluations of team members are some of the most difficult to make.

- *Definition of roles.* A diligent effort needs to be made to determine who is comfortable with and who has what responsibility for the key tasks so duplication of capabilities or responsibilities is minimized. Roles cannot be pinned down precisely for all tasks, since some key tasks and problems simply cannot be anticipated and since contributions are not always made by people originally expected to make them. Maintaining a loose, flexible, flat structure with shared responsibility and information is desirable for utilizing individual strengths, flexibility, rapid learning, and responsive decision-making.

- *Peer groups.* The support and approval of family, friends, and co-workers can be helpful, especially when adversity strikes. Reference group approval can be a significant source of positive reinforcement for a person's career choice and, thus, his or her entire self-image and identity.[18] Ideally, peer group support for each team member should be there. (If it is not, the lead entrepreneur may have to accept the additional burden of encouragement and support in hard times, a burden that can be sizeable.) Therefore, questions of whether a prospective team member's spouse is solidly in favour of his or her decision to pursue an entrepreneurial career and the sweat equity required and of whether the team member's close friends will be a source of support and encouragement or of detraction or negativism need to be considered.

Common Pitfalls

There can be difficulties in the practical implementation of these philosophies and attitudes, irrespective of the venture opportunity and the people involved. The company may come unglued before it gets started, may experience infant mortality, or may live perpetually immersed in nasty divisive conflicts and power struggles that will cripple its potential, even if they do not kill the company.

Often, a team lacks skill and experience in dealing with such difficult start-up issues, does not take the time to go through an extended "mating dance" among potential partners during the moonlighting phase before actually launching the venture, or does not seek the advice of competent advisors. As a result, such a team may be unable to deal with such sensitive issues as who gets how much ownership, who will commit what time and money or other resources, how disagreements will be resolved, and how a team member can leave or be let go. Thus, crucial early discussions among team members sometimes lead to a premature disbanding of promising teams with sound business ideas. Or in the rush to get going, or because the funds to pay for help in these areas are lacking, a team may stay together but not work through, even in a rough way, many of these issues. Such teams do not take advantage of the moonlighting phase to test the commitment and contribution made by team members. For example, to build a substantial business, a partner needs to be totally committed to the venture. The success of the venture is the partner's most important goal, and other priorities, including his or her family, come second. Another advantage of using such a shakedown period effectively is that the risks inherent in such factors as premature commitment to permanent decisions regarding salary and stock are lower.

The common approach to forming a new venture team also can be a common pitfall for new venture teams. Here, two to four entrepreneurs, usually friends or work acquaintances, decide to demonstrate their equality with such democratic trimmings as equal stock ownership, equal salaries, equal office space and cars, and other items symbolizing their peer status. Left unanswered are questions of who is in charge, who makes the final decisions, and how real differences of opinion are resolved. While some overlapping of roles and a sharing in and negotiating of decisions are desirable in new venture teams, too much looseness is debilitating. Even sophisticated buy-sell agreements among partners often fail to resolve the conflicts.

Another pitfall is a belief that there are no deficiencies in the lead entrepreneur or the management team. Or a team is overly fascinated with or overcommitted to a product idea. For example, a lead entrepreneur who is unwilling or unable to identify his or her own deficiencies and weaknesses and to add appropriate team members to compensate for these, and who further lacks an understanding of what is really needed to make a new venture grow into a successful business, has fallen into this pitfall. [19]

Failing to recognize that creating and building a new venture is a dynamic process is a problem for some teams. Therefore, such teams fail to realize that initial agreements are likely not to reflect actual contributions of team members over time, regardless of how much time one devotes to team-building tasks and regardless of the agreements team members make before start-up. In addition, they fail to consider that teams are likely to change in composition over time. Richard Testa, a leading attorney whose firm has dealt with many start-ups and with numerous venture capital firms, startled those attending a seminar on raising venture capital by saying:

> The only thing that I can tell you with great certainty about this start-up business has to do with you and your partners. I can virtually guarantee you, based on our decade plus of experience, that five years from now at least one of the founders will have left every company represented here today. [20]

Woe is the team that fails to put in place mechanisms that will facilitate and help structure graceful divorces and provide for the internal adjustments required as the venture grows.

Destructive motivations in investors, prospective team members, or the lead entrepreneur spell trouble. Teams suffer if they are not alert to signs of potentially destructive motivations, such as an early concern for power and control by a team member. In this context, it has been argued that conflict management is a central task for members of teams. A study of self-empowered teams found that how team members resolve their conflicts could affect their self-efficacy, as well as overall team performance. Team members in this study were most effective when they recognized they wanted to resolve the conflict for mutual benefit and that the goal is to help each other get what each other really needs and values, and not to try to win or to outdo each other. [21]

Finally, new venture teams may take trust for granted. Integrity is important in long-term business success, and the world is full of high-quality, ethical people; yet the real world also is inhabited by predators, crooks, sharks, frauds, and impostors. Chapter 7 contains a detailed discussion on the importance of integrity in entrepreneurial pursuits. It is paradoxical that an entrepreneur cannot succeed without trust, but he or she probably cannot succeed with blind trust either. Trust is something that is earned, usually slowly, for it requires a lot of patience and a lot of testing in the real world. This is undoubtedly a major reason why investors prefer to see teams that have worked closely together. In the area of trust, a little cynicism goes a long way, and teams that do not pay attention to detail, such as performing due diligence with respect to a person or firm, fall into this pit.

REWARDS AND INCENTIVES

Slicing the Founder's Pie

One of the most frequently asked questions from start-up entrepreneurs is: How much stock ownership should go to whom? (Chapter 9 "Financing the Venture" examines the various methods used by venture capitalists and investors to determine what share of the company is required by the investor at different rounds of investment.) Consider the recent discussions with Jed, a former student, who secured substantial early-stage funding from John Doerr of Kleiner Perkins Caufield & Byers. The advice for Jed and all others is the same.

First, start with a philosophy and set of values that boil down to this great principle: Share the wealth with those who help to create the value and thus the wealth. Once over that hurdle, you are less likely to get hung up on the percentage of ownership issue. After all, 51 percent of nothing is nothing. The key is making the pie as large as possible. Second, the ultimate goal of any venture-capital-backed company is to realize a harvest at a price 5 to 10 times the original investment, and up. Thus, the company will either be sold via an initial public offering (IPO) or to a larger company. It is useful to work backward from the capital structure at the time of the IPO to envision and define what will happen and who will get what. Most venture-capital-backed, smaller company IPOs during the robust capital markets of the late 1990s would have 12 to 15 million shares of stock outstanding after the IPO. In most situations 2.5 to 4 million shares are sold to the public (mostly to institutional investors) at $12 to $15 per share, depending on the perceived quality of the company and the robustness of the appetite for IPOs at the time. The number could be halved or doubled. Typically, the founder/CEO will own 1 to 3 million shares after the IPO, worth somewhere between $12 and $45 million. Put in this perspective, it is much easier to see why finding a great opportunity, building a great team, and sharing the wealth with widespread ownership in the team is far more important than what percentage of the company is owned.

Finally, especially for young entrepreneurs in their 20s or 30s, this will not be their last venture. The single most important thing is that it succeeds. Make this happen, and the future opportunities will be boundless. All this can be ruined if the founder/CEO simply gets greedy and overcontrolling, keeping most of the company to himself or herself, rather than creating a sizeable, shared pie.

The Reward System[22]

The reward system of a new venture includes both the financial rewards of a venture—such as stock, salary, and fringe benefits—and the chance to realize personal growth and goals, exercise autonomy, and develop skills in particular venture roles. Also, what is perceived as a reward by any single team member will vary. This perception will depend very much upon personal values, goals, and aspirations. Some may seek long-range capital gains, while others desire more short-term security and income.

The reward system established for a new venture team should facilitate the interface of the venture opportunity and the management team. It needs to flow from team formation and enhance the entrepreneurial climate of the venture and the building of an effective team. For example, being able to attract and keep high-quality team members depends, to a great extent, on financial and psychological rewards given. The skills, experience, commitment, risk, concern, and so forth, of these team members are secured through these rewards.

The rewards available to an entrepreneurial team vary over the life of a venture. While intangible rewards, such as opportunity for self-development and realization, may be available throughout, some of the financial rewards are more or less appropriate at different stages of the venture's development.

Because these rewards are so important and because, in its early stages, a venture is limited in the rewards it can offer, the total reward system over the life of the venture needs to be thought through very carefully and efforts need to be made to ensure that the venture's capacity to reward is not limited as levels of contribution change or as new personnel are added.

External issues also have an impact on the reward system created for a new venture. The division of equity between the venture and external investors will affect how much equity is available to team members. Further, the way a venture deals with these questions also will determine its credibility with investors and others, because these people will look to the reward system for signs of commitment by the venture team.

Critical Issues

Dividing ownership among the founding team, based on the philosophy and vision discussed earlier, is an early critical task for the lead entrepreneur. Investors may provide advice but will, more often than not, dump the issue squarely back in the lap of the lead entrepreneur, since whether and how these delicate ownership decisions are resolved often is seen by investors as an important litmus test. Also, the process by which a reward system is decided and the commitment of each team member to deal with problems in a way that will ensure rewards continue to reflect performance are of utmost importance. Each key team member needs to be committed to working out solutions that reflect the commitments, risks, and anticipated relative contributions of team members as fairly as possible.[23]

A good reward system reflects the goals of the particular venture and is in tune with valuations. If a venture is not seeking outside capital, outside owners need not be considered; but the same issues need to be resolved. For example, if a goal is to realize a substantial capital gain from the venture in the next 5 to 10 years, then the reward system needs to be aimed at reinforcing this goal and encouraging the long-term commitment required for its attainment.

No time-tested formulas or simple answers exist to cover all questions of how distributions should be made. However, the following issues should be considered:

- *Differentiation.* The democracy approach can work, but it involves higher risk and more pitfalls than a system that differentiates based on the value of contributions by team members. As a rule, different team members rarely contribute the same amount to the venture, and the reward system needs to recognize these differences.
- *Performance.* Reward needs to be a function of performance (as opposed to effort) during the early life of the venture and not during only one part of this period. Many ventures have been torn apart when the relative contributions of the team members changed dramatically several years after start-up without a significant change in rewards. (Vesting goes a long way toward dealing with this issue.)
- *Flexibility.* Regardless of the contribution of any team member at any given time, the probability is high that this will change. The performance of a team member may be substantially more or less than anticipated. Further, a team member may have to be replaced and someone may have to be recruited and added to the existing team. Flexibility in the reward system, including such mechanisms as vesting and setting aside a portion of stock for future adjustments, can help to provide a sense of justice.

Considerations of Timing

Division of rewards, such as the split of stock between the members of the entrepreneurial team, will most likely be made very early in the life of the venture. Rewards may be a way of attracting significant early contribution; however, it is performance over the life of the venture that needs to be rewarded.

For example, regarding equity, once the allocation of stock is decided, changes in the relative stock positions of team members will be infrequent. New team members or external investors may dilute each member's position, but the relative positions will probably remain unchanged.

However, one or more events may occur during the early years of a venture. First, a team member who has a substantial portion of stock may not perform and need to be replaced early in the venture. A key team member may find a better opportunity and quit, or a key team member could die in an accident. In each of these instances, the team will then be faced with the question of what will happen to the stock held by the team member. In each case, stock was intended as a reward for performance by the team member during the first several years of the venture, but the team member will not perform over this time period.

Several mechanisms are available to a venture when the initial stock split is so made to avoid the loss or freezing of equity. A venture can retain an option of returning stock to its treasury at the price at which it was purchased in certain cases, such as when a team member needs to be replaced. A buyback agreement also achieves this purpose.

To guard against the event that some portion of the stock has been earned and some portion will remain unearned, as when a team member quits or dies, the venture can place stock purchased by team members in escrow to be released over a two- or three-year period. Such a mechanism is called a stock-vesting agreement, and such an agreement can foster longer-term commitment to the success of the venture, while also providing a method for a civilized no-fault corporate divorce if things do not work out. Such a stock-vesting agreement is attached as a restriction on the stock certificate. Typically, the vesting agreement establishes a period of years, often four or more. During this period, the founding stockholders can "earn out" their shares. If a founder decides to leave the company before completion of the four-year vesting period, he or she may be required to sell the stock back to the company for the price originally paid for it, usually nothing. The departing shareholder, in this instance, would not own any stock after the departure. Nor would any capital gain windfall be realized by the departing founder. In other cases, founders may vest a certain portion each year, so they have some shares even if they leave. Such vesting can be weighted toward the last year or two of the vesting period. Other restrictions can give management and the board control over the disposition of stock, whether the stockholder stays or leaves the company. In essence, a mechanism such as a stock-vesting agreement confronts team members with the reality that "this is not a get-rich-quick exercise."

Other rewards, such as salary, stock options, bonuses, and fringe benefits, can be manipulated more readily to reflect changes in performance. But the ability to manipulate these is also somewhat dependent upon the stage of development of the venture. In the case of cash rewards, there is a trade-off between giving cash and the growth of the venture. Thus, in the early months of a venture, salaries will necessarily be low or nonexistent, and bonuses and other fringe benefits usually will be out of the question. Salaries, bonuses, and fringe benefits all drain cash, and until profitability is achieved, cash can always be put to use for operations. After profitability is achieved, cash payments will still limit growth. Salaries can become competitive once the venture has passed breakeven, but bonuses and fringe benefits should probably be kept at a minimum until several years of profitability have been demonstrated.

Mahshad Koohgoli advocates strict adherence to checkpoints. On the subject of timing with regard to his young venture Protecode, he revealed "We are keeping our focus. I've got 18 people in here right now. Eighteen payrolls; 18 families. I have no right to mislead them. I have no right to mislead myself. I hate to waste my time in life. Doing things quickly is very good. Something I've heard is 'you want to fail fast if you have to fail'—you don't want to drag it on for years." Koohgoli sees a statute of limitations, "If two years have gone by and nothing's happened, there's something wrong."[24] Finally, Eugene Kleiner, pioneer of venture capitalism asserts, "There is a time when panic is the appropriate response."

Considerations of Value

The contributions of team members will vary in nature, extent, and timing. In developing the reward system, particularly the distribution of stock, contributions in certain areas are of particular value to a venture, as follows:

- *Idea.* In this area, the originator of the idea, particularly if trade secrets or special technology for a prototype was developed or if product or market research was done, needs to be considered.
- *Business plan preparation.* Preparing an acceptable business plan, in terms of dollars and hours expended, needs to be considered.

- *Commitment and risk.* A team member may invest a large percentage of his or her net worth in the company, be at risk if the company fails, have to make personal sacrifices, put in long hours and major effort, risk his or her reputation, accept reduced salary, or already have spent a large amount of time on behalf of the venture. This commitment and risk need to be considered.

- *Skills, experience, track record, or contacts.* A team member may bring to the venture skills, experience, track record, or contacts in such areas as marketing, finance, and technology. If these are of critical importance to the new venture and are not readily available, these need to be considered.

- *Responsibility.* The importance of a team member's role to the success of the venture needs to be considered.

Being the originator of the idea or expending a great amount of time or money in preparing the business plan is frequently overvalued. If these factors are evaluated in terms of the real success of the venture down the road, it is difficult to justify much more than 15 to 20 percent of equity for them. Commitment and risk, skills, experience, and responsibility contribute more by far to the success of a venture.

The above list is valuable in attempting to weigh fairly the relative contributions of each team member. Contributions in each of these areas have some value; it is up to a team to agree on how to assign value to contributions and, further, to leave enough flexibility to allow for changes.

INTERNET IMPACT: TEAM

Attracting Talent

The Internet is quickly changing the economics and capabilities of the job market. The ease and low cost of posting detailed employment openings, the extremely large databases of job seekers, and the speed of candidate response have many hiring managers and entrepreneurs devoting more time than ever before to recruiting online.

Since employers can delimit résumé searches to specified skill sets, years of experience, and salary requirements with a few keystrokes, a single Internet site such as Monster.com can serve as a targeted recruiting engine that is equal to a dozen or more recruiters. Jeff Taylor, Monster.com's founder and CEO, commented, "Post an opening for somebody fluent in Japanese and English, and you're as apt to hear from applicants in Tokyo and Dublin as from those in Los Angeles. We get 11 million visitors a month, and in many cases, small businesses get as many as 400 responses from one posting."

Web sites representing professional associations such as Women in Technology International (www.witi.com) also have large databases of qualified individuals. These sites will often post job openings for a nominal fee.

Chapter Summary

1. A strong team is usually the difference between a success and a marginal or failed venture, and between a so-so and a great company.

2. Core philosophies, values, and attitudes, particularly sharing the wealth and ownership with those who create it, are key to team building.

3. The fit concept is central to anticipating management gaps and building the team.[25]

4. Numerous pitfalls await the entrepreneur in team building and need to be avoided. The lead entrepreneur and the entire team need to remain vigilant in their honest assessment of immediate and potential pitfalls.

5. Compensating and rewarding team members requires both a philosophy and technical know-how, and can have enormous impact on the odds of success.

Study Questions

1. Why is the team so important in the entrepreneurial process? How far can you get alone?

2. Describe what is meant by "team" philosophy and attitudes. Why are these important? How is this different from the quip "teamwork is everyone doing what I say."

3. What are the most critical questions an entrepreneur needs to consider in thinking through the team issues? What are some common pitfalls in team building? Can they be avoided or prepared for?

4. What are the critical rewards, compensation, and incentive issues in putting a team together? Why are these so crucial and difficult to manage?

5. How does the lead entrepreneur allocate stock ownership and options in the new venture? Who should get what ownership and why?

Mind Stretchers   *Have you considered?*

1. Think about a team in which you have been a member or a captain. What leadership and coaching principles characterized the most and least successful teams?

2. What is a team? What is its antithesis? Who is part of the team? Are suppliers and buyers included? What about competitors?

3. Even sole proprietors do not work alone. How do you see the fit between you and the team concept?

4. One expert insists that the only guarantee he can make to a start-up team is that in five years, at least one or two members will leave or be terminated. What causes this? Why will your team be different?

5. Ask five people who have worked with you in a team to give you feedback about your team-building skills.

EXERCISE   Rewards

The following exercise can help an entrepreneur devise a reward system for a new venture. In proceeding with the exercise, it is helpful to look at these issues from an investor's point of view and to imagine that the venture is in the process of seeking capital from an investor group to which a presentation was made several weeks ago and which is favourably impressed by the team and its plan for the new venture. Imagine then that this investor group would like a brief presentation (of 10 to 15 minutes) about how the team plans to reward its members and other key contributors.

Name: _____

Venture: _____

Date: _____

Part I

Part I is to be completed by each individual team member—*alone*.

Step 1   Indicate who will do what during the first year or two of your venture, what contributions each has made or will make to creating a business plan, the commitment and risk involved for each, and what unique critical skills, experience, contacts, and so forth, each brings to the venture. Try to be as specific as possible, and be sure to include yourself.

Team Member	Responsibility	Title	Contribution to Business Plan	Commitment and Risk	Unique/Critical Skills, etc.

Step 2   Indicate below the approximate salary and shares of stock (as a percent) each member should have upon closing the financing of your new venture.

Team Member	Salary	Shares of Stock (# and %)

Step 3   Indicate below what fringe benefits you believe the company should provide during the first year or two.

Team Member	Vacation	Holidays	Health/Life Insurance	Retirement Plan	Other

Step 4   List other key contributors, such as members of the board of directors, and indicate how they will be rewarded.

Name	Expertise/ Contribution	Salary	Shares of Stock (# and %)	Other

Part II

Part II involves meeting as a team to reach consensus on the responsibilities of each team member and how each will be rewarded. In addition to devising a reward system for the team and other key contributors, the team will examine how consensus was reached.

Step 1   Meet as a team and reach consensus on the above team issues and indicate the consensus solution below.

Responsibilities/Contributions				
Team Member	Responsibility	Contribution to Business Plan	Commitment and Risk	Unique/Critical Skills, etc.

Rewards		
Team Member	Salary	Shares of Stock (# and %)

Rewards (continued)						
Team Member	Title	Vacation	Holidays	Health/Life Insurance	Retirement Plan	Other

Step 2   Meet as a team and reach consensus on issues involving other key contributors and indicate the consensus solution below.

Name	Expertise/ Contribution	Salary	Shares of Stock (# and %)	Other

Step 3   Discuss as a team the following issues and indicate any important lessons and implications:

- What patterns emerged in the approaches taken by each team? What are the differences and similarities?

- How difficult or easy was it to reach agreement among team members? Did any issues bog down?

- If salaries or stock were equal for all team members, why was this so? What risks or problems might such an approach create?

- What criteria, either implicit or explicit, were used to arrive at a decision concerning salaries and stock? Why?

CASE   MATCHA MEN

Preparation Questions

1. Evaluate the composition of Brian and Mars' team? Who is part of their team and who is not?

2. Are there any elements or individuals missing from their team? What characteristics or attributes should they be looking for in order to complete their team?

3. What should Brian and Mars do next?

Tea is in Brian Takeda's blood. His childhood memories are dotted with scenes of tea ceremonies with his grandmother, and his family lineage includes more than one Japanese tea master. So in 2001, when an entrepreneurship professor at an Ontario business school challenged Takeda and fellow student Mars Koo to develop a business plan for a new venture, Takeda's thoughts turned immediately to tea. Having seen Japan's fast-growing green tea market firsthand, he felt that North America was an untapped well of opportunity. The pair built a business plan that envisioned a chain of premium, fresh-brewed loose-leaf tea retailers across Canada and the United States.

East Meets West

Their model was an elegant meeting of East and West: the high-end teas of the Japanese salon and the chado ceremony, transplanted into the accessible, high-volume retail model of the café. The concept followed the lead of chains like Starbucks and Second Cup, offering customers premium products, a space for social gathering, and a focus on customer education. As Starbucks reshaped consumer tastes a decade earlier by promoting superior arabica premium beans, so Infuze planned to cultivate a Canadian taste for premium tea, far beyond flat, forgettable supermarket varieties.

In 2002, shortly after graduation, the pair began planning for a Vancouver-area store to test their concept. Their parents thought enough of their plan that they put up the $200,000 they needed to get rolling. A short time later, Infuze Holdings had its first location—a spot in Vancouver's Gastown district, tucked amidst large hotels and shopping areas. Although cash was scarce, the company chose a high-end design group to create a sleek, Zen-inspired interior. It also hired a noted branding expert to develop a minimalist logo and packaging treatment. "It was expensive," Takeda admits. "But we always pledged to be the best at what we do, and to partner with those who are the best at what they do."

The obsession with quality extended to their products as well. When their first store opened in early 2003, Infuze offered a range of more than 50 freshly brewed loose-leaf teas. The selection included green, black, oolong and white teas, fruit and herb-infused teas, and iced tea. In each category, Infuze offered both premium and regular teas, distinguished by price (from $1.50 to $4 per cup) and by packaging. Introducing teas at super-premium price points was novel—at the time, even at chains such as Starbucks, tea was still served in bags at price levels ranging from $1.30 to $2.00. Yet Infuze's premium teas were exceptional, including rare Taiwanese oolongs and sen-

cha green teas. Even its lower-priced regular beverages used high-grade loose-leaf teas.

While Infuze had little money for marketing and promotion, its designs and products succeeded in attracting a discriminating and well-connected clientele. The founders, sensing an opportunity, began to leverage the knowledge and networks of those early customers. Within a month, Infuze-branded teas were being offered at a local boutique hotel and in tea-flavoured martinis at another stylish eatery.

Matcha

To further increase Infuze's prestige, Takeda and Koo gambled on a product that had almost no North American exposure—matcha. Matcha is a jade-green powder made by grinding shade-grown, hand-picked tea leaves and stems with granite wheels. It can be whisked with hot water for a frothy tea drink or used in blended drinks and baked goods. Matcha contains an amino acid called theanine, which is reputed to offer its users an energy boost similar to caffeine—but without causing the jitters. This tea is perhaps the world's best, and Infuze hoped that offering it would differentiate its menu and help encourage a culture of tea connoisseurship. It's also pricey. Shortly after its first store opened, Infuze launched its matcha-based drinks at prices ranging from $3.50 for a whisked cup of matcha tea to $5 for a matcha smoothie.

It wasn't long before good luck gave Takeda and Koo a boost. It turned out that many of their first customers were from the nearby offices of The Vancouver Sun. The store's uniqueness, coupled with the founders' penchant for giving customers lessons on their teas' history, cultivation, health benefits and flavour profiles, led to some immediate and favourable press coverage. The attention grew as the founders exploited their story. The media treated matcha as a made-in-Vancouver success, playing up Takeda's family history and the heresy of shilling tea in Starbucks country. Coverage continued to spread. "We've never sent out a press release," says Takeda. "We've never cold-called an editor."

Infuze had other advantages. Most significant was its exclusive distribution rights to matcha in Vancouver. In the company's planning stages, the founders secured a commitment from Aiya Corp. of Japan, the market leader in ceremonial green tea production. Side stepping usual distribution channels, Aiya pledged to offer just-in-time delivery of its high-end teas, which could otherwise be difficult to source and procure. Infuze was offered exclusivity in their area, giving its tea rooms a virtual monopoly on the green powder.

This case was written by Lukas Neville , Ph.D. student, Queen's School of Business, and Professor Elspeth J. Murray, CIBC Teaching Fellow in Entrepreneurship, Queen's School of Business, Queen's University. This case was developed with the support of the CIBC Curriculum Development Fund at the Queen's Centre for Business Venturing, for purposes of classroom discussion.

Before long, Infuze's business took a turn. Takeda and Koo knew that their pair of tea houses was too small to drive and sustain mainstream consumer demand for matcha alone. So even though their original business plan identified other retailers as a serious competitive threat, the duo found themselves supplying an increasing number of those same competitors with matcha powder. The biggest was a 40-store regional chain, which Takeda and Koo helped to develop its own matcha latte and "matcha chillo" drinks. This deal put matcha drinks into a competitor's store not five minutes away from one of their own.

Since Infuze was young, it was difficult for the founders to quantify the effects of this change in tactics—but they felt that wholesaling and retail beverage sales seemed to form a virtuous circle for the company. "Sure, we gave up being the only place in town for matcha," says Takeda. "But the more prevalent it was, the more popular it became. We were making money whether it was being sold wholesale or through our store, so it wasn't in our interests to clutch onto exclusivity on the retail side." With the chain's aggressive PR campaign, matcha grabbed national coverage. In less than six months, Infuze's bulk sales increased from 5 percent to 20 percent of gross revenue.

Even then, however, wholesale distribution was still a sideline. That changed after a meeting in late 2004. Takeda and Koo were invited to San Francisco to meet with senior decision-makers at a 500-location chain of smoothie stores. The smoothie giant was enthralled with matcha and was prepared to order it in bulk from Infuze in unprecedented volumes. It was also ready to move fast. "Product development in the beverage industry can be a year-long cycle," Takeda says. "They were ready to push it forward in three months."

But the new deal was fraught with peril. "There was nothing to stop our client from dealing with Aiya directly," said Takeda. "We were two guys in Vancouver working as middlemen between two massive corporations." And even if they could continue working with the client directly, Infuze stood to gain only a very modest markup on the cost of the bulk matcha—hardly commensurate with the resources Infuze was investing to close the deal.

By this time, Infuze had done a second round of financing. And Takeda and Koo's worries were echoed by their new investors, who insisted that Infuze's relationship with Aiya needed retooling. Infuze's management took their business case to Aiya: Infuze's bulk business was growing quickly, they had a 500-location chain waiting in the wings, but the present structure of the deal left Infuze no incentive for continuing to pursue bulk sales. Aiya responded with a "working understanding." Says Takeda: "Aiya basically promised me that we would find a fair way to share the risks and rewards of growing the matcha market. But they wouldn't commit to any details."

Aiya had a corporate culture that valued deliberation, and negotiations plodded on for months. Yet Infuze was still able to help its big, fast-moving client debut its matcha smoothie. The arrangement was held together by the good faith of Infuze's founders and two equity investments from Aiya as evidence of its commitment. Takeda, Koo, and their staff joined Aiya at trade fairs and conventions. Takeda and Koo were used to conveying matcha's value proposition clearly and concisely. "Behind the counter at Infuze, you've got 20 seconds of the customer's attention," Takeda says. They used their 20-second elevator pitch at the trade shows they attended to considerable effect. "We were getting 10 business cards for every one that Aiya's staff were getting."

New Deal

In May 2005, Aiya finally returned with a new deal for Infuze. The offer involved a five-year term, entitling Infuze to 33.3 percent of its gross margin for all sales to new or expanded Canadian and American accounts. Infuze, as a non-exclusive supplier and marketer, would be required to make "reasonable commercial efforts" to expand its own chain of branded tea houses, sell Aiya tea in its tea houses, and maximize North American sales.

The night they received Aiya's memorandum of understanding, Takeda and Koo stayed up late digesting its contents. Under its terms, Aiya and Infuze would share the cost of direct marketing and employees. Aiya would cover two-thirds of the costs and Infuze the remaining third. Infuze's spending would be subsidized by an injection of $250,000 from Aiya, in exchange for a modest share of equity. "We were ecstatic. It was an unbelievable deal," says Takeda. "When we first talked with Aiya in January, they had been talking about performance milestones, contingent on growth levels. By the time we had a written deal, there were no performance requirements." The trust built during the two companies' long courtship allowed Aiya to feel comfortable with a flexible contract free of formal obligations beyond a commitment to revenue-sharing.

But for all their enthusiasm, Takeda and Koo were daunted by the road that lay ahead: Would Infuze miss its retail opportunity by moving into wholesale? What would it need to do to switch from retail to wholesaling? And how were two guys in Vancouver going to make Americans clamour for matcha and bring industry giants to their doorstep? "It was going to be a 180-degree turnaround in the direction of our business. And we needed strategy on the fly, in real time," says Takeda.

Infuze's founders were worn out and overwhelmed. They had been successful at retailing. Their first experiments in wholesaling had been extraordinarily promising. But were they ready to switch gears mid-race?

7

ETHICAL DECISION MAKING AND THE ENTREPRENEUR

A creative man is motivated by the desire to achieve, not by the desire to beat others.

Ayn Rand

Upon completion of this chapter, you will be able to:

1. Make decisions involving ethical issues and analyze your reasons for doing so.

2. Discuss with others the ethical implications of the decisions you make and identify how they might affect you, your partners, your customers, and your competitors.

3. Recognize the importance of high ethical standards in an entrepreneurial career.

OVERVIEW OF ETHICS

Most successful entrepreneurs believe that high ethical standards and integrity are exceptionally important to long-term success. For example, a study of 128 presidents/ founders attending the Harvard Business School's Owner/President Management program were asked to name the most critical concepts, skills, and know-how for success at their companies at the time and what they would be in five years. Seventy-two percent stated that high ethical standards were the single most important factor in long-term success. A study of 1,700 MBA students from the U.S., Canada, and the U.K. by the Aspen Institute found that MBA students are concerned that their schools are not doing enough to prepare them for ethical dilemmas they may face in the business world.[1] Their concern and awareness is not surprising given the recent spate of corporate scandals. Ethical lapses like those of executives at Ravelston Corporation and Hollinger International, for example, erode the confidence in business activity at all levels. It should also be noted that business students have a marked propensity to cheat. In a study of 5,331 students in the U.S. and Canada, 56 percent of MBA students indicated that they had cheated in the past year.[2] It has been reported that 73 percent of university students admitted to "serious cheating incidents" on written work while in high school.[3] "A recent University of Guelph study has discovered that more than half the student body in Canada is cheating its way through school."[4] And research has shown that those who "engage in dishonest behaviour in their college classes were more likely to engage in dishonest behaviour on the job."[5] The Internet has made both plagiarism and catching offenders easier. Technology has aided those aspiring to break the rules; text messaging during exams and camera phones copying an exam are common tactics. Ryerson University had to deal with a situation where students were working on solutions via Facebook.[6] Some contend that much blame should be placed on the instructors and academic administrators who enable or do not properly handle dishonesty.

An article appearing in the *Journal of Business Ethics* finds that with regard to moral principles in business, "the argument is about values: are they universal or emergent? In entrepreneurship, it is about opportunities—are they discovered or constructed?" The authors of the article conclude that ethics and entrepreneurship are quite similar; both require a decision maker who has the preparation for the unexpected.[7] Entrepreneurship carries ethical challenges beyond those that may confront a manager in an established organization. While entrepreneurs may be praised as innovators contributing to society by developing new products, generating employment opportunities, and opening further possibilities—entrepreneurs are often bound through the dynamic value creation process alone and without precedent. On the other hand, the manager in an established corporation has guidance from colleagues, rules/regulations, and company culture to direct him or her through ethical obstacles.[8] The assertion follows that the tenacity to succeed may push the entrepreneur to bend his or her own personal values.[9]

In the search for profits, quite often, moral dilemmas enter the mix. Unethical behaviour is found among a range of stakeholders in the business world.[10] Financial pressures, short-term tactics, and heightened competition push entrepreneurs to do the 'wrong things,' just as they do others—including health care providers and educators. Richard Hudson of Mount Allison University and Roger Wehrell of Saint Francis Xavier University found that those pursuing a socially responsible cause often experience inferior profit margins whereas those putting profits first may be forced to push other considerations aside.[11] It becomes easier to have a "voice" where a fledgling enterprise is concerned; how much harm can you do by protesting Air Canada's corporate activity by boycotting their services or selling your few shares?

A provocative article in the *Harvard Business Review* asserted that the ethics of business were not those of society but rather those of the poker game.[12] The author of the article argued, "Most businessmen are not indifferent to ethics in their private lives, everyone will agree. My point is that in their office lives they cease to be private citizens; they become game players who must be guided by a somewhat different set of ethical standards." The author further argued that personal ethics and business ethics are often not in harmony, and by negotiation or compromise, a resolution must be reached. The article provoked a storm of response. The question remains, how are businesspeople supposed to operate in this capitalist system?

One individual has shown that hard work, determination, and high ethical standards are the proper response. Prem Watsa grew up in Hyderabad, India, and after earning a chemical engineering degree at the Indian Institute of Technology moved to Canada to study where he worked nights in order to support himself. Watsa founded Fairfax Financial Holdings, which posted over US$1.5 billion in profits for 2008. Some have labelled Prem Watsa the "Canadian Warren Buffet" and the *Globe and Mail* awarded him 2008's CEO of the Year, noting his company's success in the face of economic downturn. In challenging times, Watsa points out "a good university education is more important than ever." He has recently become Chancellor of the University of Waterloo and aims to "foster a new generation of entrepreneurs." His words of wisdom: "Stay positive and look at adversity as opportunity. Integrity, a solid work ethic and the right attitude are essential tools for tomorrow's business leaders."[13]

In addition, the law, which one might expect to be black and white, is full of thorny issues. Laws not only have authority but also limitations. Laws are made with forethought and with the deliberate purpose of ensuring justice. They are, therefore, ethical in intent and deserve respect. However, laws are made in legislatures, not in heaven. They do not anticipate new conditions; they do not always have the effect they were intended to have;

they sometimes conflict with one another; and they are, as they stand, incapable of making judgments where multiple ethical considerations hang in the balance or seem actually to war with one another. Thus, from the beginnings of recorded history in Egypt and the Middle East, a code of laws was always accompanied by a human interpreter of laws, a judge, to decide when breaking the letter of the law did not violate the spirit or situation that the law was intended to cover.

ETHICAL STEREOTYPES

The 1990s ushered in the "New Era of Entrepreneurship" worldwide. Canada, now as in the past, is seen as providing an inviting and nurturing climate for those wishing to start their own enterprises and reap the rewards. In part, this is because the provincial and federal governments have encouraged an atmosphere under which market forces, private initiative, and individual responsibility and freedom can flourish. But as has been pointed out an entrepreneur need not be a decent and law-abiding individual, a criminal can be regarded as enterprising.[14] Just as surely as there is illegal business activity, there is immoral entrepreneurship. A study published by the Canadian Council for Small Business and Entrepreneurship in 2009 compared the legitimate entrepreneur with the illegitimate entrepreneur. Whether an entrepreneur adds value to society or extracts value from society, he or she will utilize similar enterprising skills and managerial capabilities.[15]

Laws, enacted in response to society's changing perceptions of what constitutes ethical business practices, have had the desirable effect of encouraging those in many industries to develop codes of ethics—in large part because they wished to set their own rules, rather than to have rules imposed on them.

As the ethical climate of business has changed, so has the image of the entrepreneur. Most 'rags to riches' stories personify the good stereotype. Entrepreneurs doing business in the unfettered economic climate of the 19th century—the era of the robber barons, where acts of industrial sabotage were common—represent the ruthless stereotype. The exploitation of immigrant labour to build the railroads leaves an unsavoury aftertaste for today's more ethically conscious entrepreneurs.

Yet, thoughtful historians of entrepreneurship will also recall that regardless of standards by which they are judged or of the motivations attributed to them, 'great' entrepreneurs gave back to society with libraries, concert halls, and charitable foundations. Critics are much more inclined to examine and dissect the ethical behaviour of the commercial sector, rather than that of the clergy, or even of academia itself. In many comparisons, the behaviour of business moguls would look quite pure.

A touch of suspicion still tinges entrepreneurial activity, and the word *entrepreneur* may still connote to some a person who belongs to a ruthless, scheming group. In 1975, *Time* suggested that a businessman might make the best-qualified candidate for U.S. president but noted the "deep-rooted American suspicion of businessmen's motives."[16] "Anyone with previous business experience becomes immediately suspect. Certain segments think he can't make a decision in the public interest."[17] However, in 1988, the prophecy of *Time* magazine was fulfilled when George Bush, an oil entrepreneur, was elected president of the United States, and later reinforced in 2000 when his son George W. Bush, a Harvard MBA, became president. Canada has largely avoided having business leaders go into politics. In Europe, however, it is common for leaders from industry to go into politics or vice-versa. But Canada remains critical of conflicts of interest and mixed-motives (witness investigations of Brian Mulroney and Jean Chrétien).

Jeremy Hall of the University of Calgary and Philip Rosson of Dalhousie University explored entrepreneurial opportunities and ethical dilemmas. Their study divides entrepreneurship into three types: productive, unproductive, and destructive (criminal).[18] They observe that technological turbulence in particular, which creates opportunities for the newcomer and challenges incumbents as well as established regulations, may generate ethical dilemmas. From photocopier to file-sharing, technology can push the boundaries of the rules of the game. A key challenge is to be prepared for the inevitable confrontations an entrepreneur will encounter.

SHOULD ETHICS BE TAUGHT?

Just as recent years have ushered in a new era of worldwide entrepreneurship, the landscape of business ethics has redefined itself. According to Andrew Stark of the University of Toronto:

> Advocates of the new business ethics can be identified by their acceptance of two fundamental principles. While they agree with their colleagues that ethics and interest can conflict, they take that observation as the starting point, not the ending point, of an ethicist's analytical task. . . . Second, the new perspective reflects an awareness and acceptance of the messy work of mixed motives.[19]

The challenge facing this new group of business ethicists is to bridge the gap between the moral philosophers and the managers. The business ethicists talk of "moderation, pragmatism, minimalism"[20] in their attempt to "converse with real managers in a language relevant to the world they inhabit and the problems they face."[21] With this focus on the practical side of decision making, courses on ethics can be useful to entrepreneurs and all managers.

Ethics Can and Should Be Taught

Derek Bok, former president of Harvard University, argues that ethics can and should be taught by educational institutions and that this teaching is both necessary and of value:

> Precisely because its community is so diverse, set in a society so divided and confused over its values, a university that pays little attention to moral development may find that many of its students grow bewildered, convinced that ethical dilemmas are simply matters of personal opinion beyond external judgment or careful analysis.[22]

Brenda Zimmerman of York University points out that 20 years ago, doing charitable work was an extra, something on the side, but today's MBAs "want to see much greater integration between their causes and the way they make money."[23] Many are choosing a career path where the returns are not measured entirely by salary. Tal Dehtiar and Michael Brown founded MBAs Without Borders while at McMaster University with the idea that there has to be another use for all their great business knowledge.[24] The University of Toronto has NeXus—"a non-profit management consulting service established to help non-profit organizations and social enterprises build capacity, explore new revenue streams, and broaden their networks for financial and community support."[25] Ann Armstrong of the University of Toronto explains that with social entrepreneurship, "if you had to choose between the social and economic outcome, you'd pick the social."[26] It brings to altruistic ventures "the ruthless efficiency of traditional business—something typically missing from charities, non-profits, and government aid agencies. "The ratio of social benefit to invested dollar is often not very good with those organizations," according to Dirk Matten of York University. Canadian Jeff Skoll, the first president of eBay, is a big supporter of social enterprises. His Skoll Foundation, which started with about US$1 billion has backed numerous social enterprises. Skoll championed the creation of the eBay foundation, which is a philanthropic program supporting children, education, volunteerism, economic and community revitalization, as well as the natural environment.

John Shad, a former chairman of the New York Stock Exchange, gave more than $20 million to the Harvard Business School to include ethics in the MBA curriculum. J. Gregory Dees, an ethics professor at Duke University, stresses that the "primary objective of such courses is to get people thinking about issues that are easy to avoid. . . . What we want people to leave with is a commitment to raising these issues in other settings, other courses, and on the job, with [an acceptable] comfort level in doing so."[27]

In addition, we have recently seen the emergence of numerous courses on socially responsible behaviour, social entrepreneurship, and on the role of environmentally sustainable business practices. A study published in 2009 in *Business Ethics* showed that personal values of entrepreneurs translated positively into economic performance of their ventures. Socially responsible business practices towards employees, customers, and society benefited the bottom line.[28]

Integrity as Governing Ethic

Lynn Paine, a specialist in management ethics, distinguishes among avoiding legal sanctions, compliance, and the more robust standard of integrity.

> From the perspective of integrity, the task of ethics management is to define and give life to an organization's guiding values, to create an environment that supports ethically sound behavior, and to instill a sense of shared accountability among employees.[29]

Paine goes on to characterize the hallmarks of an effective integrity strategy and the strategies for ethics management (see Exhibit 7.1). Clearly, the call for ethical strategies and practices is being heard. That is good news for our society, our economy, and you!

Entrepreneurs' Perspectives

Most entrepreneurs also believe ethics should be taught. In the research project previously mentioned, entrepreneurs and chief executive officers attending a management program at the Harvard Business School were asked the question: Is there a role for ethics in business education for entrepreneurs? Of those responding, 72 percent said ethics can and should be taught as part of the curriculum. (Only 20 percent said it should not, and two respondents were not sure.)

The most prominently cited reason for including ethics was that ethical behaviour is at the core of long-term business success, because it provides the glue that binds enduring successful business and personal relationships together. In addition, the responses reflected a serious and thoughtful awareness of the fragile but vital role of ethics in entrepreneurial attainment and of the long-term consequences of ethical behaviour for a business. Typical comments were:

EXHIBIT 7.1   Strategies for Ethics Management

Characteristics of Compliance Strategy		Characteristics of Integrity Strategy	
Ethos	Conformity with externally imposed standards	**Ethos**	Self-governance according to chosen standards
Objective	Prevent criminal misconduct	**Objective**	Stable responsible conduct
Leadership	Lawyer driven	**Leadership**	Management driven with aid of lawyers, HR, others
Methods	Education, reduced discretion, auditing and controls, penalties	**Methods**	Education, leadership, accountability, organizational systems and decision processes, auditing and controls, penalties
Behavioural Assumptions	Autonomous beings guided by material self-interest	**Behavioural Assumptions**	Social beings guided by material self-interest, values, ideals, peers
Implementation of Compliance Strategy		**Implementation of Integrity Strategy**	
Standards	Criminal and regulatory law	**Standards**	Company values and aspirations, social obligations, including law
Staffing	Lawyers	**Staffing**	Executives and managers with lawyers, others
Activities	Develop compliance standards, train, and communicate	**Activities**	Lead development of company values and standards; Train and communicate; Integrate into company systems; Provide guidance and consultation; Assess values performance; Identify and resolve problems; Oversee compliance activities
Education	Compliance standards and system	**Education**	Decision making and values; Compliance standards and system

Source: Lynn Sharp Paine, "Managing for Organizational Integrity," *Harvard Business Review* 72, no. 2 (1994): 113. Copyright © by the Harvard Business School Publishing Corporation; all rights reserved.

- If the free enterprise system is to survive, the business schools better start paying attention to teaching ethics. They should know that business is built on trust, which depends upon honesty and sincerity.
- If our society is going to move forward, it won't be based on how much money is accumulated in any one person or group. Our society will move forward when all people are treated fairly—that's my simple definition of ethics. I know of several managers, presidents, etc., who you would not want to get between them and their wallets or ambitions.
- In my experience the business world is by and large the most ethical and law-abiding part of our society.
- Ethics should be addressed, considered, and thoroughly examined; it should be an inherent part of each class and course. . .; instead of crusading with ethics, it is much more effective to make high ethics an inherent part of business—and it is.

However, these views were not universally held. One entrepreneur who helped to found a large company with international operations warned: "For God's sake, don't forget that 90 percent of the businessman's efforts consist of just plain hard work." Another argument holds that certain conditions make it is easier to be ethical, perhaps even a luxury. "If you've got a job and a pension, it's a lot easier to buy organic foods." Whereas, for the poor and unemployed—survival may be the primary driver; taking the higher ground and worrying about the planet may not be a primary concern.[30]

There is also some cynicism. The 40-year-old head of a real estate and construction firm with 300 employees and $75 million in annual sales said: "There is so much hypocrisy in today's world that even totally ethical behaviour is questioned since many people think it is some new negotiating technique."

It would be unfortunate if the entrepreneur did not realize his or her potential for combining action with ethical purpose because of the suspicion that the two are unrelated or inimical. There is no reason they need be considered generically opposed. Nevertheless, in analyzing ethics, the individual can expect no substitute for his or her own effort and intelligence.

THORNY ISSUES FOR ENTREPRENEURS

Although the majority of entrepreneurs take ethics seriously, researchers in this area are still responding to David McClelland's call for inquiry: "We do not know at the present time what makes an entrepreneur more or less ethical in his dealings, but obviously there are few problems of greater importance for future research."[31] Exhibit 7.2 outlines topics for consideration. Clearly, opportunities for further research exist.

Action under Pressure

An entrepreneur will have to act on issues under pressure of time and when struggling for survival. In addition, the entrepreneur will most likely decide ethical questions that involve obligations on many sides—to customers, employees, shareholders, family, partners, himself, or a combination of these. Walking the tightrope and balancing common sense with an ethical framework is precarious.

To cope with the inevitable conflicts, an entrepreneur should develop an awareness of his or her own explicit and implicit ethical beliefs, those of his or her team and investors, and those of the milieu within which the company competes for survival. As the successful entrepreneurs quoted above believe, in the long run, succumbing to the temptations of situational ethics will, in all likelihood, result in a tumble into the quicksand, not a safety net—just ask executives at Nortel and Bre-X, or Garth Drabinsky and Myron Gottlieb, co-founders of the theatre production company Livent.

An appreciation of this state of affairs is succinctly stated by Fred Allen, chairman and president of Pitney-Bowes:

EXHIBIT 7.2   Selected Ethical Dilemmas of Entrepreneurial Management

Dilemma: Elements	Issues That May Arise
Promoter: Entrepreneurial euphoria Impression management Pragmatic versus moral considerations	What does honesty mean when promoting an innovation? Does it require complete disclosure of the risks and uncertainties? Does it require a dispassionate analysis of the situation, with equal time given to the downside as well as the upside? What sorts of influence tactics cross the line from encouragement and inducement to manipulation and coercion?
Relationship: Conflicts of interest and roles Transactional ethics Guerrilla tactics	Tension between perceived obligations and moral expectations. Changes in roles and relationships: pre- versus post-venture status. Decisions based on affiliative concerns rather than on task-based concerns. Transition from a trust-based work environment to one that is more controlled.
Innovator: "Frankenstein's problem" New types of ethical problems Ethic of change	Side effects and negative externalities force a social reconsideration of norms and values. Heightened concern about the future impact of unknown harms. Who is responsible for the assessment of risk? Inventor? Government? Market? Breaking down traditions and creating new models.
Other dilemmas: Finders-keepers ethic Conflict between personal values and business goals Unsavory business practices	Is there a fair way to divide profits when they are the result of cooperative efforts? Should the entrepreneur take all the gains that are not explicitly contracted away? Managing an intimate connection between personal choices and professional decisions. Coping with ethical pressures with creative solutions and integrity. Seeking industry recognition while not giving into peer pressure to conform.

Source: J. Gregory Dees and Jennifer A. Starr, "Entrepreneurship Through an Ethical Lens," in *The State of the Art of Entrepreneurship*, Donald L. Sexton and John D. Kasarda, eds. (Boston, MA: PWS-Kent Publishing Company, 1992).

As businessmen we must learn to weigh short-term interests against long-term possibilities. We must learn to sacrifice what is immediate, what is expedient, if the moral price is too high. What we stand to gain is precious little compared to what we can ultimately lose.[32]

Stumbles, Tumbles, and Falls from Grace

NORTEL[33]

Quick shake-ups at the top. Jean Monty was CEO from 1993 to 1997; John Roth from 1997 to 2001, during which time he lobbied the authorities for lower taxes and threatened to move Nortel to the United States, market capitalization plummeted from $398 billion to $5 billion, 60,000 employees were laid off and Roth cashed in $135 million in stock options. Frank Dunn was CEO from 2001 to 2004 when he was fired with other financial executives; Dunn came under investigation by the U.S. Securities and Exchange Commission as well as the Ontario Securities Commission, and was arrested by the RCMP in mid-2008. U.S. Admiral William Owens took the helm from 2004 to 2005 to right the sinking ship, and then Mike Zafirovski took over and steered Nortel into bankruptcy in 2009 amid calls for a new captain!

BRE-X[34]

Smoke and mirrors, no substance. Bre-X was a Canadian mining company that had a short stratospheric economic rise on prospects of discovering gold. Its stock soared from just about nothing to $285 per share and a market capitalization of $6 billion. The discovery of gold was found to be a hoax and key players went into hiding. After a fleeting tumultuous ride, investors were left holding worthless paper.

LIVENT[35,36,37]

Lights, curtain, legal action. Garth Drabinsky and Myron Gottlieb wrestled their favourite division away from Cineplex Odeon. They took a business unit that included the Pantages Theatre in Toronto and *The Phantom of the Opera*. The company went public on the TSX and within a few years and under heavy financial losses, Drabinsky and Gottlieb were escorted by security guards out the door. Live Entertainment Corporation of Canada, Inc. (Livent) subsequently filed a $225-million lawsuit against the pair. Livent went bankrupt as the RCMP launched a criminal investigation and U.S. and Canadian securities regulators began investigating the company's books. Drabinsky and Gottlieb were indicted in a New York courtroom for which they failed to appear and therefore had fugitive arrest warrants entered against them. More recently, Canadian police charged four Livent senior executives with fraud totalling nearly half a billion dollars. The Supreme Court of Canada in 2009 denied Drabinsky and Gottlieb's appeal for their civil case. In their criminal case both were convicted on two counts of fraud and one count of uttering forged documents.

Sources: "The Good, The Bad & The Ugly," *Canadian Business*, March 30, 2009; "Theatre Impresario Awaiting Sentencing on Fraud, Forgery," *CBC news*, May 14, 2009; Shannon Kari, "Months, Years Before Livent Duo Face Any Prison Time," *Financial Post*, March 25, 2009; Barbara Shecter, "Livent Dazzled Audiences, Investors While Taking on Hollywood," *Financial Post*, May 3, 2009.

Different Views

Different reactions to what is ethical may explain why some aspects of venture creation go wrong, both during start-up and in the heat of the battle, for no apparent reason. Innumerable examples can be cited to illustrate that broken partnerships often can be traced to apparent differences in the personal ethics among the members of a management team. So, too, with investors. While the experienced venture capital investor seeks entrepreneurs with a reputation for integrity, honesty, and ethical behaviour, the definition is necessarily subjective and depends in part on the beliefs of the investor himself and in part on the prevailing ethical climate in the industry sector in which the venture is involved.

Business ethics has evolved and continues to change over time. Acceptable behaviour changes, sometimes quite quickly. In the present era of transparency, Mark Wexler of Simon Fraser University observes that as a firm grows in size, "you need a lot more internal vigilance and self-auditing," while a smaller enterprise can be run as an extension of the leader's personality.[38]

Problems of Law

For entrepreneurs, situations where one law directly conflicts with another are increasingly frequent. For example, a small-business investment company got in serious financial trouble. The federal authorities stated the company should begin to liquidate its investments, because it would otherwise be in defiance of its agreement with them. However, the securities regulatory authorities stated that this liquidation would constitute unfair treatment of stockholders, due to resulting imbalance in their portfolios. After a year and a half of agonizing negotiation, the company was able to satisfy all the parties, but compromises had to be made on all sides.

Legal demands involve labour practices that mandate particular treatment of aboriginal peoples, members of visible minorities, women, and persons with disabilities. In addition, the Canadian government frequently has a campaign to promote the hiring of immigrants. And, not all laws apply to all businesses, the Employment Equity Act and Employment Equity Regulations cover 400 private sector employers and Crown corporations. These laws are based on valid ethical intent, but the administration and interpretation of them is no simple matter. Recently a number of individuals have been accused of fraudulently obtaining Aboriginal status solely to receive government contracts.

Further, unlike international laws governing commercial airline transportation, there is no international code of business ethics. When doing business abroad, entrepreneurs may find that those with whom they wish to do business have little in common with them—no common language, no common historical context for conducting business, and no common set of ethical beliefs about right and wrong and everything in between. For example, in Canada, bribing a high official to obtain a favour is considered both ethically and legally unacceptable; in many parts of the world, it is the only way to get things done. What we see as a bribe, those in other parts of the world see as a tip, like what you might give the headwaiter at a fancy restaurant for a good table.

"When in Rome" is one approach to this problem. Consulting a lawyer with expertise in international business before doing anything is another. Assuming that the object of an entrepreneur's international business venture is to make money, he or she needs to figure out some way that is legally tolerable under the laws that do apply and that is ethically tolerable personally.

Examples of the Ends-and-Means Issue

A central question in any ethical discussion concerns the extent to which a noble end may justify ignoble means—or whether using unethical means for assumed ethical ends may subvert the aim in some way. As an example of a noble end, consider the case of a university agricultural extension service whose goal was to aid small farmers to increase their crop productivity. The end was economically constructive and profit oriented only in the sense that the farmers might prosper from better crop yields. However, to continue being funded, the extension service was required to provide predictions of the annual increase in crop yield it could achieve, estimates it could not provide at the required level of specificity. Further, unless it could show substantial increases in crop yields, its funding might be heavily reduced. In this case, the extension service decided, if need be, to fudge the figures because it was felt that even though the presentation of overly optimistic predictions was unethical, the objectives of those running the organization were highly ethical and even the unethical aspects could be condoned within the context of the inability of the various groups involved to speak each other's language clearly. The funding source finally backed down in its demand, ameliorating the immediate problem. But if it had not, the danger existed that the individuals in this organization, altruistic though their intentions were, would begin to think that falsification was the norm and would forget that actions that run contrary to one's ethical feelings gradually would build a debilitating cynicism.

Another example is given in the case of a merger of a small rental-service business with a midsize conglomerate, where a law's intent was in direct opposition to what would occur if the law were enforced literally. In this case, a partner in the rental firm became involved in a severe automobile accident and suffered multiple injuries shortly before the merger and was seemingly unable to return to work. The partner also knew that the outlook for his health in the immediate future was unpredictable. For the sake of his family, he was eager to seek some of the stock acquired in the merger and make a large portion of his assets liquid. However, federal law does not allow quick profit-taking from mergers and therefore did not allow such a sale. The partner consulted the president and officers of the larger company, and they acquiesced in his plans to sell portions of his stock and stated their conviction that no adverse effect on the stock would result. Still unsure, the man then checked with his lawyer and found that the federal law in question had almost never been prosecuted. Having ascertained the risk and having probed the rationale of the law as it applied to his case, the man then sold some of the stock acquired in the merger to provide security for his family in the possible event of his incapacitation or death. Although he subsequently recovered completely, this could not have been foreseen.

In this instance, the partner decided that a consideration of the intrinsic purpose of the law allowed him to act as he did. In addition, he made as thorough a check as possible of the risks involved in his action. He was not satisfied with the decision he made, but he believed it was the best he could do at the time. One can see in this example the enormous ethical tugs-of-war that go with the territory of entrepreneurship.

An Example of Integrity

The complicated nature of entrepreneurial decisions also is illustrated in the following example. At age 27, an entrepreneur joined a new computer software firm with sales of $1.5 million as vice president of international marketing of a new division. His principal goal was to establish profitable distribution for the company's products in the major industrialized nations. Stock incentives and a highly leveraged bonus plan placed clear emphasis on profitability, rather than on volume. In one European country, the choice of distributors was narrowed to 1 from a field of more than 20. The potential distributor was a top firm, with an excellent track record and management, and the chemistry was right. In fact, the distributor was so eager to do business with the entrepreneur's company that it was willing to accept a 10-percent commission, rather than the normal 15-percent royalty. The other terms of the deal were acceptable to both parties. In this actual case, the young vice president decided to give the distributor the full 15-percent commission, even though it would have settled for less. This approach was apparently quite successful because, in five years, this international division grew from zero to $18 million in very profitable sales, and a large firm acquired the venture for $80 million. In describing his reasoning, the entrepreneur said his main goal was to create a sense of long-term integrity. He said further:

> I knew what it would take for them to succeed in gaining the kind of market penetration we were after. I also knew that the economics of their business definitely needed the larger margins from the 15 percent, rather than the smaller royalty. So I figured that if I offered them the full royalty, they would realize I was on their side, and that would create such goodwill that when we did have some serious problems down the road—and you always have them—then we would be able to work together to solve them. And that's exactly what happened. If I had exploited their eagerness to be our distributor, then it only would have come back to haunt me later on.

ETHICS REDUX

The following statements are often made, even by practising entrepreneurs: How can we think about ethics when we haven't enough time even to think about running our venture? Entrepreneurs are doers, not thinkers—and ethics is too abstract a concept to have any bearing on business realities. When you're struggling to survive, you're not worried about the means you use—you're fighting for one thing: survival.

However, the contemplation of ethical behaviour is not unlike poetry—emotion recollected in tranquillity. This chapter is intended to provide one such tranquil opportunity.

Through the decisions actually made, or not made, an individual becomes more aware of his or her own value system and how making ethical decisions can be affected by the climate in which these decisions are made. However, in the online exercise for this chapter, participants are asked only to answer questions. They are not asked to carry out an action. Between intent and action lies a large gap, which can be filled only by confronting and working through a number of ambiguous situations. Visit www.mcgrawhill.ca/olc/timmons to try the exercise and test your ethical mettle.

Chapter Summary

1. The majority of CEOs, investors, and entrepreneurs believe that a high ethical standard is the most important factor in long-term success.
2. Historically, ethical stereotypes of businesspeople ranged widely, and today the old perceptions have given way to a more aware and accepting notion of the messy work of ethical decisions.
3. Most business schools today have incorporated ethical issues into their curricula.
4. Entrepreneurs can rarely, if ever, finish a day without facing at least one or two ethical issues.
5. Ethical dilemmas challenge entrepreneurs at the most crucial moments of survival.

Study Questions

1. Many professional exams (e.g., CA, CMA, CFA) test ethics. Can ethics be tested on paper? Actual behaviour isn't being tested, so wouldn't an unethical person be able to get ethics questions correct just as likely as a truly ethical person?
2. What are the most thorny ethical dilemmas that entrepreneurs face, and why?
3. Describe an actual example of how and why taking a high ethical ground results in a good decision for business.

Mind Stretchers *Have you considered?*

1. How would you define your own ethics?
2. What was the toughest ethical decision you have faced? How did you handle it, and why? What did you learn?
3. How do you personally determine whether someone is ethical or not?
4. How would you describe the ethics of the prime minister of Canada? Would these ethics be acceptable to you from an investor, a partner, a spouse? Are the ethics of elected leaders different from those in the private sector, such as the CEO of a chartered bank or the CEO of a multinational oil company?

EXERCISE Ethics

First Part

Make decisions in the following situations.

You will not have all the background information on each situation; instead, you should make whatever assumptions you feel you would make if you were actually confronted with the decision choices described. Select the decision choice that most closely represents the decision you feel you would make personally. You should choose decision choices even though you can envision other creative solutions that were not included in the exercise.

Situation 1. You are taking a very difficult chemistry course, which you must pass to maintain your scholarship and to avoid damaging your application for graduate school. Chemistry is not your strong suit, and because of a just-below-failing average in the course, you must receive a grade of 90 or better on the final exam, which is two days away. A janitor who is aware of your plight informs you that he found the master stencil for the chemistry final in a trash barrel and saved it. He will make it available to you for a price, which is high but which you could afford. What would you do?

_____ (a) I would tell the janitor thanks, but no thanks.

_____ (b) I would report the janitor to the proper officials.

_____ (c) I would buy the exam and keep it to myself.

_____ (d) I would not buy the exam myself, but I would let some of my friends, who are also flunking the course, know that it is available.

Situation 2. You have been working on some complex analytical data for two days now. It seems that each time you think you have them completed, your boss shows up with a new assumption or another what-if question. If you only had a copy of a new software program for your personal computer, you could plug in the new assumptions and revise the estimates with ease. Then a colleague offers to let you make a copy of some software that is copyrighted. What would you do?

_____ (a) I would readily accept my friend's generous offer and make a copy of the software.

_____ (b) I would decline to copy it and plug away manually on the numbers.

_____ (c) I would decide to go buy a copy of the software myself for $300 and hope I would be reimbursed by the company in a month or two.

_____ (d) I would request another extension on an already overdue project date.

Situation 3.   Your small manufacturing company is in serious financial difficulty. A large order of your products is ready to be delivered to a key customer, when you discover that the product is simply not right. It will not meet all performance specifications, will cause problems for your customer, and will require rework in the field; but this, you know, will not become evident until after the customer has received and paid for the order. If you do not ship the order and receive the payment as expected, your business may be forced into bankruptcy. And if you delay the shipment or inform the customer of these problems, you may lose the order and also go bankrupt. What would you do?

_____ (a) I would not ship the order and place my firm in voluntary bankruptcy.

_____ (b) I would inform the customer and declare voluntary bankruptcy.

_____ (c) I would ship the order and inform the customer, after I received payment.

_____ (d) I would ship the order and not inform the customer.

Situation 4.   You are the cofounder and president of a new venture, manufacturing products for the recreational market. Five months after launching the business, one of your suppliers informs you it can no longer supply you with a critical raw material since you are not a large-quantity user. Without the raw material the business cannot continue. What would you do?

_____ (a) I would grossly overstate my requirements to another supplier to make the supplier think I am a much larger potential customer in order to secure the raw material from that supplier, even though this would mean the supplier will no longer be able to supply another, non-competing small manufacturer who may thus be forced out of business.

_____ (b) I would steal raw material from another firm (non-competing) where I am aware of a sizeable stockpile.

_____ (c) I would pay off the supplier, since I have reason to believe that the supplier could be persuaded to meet my needs with a sizeable under-the-table payoff that my company could afford.

_____ (d) I would declare voluntary bankruptcy.

Situation 5.   You are on a marketing trip for your new venture for the purpose of calling on the purchasing agent of a major prospective client. Your company is manufacturing an electronic system that you hope the purchasing agent will buy. During the course of your conversation, you notice on the cluttered desk of the purchasing agent several copies of a cost proposal for a system from one of your direct competitors. This purchasing agent has previously reported mislaying several of your own company's proposals and has asked for additional copies. The purchasing agent leaves the room momentarily to get you a cup of coffee, leaving you alone with your competitor's proposals less than an arm's length away. What would you do?

_____ (a) I would do nothing but await the man's return.

_____ (b) I would sneak a quick peek at the proposal, looking for bottom-line numbers.

_____ (c) I would put the copy of the proposal in my briefcase.

_____ (d) I would wait until the man returns and ask his permission to see the copy.

Second Part

Step 1   Based on the criteria you used, place your answers to each of the above situations along the continuum of behaviour shown below.

	Duty	Contractual	Utilitarian	Situational
Situation 1				
Situation 2				
Situation 3				
Situation 4				
Situation 5				

Step 2   After separating into teams of five to six people, record the answers made by each individual member of your team on the form below. Record the answers of each team member in each box and the team's solution in the column on the far right.

Member Name						Team Answer
Situation 1						
Situation 2						
Situation 3						
Situation 4						
Situation 5						

Step 3 Reach a consensus decision in each situation (if possible) and record the consensus that your team has reached above. Allow 20 to 30 minutes.

Step 4 Report to the entire group your team's conclusions and discuss with them how the consensus, if any, was reached. The discussion should focus on the following questions:

- Was a consensus reached by the group?
- Was this consensus difficult or easy to achieve and why?
- What kinds of ethical issues emerged?
- How were conflicts, if any, resolved, or were they left unresolved?
- What creative solutions did you find in order to solve the difficult problem without compromising your integrity?

Step 5 Discuss with the group the following issues:

- What role do ethical issues play and how important are they in the formation of a new venture management team?
- What role do ethical issues play and how important are they in obtaining venture capital? That is, how do investors feel about ethics and how important are they to them?
- What feelings bother participants most about the discussion and consensus reached? For example, if a participant believes that his or her own conduct was considered ethically less than perfect, does he or she feel a loss of self-respect or a sense of inferiority? Does he or she fear others' judgment, and so on?

Step 6 Define each group member's general ethical position and note whether his or her ethical position is similar to or different from yours:

Member Name	Position	Different/Similar

Step 7 Decide whom you would and would not want as a business partner based on their ethical positions:

Would Want	Would Not Want

CASE   TANGENT HOST: AN UNEASY PARTNERSHIP

Preparation Questions

1. How would you resolve the situation if you were Rick Peterson?

2. Should you confront Drew Fitchburg, if so how?

3. What has Rick Peterson done right and wrong?

In July 2009, Rick Peterson was contemplating the future of his company. Several new opportunities, coupled with ongoing and seemingly unsolvable problems, were causing the 27-year-old president and CEO of Tangent Host to question his involvement with what had started out as just a side-business but now occupied him full-time. Of immediate concern was the behaviour of Rick's business partner; things were off track and needed to be resolved. "I'm a bit more ambitious than Drew," confessed Rick. "I've worked hard to get this far and I'm keen to move forward. I put myself through university and graduated with honours, while Drew accumulated some certificates and credentials in the I.T. sector working a variety of odd jobs. In fairness, I probably learned from Drew's mistakes growing up a few years behind him."

Tangent Host (Tangent), an Internet services firm in Kanata, Ontario, provided database management, e-business consulting, and server collocation.[1] Tangent had grown considerably since its inception just three and a half years prior. At first the growth was an exciting surprise because Rick had not considered the business to be a possible source of stable income. His perception had changed quickly; in only months Tangent—initially run from the basement of his home—had attracted the attention of many companies with unmet needs for reliable, affordable, and innovative Internet services. More specifically, Rick had taken on several large clients that needed collocation services and had built a portfolio of over 450 clients paying monthly fees to have their Web sites and databases backed up on Tangent's servers. "I'm still hopeful we can reach 500 by the end of 2009, Rick admitted. "We had roughly 375 clients in 2008, 325 in 2007, and 225 back in 2006—our first real year on the books."

Coping with Challenges as the Venture Grows

Rick took the plunge and turned down additional work in downtown Ottawa as a federal government tech consultant and moved just west of Ottawa to Kanata (otherwise known as "Silicon Valley North"). Despite its apparent success, the firm was experiencing some difficulties and the personal costs of being an entrepreneur were becoming obvious to Rick. Tangent was in the midst of transition and these 'growing pains' preoccupied Rick's thoughts. He realized now that a firm's sales on paper were not always reflected in its bank account.

Timely collection of accounts receivable seemed to be a full-time job in its own right. Collections were unpleasant for Rick because many of Tangent's clients had become friendly with him and his partner, Drew Fitchburg, and some of them expected special treatment. At the same time, Rick considered the strength of these relationships to be the root cause of Tangent's surprising growth, as existing clients' word of mouth referrals compensated for the absence of a robust advertising budget. In fact, about a third of all new business came to Tangent this way.

Many clients had chosen to stay with Tangent even after competitors had offered lower prices. Tangent rarely had technical problems, but even after one of its servers was hacked, Tangent lost only two clients. Although no dollar value could be placed on their customers' trust in Tangent, Rick believed that having healthy client relationships was reflected in the firm's revenues—both positively and negatively. Rick explained, "Their confidence in us guarantees sales, but those relationships cut the other way too. Often we're taken advantage of by friends—they delay payment and ask for extras. A few of Tangent's old friends, worth very little to the bottom line, are high-maintenance accounts—always asking for a little more work for free."

"If Tangent were to become a serious endeavour," Rick mused, "it would have to start producing enough income to support both partners." For one thing, Rick's government job had compensated him better than Tangent seemed able to do, and Rick had been working day and night in order to run the business. Rick had begun to think that he would not be able to derive the income he desired from Tangent unless he tightened up on its cash flow, exercised greater control over costs, and doubled the firm's revenues. That, he thought, would take time, operational prudence, and innovative management.

MARKET ATTRIBUTES   The market for Tangent's two principal products, Web hosting and Web design, were characterized by intense competition among countless small firms and a few medium and large firms, all providing the same services. Firms differed in the customers they served (based on size and industries), the scope and variety of their services (Web hosting, Web design, graphics, programming, etc.), and the extent to which they used in-house resources. Many firms, including Tangent, outsourced some of their services.

Tangent struck deals with Web designers and technology consultants, paying referral fees for clients they brought to Tangent. This method of generating new clients produced over half of the firm's Web hosting revenues and had spawned several important relationships. Web site designers in Toronto, Montreal, and Ottawa typically took a 30-percent cut of hosting revenues from clients they referred to Tangent (unbeknownst to the clients). These clients ended up paying premium prices for Web hosting, and generally had little understanding of the services they purchased.

This case was written by Nicholas P. Robinson, Faculty of Law, McGill University, and Prescott C. Ensign, for purposes of classroom discussion.

[1] Collocation was the storage of identical information on different servers, typically located in different places, to ensure access to data even if one server was unavailable.

COLLECTIONS   It seemed to Rick that one of Tangent's growing problems was that "we mix business relationships with friendships." After telling one client, a construction company owner, about Tangent's collections problems, Rick received a phone call from a local collection agent offering to take care of bad debts. He worried that resorting to such means could sour Tangent's relations with customers. Rick believed that part of the blame for cash flow problems rested on the fact that payment for Web site design was received in phases. Clients paying either upon satisfactory completion of the project or at certain milestones meant that Tangent Host could be held at ransom (without compensation). Rick shared, "It's not unusual for Drew and I to have to do more work than we bargained for. Clients often demand more than what we quoted them." Rick continued, "And occasionally a client has failed to pay after a Web site is delivered for review. The worst offenders are the small margin contracts and those individuals that we know personally. We're just not attracting the high-end clients that we need to attract. Vague written contracts and the occasional oral agreement have created other problems—unpredictable revenue flow and mounting bad debt." (See Exhibit 1.)

Rick saw Tangent's rapport with clients as a double-edged sword. The personal touch had kept clients from departing despite increasingly frequent technical glitches—something Drew used to be able to prevent. "As Tangent grew we were overwhelmed by calls to our help desk." Tapping the mobile phone clipped to his belt, Rick continued, "This led us to force clients to contact us only through email." Bad debts were also taking their toll. Rick exclaimed, "I never imagined the road to Easy Street would look like this." He recently had threatened to take a client's Web site offline. Rick chuckled, "Turning off a client's email gets their attention."

AN UNEASY PARTNERSHIP   After a little over three and a half years of modest financial success with Tangent Host (see Exhibit 1), Rick's attention had begun to drift toward transforming the fledgling venture into a serious business. Rick admitted, "Right now we're amateur and I want to be big league; and I want Drew to want and work for this too. But we've got issues and obstacles to confront. Specifically, Drew's and my deteriorating relationship—he's just avoiding me more and more. He doesn't have to report to me, but I've got to know what—if anything—he's doing. I certainly keep him informed as things develop—even if it's bad news. Drew's contribution has been essential to Tangent's continuance. He possesses the technical skills, experience, and expertise needed to manage much of the business. But it's become apparent that Drew has been taking his involvement less seriously than before and now he's acting more like an employee than a partner with an interest in seeing the firm thrive."

Tangent's increasingly frequent problems with quality and reliability were an embarrassment for Rick, who saw them as consequences of Drew's poor performance. "Although the partnership agreement specified in writing that both of us would devote our full attention to the business, Drew seems to be less and less available when problems arise. After a year of him coasting, I've begun to question Drew's commitment to the firm." Rick paused and then continued, "I just don't know where we are headed. Our agreement makes no mention of an exit strategy—a way for one partner to buyout the other and bow out gracefully."

In April 2009, Rick received a curious call from Tangent's accountant, Nicolas Rowell. After briefly discussing the company's finances, Nicolas probed Rick by asking: "Why is there such a great discrepancy in income between you two?" Rick responded, "What do you mean by 'discrepancy'?" "Well," Nicolas continued, "it would seem that Drew has declared almost double the personal income from the business compared to you." This was alarming news to Rick, who had thought Drew's personal income was derived solely from Tangent Host dividends they split equally.

According to Canadian income tax practices, each partner could separately declare income and personal expenses derived from their involvement in the business. It became apparent to Rick that somehow Drew was earning far more revenue than Rick, maybe even incurring fewer expenses. The next day Rick raised the issue in conversation with Drew and learned that Drew had lumped some non-business income, derived from his personal side activities, with his income from Tangent Host. In other words, Drew had been running a smaller business in his spare time. He had built a small Internet marketing business that provided advertising services to a substantial and growing customer base. Indeed, Drew was selling banner-advertising space to Tangent's existing clients using Google AdSense.

Although uncertain if Drew's side business violated the terms of the partnership, it seemed to Rick to be a significant conflict of interest. Invariably, the tracking of Tangent clients' Web site traffic would have involved some data that Drew garnered through his position at Tangent. Drew seemed to have had so much success with his side business that it was unthinkable to Rick that Drew could be equally committed to Tangent. Sitting in his home office, Rick pondered whether it was fair for Drew to be running a second business while Tangent Host struggled to grow.

The Road Ahead

As the July sun set over the Ottawa Valley, Rick Peterson peered out the window to see its rays reflect off the river and glisten through the pine trees. He questioned again whether remaining in business with Drew was the right thing for him, and if so, what direction the company should take. He thought it undeniable that something would have to change if Tangent were to be worth the countless hours and energy he devoted to it.

EXHIBIT 1   Tangent Host Income Statements (Canadian Dollars)

	Year ended December 31, 2008	Year ended December 31, 2007	Year ended December 31, 2006
Web Hosting Sales	60,000	45,000	30,000
Web Design Sales	60,000	45,000	30,000
Domain Name Sales	1,440	1,100	750
Total Revenues	**121,440**	**91,100**	**60,750**
Expenses			
Server Lease	15,000	12,000	9,000
New Computer Charges	12,000	10,000	8,000
Software Expense	1,800	1,400	1,200
Domains Expense	1,500	1,200	1,000
Advertising	2,400	2,000	1,600
ISP Access	3,600	3,200	2,800
Personal Account (Drew)	1,440	1,300	1,200
Personal Account (Rick)	1,440	1,300	1,200
Office Supplies	1,200	1,200	1,000
Bad Debt Expense	9,000	6,500	4,000
Affiliate Fees	6,000	4,500	3,000
Toll-free Telephone Number	720	700	675
Total Expenses	**56,100**	**45,300**	**34,675**
Net Income	**65,340**	**45,800**	**26,075**

Online
LearningCentre

Find more great exercises and additional study tools on the Online Learning Centre at
www.mcgrawhill.ca/olc/timmons

PART
IV

FINANCING ENTREPRENEURIAL VENTURES

A financing strategy should be driven by corporate and personal goals, by resulting financial requirements, and ultimately by the available alternatives. In the final analysis, these alternatives are governed by the entrepreneur's relative bargaining power and skill in managing and orchestrating the fund-raising opportunities. In turn, that bargaining power is governed to a large extent by the cruelty of real time. It is governed by when the venture will run out of cash given its current cash burn rate.

More numerous alternatives for financing a company exist now than ever before. Even in the wake of economic turmoil, many contend that money remains plentiful for well-managed emerging firms with the promise of profitable growth. Savvy entrepreneurs should remain vigilant for the warnings noted here to avoid the myopic temptation to "take the money and run." The cost of money can vary considerably.

While some of these alternatives look distinct and separate, a financing strategy probably will encompass a combination of both debt and equity capital. In considering which financial alternatives are best for a venture at any particular stage of growth it is important to draw on the experience of other entrepreneurs, investors, lenders, accountants, and other professionals.

In the search for either debt or equity capital, it is important that entrepreneurs take a professional approach to selecting and presenting their ventures to both investors and lenders.

CHAPTER

8

RESOURCE REQUIREMENTS

It's almost like you see too much, because when it happens for real, everything flies at you so fast, you never get a sense of the ice and where everyone is at that one moment.

Steve Yzerman

THE ENTREPRENEURIAL APPROACH TO RESOURCES

Resources include (1) people, such as the management team, the board of directors, lawyers, accountants, and consultants; (2) financial resources; (3) assets, such as plant and equipment; and (4) a business plan and other intellectual property. Nick Bontis of McMaster University sees knowledge and know-how in people and processes as the key ingredient for a new venture to survive and ultimately thrive. Successful entrepreneurs view the need for and the ownership and management of these resources in the pursuit of opportunities differently from the way managers in many large organizations view them. This different way of looking at resources is reflected in a definition of entrepreneurship given in Chapter 1—the process of creating or seizing an opportunity *and pursuing it regardless of the resources currently controlled.*[1]

Successful entrepreneurs have a unique approach to resources.[2] The decisions on what resources are needed, when they are needed, and how to acquire them are strategic decisions that fit with the other driving forces of entrepreneurship. Entrepreneurs seek to use the minimum possible amount of all types of resources at each stage in their ventures' growth. Rather than own the resources they need, they seek to control them.

Entrepreneurs with this approach reduce some of the risk in pursuing opportunities, including:

- *Less capital.* The amount of capital required is simply smaller due to the quest for prudence. The financial exposure is therefore reduced and the dilution of the founder's equity. As Michael Dunleavy with the business law firm LaBarge Weinstein in Kanata, Ontario, admonishes: don't give away too much equity too early—otherwise there is damage to be undone in order to capture the interest of later investors.

- *Staged capital commitments.* The capital infusions are staged to match critical objectives that will signal whether it is prudent to keep going, and thus infuse the second stage of capital, or abort the venture. Both the founder's and investor's financial exposure, and dilution of equity ownership, are thereby reduced.

- *More flexibility.* Entrepreneurs who do not own a resource are in a better position to commit and decommit quickly[3] One price of ownership of resources is an inherent inflexibility. With the rapidly fluctuating conditions and uncertainty with which most entrepreneurial ventures have to contend, inflexibility can be a curse. Response times to evaluate quick changes and take action need to be short if a firm is to be competitive. Decision windows are most often small and elusive. And it is extremely difficult to predict accurately the resources that will be necessary to execute the opportunity. The entrepreneurial approach to resources permits iterations or strategic experiments in the venture process—that is, ideas can be tried and tested without committing to the ownership of all assets and resources in the business, to markets and technology that change rapidly, and so forth. For example, Howard Head says that if he had raised all the money he needed at the outset, he would have failed by spending it all too early on the wrong version of his metal ski. Consider also, for example, the inflexibility of a company that commits permanently to a certain technology, software, or management system.

- *Low sunk cost.* In addition, sunk costs are lower if the firm exercises the option to abort the venture at any point. Consider, instead, the enormous upfront capital commitment of a nuclear power plant and the cost of abandoning such a project.

- *Lower costs.* Fixed costs are lowered, thus favourably affecting breakeven. Of course, the other side of the coin is that variable costs may rise. If the entrepreneur has found an opportunity with forgiving and rewarding economics, then there still will most likely be ample gross margins in the venture to absorb cost increases.

- *Reduced risk.* In addition to reducing total exposure, other risks, such as the risk of obsolescence of the resource, are also lower. For example, venture leasing has been used by biotechnology companies as a way to supplement sources of equity financing.

While some might scoff at the practice, assuming erroneously that the firm cannot afford to buy a resource, in fact not owning a resource can provide advantages and options. These decisions are often extremely complex, involving consideration of such details as the tax implications of leasing versus buying, and so forth.

Bootstrapping Strategies: Marshalling and Minimizing Resources

Minimizing resources is referred to in colloquial terms as bootstrapping or, more formally, as a lack of resource intensity, defined as a multistage commitment of resources with a minimum commitment at each stage or decision point[4] When discussing his philosophy on bootstrapping, Greg Gianforte (who retired at the age of 33 after he and his partners sold their software business, Brightwork Development, to McAfee Associates for more than $10 million) stated, "A lot of entrepreneurs think they need money. . .when actually they haven't figured out the business equation.[5] According to Gianforte, lack of money, employees, equipment—even lack of product—is actually a huge advantage because it forces the bootstrapper to concentrate on selling to bring cash into the business. Thus, to persevere, entrepreneurs ask at every step how they can accomplish a little more with a little less and pursue the opportunity (see for yourself by trying the online exercise "How Entrepreneurs Turn Less into More" at www.mcgrawhill.ca/olc/timmons).

As was outlined in Exhibit 1.3, the opposite attitude is often evident in large institutions that usually are characterized by a trustee or custodial viewpoint. Managers in larger institutions seek to have not only enough committed resources for the task at hand but also a cushion against the tough times.

> ## Mustering Resources at Genuwine Cellars Inc.
>
> **Robb Denomme co-founded Genuwine Cellars with wood craftsman Lance Kingma. They have been building custom-made wine cellars for high-end hotels, business moguls, and celebrities worldwide. From their base in Winnipeg, Manitoba, they do their own manufacturing—something that sets them apart from competitors. Having necessary resources in-house settles well with clients and importing additional components from Asia cuts costs. Genuwine Cellars has set up a design office in Latin America for reasons of efficiency and access to skilled professionals. BDC awarded Robb a Young Entrepreneur of the Year Award and noted that in addition to lean manufacturing and an organizational structure that incorporates sales, design, and manufacturing functions: "Hiring an outside business consultant, who has become Robb's mentor, also helped."[6] Robb gives much credit to a great team of talented people. But does note that the greatest challenge he has faced as proprietor came a few years ago when he had to lay off a handful of his 50-person team because they were not dedicated.[7] Robb stated, "We always felt we needed every warm body, but after that, we were able to do more with less people. I was shocked to learn that." Robb also acknowledges the value of learning vicariously through the experience of others.**
>
> Sources: BDC "2008 YEA Winners" *BDC etc.*, January 2009; Daryl-Lynn Carlson, "Outlook 2009: Gen Y Takes Recession in Stride," *National Post*, December 29, 2008 ; Canadian Newswire, "Genuwine Cellars Captivates Discriminating Tastes—Robb Denomme Wins BDC's Young Entrepreneur Award for Manitoba," www.newswire.ca (accessed October 21, 2008).

Using Other People's Resources

Obtaining the use of other people's resources, particularly in the start-up and early growth stages of a venture, is an important approach for entrepreneurs. In contrast, large firms assume that virtually all resources have to be owned to control their use, and decisions centre around how these resources will be acquired and financed—not so with entrepreneurs.

Having the use of the resource and being able to control or influence the deployment of the resource are key. The quote at the beginning of the chapter illustrates being able to see everything unfolding quickly and sensing how it all comes together and fits into place. Scott Nichol founded 6N Silicon in September 2006 bringing his own expertise in metallurgy to tackle the purification of silicon for solar power. He located 6N Silicon "in the heart of Canada's metal processing industry, surrounded by Canada's extensive metal processing knowledge. 6N has benefited from access to considerable industry experience in processing other metals and applying collective skills to refine the 6N solution."[8]

Other people's resources can include, for example, money invested or lent by friends, relatives, business associates, or other investors. Or resources can include people, space, equipment, or other material loaned, provided inexpensively or free by customers or suppliers, or secured by bartering future services, opportunities, and the like. In fact, using other people's resources can be as simple as benefiting from free booklets and pamphlets, such as those published by many of the Big Four accounting firms, or using low-cost educational programs or government-funded management assistance programs. Extending accounts payable is one of the primary sources of working capital for many start-ups and growing firms.

How can you as an entrepreneur begin to tap into these resources? Howard Stevenson and William Sahlman suggest that you have to do "two seemingly contradictory things: seek out the best advisors—specialists if you have to—and involve them more thoroughly, and at an earlier stage, than you have in the past. At the same time, be more skeptical of their credentials and their advice."[9] A recent study found that social capital, including having an established business network and encouragement from friends and family, is strongly associated with entrepreneurial activity.[10] In addition to networking with family, friends, classmates, and advisors, the human touch enhances the relationship between the entrepreneur and the venture's advisors. Accuracy in social perception, skill at impression management, skill at persuasion and influence, and a high level of social adaptability may be relevant to the activities necessary for successful new ventures.[11] Paola Dubini of the University of Bocconi, Italy, and Howard Aldrich of the University of North Carolina have contributed to the growing body of knowledge about how these "social assets" may benefit the bottom line of a new venture; see Exhibit 8.1 for the strategic principles they have identified. However, a handful of studies have failed to demonstrate the effectiveness of networking activities on the performance of ventures.[12]

There are many examples of controlling people resources, rather than owning them. In real estate, even the largest firms do not employ top architects full-time but, rather, secure them on a project-by-project basis. Most smaller firms do not employ lawyers but obtain legal assistance as needed. Technical consultants, design engineers, and programmers are other examples. An illustration of this approach is a company that grew to $20 million in sales in about 10 years with $7,500 cash, a liberal use of credit cards, reduced income for the founders, and hard work and long hours. This company has not had to raise any additional equity capital.

bitHeads—Resources for Hire

Founded by three Bachelor of Computer Science graduates (two from the University of New Brunswick and one from the University of Windsor), the company provides software product development for large and small organizations in Canada, the U.S., and Europe. bitHeads today has 50 employees, many of whom have learned programming skills at technical college. For organizations large or small, bitHeads provides a flexible solution—immediate help with software programming, project management, or even development mentorship. It allows an organization on-demand access to resources they might not need again in the future. bitHeads specializes in VoIP, wireless, Internet, enterprise software, and more recently game development with the acquisition of a RndLabs, an independent game studio added to HeadGames, a division of bitHeads.

Source: www.bitheads.com.

An example of the opposite point of view is a proposed new venture in the iPhone applications software industry. The business plan called for about $300,000, an amount that would pay for only the development of the first products. The first priority in the deployment of the company's financial resources outlined in the business plan was to buy outright office equipment and sign a one-year lease on space costing approximately $150,000. The founders refused to consider other options, such as renting the equipment

---

EXHIBIT 8.1   Hypotheses Concerning Networks and Entrepreneurial Effectiveness

Effective entrepreneurs are more likely than others to systematically plan and monitor network activities.

- Effective entrepreneurs are able to chart their present network and to discriminate between production and symbolic ties.
- Effective entrepreneurs are able to view effective networks as a crucial aspect for ensuring the success of their company.
- Effective entrepreneurs are able to stabilize and maintain networks to increase their effectiveness and their efficiency.

Effective entrepreneurs are more likely than others to undertake actions toward increasing their network density and diversity.

- Effective entrepreneurs set aside time for purely random activities—things done with no specific problem in mind.
- Effective entrepreneurs are able to check network density, so as to avoid too many overlaps (because they affect network efficiency) while still attaining solidarity and cohesiveness.
- Effective entrepreneurs multiply, through extending the reachability of their networks, the stimuli for better and faster adaptation to change.

Source: Adapted from Paola Dubini and Howard Aldrich, "Personal and Extended Networks Are Central to the Entrepreneurial Process," *Journal of Business Venturing* 6, no. 5 (1991): 305–313.

or working from home with what they had. The company was unable to attract venture capital, even though, otherwise, it had excellent prospects. The $150,000 raised from informal private investors was not enough money to execute the opportunity, and the founders decided to give it back and abandon the venture. A more entrepreneurial team would have figured out a way to keep going under these circumstances.

The Right Stuff—Does Canada Have What It Takes?

Some contend that Canada is too conservative, resistant to innovation and risk, and stuck on its history of natural resources for competitive advantage. Michael Treacy, serial entrepreneur and strategy expert, knows that trade-offs have to be made to catch up and pursue things in a knowledge-based economy. "The only way to keep attracting work without suppressing wages," Treacy reasons, "is to improve productivity, and that means investing in innovation. Knowledge talent will be the only basis of real, sustainable competitive advantage over time."[13] According to Treacy, Canada is not prepared for a world where knowledge rules. This he finds in sizeable contrast to the U.S. where innovation thrives. "That massive, consumer-driven culture opens up a world of opportunity for new ventures, because the market recognizes and warmly receives the value of a new product or service. And the people who can provide early-stage financing are willing to back it."[14]

Some have questioned whether or not entrepreneurship is the same everywhere. In France, entrepreneurs are more often part of the "corporate" establishment, whereas in Japan "network" entrepreneurs rely on the organization of industry. The "informal" entrepreneur characterizes the entrepreneur in Africa and parts of Asia. The western notion of the entrepreneur is that of an individualist with competitive instincts not part of a collective, as in other regions where trust may be more prominent.[15]

Most contend that entrepreneurial attributes are more universal than idiosyncratic; it is the institutional environment that drives economic activity and latent behaviours. For example, recent research has shown that Labour Sponsored Venture Capital Corporations "crowd out" other types of venture capital funds, clearly frustrating one of the key governmental goals of this program.[16] These vehicles for new venture creation were supposed to foster additional financing (expand the aggregate pool of risk capital) not displace it! It is most probable that it is the incentive structures that arise from institutional arrangements that produce entrepreneurs. Finally, it should be noted that differences in entrepreneurial activity are often greater within a country (e.g., Québec vs. Saskatchewan) than between countries (e.g., Texas vs. Alberta).

Treacy concludes with that critical question about the future supply of Canadian entrepreneurs: "What are we doing to nurture them, and what are we doing to keep them here?"

OUTSIDE PEOPLE RESOURCES

Build Your Brain Trust

Building a brain trust—a group of close advisors selected for their various expertises—for your venture is a huge part of improving the "fit" vis-à-vis the Timmons Model, and managing risk and reward. The adage "it's not just what you know, it's who you know that matters" conveys the message. While networking for its own sake is ill-advised, making connections pays dividends—some of these payoffs may be delayed, options to be exercised in the future.

After assessing the venture and entrepreneur's background through a basic "Gap Analysis" and applying the Timmons Model to the venture, it becomes clear what is missing and where value can be added in during the creation, launch, and building of the enterprise. Aydin Mirzaee, founder of bOK Systems and author of the business plan in Chapter 4, was able to add Michael Cowpland of Corel and a Toronto VC to his brain trust. Aydin gained access to their knowledge, their relevant and extensive experience, and their contacts with other talent pools and capital. It was then up to Aydin, through his entrepreneurial energy, promise, and salesmanship, to capture their interest, gain their confidence, and tap into their talent. When this all comes together, drawing on the considerable strength of others, a better venture opportunity can be realized. The key is getting investors and directors to recognize high potential and see how they could personally make a large impact on the odds of success *because* they know what to do and how to do it in order to add value to this specific opportunity. The "Build Your Brain Trust," exercise at the end of this chapter will walk you through the key issues and tasks necessary to assemble a brain trust that can add maximum value to your venture.

The right advisors and brain trust members are very important parts of your extended team and provide critical value to your venture. The most successful entrepreneurs think this through *before* they launch. They know what they need to fill in the gaps that exist on the team, and they ask themselves what they don't know. They focus on identifying individuals with the know-how, experience, and networks who have access to critical talent, experience, and resources that can make the difference between success and failure. Spend enough—but not too much—time planning and looking before you leap. James Chrisman of Mississippi State University, and Ed McMullan and Jeremy Hall both of the University of Calgary studied new ventures that had outside advisors; their research showed that start-up counselling assistance was positively related to a ventures growth up to a point where more help adds less and less value (marginal returns to outside assistance), eventually adding no value and ultimately reaching a point where guided preparation was actually detrimental.[17] Jean Lorrain of the Université du Québec á Trois-Rivières and Sylvie Laferté of Télé-université du Québec find that the support needs of young entrepreneurs are unique: "young entrepreneurs experience serious personal problems. . . feel at a particular loss with respect to self-management issues, including stress and time management."[18]

Board of Directors

Initial work in evaluating the need for people resources is done when forming a new venture team (see Chapter 6). Once resource needs have been determined and a team has been selected, it will usually be necessary to obtain additional resources from outside the venture in the start-up stage and during other stages of growth as well.

The decision of whether to have a board of directors and, if the answer is yes, the process of choosing and finding the people who will sit on the board are troublesome for new ventures.[19]

The Decision   The decision of whether to have a board of directors is influenced first by the form of organization chosen for the firm. If the new venture is organized as a corporation, it must have a board of directors, which must be elected by the shareholders. There is flexibility regarding a board with other forms of organization.

In addition, certain investors will require a board of directors. Venture capitalists almost always require boards of directors and that they be represented on the boards.

Beyond that, deciding whether to involve outsiders is worth careful thought. This decision making starts with identifying missing relevant experience, know-how, and networks, and determining if the venture has current needs that can be provided by outside directors. Their probable contributions then can be balanced against the resultant greater disclosure to outsiders of plans for operating and financing the business. Also, since one responsibility of a board of directors is to appoint officers for the firm, the decision whether to have a board also is tied to financing decisions and ownership of the voting shares in the company.

Boards are dominated by company executives and venture capitalists.[20] At least half of a board's members should be outside directors in order to provide independent, outside viewpoints. When Art Spinner of Hambro International was interviewed by *INC.*, he explained:

> Entrepreneurs worry about the wrong thing. . . that the boards are going to steal their companies or take them over. Though entrepreneurs have many reasons to worry, that's not one of them. It almost never happens. In truth, boards don't even have much power. They are less well equipped to police entrepreneurs than to advise them.[21]

The expertise that members of a board can bring to a venture, at a price it can afford, can far outweigh any of the negative factors. A board can play a crucial role, so it is important to intentionally choose a board by focusing on "holes" that need to be filled. According to noted business writer, David Gumpert, "The board continually challenged us—in terms of tactics, strategy and overall business philosophy." These challenges benefited the venture by (1) preventing dumb mistakes, (2) keeping us focused on what really mattered, and (3) stopping us from getting gloomy.[22]

Selection Criteria: Add Value with Know-How and Contacts Once the decision to have a board of directors has been made—and remember that it may not be optional, it may be a legal requirement—finding the appropriate people for the board is a challenge. It is important to be objective and to select trustworthy people. Most ventures typically look to personal acquaintances of the lead entrepreneur or the team or to their lawyers, bankers, accountants, or consultants for their first outside directors. While such a choice might be the right one for a venture, the process also involves finding the right people to fill the gaps discovered in the process of forming the management team.

This issue of filling in the gaps relates to one criteria of a successful management team, intellectual honesty; that is, knowing what you know and what you need to know. In a study of boards and specifically venture capitalists' contribution to them, entrepreneurs seemed to value operating experience over financial expertise.[23]

Defining expectations and minimum requirements for board members might be a good way to get the most out of a board of directors. A "wish list" of attributes and areas of knowledge may be constructed or alternatively if a list of candidates is identified, pros and cons for each individual may be tallied. Again, one must be mindful that the whole, the sum of the individuals, is the goal. These individuals must work together.

A top-notch outside director usually spends *at least* 9 to 10 days per year on his or her responsibilities. Four days per year are spent for quarterly meetings, a day of preparation for each meeting, a day for another meeting to cope with an unanticipated issue, plus up to a day or more for various phone calls. Yearly fees are usually paid for such a commitment.

Quality directors most often become involved for the learning and professional development opportunities, rather than for the money. Compensation to board members varies widely. Fees can range from as little as $500 to $1,000 for a half- or full-day meeting to $10,000 to $30,000 per year for four to six full-day to day-and-a-half meetings, plus accessibility on a continuous basis. Directors are also usually reimbursed for their expenses incurred in preparing for and attending meetings. Shares in a start-up company, often 2 to 5 percent, or options, for 5,000 to 50,000 shares, are common incentives to attract and reward directors.

As a director of 11 companies and an advisor to two other companies, Art Spinner suggested the following as a simple set of rules to guide you toward a productive relationship with your board:

✓ Treat your directors as individual resources.
✓ Always be honest with your directors.
✓ Set up a compensation committee.
✓ Set up an audit committee.
✓ Never set up an executive committee.[24]

New ventures are finding that, for a variety of reasons, people who could be potential board members are increasingly cautious about getting involved.

Liability Motivated by an apparent wave of corporate fraud scandals that many felt could lead to a crisis of confidence in the capital marketplace, in 2002 the U.S. government passed the Sarbanes-Oxley Act (SOX). SOX requires companies to file paperwork with the Securities and Exchange Commission faster, create a more transparent means of collecting and posting financial data, maintain volumes of data, and test their procedures for posting accurate, timely information. The potential consequences of running afoul of this law are ominous, including prison time and huge fines for the company's chief officers. According to Tara Gray, of the Economics Division of the Parliamentary Research Information and Research Service, Canada's response to SOX has been to emulate it. Particularly given that many Canadian firms are listed on U.S. exchanges and must comply with SOX even when it conflicts with Canadian regulations. "Canadian firms make up the single largest group of foreign firms listed on U.S. stock exchanges."[25] But there are some stark differences between Canada and the U.S.:

✓ Securities regulation is not under federal control in Canada.
✓ A greater proportion of Canadian firms have a controlling shareholder.
✓ Many Canadian public corporations have relatively low market capitalizations.

While start-ups are usually not subject to the technical requirements of the act, the spirit of the law and emerging case law create higher disclosure standards for even small and growing firms. Audit committees sitting on start-up boards, for example, could have real SOX-like exposure.

As well, directors of a company can be held personally liable for its actions and those of its officers. A climate of litigation exists in many areas. For example, some specific grounds for liability of a director have included voting a dividend that renders the corporation insolvent, voting to authorize a loan out of corporate assets to a director or an officer who ultimately defaults, and signing a false corporate document or report. Courts have held that if a director acts in good faith, he or she can be excused from liability. However, it can be difficult for a director to *prove* that he or she has acted in good faith, especially in a start-up situation. This proof is complicated by several factors, including possibly an inexperienced management team, the financial weaknesses and cash crises that occur and demand solution, and the lack of good and complete information and records, which are necessary as the basis for action.

One solution to liability concerns is for the firm to purchase indemnity insurance for its directors. But this insurance is expensive. Despite the liability problems noted above, few enterprises report difficulty in recruiting board members. In dealing with this issue, new ventures will want to examine a possible director's attitude toward risk in general and evaluate whether this is the type of attitude the team needs to have represented.

Harassment   Outside shareholders, who may have acquired shares through a private placement or through the over-the-counter market, can have unrealistic expectations about the risk involved in a new venture, the speed at which a return can be realized, as well as the size of the return. Such shareholders are a source of continual annoyance for boards and for their companies.

Time and Risk   Experienced directors know that often it takes more time and intense involvement to work with an early-stage venture with sales of $5 million or less than with one having sales of $25 million or more, and the former is riskier. But the rewards—which may never be measured financially—are often substantial. The thrill of seeing others succeed or even simply navigate away from catastrophe can be satisfying. And we know that the initial break-in period for a start-up is crucial. Monica Diochon of St. Francis Xavier University, Teresa Menzies of Brock University, and Yvon Gasse of the Université Laval report that "sustainable operating ventures can be distinguished from others according to the activities undertaken during start-up."[26] "Outsider assistance during the early stages of a venture's development can influence its subsequent development."[27] James Chrisman and Ed McMullan both of the University of Calgary found that ventures receiving such help "had higher than expected rates of survival, growth, and innovation." The online exercise "How Entrepreneurs Turn Less into More," on the Online Learning Centre at www.mcgrawhill.ca/olc/timmons, is a great place to start.

Alternatives to a Formal Board

The use of advisors and quasi-boards can be a useful alternative to having a formal board of directors—assuming a board is not legally required.[28] A board of advisors—which may complement a board of directors—is designed to dispense advice, rather than make decisions, and therefore advisors are not exposed to personal liability. A firm can solicit objective observations and feedback from these advisors. Such informal boards can bring needed expertise, without the legal entanglements and formalities of a regular board. Also, the possible embarrassment of having to remove someone who is not serving a useful role can be avoided. Informal advisors are usually much less expensive, with honorariums of $500 to $1,000 per meeting common. Remember, however, the level of involvement of these advisors probably will be less than that of members of a formal board. The firm also does not enjoy the protection of law, which defines the obligations and responsibilities of members of a formal board.

An informal group of advisors can also be a good mechanism through which a new venture can observe a number of people in action and select one or two as regular directors. The entrepreneur gains the advantages of counsel and advice from outsiders without being legally bound by their decisions.

Legal Counsel

The Decision   Nearly all companies need and use the services of lawyers, and newly created ventures perhaps more than most. Since it is critical that entrepreneurs fully understand the legal aspects of any decisions and agreements they make, they should never completely out-source that responsibility to their lawyer. Leslie Charm, a partner in the firm Youngman & Charm, put it this way, "You must understand the meaning of any document you're consider-ing as well as your attorneys do. That's because at the end of the day, when you close that deal, you are the one who has to live with it, not your lawyers." In addition, Charm noted that lawyers should be viewed as teachers and advisors; use them to explain legalese, articulate risk and ramifications; and in negotiations, use them to push to close the deal.

Various authors describe the importance of choosing and managing legal counsel. By following some legal basics and acquiring appropriate legal services, companies can achieve better legal health, including fewer problems and lower costs over the long term.[29] Some of the legal work can be done by entrepreneurs who do not have law degrees by using self-help legal guides and pre-printed forms. However, one should not rely exclusively on these materials. Factors to consider in choosing a lawyer include availability, comfort level with the lawyer, experience level and appropriateness to the task, cost, and whether or not the lawyer knows the industry and has connections to investors and venture capital.

Just how lawyers are used by entrepreneurial ventures depends on the needs of the venture at its particular stage. Size is also a factor. As company size increases, so does the need for advice in such areas as liability, mergers, and benefit plans. Contracts and agreements were almost uniformly the predominant use by entrepreneurs, regardless of the venture's size.

Entrepreneurs will most likely need to get assistance with the following areas of the law:

- *Incorporation.* Issues such as the forgivable and non-forgivable liabilities of found-ers, officers, and directors or the form of organization chosen for a new venture are important. As tax laws and other circumstances change, they are important for more established firms as well. How important this area can be is illustrated by the case of a founder who nearly lost control of his company as a result of the legal manoeuvring of the clerk and another shareholder. The clerk and the shareholder controlled votes on the board of directors, while the founder had controlling interest in the shares of the company. The shareholder tried to call a directors' meeting and not re-elect the founder president. The founder found out about the plot and adroitly managed to call a shareholders' meeting to remove the directors first.

- *Franchising and licensing.* Innumerable issues concerning future rights, obligations, and what happens in the event of non-performance by either a franchisee or lessee or a franchisor or lessor require specialized legal advice.

- *Contracts and agreements.* Firms need assistance with contracts, licences, leases, and other such agreements such as non-compete employment agreements and those gov-erning the vesting rights of shareholders.

- *Formal litigation, liability protection, and so on.* In today's litigious climate, sooner or later most entrepreneurs will find themselves as defendants in lawsuits and require counsel.

- *Real estate, insurance, and other matters.* It is hard to imagine an entrepreneur who, at one time or another, will not be involved in various kinds of real estate transactions, from rentals to the purchase and sale of property, which require the services of a lawyer.

- *Copyrights, trademarks, patents, and intellectual property protection.* Products are hard to protect. But pushing ahead with product development before ample protection from the law is provided can be expedient in the short term but disastrous in the long term. For example, an entrepreneur—facing the loss of a $2.5 million sale of his business and uncollected fees of over $200,000 if his software was not protected—obtained an expert on the sale, leasing, and licensing of software products. The lawyer devised subtle but powerful protections, such as internal clocks in the software that shut down the software if they were not changed.

- *Employee plans.* Benefit and share ownership plans have become complicated to use effectively and to administer. They require the special know-how of lawyers to avoid common pitfalls.

- *Tax planning and review.* Too frequently the tail of the accountant's tax avoidance advice wags the dog of good business sense. Entrepreneurs who worry more about finding good opportunities to make money, rather than tax shelters, are infinitely better off.

- *Federal, provincial, and other regulations and reports.* Understanding the impact of and complying with regulations often is not easy. Violations of federal, provincial, and other regulations often can have serious consequences.

- *Mergers and acquisitions.* Specialized legal knowledge is required when buying or selling a company. Unless an entrepreneur is highly experienced and has highly qualified legal advisors in these transactions, he or she can either lose the deal or end up having to live with legal obligations that can be costly.

- *Bankruptcy law.* Many people have heard tales of entrepreneurs who did not make deposits to pay various federal and provincial taxes in order to use that cash in their business. These entrepreneurs perhaps falsely assumed that if their companies went bankrupt, the government was out of luck, just like the banks and other creditors. They were wrong. The owners, officers, and often the directors are held personally liable for those obligations.

- *Other matters.* These matters can range from assistance with collecting delinquent accounts to labour relations.

- *Personal needs.* As entrepreneurs accumulate net worth (i.e., property and other assets), legal advice in estate, tax, and financial planning is important.

Selection Criteria: Add Value with Know-How and Contacts   In a survey of the factors that enter into the selection of a law firm or a lawyer, 54 percent of the respondents said personal contact with a member of the firm was the main factor.[30] Reputation was a factor for 40 percent, and a prior relationship with the firm for 26 percent. Equally revealing was the fact that fees were mentioned by only 3 percent.

Many areas of the country have lawyers who specialize in new ventures and in firms with higher growth potential. The best place to start in selecting a lawyer is with acquaintances of the lead entrepreneur, of members of the management team, or of directors. Recommendations from accountants, bankers, and associates also are useful. Other sources are partners in venture capital firms, partners of a leading accounting firm (those who have privately owned and emerging company groups), or a provincial bar association. To be effective, a lawyer needs to have the experience and expertise to deal with specific issues facing a new venture. Hooking up with the vast resources of a large law firm or national accounting firm may be very beneficial, but we do not necessarily advise that strategy. You can usually get reasonable tax or estate-planning advice from a big law firm merely by picking up a telephone. The trade-off is that, if you are a small company and they have a dozen General Electrics as clients, you may get short shrift. One- or two-person firms can have an excellent network of specialists to refer to for problems outside their bailiwick. Use the specialist when you have to.[31]

As with members of the management team, directors, and investors, the chemistry also is important. Finally, advice to be highly selective and to expect to get what you pay for is sound. It is also important to realize that lawyers are not leaders of entrepreneurial enter-prises and that they do not usually make business judgments. Rather, they seek to provide perfect or fail-safe legal protection.

Most lawyers are paid on an hourly basis. Retainers and flat fees are sometimes paid, usually by larger ventures. The amount an enterprise pays for legal services expectedly rises as the firm grows. Many law firms will agree to defer charges or initially to provide services at a lower than normal rate to obtain a firm's business. According to Michael Dunleavy of LaBarge Weinstein, it's a good sign if your lawyer will defer payment until the venture is thriving. If your lawyer wants fees paid up front or charges market rates, it's a sign that she's less confident in your start-up's viability.

Bankers and Other Lenders

The Decision   Deciding whether to have a banker or another lender usually involves decisions about how to finance certain needs. Most companies will need the services of a banker or other lender at some time. The decision also can involve how a banker or other lender can serve as an advisor.

As with other advisors, the banker or other lender needs to be a partner, not a difficult minority shareholder. First and foremost, therefore, an entrepreneur should carefully pick the right banker or lender rather than just pick a bank or a financial institution, although picking the bank or institution is also important. Different bankers and lenders have repu-tations ranging from "excellent" to "just OK" to "not OK" in how they work with start-ups and growing enterprises. Their institutions also have reputations for how well they work with entrepreneurial companies. Ideally, an entrepreneur needs an excellent banker or lender with an excellent financial institution, although an excellent banker or lender with a just OK institution is preferable to a just OK banker or lender with an excellent institution.

For an entrepreneur to know clearly what he or she needs from a lender is an important starting point. Some will have needs that are asset-based, such as money for equipment, facilities, or inventory. Others may need working capital to fund short-term operations.

Having a business plan is invaluable preparation for selecting and working with a lender. Also, because a banker or other lender is a "partner," it is important to invite him or her to see the company in operation, to avoid late financial statements (as well as late payments and over-drafts), and to be honest and straightforward in sharing information—even if it's bad news.

Selection Criteria: Add Value with Know-How and Contracts   Bankers and other lenders are known to other entrepreneurs, lawyers, accountants, and venture capitalists. Starting with their recommendations is ideal. From among four to seven or so possibilities, an entrepreneur will find the right lender and the right institution.

Today's banking and financial services marketplace is much more competitive than in the past. There are more choices, and it is worth the time and effort to shop around.

Accountants

The Decision   The accounting profession has come a long way from the "green eyeshades" stereotype one hears reference to occasionally. Today, virtually all the larger accounting firms have discovered the enormous client potential of new and entrepreneurial ventures, and a significant part of their business strategy is to cater specifically to these firms.

Accountants often are maligned, especially after the fallout of ethical scandals. The activities that accountants engage in have grown and no longer consist of solely counting numbers.[32] Accountants who are experienced as advisors to emerging companies can provide valuable services in addition to audits and taxation advice. An experienced general business advisor can be invaluable in helping to evaluate strategy, raising debt and equity capital, facilitating mergers and acquisitions, locating directors, and even balancing business decisions with important personal needs and goals. In fact, when Prescott Ensign's wife was launching a venture her accountant advised her on much more than the simple tax questions she initially inquired about. She was given advice on partnership arrangements (and why they often don't work), incorporation, cross-border shipping, and monitoring expenses and cash flow. Accountants and others may not have "lived it"—but their second-hand experience relayed by a multitude of clients may cut across industries and stages of the venture's lifecycle.

Selection Criteria: Add Value with Know-How and Contacts   In selecting accountants, the first step is for the venture to decide whether to go with a smaller local firm, a regional firm, or one of the major accounting firms. Although each company should make its own decision, many entrepreneurs prefer working with smaller regional accounting firms, because of lower costs and better personal attention.[33] In deciding on an accountant, you will need to address several factors:[34]

- *Service.* Levels of service offered and the attention likely to be provided need to be evaluated. Chances are, for most start-ups, both will be higher in a small firm than a large one. But if an entrepreneur of a higher potential firm seeking venture capital or a strategic partner has aspirations to go public, a national firm is a good place to start.

- *Needs.* Needs, both current and future, have to be weighed against the capabilities of the firm. Larger firms are more equipped to handle highly complex or technical problems, while smaller firms may be preferable for general management advice and assistance because the principals are more likely to be involved in handling the account. In most instances, those companies in the early stages of planning or that do not plan to go public do not require a top-tier accounting firm. However, one exception to this might be those start-ups that are able to attract formal venture-capital funds from day one.[35]

- *Cost.* Most major firms will offer very cost-competitive services to start-ups with significant growth and profit potential. If a venture needs the attention of a partner in a larger firm, services of the larger firm are more expensive. However, if the firm requires extensive technical knowledge, a larger firm may have more experience and therefore be cheaper. Many early-growth phase companies are not able to afford to hire a leading national accounting firm and therefore a smaller local firm is best. However, these firms should tell you when you are ready to move on to a larger firm that provides more extensive services.[36]

- *Chemistry.* Rapport and personal interaction always is an important consideration

The recent trend in the accounting market has lead to increased competition, spiralling capital costs, declining profit margins, and an increase in lawsuits.[37] Entrepreneurs should shop around in such a buyer's market for competent accountants who provide the most suitable and appropriate services. Sources of reference for good lawyers are also sources of reference for accountants; trade groups may also provide recommendations.

Once a firm has reached any significant size, it will have many choices. The founders of one firm, which had grown to about $5 million in sales and had a strong potential to reach $20 million in sales in the next five years and eventually go public, put together a brief summary of the firm, including its background and track record, and a statement of needs for both banking and accounting services. The founders were startled by the aggressive response they received from several banks and major accounting firms.

The accounting profession is straightforward enough. Whether the accounting firm is small or large, it sells time, usually by the hour.

Consultants

The Decision[38]   Consultants are hired to solve particular problems and to fill gaps not filled by the venture team. There are many skilled consultants who can be of invaluable assistance and are a great source of "other people's resources." Advice needed can be quite technical and specific or general and far-ranging. Problems and needs also vary widely, depending upon whether the venture is just starting or is an existing business.

Start-ups usually require help with critical onetime tasks and decisions that will have lasting impact on the business. Consultants are employed by start-ups for the following reasons:

✓ To compensate for a lower level of professional experience.

✓ To target a wide market segment (possibly to do market research).

✓ To undertake projects that require a large start-up investment in equipment.[39]

These tasks and decisions might include assessing business sites, evaluating lease and rental agreements, setting up record and bookkeeping systems, finding business partners, obtaining start-up capital, and formulating initial marketing plans.

Existing businesses face ongoing issues resulting from growth. Many of these issues are so specialized that rarely is this expertise available within the venture team. Issues of obtaining market research, evaluating when and how to go about computerizing business tasks, deciding whether to lease or buy major pieces of equipment, and determining whether to change inventory valuation methods can be involved.

While it is not always possible to pinpoint the exact nature of a problem, sometimes a fresh, outside view helps when a new venture tries to determine the broad nature of its concern, such as whether it involves a personnel problem, manufacturing problem, or marketing problem, for example.

Karl Bayer, of Germany's Institute for Systems and Innovation Research, reported that the use of consultants had a negative effect on sales three to five years later. Additionally, his research found that "the work delivered by the consultants... [was] inadequate for the task."[40] He suggests that the entrepreneur can most likely find and adequately prepare a consultant so that gaps are filled and the firm benefits in the long run, but it takes diligence.

Selection Criteria: Add Value with Know-How and Contacts   Unfortunately, nowhere are the options so numerous, the quality so variable, and the costs so unpredictable as in the area of consulting. The number of people calling themselves management consultants is large and growing steadily. More than half the consultants were found to work on their own, while the remainder work for firms. In addition, government agencies employ consultants to work with businesses; various private and non-profit organizations provide management assistance to help entrepreneurs; and others, such as professors, engineers, and so forth, provide consulting services part time. Such assistance also may be provided by other professionals, such as accountants and bankers. A new and vital arena concerns Web presence. For example, Couple of Chicks e-marketing provides Internet marketing, distribution, and revenue measurement. The "chicks," Alicia Whalen of St. Catharines, Ontario, and Patricia Brusha of Mississauga, Ontario, use their expertise in search engine strategies and online metrics to boost Web site performance (www.acoupleofchicks.com).

Again, the right chemistry is critical in selecting consultants. One company president who was asked what he had learned from talking to clients of the consultant he finally hired said, "They couldn't really pinpoint one thing, but they all said they would not consider starting and growing a company without him!"

As unwieldy and risky as the consulting situation might appear, there are ways of limiting the choices. Consultants tend to have specialties; while some consultants claim wide expertise, most will indicate the kinds of situations they feel most comfortable with and skillful in handling. In seeking a consultant, consider the following:[41]

✓ Good consultants are not geographically bound; they will travel and can work via electronic means.

✓ The best referral system is word of mouth. This point cannot be stressed enough.

✓ Always check references carefully. It is important to look at the past solutions consultants have utilized.

✓ People skills are essential and therefore should be assessed when interviewing a consultant.

✓ Ask about professional affiliations and call them to verify the person is in good standing.

Three or more potential consultants can be interviewed about their expertise and approach and their references checked. Candidates who pass this initial screening then can be asked to prepare specific proposals.

A written agreement, specifying the consultant's responsibilities and objectives of the assignment, the length of time the project will take, and the type and amount of compensation, is highly recommended. Some consultants work on an hourly basis, some on a fixed-fee basis, and some on a retainer-fee basis. Huge variations in consulting costs for the same services exist. At one end of the spectrum are government agencies, which provide consultants to small businesses without charge. At the other end of the spectrum are well-known consulting firms that may charge large amounts for minimal marketing studies or technical feasibility analysis.

While the quality of many products roughly correlates with their price, this is not so with consulting services. It is difficult to judge consultants solely on the basis of the fees they charge.

FINANCIAL RESOURCES

Analyzing Financial Requirements

Once the opportunity has been assessed, once a new venture team has been formed, and once all resource needs have been identified, then is the time for a new venture to evaluate what financial resources are required and when. 6N Silicon Inc., which "makes silicon that can be combined with scrap from the chip manufacturing industry to make crystalline silicon,"[42] was able to obtain federal funding from Sustainable Development Technology Canada and get money from Ontario's Innovation Demonstration Fund. 6N raised $6 million in its first round of venture funding in July 2007, $20 million in second-round funding in April 2008, and in early 2009 another $5 million was found for equipment lease financing.

As has been noted before, there is a temptation to place the cart before the horse. Entrepreneurs are tempted to begin their evaluation of business opportunities—and particularly their thinking about formal business plans—by analyzing spreadsheets, rather than focusing first on defining the opportunity, deciding how to seize it, and then preparing the financial estimates of what is required.

However, when the time comes to analyze financial requirements, it is important to realize that cash is the lifeblood of a venture. As James Stancill, of the University of Southern California, has said: "Any company, no matter how big or small, moves on cash, not profits. You can't pay bills with profits, only cash. You can't pay employees with profits, only cash."[43] Financial resources are almost always limited, and important and significant trade-offs need to be made in evaluating a company's needs and the timing of those needs.

Spreadsheets   Computers and spreadsheet programs are tools that save time and increase productivity and creativity enormously. Spreadsheets are nothing more than pieces of accounting paper adapted for use with a computer.

The origins of the first spreadsheet program, VisiCalc, reveal its relevance for entrepreneurs. It was devised by business school student Dan Bricklin. Faced with analyzing pro forma income statements and balance sheets, cash flows, and breakevens for his cases, he was asked the question: "What if you assumed such and such?"

The major advantage of using spreadsheets to analyze capital requirements is having the ability to quickly examine different scenarios. This takes on particular relevance also when one considers, as James Stancill points out, "Usual measures of cash flow-net income plus depreciation (NIPD) or earnings before interest and taxes (EBIT) give a realistic indication of a company's cash position only during a period of steady sales."[44]

Take cash flow projections, for example. An entrepreneur could answer a question such as, What if sales grow at just 5 percent, instead of 15 percent, and what if only 50 percent, instead of 65 percent, of amounts billed are paid in 30 days? The impact on cash flow of changes in these projections can be seen.

The same what-if process also can be applied to pro forma income statements and balance sheets, budgeting, and breakeven calculations. To illustrate, by altering assumptions about revenues and costs such that cash reaches zero, breakeven can be analyzed. Thus, for example, return merchandise authorization (RMA) assumptions could be used as comparative boundaries for testing assumptions about a venture.

An example of how computer-based analysis can be of enormous value is the experience of a colleague who was seriously considering starting a new publishing venture. His analysis of the opportunity was encouraging, and important factors such as relevant experience and commitment by the lead entrepreneur were there. Assumptions about fixed and variable costs, market estimates, and probable start-up resource requirements had also been assembled. What needed to be done next was to generate detailed monthly cash flows to determine more precisely the economic character of the venture, including the impact of the quite seasonal nature of the business, and to determine the amount of money needed to launch the business and the amount and timing of potential rewards. In less than three hours, the assumptions about revenues and expenditures associated with the start-up were entered into a computer model. Within another two hours, he was able to see what the venture would look like financially over the first 18 months and then to see the impact of several different what-if scenarios. The net result was that the new venture idea was abandoned because the amount of money required appeared to outweigh the potential.

The strength of computer-based analysis is also a source of problems for entrepreneurs who place the "druther" before the fact. As the quote from Yzerman at the start of the chapter makes clear, with so many moving parts, analysis that is not grounded in sound perceptions about an opportunity is most likely to be confused.

INTERNET IMPACT: RESOURCES

Extending Your Network

An entrepreneur can greatly increase his or her reach for resources via the Internet. The Web offers a platform for which many tools are available (e.g., LinkedIn, Xing, Yahoo! Kickstart, Plaxo, Jigsaw, and Spoke). Nick Bontis is the Chief Knowledge Officer of Knexa, founded in 1999 as an online auction for knowledge. Knexa evolved to provide knowledge exchange tools. Online groups and bulletin boards might also be a source for answers to challenges new ventures and their leaders face (e.g., Brightspark and Innovation Resource Centre). And if you are short of ideas, check out Springwise.com, which "scans the globe for the most promising business ventures, ideas, and concepts."[45] Springwise is the brainchild of Reiner Evers, the creator of Trendwatching.com, a site devoted to spotting and tracking "the most promising consumer trends, insights, and related hands-on business ideas."[46]

In addition to intellectual resources the Web provides access to physical and financial assets (e.g., VenCorps, Alibaba, and Tradekey). Whether sourcing capital or equipment, just about anything can be found with some patience and a systematic search. Whether opening a restaurant or a carwash, used appliances and tools can readily be found. It is now even possible to pitch your idea and broadcast it on the Internet (e.g., Under the Radar).

Fund-raising for Nonprofits

A dynamic online service model has emerged that is changing the way nonprofits conduct their fund-raising auctions. Charity auctions, which account for millions of dollars in charitable giving in Canada, often attract high-income individuals and freely donated, high-quality items. But coordinating and staffing those venues has always been a challenge, particularly since volunteer turnover requires the retraining of a majority of the workforce each time an auction is held. In addition, physical auctions are typically catered affairs that are attended by only a small percentage of an organization's support base. Tom Williams of Victoria, British Columbia, has started GiveMeaning.com, a site that hosts fund-raising pages and serves as a system for charities seeking support and those wishing to make online donations. CanadaHelps.org is a donation portal for 83,000 charities that can be browsed under a number of categories. It was created in 2000 by Queen's University students Matthew Choi, Ryan Little, and Aaron Pereira to help charities reduce overhead costs and since its inception, it has facilitated $60 million in donations.

Chapter Summary

1. Successful entrepreneurs use ingenious boot-strapping approaches to marshalling and minimizing resources.

2. Control of resources rather than ownership of resources is the key to a "less is more" resource strategy.

3. Entrepreneurs are also creative in identifying other people's money and resources, thereby spreading and sharing the risks.

4. Building a brain trust of the right mentors, advisors, and coaches is one of the entrepreneur's most valuable "secret weapons."

5. Selecting outside advisors, directors, and other professionals boils down to one key criterion: Do they add value through their know-how and networks?

6. Today, access to financial and non-financial resources is greater than ever before and is increasing because of the Internet.

Study Questions

1. Entrepreneurs think and act ingeniously when it comes to resources. What does this mean and why is it so important?

2. Describe at least two creative bootstrapping examples you know of.

3. In selecting outside advisors, a board, consultants, and others, what are the most important criteria, and why?

Mind Stretchers   *Have you considered?*

1. Many successful entrepreneurs and private investors say it is just as bad to start out with too much money as it is too little. Why is this so? Can you find some examples?

2. It is said that money is the least important part of the resource equation and of the entrepreneurial process. Why is this so?

3. Within the first six months of start-up, which strategies will enable the entrepreneur to conserve cash and stretch resources?

EXERCISE   Build Your Brain Trust

Building a cadre of mentors, advisors, coaches, and directors can be the difference between success and failure in a venture. Building this brain trust will require your professionalism, thoroughness, salesmanship, and tenacity. You gain the trust and confidence of these mentors through your performance and integrity.

This exercise is intended to provide a framework and key steps in thinking through your requirements and developing a brain trust for your ventures.

Part I: Gap and Fit Analysis vis-à-vis the Timmons Model

1. At each phase of development of a venture, different know-how and access to experience, expertise, and judgment external to the founding team are often required. A key risk-reward management tool is the gap and fit analysis using the model.
   - Who has access to key know-how and resources that we do not?
   - What is missing that we have to have to obtain a very good chance?
   - Who can add the most value, insights, and solid experience to the venture now, in the next two years; and how?
   - Who are the smartest, most insightful people given what we are trying to do?
   - Who has the most valuable perspective and networks that could help the venture or in an area that you know least about?

2. Break down the Timmons Model to focus on each dimension.
   - Core opportunity: If they are not on your team now, who are the people who know more than anyone else on the planet about: the revenue and cost model, and underlying drivers and assumptions; how to price, get sales, marketing, customer service, and distribution; IT and e-business; the competition; the free cash flow characteristics and economics of the business?

- Resources: Who can help you get the necessary knowledge of and access to people, networks, money, and key talent?
- Team: Who has 10 to 20 years more experience and scar tissue than you do in building a venture from ground zero?

- Context: Who understands the context, changes, and timing of the venture in terms of the capital markets, any key regulatory requirements, and the internal drivers of the industry/technology/market?

3. Conclusions: What and who can make the biggest difference in the venture? Usually just one to three key people or resources can make a huge difference.

Part II: Identify and Build the Brain Trust

1. Once you've figured out what and who can make the greatest difference, you need to arrange for an introduction. Faculty, family, friends, roommates, and the like are good places to start.

2. If you can't get the introductions, then you have to go with your wits and creativity to get a personal meeting.
   - Be highly prepared and articulate.
   - Send an executive summary and advance agenda.
   - Know the reasons and benefits that will be most appealing to this person.
   - Follow up and follow through: send a handwritten note, not just another email.

3. Ask for blunt and direct feedback to such questions as:
   - What have we missed here? What flaws do you see in our team, our marketing plan, our financial requirements, our strategy, etc.?

- Are there competitors we don't know about?
- How would you compete with me?
- Who would reject and accept us for an investment? Why?
- Who have we missed?
- Who else should we talk with?

You will gain significant insight into yourself and your venture, as well as how knowledgeable and insightful the potential brain trust member is about your business, from the questions he or she asks, and from your own. You will soon know whether the person is interested and can add value.

4. Grow the brain trust to grow the venture. Think two years ahead and add to the brain trust people who have already navigated the difficult waters you expect to travel.

| CASE | WANT BEVERAGES |

Preparation Questions

1. In terms of resources, what are Want Beverages' strengths? What resources are missing?

2. Evaluate the financial situation of Want Beverages.

3. What goals do Bill and Angela Moffat have for Want Beverages? Can they go after competitors like RedBull? If so, how?

In July 2006, as Bill and Angela Moffat looked back at the first year of operations for Want Beverages (www.wantbeverages. com) and looked ahead to their plans for the coming year, they realized that there were many decisions that needed to be made. The owners of the Burlington, Ontario-based beverage company could clearly picture where they wanted the company to be several years in the future, but the path to get there was not as clear. What should they do in the upcoming year to increase sales to a level that would ensure success in achieving their long-term goals? Due to the dynamics of the industry they felt they needed to move quickly but a lack of resources, both people and money, was limiting their growth potential. So far they had financed Want from personal savings and lines of credit but they now needed more secure financing arrangements. They were

not sure what would be the best source of funds but they were sure that any lender or investor would want to see a detailed marketing plan for the next two or three years.

Background

For years the Moffats had represented a number of clothing and shoe companies, calling on stores throughout Ontario. They called their business Spellbound. While Spellbound was very successful, Bill and Angela felt there was an opportunity for them to build a company of their own. The companies they represented sold some of the most popular lines of clothing and footwear targeted at the action sports market but the Moffats realized that their personal chances for long-term success were dependent on those companies. This had become more obvious

---

This case was written by David Rose, Hugh Munro, and Lisa Giguere of Wilfrid Laurier University, Business & Economics, for purposes of classroom discussion.

to them in a few cases where a manufacturer had made decisions that might have been best for the company but were not in the best interests of Spellbound. The Moffats' goal was to have Want become a strong, profitable business that could support them and their young family without depending on Spellbound.

Since Spellbound's target market was young, action sports lovers Bill and Angela had developed a strong relationship with retailers across Ontario who served this market. They could see an opportunity to develop a beverage brand to appeal to this market. According to Bill:

> The average teenager only buys two or three shirts a year, but the same person buys 24 beverages per month. If we can become the beverage company that the young action sports crowd can call their own, we have an opportunity to build a very large market.

Using the insights that they had gained from their Spellbound experience, the Moffats launched their new company, Want Beverages, in June 2005. Their first product was a Berry-flavoured energy drink but they were determined to be a beverage company that targeted the 14 to 24-year-old, action sports crowd, rather than an energy drink company. In May 2006 they launched two new energy drink flavours, Lemonade and Lemonade Lite, as well as bottled water. Retailing for $1.00 per bottle, including tax, the bottled water would not provide the same profit margins for Want or the retailers, but the Moffats thought it was important to have it as part of their product offering. Now, loyal consumers in the target market could drink Want products more often than just the one or two energy drinks they would consume in a day. In the future they still planned to add an electrolyte drink and perhaps other beverages that would appeal to the target audience, for example, iced tea. They dreamed of becoming the brand that the target audience, throughout North America, would think of whenever they reached for a beverage. A critical component of the Want brand would be the commitment to give 15 cents from every bottle Want sold[1] to support action sports, for example, local skateparks, snowboard hills, and BMX trails.

Sales to early July were encouraging, with revenue of $35,000 so far in 2006, representing sales of 1,200 cases of energy drinks and water. These sales occurred mainly in a six-week period, as sales had been minimal in March and April due to a lack of inventory while Want was getting production underway for the launch of Lemonade and Lemonade Lite.

The Energy Drink Market

DISTRIBUTION The first retailers to carry Want Beverages were stores that catered to the action sports crowd. Skateboard and snowboard shops were the primary targets in the first year. Want provided these retailers with a Want branded counter-top refrigerator along with promotional materials. Since this was the only beverage carried in most of these stores, the store employees were frequent buyers of Want products and in many cases became advocates for the brand.

Selling through outlets that did not traditionally sell beverages was not without problems. Some retailers would not carry the Want product because they did not feel they could control the 'disappearance' of the product. As one store owner remarked:

> If I put a Want refrigerator on the counter, I know that each of my staff will have one bottle each day. At the end of the week I will have no product left in the refrigerator, but I am pretty

sure I won't have as much money as I should. It will be a big job to figure out who is paying and who isn't.

Another issue that resulted from distributing through these non-traditional outlets was the different markups and payment terms that were common in the snowboard and skateboard accessory business. While convenience stores were accustomed to paying for their beverages on short terms or even COD, other retailers were used to receiving 30 or 60-day terms. As well, 50-percent margins were not uncommon in clothing and shoe stores while convenience stores were accustomed to 20 to 35 percent margins.

West 49, the largest Canadian action sports retail chain with close to 100 stores located in malls across the country, had just recently decided to carry Want beverages in all locations, instantly giving Want national distribution. Want beverages had been available at 16 West 49 locations in 2005 on a trial basis. Based on the results at these test locations, they had decided to stock Want in all of their stores in 2006. While Want had to provide a refrigerator for each West 49 location, the retailer committed to an initial order of 10 cases per store and West 49 looked after distribution. Want only had to deliver the refrigerators and product to West 49's warehouse in Burlington, Ontario, just minutes from Want's Burlington warehouse.

Bars were also becoming an important part of Want's distribution, given the popularity of energy drinks mixed with alcohol, usually vodka. In busy bars, where the staff was actively promoting Want, sales could be in the seven or eight cases per week range. Bill attributed Want's success in bars to the unique flavour, a much lower price than for other energy drinks, and a good relationship with bar staff. This last point was important, according to Bill:

> If the staff isn't pushing our product, it hurts both Want and the bar. If a customer asks for a 'Red Bull and Vodka' and the bartender says 'We only have Want' the customer will likely switch to another drink, for example beer or wine. But if the bartender is positive about Want, there is a good chance the customer will be very pleased to pay a lower price for Want.

For all of the Ontario stores, Bill personally delivered the product, often in conjunction with calling on Spellbound's accounts. So far, the vehicle expenses were paid through Spellbound rather than Want, unless the trip was only for Want business. This arrangement was very convenient in the beginning but Want would eventually have to start paying the distribution costs as the Want business increased and Spellbound stayed the same or declined.

MANUFACTURING Want's products were bottled by a contract manufacturer, based on a recipe developed and strictly controlled by the Moffats. This bottler had been selected because they were willing to produce batches of as few as five pallets (585 cases) and they had a flexible production schedule so an order could be produced with as little as two weeks lead time. However, in exchange for the low volume requirement, the bottler charged $7.25 per case and insisted on being paid in advance. Since the Moffats were 'bootstrapping' the Want operation, attempting to operate without any external financing, the lack of credit terms created cash flow issues, particularly since most retailers were demanding 30 or 60-day terms.

There were other, cheaper manufacturing options. The Moffats knew of several bottlers who would produce the

---

[1] In order to keep the retail price at $1.00, Want was only able to donate five cents per bottle of water sold.

product for $2.50 per case, and would probably give at least 30-day terms, but their minimum quantity was usually 40,000 cases per batch. That was a lot of product to commit to buying, considering that total Want sales in 2005 were only 750 cases. There were also storage constraints given the 6,000 case capacity of the new Want warehouse. Finally, there was also a question of reliability. As Bill pointed out:

> The other bottlers are all reputable companies but we have never dealt with them. When I place an order with our current supplier I am very confident that the order will arrive on time. Right now I am focusing on building brand awareness and increasing distribution. Sure, it would be cheaper to deal with other bottlers, but right now I just don't have time to be worrying about whether the order will arrive on time or not.

(See Exhibits 1 and 2 for Want Beverages Inc. financial information.)

Promotion

The Moffats felt that Want's market strength would come from the fact that they focused on the Canadian action sports industry. They were convinced that action and extreme sports in Canada had only been slightly targeted by other beverage companies, all of which were U.S. based, and none of those companies were 'giving back' to the industry in the way that Want was doing with the 15 cent per bottle donation. Want was very grassroots, sponsoring up-and-coming athletes and participating in small, community events. Much of Want's advertising and promotion activity involved participating in sporting events including wakeboarding, skateboarding, and snowboarding functions. In 2006 more emphasis was also being placed on mountain biking, with Want sponsoring the Ontario Cup Downhill Mountain Bike Race series as well as sponsoring one of the downhill racing teams. By being present at local events, Bill and Angela felt they had direct access to their target market and could get a good grasp on what their ultimate consumer liked and disliked. As Bill and Angela explained:

> A number of bar promotions had been held and more were planned. At these events, Bill and/or Angela would set up a sampling area in the bar. They would bring their own Want product but had to buy vodka from the bar, at a cost of anywhere from $80 to $150 per bottle, depending on the bar. Using 15 ml. (one-half ounce) shots of vodka allowed them to serve 80 samples from an 1140-ml (40-ounce) bottle of vodka.

Staffing

The Moffats felt that a big part of building the Want brand involved getting out to places where the target market could be found. In summer 2005 they participated in 15 large, action sports events where they would set up a tent and spend an entire day. At the events, the Moffats were careful to control costs as much as possible. Rather than give away full bottles of product, they only gave one or two-ounce samples. They knew that other companies had teams of samplers who were hired specifically to attend events, but they often saw them putting little effort into their sampling and giving away far too much free product. Bill was certain that he needed to be at each event to control costs and to make sure that maximum value was reaped from the event, even if it meant limiting the number of events that could be sponsored. At many of these events they also met retailers who were interested in carrying their product.

The Moffats were considering whether they should hire additional sales staff and how they should pay them. They were considering hiring a full-time sales representative with knowledge of the industry, who they felt might cost about $50,000 per year including salary, a small commission based on sales and travel expenses. The new sales representative would be expected to attend sporting events and bar promotions either with or instead of the Moffats. This would allow Bill and Angela to focus more on other areas of the business including manufacturing, distribution, finance, and strategic planning. They also wondered if a better plan would be to have a number of sales representatives working on a straight commission basis. For example, they might get $50 for setting up a new retail account with a refrigerator and an initial order of five cases of product, and then $3.00 per case for all subsequent orders that they sold and delivered. Bill and Angela wondered if there were more people operating Spellbound-type businesses who would be interested in selling Want beverages in addition to their other product lines.

Finance

Since the Moffats were still operating Spellbound, they had not taken a salary from Want yet and had used their personal savings to pay for Want expenses that were over and above sales revenues. They were now at the point where a lack of cash was limiting their growth opportunities. Each time a new store agreed to begin selling Want products, except for convenience stores and bars, the store was given a counter-top refrigerator at no charge, provided they purchased at least 10 cases of product. The refrigerators originally cost $250 each, including Want logos, and the Moffats had to pay for the refrigerators six weeks before they were scheduled for production. For 2006, they had modified the design of the refrigerator and logos, and they had negotiated a better arrangement with the manufacturer so they were now paying only $150 per refrigerator with payment due on delivery.

The Moffats were uncertain about what the best financing source might be. Securing a bank loan would be an attractive option. However, the company had few assets that could be used to secure a loan and no track record of profitability so it would be difficult to convince a bank to lend Want the necessary money. The interest on a loan would also increase the company's breakeven point. An equity investor might be a better idea, but Bill and Angela were reluctant to have a partner who might not share their vision for the company. If they did decide to look for an equity investor they wondered what sort of investor they should be looking for and how much of the company they would need to give up. It was difficult to calculate a value for a start-up with limited revenues and no profits, as the value of the firm was really dependent on future activities. One approach could be to estimate the value of the firm at some point in the future and then calculate the net present value (NPV) of that figure at the time the investment was received. The amount of the required investment could then be converted to a percent ownership. The discount rate used to calculate the NPV would depend on the return that the investor wanted to achieve. In the end, the value would depend on negotiations between what the investor would be willing to offer and what the Moffats would be willing to accept.

The Future

Bill and Angela were concerned about the future of Want Beverages. Although they were still operating Spellbound and did not currently need to take a salary from Want, they hoped to be able to do so in the future. As they considered all that had happened so far, they wondered what the best plan would be to build Want into the profitable business that they knew it could be.

EXHIBIT 1   Want Beverages Inc.

INCOME STATEMENT 4/12/05–12/31/05	(Canadian Dollars)
Gross Sales	18,610.46
Cost of Goods Sold	13,042.19
Gross Profit	5,568.27
Expenses	
Advertising	500.00
Amortization	1,847.00
Bank Charges & Interest	1,145.68
Event Fees & Equipment incl. trailer	10,162.01
Miscellaneous	846.72
Promotional Supplies	2,689.77
Promotional Cases for Events (used as event admission)	5,087.62
Promotional Cases for Team Riders	3,963.74
Promotional Cases for Sampling	2,123.18
Rent	4,565.16
Supplies	1,274.97
Telephone & Utilities	2,069.07
Travel, Meals & Entertainment	2,597.59
Total Expenses	**38,872.51**
Net Income (Loss)	**−33,304.24**

BALANCE SHEET As at 12/31/05	(Canadian Dollars)
ASSETS	
Current Assets	
Accounts Receivable	7,930.20
Inventory	11,133.90
GST	2,865.04
	21,929.14
Capital Assets	
Refrigerators (Less accum. amortization)	15,005.52
TOTAL ASSETS	**36,934.66**
Current Liabilities	
Demand Loan and Overdraft	40,996.53
Accounts Payable: Spellbound	15,617.03
Accounts Payable: Suppliers	13,625.34
TOTAL LIABILITIES	**70,238.90**
EQUITY	
Capital Stock	2.00
Retained Earnings	−33,304.24
TOTAL LIABILITIES & EQUITY	**36,934.66**

Source: Want company records. Figures may have been disguised for confidentiality.

EXHIBIT 2   Want Beverages Inc.'s Price and Cost Information

	Per 24 Bottle Case	Per Bottle
Suggested Retail Price (including tax)		$2.50
Selling Price to Retailer	$30.00	$1.25
Production Costs:		
Bottling Fee	$7.25	$0.30
Bottles	$3.84	$0.16
Labels	$1.77	$0.07
Ingregients	$1.21	$0.05
Donations	$3.60	$0.15
Total Production Costs	$17.67	$0.73
Gross Margin	$12.33	$0.52

Source: Want company records. Figures may have been disguised for confidentiality.

Find more great exercises and additional study tools on the Online Learning Centre at
www.mcgrawhill.ca/olc/timmons

C · H · A · P · T · E · R

9

FINANCING THE VENTURE

Happiness to an entrepreneur is a positive cash flow.

Fred Adler
Venture Capitalist

Upon completion of this chapter, you will be able to:

1. Describe critical issues in financing new ventures.

2. Discuss the difference between entrepreneurial finance and conventional managerial or corporate finance.

3. Appreciate the process of crafting financial and fund-raising strategies and the critical variables involved, including identifying the financial life cycles of new ventures, a financial strategy framework, and investor preferences.

4. Understand the capital markets food chain and its implications.

5. Identify informal and formal investment sources of equity capital.

6. Learn how to be vigilant in finding, contacting, and dealing with equity investors.

7. See how venture capital investors make decisions.

VENTURE FINANCING: THE ENTREPRENEUR'S ACHILLES' HEEL

There are three core principles of entrepreneurial finance: (1) more cash is preferred to less cash, (2) cash sooner is preferred to cash later, and (3) less-risky cash is preferred to more-risky cash. While these principles seem simple enough, entrepreneurs, chief executive officers, and division managers often seem to ignore them. To these individuals, financial analysis seems intimidating, regardless of the size of the company. Even management teams, comfortable with the financial issues, may not be adept at linking strategic and financial decisions to their companies' challenges and choices.

Financial Management Myopia: It Can't Happen to Me

Financial management myopia is a combination of self-delusion and just plain not understanding the complex dynamics and interplay between financial management and business strategy. Why is this so?

237

Getting Beyond "Collect Early, Pay Late"   During our 40-plus years as educators, authors, directors, founders, and investors in entrepreneurial companies, we have met a few thousand entrepreneurs and managers, company founders, presidents, and the chief executive officers of middle-market companies. By their own admission, they felt uniformly uncomfortable, if not downright intimidated and terrified, by their lack of expertise in financial analysis and its relationship to management and strategy. The vast majority of entrepreneurs and non-financial managers are disadvantaged. Beyond "collect early, pay late," there is precious little sophistication and an enormous level of discomfort when it comes to these complex and dynamic financial interrelationships. Even good managers who are revelling in major sales increases and profit increases often fail to realize until it's too late the impact increased sales have on the cash flow required to finance the increased receivables and inventory.

The Spreadsheet Mirage   It is hard to imagine any entrepreneur who would not want ready answers to many financial vigilance questions, such as in Exhibit 9.1. Until now, however, getting the answers to these questions was a rarity. If the capacity and information are there to do the necessary analysis (and all too often they are not), it can take up to several weeks to get a response. In this era of spreadsheet mania, more often than not, the answers will come in the form of a lengthy report with innumerable scenarios, pages of numbers, backup exhibits, and possibly a presentation by a staff financial analyst, controller, or chief financial officer.

Too often the barrage of spreadsheet exhibits is really a mirage. What is missing? Traditional spreadsheets can only report and manipulate the data. The numbers may be there, the trends may be identified, but the connections and interdependencies between financial structure and business decisions inherent in key financial questions may be missed. As a result, gaining true insights and getting to creative alternatives and new solutions may be painfully slow, if not interminable. By themselves, spreadsheets cannot model the more complex financial and strategic interrelationships that entrepreneurs need to grasp. And for the board of directors, failure to get this information would be fatal and any delay would mean too little and too late. Such a weakness in financial know-how becomes life threatening for entrepreneurs such as those noted earlier, when it comes to anticipating the financial and risk-reward consequences of their business decisions. During a financial crisis, such a weakness can make an already dismal situation worse.

EXHIBIT 9.1   The Crux of It: Anticipation and Financial Vigilance

To avoid some of the great tar pits like the ones described earlier, entrepreneurs need answers to questions that link strategic business decisions to financial plans and choices. The crux of it is anticipation: *What is most likely to happen? When? What can go right along the way? What can go wrong? What has to happen to achieve our business objectives and to increase or to preserve our options?* Financially savvy entrepreneurs know that such questions trigger a process that can lead to creative solutions to their financial challenges and problems. At a practical level, financially astute entrepreneurs and managers maintain vigilance over numerous key strategic and financial questions:

- What are the financial consequences and implications of crucial business decisions such as pricing, volume, and policy changes affecting the balance sheet, income statement, and cash flow? How will these change over time?
- How can we measure and monitor changes in our financial strategy and structure from a management, not just a GAAP, perspective?
- What does it mean to grow too fast in our industry? How fast can we grow without requiring outside debt or equity? How much capital is required if we increase or decrease our growth by X percent?
- What will happen to our cash flow, profitability, return on assets, and shareholder equity if we grow faster or slower by X percent?
- How much capital will this require? How much can be financed internally and how much will have to come from external sources? What is a reasonable mix of debt and equity?
- What if we are 20% less profitable than our plan calls for? Or 20% more profitable?
- What should be our focus and priorities? What are the cash flow and net income breakeven points for each of our product lines? For our company? For our business unit?
- What about our pricing, our volume, and our costs? How sensitive are our cash flow and net income to increases or decreases in price, variable costs, or volume? What price/volume mix will enable us to achieve the same cash flow and net income?
- How will these changes in pricing, costs, and volume affect our key financial ratios and how will we stack up against others in our industry? How will our lenders view this?
- At each stage—start-up, rapidly growing, stagnating, or mature company—how should we be thinking about these questions and issues?

Time and again, the financially fluent and skillful entrepreneurs push what would otherwise be an average company toward and even beyond the brink of greatness. Clearly, financially knowledgeable CEOs enjoy a secret competitive weapon that can yield a decisive edge over less financially skilled entrepreneurs.

Critical Financing Issues

Exhibit 9.2 illustrates the central issues in entrepreneurial finance. These include the creation of value, the slicing and dividing of the value pie among those who have a stake or have participated in the venture, and the handling of the risks inherent in the venture. Developing financing and fund-raising strategies, knowing what alternatives are available, and obtaining funding are tasks vital to the survival and success of most higher potential ventures.

As a result, entrepreneurs face certain critical issues and problems, which influence the financing of entrepreneurial ventures, such as:

- *Creating value.* Who are the constituencies for whom value must be created or added to achieve a positive cash flow and to develop harvest options?
- *Slicing the value pie.* How are deals, both for start-ups and for the purchases of existing ventures, structured and valued, and what are the critical tax consequences of different venture structures? What is the legal process and what are the key issues involved in raising outside risk capital?
- *Selling the idea.* How do entrepreneurs make effective presentations of their business plans to financing and other sources? What are some of the nastier pitfalls, minefields, and hazards that need to be anticipated, prepared for, and responded to? How critical and sensitive is timing in each of these areas?

EXHIBIT 9.2   Central Issues in Entrepreneurial Finance

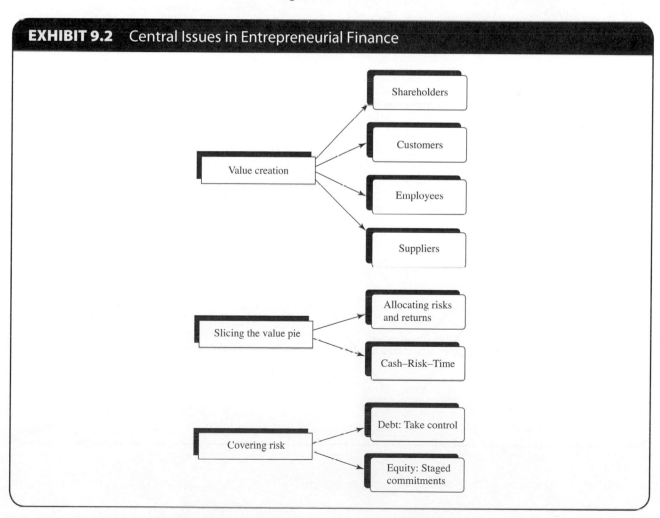

- *Covering risk.* How much money is needed to start, acquire, or expand the business, and when, where, and how can it be obtained on acceptable terms? What sources of risk and venture capital financing—equity, debt, and other innovative types—are available, and how is appropriate financing negotiated and obtained?
- Who are the financial contacts and networks that need to be accessed and developed?
- How do successful entrepreneurs marshal the necessary financial resources and other financial equivalents to seize and execute opportunities, and what pitfalls do they manage to avoid, and how?
- Can a staged approach to resource acquisition mitigate risk and increase return?

A clear understanding of the financing requirements is especially vital for new and emerging companies because new ventures go through financial 'hell' compared to existing firms, both smaller and larger, that have a customer base and revenue stream. In the early going, new firms are gluttons for capital, yet are usually not very debt-worthy. To make matters worse, the faster they grow, the more gluttonous is their appetite for cash.

This phenomenon is best illustrated in Exhibit 9.3 where loss as a percentage of initial equity is plotted against time.[1] The shaded area represents the cumulative cash flow of 157 companies from their inception. For these firms, it took 30 months to achieve operating breakeven and 75 months (or going into the seventh year) to recover the initial equity. As can be seen from the illustration, *cash goes out for a long time before it starts to come in.* This phenomenon is at the heart of the financing challenges facing new and emerging companies.

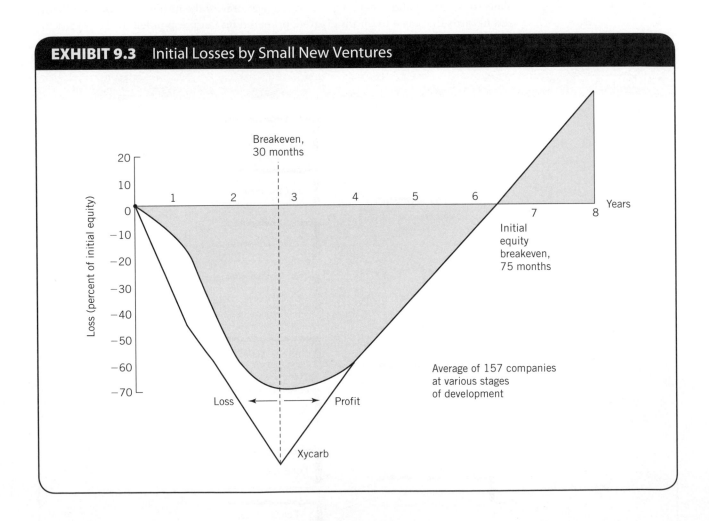

EXHIBIT 9.3   Initial Losses by Small New Ventures

Entrepreneurial Finance: The Owner's Perspective

If an entrepreneur who has had responsibility for financing in a large established company and in a private emerging firm is asked whether there are differences between the two, the person asking will get an earful. While there is some common ground, there are both stark and subtle differences, both in theory and in practice, between entrepreneurial finance as practised in higher potential ventures and corporate or administrative finance, which usually occurs in larger, publicly traded companies. Further, there are important limits to some financial theories as applied to new ventures.

Students and practitioners of entrepreneurial finance have always been dubious about the reliability and relevance of much of so-called modern finance theory, including the capital asset pricing model (CAPM), beta, and so on.[2] Apparently, this skepticism is gaining support from a most surprising source, corporate finance theorists. As reported in a *Harvard Business Review* article:

> One of the strongest attacks is coming from a man who helped launch modern finance, University of Chicago Professor Eugene Fama. His research has cast doubt on the validity of a widely used measure of stock volatility: beta. One group, however, eschews the scientific approach altogether, arguing that investors aren't always rational and that managers' constant focus on the markets is ruining corporate America. In their view, the highly fragmented U.S. financial markets do a poor job of allocating capital and keeping tabs on management.[3]

Challenging further the basic assumptions of corporate finance, the author continued: "These three concepts, the efficient market hypothesis, portfolio theory, and CAPM, have had a profound impact on how the financial markets relate to the companies they seek to value. . . . They have derailed and blessed countless investment projects."[4] Nancy Nichols, concluded that "despite tidy theories, there may be no single answer in a global economy."[5]

It is especially noteworthy that even the most prestigious of modern finance theorists, prominent Nobel laureate Robert Merton of Harvard University, may have a lot to learn. His works and theories of finance were the basis for Long Term Capital Management, Inc. The total collapse of that firm in the late 1990s threatened to topple the entire financial system.

Acquiring knowledge of the limits of financial theories, of differences in the domain of entrepreneurial finance, and of understanding the implications is a core task for entrepreneurs. To begin to appreciate the character and flavour of these limits and differences, consider the following sampling.

Cash Flow and Cash Cash flow and cash are the king and queen of entrepreneurial finance. Accrual-based accounting, earnings per share, or creative and aggressive use of the tax legislation and testing rules of the securities regulatory bodies are not. Just ask Enron or Nortel!

Time and Timing Financing alternatives for the financial health of an enterprise are often more sensitive to, or vulnerable to, the time dimension. In entrepreneurial finance, time for critical financing moves often is shorter and more compressed, the optimum timing of these moves changes more rapidly, and financing moves are subject to wider, more volatile swings from lows to highs and back.

Capital Markets Capital markets for more than 95 percent of the financing of private entrepreneurial ventures are relatively imperfect, in that they are frequently inaccessible, unorganized, and often invisible. Virtually all the underlying characteristics and assumptions that dominate such popular financial theories and models as the capital asset pricing model simply do not apply, even up to the point of a public offering for a small company. In reality, there are so many and such significant information, knowledge, and market gaps and asymmetries that the rational, perfect market models suffer enormous limitations.

Emphasis Capital is one of the least important factors in the success of higher potential ventures. Rather, higher potential entrepreneurs seek not only the best deal but also the backer who will provide the most value in terms of know-how, wisdom, counsel, and help. In addition, higher potential entrepreneurs invariably opt for the value added (beyond money), rather than just the best deal or share price.

Strategies for Raising Capital   Strategies that optimize or maximize the amount of money raised can actually increase risk in new and emerging companies, rather than lower it. Thus, the concept of "staged capital commitments," whereby money is committed for a 3- to 18-month phase and is followed by subsequent commitments based on results and promise, is a prevalent practice among venture capitalists and other investors in higher potential ventures. Similarly, wise entrepreneurs may refuse excess capital when the valuation is less attractive and when they believe that valuation will rise substantially.

Downside Consequences   Consequences of financial strategies and decisions are eminently more personal and emotional for the owners of new and emerging ventures than for the managements of large companies. The downside consequences for such entrepreneurs of running out of cash or failing are monumental and relatively catastrophic, since personal guarantees of bank or other loans are common. Contrast these situations with that of the 100 highest paid executives in Canada. The average one of these 100 CEOs has earned as much by January 2 at 9:46 a.m. (assuming he or she works 9 to 5) as the average Canadian earns in a full year. By the end of the workday on January 2, the average of the 100 top-paid CEOs in Canada will have earned $70,000. The highest paid Canadian executive will have earned more than $570,000 in those two days of work. "The average of the top 100 CEOs is paid as much in a year as 238 average Canadians. . . . The highest paid CEO makes as much as a small town—1,969 people—working at the average of wages and salaries, or 4,696 people working full-year at the minimum wage."[6] With much of these compensation packages independent of performance, the downside for these executives is obviously quite low.

Risk-Reward Relationships   While the high-risk/high-reward and low-risk/low-reward relationship (a so-called law of economics and finance) works fairly well in efficient, mature, and relatively perfect capital markets (e.g., those with money market accounts, deposits in credit unions, widely held and traded stocks and bonds, certificates of deposit), the opposite occurs too often in entrepreneurial finance to permit much comfort with this law. Some of the most profitable, highest return venture investments have been quite low-risk propositions from the outset. Many leveraged buyouts using extreme leverage are probably much more risky than many start-ups. Yet, the way the capital markets price these deals is just the reverse. The reasons are anchored in the second and third points noted above—timing and the asymmetries and imperfections of the capital markets for deals. Entrepreneurs or investors who create or recognize lower risk/very high-yield business propositions, before others jump on the Brink's truck, will defy the laws of economics and finance.

Valuation Methods   Established company valuation methods, such as those based on discounted cash flow models used in Wall Street and Bay Street mega deals, seem to favour the seller, rather than the buyer, of private emerging entrepreneurial companies. A seller loves to see an investment banker show up with a notebook computer and then proceed to develop "the 10-year discounted cash flow stream." The assumptions normally made and the mind-set behind them are irrelevant or grossly misleading for valuation of smaller private firms because of dynamic and erratic historical and prospective growth curves.

Conventional Financial Ratios   Current financial ratios are misleading when applied to most private entrepreneurial companies. For one thing, entrepreneurs often own more than one company at once and move cash and assets from one to another. For example, an entrepreneur may own real estate and equipment in one entity and lease it to another company. Use of different fiscal years compounds the difficulty of interpreting what the balance sheet really means and the possibilities for aggressive tax avoidance. Further, many of the most important value and equity builders in the business are off the balance sheet or are hidden assets: the excellent management team; the best scientist, technician, or designer; know-how and business relationships that cannot be bought or sold, let alone valued for the balance sheet.

Goals   Creating value over the long term, rather than maximizing quarterly earnings, is a prevalent mind-set and strategy among highly successful entrepreneurs. Since profit is more than just the bottom line, financial strategies are geared to build value, often at the expense of short-term earnings. The growth required to build value often is heavily self-financed, thereby eroding possible accounting earnings.

DETERMINING CAPITAL REQUIREMENTS

How much money does my venture need? When is it needed? How long will it last? Where and from whom can it be raised? How should this process be orchestrated and managed? These are vital questions to any entrepreneur at any stage in the development of a company. These questions are answered in the next two sections.

Financial Strategy Framework

The financial strategy framework shown in Exhibit 9.4 is a way to begin crafting financial and fund-raising strategies. The exhibit provides a flow and logic with which an otherwise confusing task can be met. *The opportunity leads and drives the business strategy, which in turn drives the financial requirements, the sources and deal structures, and the financial strategy.* (Again, until this part of the exercise is well-defined, developing spreadsheets and "playing with the numbers" is just that—playing.)

Once an entrepreneur has defined the core of the market opportunity and the strategy for seizing it (of course, these may change, even dramatically), he or she can begin to examine the financial requirements in terms of (1) asset needs (for start-up or for expansion facilities, equipment, research and development, and other apparently onetime expenditures) and

EXHIBIT 9.4   Financial Strategy Framework

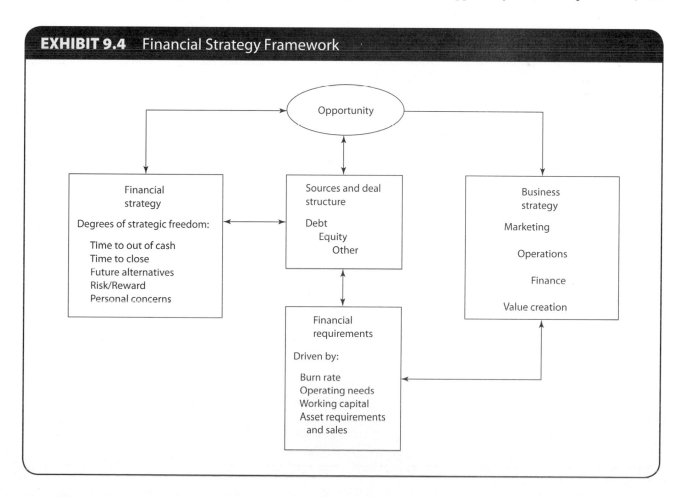

(2) operating needs (i.e., working capital for operations). This framework leaves ample room for crafting a financial strategy, for creatively identifying sources, for devising a fund-raising plan, and for structuring deals.

Each *fund-raising strategy*, along with its accompanying deal structure, commits the company to actions that incur actual and real-time costs and may enhance or inhibit future financing options. Similarly, each source has particular requirements and costs—both apparent and hidden—that carry implications for both financial strategy and financial requirements. The premise is that successful entrepreneurs are aware of potentially punishing situations, and that they are careful to "sweat the details" and proceed with a certain degree of wariness as they evaluate, select, negotiate, and craft business relationships with potential funding sources. In doing so, they are more likely to find the right sources, at the right time, and on the right terms and conditions. They are also more likely to avoid potential mismatches, costly sidetracking for the wrong sources, and the disastrous marriage to these sources that might follow.

Certain changes in the economic climate, such as the aftershocks felt following March 2000, October 1987, and Fall 2008, cause repercussions across financial markets and institutions serving smaller companies. These take the form of greater caution by both lenders and investors as they seek to increase their protection against risk. When the financial climate becomes harsher, an entrepreneur's capacity to devise financing strategies and to effectively deal with financing sources can be stretched to the limit and beyond. Also, certain lures of cash that come in unsuspecting ways turn out to be a punch in the wallet. Later in this chapter we cover some of these potentially fatal lures and some of the issues and considerations needed to recognize and avoid these traps while devising a fund-raising strategy and evaluating and negotiating with different sources.

Free Cash Flow: Burn Rate, OOC, and TTC

The core concept in determining the external financing requirements of the venture is free cash flow. Three vital corollaries are the burn rate (projected or actual), time to OOC (when will the company be Out Of Cash), and TTC (or the Time To Close the financing and have the cheque clear). These have a major impact on the entrepreneur's choices and relative bargaining power with various sources of equity and debt capital, which is represented in Exhibit 9.5. Chapter 10 addresses the details of deal structuring, terms, conditions, and covenants.

EXHIBIT 9.5   Entrepreneur's Bargaining Power Based on Time to Out of Cash

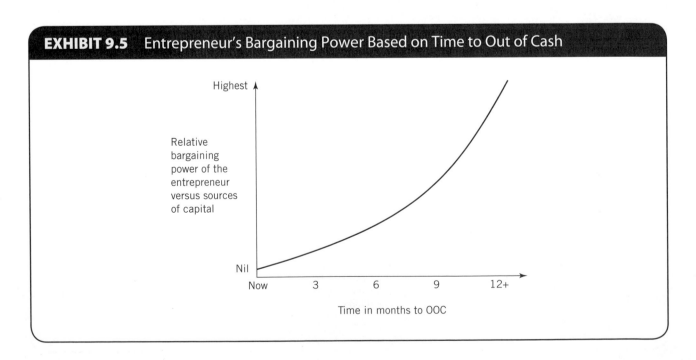

The message is clear: If you are out of cash in 90 days or less, you are at a major disadvantage. OOC even in six months is perilously soon. But if you have a year or more, the options, terms, price, and covenants that you will be able to negotiate will improve dramatically. The implication is clear: Ideally, raise money when you do not need it.

The cash flow generated by a company or project is defined as follows:

	Earnings before interest and taxes (EBIT)
Less	Tax exposure (tax rate times EBIT)
Plus	Depreciation, amortization, and other non-cash charges
Less	Increase in operating working capital
Less	Capital expenditures

Economists call this result free cash flow. The definition takes into account the benefits of investing, the income generated, and the cost of investing, the amount of investment in working capital and plant and equipment required to generate a given level of sales and net income.

The definition can fruitfully be refined further. Operating working capital is defined as:

	Transactions cash balances
Plus	Accounts receivable
Plus	Inventory
Plus	Other operating current assets (e.g., prepaid expenses)
Less	Accounts payable
Less	Taxes payable
Less	Other operating current liabilities (e.g., accrued expenses)

Finally, this expanded definition can be collapsed into a simpler one:[7]

	Earnings before interest but after taxes (EBIAT)
Less	Increase in net total operating capital (FA + WC)

where the increase in net total operating capital is defined as:

	Increase in operating working capital
Plus	Increase in net fixed assets

CRAFTING FINANCIAL AND FUND-RAISING STRATEGIES

Critical Variables

When financing is needed, a number of factors affect the availability of the various types of financing, and their suitability and cost:

- Accomplishments and performance to date.
- Investor's perceived risk.
- Industry and technology.
- Venture upside potential and anticipated exit timing.
- Venture anticipated growth rate.
- Venture age and stage of development.
- Investor's required rate of return or internal rate of return.
- Amount of capital required and prior valuations of the venture.
- Founders' goals regarding growth, control, liquidity, and harvesting.
- Relative bargaining positions.
- Investor's required terms and covenants.

Numerous other factors, especially an investor's or lender's view of the quality of a business opportunity and the management team, will also play a part in a decision to invest in or lend to a firm.

Generally, a company's operations can be financed through debt and some form of equity financing.[8] Moreover, it is generally believed that a new or existing business needs to obtain both equity and debt financing if it is to have a sound financial foundation for growth without excessive dilution of the entrepreneur's equity.

Short-term debt (i.e., debt incurred for one year or less) usually is used by a business for working capital and is repaid out of the proceeds of its sales. Longer-term borrowings (i.e., term loans of one to five years or long-term loans maturing in more than five years) are used for working capital and/or to finance the purchase of property or equipment that serve as collateral for the loan. Equity financing is used to fill the non-bankable gaps, preserve ownership, and lower the risk of loan defaults.

However, a new venture just starting operations will have difficulty obtaining either short-term or longer-term bank debt without a substantial cushion of equity financing or long-term debt that is subordinated or junior to all bank debt.[9] As far as a lender is concerned, a start-up has little proven capability to generate sales, profits, and cash to pay off short-term debt and even less ability to sustain profitable operations over a number of years and retire long-term debt. Even the underlying protection provided by a venture's assets used as loan collateral may be insufficient to obtain bank loans. Asset values can erode with time; in the absence of adequate equity capital and good management, they may provide little real loan security to a bank.

A bank may lend money to a start-up to some maximum debt-to-equity ratio. As a rough rule, a start-up may be able to obtain debt for working capital purposes that is equal to its equity and subordinated debt. A start-up can also obtain loans through such avenues as Business Development Bank of Canada, manufacturers and suppliers, or leasing.

An existing business seeking expansion capital or funds for a temporary use has a much easier job obtaining both debt and equity. Sources such as banks, professional investors, and leasing and finance companies often will seek out such companies and regard them as important customers for secured and unsecured short-term loans or as good investment prospects. Furthermore, an existing and expanding business will find it easier to raise equity capital from private or institutional sources and to raise it on better terms than the start-up.

Awareness of criteria used by various sources of financing—whether for debt, equity, or some combination of the two—that are available for a particular situation is central to devise a time-effective and cost-effective search for capital.

Financial Life Cycles

One useful way to begin identifying equity financing alternatives, and when and if certain alternatives are available, is to consider what can be called the financial life cycle of firms. Exhibit 9.6 shows the types of capital available over time for different types of firms at different stages of development (i.e., as indicated by different sales levels).[10] It also summarizes, at different stages of development (research and development, start-up, early growth, rapid growth, and exit), the principal sources of risk capital and costs of risk capital.

As can be seen in the exhibit, sources have different preferences and practices, including how much money they will provide, when in a company's life cycle they will invest, and the cost of the capital or expected annual rate of return they are seeking. The available sources of capital change dramatically for companies at different stages and rates of growth, and there will be variations in different parts of the country.

Many of the sources of equity are not available until a company progresses beyond the earlier stages of its growth. Some sources available to early-stage companies, especially personal sources, friends, and other informal investors or angels, will be insufficient to meet the financing requirements generated in later stages if the company continues to grow successfully.

Another key factor affecting the availability of financing is the upside potential of a company. Of the new businesses of all kinds expected to launch in Canada in the coming year, probably 5 percent or fewer will achieve the growth and sales levels of high potential

EXHIBIT 9.6   Financing Life Cycles

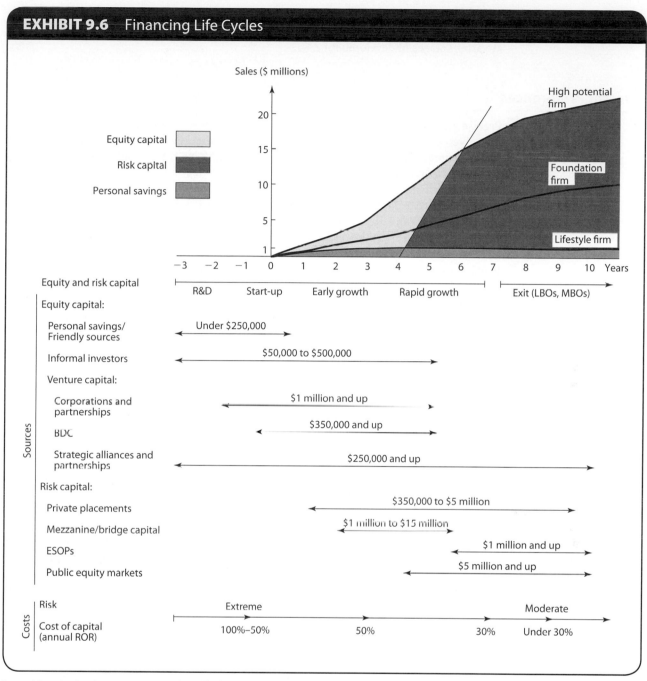

Source: Adapted and updated from W. H. Wetzel, Jr., "The Cost and Availability of Credit and Risk Capital in New England," in *A Region's Struggling Savior: Small Business in New England*, J. A. Timmons and D. E. Gumpert, eds. (Waltham, MA: Small Business Foundation of America, 1979).

firms. Foundation firms will total about 8 to 12 percent of all new firms, which will grow more slowly but exceed $1 million in sales and may grow to $5 to $15 million. Remaining are the traditional, stable lifestyle firms. High potential firms (those that grow rapidly and are likely to exceed $20 to $25 million or more in sales) are strong prospects for a public offering and have the widest array of financing alternatives, including combinations of debt and equity and other alternatives (which are noted later), while foundation firms have fewer, and lifestyle firms are limited to the personal resources of their founders and whatever net worth or collateral they can accumulate.

In general, investors believe the younger the company, the more risky the investment. This is a variation of the old saying in the venture capital business: The lemons ripen in two-and-a-half years, but the plums take seven or eight.

While the timeline and dollar limits shown are only guidelines, they do reflect how these money sources view the riskiness, and thus the required rate of return, of companies at various stages of development.

Investor Preferences

Precise practices of investors or lenders may vary between individual investors or lenders in a given category, may change with the current market conditions, and may vary in different areas of the country from time to time. Identifying realistic sources and developing a fund-raising strategy to tap them depend upon knowing what kinds of investments investors or lenders are seeking. While the stage, amount, and return guidelines noted in Exhibit 9.6 can help, doing the appropriate homework in advance on specific investor or lender preferences can save months of wild-goose chases and personal cash, while significantly increasing the odds of successfully raising funds on acceptable terms.

In the wake of the global recession, Canadian VC financing has mostly vanished. Financing from south of the border has also retreated. Joshua Geist of Geminare notes, "We would not have a problem getting a deal done in Canada, but the deal would be so poor, and there would be so little value out of it for the company that I already know this isn't for us." "VCs are having a hard time exiting earlier deals to extract cash and with the cash on hand that is being doled out carefully to existing picks. The historically biggest players, big pension funds, have switched to adding private equity buyouts to their portfolios and not backing new ventures seeking risk capital. And those still in the game 'think long and hard' before putting a deal together," says Mike Middleton of Q1 Capital Partners. [11] For Canada, tougher times lead to tougher deals. On their website, inventureLab (www.inventurelab.com) proclaims in big bold letters that "Venture capital is broken." They argue that "The priorities of venture capital do not help innovators build value. Their need for deal flow and rapid exits is not aligned with the process of transforming innovations into businesses, nor with the interests of the creators of the intellectual property." Providing business and sector expertise, inventureLab's approach is to focus on the needs of inventors and investors and create new paths to market for an innovation.

THE CAPITAL MARKETS FOOD CHAIN

Consider the capital markets for equity as a "food chain," whose participants have increasing appetites in terms of the deal size they want to acquire (Exhibit 9.7). This framework can help entrepreneurs identify and appreciate the various sources of equity capital at various stages of the venture's development, the amount of capital they typically provide, and the portion of the company and share price one might expect should the company eventually have an initial public offering (IPO) or trade sale.

The bottom row in Exhibit 9.7 shows this ultimate progression from R&D stage to IPO, where the capital markets are typically willing to pay $12 to $18 per share for new issues of small companies. Obviously, these prices are lower when the so-called IPO window is tight or closed, such as after the dot-com bubble. Prices for the few offerings that did exist (1 to 3 per week versus more than 50 per week in June 1996) were $5 to $9 per share. In hot IPO periods, 1999 for instance, offering prices reached as high as $20 per share and more. The modest revival that began in late 2003 continued into 2005. More recently, again the IPO markets suffered a severe decline and were basically shut down after the market trouble and economic turmoil beginning in late 2008, continuing through 2009 and well into 2010. In the third quarter of 2008 no private companies went public in Canada—no IPOs at all. In the first half of 2008 there were 53 public equity issues sold to Canadian investment markets with a value of $680 million—a fraction of what occurred in the boom years between 1996 and 1999.

One of the toughest decisions for the founders is whether to give up equity, and implicitly control, to have a run at creating very significant value. The row, "% company owned at IPO," shows that by the time a company goes public, the founders may have sold 70 to 80 percent or more of their equity. As long as the market capitalization of the company is

EXHIBIT 9.7   The Capital Markets Food Chain for Entrepreneurial Ventures

Stage of Venture	R&D	Seed	Launch	High Growth
Enterprise Value at Stage	Less than $1 million	$1–$5 million	$1–$5 million	More than $100 million
Sources	Founders High Net Worth Individuals FFF* SR&ED	FFF* Angel Funds Seed Funds SR&ED	Venture Capital Series A, B, C… Strategic Partners Very High Net Worth Individuals Private Equity	IPOs Strategic Acquirers Private Equity
Amount of Capital Invested	Less than $50,000–$200,000	$10,000–$500,000	$500,000–$20 million	$10–$50 million-plus
% Company Owned at IPO	10–25%	5–15%	40–60% by prior investors	15–25% by public
Share Price	$.01–$.50	$.50–$1.00	$1.00–$8.00	$12–$18
Number†	1–5 million	1–3 million	3–5 million	5–10 million

*Friends, families, and fools.
†At post–IPO

at least $100 million or more, the founders have created significant value for investors and themselves. During the peak of the dot-com mania, companies went public with market capitalizations of $1 to $2 billion and more. Founders' shares on paper were at least initially worth $200 to $400 million and more. These were truly staggering, unprecedented valuations, which were not sustainable.

In the remainder of the chapter, we will discuss these various equity sources and how to identify and deal with them. Exhibit 9.8 summarizes the venture capital food chain. In the first three rounds, series A, B, C, one can see that on average, the amount of capital invested was quite substantial: $1–$4 million, $6–$10 million, and $10–$15 million.

COVER YOUR EQUITY

One of the toughest trade-offs for any young company is to balance the need for start-up and growth capital with preservation of equity. Holding on to as much as you can for as long as you can is generally good advice for entrepreneurs. As was evident in Exhibit 9.6, the earlier the capital enters, regardless of the source, the more costly it is. Creative bootstrapping strategies can be great preservers of equity, as long as such parsimony does not slow the venture's progress so much that the opportunity weakens or disappears.

EXHIBIT 9.8   The Venture Capital Food Chain for Entrepreneurial Ventures

Venture Capital Series A, B, C, … (Average size of round): Example of three staged rounds

Round* { "A" @ $1–4 million—Start-up
"B" @ $6–10 million—Product development
"C"** @ $10–15 million—Shipping product

*Valuations vary markedly by industry.
**Valuations vary by region and venture capital cycle.

Three central issues should be considered when beginning to think about obtaining risk capital: (1) Does the venture need outside equity capital? (2) Do the founders want outside equity capital? and finally, (3) Who should invest? While these three issues are at the centre of the management team's thinking, it is also important to remember that a smaller percentage of a larger pie is preferred to a larger percentage of a smaller pie. Or as one entrepreneur stated, "I would rather have a piece of a watermelon than a whole raisin."[12]

After reviewing the online Venture Opportunity Screening Exercises, the business plan for Chapter 4, and the free cash flow equations (including OOC, TTC, and breakeven) from earlier in this chapter, it may be easier to assess the need for additional capital. Deciding whether the capital infusion will be debt or equity is situation specific, and it may be helpful to be aware of the trade-offs involved; see Chapter 11 for an introduction to debt capital. In the majority of the high-technology start-ups and early-stage companies, some equity investment is normally needed to fund research and development, prototype development and product marketing, launch, and early losses.

Once the need for additional capital has been identified and quantified, the management team must consider the desirability of an equity investment. As was mentioned in Chapter 8, bootstrapping continues to be an attractive source of financing. Many entrepreneurs suggest getting customers to pay quickly.[13] Entrepreneurs in certain industries can tap vendors by getting them to extend credit.[14] Such credit is termed "spontaneous" financing and arises in the normal course of business activity. While it may appear a blessing at the time, tables can turn. Air Canada is "perilously close to violating debt covenants. When its cash holdings fall below $900 million, for example, its credit card processing company can withhold a portion of ticket sales."[15] And the threshold is expected to rise to $1.3 billion—while its current reserves hover around $1 billion. Standard and Poor's recently downgraded the airline's debt, adding greater pressure.

An equity investment requires that the management team firmly believes that investors can and will add value to the venture. With this belief, the team can begin to identify those investors who bring expertise to the venture. Cash flow versus high rate of return required is an important aspect of the "equity versus other" financing decision.

Deciding *who* should invest is a process more than a decision. The management team has a number of sources to consider. There are both informal and formal investors, private and public markets. The single most important criterion for selecting investors is what they can contribute to the value of the venture—beyond just funding. Angels or wealthy individuals are often sought because the amount needed may be less than the minimum investment required by formal investors (i.e., venture capitalists and private placements). Whether a venture capitalist would be interested in investing can be determined by the amount needed and the rate of return expected.

TIMING

There are two times for a young company to raise money; when there is lots of hope, or lots of results, but never in between.

Georges Doriot
Venture Capitalist

Timing is also critical. A venture should not wait to look for capital until it has a serious cash shortage. For a start-up, especially one with no experience or success in raising money, it is unwise to delay seeking capital because it is likely to take six months or more to raise money. In addition to the problems with cash flow, the lack of planning implicit in waiting until there is a cash shortage can undermine the credibility of a venture's management team and negatively impact its ability to negotiate with investors.

But if a venture tries to obtain equity capital too early, the equity position of the founders may be unnecessarily diluted and the discipline instilled by financial leanness may be eroded inadvertently.

ANGELS AND INFORMAL INVESTORS

Who They Are

Wealthy individuals are an important source of capital for start-up and emerging businesses today. They have made it on their own, have substantial business and financial experience, and are likely to be in their 40s or 50s. They are also well educated; 95 percent hold university degrees, and 51 percent have graduate degrees. Of the graduate degrees, 44 percent are in a technical field and 35 percent are in business or economics.

Since the typical informal investor will invest from $10,000 to $250,000 in any one deal, informal investors are particularly appropriate for the following:[16]

- Ventures with capital requirements of between $50,000 and $500,000.
- Ventures with sales potential of between $2 and $20 million within 5 to 10 years.
- Small, established, privately held ventures with sales and profit growth of 10 to 20 percent per year, a rate that is not rapid enough to be attractive to a professional investor, such as a venture capital firm.
- Special situations, such as very early financing of high-technology inventors who have not developed a prototype.
- Companies that project high levels of free cash flow within three to five years.

These investors may invest alone or in syndication with other wealthy individuals, may demand considerable equity for their interests, or may try to dominate ventures. They also can get very impatient when sales and profits do not grow as they expected.

Usually, these informal investors will be knowledgeable and experienced in the market and technology areas in which they invest. If the right angel is found, he or she will add a lot more to a business than just money. As an advisor or director, his or her savvy, know-how, and contacts that come from having "made it" can be far more valuable than the $10,000 to $250,000 invested. The New Brunswick Small Business Investor Tax Credit gives a 30-percent tax break on investment amounts up to $80,000. The Yukon Small Business Investment Tax Credit grants a 24-percent break on investments of $100,000 or less. Generally, the evaluations of potential investments by such wealthy investors tend to be less thorough than those undertaken by organized venture capital groups, and such non-economic factors as the desire to be involved with entrepreneurship may be important to their investment decisions. There is a clear geographic bias of working within a one-hour driving radius of the investor's base. For example, a successful entrepreneur may want to help other entrepreneurs get started, or a wealthy individual may want to help build new businesses in his or her community.

Finding Informal Investors

Finding these backers is not easy. One expert noted: "Informal investors, essentially individuals of means and successful entrepreneurs, are a diverse and dispersed group with a preference for anonymity. Creative techniques are required to identify and reach them."[17] The Internet has provided entrepreneurs with an effective method of locating such investors. Formal sources such as Garage Technology Ventures and Brightspark Capital provide invaluable advice, assistance, and information regarding potential investors and help forge the link between investors and entrepreneurs seeking capital.

Invariably, financial backers are also found by tapping an entrepreneur's own network of business associates and other contacts. Other successful entrepreneurs know them, as do many tax attorneys, accountants, bankers, and other professionals. Apart from serendipity, the best way to find informal investors is to seek referrals from lawyers, accountants, business associates, university faculty, and entrepreneurs who deal with new ventures and are likely to know such people. Because such investors learn of investment opportunities from their business associates, fellow entrepreneurs, and friends, and because many informal investors invest together in a number of new venture situations, one informal investor contact can lead the entrepreneur to contacts with others.

In most larger cities, there are law firms and private placement firms that syndicate investment packages as offerings to networks of private investors. They may raise from several hundred thousand dollars to several million. The National Angel Capital Organization (www.angelinvestor.ca) is the national clearinghouse and lists 25 angel networks, but many angels fly under the radar. New Brunswick has only one readily identifiable angel network, which is not even included in the national registry. That New Brunswick angel network counts 25 individual angels, which completed two deals in 2007 for $1.1 million.[18] Manitoba, Newfoundland and Labrador, Quebec, and Saskatchewan each have only one network identified in the NACO directory.

Contacting Investors

If an entrepreneur has obtained a referral, he or she needs to get permission to use the name of the person making a referral when the investor is contacted. A meeting with the potential investor then can be arranged. At this meeting, the entrepreneur needs to make a concise presentation of the key features of the proposed venture by answering the following questions:

- What is the market opportunity?
- Why is it compelling?
- How will/does the business make money?
- How soon can the business reach positive cash flow?
- Why is this the right team at the right time?
- How does an investor exit the investment?

After the dot-com crash, investors throughout the capital markets food chain returned to these fundamental basics for evaluating potential deals. And the drought following the financial meltdown in late 2008 was expected to subside as investors cautiously test the waters once again in 2010 and generate confidence and momentum.

Entrepreneurs need to avoid meeting with more than one informal investor at the same time. Meeting with more than one investor often results in any negative viewpoints raised by one investor being reinforced by another. It is also easier to deal with negative reactions and questions from only one investor at a time. Like a wolf on the hunt, if an entrepreneur isolates one target "prey" and then concentrates on closure, he or she will increase the odds of success.

Whether or not the outcome of such a meeting is continued investment interest, the entrepreneur needs to try to obtain the names of other potential investors from this meeting. If this can be done, the entrepreneur will develop a growing list of potential investors and will find his or her way into one or more networks of informal investors. If the outcome is positive, often the participation of one investor who is knowledgeable about the product and its market will trigger the participation of other investors.

Evaluation Process

An informal investor will want to review a business plan, meet the full management team, see any product prototype or design that may exist, and so forth. The investor will conduct background checks on the venture team and its product potential, usually through someone he or she knows who knows the entrepreneur and the product. The process is not dissimilar to the due diligence of the professional investors (see below) but may be less formal and structured. The new venture entrepreneur, if given a choice, would be wise to select an informal investor who can add knowledge, wisdom, and networks as an advisor and whose objectives are consistent with those of the entrepreneur.

The Decision

If the investor decides to invest, he or she will have an investment agreement drafted by an attorney. This agreement may be somewhat simpler than those used by professional investors, such as venture capital firms. All the cautions and advice about investors and investment agreements that are discussed later in the chapter apply here as well.

Most likely, the investment agreement with an informal investor will include some form of a "put," whereby the investor has the right to require the venture to repurchase his or her stock after a specified number of years at a specified price. If the venture is not harvested, this put will provide an investor with a cash return.

For access to important documents for venture agreements, please visit the Online Learning Centre (www.mcgrawhill.ca/olc/timmons) for downloadable sample term sheets.

Will It Float?

Late-night television host, David Letterman, had a segment testing various items to see if they would float. To much fanfare, the item would be presented, analyzed, and a verdict would be reached before being dropped in a large tank of water for the real test. The verdict is still out on whether or not these entrepreneurs and their ideas will receive funding.

A BETTER MOUSETRAP

Frank Naumman of Waterloo, Ontario, has added a light emitting diode to his mousetrap as an indicator of whether or not it has been triggered. Although the modern mousetrap has been around since at least the 1880s, the last patent filing for an improved mousetrap was in 1993.[19]

ENERGY GENERATOR

Thane Heins of Almonte, Ontario, has developed "Perepeteia" what some say may be a perpetual motion machine. While these claims may be grandiose, the efficiency of his generator has caught the attention of scientists, the YouTube community, and at least one investor.[20]

DRYWALL FASTENER

Sean Ledoux of North Bay, Ontario, has come up with the idea of a single broad-headed screw to attach two drywall sheets to a wall instead of two screws, one on each side of the seam. He also has modified the screw threads but won't reveal details. Sean is already in talks to license the invention to Robertson Inc.—the founder of which lays claim to the creation of the square-notched screw.[21]

MASCARA REMOVER

Robyn Mumford of Cobourg, Ontario, has designed a device that removes mascara just from the eyelashes without having to rub the sensitive skin around the eyes. Though the potential is huge, Anthony Gussin of Nytric, an innovation consulting company—points out that it will take "considerable financial resources to develop."[22]

TRAILER HITCH ALIGNER

Ortwin Groh of Chilliwak, British Columbia, has developed a trailer-hitch alignment system to aid in backing up a vehicle in order to make proper contact to attach a trailer before towing. One piece attaches to the vehicle's bumper and another piece attaches to the trailer and then the driver lines them up in the mirrors while backing up the vehicle.[23]

TRAILER HITCH ALIGNER

Dave Underwood of London, Ontario, has the "Hitch Docker" to quickly, easily, efficiently line up and hook up a trailer with no damage to your bumper—guaranteed.[24] He has already had success across Ontario and his product is available through several specialty Internet firms based in the United States, but Dave is still seeking backing to make it big (e.g., Canadian Tire and Wal-Mart).

TRAILER HITCH ALIGNER

Jack Julicher of Bowmanville, Ontario, has patented the "Easy-Hitch" to "allow you to safely, and without hassle, hitch up any type of trailer system to your vehicle."[25] One telescopic rod with flashing light attached to the hitch-ball on the vehicle while another telescopic rod with flashing light attaches to the trailer. This permits visibility to insure alignment while backing up the vehicle. Jack and his wife were featured on *Dragons' Den* on CBC Television.

Sources: Joe Castaldo, "The Next Great Canadian Idea: A Better Mousetrap," *Canadian Business*, July 11, 2008; Sharda Prashad, "The Next Great Canadian Idea: Peripiteia Generator," *Canadian Business*, July 11, 2008; Andrew Wahl, "Semifinalist 3: Drywall Fastener," *Canadian Business*, June 4, 2007; Zena Olijnyk, "Semifinalist 2: Mascara Remover," *Canadian Business*, June 4, 2007; Joe Castaldo, "Semifinalist 1: Trailer Hitch Aligner," *Canadian Business*, June 4, 2007; www.hitchdocker.com; www.easyhitch.net.

VENTURE CAPITAL: GOLD MINES AND TAR PITS

There are only two classes of investors in new and young private companies: value-added investors and all the rest. If all you receive from an investor, especially a venture capitalist or a substantial private investor, is money, then you may not be getting a bargain. One of the keys to raising risk capital is to seek investors who will truly add value to the venture well beyond the money. Research and practice show that investors may add or detract value in a young company. Therefore, carefully screening potential investors to determine how they might fill some gaps in the founders' know-how and networks can yield significant results. Adding key management, new customers or suppliers, or referring additional investment are basic ways to add value.

A young founder of an international telecommunications venture landed a private investor who also served as an advisor. The following are examples of how this private investor provided critical assistance: introduced the founder to other private investors, to foreign executives (who became investors and helped in a strategic alliance), to the appropriate legal and accounting firms; served as a sounding board in crafting and negotiating early rounds of investments; and identified potential directors and other advisors familiar with the technology and relationships with foreign investors and cross-cultural strategic alliances.

Numerous other examples exist of venture capitalists' being instrumental in opening doors to key accounts and vendors that otherwise might not take a new company seriously. Venture capitalists may also provide valuable help in such tasks as negotiating original equipment manufacturer (OEM) agreements or licensing or royalty agreements, making key contacts with banks and leasing companies, finding key people to build the team, helping to revise or to craft a strategy.

It is always tempting for an entrepreneur desperately in need of cash to go after the money that is available, rather than wait for the value-added investor. These quick solutions to the cash problem usually come back to haunt the venture.

WHAT IS VENTURE CAPITAL?[26]

The word *venture* suggests that this type of capital involves a degree of risk and even something of a gamble. Specifically, "The venture capital industry supplies capital and other resources to entrepreneurs in business with high growth potential in hopes of achieving a high rate of return on invested funds."[27] The whole investing process involves many stages, which are represented in Exhibit 9.9. Throughout the investing process, venture capital firms seek to add value in several ways: identifying and evaluating business opportunities, including management, entry, or growth strategies; negotiating and closing the investment; tracking and coaching the company; providing technical and management assistance; and attracting additional capital, directors, management, suppliers, and other key stakeholders and resources.

The process begins with the conception of a target investment opportunity or class of opportunities, which leads to a written proposal or prospectus to raise a venture capital fund. Once the money is raised, the value creation process moves from generating deals to crafting and executing harvest strategies and back to raising another fund. The process usually takes up to 10 years to unfold, but exceptions in both directions often occur.

EXHIBIT 9.9   Venture Capital Investing Process

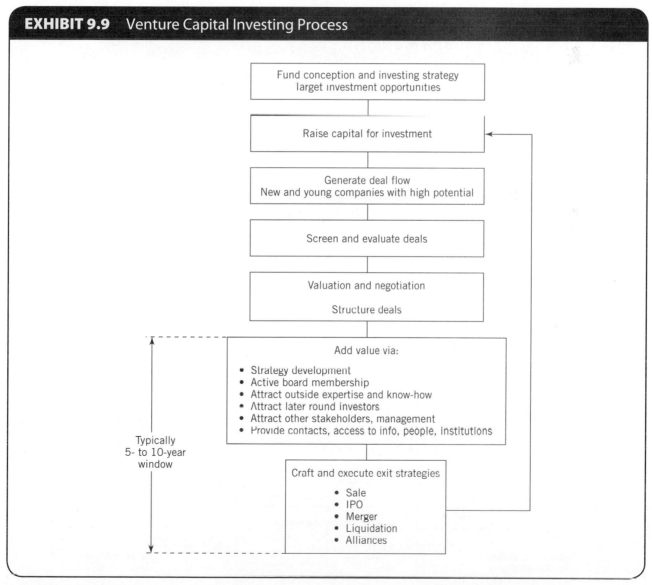

Source: William D. Bygrave and Jeffry A. Timmons, *Venture Capital at the Crossroads* (Boston, MA: Harvard Business School Publishing, 1992).

THE VENTURE CAPITAL INDUSTRY

Although the roots of venture capital can be traced from investments made by wealthy families in the 1920s and 1930s, the venture capital industry did not experience a growth spurt until the 1980s, when the industry took off. Before 1980, venture capital investing activities could be called dormant; but in the 1980s the industry roared up. The sleepy cottage industry of the 1970s was transformed into a vibrant, at times frenetic, occasionally myopic, and dynamic market for private risk and equity capital in the 1980s. And it was deals galore through the 1990s with year after year reaching ever-higher levels through 2000. A sobering wake-up came in 2001 and the brakes came on hard in the ensuing years. Due diligence increased to six or eight months, closer to historical norms, rather than the 45 days or less during the dot-com feeding frenzy. Things gained momentum and in subsequent years the money started to flow once again—until everything came apart with the economic turmoil that began in late 2008 and continued on into 2010.

The stark reality of all this is that the venture capital cycle—much like real estate—seems to repeat itself. Scarcity of capital leads to high returns, which attracts an overabundance of new capital, which drives returns down. The meltdown side of the venture capital and private equity markets can be expected with the certainty—though fortunately not frequency—as the change of seasons.

THE VENTURE CAPITAL PROCESS

Exhibit 9.10 represents the core activities of the venture capital process. At the heart of this dynamic flow is the collision of entrepreneurs, opportunities, investors, and capital.[28] Because the venture capitalist brings, in addition to money, experience, networks, and industry contacts, a professional venture capitalist can be very attractive to a new venture. Moreover, a venture capital firm has deep pockets and contacts with other groups that can facilitate the raising of money as the venture develops.

EXHIBIT 9.10   Flows of Venture Capital

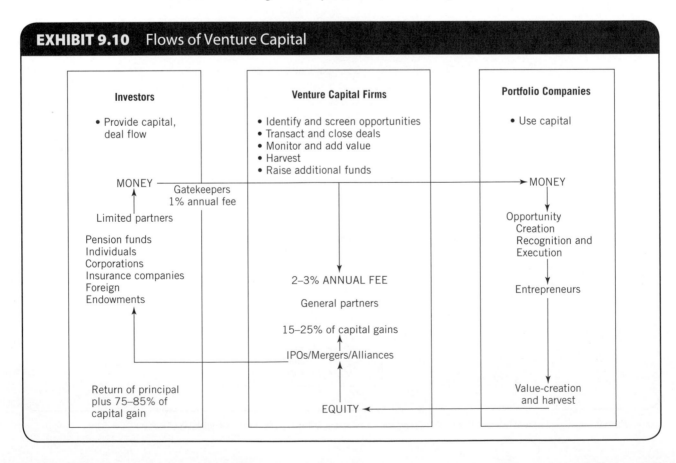

The venture capital process occurs in the context of mostly private, quite imperfect capital markets for new, emerging, and middle-market companies (i.e., those companies with $5 to $200 million in sales). The availability and cost of this capital depend on a number of factors:

- Perceived risk, in view of the quality of the management team and the opportunity.
- Industry, market, attractiveness of the technology, and fit.
- Upside potential and downside exposure.
- Anticipated growth rate.
- Age and stage of development.
- Amount of capital required.
- Founders' goals for growth, control, liquidity, and harvest.
- Fit with investors' goals and strategy.
- Relative bargaining positions of investors and founders given the capital markets at the time.

However, no more than 2 to 4 percent of those contacting venture capital firms receive financing from them. Despite the increase in funds in the recent boom years, observers comment that the repeat fund-raisers "stay away from seed and early-stage investments largely because those deals tend to require relatively small amounts of capital, and the megafunds, with $500 million-plus to invest, like to make larger commitments."[29] Further, an entrepreneur may give up 15 to 75 percent of his or her equity for seed/start-up financing. Thus, after several rounds of venture financing have been completed, an entrepreneur may own no more than 10 to 20 percent of the venture.

The venture capitalists' stringent criteria for their investments limit the number of companies receiving venture capital money. Venture capital investors look for ventures with very high growth potential where they can quintuple their investment in five years; they place a very high premium on the quality of management in a venture; and they like to see a management team with complementary business skills headed by someone who has previous entrepreneurial or profit-and-loss (P&L) management experience. In fact, these investors are searching for the "superdeal." Superdeals meet the investment criteria outlined in Exhibit 9.11.

Identifying Venture Capital Investors

Venture capital corporations or partners have an established capital base and professional management. Their investment policies cover a range of preferences in investment size and the maturity, location, and industry of a venture. Capital for these investments can be provided by one or more wealthy families, one or more financial institutions (e.g., insurance companies or pension funds), and wealthy individuals. Most are organized as limited partnerships, in which the fund managers are the general partners and the investors are the limited partners. Today, most of these funds prefer to invest from $2 to $5 million or more. Although some of the smaller funds will invest less, most of their investments are in the range of $500,000 to $1.5 million. Some of the so-called megafunds with more than $500 million to invest do not consider investments of less than $5 to $10 million. The investigation and evaluation of potential investments by venture capital corporations and partnerships are thorough and professional. Most of their investments are in high-technology businesses, but many will consider investments in other areas.

Sources and Guides   If an entrepreneur is searching for a venture capital investor, a good place to start is with Canada's Venture Capital and Private Equity Association (www.cvca.ca), which has a membership directory of venture capital firms. CVCA boasts over 1,700 members with over $75 billion in capital under management in three domains: buyout, mezzanine, and venture capital. Entrepreneurs also can seek referrals from accountants, lawyers, investment and commercial bankers, and businesspeople who are knowledgeable about professional investors. Especially good sources of information are other entrepreneurs who have recently tried, successfully or unsuccessfully, to raise money.

EXHIBIT 9.11   Characteristics of the Classic Superdeal from the Investor's Perspective

Mission

- Build a highly profitable and industry-dominant market leading company.
- Go public or merge within four to seven years at a high price-earnings (P/E) multiple.

Complete Management Team

- Led by industry "superstar."
- Possess proven entrepreneurial, general management, and P&L experience in the business.
- Have leading innovator or technologies/marketing head.
- Possess complementary and compatible skills.
- Have unusual tenacity, imagination, and commitment.
- Possess reputation for high integrity.

Proprietary Product or Service

- Has significant competitive lead and "unfair" and sustainable or defensible advantages.
- Has product or service with high value-added properties resulting in early payback to user.
- Has or can gain exclusive contractual or legal rights.

Large, Robust, and Sustainable Market

- Will accommodate a $100-million entrant in five years.
- Has sales currently at $200 million, or more, and growing at 25% or more per year.
- Has no dominant competitor now.
- Has clearly identified customers and distribution channels.
- Possesses forgiving and rewarding economics, such as:
  - Gross margins of 40 to 50%, or more.
  - 10% or more profit after tax.
  - Early positive cash flow and breakeven sales.

Deal Valuation and ROR

- Has "digestible" first-round capital requirements (i.e., greater than $1 million and less than $10 million).
- Able to return 10 times original investment in five years at P/E of 15 times or more.
- Has possibility of additional rounds of financing at substantial mark-up.
- Has anti-dilution and IPO subscription rights and other identifiable harvest/liquidity options.

Source: William D. Bygrave and Jeffry A. Timmons, *Venture Capital at the Crossroads* (Boston, MA: Harvard Business School Publishing, 1992).

Sometimes professional investors find entrepreneurs. Rather than wait for a deal to come to them, a venture capital investor may decide on a product or technology it wishes to commercialize and then put its own deal together. Michael Dunleavy and his fellow partners at Labarge Weinstein are always on the lookout for great companies to launch. They attend new technology showcases and other venues to discover the next great entrepreneurs who have not yet been called up to the big league.

What to Look For   Entrepreneurs are well advised to screen prospective investors to determine the appetites of such investors for the stage, industry, technology, and capital requirements proposed. It is also useful to determine which investors have money to invest, which are actively seeking deals, and which have the time and people to investigate new deals. Depending on its size and investment strategy, a fund that is a year or two old will generally be in an active investing mode.

Early-stage entrepreneurs need to seek investors who (1) are considering new financing proposals and can provide the required level of capital; (2) are interested in companies at the particular stage of growth; (3) understand and have a preference for investments in the particular industry (i.e., market, product, technology, or service focus); (4) can provide good business advice, moral support, and contacts in the business and financial community; (5) are reputable, fair, and ethical and with whom the entrepreneur gets along; and (6) have successful track records of 10 years or more advising and building smaller companies.[30]

Entrepreneurs can expect a number of value-added services from an investor. Ideally, the investor should define his or her role as a coach, thoroughly involved, but not a player. In terms of support, investors should have both patience and bravery. The entrepreneur should be able to go to the investor when he or she needs a sounding board, counselling, or an objective, detached perspective. Investors should be helpful with future negotiations, financing, private and public offerings, as well as in relationship building with key contacts.

What to Look Out For   There are also some things to be wary of in finding investors. These warning signs are worth avoiding unless an entrepreneur is so desperate that he or she has no real alternatives.

- *Attitude.* Entrepreneurs need to be wary if they cannot get through to a general part ner in an investment firm and keep getting handed off to a junior associate, or if the investor thinks he or she can run the business better than the lead entrepreneur or the new venture team.
- *Overcommitment.* Entrepreneurs need to be wary of lead investors who indicate they will be active directors but who also sit on the boards of six to eight other start-up and early-stage companies or are in the midst of raising money for a new fund.
- Inexperience. Entrepreneurs need to be wary of dealing with venture capitalists who have an MBA; are under 30 years of age; have worked only on Bay Street or as a consultant; have no operating, hands-on experience in new and growing companies; and have a predominantly financial focus.
- *Unfavourable reputation.* Entrepreneurs need to be wary of funds that have a reputation for early and frequent replacement of the founders or those where more than one-fourth of the portfolio companies are in trouble or failing to meet projections in their business plans.
- *Predatory pricing.* During adverse capital markets, investors who unduly exploit these conditions by forcing large share price decreases in the new firms and punishing terms on prior investors do not make the best long-term financial partners.

How to Find Out   How does the entrepreneur learn about the reputation of the venture capital firm? The best source is the CEO/founders of prior investments. Besides the successful deals, ask for the names and phone numbers of CEOs the firm invested in whose results were only moderate to poor, and where the portfolio company had to cope with significant adversity. Talking with these CEOs will reveal the underlying fairness, character, values, ethics, and potential of the venture capital firm as a financial partner, as well as how it practises its investing philosophies. It is always interesting to probe regarding the behaviour at pricing meetings.

Dealing with Venture Capitalists[31]

Don't forget that venture capitalists see lots of business plans and proposals, sometimes 100 or more a month. Typically, they invest in only one to three of these. The following suggestions may be helpful in working with them.

If possible, obtain a personal introduction from someone that is well-known to the investors (a director or founder of one of their portfolio companies, a limited partner in their fund, a lawyer or accountant who has worked with them on deals) and who knows you well. After identifying the best targets, you should create a market for your company by marketing it. Have several prospects. Be vague about who else you are talking with. You can end up with a rejection from everyone if the other firms know who was the first firm that turned you down. Beware, it is often just as hard to get a "no" as to get a "yes." You can waste an enormous amount of time before getting there.

When pushed by the investors to indicate what other firms/angels you are talking to, simply put it this way: "All our advisors believe that information is highly confidential to the company, and our team agrees. We are talking to other high quality investors like yourselves. The ones with the right chemistry who can make the biggest difference in our company and are prepared to invest first will be our partner. Once we have a term sheet and deal on the table, if you also want co-investors we are more than happy to share these other investors' names." Failing to take such a tack usually puts you in an adverse negotiating position.

Most investors who have serious interest will have some clear ideas about how to improve your strategy, product line, positioning, and a variety of other areas. This is one of the ways they can add value—if they are right. Consequently, you need to be prepared for them to take apart your business plan and to put it back together. They are likely to have their own format and their own financial models. Working with them on this is a good way to get to know them.

Never lie. As one entrepreneur put it, "You have to market the truth, but do not lie." Do not stop selling until the money is in the bank. Let the facts speak for themselves. Be able to deliver on the claims, statements, and promises you make or imply in your business plan and presentations. Tom Huseby of SeaPoint Ventures adds some final wisdom: "It's much harder than you ever thought it could be. You can last much longer than you ever thought you could. They have to do this for the rest of their lives!" Finally, never say no to an offer price. There is an old saying that your first offer may be your best offer.

Questions the Entrepreneur Can Ask

The presentation to investors when seeking venture capital is demanding and pressing, which is appropriate for this high-stakes game. Venture capitalists have an enormous legal and fiduciary responsibility to their limited partners, not to mention their powerful self-interest. Therefore, they are thorough in their due diligence and questioning to assess the intelligence, integrity, nimbleness, and creativity of the entrepreneurial mind in action (see Chapter 1).

Once the presentation and question-answer session is complete, the founders can learn a great deal about the investors and enhance their own credibility by asking a few simple questions:

- Tell us what you think of our strategy, how we size up the competition, and our game plan. What have we missed? Who have we missed?
- Are there competitors we have overlooked? How are we vulnerable and how do we compete?
- How would you change the way we are thinking about the business and planning to seize the opportunity?
- Is our team as strong as you would like? How would you improve this and when?
- Give us a sense of what you feel would be a fair range of value for our company if you invested \$_____?

Their answers will reveal how much they have done and how knowledgeable they are about your industry, technology, competitors, and the like. This will provide robust insight as to whether and how they can truly add value to the venture. At the same time, you will get a better sense of their forthrightness and integrity: Are they direct, straightforward, but not oblivious to the impact of their answers? Finally, these questions can send a very favourable message to investors: Here are entrepreneurs who are intelligent, open-minded, receptive, and self-confident enough to solicit our feedback and opinions even though we may have opposing views.

Due Diligence: A Two-Way Street

It can take several weeks or even months to complete the due diligence on a start-up, although if the investors know the entrepreneurs, it can go much more quickly. The verification of facts, backgrounds, and reputations of key people, market estimates, technical capabilities of the product, proprietary rights, and the like is a painstaking investigation for investors. They will want to talk with your directors, advisors, former bosses, and previous partners. Make it as easy as possible for them by having very detailed résumés and lists of

10 to 20 references (with phone numbers and addresses) such as former customers, bankers, vendors, and so on, who can attest to your accomplishments. Prepare extra copies of published articles, reports, studies, market research, contract, or purchase orders, technical specifications, and the like that can support your claims.

One recent research project examined how 86 venture capital firms nationwide conducted their intensive due diligence. To evaluate the opportunity, the management, the risks, the competition, and to weigh the upside against the downside, firms spent from 40 to 400 hours, with the typical firm spending 120 hours. That is nearly three weeks of full-time effort. At the extreme, some firms engaged in twice as much due diligence.[32] Central to this investigation were careful checks of the management's references and verification of track record and capabilities.

While all this is going on, do your own due diligence on the venture fund. Ask for the names and phone numbers of some of their successful deals, some that did not work out, and the names of any presidents they ended up replacing. Who are their legal and accounting advisors? What footprints have they left in the sand regarding their quality, reputation, and record in truly adding value to the companies in which they invest? Finally, the chemistry between the management team and the general partner that will have responsibility for the investment and, in all likelihood, a board seat is crucial. If you do not have a financial partner you respect and can work closely with, then you are likely to regret ever having accepted the money.

OTHER EQUITY SOURCES

Business Development Bank of Canada (BDC)

Promoting small and medium-sized enterprises by guaranteeing long-term loans, venture capital, and subordinate financing, Business Development Bank of Canada has been supporting start-up and high-potential ventures since 1944 (see Exhibit 9.12). According to their Web site:

- **BDC *Financing*** clients accepted $2.9 billion new loans through some 9,100 transactions. Income totalled $160.9 million in fiscal 2008. The closing portfolio, before allowance for credit losses, rose to $10.0 billion, an increase of $886 million, or nearly 10 percent over 2007.

- **BDC *Subordinate Financing*** clients accepted $97.4 million through 107 transactions executed by way of a limited partnership with the Caisse de dépôt et placement du Québec. BDC's share of the transactions accounted for $48.7 million in fiscal 2008. As of March 31, 2008, BDC's Subordinate Financing portfolio stands at a fair value of $156.2 million, a 5.3-percent increase over last year.

- **BDC *Venture Capital*** authorized 85 direct investments for a total of $105.5 million. It also authorized investments of $25 million in two funds.

- **BDC *Consulting*** revenues reached $24.8 million. In 2008, 2,770 mandates were started. BDC Consulting offers entrepreneurs tailored, affordable, high-quality services to help them become more competitive.

Leading as a development bank, BDC pays special attention to start-ups, innovators, fast growth companies, manufacturers, and exporters who face lower financing approval rates. BDC also pays special attention to entrepreneurs who are working to commercialize the fruits of research and development—university or lab discoveries—to create innovative products and globally successful companies in sectors such as life sciences and information technology.

Over the past six years, about 14 percent of BDC authorizations went to clients in the start-up phase. Market data shows that approximately 5 percent of Canadian businesses are start-ups. BDC finds that after five years, 67 percent of the start-up businesses it supported survive, compared to the Statistics Canada industry benchmark of 36 percent.

EXHIBIT 9.12   Business Development Bank of Canada

- BDC Venture Capital is a Canadian leader in the critically important early-stage (including seed) investment phase. In fiscal 2009, BDC made 58 percent of the dollar value of its direct investments in early-stage firms. That figure compares with the industry average of 44 percent. In 2009, direct seed investments in Canada totalled $64.1 million.
- BDC offers subordinate financing, a hybrid financing that combines debt and equity features, to entrepreneurs who need working capital to grow their businesses but do not have the tangible security that conventional lenders require, or who do not want to dilute their ownership of the firm.
- Women entrepreneurs lead businesses of all sizes in all sectors. They also enter the small business marketplace at twice the rate men do. Over the past two decades, their number has more than doubled. BDC has more than 7,000 women clients, almost twice as many as it did a decade ago. Women represent about one quarter of BDC's client roster.
- Young entrepreneurs lead about 9 percent of Canadian small businesses. Many of them find it hard to secure financing because they have limited net worth, little or no managerial experience, and have no proven track record. In fiscal 2009, through 22 Entrepreneurship Centres across Canada, BDC granted $190 million worth of loans to young entrepreneurs across the country.
- BDC maintains formal partnerships with more than 200 Community Futures Development Corporations, a cross-country network of contact points located mostly in rural areas. These partnerships enable BDC to reach entrepreneurs who live near these centres. Using this network, BDC supported more than 800 entrepreneurs in 2009.
- BDC helps promote economic development in Aboriginal communities through a grassroots approach called the Circle of Entrepreneurial Success. This strategy delivers management training, ongoing mentorship, and loans of $5,000 to $20,000, with terms that vary depending on the cash flow expectations for the project.

Source: Business Development Bank of Canada, Annual report 2009, www.bdc.ca.

Scientific Research and Experimental Development Tax Credit Program

The risk and expense of conducting serious research and development are often beyond the means of start-ups and small businesses. For about 25 years, the SR&ED federal tax incentive program has encouraged companies to invest in and pursue innovation, by offering tax credits of up to 35 percent on the first $2 million of qualified expenditures and 20 percent on amounts over that cap. In addition, provincial incentives vary from nothing to 20 percent. The Canada Revenue Agency administers the program and receives claims from over 11,000 enterprises, three-quarters of whom are small with claims varying from $20,000 to $2 million.

Corporate Venture Capital

While corporate venture capitalists are similar to traditional VCs in that they look for promising young companies on the verge of a spike in sales, corporations tend to be more risk-averse and specialized. Business investing is highly cyclical in nature and follows a pattern of ebb and flow. Since investing in a relevant technology can reduce the costs of their own research and development, fit is usually an important aspect of the funding decision. When working with corporate funding sources, make sure you consider the corporation's philosophy and culture, as well as their investment track record with small businesses before agreeing to any deal.

Mezzanine Capital

At the point where the company has overcome many of the early-stage risks, it may be ready for mezzanine capital.[33] The term *mezzanine financing* refers to capital that is between senior debt financing and common stock. In some cases it takes the form of redeemable preferred stock, but in most cases it is subordinated debt that carries an equity "kicker" consisting of warrants or a conversion feature into common stock. This subordinated-debt capital has many characteristics of debt but also can serve as equity to underpin senior debt. It is generally unsecured, with a fixed coupon and maturity of 5 to 10 years. A number of variables are involved in structuring such a loan: the interest rate, the amount and form of the equity, exercise/conversion price, maturity, call features, sinking fund, covenants, and put/call options. These variables provide for a wide range of possible structures to suit the needs of both the issuer and the investor.

Offsetting these advantages are a few disadvantages to mezzanine capital compared to equity capital. As debt, the interest is payable on a regular basis, and the principal must be repaid, if not converted into equity. This is a large claim against cash and can be burdensome if the expected growth and/or profitability does not materialize and cash becomes tight. In addition, the subordinated debt often contains covenants relating to net worth, debt, and dividends.

Mezzanine investors generally look for companies that have a demonstrated performance record, with revenues approaching $10 million or more. Because the financing will involve paying interest, the investor will carefully examine existing and future cash flow and projections.

Mezzanine financing is utilized in a wide variety of industries, ranging from basic manufacturing to high technology. As the name implies, however, it focuses more on the broad middle spectrum of business, rather than on high-tech, high-growth companies. Specialty retailing, broadcasting, communications, environmental services, distributors, and consumer or business service industries are more attractive to mezzanine investors.

Private Placements

Private placements are an attractive source of equity capital for a private company that for whatever reason has ruled out the possibility of going public. If the goal of the company is to raise a specific amount of capital in a short time, this equity source may be the answer. In this transaction, the company offers stock to a few private investors, rather than to the public as in a public offering. A private placement requires little paperwork compared to a public offering.

If the company's management team knows of enough investors, then the private placement could be distributed among a small group of friends, family, relatives, or acquaintances. Or the company may decide to have a broker circulate the proposal among a few investors who have expressed an interest in small companies. The following four groups of investors might be interested in a private placement:[34]

1. Let us say you manufacture a product and sell to dealers, franchisors, or wholesalers. These are the people who know and respect your company. Moreover, they depend on you to supply the product they sell. They might consider it to be in their interest to buy your stock if they believe it will help assure continuation of product supply, and perhaps give them favoured treatment if you bring out a new product or product improvement. One problem is when one dealer invests and another does not; can you treat both fairly in the future? Another problem is that a customer who invests might ask for exclusive rights to market your product in a particular geographical area, and you might find it hard to refuse.

2. A second group of prospective buyers for your stock are those professional investors who are always on the lookout to buy a good, small company in its formative years, and ride it to success. Very often, these sophisticated investors choose an industry and a particular product or service in that industry they believe will become hot and then focus 99 percent of their attention on the calibre of the management. If your management, or one key individual, has earned a high reputation as a star in management, technology, or marketing, these risk-minded investors tend to flock to that person. (The high-tech industry is an obvious example.) Whether your operation meets their tests for stardom as a hot field may determine whether they find your private placement a risk to their liking.

3. Other investors are searching for opportunities to buy shares of smaller growth companies in the expectation that the company will soon go public and they will benefit as new investors bid the price up, as often happens. For such investors, news of a private placement is a tip-off that a company is on the move and worth investigating, always with an eye on the possibility of its going public.

4. Private placements also often attract venture capitalists who hope to benefit when the company goes public or when the company is sold. To help ensure that happy development, these investors get seriously active at the level of the board of directors, where their skill and experience can help the company reach its potential.

Initial Public Stock Offerings

Commonly referred to as an IPO, an initial public offering raises capital through provincially registered and underwritten sales of the company's shares. Numerous federal and provincial securities laws and regulations govern these offerings; thus, it is important that management consult with lawyers and accountants who are familiar with the current regulations.

In the past, such as during strong bull markets for new issues, it was possible to raise money for an early-growth venture or even for a start-up. These boom markets are easy to identify because the number of new issues jump astoundingly. The flip side is that sharp decreases follow just as quickly as investor enthusiasm grinds to a halt. In these more difficult financial environments, such as following the 2008 recession, the new-issues market became very quiet for entrepreneurial companies. As a result, exit opportunities are limited. In addition, it becomes very difficult to raise money for early-growth or even more mature companies from the public market.

The more mature a company is when it makes a public offering, the better the terms of the offering. A higher valuation can be placed on the company, and less equity will be given up by the founders for the required capital.

There are a number of reasons an entrepreneurial company would want to go public. The following are some of the advantages:

- To raise more capital with less dilution than occurs with private placements or venture capital.
- To improve the balance sheet and/or to reduce or to eliminate debt, thereby enhancing the company's net worth. To obtain cash for pursuing opportunities that would otherwise be unaffordable.
- To access other suppliers of capital and to increase bargaining power, as the company pursues additional capital when it needs it least.
- To improve credibility with customers, vendors, key people, and prospects. To give the impression: "You're in the big leagues now."
- To achieve liquidity for owners and investors.
- To create options to acquire other companies with a tax-free exchange of stock, rather than having to use cash.
- To create equity incentives for new and existing employees.

Notwithstanding the above, IPOs can be disadvantageous for a number of reasons:

- The legal, accounting, and administrative costs of raising money via a public offering are more disadvantageous than other ways of raising money.
- A large amount of management effort, time, and expense are required to comply with securities regulations and reporting requirements and to maintain the status of a public company. This diversion of management's time and energy from the tasks of running the company can hurt its performance and growth.
- Management can become more interested in maintaining the price of the company's stock and computing capital gains than in running the company. Short-term activities to maintain or increase a current year's earnings can take precedence over longer-term programs to build the company and increase its earnings.
- The liquidity of a company's stock achieved through a public offering may be more apparent than real. Without a sufficient number of shares outstanding and a strong "market maker," there may be no real market for the stock and, thus, no liquidity.
- The investment banking firms willing to take a new or unseasoned company public may not be the ones with whom the company would like to do business and establish a long-term relationship.

Private Placement after Going Public[35]

Sometimes a company goes public and then, for any number of reasons that add up to bad luck, the high expectations that attracted lots of investors early on turn sour. Your financial picture worsens; there is a cash crisis; down goes the price of your stock in the public marketplace. You find that you need new funds to work your way out of difficulties, but public investors are disillusioned and not likely to cooperate if you bring out a new issue.

Still, other investors are sophisticated enough to see beyond today's problems; they know the company's fundamentals are sound. While the public has turned its back on you, these investors may be receptive if you offer a private placement to tide you over. In such circumstances, you may use a wide variety of securities—common stock, convertible preferred stock, convertible debentures. There are several types of exempt offerings, usually described by reference to the securities regulation that applies to them.

Employee Stock Ownership Plans (ESOPs)

ESOPs are another potential source of funding used by existing companies that have high confidence in the stability of their future earnings and cash flow. An ESOP is a program in which the employees become investors in the company, thereby creating an internal source of funding. "The combination of being able to invest in employer stock and to benefit from its many tax advantages make the ESOP an attractive tool."[36] The ESOP Association of Canada claims that enterprises with ESOPs have higher profit growth, higher profit margins, increased productivity, and better returns on both total equity as well as capital (www.espop-canada.com).

Keeping Current about Capital Markets

One picture is vivid from all this: Capital markets, especially for closely held, private companies right through the initial public offering, are very dynamic, volatile, asymmetrical, and imperfect. Keeping abreast of what is happening in the capital markets in the six to 12 months before a major capital infusion can save invaluable time and hundreds of thousands and occasionally millions of dollars. Below are listed the best sources currently available to keep you informed:

✓ Canada's Venture Capital & Private Equity Association (www.cvca.ca).
✓ Guide for Canadian companies looking to access the U.S. capital markets (www.osler.com/resources.aspx?id=11930).
✓ Raising Capital in Canada (www.bowne.com/securitiesconnect/pubs_raising_capital.asp).
✓ *Venture Capital Journal* (www.vcjnews.com).
✓ *Red Herring*, a Silicon Valley magazine.

Chapter Summary

1. Cash flow is king and cash is queen. Happiness is a positive cash flow. More cash is preferred to less cash. Cash sooner is preferred to cash later. Less-risky cash is preferred to more-risky cash.

2. Financial know-how, issues, and analysis are often the entrepreneurs' Achilles' heels.

3. Entrepreneurial finance is the art and science of quantifying value creation, slicing the value pie, and managing and covering financial risk.

4. Determining capital requirements, crafting financial and fund-raising strategies, and managing and orchestrating the financial process are critical to new venture success.

5. Harvest strategies are as important to the entrepreneurial process as value creation itself. Value that is unrealized may have no value.

6. Appreciating the capital markets as a food chain looking for companies to invest in is key to understanding motivations and requirements.

7. Entrepreneurs have to determine the need for outside investors, whether they want outside investors, and if so whom.

8. Canada's unique capital markets include a wide array of private investors, from "angels" to venture capitalists.

9. The search for capital can be very time consuming, and whom you obtain money from is more important than how much (i.e., identifying gold mines and avoiding tar pits).

10. It is said that the only thing that is harder to get from a venture capitalist than a "yes" is a "no."

11. Entrepreneurs who know what and whom to look for—and look out for—increase their odds for success.

Study Questions

1. Define the following and explain why they are important: burn rate, free cash flow, OOC, TTC, financial management myopia, spreadsheet mirage.

2. Why is entrepreneurial finance simultaneously both the least and most important part of the entrepreneurial process? Explain this paradox.

3. What factors affect the availability, suitability, and cost of various types of financing? Why are these factors critical?

4. Why do financially savvy entrepreneurs ask the financial and strategic questions in Exhibit 9.1? Can you answer these questions for your venture?

5. What does one look for in an investor, and why?

6. How can the founders prepare for the due diligence and evaluation process?

7. Describe the venture capital investing process and its implications for fund-raising.

8. What other sources of capital are available and how are these accessed?

9. Explain the capital markets food chain and its implications for entrepreneurs and investors.

Mind Stretchers   *Have you considered?*

1. With regard to your new venture, to what extent might you be suffering from financial myopia and spreadsheet mirage?

2. People who believe that you first have to have money, in large amounts, to make money are naive and ignorant. Why is this so? Do you agree?

3. Who do you need to get to know well to strengthen the entrepreneurial finance know-how on your team?

4. Some entrepreneurs say you shouldn't raise venture capital unless you have no other alternative. Do you agree or disagree, and why?

5. Identify a founder/CEO who has raised outside capital, and was later fired by the board of directors. What are the lessons here?

6. How do venture capitalists make money? What are the economics of venture capital as a business?

| CASE | SANDVINE INC. |

Preparation Questions

1. Evaluate the company. How much do you believe the company is worth?

2. From an investor's perspective, please make specific recommendations regarding financing.

3. What specific actions would you propose be taken and when?

In late September 2003 Dave Caputo, president and CEO of Waterloo, Ontario-based Sandvine Inc., was considering what recommendations he should make at the upcoming senior management meeting. In business only 28 months, Sandvine had developed two exciting new products designed to increase the profitability of Internet Service Providers (ISPs). The first allowed ISPs to reduce costs by better managing the exploding volumes of peer-to-peer (P2P) network traffic they were forced to handle as a result of their subscribers' increasing use of P2P file sharing. The second provided a means for the ISPs to increase their revenues by offering their subscribers a suite of network-based services such as virus protection, content filtering, and firewalls, (i.e., subscriber services).

The company was scoring some important successes in the early-stage commercialization of its products, and had high hopes of delivering a 'home run' for its investors. But there were issues. Caputo was uncertain about the sustainability of heavy P2P-generated traffic volumes in light of a growing propensity among copyright holders to take legal action against unauthorized copying of music files. At the same time, he was becoming increasingly concerned about Sandvine's ability to compete in the subscriber services arena in the face of large, well-known competition.

At the senior management meeting scheduled for October 2, Caputo wanted to outline his suggestions to the team about the way forward. Before he could do this, though, he needed to answer some important strategic questions. Should Sandvine remain committed to both product areas, should they focus on just one (and if so, which one), or should they pursue a third, as yet unknown alternative? Overlaid on these concerns was the question of geographic expansion. With sales offices in Europe, and a new office just opened in Hong Kong, were they over-stretching their limited resources, or was it crucial to aggressively pursue quick worldwide adoption of Sandvine's unique technology?

Background

Sandvine's origins could be traced back to 1997, when video networking equipment maker PixStream was started in Waterloo, Ontario, with just $3 million of seed money. PixStream was so successful that it was sold to Cisco Systems for $554 million just as the tech bubble burst in 2001. Cisco shut down PixStream four months later, with a layoff of 220 staff, as part of a massive global restructuring. The layoffs were especially troubling to Caputo, who had known many of the staff since the company's birth. Young engineers and tech workers who had started out in sneakers and t-shirts had now developed and matured. Increasingly, family portraits were replacing Smashing Pumpkins posters at their cubicles. More importantly, many of these folks were talented people who had been responsible for the dazzling success of PixStream.

Caputo was not the only one concerned about the breakup of the talented PixStream team. Within hours of Cisco announcing the closure of PixStream, Caputo had received a call from one of the original PixStream investors. His question was simple: "What are you going to do, Dave, to keep the team together?" Caputo's response was to huddle with four other PixStream leaders to see what could be done. With the blessing of Cisco and in advance of PixStream's closure, the team met with venture capital groups (VCs) to plant the seeds for what would ultimately become Sandvine. Within weeks, Celtic House, VenGrowth, TechCapital Partners, and BDC had agreed to invest in the new venture. The terms of the deal were almost unbelievable and reflected the incredible strength of the PixStream team. 'Sign the talent . . . then find the product' was an unorthodox approach to financing even tech start-ups, but the five soon-to-be ex-Cisco managers had so impressed the VCs that they were willing to break with tradition. By the time the dust settled Caputo had succeeded in brokering one of the largest seed-round placements in Canadian history and $19.5 million was in the bank. Sandvine was founded on August 31, 2001, the day after Cisco closed PixStream.

Products

As the team was being formed, the founders began the search for products that would provide Sandvine with an opportunity to develop a competitive advantage, and offer a large enough market opportunity to justify the large investment in the company. The group shared a belief in what they thought was an absolute truth: that the Internet would continue to grow and that this reality should frame new product ideas. They also recognized that they had a unique team of software and hardware developers with some very specific skills. With backgrounds that included, in many cases, experience at PixStream, they

This case was written by Detlev Nitsch, David Rose, and Josephine McMurray of Wilfrid Laurier University, Business & Economics, for purposes of classroom discussion.

www.mcgrawhill.ca/olc/timmons

had the expertise to develop tools that could analyze a thick data stream and determine what to do with its various components. Some other firms could do this too, but what set the Sandvine team apart was their ability to develop products that could perform these functions in real-time, while the traffic was flowing, as opposed to post-hoc analysis done offline. These unique capabilities were the reason it had been so important to keep the team together. After interviewing experts, visiting customers, buying market research, analyzing potential competitors and searching patents for conflicts and undeveloped ideas the team decided that the best opportunities involved products that would improve the profitability of ISPs.

After the product category decision was made, development efforts led to two ready-for-market products in the Sandvine stable:

1. The PPE 8200 Peer-to-Peer Element rearranged peer-to-peer traffic and ensured that each peer-to-peer search was directed down the least costly network path, hence saving ISPs from excessive bandwidth expenses.

2. The Sandvine Subscriber Services Cluster™ provided ISPs with a turnkey solution that would allow them to offer content filtering, virus scanning, and firewall protection to their subscribers.

Both products were designed to be highly scalable so that, from a customer's perspective, keeping pace with growth simply involved adding another unit of the same element to support additional users or bandwidth. All development would be performed in-house, and component manufacturing would be outsourced, with final assembly and testing taking place in Sandvine's Waterloo facility.

The Internet Service Provider Industry

The ISP industry was vast, and approached perfect competition due to the large number of service providers and ease of access for buyers. ISPs provided access to the Internet in one of two ways. Customers could purchase dial-up service through telephone lines, or they could utilize faster, always-on, broadband technology with either telephone wires or cable. The industry in 2003 was populated by competitors who were distinguishable on many dimensions. Some ISPs were large providers with links to telephone companies (e.g., Bell's Sympatico) or cable firms (e.g., Rogers, COGECO). Others were relatively small local companies that sold Internet access to customers in a small geographic area.

Value Added Subscriber Services

Many ISPs hoped that providing network-based subscriber services such as Internet firewalls, anti-virus protection, and content filtering, in addition to the basic services, would allow them to create a lucrative monthly revenue stream. Some observers felt that the ISP industry might have the same experience as the telephone market, where competition had been just as intense and where high-margin services such as call waiting, call display, and voice mail had provided a powerful up-sell to kick-start stagnating revenues. These services had continued to be extremely profitable for the telephone service providers, as they had been able to increase prices several times without losing many subscribers. It appeared that customers had little interest in re-evaluating their purchase decision once they had grown accustomed to their new telephone features.

Peer to Peer

Sandvine knew that it was their P2P traffic management product that would command the initial attention of ISPs and get their foot in the door. P2P file sharing activity was threatening to swamp ISPs in a torrent of off-network traffic. According to some estimates, as much as 65 percent of total Internet bandwidth usage was now devoted to P2P traffic. This was creating a growing and unacceptably large monthly expense for ISPs. When a P2P client connected to other P2P clients on the network, most of the time the client they connected with was outside their ISP's network. ISPs paid companies such as MCI, WorldCom, Sprint, and AT&T a fee every time traffic left their networks, so anything that might reduce these fees would be attractive. The Sandvine solution used a concept of the lowest cost network path by first hunting on the ISP's own network for the requested share and leaving to search the Internet only if the target was not found internally.

Marketing Strategy

In Caputo's opinion there was a limit to the size of the P2P market. He thought that the subscriber services market was really Sandvine's most attractive opportunity, in terms of both market size and longevity, but would be more difficult to penetrate. Since the subscriber services bundle needed to be installed 'in-line', between the Internet and the user, they were 'mission-critical' products for ISPs. A failure in the Sandvine Subscriber Services Cluster had the potential to shut down an ISP's entire network, which was a risk that Caputo felt ISPs would be unwilling to place under the control of an unproven supplier. Sandvine's P2P element, on the other hand, operated as an adjunct to the ISP's network. A failure would not shut down the ISP's network and thus represented a much lower risk to the ISP's business.

Clearly there was a market, yet Sandvine knew they would have to work closely with their ISP clients to help them educate the end-users. Because of the number of ISPs and Internet users in North America, it seemed clear that Sandvine should concentrate selling efforts initially on that market. However, global development was opening up huge opportunities in Europe and Asia. This led to Sandvine opening a U.K office in January 2003 and planning an Asian entry later in 2003, to take advantage of first mover status on their technology.

For both the P2P element and the Subscriber Services cluster, ISPs should have a payback period of less than four months.

The Company

The company had grown very quickly over the past year. There were now 78 employees, organized as follows:

- 43 engineers working on hardware, software, firmware and IT.
- 15 worked primarily on the P2P traffic-management, while 28 were assigned to subscriber services.
- 17 sales and marketing staff in product management, support and business development.
- 12 manufacturing and testing staff.
- 3 people in finance.
- 3 sales representatives in the U.K., Canada, and the United States.

Caputo had deliberately constructed an organization designed to place the customer first, and where there was transparency in decision-making with little to no political maneuvering. He called his approach the "Sandvine Way" and believed that it would help the company build a distinctive, competitive advantage. Caputo hoped to create an infrastructure that would scale easily as the company grew, without losing the informal, creative, and dynamic spirit that usually characterized start-up technology companies. This intangible was the very first thing that had been lost when Cisco had taken over PixStream. Overnight, effective decision-makers were rendered inoperable as control shifted to the larger entity, with its disparate geographic units and different bureaucracy. Caputo had learned from the Cisco experience that without a common understanding of what was expected of people and what activities were valued, scarce resources would be wasted as the company grew.

Jenn Patterson, the new manager of Human Resources, was a PixStream "grad." Like Caputo, she had been with the company from its birth to its demise and truly understood its distinctive culture. Caputo called on Patterson to work with him to create a simple plan—to begin working on a deliberate culture, a model that would allow the management team to clearly and doggedly communicate their vision of the organization. The "Sandvine Way" was the collective vision of Caputo, Patterson, and other members of the management team and included eight 'truths' that were to be acted on and understood clearly.

Sandvine's five founders remained solidly aligned with their technical mission, but more particularly, having been through the PixStream sale, were aware that there was a point where engineering had to step back to allow the sales and marketing staff to ramp up the company and its products for commercialization.

Financial

Currently the company had a cash 'burn rate' of approximately $700,000 per month (estimated at $100,000 per year per employee in Waterloo and $150,000 for European employees). The original $19 million had been augmented with another successful round of financing. To date, marketing expenses remained modest with an emphasis on production of roadmaps, white papers, trade show attendance and PR related to industry analysts. It was estimated that the marketing budget was less than $200,000 per year, in addition to the payroll expense for employees working in that area.

Current Situation

Sandvine had just recruited three highly respected sales professionals who were well known in the industry. Each had been given responsibility for one of three regions: Canada, the U.S., and the United Kingdom. Chris Colman had opened the new U.K. office in Basingstoke, Hampshire, in January 2003, as managing director, Sales and Business Development responsible for establishing Sandvine's Europe, Middle East, and Africa (EMEA) division. This was Sandvine's first office outside North America, but they planned to venture into the Asian market with an office in Hong Kong later in 2003.

An inside sales manager helped to direct the overall sales effort, and nurtured and managed a sophisticated Customer Relationship Management (CRM) system. This system allowed Sandvine to input customer information, competitive intelligence, details of competitors, and buyer organization charts in

an effort to scout competitors' activities and bid intelligently on proposals.

At the beginning of July 2003, one P2P customer had converted from 'trial user' to 'buyer.' Explaining the reasons for their purchase, the customer said:

> The Sandvine unit integrates easily with our existing infrastructure, and their approach dramatically improves our ability to control the cost impact of P2P on the network. At the same time, it respects our broadband customers' expectations of quality and consistency. Our company's technicians were impressed with the knowledge of the Sandvine engineers and the willingness they showed in fine-tuning the device to optimize performance.

There were a further 15 active trial sites for the P2P elements in Canada and the U.S., in addition to six that were under way in EMEA. There was considerable confidence that all the trials would be successfully converted to sales in the near future. The subscriber services clusters were also on trial. The company was expecting to very shortly announce that two major customers would install their products.

From what Caputo had recently heard from the market, it appeared that smaller competitors in subscriber services were not about to give up without a fight. His assessment of the competitive threat was that Symantec and McAfee were not the only ones he needed to worry about:

> Companies that most people likely never heard of, such as F-Secure, Zone, Trend Micro, ZK and others are fighting the gorillas with the only weapon they have . . . price. Customers have told us they have hard quotes for three or more services (such as anti-virus, firewall, parental control, spam elimination, pop-up elimination) for $1.00. Not per month, but for a year!

The attractiveness of the P2P market was also less than certain. In May 2003, Kazaa Media Desktop had become the world's most downloaded software, having overtaken the previous record-holder, ICQ, by reaching 230,309,616 worldwide downloads. Kazaa was distributed without charge and enabled its users to download more licensed content than any other application.[1] The official story was 'downloading licensed content', but the Internet set wasn't propelling Kazaa, Grokster, Gnutella, and other file sharing software into the record books by downloading copies of MS Office. Kazaa helped users share their favourite music, the latest movies and the hottest new apps.

Around the same time, another media item brought the following news from Apple: *The revolutionary* iTunes Music Store puts 200,000 songs at your fingertips. It's built right into iTunes 4 and lets you search or browse genres, new releases, exclusives and more. Preview any song for free. When you find a song you want, buy it for just 99¢. It's what music lovers have been waiting for: a music store with Apple's legendary ease of use, offering a hassle-free way to preview, buy, and download music online quickly and easily for just 99¢ a song, Apple claimed it could make the whole music buying experience easier. Steve Jobs, CEO of Apple, was convinced that the music industry was about to turn a corner in the copyright war. With the government shutting down pirate Web sites and the record industry now going after individuals for alleged

---

[1] "Kazaa Media Desktop Sets Most Downloaded Software Record," www.kazaa.com/us/news/.

piracy, the Apple chief believed digital theft was becoming more complicated and more risky.

If legal purchases became simple and cheap, Caputo wondered if music fans would overwhelmingly migrate to legitimate services? He found these new developments in the entertainment industry extremely troubling. This was not quite the 'order' that he had expected to emerge in the chaotic and random P2P market. If Apple was just the first of a new breed of legitimate services that sold music affordably, conveniently, and legally, how would this affect Sandvine?

Conclusion

Despite significant progress since the company's formation, Caputo was worried. Product development had taken longer than expected, and while he was confident that Sandvine would retain its first mover advantage he wondered if the bottom was now falling out of the P2P market. If this occurred, what would be the implications for Sandvine's marketing strategy of using this product as a 'foot in the door' to build credibility and relationships in the industry? And on the subscriber services side,

would ISPs be able to persuade their customers of the value of Internet-based value-added services?

What would Sandvine do if the music industry made music cheap, affordable, and conveniently available through their Web sites? Would ISPs bother with Web-based services without the P2P broadband cost savings? Would consumers buy into the concept of Web-based value-added services? Sandvine's P2P software development had now been stopped and most of the engineering staff was concentrating their efforts on the subscriber services cluster. But any more changes to the strategic plan would have wide-ranging implications for all the functional areas, as well as for the firm's organization structure, staffing, leadership, and culture. For example, how important to the future success of the firm was the "Sandvine Way," and would it be possible to stay true to its key precepts in the face of possible reversals of fortune? "Well", Caputo thought, "I have a week to think about this before the next management meeting. One thing's for sure, though, the next 12 months are going to be an interesting ride!"

Find more great exercises and additional study tools on the Online Learning Centre at
www.mcgrawhill.ca/olc/timmons

C·H·A·P·T·E·R

10

THE DEAL: VALUATION, STRUCTURE, AND NEGOTIATION

When one door closes another door opens; but we so often look so long and so regretfully upon the closed door that we do not see the ones which open for us.

Alexander Graham Bell

THE ART AND CRAFT OF VALUATION

The entrepreneur's and private investor's world of finance is very different from the corporate finance arena where public companies jostle and compete in well-established capital markets. The private company and private capital world of entrepreneurial finance is more volatile, more imperfect, and less accessible than corporate capital markets. The sources of capital are very different. The companies are much younger, more dynamic, and the environment more rapidly changing and uncertain. The consequences, for entrepreneurs and investors alike, of this markedly different context are profound. Cash flow is king, and beta coefficients and elegant corporate financial theories are irrelevant. Also, liquidity and timing are everything, and there are innumerable, unavoidable conflicts between users and suppliers of capital. Finally, the determination of a company's value is elusive and more art than science.

WHAT IS A COMPANY WORTH?

The answer: It all depends! Unlike the market for public companies, where millions of shares are traded daily and the firm's market capitalization (total shares outstanding times the price per share) is readily determined, the market for private companies is very imperfect.

Determinants of Value

The criteria and methods applied in corporate finance to value companies traded publicly in the capital markets, when cavalierly applied to entrepreneurial companies, have severe limitations. The ingredients to the entrepreneurial valuation are cash, time, and risk. In Chapter 9 you determined the burn rate, OOC, and the TTC for your venture, so it is not hard to infer that the amount of cash available and the cash generated will play an important role in valuation. Similarly, Exhibit 9.5 showed that time also plays an influential role. Finally, risk or perception of risk contributes to the determination of value. The old adage, "The greater the risk, the greater the reward" plays a considerable role in how investors size up the venture.

Long-Term Value Creation versus Quarterly Earnings

The core mission of the entrepreneur is to build the best company possible and, if possible, to create a great company. This is the single surest way of generating long-term value for all the stakeholders and society. Such a mission has quite different strategic imperatives than one aimed solely at maximizing quarterly earnings to attain the highest share price possible given price/earnings ratios at the time. More will be said about this in Chapter 15.

Psychological Factors Determining Value

Time after time companies are valued at preposterous multiples of any sane price/earnings or sales ratios. In the best years, with the bull market charging ahead, equities trading on the Toronto Stock Exchange were trading at nearly 20 times earnings. The stocks of many of these companies were being traded at 50 or more times earnings and several were at 95 to 100 times earnings and six to seven times sales! Even more extreme valuations were seen during the peak of the so-called dot-com bubble from 1998 to early 2000. Some companies were valued at 100 times revenue and more during this classic frenzy. High multiples did come back down but then pressed into 2005 and beyond until the rude awakening of late 2008 and early 2009. In mid-2005, the TSX composite index was at nearly 20 times earnings but by Fall 2008, the P/E ratio for the Toronto Stock Exchange index was at half its former glory.

Often, behind extraordinarily high valuations is a psychological wave, a combination of euphoric enthusiasm for a fine company, exacerbated by greed and fear of missing the run up. The same psychology can also drive prices to undreamed of heights in private companies. The Bre-X fiasco is one such story that did not end well.

A Theoretical Perspective

Establishing Boundaries and Ranges, Rather than Calculating a Number   Valuation is much more than science, as can be seen from the examples just noted. As will be seen shortly, there are at least a dozen different ways of determining the value of a private company. A lot of assumptions and a lot of judgment calls are made in every valuation exercise. In one instance, for example, an entrepreneur consulted 13 experts to determine how much he should bid for the other half of a $10 million in sales company. The answer ranged from $1 to $6 million. He subsequently acquired the other half for $3.5 million.

Tom Culligan and Frank O'Dea started Second Cup in 1975 in a shopping mall in the outskirts of Toronto. The venture grew and eventually Frank O'Dea delivered a shotgun clause to his partner (an offer to buy out the partner at a specified price; the partner must either sell or buy out the other partner at that offer price) and Tom Culligan decided to buy rather than sell.

It can be a serious mistake, therefore, to approach the valuation task in hopes of arriving at a single number or even a narrow range. All you can realistically expect is a range of values with boundaries driven by different methods and underlying assumptions for each. Within that range, the buyer and the seller need to determine the comfort zone of each. At what point are you basically indifferent to buying and selling? Determining your point of indifference can be an invaluable aid in preparing you for negotiations to buy or sell.

Investor's Required Rate of Return

Various investors will require a different rate of return (ROR) for investments in different stages of development and will expect holding periods of various lengths. For example, Exhibit 10.1 summarizes, as ranges, the annual rates of return that venture capital investors seek on investments by stage of development and how long they expect to hold these investments. Several factors underlie the required ROR on a venture capital investment, including premiums for systemic risk, illiquidity, and value added. Of course, these can be expected to vary regionally and from time to time as market conditions change, because the investments are in what are decidedly imperfect capital market niches to begin with.

Investor's Required Share of Ownership

The rate of return required by the investor determines the investor's required share of the ownership, as Exhibit 10.2 illustrates. The future value of a $1-million investment at 50 percent compounded is $1 million $\times$ (1.5)5 = $1 million $\times$ 7.59 = $7.59 million. The future value of the company in Year 5 is profit after tax $\times$ price/earnings ratio = $1 million $\times$ 15 = $15 million. Thus, the share of ownership required in Year 5 is:

$$\frac{\text{Future value of the investment} = \$7.59 \text{ million}}{\text{Future value of the company} = \$15.00 \text{ million}} = 51\%$$

One can readily see that by changing any of the key variables, the results will change accordingly.

If the venture capitalists require the RORs mentioned earlier, the ownership they also require is determined as follows: In the start-up stage, 25 to 75 percent for investing all of the required funds; beyond the start-up stage, 10 to 40 percent, depending on the amount invested, maturity, and track record of the venture; in a seasoned venture in the later rounds of investment, 10 to 30 percent to supply the additional funds needed to sustain its growth.

EXHIBIT 10.1   Rate of Return Sought by Venture Capital Investors

Stage	Annual Rate of Return (%)	Typical Expected Holding Period (years)
Seed and start-up	50–100% or more	More than 10
First stage	40–60	5–10
Second stage	30–40	4–7
Expansion	20–30	3–5
Bridge and mezzanine	20 30	1 3
LBOs	30–50	3–5
Turnarounds	50	3–5

EXHIBIT 10.2   Investor's Required Share of Ownership under Various ROR Objectives

Assumptions:
  Amount of initial start-up investment = $1 million   Year 5 After-tax profit = $1 million
  Holding period = 5 years   Year 5 Price/earnings ratio = 15
  Required rate of return = 50%
Calculating the required share of ownership:

Price/Earning Ratio	Investor's Return Objective (Percent/Year Compounded)			
	30%	40%	50%	60%
10×	37%	54%	76%	106%
15×	25	36	51	70
20×	19	27	38	52
25×	15	22	30	42

THE THEORY OF COMPANY PRICING

In Chapter 9, we introduced the concept of the food chain, which we have included here as Exhibit 10.3. This chart depicts the evolution of a company from its idea stage through an initial public offering (IPO). The appetite of the various sources of capital—from family, friends, and angels, to venture capitalists, strategic partners, and the public markets—varies by company size, stage, and amount of money invested. We argue that entrepreneurs who understand these appetites and the food chain are better prepared to focus their fund-raising strategies on more realistic sources, amounts, and valuations. Economic conditions too play a role. Gregory Smith, president of Canada's Venture Capital and Private Equity Association believes, "It is not surprising that the buyout industry's investment and fund-raising levels have subsided in the first quarter. The worldwide economic crisis that began in Q4 2008 continued in Q1 2009 and our industry, in common with most economic sectors, has not been immune from its effects."[1] But Smith remains optimistic, Canadian financial institutions are strong, with most still having "considerable capital available for deployment." They are just choosing to cautiously remain on the sidelines. However, the harsh reality was not encouraging; half as many deals in Q1 2009 compared to Q1 2008 and the average buy-out was for less than one-quarter of the value of the average deal a year prior.

The Theory of Company Pricing is simplistically depicted in Exhibit 10.4. In the ideal scenario, a venture capital investor envisions two to three rounds, starting at a $1.00 per share equivalent, then a four to five times mark-up to Series B, followed by a double mark-up to Series C, and then doubling that $8.00 round at an IPO. This generic pattern would characterize the majority of deals that succeeded to an IPO, but there are many variations to this central tendency. In truth, many factors can affect this theory.

THE REALITY

The past 25 years have seen the venture capital industry explode from investing only $5 to $10 million per year to nearly $6 billion in 2000 before things slowed precipitously. Exhibit 10.5 on p. 276 shows how the many realities of the capital marketplace are at work, and how current market conditions, deal flow, and relative bargaining power influence the actual deal struck. Exhibit 10.6 on p. 277 shows how the dot-com explosion and the plummeting of the capital markets led to much lower values for private companies. The S&P/TSX Composite Index fell from nearly 11,500 in September 2000 to half that by October 2002. The market rebounded and record levels were seen again, breaking 13,000 in 2006, breaking 14,000 in 2007, and 15,155 in June 2008 before landing at 7,647 in November 2008—nearly a 50-percent drop!

EXHIBIT 10.3   The Capital Markets Food Chain for Entrepreneurial Ventures

	Stage of Venture			
	R&D	**Seed**	**Launch**	**High Growth**
Enterprise Value at Stage	Less than $1 million	$1–$5 million	$1–$50 million-plus	More than $100 million
Sources	Founders High net worth individuals FFF* SR&ED	FFF* Angel funds Seed funds SR&ED	Venture capital Series A, B, C…† Strategic partners Very high net worth individuals Private equity	IPOs Strategic acquirers Private equity
Amount of Capital Invested	Less than $50,000–$200,000	$10,000–$500,000	$500,000–$20 million	$10–$50 million plus
% Company Owned at IPO	10–25%	5–15%	40–60% by prior investors	15–25% by public
Share Price and Number‡	$.01–$.50 1–5 million	$.50–$1.00 1–3 million	$1.00–$8.00 3–5 million	$12–$18-plus 5–10 million

*Friends, families, and fools
†Venture capital series A, B, C, …(average size of round)

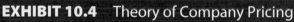

Round   { "A" @ $3–5 million—start-up
          "B" @ $5–10 million—product development
          "C"** @ $10 million—shipping product

Valuations vary markedly by industry
Valuations vary by region and VC cycle
‡ At post–IPO

EXHIBIT 10.4   Theory of Company Pricing

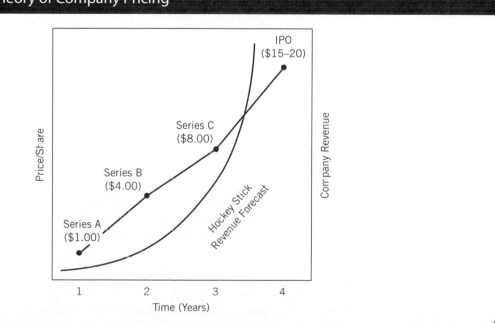

EXHIBIT 10.5   The Reality

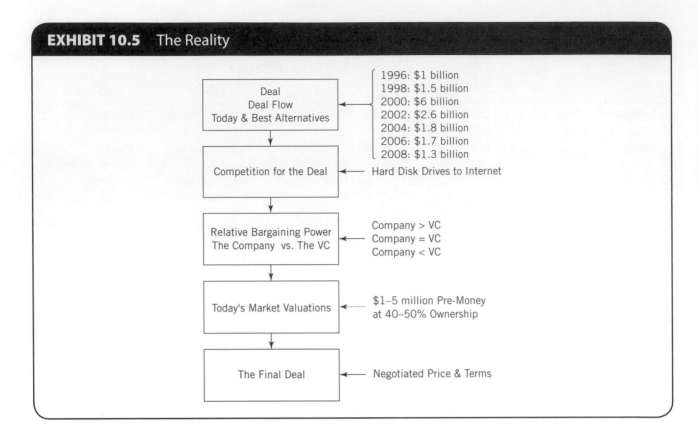

The Down Round or Cram Down

In this environment, which existed after the October 1987 stock market crash, after the dot-com bubble burst, and after the economic meltdown in late 2008, entrepreneurs face rude shocks in the second or third round of financing. Instead of a substantial four or even five times increase in the valuation from Series A to B, or B to C, they are jolted with what is called a "cram down" round: The price is typically one-fourth to two-thirds of the last round, as shown in Exhibit 10.6. This severely dilutes the founders' ownership, as investors are normally protected against dilution. Founder dilution as a result of failing to perform is one thing, but dilution because the TSX and IPO markets collapse seems rudely unfair. But that is part of the reality of valuation.

Take, for example, two excellent young companies, one launched in 2002 and one in 2003. By mid-2004, the first had secured two rounds of venture financing, was on target to exceed $20 million in revenue, and was seeking a $25-million round of private equity. The previous round was at $4.50 per share. The Series C round was priced at $2.88 per share, a 36-percent discount from the prior round. The second company met or exceeded all its business plan targets and was expected to achieve $25 million of EBITDA in 2004. Its prior Series B round was priced at $8.50 per share. The new Series C was set at $6.50 per share, or nearly a 24-percent discount.

In many financings of late, onerous additional conditions were imposed, such as a three to five times return to the Series C investors *before* Series A or B investors receive a dime! Both the founders and early-round investors are severely punished by such cram-down financings. The principle of the last money in governing the deal terms still prevails.

One can sense just how vulnerable and volatile the valuation of a company can be in these imperfect markets when external events, such as a stock market collapse, trigger a downward spiral. One also gains a new perspective on how critically important timing is. Even these two strongly performing companies in the preceding example were crammed down. Imagine those companies that didn't meet their plans: They were pummelled, if financed at all. What a startling reversal from the dot-com boom in 1998–1999 when companies at *concept stage* (with no product, no identifiable or defensible model of how they would make money or even breakeven, and no management team with proven experi-

EXHIBIT 10.6   The Reality: The Down Round

#1: 3–4 million shares at $1–$1.50 per share leads to $3–5 million round
#2: 6–10 million shares at $.25–$.50 per share leads to $2–3 million round

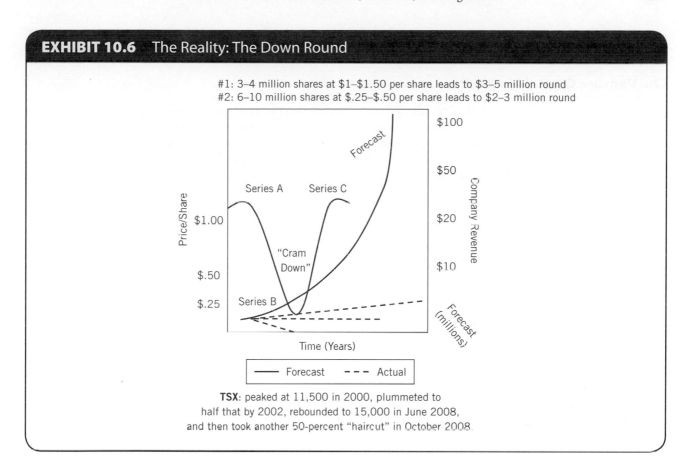

TSX: peaked at 11,500 in 2000, plummeted to
half that by 2002, rebounded to 15,000 in June 2008,
and then took another 50-percent "haircut" in October 2008.

ence) raised $20, $50, $70 million, and more *and* had an IPO with multibillion-dollar valuations. History asks: What is wrong with this picture! History also offers the answer: Happiness is still a positive cash flow!

Improved Valuations or Bouncing Back

As we saw in the last chapter, both the number of deals and average investment per deal slowly increase following a downturn. Valuations were rising, and the punishing cram down rounds with severe preferential returns had become the exception rather than the norm. There was a general sense that the capital climate was improving. One of the laws of physics, is that for every action there is an equal and opposite reaction. We hope that the same holds true in the financial world and that rebounds, such as following the late 2008 to 2010 economic turmoil, prove to be strong and sustained. Gregory Smith, president of the CVCA, gives a rallying cry: "We are at a crisis point in Canada's venture industry. At several levels, the data conclusively demonstrate that there is a venture capital financing 'gap' in Canada, and this means Canada's ability to drive innovation will weaken and we will see the overall economy suffer. Time is critical and we must act now. After all, the impact of venture-backed companies on the Canadian economy is significant, they generate jobs, contribute to the GDP and... they grow 5 times faster than the overall economy."[2] The CVCA and Thompson Reuters reported that "New commitments of capital going to domestic venture capital funds totalled a mere $149 million, which is 74.4 percent lower than the $418 million committed during the same period in 2008. These numbers are in stark contrast to the situation in the U.S. where a total of US$4.3 billion was raised in Q1 2009, 39 percent below the US$7.1 billion raised in Q1 2008."[3] Gregory Smith indicates, "This fundraising gap with the U.S. must be addressed if Canada is to compete in the knowledge-based economy of the future. Venture capital is the lifeblood of Canada's industries of tomorrow and the shortage of venture capital will have a profound impact on our ability to take a leadership role in those industries ranging from information technologies to cleantech upon which a prosperous future depends."[4]

VALUATION METHODS

The Venture Capital Method[5]

This method is appropriate for investments in a company with negative cash flows at the time of the investment, but which in a number of years is projected to generate significant earnings. As discussed in Chapter 9, venture capitalists are the most likely professional investors to partake in this type of an investment, thus the reference to the venture capital method. The steps involved in this method are as follows:

1. Estimate the company's *net income* in a number of years, at which time the investor plans on harvesting. This estimate will be based on sales and margin projections presented by the entrepreneur in his or her business plan
2. Determine the appropriate *price-to-earnings ratio*, or P/E ratio. The appropriate P/E ratio can be determined by studying current multiples for companies with similar economic characteristics.
3. Calculate the projected *terminal value* by multiplying net income and the P/E ratio.
4. The terminal value can then be discounted to find the *present value* of the investment. Venture capitalists use discount rates ranging from 35 to 80 percent, because of the risk involved in these types of investments.
5. To determine the investor's *required percentage of ownership*, based on their initial investment, the initial investment is divided by the estimated present value.

   To summarize the above steps, the following formula can be used:

   $$\text{Final ownership required} = \frac{\text{Required future value (investment)}}{\text{Total terminal value}}$$

   $$= \frac{(1 + IRR)^{years} \text{(investment)}}{\text{P/E ratio (terminal net income)}}$$

6. Finally, the number of shares and the share price must be calculated by using the following formula:

   $$\text{New shares} = \frac{\text{Percentage of ownership required by the investor}}{1 - \text{Percentage of ownership required by the investor} \times \text{old shares}}$$

By definition, the share price equals the price paid divided by the number of shares. This method is commonly used by venture capitalists because they make equity investments in industries often requiring a large initial investment with significant projected revenues; in addition, the percentage of ownership is a key issue in the negotiations.

The Fundamental Method

This method is simply the present value of the future earnings stream (see Exhibit 10.7).

The First Chicago Method[6]

Another alternative valuation method, developed at First Chicago Corporation's venture capital group, employs a lower discount rate, but applies it to an expected cash flow. That expected cash flow is the average of three possible scenarios, with each scenario weighted according to its perceived probability. The equation to determine the investor's required final ownership is:

$$\text{Required final ownership} = \frac{\text{Future value of investment} - \text{Future value of non-IPO cash flow}}{\text{Probability (of success) (Forecast terminal value)}}$$

EXHIBIT 10.7 Example of the Fundamental Method

Hitech, Inc.

Year	Revenue Growth (%)	Revenue (millions)	After-Tax Margin (%)	After-Tax Profit (millions)	Present Value Factor	Present Value of Each Year's Earnings (millions)
1	50%	$3.00	-0-	-0-	1.400	-0-
2	50	4.50	4.0%	$0.18	1.960	$0.09
3	50	6.75	7.0	0.47	2.744	0.17
4	50	10.13	9.0	0.91	3.842	0.24
5	50	15.19	11.0	1.67	5.378	0.31
6	40	21.26	11.5	2.45	7.530	0.33
7	30	27.64	12.0	3.32	10.541	0.32
8	20	33.17	12.0	3.98	14.758	0.27
9	15	38.15	12.0	4.58	20.661	0.22
10	10	41.96	12.0	5.03	28.926	0.17
Total present value of earnings in the super-growth period						2.12
Residual future value of earnings stream				$63.00	28.926	2.18
Total present value of company						4.30

This formula[7] differs from the original basic venture capital formula in two ways: (1) the basic formula assumes there are no cash flows between the investment and the harvest in Year 5; the future value of the immediate cash flows is subtracted from the future value of the investment because the difference between them is what must be made up for out of the terminal value; and (2) the basic formula does not distinguish between the forecast terminal value and the expected terminal value. The traditional method uses the forecast terminal value, which is adjusted through the use of a high discount rate. The formula employs the expected value of the terminal value. Exhibit 10.8 is an example of using this method.

EXHIBIT 10.8 Example of the First Chicago Method

	Success	Sideways Survival	Failure
1. Revenue growth rate (from base of $2 million)	60%	15%	0%
2. Revenue level after 3 years	$8.19 million	$3.04 million (liquidation)	$2 million
3. Revenue level after 5 years	$20.97 million (IPO)	$4.02 million	
4. Revenue level after 7 years		$5.32 million (acquisition)	
5. After-tax profit margin and earnings at liquidity	15%; $3.15 million	7%; $.37 million	
6. Price-earnings ratio at liquidity	17	7	
7. Value of company liquidity	$53.55 million	$2.61 million	$.69 million
8. Present value of company using discount rate of 40%	$9.96 million	$.25 million	$.25 million
9. Probability of each scenario	.4	.4	.2
10. Expected present value of the company under each scenario	$3.98 million	$.10 million	$.05 million
11. Expected present value of the company		$4.13 million	
12. Percentage ownership required to invest $2.5 million		60.5%	

Ownership Dilution[8]

The previous example is unrealistic because in most cases, several rounds of investments are necessary to finance a high-potential venture. Take, for instance, the pricing worksheet presented in Exhibit 10.9 in which three financing rounds are expected. In addition to estimating the appropriate discount rate for the current round, the first-round venture capitalist must now estimate the discount rates that are most likely to be applied in the following rounds, which are projected for Years 2 and 4. Although a 50-percent rate is still appropriate for Year 0, it is estimated that investors in Hitech, Inc., will demand a 40-percent return in Year 2 and a 25-percent return in Year 4. The final ownership that each investor must be left with, given a terminal price/earnings ratio of 15, can be calculated using the basic valuation formula:

Round 1

$$\frac{\text{Future value (Investment)}}{\text{Terminal value (Company)}} = \frac{1.50^5 \times \$1.5 \text{ million}}{15 \times \$2.5 \text{ million}} = 30.4\% \text{ ownership}$$

Round 2

$$(1.40^3 \times \$1 \text{ million}) / (15 \times \$2.5 \text{ million}) = 7.3\%$$

Round 3

$$(1.25^1 \times \$1 \text{ million}) / (15 \times \$1.5 \text{ million}) = 3.3\%$$

Discounted Cash Flow

In a simple discounted cash flow method, three time periods are defined: (1) Years 1–5; (2) Years 6–10; and (3) Year 11 to infinity.[9] The necessary operating assumptions for each period are initial sales, growth rates, EBIAT/sales, and (net fixed assets + operating working capital)/ sales. While using this method, one should also note relationships and trade-offs. With these assumptions, the discount rate can be applied to the weighted average cost of capital (WACC).[10] Then the value for free cash flow (Years 1–10) is added to the terminal value. This terminal value is the growth perpetuity.

EXHIBIT 10.9   Example of a Three-Stage Financing

Hitech, Inc. (numbers in thousands)						
	Year 0	Year 1	Year 2	Year 3	Year 4	Year 5
Revenues	500	1,250	2,500	5,000	8,100	12,800
New income	(250)	(62)	250	750	1,360	2,500
Working capital at 20%	100	250	500	1,000	1,600	2,560
Fixed assets at 40%	200	500	1,000	2,000	3,200	5,120
Free cash flow	(550)	(512)	(500)	(750)	(440)	(380)
Cumulative external financial need	500	1,653	1,543	2,313	2,753	3,133
Equity issues	1,500	0	1,000	0	1,000	0
Equity outstanding	1,500	1,500	2,500	2,500	3,500	3,500
Cash balance	950	436	938	188	748	368
Assume: long-term IRR required each round by investors	50%	45%	40%	30%	25%	20%

Source: William A. Sahlman, "A Method for Valuing High-Risk, Long-Term Investments," Harvard Business School Note 9-288-006.

Other Rule-of-Thumb Valuation Methods

Several other valuation methods are also employed to estimate the value of a company. Many of these are based on similar, most recent transactions of similar firms, established by a sale of the company, or a prior investment. Such comparables may look at several different multiples, such as earnings, free cash flow, revenue, EBIT, and book value. Knowledgeable investment bankers and venture capitalists make it their business to know the activity in the current marketplace for private capital and how deals are being priced. These methods are used most often to value an existing company, rather than a start-up, since there are so many more knowns about the company and its financial performance.

TAR PITS FACING ENTREPRENEURS

There are several inherent conflicts between entrepreneurs or the users of capital and investors or the suppliers of capital.[11] While the entrepreneur wants to have as much time as possible for the financing, the investors want to supply capital just in time or to invest only when the company needs the money. Entrepreneurs should be thinking of raising money when they do not need it, while preserving the option to find another source of capital.

Similarly, users of capital want to raise as much money as possible, while the investors want to supply just enough capital in staged capital commitments. The investors, such as venture capitalists, use staged capital commitments to manage their risk exposure over 6- to 12-month increments of investing.

In the negotiations of a deal, the entrepreneur sometimes becomes attracted to a high valuation with the sentiment "My price, your terms." The investors will generally attempt to change this opinion because it is their capital. The investors will thus focus on a low valuation, with the sentiment, "My price *and* my terms."

This tension applies not only to financial transactions but also to the styles of the users versus the styles of the suppliers of capital. The users value their independence and treasure the flexibility their own venture has brought them. However, the investors are hoping to preserve their options as well. These options usually include both reinvesting and abandoning the venture.

These points of view also clash in the composition of the board of directors, where the entrepreneur seeks control and independence, and the investors want the right to control the board if the company does not perform as well as was expected. This sense of control is an emotional issue for most entrepreneurs, who want to be in charge of their own destiny. Prizing their autonomy and self-determination, many of these users of capital would agree with the passion Walt Disney conveyed in this statement: "I don't make movies to make money. I make *money* to make movies." The investors may believe in the passions of these users of capital, but they still want to protect themselves with first refusals, initial public offering rights, and various other exit options.

The long-term goals of the users and suppliers of capital may also be contradictory. The entrepreneurs may be content with the progress of their venture and happy with a single or double. It is their venture, their baby; if it is moderately successful, many entrepreneurs believe they have accomplished a lot. The investors will not be quite as content with moderate success, but instead want their capital to produce extraordinary returns—they want a home run from the entrepreneur. Thus, the pressures put on the entrepreneur may seem unwarranted to the entrepreneur, yet necessary for the investor.

These strategies contradict each other when they are manifested in the management styles of the users and providers of capital. While the entrepreneur is willing to take a calculated risk or is working to minimize or avoid unnecessary risks, the investor has bet on the art of the exceptional and thus is willing to bet the farm everyday.

Entrepreneurs possess the ability to see opportunities and, more importantly, to seize those opportunities. They possess an instinctual desire to change, to adapt, or to de-commit in order to seize new opportunities. Yet the investors are looking for clear steady progress, as projected in the business plan, which leaves little room for surprises.

Finally, the ultimate goals may differ. The entrepreneur who continues to build his or her company may find operating a company enjoyable. At this point, the definition of success both personally and for the company may involve long-term company building, such that a sustainable institution is created. But the investors will want to cash out in two to five years, so that they can reinvest their capital in another venture.

STAGED CAPITAL COMMITMENTS[12]

Venture capitalists rarely, if ever, invest all the external capital that a company will require to accomplish its business plan; instead they invest in companies at distinct stages in their development. As a result, each company begins life knowing that it has only enough capital to reach the next stage. By staging capital, the venture capitalists preserve the right to abandon a project whose prospects look dim. The right to abandon is essential because an entrepreneur will almost never stop investing in a failing project as long as others are providing capital.

Staging the capital also provides incentives to the entrepreneurial team. Capital is a scarce and expensive resource for individual ventures. Misuse of capital is very costly to venture capitalists but not necessarily to management. To encourage managers to conserve capital, venture capital firms apply strong sanctions if it is misused. These sanctions ordinarily take two basic forms. First, increased capital requirements invariably dilute management's equity share at an increasingly punitive rate. Second, the staged investment process enables venture capital firms to shut down operations. The credible threat to abandon a venture, even when the firm might be economically viable, is the key to the relationship between the entrepreneur and the venture capitalists. By denying capital, the venture capitalist also signals other capital suppliers that the company in question is a bad investment risk.

Short of denying the company capital, venture capitalists can discipline wayward managers by firing or demoting them. Other elements of the stock purchase agreement then come into play. For example, the company typically has the right to repurchase shares from departing managers, often at prices below market value, and vesting schedules limit the number of shares employees are entitled to if they leave prematurely. Finally, non-compete clauses can impose strong penalties on those who leave, particularly if their human capital is closely linked to the industry in which the venture is active.

Entrepreneurs accept the staged capital process because they usually have great confidence in their own abilities to meet targets. They understand that if they meet those goals, they will end up owning a significantly larger share of the company than if they had insisted on receiving all of the capital up front.

Learn the VC's Buttons and Push Them

Avrio Ventures looks for growth stage industrial bio-products, nutraceutical ingredients, and food technology enterprises. In 2009 Avrio closed a Series A round investment into Manitoba Harvest in order to support Manitoba Harvest's rapid growth in channels of distribution, research, and new product development. Manitoba Harvest needed the capital to realize market opportunities and broaden their line of hemp-based nutraceuticals and natural foods.

Avrio looks for particular attributes in ventures it is considering and lists its investment criteria as:

- An experienced growth-oriented management team
- A sustainable competitive advantage either through proven science, proprietary intellectual property, or a strong brand franchise
- A large addressable market opportunity or a high-growth niche market segment
- A sound business model
- An entrepreneurial desire to build an enduring, world class organization

Avrio Ventures "focuses on commercialization and growth stage investments. Typically, the use of proceeds is to commercialize products, initiate product rollouts, expand distribution and market presence, or fund growth (organically or through acquisitions). Avrio will invest up to $10 million over the life of any single portfolio company. The Avrio team is patient, recognizing that successful companies require support over at least five years to realize their potential value. If your company meets these criteria, please submit a business plan."[13]

STRUCTURING THE DEAL

What Is a Deal?[14]

Deals are defined as economic agreements between at least two parties. In the context of entrepreneurial finance, most deals involve the allocation of cash flow streams (with respect to both amount and timing), the allocation of risk, and hence the allocation of value between different groups. For example, deals can be made between suppliers and users of capital, or between management and employees of a venture.

A Way of Thinking about Deals over Time   To assess and to design long-lived deals, William Sahlman of the Harvard Business School suggests the following series of questions as a guide for deal makers in structuring and in understanding how deals evolve:[15]

- Who are the players?
- What are their goals and objectives?
- What risks do they perceive and how have these risks been managed?
- What problems do they perceive?
- How much do they have invested, both in absolute terms and relative terms, at cost and at market value?
- What is the context surrounding the current decision?
- What is the form of their current investment or claim on the company?
- What power do they have to act? To precipitate change?
- What real options do they have? How long does it take them to act?
- What credible threats do they have?
- How and from whom do they get information?
- How credible is the source of information?
- What will be the value of their claim under different scenarios?
- How can they get value for their claims?
- To what degree can they appropriate value from another party?
- How much uncertainty characterizes the situation?
- What are the rules of the game (e.g., tax, legislative)?
- What is the context (e.g., state of economy, capital markets, industry specifics) at the current time? How is the context expected to change?

The Characteristics of Successful Deals[16]   While deal making is ultimately a combination of art and science, it is possible to describe some of the characteristics of deals that have proven successful over time:

- They are simple.
- They are robust (they do not fall apart when there are minor deviations from projections).
- They are organic (they are not immutable).

- They take into account the incentives of each party to the deal under a variety of circumstances.
- They provide mechanisms for communications and interpretation.
- They are based primarily on trust rather than on legalese.
- They are not patently unfair.
- They do not make it too difficult to raise additional capital.
- They match the needs of the user of capital with the needs of the supplier.
- They reveal information about each party (e.g., their faith in their ability to deliver on the promises).
- They allow for the arrival of new information before financing is required.
- They do not preserve discontinuities (e.g., boundary conditions that will evoke dysfunctional behaviour on the part of the agents of principals).
- They consider the fact that it takes time to raise money.
- They improve the chances of success for the venture.

The Generic Elements of Deals   A number of terms govern value distribution, as well as basic definitions, assumptions, performance incentives, rights, and obligations. The deal should also cover the basic mechanisms for transmitting timely, credible information. Representations and warranties, plus negative and positive covenants, will also be part of the deal structure. Additionally, default clauses and remedial action clauses are appropriate in most deals.

Tools for Managing Risk/Reward   In a deal, the claims on cash and equity are prioritized by the players. Some of the tools available to the players are common stock, partnerships, preferred stock (dividend and liquidation preference), debt (secured, unsecured, personally guaranteed, or convertible), performance conditional pricing (ratchets or positive incentives), puts and calls, warrants, and cash. Some of the critical aspects of a deal go beyond just the money:[17]

- Number, type, and mix of stocks (and perhaps of stock and debt) and various features that may go with them (such as puts) that affect the investor's rate of return.
- The amounts and timing of takedowns, conversions, and the like.
- Interest rates on debt or preferred shares.
- The number of seats, and who actually will represent investors, on the board of directors.
- Possible changes in the management team and in the composition of the board.
- Registration rights for investor's stock (in the case of a registered public offering).
- Right of first refusal granted to the investor on subsequent private placements or an IPO.
- Employment, non-compete, and proprietary rights agreements.
- The payment of legal, accounting, consulting, or other fees connected with putting the deal together.
- Specific performance targets for revenues, expenses, market penetration, and the like, by certain target dates.

Understanding the Bets

Deals, because they are based on cash, risk, and time, are subject to interpretation. The players' perceptions of each of these factors contribute to the overall valuation of the venture and the subsequent proposed deal. As was described earlier, there are a number of different ways to value a venture, and these various valuation methods contribute to the complexity of deals. Consider, for instance, the following term sheets:[18]

- A venture capital firm proposes to raise $150 to $200 million to acquire and build an enterprise. The venture capital firm will commit between $15 and $30 million in equity and will lead in raising senior and subordinated debt to buy licences. Licensees will have to claim about 30 percent of the future equity value in the new company, the venture capital firm will claim 60 percent (subordinated debt claim is estimated at 10 percent), and management will get 5 to 10 percent of the future equity but only after all prior return targets have been achieved. The venture capital firm's worst-case scenario will result in 33 percent ROR to the firm, 9 percent ROR to licensees, and 0 percent for management. The non-compete agreements extend for 12 years, in addition to the vesting.

- An entrepreneur must decide between two deals:

  Deal A: A venture capital firm will lead a $3-million investment and requires management to invest $1 million. Future gains are to be split 50-50 after the venture capital firm has achieved a 25-percent ROR on the investment. Other common investment provisions also apply (vesting, employment agreements, etc.). The venture capital firm has the right of first refusal on all future rounds and other deals management may find.

  Deal B: Another venture capital firm will lead a $4-million investment. Management will invest nothing. The future gains are to be split 75 percent for the venture capital firm and 25 percent for management on a side-by-side basis. Until the venture achieves positive cash flow, this venture capital firm has the right of first refusal on future financing and deals management may find.

- A group of very talented money managers is given $40 million in capital to manage. The contract calls for the managers to receive 20 percent of the excess return on the portfolio over the government bond return. The contract runs for five years. The managers cannot take out any of their share of the gains until the last day of the contracts (except to pay taxes).

While reading and considering these deals, try to identify the underlying assumptions, motivations, and beliefs of the individuals proposing the deals. Following are some questions that may help in identifying the players' bets.

- What is the bet?
- Who is it for?
- Who is taking the risk? Who receives the rewards?
- Who should be making these bets?
- What will happen if the entrepreneurs exceed the venture capitalists' expectations? What if they fall short?
- What are the incentives for the money managers? What are the consequences of their success or failure to perform?
- How will the money managers behave? What will be their investing strategy?

Some of the Lessons Learned: The Dog in the Suitcase

A few years ago a friend, living in an Edmonton, Alberta high-rise, called in great distress. Her beloved barkless dog had died in the middle of the night. She wanted a decent burial for the dog, but since it was the dead of winter, she did not know what to do. It was suggested that she contact a pet cemetery in nearby St. Albert and take the dog there. It would be frozen until spring, at which time it would be properly buried.

She gathered her courage, placed the dog in a suitcase, and headed down the elevator to the outdoors. As she struggled toward the nearest intersection to catch a cab, a young man noticed her struggle and offered to help. Puffing by now, she sized up the young man quickly and accepted his offer to carry the bag. In no time, she turned to find the young man sprinting down the street with her suitcase. Imagine the look on the faces of the young man and his buddies when they opened the suitcase and discovered the loot!

The moral of this story is that raising capital can have all the surprises of a dog in the suitcase for the entrepreneur. The following tips may help to minimize many of these surprises:

- Raise money when you do not need it.
- Learn as much about the process and how to manage it as you can.
- Know your relative bargaining position.

- If all you get is money, you are not getting much.
- Assume the deal will never close.
- Always have a backup source of capital.
- The legal and other experts can blow it—sweat the details yourself!
- Users of capital are invariably at a disadvantage in dealing with the suppliers of capital.
- If you are out of cash when you seek to raise capital, suppliers of capital will eat you for lunch.
- Start-up entrepreneurs are raising capital for the first time; suppliers of capital have done it many times, everyday, for a living.

NEGOTIATIONS

Negotiations have been defined by many experts in a variety of ways, as the following examples demonstrate. Herb Cohen, the author of *You Can Negotiate Anything*, defines negotiations as "a field of knowledge and endeavor that focuses on gaining the favor of people from whom we want things"[19] or similarly, as "the use of information and power to affect behavior within a 'web of tension.'"[20] Other experts in the field of negotiations, Roger Fisher and William Ury, assert that negotiations are a "back-and-forth communication designed to reach an agreement when you and the other side have some interests that are shared and others that are opposed."[21]

What Is Negotiable?

Far more is negotiable than entrepreneurs think.[22] For instance, a normal ploy of the lawyer representing the investors is to insist, matter of factly, that "this is our boilerplate" and that the entrepreneur should take it or leave it. It is possible for an entrepreneur to negotiate and craft an agreement that represents his or her needs.

During the negotiation, the investors will be evaluating the negotiating skills, intelligence, and maturity of the entrepreneur. The entrepreneur has precisely the same opportunity to size up the investor. If the investors see anything that shakes their confidence or trust, they probably will withdraw from the deal. Similarly, if an investor turns out to be arrogant, hot-tempered, unwilling to see the other side's needs and to compromise, and seems bent on getting every last ounce out of the deal by locking an entrepreneur into as many of the "burdensome clauses" as is possible, the entrepreneur might want to withdraw.

Throughout the negotiations, entrepreneurs need to bear in mind that a successful negotiation is one in which both sides believe they have made a fair deal. The best deals are those in which neither party wins and neither loses, and such deals are possible to negotiate. This approach is further articulated in the works of Fisher and Ury, who have focused neither on soft nor hard negotiation tactics, but rather on principled negotiation, a methodical approach. This method asserts that the purpose of negotiations is "to decide issues on their merits rather than through a haggling process focused on what each side says it will and won't do. It suggests that you look for mutual gains wherever possible, and that where your interests conflict, you should insist that the result be based on some fair standards independent of the will of either side."[23] They continue to describe principled negotiations in the following four points:

✓ *People*: Separate the people from the problem.

✓ *Interests*: Focus on interests, not positions.

✓ *Options*: Generate a variety of possibilities before deciding what to do.

✓ *Criteria*: Insist that the result be based on some objective standard.

Others have spoken of this method of principled negotiation. Generally the adage holds to treat others as you would like to be treated. For example, Mario Lemieux states, "One thing I hate is people screaming at me. If you want me to do something, talk to me. When someone screams at me to hurry up, I slow down."

The Specific Issues Entrepreneurs Typically Face[24]

Whatever method you choose in your negotiations, the primary focus is likely to be on how much the entrepreneur's equity is worth and how much is to be purchased by the investor's investment. Even so, numerous other issues involving legal and financial control of the company and the rights and obligations of various investors and the entrepreneur in various situations may be as important as valuation and ownership share. Not the least of which is the value behind the money—such as contacts and helpful expertise, additional financing when and if required, and patience and interest in the long-term development of the company—that a particular investor can bring to the venture. The following are some of the most critical aspects of a deal that go beyond "just the money":

- Number, type, and mix of stocks (and perhaps of stock and debt) and various features that may go with them (such as puts) that affect the investor's rate of return.
- The amounts and timing of takedowns, conversions, and the like.
- Interest rate on debt or preferred shares.
- The number of seats, and who actually will represent investors, on the board of directors.
- Possible changes in the management team and in the composition of the board of directors.
- Registration rights for investor's stock (in case of a registered public offering).
- Right of first refusal granted to the investor on subsequent private or initial public stock offerings.
- Stock vesting schedule and agreements.
- The payment of legal, accounting, consulting, or other fees connected with putting the deal together.

Entrepreneurs may find some subtle but highly significant issues negotiated. If they, or their attorneys, are not familiar with these, they may be missed as just boilerplate when, in fact, they have crucial future implications for the ownership, control, and financing of the business. Some issues that can be burdensome for entrepreneurs are:

- *Co-sale provision.* This is a provision by which investors can tender their shares of their stock before an initial public offering. It protects the first-round investors but can cause conflicts with investors in later rounds and can inhibit an entrepreneur's ability to cash out.
- *Ratchet anti-dilution protection.* This enables the lead investors to get for free additional common stock if subsequent shares are ever sold at a price lower than originally paid. This protection allows first-round investors to prevent the company from raising additional necessary funds during a period of adversity for the company. While nice from the investor's perspective, it ignores the reality that, in distress situations, the last money calls the shots on price and deal structure.
- *Washout financing.* This is a strategy of last resort, which wipes out all previously issued stock when existing preferred shareholders will not commit additional funds, thus diluting everyone.
- *Forced buyout.* Under this provision, if management does not find a buyer or cannot take the company public by a certain date, then the investors can proceed to find a buyer at terms they agree upon.
- *Demand registration rights.* Here, investors can demand at least one IPO in three to five years. In reality, such clauses are hard to invoke because the market for new public stock issues, rather than the terms of an agreement, ultimately governs the timing of such events.
- *Piggyback registration rights.* These grant to the investors (and to the entrepreneur, if he or she insists) rights to sell stock at the IPO. Since the underwriters usually make this decision, the clause normally is not enforceable.
- *Key-person insurance.* This requires the company to obtain life insurance on key people. The named beneficiary of the insurance can be either the company or the preferred shareholders.

The Term Sheet

Regardless of whether you secure capital from angels or venture capitalists, you will want to be informed and knowledgeable about the terms and conditions that govern the deal you sign. Many experienced entrepreneurs will argue that the terms and who your investor is are more important than the valuation. Today, the technical sophistication in deal structures creates an imperative for entrepreneurs and their legal counsel: if you don't know the details you will get what you deserve—not what you want.

To illustrate this point, consider the choice among four common instruments: (1) fully participating preferred stock, (2) partially participating preferred stock (4× return), (3) common preference ($1.00/share to common), and (4) non-participating preferred stock. Then, consider a $200-million harvest realized either through an IPO or an acquisition by another company. Why does any of this matter? Aren't these details better left to the legal experts?

Consider the economic consequences of each of these deal instruments under the two harvest scenarios in Exhibit 10.10. The graph shows there can be up to a $24-million difference in the payout received, even though, in the example, there are equal numbers of shares of common stock, typically owned by the founders, and preferred stock, owned by investors. The acquisition exit is more favourable to investors, especially since periodically the IPO market is closed to new companies.

Black Box Technology, Inc., Term Sheet

The best single presentation and discussion we have seen of the deal structure, term sheet contents, and their implications for negotiating the deal is presented in Black Box Technology, Inc.—Term Sheet (available on the Online Learning Centre at www. mcgrawhill.ca/olc/timmons). This was developed by the former Boston law firm of Testa, Hurwitz & Thibeault, LLP. We highly recommend its careful reading before any negotiations with private investors and selecting very experienced counsel. "Getting a term sheet

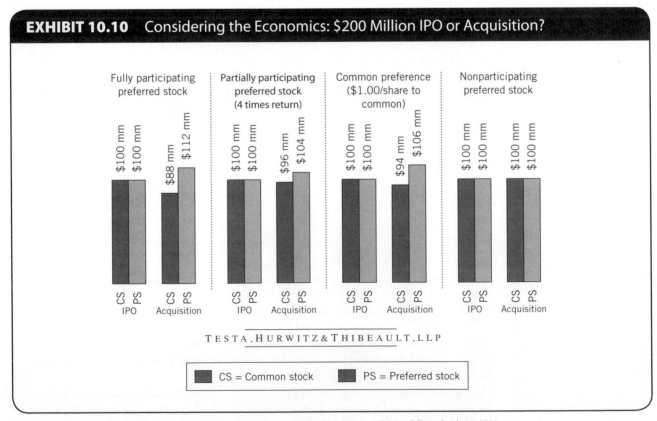

EXHIBIT 10.10   Considering the Economics: $200 Million IPO or Acquisition?

Source: Testa, Hurwitz & Thibeault, LLP, presentation by Heather M. Stone and Brian D. Goldstein at Babson College, October 3, 2001.

from an investor is like getting an invitation to the Prom in January—you've got a long way to go before you dance" according to start-up lawyer Ryan Roberts. [25] "VCs love to be the first to be second. They don't want to be the first to issue a term sheet, but will issue one quickly once someone else has," observes Mark Davis of DFJ Gotham Ventures. [26]

TRAPS

Strategic Circumference

Each fund-raising strategy sets in motion some actions and commitments by management that will eventually scribe a strategic circumference around the company in terms of its current and future financing choices. These future choices will permit varying degrees of freedom as a result of the previous actions. Those who fail to think through the consequences of a fund-raising strategy and the effect on their degrees of freedom fall into this trap.

While it is impossible to avoid strategic circumference completely, and while in some cases scribing a strategic circumference is clearly intentional, others may be unintended and, unfortunately, unexpected. For example, a company that plans to remain private or plans to maintain a 1.5 to 1.0 debt-to-equity ratio has intentionally created a strategic circumference.

Legal Circumference

Many people have an aversion to becoming involved in legal or accounting minutiae. Many believe that since they pay sizeable professional fees, their advisors should and will pay attention to the details.

Legal documentation spells out the terms, conditions, responsibilities, and rights of the parties to a transaction. Because different sources have different ways of structuring deals, and because these legal and contractual details come at the *end* of the fund-raising process, an entrepreneur may arrive at a point of no return, facing some very onerous conditions and covenants that are not only very difficult to live with, but also create tight limitations and constraints—legal circumference—on future choices that are potentially disastrous. Entrepreneurs cannot rely on lawyers and advisors to protect them in this vital matter.

To avoid this trap, entrepreneurs need to have a fundamental precept: "The devil is in the details." It is very risky for an entrepreneur *not* to carefully read final documents and very risky to use a lawyer who is *not* experienced and competent. It also is helpful to keep a few options alive and to conserve cash. This also can keep the other side of the table more conciliatory and flexible.

Attraction to Status and Size

It seems there is a cultural attraction to higher status and larger size, even when it comes to raising capital. Simply targeting the largest or the best-known or most-prestigious firms is a trap entrepreneurs often fall into. These firms are often most visible because of their size and investing activity and because they have been around a long time. Yet, as the venture capital industry has become more heterogeneous, as well as for other reasons, such firms may or may not be a good fit.

Take, for example, an entrepreneur who had a patented, innovative device that was ready for use by manufacturers of semiconductors. He was running out of cash from an earlier round of venture capital investment and needed more money for his device to be placed in test sites and then, presumably, into production. Although lab tests had been successful, his prior backers would not invest further because he was nearly two years behind schedule in his business plan. For a year, he concentrated his efforts on many of the largest and most well-known firms and celebrities in the venture capital business, but to no avail. With the help of outside advice, he then decided to pursue an alternative fund-raising strategy. First, he listed firms that were most likely prospects as customers for the device. Next, he sought to identify investors who already had investments in this potential customer base, because it was thought that these would be the most likely potential backers since they would be the most informed about his technology, its potential value-added properties, and any potential competitive advantages the company could achieve. Less than a dozen venture capital firms were identified (from among a pool of over 700, at the time), yet none had been contacted previously by this entrepreneur. In fact, many were virtually unknown to him, even though they were very active investors in the industry. In less than three months, offers were on the table from three of these and the financing was closed.

It is best to avoid this trap by focusing your efforts toward financial backers, whether debt or equity, who have intimate knowledge and first-hand experience with the technology, marketplace, and networks of expertise in the competitive arena. Focus on those firms with relevant know-how that would be characterized as a good match.

Unknown Territory

Venturing into unknown territory is another problem. Entrepreneurs need to know the terrain in sufficient detail, particularly the requirements and alternatives of various equity sources. If they do not, they may make critical strategic blunders and waste time.

Douglas Cumming of the University of Alberta observes that in Canada "there is no single unique optimal form of venture finance." This is in contrast to the United States where tax laws lead to convergence on only one security. Canada's mix of financing instruments match up with the entrepreneurial firm depending upon its unique attributes and needs. Cumming finds that in Canada, "seed stage firms are more likely to be financed with either straight preferred equity than convertible preferred equity. Seed stage firms were also less likely to be financed with straight debt, convertible debt, or mixes of debt and common equity"—nascent firms without cash flows are simply less suited for debt finance. Whereas, high-tech firms are likely to be financed through convertible preferred equity.[27]

For example, a venture that is not a "mainstream venture capital deal" may be overvalued and directed to investors who are not a realistic match, rather than being realistically valued and directed to small and more specialized funds, private investors, or potential strategic partners. The preceding example is a real one. The founders went through nearly $100,000 of their own funds, strained their relationship to the limit, and nearly had to abandon the project.

Another illustration of a fund-raising strategy that was ill conceived and, effectively, a lottery—rather than a well-thought-out and focused search—is a venture in the fibre optics industry we'll call Opti-Com.[28] Opti-Com was a spin-off as a start-up from a well-known public company in the industry. The management team was entirely credible, but members were not considered superstars. The business plan suggested the company could achieve the magical $50 million in sales in five years, which the entrepreneurs were told by an outside advisor was the minimum size that venture capital investors would consider. The plan proposed to raise $750,000 for about 10 percent of the common stock of the company. Realistically, since the firm was a custom supplier for special applications, rather than a provider of a new technology with a significant proprietary advantage, a sales estimate of $10 to $15 million in five years would have been more plausible. The same advisor urged that their business plan be submitted to 12 mainstream venture capital firms in the immediate vicinity. Four months later, they had received 12 rejections. The entrepreneurs then were told to "go see the same quality of venture capital firms in New York." A year later, the founders were nearly out of money and had been unsuccessful in their search for capital. When redirected away from mainstream venture capitalists to a more suitable source, a small fund specifically created in the area to provide risk capital for emerging firms that might not be robust enough to attract conventional venture capital but would be a welcome addition to the economic renewal of the province, the fit was right. Opti-Com raised the necessary capital, but at a valuation much more in line with the market for start-up deals.

Opportunity Cost

The lure of money often leads to a common trap—the opportunity cost trap. An entrepreneur's optimism leads him or her to the conclusion that with good people and products (or services), there has to be a lot of money out there with "our name on it!" In the process, entrepreneurs tend to grossly underestimate the real costs of getting the cash in the bank. Further, entrepreneurs also underestimate the real time, effort, and creative energy required. Indeed, the degree of effort fund-raising requires is perhaps the least appreciated aspect in obtaining capital. In both these cases, there are opportunity costs in expending these resources in a particular direction when both the clock and the calendar are moving.

For a start-up company, for instance, founders can devote nearly all their available time for months to seeking out investors and telling their story. It may take six months or more to get a "yes" and up to a year for a "no." In the meantime, a considerable amount of cash and human capital has been flowing out, rather than in, and this cash and capital might have been better spent elsewhere.

One such start-up began its search for venture capital and within 12 months the founders had exhausted $100,000 of their own seed money and had quit their jobs to devote themselves full time to the effort. Yet they were unsuccessful after approaching more than 35 sources of capital. The opportunity costs are clear.

There are opportunity costs, too, in existing emerging companies. In terms of human capital, it is common for top management to devote as much as half of its time trying to raise a major amount of outside capital. Again, this requires a tremendous amount of emotional and physical energy as well, of which there is a finite amount to devote to the daily operating demands of the enterprise. The effect on near-term performance is invariably negative. In addition, if expectations of a successful fund-raising effort are followed by a failure to raise the money, morale can deteriorate and key people can be lost.

Significant opportunity costs are also incurred in forgone business and market opportunities that could have been pursued. Take, for example, the start-up firm noted above. When asked what level of sales the company would have achieved in the year had it spent the $100,000 of the founders' seed money on generating customers and business, the founder answered without hesitation, "We'd be at $1 million sales by now, and would probably be making a small profit."

Underestimation of Other Costs

Entrepreneurs tend to underestimate the out-of-pocket costs associated with both raising the money and living with it. There are incremental costs after a firm becomes a public company. The Canadian regulatory bodies require periodic audited financial statements and various reports, there are outside directors' fees and liability insurance premiums, there are legal fees associated with more extensive reporting requirements, and so on. These can add up quickly, often to $100,000 or more annually.

Another "cost" that can be easily overlooked is of the disclosure that may be necessary to convince a financial backer to part with his or her money. An entrepreneur may have to reveal much more about the company and his other personal finances than he or she ever imagined. Thus, company weaknesses, ownership and compensation arrangements, personal and corporate financial statements, marketing plans and competitive strategies, and so forth may need to be revealed to people whom the entrepreneur does not really know and trust, and with whom he or she may eventually not do business. In addition, the ability to control access to the information is lost.

Greed

The entrepreneur—especially one who is out of cash, or nearly so—may find the money irresistible. One of the most exhilarating experiences for an entrepreneur is the prospect of raising that first major slug of outside capital, or obtaining that substantial bank line needed for expansion. If the fundamentals of the company are sound, however, then there is money out there.

Being Too Anxious

Usually, after months of hard work finding the right source and negotiating the deal, another trap awaits the hungry but unwary entrepreneur, and all too often the temptation is overwhelming. It is the trap of believing that the deal is done and terminating discussions with others too soon. Entrepreneurs fall into this trap because they want to believe the deal is done with a handshake (or perhaps with an accompanying letter of intent or an executed term sheet).

A masterful handling of such a situation occurred when an entrepreneur and a key vice president of a company with $30 million in sales had been negotiating with several venture capitalists, three major strategic partners, and a mezzanine source for nearly six months. The company was down to 60 days' worth of cash, and the mezzanine investors knew it. They offered the entrepreneur $10 million as a take-it-or-leave-it proposition. The vice president, in summarizing the company's relative bargaining position, said, "It was the only alternative we had left; everything else had come to rest by late last month and the negotiations with the three major companies had not reached serious stages. We felt like they were asking too much, but we needed the money." Yet the two had managed to keep this weakness from being apparent to the mezzanine. Each time negotiations had been scheduled, the entrepreneur had made sure he also had scheduled a meeting with one of the other larger companies for later that afternoon (a two-hour plane ride away). In effect, he was able to create the illusion that these discussions with other investors were far more serious than they actually were. The deal was closed on terms agreeable to both. The company went public six months later and is still highly successful today.

Impatience

Another trap is being impatient when an investor does not understand quickly, and not realizing each deal has velocity and momentum.

The efforts of one management group to acquire a firm in the cellular phone business being sold by their employers provides an example. As members of the management team, they were the first to know in May that the company was going to be sold by its owners. By early July, the investment bankers representing the sellers were expected to have the offering memorandum ready for the open market. To attempt to buy the company privately would require the team to raise commitments for approximately $150 million in three to four weeks, hardly enough time to put together even a crude business plan, let alone raise such a substantial sum. The train was moving at 200 kilometres per hour and gaining speed each day. The founders identified five top-notch, interested venture capital and leveraged buyout firms and sat down with representatives of each to walk through the summary of the business plan and the proposed financing. One excellent firm sent an otherwise very experienced and capable partner, but his questioning indicated just how little he knew about this business. The team knew they had to look elsewhere.

Had the group been too impatient simply because the train was moving so quickly, they would have exposed themselves to additional risk. That potential investor had a serious lack of elementary knowledge of the industry and the business model, and had not done his homework in advance. If they had waited for this investor to become knowledgeable about the business, it would have been too late.

Take-the-Money-and-Run Myopia

A final trap in raising money for a company is a take-the-money-and-run myopia that invariably prevents an entrepreneur from evaluating one of the most critical longer-term issues—to what extent can the investor add value to the company beyond the money? Into this trap falls the entrepreneur who does not possess a clear sense that his or her prospective financial partner has the relevant experience and know-how in the market and industry area, the contacts the entrepreneur needs but does not have, the savvy and the reputation that adds value in the relationship with the investor—and yet takes the money.

As has been said before, the successful development of a company can be critically affected by the interaction of the management team and the financial partners. If an effective relationship can be established, the value-added synergy can be a powerful stimulant for success. Many founders overlook the high value-added contributions that some investors are accustomed to making and erroneously opt for a "better deal."

Tables Turn in Times of Turmoil

In 2009, the tables were turning on the VCs and they were begging hard for money. Upstream from VC money exists a variety of institutional and other investors. The venture funds were simply dry, all tapped out and upstream was nervous and sitting tight. At that point, two of Canada's biggest firms, VenturesWest and Celtic House, were stalled in their own fundraising and had to suspend venture-funding activity.[29]

For Brightspark it has meant a reversal for new life. Brightspark was founded in 1999 with two parts: a software start-up incubator and VC. The VC arm invested in what came out of the other half. The incubator half (Brightspark Labs) was disbanded in 2002 having placed its employees and ideas in the real world while the other half (Brightspark Ventures) was going strong. In 2009, under dire economic conditions Brightspark was forced to start building software and launching—rather than funding—new ventures. Mark Skapinker, co-founder of Brightspark, said "We decided to go back to basics." The firm launched three Web-based businesses, all of which share a common architecture. Why would a VC firm launch its own businesses? "While it might seem counterintuitive for a VC firm to dream up, develop, fund, and launch its own companies, for the entrepreneurial veterans at Brightspark it's merely a case of doing what comes naturally."[30] "We hope that we are showing the market that great tech companies can be created and grown in the face of a brutal VC and financial market."[31]

Sources: Timothy Hay, "O Canada VC, We Stand On Guard for Thee," *Wall Street Journal*, April 3, 2009; Mark Skapinker, "Say It Like You See It," www.blog.brightspark.com (accessed April 4, 2009); Canadian Venture Capital Association, "Venture Capital Investment Continued to Fall in Q1 2009," Press Release, May 12, 2009.

INTERNET IMPACT: RESOURCES

Real Estate Marketing and Sales

The Internet enables buyers and sellers of real estate to bypass agents whose function has been to collect data from many sources and make it available to end-users. In that way, online resources are quickly changing the basis for competing and creating value in the real estate industry. Gone are the days where local agents—armed with the latest proprietary Multiple Listing Service (MLS) data—were the gatekeepers and purveyors of up-to-date information on available properties, community aspects, and comparative pricing.

Instead of spending weekends with a broker—or driving around town looking for "for sale" signs and open houses—buyers can now conduct detailed searches on MLS portals like www.realtor.com, and on sale-by-owner sites like www.bytheowner.com. For buyers looking to relocate or purchase secondary properties far from their current home, the Internet has become a powerful resource.

Despite many dire predictions in the early days of the Internet, it is unlikely that these online capabilities will ever do away with the need for professional intermediaries in the complex—and often emotional—purchase of real estate. However, as their commissions shrink along with the scope of the services they are being expected to provide, the success factor for real estate agents will be in taking on a value added consultative role in the overall process.

Chapter Summary

1. There is rarely a "fair fight" between users (entrepreneurs) and suppliers (investors) of capital. Entrepreneurs need to be prepared by learning how the capital markets determine valuation risk.

2. Several valuation methods are used to arrive at value for a company, the venture capital method being the most common.

3. Investors prefer to stage their capital commitments, thereby managing and containing the risk, and preserving their options to invest further or cease.

4. Numerous potential conflicts exist between users and suppliers of capital, and these require appreciation and managing. The economic consequences can be worth millions to founders.

5. Successful deals are characterized by careful thought and sensitive balance among a range of important issues.

6. Deal structure can make or break an otherwise sound venture, and the devil is always in the details.

7. Negotiating the deal is both art and science, and also can make or break the relationship.

8. The entrepreneur encounters numerous strategic, legal, and other traps during the fund-raising cycle and needs awareness and skill in coping with them. And advisors (Chapter 8) can help.

Study Questions

1. Why can there be such wide variations in the valuations investors and founders place on companies? What are the determinants of value? What is a company worth: explain the theory and the reality of valuation.

2. Define and explain why the following are important: long-term value creation, investor's required IRR, investor's required share of ownership, discounted cash flow, and deal structure in fund-raising.

3. Explain five prevalent methods used in valuing a company and their strengths and weaknesses, given their underlying assumptions.

4. What is a staged capital commitment, and why is it important?

5. What is a "cram down" or "down round"?

6. What are some of the inherent conflicts between investors and entrepreneurs, and how and why can these affect the venture's odds for success?

7. What are the most important questions and issues to consider in structuring a deal? Why?

8. What issues can be negotiated in a venture investment, and why are these important?

9. What are the pitfalls and traps in fund-raising, and why do entrepreneurs sometimes fail to avoid them?

Mind Stretchers   *Have you considered?*

1. Who should and should not have outside investors in their companies?

2. It is said that a good deal structure cannot turn a bad business into a good one, but many a good business has been killed by a bad deal structure. Why is this so? Find an example of each.

3. What beliefs and assumptions are revealed by the "bets" made in different deals?

4. What is a good deal? Why?

5. Is venture capital always structured to the advantages of the money lenders? Why?

CASE	TERRACYCLE INC.

Preparation Questions

1. Is TerraCycle 'VC-able'?
2. Is Carrot Capital the right fit for TerraCycle?
3. Should they take the deal anyway? Do they have a choice?

There was a bright burst of flashbulbs as Tom Szaky signed the electronic screen and pushed the button to signal the start of the NASDAQ's trading day. With his tousled bedhead, wearing a blazer over a T-shirt, the 21-year-old was visibly different from the CEOs, celebrities, and statespeople that usually preside over the market opening.

Szaky was a student on a leave of absence from Princeton University. He had put his studies on hold to found Terracycle, a New Jersey-based start-up that manufactured organic plant fertilizer from worm excrement. A week earlier, he'd pitched the concept to a panel of venture capitalists as part of the Carrot Capital Education Foundation Business Plan Challenge. His top performance in that competition earned him the right to ring the opening bell.

But it didn't stop there. Taking top honours also put Terracycle in line for up to US$1 million in seed funding from Carrot Capital, a New York-based venture capital company. Szaky next met with Carrot's managing director, setting up sessions for both companies to start conducting due diligence. While the judges had been enthusiastic about Terracycle's business model, an offer of VC funding was contingent on a closer inspection of the company's plans.

Szaky knew the stakes were high. With just $500 in the bank and $5,000 coming in from another business-plan competition, Terracycle had barely enough cash to stay alive for another month. With no other venture capital deals on the horizon, Szaky and his six fellow staffers had only a few short weeks to either proceed with financing from Carrot—or find another way ahead with only their scarce bootstrapped cash to rely on.

"Worm Poop"

Just over a week later, Szaky found himself in more familiar, but less glamorous, surroundings. His brow glistening with sweat, he grunted with exertion as he shovelled compost from a metal biocomposter into a platformed worm gin in Princeton, N.J. Beside him was Bill Gillum, a former Bell Labs scientist with a Ph.D. in inorganic chemistry, who alternated between shovelling and adjusting settings on the biocomposter's computer.

The biocomposter and gin were two parts of a prototype system for producing nutrient rich vermicompost on a large scale. The prototype was the latest step in a grand vision that had begun years earlier when Szaky took a road trip to Montreal. There, he had been impressed by the wriggling fertilizer factory installed under his Montreal friend's kitchen counter—a miniature vermicompost operation, where a bucket of red worms converted the house's kitchen waste into nutrient-rich plant food for the garden.

Now Szaky and Gillum were tinkering with an industrial-scale version of that same concept. A far cry from the kitchen-cupboard bucket, Terracycle's system used tens of thousands of worms, capable of producing thousands of pounds of fertilizer. Raw organic waste—from coffee grounds to paper sludge— was first heated and oxygenated to eliminate any harmful bacteria; then it was fed into a biotransformer, where red worms would chew through it, excreting nutrient-rich vermicompost castings in the process.

The final step saw these castings—"worm poop," in the candid language of Terracycle's founders—separated to remove any worms or undigested waste. The product could be bagged directly as a solid, or brewed and packaged as a liquefied plant food. This innovative separation and brewing process allowed the fertilizer to retain its nutrients on the shelf for years—a considerable improvement over the kitchen-cupboard system, whose output would lose its nutrients after only weeks.

Their working prototype could produce and bottle up to 80 half-litre containers per week—if Terracycle's staff chipped in enough manual labour. Often, they would spend their mornings in meetings, and then spend afternoons shovelling organic waste into the gin. The end product was bottled in spartan containers—the company had yet to settle on packaging design or a product name. Based on Bill's own anecdotal experience, the company's plant food was at least as effective as its chemical counterparts, such as Miracle-Gro.

Terracycle badly needed capital to turn the prototype into a working production facility. To convert a warehouse space in Trenton, N.J., into a fully functional production facility capable of producing 100,000 750-millilitre bottles per week would require $300,000; to scale up to 215,000 bottles per week, they would need $850,000 in facility upgrades and bottling and brewing equipment. The company also needed to undertake rigorous product testing—a process that, for each product, would take six months and cost $60,000 at Rutgers, the state university of New Jersey.

Terracycle had been focused on producing a liquid indoor plant food, but a number of other products were possible. Once the earthworm castings had been produced, they could be packaged in their solid form to be used as pellet fertilizers or growth media (soil substitute). Alternately, the castings could be brewed in distilled water to produce a sprayable liquid. Products for specialty applications such as rose bushes could be developed with small changes to the composition of the worms' organic-waste diet. And the company had a range of bottling options, from a spray applicator on small bottles for indoor use to a hose applicator affixed to a large jug for lawns and outdoor plants.

This case was written by Lukas Neville, Ph.D. student, Queen's School of Business, and Professor Elspeth J. Murray, CIBC Teaching Fellow in Entrepreneurship, Queen's School of Business, Queen's University. This case was developed with the support of the CIBC Curriculum Development Fund at the Queen's Centre for Business Venturing, for purposes of classroom discussion.

www.mcgrawhill.ca/olc/timmons

First Product

Responsibility for setting product lines fell to Robin Tator. Tator, the company's vice-president of marketing and sales, had given Szaky one of his very first jobs as a teen. Tator had joined the firm early in its development and had been dividing his time between Ontario and New Jersey ever since, steering sales and distribution efforts on both sides of the border.

Terracycle had already tentatively selected its first product: a sprayable, all-purpose indoor plant food aimed at the consumer market. Pricing was designed to match larger competitors like Miracle-Gro. While Terracycle couldn't match the scale economies of its competitors, the production process for its vermicompost was far less expensive than the energy-intensive production of chemical fertilizer products.

The size of the fertilizer and media market was appealing—in the United States alone, it was a US$6-billion segment of the US$37-billion lawn and garden market. But the segment was beset by sluggish growth—no more than 5 percent annually—and dominated by a handful of industry Goliaths. Scotts' Miracle-Gro controlled at least 35 percent of the consumer lawn and garden market—and had an even tighter grip on the all-purpose fertilizer market.

Tator considered the organic market a green field of opportunity: The market was small—perhaps $400 million—for "designer" soils and premium plant food, but it was growing at a rate of 16 percent per year. Sales of organic products, which made up at best 10 percent of the overall lawn and consumables market, had grown well over 400 percent between 1997 and 2002. Though one competitor, Schultz, had made tentative steps into the market and Scotts was planning an organic line, the organic market was still dominated by small, regionally focused competitors.

Tator advocated a consumer focus, even though the agricultural and commercial markets offered higher margins. First, he expected indoor home users to respond positively to the product's safe, non-chemical formulation. Second, he anticipated that consumers would more readily try out the Terracycle product—while agricultural users, whose livelihood depended on the product's efficacy, would take longer to experiment with and adopt the product.

Terracycle vs. Carrot

While Terracycle refined its production process and planned for its product rollout, however, the relationship with its potential financier began to sour. The discussions were conducted by Szaky, CFO Doug Feltman, and interim CEO Thomas Pyle. Feltman had joined the team after serving as CFO of market-ing firm Grey Worldwide. Pyle's career in banking included senior roles at Deutsche Bank, Chase Manhattan, and Skandinaviska Enskilda Banken.

Despite their resumes, the financial projections they presented reflected both the company's embryonic stage of development and the fact that the leadership was balancing dozens of competing priorities. Their submissions included neither detailed cash-flow projections nor a proposed use of proceeds for the financing round.

Carrot wanted more. It needed a clear picture of what stage of development the young company would reach with its round of financing. Szaky and partners soon discerned that the financing would be tranched—delivered in stages—based on set metrics for sales, development, and hiring. Having attributed their survival thus far to their adaptability, the Terracycle team worried that set metrics would limit their flexibility in the face of unpredictable change.

Terracycle and its prospective investors also clashed on spending priorities. The company had budgeted relatively modest amounts for marketing, preferring to build sales through guerrilla marketing and a network of unpaid student interns. They also planned to place the management team—who had been sleeping at the office and drawing meagre, infrequent paycheques—on salary. Carrot expected, by contrast, investments into professional branding and marketing. They considered the intern program an unacceptable distraction.

The VC also wanted to rethink the management line-up. In a letter, Carrot allowed that the management members were smart and capable, but argued they were the wrong people for the company. Carrot wanted to hire start-up veterans with deeper experience in consumer products and retail marketing. Those who were left, Carrot made clear, would be expected to continue working at modest salaries or for equity alone.

Carrot, as an act of good faith, was willing to keep the company afloat with a $20,000 bridge loan and agreed to give it additional time to work out a deal. But Terracycle's managers were skeptical, sensing a gulf between their vision and Carrot's aims. On top of those substantive challenges, Szaky felt uneasy with Carrot on a gut level, as if he was being cloistered from his team during the high-intensity negotiations with the VC.

Butting heads with Carrot over both strategy and spending, Terracycle was in an unenviable position. It would be months before they had a saleable product ready. Their coffers were empty. The company had some embryonic relationships with individual investors—enough, perhaps, to cobble together enough funding to survive a few more months—but there was still a very good chance that it would not survive if they rejected the venture capital deal.

11

OBTAINING DEBT CAPITAL[1]

Leveraging a company is like driving your car with a sharp stick pointed at your heart through the steering wheel. As long as the road is smooth it works fine. But hit one bump in the road and you may be dead.

Warren Buffet

RESULTS EXPECTED

Upon completion of this chapter, you will be able to:

1. Identify sources of debt and how to access them in today's capital markets.

2. Describe the lender's perspective and criteria in making loans, how to prepare a loan proposal, and how to negotiate a loan.

3. Understand the key aspects of managing and orchestrating the acquisition of debt capital.

4. Discuss how lenders estimate the debt capacity of a company.

5. Identify tar pits entrepreneurs need to avoid in considering debt.

Market cycles impact credit availability—often creating a lack thereof—for emerging companies. After a market meltdown (such as in 2000 and again in 2009), many old rules disappeared and a harsher banking climate once again appeared. This chapter aims at preparing you to cope better with those realities in the debt capital markets. And as debt markets improve, and they always do, lessons learned here will provide important competitive advantages.

A CYCLICAL PATTERN: THE GOOD OLD DAYS RETURN BUT FADE AGAIN

For entrepreneurs and their investors, the punishing credit crunch and stagnant equity markets give way to robust capital markets and once again are beaten down. Interest rates fluctuate and the credit environment turns from friend to foe in a short timeframe. The availability of bank loans and competition among banks changes dramatically from pursuer of entrepreneurs to playing hard to get. And as Jean-Etienne de Bettignies and James

Brander, both of the University of British Columbia observe: "With bank finance, the entrepreneur keeps full control of the firm and has efficient incentives to exert effort." This may not be the case with venture capital finance—the subject of the previous chapter.[2]

Regardless of the credit environment lenders are becoming more savvy in seeking growth companies with the potential to assert themselves in the new economy. When times are good, bank presidents and loan officers aggressively seek entrepreneurial companies as prospective clients. They work with local universities and business development associations to sponsor seminars, workshops, and small business fairs, all to cultivate entrepreneurial customers. This is a very welcome credit climate for entrepreneurs. In a more severe credit crunch, regardless of interest rates, money slows, lenders turn reluctant and are less encouraging. The availability of credit is cyclical, the good times will return and fade, but remember that the fundamentals of credit don't change that much.

A Word of Caution

History suggests a favourable credit environment can and will change, sometimes suddenly. When a credit climate reverses itself, personal guarantees come back. Even the most creditworthy companies with enviable records for timely repayment of interest and principal could be asked to provide personal guarantees by the owners. In addition, there could be a phenomenon viewed as a perversion of the debt capital markets. As a credit crunch becomes more severe, banks face their own illiquidity problems. To cope with their own balance sheet dissipation, banks can and might call the best loans first. Thousands of high quality smaller companies can be stunned and debilitated by such actions. Also, as competition among banks lessens, pricing and terms can become more onerous as the economy continues in a period of credit tightening. Debt reduction could then become a dominant financial strategy of small and large companies alike.

The Lender's Perspective

Lenders have always been wary capital providers. Because banks may earn as little as a 1-percent net profit on total assets, they are especially sensitive to the possibility of a loss. If a bank writes off a $1-million loan to a small company, it must then be repaid an incremental $100 million in profitable loans to recover that loss.

Yet, lending institutions are businesses and seek to grow and improve profitability as well. They can do this only if they find and bet on successful, young, growing companies. Historically, points and fees charged for making a loan have been a major contributor to bank profitability. During parts of the credit cycle, banks may seek various sweeteners to make loans. Take, for instance, a lending proposal for a company seeking a $15-million five-year loan. In addition to the up-front origination fees and points, the bank further proposed a YES, or yield enhancement security, as part of the loan. This additional requirement would entitle the bank to receive an additional $3-million payment from the company once its sales exceeded $10 million and it was profitable, or if it was sold, merged, or taken public. While this practice hasn't happened frequently in the current economic climate, it could be revived, depending on the cycle.

SOURCES OF DEBT CAPITAL[3]

The principal sources of borrowed capital for new and young businesses are trade credit, commercial banks, finance companies, factors, and leasing companies.[4] Start-ups have more difficulty borrowing money than existing businesses because they don't have assets or a track record of profitability and/or a positive cash flow. Nevertheless, start-ups managed by an entrepreneur with a track record and with significant equity in the business who can present a sound business plan can borrow money from one or more sources. Still, if little equity or collateral exists, the start-up won't have much success with banks.

The availability of such debt for high-tech start-ups can sometimes depend on where a business is located. Debt and leases as well as equity capital can be more available to start-up companies in such hotbeds of entrepreneurial activity as, say, in the prairies. The hotbed areas also feature close contact between venture capital firms and the high-technology-focused lending officers of banks. This contact tends to make it easier for start-ups and early-stage companies to borrow money, although banks rarely lend to new ventures. But even in these hotbeds, very few banks are active in this start-up environment.

The advantages and disadvantages of these sources, summarized in Exhibit 11.1, are basically determined by such obvious dimensions as the interest rate or cost of capital, the key terms, the conditions and covenants, and the fit with the owner's situation and the company's needs at the time.[5] How good a deal you can strike is a function of your relative bargaining position and the competitiveness among the alternatives.

Ultimately, most important is the person with whom you will be dealing, rather than the amount, terms, or institution. You will be better off seeking the right banker (or other provider of capital) than just the right bank. Once again, the industry and market characteristics, and the stage and health of the firm in terms of cash flow, debt coverage, and collateral are central to the evaluation process. Exhibit 11.2 summarizes the term of financing available from these different sources. Note the difficulty in finding sources for more than one year of financing.

Finally, an enduring question entrepreneurs ask is, What is bankable? How much money can I expect to borrow based on my balance sheet? Exhibit 11.3 summarizes some general guidelines in answer to this question. Because most loans and lines of credit are asset-based loans, knowing the lender's guidelines is very important. The percentages

EXHIBIT 11.1   Debt Financing Sources for Types of Business

Source	Start-up Company	Existing Company
Trade credit	Yes	Yes
Finance companies	Occasionally, with strong equity	Yes
Commercial banks	Rare (if assets are available)	Yes
Factors	Depends on nature of the customers	Yes
Leasing companies	Difficult, except for start-ups with venture capital	Yes
Credit unions	Depends on strength of personal guarantee	Real estate and asset-based companies
Insurance companies	Rare, except alongside venture capital	Yes, depending on size

Source: Jeffry A. Timmons, *Financing and Planning the New Venture* (Acton, MA: Brick House Publishing Company, 1990).

EXHIBIT 11.2   Debt Financing Sources by Term of Financing

Source	Short	Medium	Long
Trade credit	Yes	Yes	Possible
Commercial banks	Most frequently	Yes (asset-based)	Rare (depends on cash flow predictability)
Factors	Most frequently	Rare	No
Leasing companies	No	Most frequently	Some
Credit unions	Yes	Yes	Real estate and other asset-based companies
Insurance companies	Rare	Rare	Most frequently

Source: Jeffry A. Timmons, *Financing and Planning the New Venture* (Acton, MA: Brick House Publishing Company, 1990), p. 34.

EXHIBIT 11.3   What Is Bankable? Specific Lending Criteria

Security	Credit Capacity
Accounts receivable	70–85% of those less than 90 days of acceptable receivables
Inventory	20–70% depending on obsolescence risk and saleability
Equipment	60–70% of market value (less if specialized)
Chattel mortgage*	80% or more of auction appraisal value
Conditional sales contract	60–70% or more of purchase price
Plant improvement loan	50–70% of appraised value or cost

Source: Jeffry A. Timmons, *Financing and Planning the New Venture* (Acton, MA: Brick House Publishing, 1990).

*A lien on assets other than real estate backing a loan.

of key balance sheet assets that are often allowable as collateral are only ranges and will vary from region to region, for different types of businesses, and for stages in the business cycle. For instance, non-perishable consumer goods versus technical products that may have considerable risk of obsolescence would be treated very differently in making a loan collateral computation. If the company already has significant debt and has pledged all its assets, there may not be much room for negotiations. A bank with full collateral in hand for a company having cash flow problems is unlikely to give up such a position to enable the company to attract another lender, even though the collateral is more than enough to meet these guidelines.

Trade Credit[6]

Trade credit is a major source of short-term funds for small businesses. Trade credit represents 30 to 40 percent of the current liabilities of non-financial companies, with generally higher percentages in smaller companies. It is reflected on the balance sheet as accounts payable, or sales payable-trade.

If a small business is able to buy goods and services and be given, or take, 30, 60, or 90 days to pay for them, that business has essentially obtained a loan of 30 to 90 days. Many small and new businesses are able to obtain such trade credit when no other form of debt financing is available to them. Suppliers offer trade credit as a way to get new customers, and often build the bad debt risk into their prices. Additionally, channel partners who supply trade credit often do so with more industry-specific knowledge than can be obtained by commercial banks.[7] Such credit is often termed *spontaneous credit* and is "subject to gradual and automatic modification in direct relation to the volume of business and profitability."[8]

The ability of a new business to obtain trade credit depends on the quality and reputation of its management and the relationships it establishes with its suppliers. Continued late payment or non-payment may cause suppliers to cut off shipments or ship only on a COD basis. A key to keeping trade credit open is to continually pay some amount, even if not the full amount. Also, the real cost of using trade credit can be very high; for example, the loss of discounts for prompt payment. Because the cost of trade credit is seldom expressed as an annual amount, it should be analyzed carefully, and a new business should shop for the best terms.

Trade credit may take some of the following forms: extended credit terms; special or seasonal datings, where a supplier ships goods in advance of the purchaser's peak selling season and accepts payment 90 to 120 days later during the season; inventory on consignment, not requiring payment until sold; and loan or lease of equipment.

Commercial Bank Financing

Canadian chartered banks prefer to lend to existing businesses that have a track record of sales, profits, and satisfied customers, and a current backlog of orders. Their concern about the high failure rates in new ventures can make banks less than enthusiastic about making loans to such firms. They like to be lower-risk lenders, which is consistent with their profit margins. For their protection, they look first to positive cash flow and then to collateral, and in new and young enterprises (depending on the credit environment) they are likely to require personal guarantees of the owners. Like equity investors, commercial banks place great weight on the quality of the management team.

Notwithstanding these factors, certain banks do, rarely, make loans to start-ups or young businesses that have strong equity financings from venture capital firms. This has been especially true in centres of entrepreneurial and venture capital activity.

Commercial banks are the primary source of debt capital for existing (not new) businesses. Small business loans may be handled by a bank's small business loan department or through credit scoring (where credit approval is done "by the numbers"). Your personal credit history will also impact the credit-scoring matrix. Larger loans may require the approval of a loan committee. If a loan exceeds the limits of a local bank, part or the entire loan amount will be offered to "correspondent" banks in neighbouring communities and nearby financial centres. This correspondent network enables the smaller banks in rural areas to handle loans that otherwise could not be made.

Most of the loans made by Canadian chartered banks are for one year or less. Some of these loans are unsecured, while receivables, inventories, or other assets secure others. Commercial banks also make a large number of intermediate-term loans (or term loans) with a maturity of one to five years. On about 90 percent of these term loans, the banks require collateral, generally consisting of stocks, machinery, equipment, and real estate. Most term loans are retired by systematic, but not necessarily equal payments over the life of the loan. Apart from real estate mortgages and loans guaranteed by the Business Development Bank of Canada or a similar organization, commercial banks make few loans with maturities greater than five years.

Banks also offer a number of services to the small business, such as computerized payroll preparation, letters of credit, international services, lease financing, and money market accounts.

According to a World Economic Forum report released in October 2008, Canada has the world's soundest banking system.

The Canadian Angle

Richard Kinlough and Bill Holy of CIT Corporate Finance, Canada state in the official journal of the Canadian Venture Capital and Private Equity Association that "the mid-market never got as frothy as in the U.S., likely the result of our conservative banking system. Total leverage never reached the 6s, peaking at around 5x total, with senior pricing in the BA+250 to 300 range. . . which was about as borrower-friendly as it got in Canada. Because the mid-market was not as aggressive as in the U.S., the correction was not as severe. By the end of Q4 2008, pricing increased 100bps to BA+400 while total leverage came down a turn to around 4.0x"

"BA" stands for Banker's Acceptance and is a short-term credit note generated for investment purposes and guaranteed by a bank. BAs are discounted from face value and traded in secondary markets. Banker's Acceptances are similar to government-backed debt (e.g., treasury bills) and are generally found in money market funds.

100, 200, 300, 400 refers to 1, 2, 3, 4 percent. 100bps similarly refers to 100 basis points or 1 full percent; a basis point is 1/100 of a percent.

Kinlough and Holy go on to state, "In Canada, liquidity is less constrained and lending terms are set at levels that send an 'open for business' signal. But just like in the U.S., the market has become a bit more conservative and pricey.

Senior leverage is around 2.5x to 3.0x, priced at BA+450. Total leverage is in the 4.0x range and should remain there for the foreseeable future."[9]

What this assessment means is that by being a bit behind the more risk tolerant U.S. banking practices became good news for the Canadian banking sector. Canadian firms were not allowed to play the leverage games that firms in the U.S. played—thus avoiding driving with the sharp stick on the steering wheel that Warren Buffet warned of in this chapter's opening quote. Or in reference to another Warren Buffet quote: "It is only when the tide goes out that you know who was swimming naked." Prime Minister Harper stated, "The global economic crisis has revealed quite a few skinny-dippers, but Canada is not one of them."[10] This Canadian austerity means that the highs and lows are avoided in favour of a moderate approach, which is not without critics—particularly in times of economic growth and free-flowing capital. It was over 25 years ago that Ben Bernanke, now Chairman of the U.S. Federal Reserve, noted that during the Great Depression (1930–1933) Canada avoided the catastrophic bank failures as plagued the U.S.[11]

Sources: Richard Kinlough and Bill Holy, "The Debt Market," *Private Capital*, Spring 2009; "Canada Will Emerge from Slump Faster, Stronger: PM," CBC News, March 10, 2009; Ben S. Bernanke, "Nonmonetary Effects of the Financial Crisis in the Propagation of the Great Depression," *American Economic Review* 73, no. 3 (1983): 257–276.

Line of Credit Loans

A line of credit is a formal or informal agreement between a bank and a borrower concerning the maximum (and sometimes minimum, e.g., $10,000) loan a bank will allow the borrower for a one-year period. Often the bank will charge a fee of a certain percent of the line of credit for a definite commitment to make the loan when requested.

Line of credit funds are used for such seasonal financings as inventory build-up and receivable financing. These two items are often the largest and most financeable items on a venture's balance sheet. It is general practice to repay these loans from the sales and reduction of short-term assets that they financed. Lines of credit can be unsecured, or the bank may require a pledge of inventory, receivables, equipment, or other acceptable assets. Unsecured lines of credit have no lien on any asset of the borrower and no priority over any trade creditor, but the banks may require that all debt to the principals and stockholders of the company be subordinated to the line of credit debt.

The bank will expect the borrower to pay off his or her open loan within a year and to hold a zero loan balance for one to two months. This is known as "resting the line" or "cleaning up." Canadian chartered banks may also generally require that a borrower maintain a chequing account at the bank with a minimum ("compensating") balance of 5 to 10 percent of the outstanding loan.

For a large, financially sound company, the interest rates for a "prime risk" line of credit will be quoted at the prime rate. A small, more risky, firm may be required to pay a higher rate. The true interest calculations should also reflect the multiple fees that may be added to the loan. Any compensating-balance or resting-the-line requirements or other fees will also increase effective interest rates.

Time-Sales Finance

Many dealers or manufacturers who offer instalment payment terms to purchasers of their equipment cannot themselves finance instalment or conditional sales contracts. In such situations, they sell and assign the instalment contract to a bank or sales finance company. (Some very large manufacturers do their own financing through captive finance companies. Most small retailers merely refer their customer instalment contracts to sales finance companies, which provide much of this financing, and on more flexible terms.)

From the manufacturer or dealer's point of view, time-sales finance is a way of obtaining short-term financing from long-term instalment accounts receivable. From the purchaser's point of view, it is a way of financing the purchase of new equipment.

Under time-sales financing, the bank purchases instalment contracts at a discount from their full value and takes as security an assignment of the manufacturer/dealer's interest in the conditional sales contract. In addition, the bank's financing of instalment note receivables includes recourse to the seller in the event of loan default by the purchaser. Thus, the bank has the payment obligation of the equipment purchaser, the manufacturer/dealer's security interest in the equipment purchased, and recourse to the manufacturer/dealer in the event of default. The bank also withholds a portion of the payment (5 percent or more) as a dealer reserve until the note is paid. Since the reserve becomes an increasing percentage of the note as the contract is paid off, an arrangement is often made when multiple contracts are financed to ensure that the reserve against all contracts will not exceed 20 percent or so.

The purchase price of equipment under a sales financing arrangement includes a "time-sales price differential" (e.g., an increase to cover the discount, typically 6 to 10 percent) taken by the bank that does the financing. Collection of the instalments may be made directly by the bank or indirectly through the manufacturer/dealer.

Term Loans

Bank term loans are generally made for periods of one to five years, and may be unsecured or secured. Most of the basic features of bank term loans are the same for secured and unsecured loans.

Term loans provide needed growth capital to companies. They are also a substitute for a series of short-term loans made with the hope of renewal by the borrower. Banks make these generally on the basis of predictability of positive cash flow.

Term loans have three distinguishing features: Banks make them for periods of up to five years (and occasionally more); periodic repayment is required; and agreements are designed to fit the special needs and requirements of the borrower (e.g., payments can be smaller at the beginning of a loan term and larger at the end).

Because term loans do not mature for a number of years, during which time the borrower's situation and fortunes could change significantly, the bank must carefully evaluate the prospects and management of the borrowing company. Even the protection afforded by initially strong assets can be wiped out by several years of heavy losses. Term lenders stress the entrepreneurial and managerial abilities of the borrowing company. The bank will also carefully consider such things as the long-range prospects of the company and its industry, its present and projected profitability, and its ability to generate the cash required to meet the loan payments, as shown by past performance. Pricing for a term loan may be higher, reflecting a perceived higher risk from the longer term.

To lessen the risks involved in term loans, a bank will require some restrictive covenants in the loan agreement. These covenants might prohibit additional borrowing, merger of the company, payment of dividends, sales of assets, increased salaries to the owners, and the like. Also, the bank will probably require financial covenants to provide early warning of deterioration of the business, like debt to equity and cash flow to interest coverage.

Chattel Mortgages and Equipment Loans

Assigning an appropriate possession (chattel) as security is a common way of making secured term loans. The chattel is any machinery, equipment, or business property that is made the collateral of a loan in the same way as a mortgage on real estate. The chattel remains with the borrower unless there is default, in which case the chattel goes to the bank. A lien charge against the title is registered with the province.[12] Generally, credit against machinery and equipment is restricted primarily to new or highly serviceable and saleable used items.

Conditional Sales Contracts

Conditional sales contracts are used to finance a substantial portion of the new equipment purchased by businesses. Under a sales contract, the buyer agrees to purchase a piece of equipment, makes a nominal down payment, and pays the balance in instalments over a period of from one to five years. Until the payment is complete, the seller holds title to the equipment. Hence, the sale is conditional upon the buyer's completing the payments.

A sales contract is financed by a bank that has recourse to the seller should the purchaser default on the loan. This makes it difficult to finance a purchase of a good piece of used equipment at an auction. No recourse to the seller is available if the equipment is purchased at an auction; the bank would have to sell the equipment if the loan goes bad. Occasionally, a firm seeking financing on existing and new equipment will sell some of its equipment to a dealer and repurchase it, together with new equipment, in order to get a conditional sales contract financed by a bank.

The effective rate of interest on a conditional sales contract is high, running to as much as 15 to 18 percent if the effect of instalment features is considered. The purchaser/borrower should make sure the interest payment is covered by increased productivity and profitability resulting from the new equipment.

Plant Improvement Loans

Loans made to finance improvements to business properties and plants are called plant improvement loans. They can be intermediate and long term and are generally secured by a first or second mortgage on that part of the property or plant that is being improved.

Commercial Finance Companies

The commercial bank is generally the lender of choice for a business. But when the bank says no, commercial finance companies, which aggressively seek borrowers, are a good option. They frequently lend money to companies that do not have positive cash flow, although commercial finance companies will not make loans to companies unless they consider them viable risks. In tighter credit economies, finance companies are generally more accepting of risk than are banks.

The primary factors in a bank's loan decision are the continuing successful operation of a business and its generation of more than enough cash to repay a loan. By contrast, commercial finance companies lend against the liquidation value of assets (receivables, inventory, equipment) that it understands, knows how and where to sell, and whose liquidation value is sufficient to repay the loan. Banks today own many of the leading finance companies. As a borrower gains financial strength and a track record, transfer to more attractive bank financing can be easier.

In the case of inventories or equipment, liquidation value is the amount that could be realized from an auction or quick sale. Finance companies will generally not lend against receivables more than 90 days old, federal or provincial government agency receivables (against which it is very difficult to perfect a lien and payment is slow), or any receivables whose collection is contingent on the performance of a delivered product.

Because of the liquidation criteria, finance companies prefer readily saleable inventory items such as electronic components or metal in such commodity forms as billets or standard shapes. Generally, a finance company will not accept inventory as collateral unless it also has receivables. Equipment loans are made only by certain finance companies and against such standard equipment as lathes, milling machines, and the like. Finance companies, like people, have items in which they are more comfortable and therefore would extend more credit against certain kinds of collateral.

How much of the collateral value will a finance company lend? Generally, 70 to 85 percent of acceptable receivables under 90 days old, 20 to 70 percent of the liquidation value of raw materials and/or finished goods inventory that are not obsolete or damaged, and

60 to 70 percent of the liquidation value of equipment, as determined by an appraiser, is acceptable. Receivables and inventory loans are for one year, while equipment loans are for three to seven years.

All these loans have tough prepayment penalties: Finance companies do not want to be immediately replaced by banks when a borrower has improved its credit image. Generally, finance companies require a three-year commitment to do business with them, with prepayment fees if this provision is not met.

The data required for a loan from a finance company includes all that would be provided to a bank, plus additional details for the assets being used as collateral. For receivables financing, this includes detailed aging of receivables (and payables) and historical data on sales, returns, or deductions (all known as dilution), and collections.

For inventory financing, it includes details on the items in inventory, how long they have been there, and their rate of turnover. Requests for equipment loans should be accompanied by details on the date of purchase, cost of each equipment item, and appraisals, which are generally always required. These appraisals must be made by acceptable (to the lender) outside appraisers.

The advantage of dealing with a commercial finance company is that it will make loans that banks will not, and it can be flexible in lending arrangements. The price a finance company exacts for this is an interest rate anywhere from 0 to 6 percent over that charged by a bank, prepayment penalties, and, in the case of receivables loans, recourse to the borrower for unpaid collateralized receivables.

Because of their greater risk taking and asset-based lending, finance companies usually place a larger reporting and monitoring burden on the borrowing firm to stay on top of the receivables and inventory serving as loan collateral. Personal guarantees will generally be required from the principals of the business. A finance company or bank will generally reserve the right to reduce the percentage of the value lent against receivables or inventory if it gets nervous about the borrower's survivability.

Factoring

Factoring is a form of accounts receivable financing. However, instead of borrowing and using receivables as collateral, the receivables are sold, at a discounted value, to a factor. Factoring is accomplished on a discounted value of the receivables pledged. Invoices that do not meet the factor's credit standard will not be accepted as collateral. (Receivables more than 90 days old are not normally accepted.) A bank may inform the purchaser of goods that the account has been assigned to the bank, and payments are made directly to the bank, which credits them to the borrower's account. This is called a notification plan. Alternatively, the borrower may collect the accounts as usual and pay off the bank loan; this is a non-notification plan.

Factoring can make it possible for a company to secure a loan that it might not otherwise get. The loan can be increased as sales and receivables grow. However, factoring can have drawbacks. It can be expensive, and trade creditors sometimes regard factoring as evidence of a company in financial difficulty, except in certain industries.

In a standard factoring arrangement, the factor buys the client's receivables outright, without recourse, as soon as the client creates them, by shipment of goods to customers. Although the factor has recourse to the borrowers for returns, errors in pricing, and so on, the factor assumes the risk of bad debt losses that develop from receivables it approves and purchases. Many factors, however, provide factoring only on a recourse basis.

Cash is made available to the client as soon as proof is provided (old-line factoring) or on the average due date of the invoices (maturity factoring). With maturity factoring, the company can often obtain a loan of about 90 percent of the money a factor has agreed to pay on a maturity date. Most factoring arrangements are for one year.

Factoring can also be on a recourse basis. In this circumstance, the borrower must replace unpaid receivables after 90 days with new current receivables to allow the borrowings to remain at the same level.

Factoring fits some businesses better than others. For a business that has annual sales volume in excess of $300,000 and a net worth over $50,000 that sells on normal credit terms to a customer base that is 75-percent credit rated, factoring is a real option. Factoring has become almost traditional in such industries as textiles, furniture manufacturing, clothing manufacturing, toys, shoes, and plastics.

The same data required from a business for a receivable loan from a bank are required by a factor. Because a factor is buying receivables with no recourse, it will analyze the quality and value of a prospective client's receivables. It will want a detailed aging of receivables plus historical data on bad debts, return, and allowances. It will also investigate the credit history of customers to whom its client sells and establish credit limits for each customer. The business client can receive factoring of customer receivables only up to the limits so set.

The cost of financing receivables through factoring is higher than that of borrowing from a bank or a finance company. The factor is assuming the credit risk, doing credit investigations and collections, and advancing funds. A factor generally charges up to 2 percent of the total sales factored as a service charge.

There is also an interest charge for money advanced to a business, usually 2 to 6 percent above prime. A larger, established business borrowing large sums would command a better interest rate than the small borrower with a one-time, short-term need. Finally, factors withhold a reserve of 5 to 10 percent of the receivables purchased.

Factoring is not the cheapest way to obtain capital, but it does quickly turn receivables into cash. Moreover, although more expensive than accounts receivable financing, factoring saves its users credit agency fees, salaries of credit and collection personnel, and maybe bad debt write-offs. Factoring also provides credit information on collection services that may be better than the borrower's.

Leasing Companies

The leasing industry has grown substantially in recent years, and lease financing has become an important source of medium-term financing for businesses. There are hundreds of leasing companies in Canada. In addition, many commercial banks and finance companies have leasing departments. Some leasing companies handle a wide variety of equipment, while others specialize in certain types of equipment—machine tools, electronic test equipment, and the like.

Common and readily resalable items such as automobiles, trucks, computers, and office furniture can be leased by both new and existing businesses. However, the start-up will find it difficult to lease other kinds of industrial, computer, or business equipment without providing a letter of credit or a certificate of deposit to secure the lease, or personal guarantees from the founders or from a wealthy third party.

An exception to this condition is high-technology start-ups that have received substantial venture capital. Some of these ventures have received large amounts of lease financing for special equipment from equity-oriented lessors, who receive some form of stock purchase rights in return for providing the start-up's lease line. Like many financing options, availability of venture leasing may be reduced significantly in tight money markets.

Generally, industrial equipment leases have a term of three to five years, but in some cases may run longer. There can also be lease renewal options for 3 to 5 percent per year of the original equipment value. Leases are usually structured to return the entire cost of the leased equipment plus finance charges to the lessor, although some so-called operating leases do not, over their term, produce revenues equal to or greater than the price of the leased equipment.

Typically, an up-front payment is required of about 10 percent of the value of the item being leased. The interest rate on equipment leasing may be more or less than other forms of financing, depending on the equipment leased, the credit of the lessee, and the time of year.

Leasing credit criteria are very similar to the criteria used by commercial banks for equipment loans. Primary considerations are the value of the equipment leased, the justification of the lease, and the lessee's projected cash flow over the lease term.

Should a business lease equipment? Leasing has certain advantages. It enables a young or growing company to conserve cash and can reduce its requirements for equity capital.

Leasing can also be a tax advantage, because payments can be deducted over a shorter period than can depreciation.

Finally, leasing provides the flexibility of returning equipment after the lease period if it is no longer needed or if it has become technologically obsolete. This can be a particular advantage to high-technology companies.

Leasing may or may not improve a company's balance sheet, because accounting practice currently requires that the value of the equipment acquired in a capital lease be reflected on the balance sheet. Operating leases, however, do not appear on the balance sheet. Generally, this is an issue of economic ownership rather than legal ownership. If the economic risk is primarily with the lessee, it must be capitalized and it therefore goes on the balance sheet along with the corresponding debt. Depreciation also follows the risk, along with the corresponding tax benefits. Start-ups that don't need such tax relief should be able to acquire more favourable terms with an operating lease.

BEFORE THE LOAN DECISION[13]

Choosing a bank and, more specifically, a banker is one of the more important decisions a new or young business will make. Entrepreneurs seeking to develop a constructive banking relationship should note:

✓ *Industry experience is critical.* Choose a banker who understands your particular industry. They will have other clients in the same industry and may serve as a valuable resource for networking and service professionals with relevant experience. In the case of funding requests, bankers with industry knowledge are more apt to make a quick and reasoned determination.

✓ *Understand their business model.* Every bank has different criteria with regard to working with new ventures and their lending decisions are largely based on quantitative credit scoring metrics. The entrepreneur needs to have an understanding of how a particular bank works and determine whether that model is a fit with his or her venture.

✓ *Understand who you're dealing with.* Bankers are relationship managers whose job is to support their clients—including expediting the approval of loans and credit lines that fit with their bank's lending criteria. Like a lot of good vendors, the best of them have specialized knowledge, excellent contacts, and will take a genuine interest in your business.

Much of the following discussion of lending practices and decisions applies to commercial finance company lenders as well as to banks. A good lender relationship can sometimes mean the difference between the life and death of a business during difficult times. There have been cases where one bank has called its loans to a struggling business, causing it to go under, and another bank has stayed with its loans and helped a business to survive and prosper.

Those banks that will not make loans to start-ups and early-stage ventures generally cite the lack of operating track record as the primary reason for turning down a loan. Lenders that make such loans usually do so for previously successful entrepreneurs of means or for firms backed by investors with whom they have had prior relationships and whose judgment they trust (e.g., established venture capital firms when they believe that the venture capital company will invest in the next round).

In centres of high technology and venture capital, the main officers of the major banks will have one or more high technology lending officers who specialize in making loans to early-stage, high-technology ventures. Through much experience, these bankers have come to understand the market and operating idiosyncrasies, problems, and opportunities of such ventures. They generally have close ties to venture capital firms and will refer entrepreneurs to such firms for possible equity financing. The venture capital firms, in turn, will refer their portfolio ventures to the bankers for debt financing.

What should an entrepreneur consider in choosing a lender? What is important in a lending decision? How should entrepreneurs relate to their lenders on an ongoing basis? In many ways, the lender's decision is similar to that of the venture capitalist. The goal is to make money for his or her company, through interest earned on good loans. The lender fears losing money by making bad loans to companies that default on their loans. To this end, he or she avoids risk by building in every conceivable safeguard. The lender is concerned with the client company's loan coverage, its ability to repay, and the collateral it can offer. Finally, but most important, he or she must judge the character and quality of the key managers of the company to whom the loan is being made.

Exhibit 11.4 outlines the key steps in obtaining a loan. Because of the importance of a banking relationship, an entrepreneur should shop around before making a choice. The criteria for selecting a bank should be based on more than just loan interest rates. Equally important, entrepreneurs should not wait until they have a dire need for funds to try to establish a banking relationship. The choice of a bank and the development of a banking relationship should begin when you do not urgently need the money. When an entrepreneur faces a near-term financial crisis, the venture's financial statements are at their worst and the banker has good cause to wonder about management's financial and planning skills—all to the detriment of the entrepreneur's chance of getting a loan.

Entrepreneurship experts Gordon Baty and James Stancill of the University of Southern California each describe factors that are especially important to an entrepreneur in selecting a bank.[14] The bank selected should be big enough to service a venture's foreseeable loans but not so large as to be relatively indifferent to your business. Banks differ greatly in their desire and capacity to work with small firms. Some banks have special small business loan officers and regard new and early-stage ventures as the seeds of very large future accounts. Other banks see such new venture loans as merely bad risks. Does the bank tend to call or reduce its

---

EXHIBIT 11.4   Key Steps in Obtaining a Loan

Before choosing and approaching a banker or other lender, the entrepreneur and his or her venture team should prepare by taking the following steps:

- Decide how much growth they want, and how fast they want to grow, observing the dictum that financing follows strategy.
- Determine how much money they require, when they need to have it, and when they can pay it back. To this end, they must:
  - Develop a schedule of operating and asset needs.
  - Prepare a real-time cash flow projection.
  - Decide how much capital they need.
  - Specify how they will use the funds they borrow.
- Revise and update the "corporate profile" in their business plan. This should consist of:
  - The core ingredients of the plan in the form of an executive summary.
  - A history of the firm (as appropriate).
  - Summaries of the financial results of the past three years.
  - Succinct descriptions of their markets and products.
  - A description of their operations.
  - Statements of cash flow and financial requirements.
  - Descriptions of the key managers, owners, and directors.
  - A rundown of the key strategies, facts, and logic that guide them in growing the corporation.
- Identify potential sources for the type of debt they seek, and the amount, rate, terms, and conditions they seek.
- Select a bank or other lending institution, solicit interest, and prepare a presentation.
- Prepare a written loan request.
- Present their case, negotiate, and then close the deal.
- After the loan is granted, borrowers should maintain an effective relationship with the lending officer.

Source: Jeffry A. Timmons, *Financing and Planning the New Venture* (Acton, MA: Brick Housing Publishing, 1990).

loans to small businesses that have problems? When it has less capital to lend will it cut back on small business loans and favour older, more solid customers? Is the bank imaginative, creative, and helpful when a venture has a problem? To quote Baty, "Do they just look at your balance sheet and faint or do they try to suggest constructive financial alternatives?"

Has the bank had lending experience in your industry? If it has, your chances of getting a loan are better, and the bank will be more tolerant of problems and better able to help you exploit your opportunities. Is there good personal chemistry between you and your prospective lending officer? Remember, the person you talk to and deal with is the bank. Does this person know your industry and competition? Can this officer competently explain your business, technology, and uniqueness to other loan officers? Is he or she experienced in administering loans to smaller firms? Can you count on this person consistently? Does he or she have a good track record? Does his or her lending authority meet or exceed your needs? Does he or she have a reputation for being reasonable, creative, and willing to take a sound risk?

How does an entrepreneur go about evaluating a bank? First, the entrepreneur should consult accountants, lawyers, and other entrepreneurs who have had dealings with the bank. The advice of entrepreneurs who have dealt with a bank through good and bad times can be especially useful. Second, the entrepreneur should meet with loan officers at several banks and systematically explore their attitudes and approaches to their business borrowers. Who meets with you, for how long, and with how many interruptions can be useful measures of a bank's interest in your account. Finally, ask for small business references from their list of borrowers and talk to the entrepreneurs of those firms. Throughout all of these contacts and discussions, check out particular loan officers as well as the viability of the bank itself; they are a major determinant of how the bank will deal with you and your venture.

Approaching and Meeting the Banker

Obtaining a loan is, among other things, a sales job. Many borrowers tend to forget this. An entrepreneur with an early-stage venture must sell himself or herself as well as the viability and potential of the business to the banker. This is much the same situation that the early-stage entrepreneur faces with a venture capitalist.

The initial contact with a lender will likely be by telephone. The entrepreneur should be prepared to describe quickly the nature, age, and prospects of the venture, the amount of equity financing and who provided it; the prior financial performance of the business; the entrepreneur's experience and background; and the sort of bank financing desired. A referral from a venture capital firm, a lawyer or accountant, or other business associate who knows the banker can be very helpful.

If the loan officer agrees to a meeting, he or she may ask that a summary loan proposal, description of the business, and financial statements be sent ahead of time. A well-prepared proposal and a request for a reasonable amount of equity financing should pique a banker's interest.

The first meeting with a loan officer will likely be at the venture's place of business. The banker will be interested in meeting the management team, seeing how team members relate to the entrepreneur, and getting a sense of the financial controls and reporting used and how well things seem to be run. The banker may also want to meet one or more of the venture's equity investors. Most of all, the banker is using this meeting to evaluate the integrity and business acumen of those who will ultimately be responsible for the repayment of the loan.

Throughout meetings with potential bankers, the entrepreneur must convey an air of self-confidence and knowledge. If the banker is favourably impressed by what has been seen and read, he or she will ask for further documents and references and begin to discuss the amount and timing of funds that the bank might lend to the business. Exhibit 11.5 provides a snapshot of the relationship between Canadian banks and entrepreneurs. An additional resource worth examining is "Dealing with your banker and other lenders," which can be found at www.canadabusiness.ca; simply type "banker" into the search box.

EXHIBIT 11.5   Fast Facts about Small and Medium-Sized Enterprises (SMEs) and Canada's Banks

▶ Banks authorized $85 billion in financing to 1.2 million SMEs in 2007
▶ 72% of SMEs use a bank as their main financial institution
▶ 65% use the same financial institution for personal and business banking
▶ Access to credit and a face-to-face relationship are identified as the most important factors between SMEs and their banks
▶ 72% of SMEs maintain a credit relationship with a financial institution
▶ 51% of SMEs have held a credit relationship with their financial institution for more than 10 years
▶ 38% have more than four credit relationships

Source: Canadian Bankers Association, www.cba.ca.

What the Banker Wants to Know[15]

You first need to describe the business and its industry. Exhibit 11.6 suggests how a banker "sees a company" may differ from what the entrepreneur might say. What are you going to do with the money? Does the use of the loan make business sense? Should some or all of the money required be equity capital rather than debt? For new and young businesses, lenders do not like to see total debt-to-equity ratios greater than one. The answers to these questions will also determine the type of loan (e.g., line of credit or term).

1. How much do you need? You must be prepared to justify the amount requested and describe how the debt fits into an overall plan for financing and developing the business. Further, the amount of the loan should have enough cushion to allow for unexpected developments (see Exhibit 11.7).

2. When and how will you pay it back? This is an important question. Short-term loans for seasonal inventory build-ups or for financing receivables are easier to obtain than long-term loans, especially for early-stage businesses. How the loan will be repaid is the bottom-line question. Presumably you are borrowing money to finance activity that will generate enough cash to repay the loan. What is your contingency plan if things go wrong? Can you describe such risks and indicate how you will deal with them?

3. What is the secondary source of repayment? Are there assets or a guarantor of means?

EXHIBIT 11.6   How Your Banker Interprets the Income Statement

Sales	What do you sell?
	Whom do you sell to?
Cost of goods	How do you buy?
	What do you buy?
	Whom do you buy from?
Gross margin	Are you a supermarket or a boutique?
Selling	How do you sell and distribute the product?
G&A: General and Administration	How much overhead and support is needed to operate?
R&D	How much is reinvested in the product?
Operating margins	Dollars available before financing costs?
Interest expense	How big is this fixed nut?
Profit before taxes	Do you make money?
Taxes	Corporation or not?
Profit after taxes	How much and to whom?
Dividends/withdrawals	How much money is left in the company?

Source: This exhibit was created by Kathie S. Stevens and Leslie Charm as part of a class discussion and is part of a presentation titled "Cash Is King, Assets Are Queen, and Everybody Is Looking for an Ace in the Hole." Ms. Stevens is former chief lending officer and member of the credit committee for a Boston bank.

EXHIBIT 11.7   Sample of a Summary Loan Proposal

Date of request:	May 30, 2010	
Borrower:	Cole Graham & Sons, Inc.	
Amount:	$4,200,000	
Use of proceeds:	A/R, up to	$1,600,000
	Inventory, up to	824,000
	WIP, up to	525,000
	Marketing, up to	255,000
	Ski show specials	105,000
	Contingencies	50,000
	Officer loans due	841,000
		$4,200,000
Type of loan:	Seasonal revolving line of credit	
Closing date:	June 15, 2010	
Term:	One year	
Rate:	Prime plus $1/2$ percent, no compensating balances, no points or origination fees.	
Takedown:	$500,000 at closing	
	$1,500,000 on August 1, 2010	
	$1,500,000 on October 1, 2010	
	$700,000 on November 1, 2012	
Collateral:	70 percent of acceptable A/R under 90 days	
	50 percent of current inventory	
Guarantees:	None	
Repayment schedule:	$4,200,000 or balance on anniversary of note	
Source of funds for repayment:	a. Excess cash from operations (see cash flow).	
	b. Renewable and increase of line if growth is profitable.	
	c. Conversion to three-year note.	
Contingency source:	a. Sale and leaseback of equipment.	
	b. Officer's loans (with a request for a personal guarantee).	

Source: Updated and adapted from Jeffry A. Timmons, *Financing and Planning the New Venture* (Acton, MA: Brick House Publishing, 1990).

4. When do you need the money? If you need the money tomorrow, forget it. You are a poor planner and manager. On the other hand, if you need the money next month or the month after, you have demonstrated an ability to plan ahead, and you have given the banker time to investigate and process a loan application. Typically, it is difficult to get a lending decision in less than three weeks (some smaller banks have once-a-month credit meetings).

One of the best ways for all entrepreneurs to answer these questions is from a well-prepared business plan. This plan should contain projections of cash flow, profit and loss, and balance sheets that will demonstrate the need for a loan and how it can be repaid. Particular attention will be given by the lender to the value of the assets and the cash flow of the business, and to such financial ratios as current assets to current liabilities, gross margins, net worth to debt, accounts receivable and payable periods, inventory turns, and net profit to sales. The ratios for the borrower's venture will be compared to averages for competing firms to see how the potential borrower measures up to them.

For an existing business, the lender will want to review financial statements from prior years prepared or audited by a CA, a list of aged receivables and payables, the turnover of inventory, and lists of key customers and creditors. The lender will also want to know that all tax payments are current. Finally, he or she will need to know details of fixed assets and any liens on receivables, inventory, or fixed assets.

The entrepreneur-borrower should regard his or her contacts with the bank as a sales mission and provide data that are required promptly and in a form that can be readily understood. The better the material entrepreneurs can supply to demonstrate their business credibility, the easier and faster it will be to obtain a positive lending decision. The entrepreneur should also ask, early on, to meet with the banker's boss. This can go a long way to help obtain financing. Remember you need to build a relationship with a bank, and not just a banker.

Specialist Banks for Lenders

There exist investment banks that focus on particular industries or geographic locales. Brett Wilson, as seen on CBC's *Dragons' Den*, was born in North Battleford, Saskatchewan, and began working at mainstream investment banks. He eventually went out on his own and co-founded Wilson Mackie & Co. and later FirstEnergy Capital Corp. to provide banking services to Canada's oil and gas enterprises. Following these successes he launched Prairie Merchant Corp.—a private bank for high-potential enterprises in energy, agriculture, real estate, sports, and entertainment. With singer Beverly Mahood, Brett Wilson has formed BPM Entertainment Corp. to seize investment opportunities in the entertainment world.[16]

There have even been calls for the creation of more Canadian investment banks. Such as to lend capital to those interested in taking over assets in Hamilton, Ontario to create a steel company. The same could be done for the auto industry. The rationale: let the assets fall where they may and see if enterprises emerge, and back those with bank loans.[17]

Sources: Tom Keyser, "Rebel With a Cause," www.albertaventures.com, December 1, 2008; Duncan Cameron, "Needed: The Canadian Investment Bank," www.rabble.ca, May 12, 2009; University of Saskatchewan, "100 Alumni of Influence," www.usask.ca/100/alumni/brett_wilson.php (accessed July 8, 2009).

THE LENDING DECISION

One of the significant changes in today's lending environment is the centralized lending decision. Traditionally, loan officers might have had up to several million dollars of lending authority and could make loans to small companies. Besides the company's creditworthiness as determined by analysis of its past results via the balance sheet, income statement, cash flow, and collateral, the lender's assessment of the character and reputation of the entrepreneur was central to the decision. As loan decisions are made increasingly by loan committees or credit scoring, this face-to-face part of the decision process has given way to deeper analysis of the company's business plan, cash flow drivers and dissipaters, competitive environment, and the cushion for loan recovery given the firm's game plan and financial structure.

The implication for entrepreneurs is a demanding one: You can no longer rely on your salesmanship and good relationship with your loan officer alone to continue to get favourable lending decisions. You, or the key team member, need to be able to prepare the necessary analysis and documentation to convince people (you may never meet) that the loan will be repaid. You also need to know the financial ratios and criteria used to compare your loan request with industry norms and to defend the analysis. Such a presentation can make it easier and faster to obtain approval of a loan because it gives your relationship manager the ammunition to defend your loan request.

Lending Criteria

First and foremost, as with equity investors, the quality and track record of the management team will be a major factor. Historical financial statements, which show three to five years of profitability, are also essential. Well-developed business projections that articulate the company's sales estimates, market niche, cash flow, profit projections, working capital, capital expenditure, uses of proceeds, and evidence of competent accounting and control systems are essential.

In its simplest form, what is needed is analysis of the available collateral, based on guidelines such as those shown in Exhibit 11.3, and of debt capacity determined by analysis of the coverage ratio once the new loan is in place. Interest coverage is calculated as earnings before interest and taxes divided by interest (EBIT/interest). A business with steady, predictable cash flow and earnings would require a lower coverage ratio (say, in the range of two) than would a company with a volatile, unpredictable cash flow stream, for example, a high-technology company with risk of competition and obsolescence (which might require a coverage ratio of five or more). The bottom line, of course, is the ability of the company to repay both interest and principal on time.

Loan Restrictions[18]

A loan agreement defines the terms and conditions under which a lender provides capital. With it, lenders do two things: try to assure repayment of the loan as agreed and try to protect their position as creditor. Within the loan agreement (as in investment agreements) there are negative and positive covenants. Negative covenants are restrictions on the borrower; for example, no further additions to the borrower's total debt, no pledge to others of assets of the borrower, and no payment of dividends or limitation on owners' salaries.

Positive covenants define what the borrower must do. Some examples are maintenance of some minimum net worth or working capital, prompt payment of all federal and provincial taxes, adequate insurance on key people and property, repayment of the loan and interest according to the terms of the agreement, and provision to the lender of periodic financial statements and reports.

Some of these restrictions can hinder a company's growth, such as a flat restriction on further borrowing. Such a borrowing limit is often based on the borrower's assets at the time of the loan. However, rather than stipulating an initially fixed limit, the loan agreement should recognize that as a business grows and increases its total assets and net worth, it will need and be able to carry the additional debt required to sustain its growth; however, banks (especially in tighter credit periods) will still put maximums after allowed credit as it gives them another opportunity to recheck the loan. Similarly, covenants that require certain minimums on working capital or current ratios may be very difficult, for example, for a highly seasonal business to maintain at all times of the year. Only analysis of past financial monthly statements can indicate whether such a covenant can be met.

> ### Canwest Global Communications in Crisis
>
> The Winnipeg-based media conglomerate was "scrambling to cut costs and reduce debt" in hopes of appeasing banks and other nervous lenders. The lenders conditions were not being met: "The covenants require Canwest to stick below numbers that measure the company's financial leverage." With quarterly figures revealing bad news, credit was permanently reduced to $112 million from $300 million and certain borrowing requirements had to be waived. But with $92 million already drawn, Canwest has little breathing room. "And if the company's cash runs out, it could face an extreme makeover in CCAA." The Companies' Creditors Arrangement Act permits financially troubled enterprises to restructure and hopefully avoid bankruptcy.
>
> "President and CEO Leonard Asper, whose family controls Canwest, blames the tanking economy." But Chris Diceman, a senior VP of DBRS, indicates "management should have focused on paying down debt. . . Instead, Canwest

embarked on international expansion." Too much leverage at an inopportune time was catching up with them. "The company's shares have lost 95 percent of their value in a year." Falling from $4 to 20¢ per share; it should be noted that $4 itself was a fair distance from share prices of over $20 in 2000, $15 in 2005, and about $11 in 2007. And if Canwest heads toward bankruptcy and the courts takeover "that would likely mean an end to the Asper family's control."[19]

After missing a $30-million interest payment earlier in 2009, Canwest failed to make $10 million in debt payments at the end of May 2009. Acknowledging it was in default it moved to negotiate "broader restructuring of its finances."[20] Grappling with $3.9 billion in debt during an economic recession cannot be easy.[21]

It was years prior that Canwest developed an appetite for debt. Numerous expensive acquisitions seemed like a good idea at the time. Driving along on a smooth road on a sunny day with a sharp stick on the steering wheel may not have seemed threatening at the time, but Warren Buffet's wisdom about leverage comes through now that the driving conditions are looking treacherous and economic uncertainty looms. Canwest filed for bankruptcy in late 2009.

Sources: Calvin Leung, "The Good, The Bad & The Ugly," *Canadian Business*, March 30, 2009; "Most Actively Traded Companies on Canadian Stock Markets," *Canadian Free Press*, May 30, 2009; "Canwest Media Gets Bondholder Reprieve," *United Press International*, May 21, 2009.

Covenants to Look For

Before borrowing money, an entrepreneur should decide what sorts of restrictions or covenants are acceptable. Lawyers and accountants of the company should be consulted before any loan papers are signed. Some covenants are negotiable (this changes with the overall credit economy), and an entrepreneur should negotiate to get terms that the venture can live with next year as well as today. Once loan terms are agreed upon and the loan is made, the entrepreneur and the venture will be bound by them. If the bank says, "Yes, but . . ."

- Wants to put constraints on your permissible financial ratios.
- Stops any new borrowing.
- Wants a veto on any new management.
- Disallows new products or new directions.
- Prevents acquiring or selling any assets.
- Forbids any new investment or new equipment.

What follows are some practical guidelines about personal guarantees: when to expect them, how to avoid them, and how to eliminate them.

Personal Guarantees and the Loan

Personal guarantees may be required of the "lead" entrepreneur or, more likely, shareholders of significance (more than 10 percent) who are also members of the senior management team. Also, personal guarantees are often "joint and severable"—meaning that each guarantor is liable for the total amount of the guarantee.

When to Expect Them
- If you are under collateralized.
- If there are shareholder loans or lots of "due to" and "due from" officer accounts.
- If you have had poor or erratic performance.
- If you have management problems.
- If your relationship with your banker is strained.
- If you have a new loan officer.
- If there is turbulence in the credit markets.
- If there has been a wave of bad loans made by the lending institution, and a crackdown is in force.
- If there is less understanding of your market.

How to Avoid Them	•	Good to spectacular performance.
	•	Conservative financial management.
	•	Positive cash flow over a sustained period.
	•	Adequate collateral.
	•	Careful management of the balance sheet.

How to Eliminate	•	See "How to Avoid Them."
Them (if you	•	Develop a financial plan with performance targets and a timetable.
already have them)	•	Negotiate elimination *upfront* when you have some bargaining chips, based on certain performance criteria.
	•	Stay active in the search for backup sources of funds.

Building a Relationship

After obtaining a loan, entrepreneurs should cultivate a close working relationship with their bankers. Too many businesspeople do not see their lending officers until they need a loan. The astute entrepreneur will take a much more active role in keeping a banker informed about the business, thereby improving the chances of obtaining larger loans for expansion and cooperation from the bank in troubled times.

Some of the things that should be done to build such a relationship are fairly simple.[22] In addition to monthly and annual financial statements, bankers should be sent product news releases and any trade articles about the business or its products. The entrepreneur should invite the banker to the venture's facility, review product development plans and the prospects for the business, and establish a personal relationship with him or her. If this is done, when a new loan is requested, the lending officer will feel better about recommending its approval.

What about bad news? Never surprise a banker with bad news; make sure he or she sees it coming as soon as you do. Unpleasant surprises are a sign that an entrepreneur is not being candid with the banker or that management does not have the business under the proper control. Either conclusion by a banker is damaging to the relationship.

If a future loan payment cannot be met, entrepreneurs should not panic and avoid their bankers. On the contrary, they should visit their banks and explain why the loan payment cannot be made and say when it will be made. If this is done before the payment due date and the entrepreneur–banker relationship is good, the banker may go along. What else can he or she do? If an entrepreneur has convinced a banker of the viability and future growth of a business, the banker really does not want to call a loan and lose a customer to a competitor or cause bankruptcy. The real key to communicating with a banker is candidly to inform but not to scare. In other words, entrepreneurs must indicate that they are aware of adverse events and have a plan for dealing with them.

To build credibility with bankers further, entrepreneurs should borrow before they need to and then repay the loan. This will establish a track record of borrowing and reliable repayment. Entrepreneurs should also make every effort to meet the financial targets they set for themselves and have discussed with their banker. If this cannot be done, the credibility of the entrepreneur will erode, even if the business is growing.

Bankers have a right to expect an entrepreneur to continue to use them as the business grows and prospers, and not to go shopping for a better interest rate. In return, entrepreneurs have the right to expect that their bank will continue to provide them with needed loans, particularly during difficult times when a vacillating loan policy could be dangerous for a business's survival.

Handling a Banker or Other Lender

1. Your banker is your partner, not a difficult minority shareholder.
2. Be honest and straightforward in sharing information.
3. Invite the banker to see your business in operation.

4. Always avoid overdrafts, late payments, and late financial statements.
5. Answer questions frankly and honestly. *Tell the truth.* Lying is illegal and undoubtedly violates loan covenants.
6. Understand the business of banking.
7. Have an "Ace in the Hole."

WHAT TO DO WHEN THE BANK SAYS NO

What do you do if the bank turns you down for a loan? Regroup, and review the following questions.

1. Does the company really need to borrow now? Can cash be generated elsewhere? Tighten the belt. Are some expenditures unnecessary? Sharpen the financial pencil: be lean and mean.
2. What does the balance sheet say? Are you growing too fast? Compare yourself to published industry ratios to see if you are on target.
3. Does the bank have a clear and comprehensive understanding of your needs? Did you really get to know your loan officer? Did you do enough homework on the bank's criteria and their likes and dislikes? Was your loan officer too busy to give your borrowing package proper consideration? A loan officer may have 50 to as many as 200 accounts. Is your relationship with the bank on a proper track?
4. Was your written loan proposal realistic? Was it a normal request, or something that differed from the types of proposals the bank usually sees? Did you make a verbal request for a loan, without presenting any written backup?
5. Do you need a new loan officer, or a new bank? If your answers to the above questions put you in the clear, and your written proposal was realistic, call the head of the commercial loan department and arrange a meeting. Sit down and discuss the history of your loan effort, the facts, and the bank's reasons for turning you down.
6. Who else might provide this financing (ask the banker who turned you down)?

You should be seeing multiple lenders at the same time so you don't run out of time or money.

TAR PITS: ENTREPRENEURS BEWARE

Modern corporate financial theory has preached the virtues of zero cash balances and the use of leverage to enhance return on equity. When applied to closely held companies whose dream is to last forever, such thinking can be extremely destructive. The excessive leverage used by so many larger companies was apparently just not worth the risk: Two-thirds of the LBOs done in the 1980s have ended up in serious trouble. The serious erosion of IBM began about the same time as the company acquired debt on its balance sheet for the very first time, in the early 1980s. This problem was manifested in the acquisition binges of the early 1990s and in the high-technology feeding frenzy of the late 1990s. Following the 2000–2003 downturn, LBOs once again emerged as a popular growth vehicle. The same can be expected after the economic turmoil that began in late 2008 and pushed on into 2010 subsides and those on the inside embrace risk thinking they know better and can do better.

Beware of Leverage: The ROE Mirage

According to the theory, one can significantly improve return on equity (ROE) by utilizing debt. Thus, the present value of a company would also increase significantly as the company went from a zero debt-to-equity ratio to 100 percent, as shown in Exhibit 11.8. On closer examination, however, such an increase in debt only improves the present value, given

EXHIBIT 11.8   Total Present Value

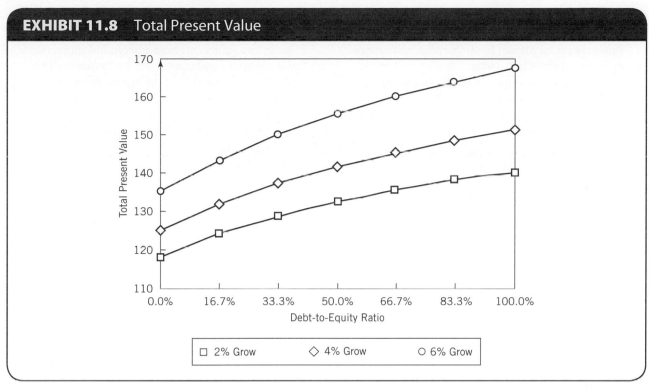

Source: William A. Sahlman, "Note on Free Cash Flow Valuation Models," Harvard Business School, 2003.

the 2 to 8 percent growth rates shown, by 17 to 26 percent. If the company gets into any trouble—and the odds of that happening sooner or later are very high—its options and flexibility become very seriously constrained by the covenants of the senior lenders. Leverage creates an unforgiving capital structure, and the potential additional ROI often is not worth the risk. If the upside is worth risking the loss of the entire company should adversity strike, then go ahead. This is easier said than survived, however.

Ask any entrepreneur who has had to deal with the workout specialists in a bank and you will get a sobering, if not frightening, message: It is hell and you will not want to do it again.

Neither a Lender Nor a Borrower Be, But If You Must . . .

Canadian billionaire investor and philanthopist, Stephen Jarislowsky repeats the words of Shakespeare "neither a borrower nor a lender be,"[23] which is actually very good advice for early-stage entrepreneurs in this time of "economic war."[24] Thus, the following may serve as useful tips if you must borrow:

1. Borrow when you do not need it (which is the surest way to accomplish No. 2).
2. Avoid personal guarantees. Put caps and time limits on the amounts based on performance milestones, such as achieving certain cash flow, working capital, and equity levels. Also, don't be afraid in many markets to offer your guarantee and then negotiate ways to get it back in whole or in part!
3. The devil is in the details. Read each loan covenant and requirement carefully—only the owner can truly appreciate their consequences.
4. Try to avoid or modify so-called hair-trigger covenants, such as: "If there is any change or event of any kind that can have any materially adverse effect on the future of the company, the loan shall become due and payable."
5. Be conservative and prudent.

Chapter Summary

1. Business cycles impact lending cycles, with more or less restrictive behaviour.

2. Start-ups are generally not candidates for bank credit, but numerous sources of debt capital are available once profitability and a decent balance sheet are established.

3. Managing and orchestrating the banking relationship before and after the loan decision is a key task for entrepreneurs.

4. Knowing the key steps in obtaining a loan as well as selecting a banker and bank that can add value and improve your odds.

5. Loan covenants can have a profound impact on how you can and cannot run the business. The devil is in the details of the loan agreement.

6. For the vast majority of small companies, leverage works only during the most favourable economic booms of credit availability. Leverage is a disaster if business turns sour.

7. When the bank says no to a loan request, several key questions need to be addressed in an effort to reverse the decision; or you need to seek sources of credit other than banks.

Study Questions

1. Define and explain the following, and why they are important: sources of debt financing, trade credit, line of credit, accounts receivable financing, time-sales factoring, commercial finance company.

2. What security can be used for a loan, and what percentage of its value do banks typically lend?

3. What are the things to look for in evaluating a lender, and why are these important?

4. What does "value-added banker" mean, and how and why is this crucial?

5. What criteria do lenders use to evaluate a loan application, and what can be done before and after the loan decision to facilitate a loan request?

6. What restrictions and covenants might a lender require, and how and why should these be avoided whenever possible?

7. What issues need to be addressed to deal with a loan request rejection?

8. Why do entrepreneurs in smaller enterprises need to be especially wary of leverage?

9. At what stages should a venture borrow money?

Mind Stretchers   *Have you considered?*

1. With the recent "credit crunch," capital is scarce. You have knocked on the doors of quite a few banks and had your loan applications denied. What next? Do you keep trying traditional lending options? What about an Internet or off-shore bank? Someone gives you the name of a guy in Las Vegas that can front you some cash off the books, do you follow up?

2. Why is Warren Buffet so wary about leverage?

3. Can you calculate the debt capacity of your proposed venture three to four years hence if it achieves positive cash flow and profitability?

CASE	JACK DEFOE, INC.

Instruction:

This case calls for you to play the role of the banker and decide what action if any should be taken. You are asked to calculate a second year's set of financial ratios and then analyze the firm from the point of view of John Davidge, Jack Defoe's branch bank manager.

John Davidge's problem (see Bank Interbranch Memo) is that Jack Defoe has written cheques for an amount exceeding the money Jack Defoe, Inc. has in its bank account plus the maximum credit line John has the authority to approve. John honoured those cheques, placing him in a precarious position with his superior. With Jack out of the country, John's other choice was to refuse to honour the cheques, which could have brought down the firm. In placing John Davidge in this distressing position, Jack Defoe has demonstrated either a lack of business ethics or a lack of management competence.

In making a lending decision, a banker normally considers four factors that we call the Four C's. These are Capacity to repay, Collateral, Character of the borrower, and business Conditions. A bank normally borrows the money it lends from depositors and purchasers of guaranteed investment certificates, which are similar to bonds. It then lends this money to borrowers such as Jack Defoe, Inc. The bank has very little spread between the borrowing and lending rates, traditionally about three percentage points. Thus it can afford very little risk and must be comfortable with each one of the Four Cs. Three out of four is not good enough. Following are explanations of the meaning of the Four Cs.

Capacity to Repay. This refers to the ability of the borrower to generate cash flows sufficient to pay the interest on the loan and to also repay the principal in a reasonable time frame.

Collateral. This refers to the amount and quality of the assets the bank takes as collateral. This collateral can be seized by the bank and sold to recover the interest and principal of the loan if the loan fails. Having to collect on a loan by resorting to seizing assets of the borrower is considered a failed loan from the bank's point of view, and would only be done as a last resort.

Character of the borrower. This refers to the credit record, demonstrated business acumen and other personal traits of the person responsible for the interest payments and the loan repayment, in this case Jack Defoe.

Business Conditions. This refers to the nature and prospects of the business borrowing the money. The key question is, "Is this a business area in which the bank wants to have its money? Will this business sector thrive and grow?"

Use these criteria in your evaluation of Jack Defoe, Inc.

Bank Interbranch Memo

From:	Don James, Loans Manager
Sent:	Friday, December 19, 2008 — 2:44 PM
To:	John Davidge, Branch Manager
Subject:	Jack Defoe Inc.

Hello John,

This account has been outstanding for three years without repayment and has grown in the past year from $6,300 to $27,840 (including overdraft). This account exceeds your $25,000 discretionary limit and must be referred to your Loans Supervisor.

Please forward your file along with your analysis and recommendations on this account.

Don

Background (abstracted from file)

Jack Defoe Inc. is a small business manufacturing components for computer monitors. The process and production equipment are highly specialized and were developed by the president and principal shareholder, Jack Defoe. Product quality is reputedly high and the product commands a premium price.

Despite the premium price, the company has been expanding sales rapidly. It has a significant market share in North America. Jack Defoe spent time in Europe and Japan this past year and is enthusiastic about export opportunities beyond North America. He has received token orders.

Until the beginning of 2008, production was carried out in a large double garage. Commencing about April 1, operations were moved to rented premises in an industrial park. Reason for the move was insufficient space. At that time most of the fixed assets were replaced, because the old assets could not meet the required production levels. The Company sold the excess fixed assets for $4,500.

Jack Defoe owns 1,500 shares in Jack Defoe Inc. He is 32 years old and is trained as an engineering technician. He is married with three children. Substantially all his personal resources are invested in the business. His wife owns the family home, which is heavily mortgaged.

Mrs. Anne Defoe, Jack's mother, owns 500 shares in Jack Defoe Inc. acquired in 2008 in exchange for a note payable of $18,000. This is believed to be a substantial part of her personal resources. The conversion was made at our request.

A total of $3,000 in dividends were paid in 2008, to give Mrs. Anne Defoe a small return on her investment. No dividends were paid in 2006 or 2007.

Jack Defoe is in Japan at this time and cannot be reached before this analysis is due.

REQUIRED: Prepare your analysis, including statements of changes in financial position.

This case was written by Don B. Smith, Wilfrid Laurier University, Business & Economics, for purposes of classroom discussion.

EXHIBIT 1

Jack Defoe Inc.
Balance Sheet as at November 30, 2008

ASSETS			LIABILITIES		
Current Assets			**Current Liabilities**		
Accounts Receivable	$45,870		Bank overdraft		$3,840
Less allow. doubtful ac.	3,720	$42,150	Demand loan		16,000
			Accounts payable		16,190
Inventories			Accrued wages		120
Raw Materials	$35,670		Income tax payable		11,460
Finished Goods	10,680	46,350	Total current liabilities		$47,610
Prepaid rent (current)		1,500	**Long Term Liabilities**		
Total current assets		$90,000	Note payable—bank		8,000
Long Term Assets			**SHAREHOLDER EQUITY**		
Deposit on machine		3,000	Common stock 2,000		
Prepaid rent (over 1 year)		3,000	Shares outstanding	$31,500	
			Retained Earnings		
Machinery & equipment	$42,200		Opening balance	$9,760	
Less accum. deprec.	5,960	36,240	Net income for year	38,370	
			Closing balance	$48,130	
			Less dividends	3,000	
				$45,130	76,630
		$132,240			$132,240

EXHIBIT 2   Jack Defoe Inc.
            Income Statement for the Year Ended November 30, 2008

Sales		$388,440
Less Cost of Goods Sold		270,555
Gross Profit		$117,885

Selling & Administrative Expenses

Salary	$42,000	
Travel & entertainment	10,830	
Bad debts	1,990	
Telephone	2,540	
Interest	4,580	
Loss on disposal of equipment	5,725	
Other expense	390	
		68,055

Net Profit Before Income Taxes

Less income taxes		$49,830
		11,460
Net Profit After Income Taxes		**$38,370**

Details of Cost of Goods Sold for the Year Ended November 30, 2008

Finished Goods Inventory December 1, 2007		$9,450

Cost of Goods Manufactured

Raw materials December 1, 2007	$17,460	
Purchases during year	192,810	
	$210,270	
Raw materials November 30, 2008	35,670	
Raw materials used	$174,600	

Manufacturing Expenses

Direct labour	$51,510	
Production supplies	6,300	
Depreciation on equipment	4,635	
Maintenance	7,200	
Building rent	14,400	
Electricity	5,880	
Miscellaneous production	7,260	271,785
Cost of goods available for sale		$281,235
Finished goods Inventory November 30, 2008		10,680
Cost of goods sold during the year		**$270,555**

EXHIBIT 3

Jack Defoe Inc.
Balance Sheet as at November 30, 2007

ASSETS			LIABILITIES		
Current Assets			**Current Liabilities**		
Cash in bank		$2,010	Demand loan		$6,300
Accounts Receivable	$19,720		Rent payable		600
Less allow. doubtful ac.	3,300	$16,420	Accounts payable		6,030
			Accrued wages		4,050
Inventories			Total current liabilities		$16,980
Raw Materials	$17,460				
Finished Goods	9,450	26,910	**Long Term Liabilities**		
Total current assets		$45,340	Note payable—A. Defoe		18,000
Long Term Assets			**SHAREHOLDER EQUITY**		
Machinery & equipment	$19,500		Common stock 1,500		
Less accum. deprec.	6,600	12,900	Shares outstanding	$13,500	
			Retained Earnings		
			Opening balance (deficit)	$(10,490)	
			Net income for year	20,250	
			Closing balance	$9,760	23,260
		$58,240			$58,240

Note: No income tax was payable on account of 2007 operations because of losses carried forward.

EXHIBIT 4	Jack Defoe Inc.	
	Income Statement for the Year Ended November 30, 2007	

Sales		$192,210
Less Cost of Goods Sold		116,640
Gross Profit		$75,570

Selling & Administrative Expenses

Salary	$40,000	
Travel & entertainment	7,740	
Bad debts	1,170	
Telephone	1,110	
Interest	4,010	
Other expense	1,290	55,320

Net Profit for the year		$20,250

Details of Cost of Goods Sold for the Year Ended November 30, 2007

Finished Goods Inventory December 1, 2006		$5,700

Cost of Goods Manufactured

Raw materials December 1, 2006	$7,860	
Purchases during year	87,600	
	$95,460	
Raw materials November 30, 2007	17,460	
Raw materials used	$78,000	

Manufacturing Expenses

Direct labour	$23,640	
Production supplies	1,980	
Depreciation on equipment	2,700	
Maintenance	2,550	
Building rent	3,600	
Electricity	2,730	
Miscellaneous production	5,190	120,390

Cost of goods available for sale		$126,090
Finished goods Inventory November 30, 2007		9,450
Cost of goods sold during the year		**$116,640**

EXHIBIT 5   Jack Defoe Inc.
Balance Sheet as at November 30, 2006

ASSETS			LIABILITIES		
Current Assets			**Current Liabilities**		
Cash in bank		$605	Rent payable		1,800
Accounts Receivable	$10,545		Accounts payable		8,870
Less allow. doubtful ac.	2,600	$7,945	Accrued wages		2,150
			Total current liabilities		$12,820
Inventories					
Raw Materials	$7,860		**Long Term Liabilities**		
Finished Goods	5,700	13,560	Note payable—A. Defoe		14,000
Total current assets		$22,110			
			SHAREHOLDER EQUITY		
Long Term Assets			Common stock 1,500		
Machinery & equipment	$11,620		Shares outstanding	$13,500	
Less accum. deprec.	3,900	7,720	**Retained Earnings**		
			Opening balance (deficit)	$(8,730)	
			Net income for year	(1,760)	
			Closing balance	$(10,490)	3,010
		$29,830			$29,830

Note: No income tax was payable on account of 2007 operations because of losses carried forward.

EXHIBIT 6	Jack Defoe Inc.

Income Statement for the Year Ended November 30, 2006

Sales		$128,970
Less Cost of Goods Sold		81,310
Gross Profit		$47,660
Selling & Administrative Expenses		
Salary	$36,000	
Travel & entertainment	7,610	
Bad debts	950	
Telephone	1,095	
Interest	2,135	
Other expense	1,630	49,420
Net Profit for the year		$(1,760)

Details of Cost of Goods Sold for the Year Ended November 30, 2006

Finished Goods Inventory December 1, 2005		$3,825
Cost of Goods Manufactured		
Raw materials December 1, 2005	$5,320	
Purchases during year	54,210	
	$59,530	
Raw materials November 30, 2006	7,860	
Raw materials used	$51,670	
Manufacturing Expenses		
Direct labour	$14,880	
Production supplies	1,830	
Depreciation on equipment	2,140	
Maintenance	2,525	
Building rent	3,600	
Electricity	2,315	
Miscellaneous production	4,225	83,185
Cost of goods available for sale		$87,010
Finished goods Inventory November 30, 2006		5,700
Cost of goods sold during the year		**$81,310**

EXHIBIT 7
Jack Defoe Inc.
Cash Flow Statement for the Year Ended November 30, 2008

	Sources	Uses	Incr.(Decr)
Net Income From Operations	$38,370		
Add back Depreciation	4,635		
Loss on disposal of equipment	5,725		$48,730
Changes in Working Capital			
Accounts payable increase	$10,160		
Income tax payable increase	11,460		
Accounts receivable increase		$25,730	
Raw materials increase		18,210	
Finished goods increase		1,230	
Prepaid rent increase		4,500	
Rent payable decrease		600	
Accrued wages decrease		3,930	
	$21,620	$54,200	(32,580)
Cash from operations			**$16,150**
Investing Activities			
Sale of old equipment	$4,500		
Deposit on new equipment		$3,000	
Purchase of new equipment		38,200	
	$4,500	$41,200	(36,700)
Financing Activities			
Demand loan—Bank	$9,700		
Note payable—Bank	8,000		
Issue of common shares	18,000		
Retired note payable		$18,000	
Dividend paid		3,000	
	$35,700	$21,000	14,700
Decrease in cash			**$(5,850)**

EXHIBIT 8	Jack Defoe Inc.		
	Cash Flow Statement for the Year Ended November 30, 2007		

	Sources	Uses	Incr.(Decr)
Net Income From Operations	$20,250		
Add back Depreciation	2,700		$22,950
Changes in Working Capital			
Accrued wages increase	$1,900		
Accounts receivable increase		$8,475	
Raw materials increase		9,600	
Finished goods increase		3,750	
Rent payable decrease		1,200	
Accounts payable decrease		2,840	
	$1,900	$25,865	(23,965)
Cash from operations (deficit)			**$(1,015)**
Investing Activities			
Purchase of new equipment		$7,880	(7,880)
Financing Activities			
Demand loan—Bank	$6,300		
Note payable	4,000		
	$10,300		10,300
Increase in cash			**$1,405**

EXHIBIT 9

Jack Defoe Inc.
Ratio Calculations

Liquidity Ratios		2007 Input	2007 Result	Measure	2008 Input	2008 Result
Current Ratio	$\dfrac{\text{Current Assets}}{\text{Current Liabilities}}$	$\dfrac{45{,}340}{16{,}980}$	2.67	to 1		
Acid Test	$\dfrac{\text{Quick Assets}}{\text{Current Liabilities}}$	$\dfrac{18{,}430}{16{,}980}$	1.09	to 1		
Working Capital	Current Assets − Current Liabilities	45,340 − 16,980	28,360	$		
Accounts Receivable Turnover	$\dfrac{\text{Annual Credit Sales}}{\text{Accounts Receivable}}$	$\dfrac{192{,}210}{16{,}420}$	11.71	times		
Average Collection Period	$\dfrac{\text{Accounts Receivable} \times 365}{\text{Annual Credit Sales}}$	$\dfrac{16{,}420 \times 365}{192{,}210}$	31.18	days		
Inventory Turnover	$\dfrac{\text{Cost of Goods Sold}}{\text{Average Inventory}}$	$\dfrac{116{,}640}{(13{,}560 + 26{,}912)/2}$	5.76	times		
Age of Inventory	$\dfrac{\text{Average Inventory} \times 365}{\text{Cost of Goods Sold}}$	$\dfrac{(13{,}560 + 26{,}912)/2 \times 365}{116{,}640}$	63.32	days		
Age of Payables	$\dfrac{\text{Accounts Payable} \times 365}{\text{Raw Materials Purchases}}$	$\dfrac{6{,}030 \times 365}{87{,}600}$	25.13	days		
Profitability Ratios						
Gross Profit Margin	$\dfrac{\text{Gross Profit} \times 100}{\text{Sales}}$	$\dfrac{75{,}570 \times 100}{192{,}210}$	39.3	percent		
Net Profit Margin	$\dfrac{\text{Net Profit} \times 100}{\text{Sales}}$	$\dfrac{20{,}250 \times 100}{192{,}210}$	10.5	percent		
Return on Equity	$\dfrac{\text{Net Income} \times 100}{\text{Total Shareholder Equity}}$	$\dfrac{20{,}250 \times 100}{23{,}260}$	87.1	percent		
Return on Tangible	$\dfrac{\text{Net Income} \times 100}{\text{Total Tangible Assets}}$	$\dfrac{20{,}250 \times 100}{58{,}240}$	34.8	percent		

Online **Learning**Centre

Find more great exercises and additional study tools on the Online Learning Centre at
www.mcgrawhill.ca/olc/timmons

PART

V

START-UP AND BEYOND

Under conditions of rapid growth, entrepreneurs face unusual paradoxes and challenges as their companies grow and the leadership modes required by these companies change.

Whether they have the adaptability and resiliency in the face of swift developments to grow fast enough as leaders and whether they have enough courage, wisdom, and discipline to balance controlled growth with growing fast enough to keep pace with the competition and industry turbulence will become crystal clear.

Entrepreneurs face enormous pressures and physical and emotional wear and tear during the rapid growth of their companies. It goes with the territory. Entrepreneurs after start-up find that "it" has to be done now, that there is no room to falter, and that there are no "runners-up." Those who have a personal entrepreneurial strategy, who are healthy, who have their lives in order, and who know what they are signing up for fare better than those who do not.

Among all the stimulating and exceedingly difficult challenges entrepreneurs face—and can meet successfully—none is more liberating and exhilarating than a successful harvest. Perhaps the point is made best in one of the final lines of the musical *Oliver*: "In the end, all that counts is in the bank, in large amounts!"

Obviously, money is not the only thing, or everything. But money can ensure both independence and autonomy to do what you want to do, mostly on your terms, and can significantly increase the options and opportunities at your discretion. While value creation was the goal, the measure of success is wealth creation, and how one chooses to distribute and use that wealth. In effect, for entrepreneurs, net worth is the final scorecard of the value creation process.

12

LEADING RAPID GROWTH: ENTREPRENEURSHIP BEYOND START-UP[1]

You can fight without ever winning, but never ever win without a fight.

Neil Peart
Musician, Author

Upon completion of this chapter, you will be able to:

1. Discuss how higher-potential, rapidly growing ventures have invented new organizational paradigms to replace brontosaurus capitalism.

2. Describe how higher-potential ventures "grow up big" and the special problems, organization, and leadership requirements of rapid growth.

3. Examine new research on the leadership practices that distinguish high growth companies.

4. Explore concepts of organizational culture and climate, and how entrepreneurial leaders foster favourable cultures.

5. Identify specific signals and clues that can alert entrepreneurial leaders to impending crises and approaches to solve these.

INVENTING NEW ORGANIZATIONAL PARADIGMS

At the beginning of this text we examined how nimble and fleet-footed entrepreneurial firms have supplanted aging corporate giants with new leadership approaches, a passion for value creation, and an obsession with opportunity that have been unbeatable in the marketplace for talent and ideas. These entrepreneurial ventures have experienced rapid to explosive growth and have become the investments of choice of the venture capital community.

Because of their innovative nature and competitive breakthroughs, entrepreneurial ventures have demonstrated a remarkable capacity to invent new paradigms of organization and management. They have abandoned the organizational practices and structures typical of the industrial giants from the post-World War II era to the 1990s. One could characterize those approaches thus: What they lacked in creativity and flexibility to deal with ambiguity and rapid change, they made up for with rules, structure, hierarchy, and quantitative analysis.

The epitome of this pattern is the Hay System, which by the 1980s became the leading method of defining and grading management jobs in large companies. Scoring high with "Hay points" was the key to more pay, a higher position in the hierarchy, and greater power. The criteria for Hay points include number of people who are direct reports, value of assets under management, sales volume, number of products, square feet of facilities, total size of one's operating and capital budget, and the like. One can easily see who gets ahead in such a system: Be bureaucratic, have the most people and largest budget, increase head count and levels under your control, and think up the largest capital projects. Missing in the criteria are all the basic components of entrepreneurship we have seen in this book: value creating, opportunity creating and seizing, frugality with resources, bootstrapping strategies, staged capital commitments, team building, achieving better fits, and juggling paradoxes.

Contrast the multilayered, hierarchical, military-like levels of control and command that characterize traditional capitalism with the common patterns among entrepreneurial firms: they are flat—often only one or two layers deep—adaptive, and flexible; they look like interlocking circles rather than ladders; they are integrative around customers and critical missions; they are learning- and influence-based rather than rank- and power-based. People lead more through influence and persuasion, which are derived from knowledge and performance rather than through formal rank, position, or seniority. They create a perpetual learning culture. They value people and share the wealth with people who help create it.

Entrepreneurial Leaders Are Not Administrators or Managers

In the growing business, owner-entrepreneurs focus on recognizing and choosing opportunities, allocating resources, motivating employees, and maintaining control—while encouraging the innovative actions that cause a business to grow. In a new venture the entrepreneur's immediate challenge is to learn how to dance with elephants without being trampled to death! Once beyond the start-up phase, the ultimate challenge of the entrepreneur is to develop the firm to the point where it is able to lead the elephants on the dance floor.

Distinguished business scholar Henry Mintzberg believes that most MBA programs encourage the wrong behaviour and develop the wrong skills.[2] The standard business education compartmentalizes the functions into discrete silos, whereas, it should be integrative. Mintzberg finds little signs that this is appreciated or understood. Like medicine, like engineering, it is a "practice, which is fed by intuition. In a practice, one achieves mastery in the doing and has to pull together disparate knowledge to apply to situations at hand."[3] Steven Dunphy and David Meyer find evidence of differences in the roles of entrepreneurs and managers.[4] Such differences may help to explain the stagnancy and eventual demise of brontosaurus capitalism. Until the 1980s, virtually all the cases, problems, and lectures in MBA programs were about large, established companies.

LEADING PRACTICES OF HIGH GROWTH COMPANIES[5]

In Chapter 2, we examined a summary of research conducted on fast growth companies to determine the leading practices of these firms. Now, this research will likely take on new meaning to the reader. As one examines each of these four practice areas—marketing, finance, management, and planning—one can see the practical side of how fast growth entrepreneurs pursue opportunities; devise, manage, and orchestrate their financial strategies; build a team with collaborative decision making; and plan with vision, clarity, and flexibility. Clearly, rapid growth is a different game, requiring an entrepreneurial mind-set and skills.

GROWING UP BIG

Stages of Growth Revisited

Higher potential ventures do not stay small very long. While an entrepreneur may have done a good job of assessing an opportunity, forming a new venture team, marshalling resources, planning, and so forth, leading and growing such a venture is a different game.

Ventures in the high growth stage face the problems discussed in Chapter 5. These include forces that limit the creativities of the founders and team; that cause confusion and resentment over roles, responsibilities, and goals; that call for specialization and therefore erode collaboration; that require operating mechanisms and controls; and more.

Recall also that founders of rapidly growing ventures are usually relatively inexperienced in launching a new venture and yet face situations where time and change are compounded and where events are nonlinear and nonparametric. Usually, structures, procedures, and patterns are fluid, and decision making needs to follow counterintuitive and unconventional patterns.

Chapter 5 discussed the stages or phases companies experience during their growth. Recall that the first three years before start-up are called the research-and-development (R&D) stage; the first three years, the start-up stage; years 4 through 10, the early-growth stage; the 10th year through the 15th or so, maturity; and after the 15th year, stability stage. These time estimates are approximate and may vary somewhat.

Various models, and our previous discussion, depicted the life cycle of a growing firm as a smooth curve with rapidly ascending sales and profits and a levelling off toward the peak and then dipping toward decline.

In truth, however, very few, if any, new and growing firms experience such smooth and linear phases of growth. If the actual growth curves of new companies are plotted over their first 10 years, the curves will look far more like the ups and downs of a roller-coaster ride than the smooth progressions usually depicted. Over the life of a typical growing firm, there are periods of jerks, bumps, hiccups, indigestion, and renewal interspersed with periods of smooth sailing. Sometimes there is continual upward progress through all this, but with others, there are periods where the firms seem near collapse or at least in considerable peril. Ed Marram, an entrepreneur and educator for 35 years, characterizes the five stages of a firm as Wonder, Blunder, Thunder, Plunder, Asunder (see Exhibit 12.1).

EXHIBIT 12.1   Growth Stages

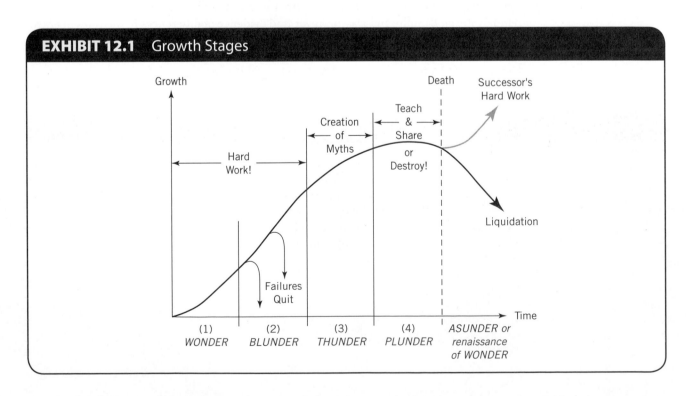

Wonder is the period that is filled with uncertainty about survival. Blunder is a growth stage when many firms stumble and fail. The Thunder stage occurs when growth is robust and the entrepreneur has built a solid new venture team. Cash flow is robust during Plunder, but in Asunder the firm needs to renew or will decline.

Core Leadership Mode

As was noted earlier, changes in several critical variables determine just how frantic or easy transitions from one stage to the next will be. As a result, it is possible to make some generalizations about the main leadership challenges and transitions that will be encountered as the company grows. The core leadership mode is influenced by the number of employees a firm has, which is in turn related to its dollar sales.[6]

Recall, as shown in Exhibit 5.3, that until sales reach approximately $5 million and employees number about 25, the core leadership mode is one of *doing*. Between $5 and $15 million in sales and 25 to 75 employees, the core leadership mode is *leading*. When sales exceed $10 million and employees number over 75, the core leadership mode is *leading team leaders*. Obviously, these revenue and employment figures are broad generalities. The number of people is an indicator of the complexity of the leadership task, and suggests a new wall to be scaled, rather than a precise point.

Sales per employee (SPE) can vary widely among firms, by virtue of an online model and a tremendously effective supply chain management system, Apple Canada can generate a higher SPE than a real estate–based service business.

SPE numbers are boundaries, constantly moving as a result of inflation and competitive dynamics. SPE figures can illustrate how a company stacks up in its industry, but remember that the number is a relative measurement. Business Development Bank of Canada also reminds that the costs attributed to making those sales must be considered.[7] Explosive sales per employee was one of the failed promises of the Internet, and to some extent the irrational dot-com valuations of the late 1990s were an anticipation of technology massively leveraging variable employee expense.

The central issue facing entrepreneurs in all sorts of businesses is this: As the size of the firm increases, the core leadership mode likewise *changes from doing to leading to leading leaders*.

During each growth stage of a firm, there are entrepreneurial crises, or hurdles, that most firms will confront. Exhibit 12.2 and the following discussion consider by stage some indications of crisis.[8] As the exhibit shows, for each fundamental driving force of entrepreneurship, a number of "signals" indicate crises are imminent. While the list is long, these are not the only indicators of crises—only the most common. Each of these signals does not necessarily indicate that particular crises will happen to every company at each stage, but when the signals are there, serious difficulties cannot be too far behind.

EXHIBIT 12.2   Crises and Symptoms

Pre-Start-up (Years – 3 to 0)

Entrepreneurs:

Focus. Is the founder really an entrepreneur, bent on building a company, or an inventor, technical dilettante, or the like?

Selling. Does the team have the necessary selling and closing skills to bring in the business and make the plan—on time?

Management. Does the team have the necessary management skills and relevant experience, or is it overloaded in one or two areas (e.g., the financial or technical areas)?

Ownership. Have the critical decisions about ownership and equity splits been resolved, and are the members committed to these?

Opportunity:

Focus. Is the business really user-, customer-, and market-driven (by a need), or is it driven by an invention or a desire to create?

Customers. Have customers been identified with specific names, addresses, and phone numbers, and have purchase levels been estimated, or is the business still only at the concept stage?

EXHIBIT 12.2   Crises and Symptoms (continued)

Supply. Are costs, margins, and lead times to acquire supplies, components, and key people known?

Strategy. Is the entry plan a shotgun and cherry-picking strategy, or is it a rifle shot at a well-focused niche?

Resources:

Resources. Have the required capital resources been identified?

Cash. Are the founders already out of cash (OOC) and their own resources?

Business plan. Is there a business plan, or is the team "hoofing it"?

Start-up and Survival (Years 0 to 3)

Entrepreneurs:

Leadership. Has a top leader been accepted, or are founders vying for the decision role or insisting on equality in all decisions?

Goals. Do the founders share and have compatible goals and work styles, or are these starting to conflict and diverge once the enterprise is under way and pressures mount?

Leadership. Are the founders anticipating and preparing for a shift from doing to leading and letting go—of decisions and control—that will be required to make the plan on time?

Opportunity:

Economics. Are the economic benefits and payback to the customer actually being achieved, and on time?

Strategy. Is the company a one-product company with no encore in sight?

Competition. Have previously unknown competitors or substitutes appeared in the marketplace?

Distribution. Are there surprises and difficulties in actually achieving planned channels of distribution on time?

Resources:

Cash. Is the company facing a cash crunch early as a result of not having a business plan (and a financial plan)? That is, is it facing a crunch because no one is asking: When will we run out of cash? Are the owners' pocketbooks exhausted?

Schedule. Is the company experiencing serious deviations from projections and time estimates in the business plan? Is the company able to marshal resources according to plan and on time?

Early Growth (Years 4 to 10)

Entrepreneurs:

Doing or leading. Are the founders still just doing, or are they leading the team for results by a plan? Have the founders begun to delegate and let go of critical decisions, or do they maintain veto power over all significant decisions?

Focus. Is the mind-set of the founders operational only, or is there some serious strategic thinking going on as well?

Opportunity:

Market. Are repeat sales and sales to new customers being achieved on time, according to plan, and because of interaction with customers, or are these coming from the engineering, R&D, or planning group? Is the company shifting to a marketing orientation without losing its killer instinct for closing sales?

Competition. Are price and quality being blamed for loss of customers or for an inability to achieve targets in the sales plan, while customer service is rarely mentioned?

Economics. Are gross margins beginning to erode?

Resources:

Financial control. Are accounting and information systems and control (purchasing orders, inventory, billing, collections, cost and profit analysis, cash management, etc.) keeping pace with growth and there when they are needed?

Cash. Is the company always out of cash—or nearly OOC, and is no one asking when it will run out, or is sure why or what to do about it?

Contacts. Has the company developed the outside networks (directors, contacts, etc.) it needs to continue growth?

Maturity (Years 10 to 15 plus)

Entrepreneurs:

Goals. Are the partners in conflict over control, goals, or underlying ethics or values?

Health. Are there signs that the founders' marriages, health, or emotional stability are coming apart (i.e., are there extramarital affairs, drug and/or alcohol abuse, or fights and temper tantrums with partners or spouses)?

Teamwork. Is there a sense of team building for a "greater purpose," with the founders now leading leaders, or is there conflict over control of the company and disintegration?

EXHIBIT 12.2   Crises and Symptoms (continued)

Opportunity:

Economics/competition. Are the products and/or services that have gotten the company this far experiencing unforgiving economics as a result of perishability, competitor blind sides, new technology, or off-shore competition, and is there a plan to respond?

Product encore. Has a major new product introduction been a failure?

Strategy. Has the company continued to cherry-pick in fast-growth markets, with a resulting lack of strategic definition (which opportunities to say no to)?

Resources:

Cash. Is the firm OOC again?

Development/information. Has growth gotten out of control, with systems, training, and development of new leaders failing to keep pace?

Financial control. Have systems continued to lag behind sales?

Harvest/Stability (Years 15 to 20 plus)

Entrepreneurs:

Succession/ownership. Are there mechanisms in place to provide for succession and the handling of very tricky ownership issues (especially family)?

Goals. Have the partners' personal and financial goals and priorities begun to conflict and diverge? Are any of the founders simply bored or burned out, and are they seeking a change of view and activities?

Entrepreneurial passion. Has there been an erosion of the passion for creating value through the recognition and pursuit of opportunity, or are turf-building, acquiring status and power symbols, and gaining control favoured?

Opportunity:

Strategy. Is there a spirit of innovation and renewal in the firm (e.g., a goal that half the company's sales come from products or services less than five years old), or has lethargy set in?

Economics. Have the core economics and durability of the opportunity eroded so far that profitability and return on investment are nearly as low as that for the Fortune 500?

Resources:

Cash. Has OOC been solved by increasing bank debt and leverage because the founders do not want—or cannot agree—to give up equity?

Accounting. Have accounting and legal issues, especially their relevance for wealth building and estate and tax planning, been anticipated and addressed? Has a harvest concept been part of the long-range planning process?

The Problem in Rate of Growth

Difficulties in recognizing crisis signals and developing appropriate mitigating measures are compounded by rate of growth itself. The faster the rate of growth, the greater the potential for difficulty; this is because of the various pressures, chaos, confusion, and loss of control. It is not an exaggeration to say that these pressures and demands increase geometrically, rather than in a linear way (see discussion in Chapter 5).

Growth rates affect all aspects of a business. Thus, as sales increase, as more people are hired, and as inventory increases, sales outpace manufacturing capacity. Facilities are then increased, people are moved between buildings, accounting systems and controls cannot keep up, and so on. The cash burn rate accelerates. As such acceleration continues, learning curves do the same. Worst of all, cash collections lag behind, as shown in Exhibit 12.3.

Distinctive issues caused by rapid growth were raised with the founders and presidents of rapidly growing companies—companies with sales of at least $1 million and growing in excess of 30 percent per year. These founders and presidents pointed to the following:

- *Opportunity overload.* Rather than lacking enough sales or new market opportunities (a classic concern in mature companies) these firms faced an abundance. Choosing from among these was a problem.

- *Abundance of capital.* While most stable or established smaller or medium-size firms often have difficulties obtaining equity and debt financing, most of the rapidly growing firms were not constrained by this. The problem was, rather, how to evaluate investors as "partners" and the terms of the deals with which they were presented.

EXHIBIT 12.3   Spend-Rate/Orders/Collection Leads and Lags

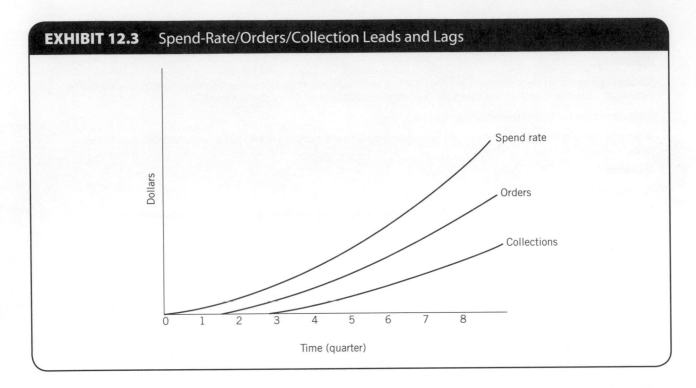

- *Misalignment of cash burn and collection rates.* These firms all pointed to problems of cash burn rates racing ahead of collections. They found that unless effective integrated accounting, inventory, purchasing, shipping, and invoicing systems and controls are in place, this misalignment can lead to chaos and collapse. One firm, for example, had tripled its sales in three years from $5 to $16 million. Suddenly, its president resigned, insisting that, with the systems that were in place, the company would be able to grow to $100 million. However, the computer system was disastrously inadequate, which compounded other management weaknesses. It was impossible to generate any believable financial and accounting information for many months. Losses of more than $1 million annually mounted, and the company's lenders panicked. To make matters worse, the auditors failed to stay on top of the situation until it was too late and were replaced. While the company has survived, it has had to restructure its business and has shrunk to $6 million in sales, to pay off bank debt and to avoid bankruptcy. Fortunately, it is recovering.
- *Decision making.* Many of the firms succeeded because they executed functional day-to-day and week-to-week decisions, rather than strategizing. Strategy had to take a back seat. Many of the representatives of these firms argued that in conditions of rapid growth, strategy was only about 10 percent of the story.
- *Expanding facilities and space . . . and surprises.* Expansion of space or facilities is a problem and one of the most disrupting events during the early explosive growth of a company. Leaders of many of these firms were not prepared for the surprises, delays, organizational difficulties, and system interruptions that are spawned by such expansion.

Industry Turbulence

The problems just discussed are compounded by the amount of industry turbulence surrounding the venture. Firms with higher growth rates are usually found in industries that are also developing rapidly. In addition, there are often many new entrants, both with competing products or services and with substitutes.

The effects are many. Often, prices fluctuate. The turbulence in the semiconductor industry is a good example. From June 1984 to June 1985, the price to original equipment manufacturers (OEMs) of 64K memory chips fell from $2.50 each to 50 cents. The price to

OEMs of 256K chips fell from $15 to $3. The same devastating industry effect manifested in the years 2000–2002 when cellular airtime pricing plunged by more than 50 percent. And more recently the price for flat screens (LCD, plasma, etc.) has plummeted. Imagine the disruption this caused in marketing and sales projections, in financial planning and cash forecasting, and the like, for firms in these industries. Often, too, there are rapid shifts in cost and experience curves. The consequences of missed steps in growing a business are profound.

THE IMPORTANCE OF CULTURE AND ORGANIZATIONAL CLIMATE

Six Dimensions

The organizational culture and climate, either of a new venture or of an existing firm, are critical in how well the organization will deal with growth. Studies of performance in large businesses that used the concept of organizational climate (i.e., the perceptions of people about the kind of place it is to work) have led to two general conclusions.[9] First, the climate of an organization can have a significant impact on performance. Further, climate is created both by the expectations people bring to the organization and by the practices and attitudes of the key managers.

The climate notion has relevance for new ventures, as well as for entrepreneurial efforts in large organizations. An entrepreneur's style and priorities—particularly how he or she manages tasks and people—are well known by the people being managed and affect performance. Recall the entrepreneurial climate described by Roger Enrico of Pepsi, where the critical factors included setting high performance standards by developing short-run objectives that would not sacrifice long-run results, providing responsive personal leadership, encouraging individual initiative, helping others to succeed, and developing individual networks for success.

Evidence suggests that superior teams function differently than inferior teams in their setting priorities, in resolving leadership issues, in what and how roles are performed by team members, in attitudes toward listening and participation, and in dealing with disagreements. Further, evidence suggests that specific approaches to management can affect the climate of a growing organization. For example, gains from the motivation, commitment, and teamwork, which are anchored in a consensus approach to management, while not immediately apparent, are striking later. At that time, there is swiftness and decisiveness in actions and in follow-through, since the negotiating, compromising, and accepting of priorities are history. Also, new disagreements that emerge generally do not bring progress to a halt because there is both high clarity and broad acceptance of overall goals and underlying priorities. Without this consensus, each new problem or disagreement often necessitates a time-consuming and painful confrontation and renegotiation simply because it was not done initially.

Organizational climate can be described along six basic dimensions:

- *Clarity.* The degree of organizational clarity in terms of being well organized, concise, and efficient in the way that tasks, procedures, and assignments are made and accomplished.
- *Standards.* The degree to which management expects and puts pressure on employees for high standards and excellent performance.
- Commitment. The extent to which employees feel committed to the goals and objectives of the organization.
- *Responsibility.* The extent to which members of the organization feel responsibility for accomplishing their goals without being constantly monitored and second-guessed.
- *Recognition.* The extent to which employees feel they are recognized and rewarded (non-monetarily) for a job well done, instead of only being punished for mistakes or errors.
- *Esprit de corps.* The extent to which employees feel a sense of cohesion and team spirit, of working well together.

Bella Dance Academy

"Lina Ball has taken her passion for dance and built it into a thriving business that is growing by leaps and bounds."[10] With an opening like that on the Canadian Newswire, Lina Ball received much attention when she won BDC's Young Entrepreneur of the Year Award for the Northwest Territories. Born and raised in Nanaimo, British Columbia, where she began dancing at the age of three, two decades later Lina Ball moved with her husband in 2003 and opened Bella Dance Academy in Yellowknife in a warehouse with high ceilings. To promote her dance school she did it all. That first season she offered ballet, tap, jazz, modern, and hip hop classes. Students ranged from 16 months to 65 years old. In addition to teaching 120 students in 25 different classes singlehandedly, "I did everything and anything I could to promote the classes that first year. I worked at festivals, handed out flyers, did a mail-out, ran radio and newspaper advertising, talked to daycares and schools—just anything." In the second year Lina added four instructors as the number of students and classes grew.[11] In late 2008 they moved to a new location with two studios. Adding more instructors to her staff, additional challenges were faced. Clearly Lina was not simply doing, she had to lead her team and create a culture of those who shared her passion. The Canadian Newswire reported that "Lina's business plan has been carefully thought out" and quotes her as saying: "We set goals every year and we've always met our enrollment numbers. It's really important to me to increase at a steady pace, but also to keep the quality of the programs and to create a positive environment for the students." Lina notes staffing in a remote location is a problem: "It takes at least a year to train a student to teach, and most of the kids leave Yellowknife after they graduate. So I train them for a year to teach for one or two years and then they're gone. That's been hard." But her Bella Dance Academy has recently benefited from an instructor that in 2009 tried out for CTV's "So You Think You Can Dance" and returned to teaching.[12] Lina and her dancers of all ages and abilities have become part of the community performing throughout the year for public events and at a seniors' residence. Bella Dance Academy (www.belladance.ca) also puts on its own recitals and shows, e.g., *Nutcracker*.

Sources: "Lina Ball Has Yellowknife Dancing! Owner of Bella Dance Academy Wins BDC's Young Entrepreneur Award for the Northwest Territories," *Canadian Newswire*, October 21, 2008; Daron Letts, "Hip Hop is On Top," *Northern News Service*, September 10, 2008; Daron Letts, "Dancer Mum on Results of Her Star Audition," *Northern News Service*, April 24, 2009.

Approaches to Entrepreneurial Leadership

In achieving the entrepreneurial culture and climate described above, certain approaches to leadership (also discussed in Chapter 5) are common across core leadership modes. David Halabisky, Erwin Dreessen, and Chris Parsley all of the Small Business Policy Branch of Industry Canada concede that entrepreneurial behaviour may be the "most crucial component in determining the growth path of a firm."[13]

Entrepreneurial Leadership   No single leadership pattern seems to characterize successful ventures. Leadership may be shared, or informal, or a natural leader may guide a task. What is common, however, is an individual who defines and gains agreements on who has what responsibility and authority and who does what with and to whom. Roles, tasks, responsibilities, accountabilities, and appropriate approvals are defined.

There is no competition for leadership in these organizations, and leadership is based on expertise, not authority. Emphasis is placed on performing task-oriented roles, but someone invariably provides for "maintenance" and group cohesion by good humour and wit. Further, the leader does not force his or her own solution on the team or exclude the involvement of potential resources. Instead, the leader understands the relationships among tasks and between the leader and his or her followers and is able to lead in those situations where it is appropriate, including managing actively the activities of others through directions, suggestions, and so forth.

This approach is in direct contrast to the communal approach, where two to four entrepreneurs, usually friends or work acquaintances, leave unanswered such questions as who is in charge, who makes the final decisions, and how real differences of opinion are resolved. While some overlapping of roles and a sharing in and negotiating of decisions are desirable in a new venture, too much looseness is debilitating.

This approach also contrasts with situations where a self-appointed leader takes over, where there is competition for leadership, or where one task takes precedence over other tasks.

Consensus Building   Leaders of most successful new ventures define authority and responsibility in a way that builds motivation and commitment to cross-departmental and corporate goals. Using a consensus approach to management requires working with peers and with the subordinates of others (or with superiors) outside formal chains of command and balancing multiple viewpoints and demands.

In the consensus approach, the founder is seen as willing to relinquish his or her priorities and power in the interests of an overall goal, and the appropriate people are included in setting cross-functional or cross-departmental goals and in making decisions. Participation and listening are emphasized.

In addition, the most effective individuals are committed to dealing with problems and working problems through to agreement by seeking a reconciliation of viewpoints, rather than emphasizing differences, and by blending ideas, rather than playing the role of hard-nose negotiator or devil's advocate to force their own solution. There is open confrontation of differences of opinion and a willingness to talk out differences, assumptions, reasons, and inferences. Logic and reason tend to prevail, and there is a willingness to change opinions based on consensus.

Communication   The most effective leaders share information and are willing to alter individual views. Listening and participation are facilitated by such methods as circular seating arrangements, few interruptions or side conversations, and calm discussion versus many interruptions, loud or separate conversations, and so forth, in meetings.

Encouragement   Successful leaders build confidence by encouraging innovation and calculated risk-taking, rather than by punishing or criticizing what is less than perfect, and by expecting and encouraging others to find and correct their own errors and to solve their own problems. Their peers and others perceive them as accessible and willing to help when needed, and they provide the necessary resources to enable others to do the job. When it is appropriate, they go to bat for their peers and subordinates, even when they know they cannot always win. Further, differences are recognized and performance is rewarded.

Trust   The most effective leaders are perceived as trustworthy and straightforward. They do what they say they are going to do; they are not the corporate rumour carriers; they are more open and spontaneous, rather than guarded and cautious with each word; and they are perceived as being honest and direct. They have a reputation of getting results and become known as the creative problem solvers who have a knack for blending and balancing multiple views and demands.

Development   Effective leaders have a reputation for developing human capital (i.e., they groom and grow other effective leaders by their example and their mentoring). As noted in Chapter 5, Bradford and Cohen distinguish between the heroic leader, whose need to be in control in many instances actually may stifle cooperation, and the post-heroic leader, a developer who actually brings about excellence in organizations by developing entrepreneurial middle management. If a company puts off developing middle management until price competition appears and its margins erode, the organization may come unravelled. Linking a plan to grow human capital at the middle management and the supervisory levels with the business strategy is an essential first step.

ENTREPRENEURSHIP FOR THE 21ST CENTURY: BIG BREAKTHROUGHS

Extraordinary individuals and enterprises have been built in recent years and contributed to the entrepreneurial revolution: Austin Hill's slew of ventures, including most recently Akoha; Gabrielle Chevalier has brought her company Solutions 2 GO to $500 million in annual revenue in just four years; Nina Gupta envisions taking Greenlite public and to $100 million in annual sales; Doug and Danny Elder aim to take their already successful promotional events "on tour" to other Western Canadian cities. These entrepreneurs created "high standard, perpetual learning cultures," which create and foster a "chain of greatness." The lessons from such great entrepreneurial leaders and enterprises provide a blueprint for entrepreneurship in the 21st century. They set the standard and provide a tangible vision of what is possible. Not surprisingly, the more exciting, faster growing, and more profitable companies in Canada today share striking similarities.

Austin Hill

Serial entrepreneur and angel investor, Austin Hill was born in Ottawa in 1973 and grew up in Calgary, where he developed a passion for computer technology. He created his first venture Cyberspace Data Security when he was 17 years old. In 1994, Hill started an Internet provider in Montreal called Infobahn Online Services with his brother. They merged with another ISP to create TotalNet, which they sold in 1997.

In 1997, with his brother and father, Austin Hill launched Zero-Knowledge Systems and raised $65 million in venture capital. He played a vital role for a decade including running a spinout "Synomos" that ultimately failed in 2005, the same year that Zero-Knowledge Systems changed its name to Radialpoint. "We wanted the world to know what we stood for—power to the people—privacy for all—we were passionate about changing the way the future would look. We were social entrepreneurs believing that we could both make a profitable company and a contribution to the betterment of society at the same time."[14] Their recruiting included a mobile billboard driven past Montreal software companies with the enticing phrase "wanna make Internet history?" After much turmoil, including "reducing head count by the hundreds because of undisciplined growth," in early 2003 Zero-Knowledge started to generate positive cash flow.

In his blog, Austin Hill points out:

> The process of building innovative enterprises requires experimentation and failure. How much experimentation is a function of risk appetite and cost of money. The cost of money was incredibly low and the risk appetite for technology stocks were so much in abundance that we were fielding random calls from retail investors looking to buy stock or get on a waiting list for the IPO for almost 2 years before we even had revenue.
>
> We proved ourselves able to play by the rules of that time and raised money and built real products and teams in a way that the market was rewarding (getting big fast, become the market leader by the size of your brain trust and the broad range of your opportunities).
>
> When the rules of the market changed, we changed with them and made sure we could continue to work with customers finding a business model and customer profile that would grow with us. We made a lot of mistakes that in hindsight now seem obvious. But we rushed into our mistakes recognizing them as valuable lessons and we were eager students.
>
> When we started Zero-Knowledge my internal email signature carried the phrase "Make new mistakes more often." Our team culture helped us to react and evolve as we saw new opportunities, identified failing products and responded to the dramatic shifts that occurred in the capital markets.

Gabrielle Chevalier

The owner of Mississauga, Ontario-based Solutions 2 GO Inc., Gabrielle Chevalier was ranked number two on a list of the top 100 women entrepreneurs in Canada in 2007 and again in 2008. With revenue growth from $37 million in 2004 to $453 million in 2008, Solutions 2 GO is a video game distributor carrying hundreds of titles by Nintendo, Sony, and Microsoft. A typical day calls for processing up to 10,000 orders from clients that include major Canadian retailers such as Wal-Mart, HMV, Blockbuster, Future Shop, and Best Buy. According to Chevalier, "In our business, we exist solely to connect manufacturers and retailers. Neither will accept any excuses from us. As a start-up with very aggressive growth plans, Solutions 2 GO wanted an IT partner who was knowledgeable, experienced, and responsive."[15] Gabrielle Chevalier chose Lynn Cooke's 360 Visibility Inc.—also listed on Canada's Top Women Entrepreneurs. Cooke co-founded 360 Visibility in 2003 "around a vision of providing all enterprise participants in a client organization with the information they need to make swift, well-informed, coordinated, and above all profitable business decisions." Lynn Cooke must be on the right track because 360 Visibility experienced three-year revenue growth of 883 percent.

Nina Gupta

Another one of Canada's Top Women Entrepreneurs, Nina Gupta, is at the helm of Greenlite—a leading manufacturer of energy efficient lighting products created in 1996 when her instincts told her that "North America's lighting business was going green." Based on years of experience in the family's automotive lighting business, she ventured into the residential and industrial lighting sector.[16] Those instincts have paid off as Greenlite revenues broke $30 million in 2008, a fair jump from $6 million just four years prior. Beyond promoting her product she is a social activist, her goal is to encourage us to switch to CFLs (compact fluorescent light bulbs) thus saving the natural environment. She also boasts of Greenlite's workforce being 80 percent female. Nina Gupta describes herself as "tenacious, hard working, focused, and honest." And admits to being "a compulsive neurotic list maker writing down plans for everything." In the future she hopes that "a public offering will raise enough money to purchase factories and assembly facilities to become a $100-million company in the next five years."

Doug and Danny Elder

Two brothers, Doug and Danny, established Off Axis in 2001 in Regina, Saskatchewan to cater to the "lifestyles of both males and females in the boarding culture." While they have a sizeable physical inventory with snowboards, skateboards, wakeboards, footwear, clothing, and accessories as well as a solid Web site, their real breakthrough was the events they put on to promote their business and the lifestyle of the sports. In 2008, BDC gave the Elders a Young Entrepreneur Award noting that the two had their finger on the pulse of Regina's youth culture and much of their success was due to stellar 'guerilla' marketing tactics. The events Doug and Danny organized got bigger and bigger, attracting big-name corporate sponsors "eager to capitalize on the Elders' expertise in youth marketing."[17] Off Axis' multi-day Jibfest and Summer Invasion events "attract well over 10,000 attendees and include vendor villages featuring a wide variety of youth-related items."[18] Off Axis was associated with a wakeboarding school near Regina, which hosted the National Wakeboard Championships in 2008 and Doug and Danny were contemplating an event tour with stops in various Western Canadian cities appealing to their demographic—15 to 24-year-olds.

The Chain of Greatness

As we reflect on these great individuals and enterprises, we can see that there is clearly a pattern here, with some common denominators in both the ingredients and the process. This chain of greatness becomes reinforcing and perpetuating (see Exhibit 12.4). Leadership that instills across the company a vision of greatness and an owner's mentality is a common beginning. A philosophy of perpetual learning throughout the organization accompanied by high standards of performance is key to the value-creating entrepreneurial cultures at the three firms. A culture that teaches and rewards teamwork, improvement, and respect for each other provides the oil and glue to make things work. Finally, a fair and generous short- and long-term reward system, as well as the necessary education to make sure that everyone knows and can use the numbers, creates a mechanism for sharing the wealth with those who contributed to it. The results speak for themselves: extraordinary levels of personal, professional, and financial achievement.

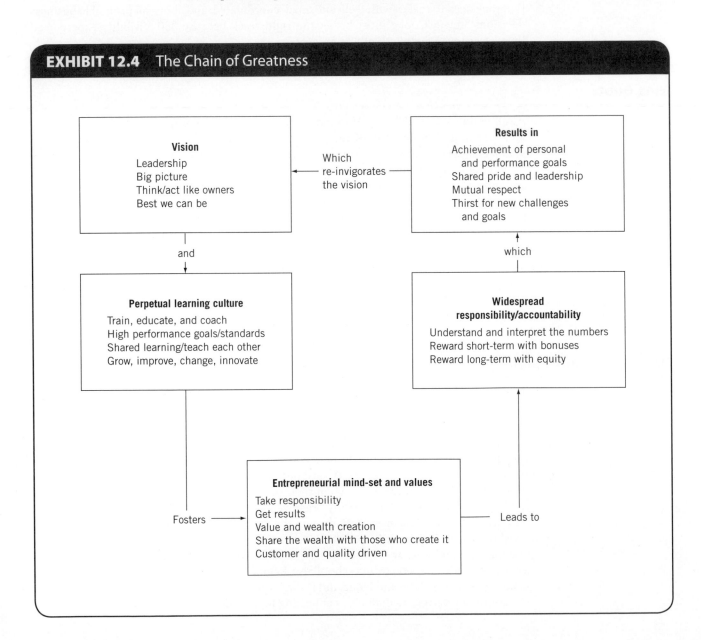

EXHIBIT 12.4   The Chain of Greatness

Vision
Leadership
Big picture
Think/act like owners
Best we can be

Which re-invigorates the vision

Results in
Achievement of personal and performance goals
Shared pride and leadership
Mutual respect
Thirst for new challenges and goals

and

which

Perpetual learning culture
Train, educate, and coach
High performance goals/standards
Shared learning/teach each other
Grow, improve, change, innovate

Widespread responsibility/accountability
Understand and interpret the numbers
Reward short-term with bonuses
Reward long-term with equity

Fosters

Leads to

Entrepreneurial mind-set and values
Take responsibility
Get results
Value and wealth creation
Share the wealth with those who create it
Customer and quality driven

Chapter Summary

1. The demands of rapid growth have led to the development of new organizational and leadership paradigms.

2. The entrepreneurial organization today is flatter, faster, more flexible and responsive, and copes readily with ambiguity and change. It is the opposite of the hierarchy, layers of management, and the more-is-better syndrome prevalent in brontosaurus capitalism.

3. Entrepreneurs in high-growth firms distinguish themselves with leading entrepreneurial practices in marketing, finance, management, and planning.

4. As high-potential firms "grow up big" they experience stages (Wonder, Blunder, Thunder, Plunder, Asunder or Wonder redux), each with its own special challenges and crises, which are compounded the faster the growth.

5. Establishing a culture and climate conducive to entrepreneurship is a core task for the venture team.

6. A chain of greatness characterizes some break-through approaches to entrepreneurial leadership.

Study Questions

1. Why have old hierarchical management paradigms given way to new organizational paradigms?

2. What special problems and crises can new ventures expect as they grow? Why do these occur?

3. Explain the stages many ventures experience and why these are unique.

4. What role does the organizational culture and climate play in a rapidly growing venture?

Why are many large companies unable to create an entrepreneurial culture?

5. What is the chain of greatness and why can entrepreneurs benefit from the concept? Can it be used to diagnose and correct a bad situation?

6. Why is the rate of growth the central driver of the organization challenges a growing venture faces?

Mind Stretchers   *Have you considered?*

1. Many large organizations are now attempting to reinvent themselves. What will be the biggest challenge in this process, and why?

2. How fast should a company grow? How fast is too fast, organizationally and financially?

3. In your ideal world, how would you describe what it is like to live and work within the perfect entrepreneurial organization?

4. Do you have what it takes to lead a rapid-growth enterprise? Will you know when to do less, trust others, and lead more?

CASE   WATCH THAT NEXT STEP

Richard Ivey School of Business
The University of Western Ontario
Ivey | Research and Development

Preparation Questions

1. Make a list of the positive and negative signs of growth at Avalon Electronics.

2. What should Wally Haas' priorities be?

3. What are the next hurdles? Will they be organizational, financial, or technical?

Wally Haas had much to celebrate as 2007 slipped into 2008. As he welcomed the new year, he could proudly look back on a banner performance at his firm, St. John's, N.L.-based Avalon

Microelectronics. Haas had founded the company—a maker of specialized software for microchips used in high-speed data transfer—just four years earlier as a tiny start-up in a remote

This case was written by Ken Mark, Eric Morse, Stewart Thornhill, and Mary Weil, Pierre L. Morrissette Institute for Entrepreneurship, Richard Ivey School of Business, University of Western Ontario, for purposes of classroom discussion.

location with little more than a good idea. Over the past 12 months, it had generated sales of $1.5 million, a ten-fold increase from the year before. Better yet, Haas was projecting sales to grow as much as 40 percent in 2008, a pace he expected to maintain for several years to come.

But even as the metaphorical champagne flowed, Haas knew that the outlook for Avalon wasn't all wine and roses. Serious issues were beginning to emerge, and Haas's company was struggling to keep up as demand for its products and services began to outstrip the company's capacity. Much to Haas's chagrin, Avalon was starting to turn down business. Fortunately, Haas's market position was protected for the time being as there were no direct competitors in Avalon's niche to snatch the clients the company couldn't take on right away. But Haas was certain that it was only a matter of time before someone would try. The only solution to his problem was to expand Avalon, fast. The question was, how—and where?

"I'm worried about the near future," Haas would say when asked about his business. "What happens when firms in our space start to encroach on our turf? We may be growing at 40 percent a year, but what happens five years down the road if our competitors are growing at 400 percent a year?"

Haas's capacity problems stemmed from the fact that he'd had a hard time convincing software engineers to leave major industry centres and move to Newfoundland to join his company. Few that had been trained in North America or Europe had been tempted by his overtures, mainly because they could earn higher salaries and work for larger, more prestigious companies in tech-savvy cities like Ottawa and San Francisco. Avalon had attracted international interest from engineers in developing countries, such as India and China. But Haas—a native Newfoundlander who'd spent 12 years in Ottawa with Nortel Networks and PMC Sierra before returning home to start Avalon—worried that most of these candidates were more interested in getting to Canada and acquiring citizenship than in working specifically for Avalon. They might be willing to start out in St. John's, but he feared they would leave for other cities as soon as they acquired legal status to remain in the country. Understandably, Haas was reluctant to invest in a hire only to see that person move on as soon as the opportunity presented itself.

One solution to his problem was to open a second Avalon design centre in an established tech hub, where it would be in the middle of existing talent pools. But where? Haas had been investigating the issue and had yet to come to any firm conclusions. He could, for instance, open a design centre in California's famed Silicon Valley, but that would be expensive due to the salary expectations of local engineers, whose skills were already in high demand and richly compensated. A cheaper option would be to open an office in an Asian hub. But whatever cost savings Haas would realize overseas would be offset by lower productivity. A third option, going to Ottawa, would strike a balance between cost and productivity, but even then Haas would have to find a manager to run the office while he managed headquarters in St. John's. No matter where he was located, he would need someone he could trust fully and completely.

Even if Haas resolved these issues, the very nature of Avalon's work would make it difficult to move some of its operations. Avalon develops what are known as "IP cores." Essentially, these cores are bits of software that enable inexpensive, generic microchips to perform customized functions. This allows firms in the data-transfer business, such as Nortel or Cisco, to buy off-the-shelf chips—at less cost than buying or developing their own custom chips—and then program them in ways to differentiate their hardware products from those of competitors. The work is highly collaborative, Haas says, meaning that it would be difficult for Avalon to function with geographically dispersed teams. And if this is true for branching out in Canada, it's doubly so for setting up in another country. "We need to consider factors like cultural proximity," he says. "We may speak the same language as engineers in other countries, but we rely on different expressions and have different expectations."

If Haas had one advantage as he confronted his expansion issues, it was his familiarity with the challenges of running a software company in a region better known for its troubled fishery and booming energy sector than its technological prowess. He had already overcome a number of them in getting Avalon this far. When it came to financing his new venture back in 2004, for example, Haas was certain he was onto a good thing and he saw the potential for decades of growth. But because his idea tapped a new area of expertise—and because he was proposing an unusual business for Newfoundland—he found it difficult to attract investors.

Tenacity paid off, though, and Haas was eventually able to secure government financing, using his personal investment in Avalon as leverage, as well as the company's acceptance into a local tech business incubator. Within a year, Avalon released its first product. Before long it was winning customers with large and deep pockets. Soon, however, Avalon found itself operating at maximum capacity—and then beyond, leaving Haas to greet the new year in a quandary: "We just can't find enough qualified engineers. Should we only expand in St. John's or should we open an office in Ottawa, or Silicon Valley or Asia? We're growing fast, but we could be growing much faster."

Find more great exercises and additional study tools on the Online Learning Centre at **www.mcgrawhill.ca/olc/timmons**

C·H·A·P·T·E·R

13

FRANCHISING

Franchisees are chosen based on a number of criteria, including entrepreneurial drive.

Don Schroeder
President and CEO, Tim Hortons

It's possible, if the economics are right . . . When you build a great franchise it can be a lot of fun.

Dan Aykroyd
Actor

Upon completion of this chapter, you will be able to:

1. Understand what franchising is and discuss the nature of the role of the franchisor and the franchisee.

2. Explore the process of becoming a franchisor.

3. Compare the profile of a successful franchisee to the profile of a successful entrepreneur.

4. Describe a basic screening method for evaluating franchises with a higher success probability.

5. Analyze the franchise relationship model and its use as a guide for developing a high-potential franchise.

INTRODUCTION

In this chapter we will explore what franchising is and how well it fits the Timmons Model definition of entrepreneurship. We will consider the scope of franchising and examine the criteria for determining a franchise's stature, from the perspective of an existing or prospective franchisor. We will present several templates and models that can be helpful in conducting due diligence on a franchise opportunity.

Let us consider how well franchising fits our definition of entrepreneurship from Chapter 1. Just as the focus of our definition of entrepreneurship is opportunity recognition for the purpose of wealth creation, so too is the focus of franchising. Franchising offers a thoughtful system for reshaping and executing a delivery system designed to extract maximum value from the opportunity. Just as opportunity, thought, and action are essential elements of an entrepreneurial venture, so too are they important components of a franchise opportunity. Franchising also fulfills our definition of entrepreneurship because each partner understands the expectation for wealth of the other and they work together toward that goal; their "bond" is sealed as partners in the franchise alliance.

Franchising is, at its core, a partnership between two organizations, the franchisor and the franchisee. The successful franchise relationship defines and exploits an opportunity as a team. The franchisor is the concept innovator who grows by seeking partners or franchisees to operate the concept in local markets. A franchisor can be born when at least one company store exists and the opportunity has been beta tested. Once the concept is proven, the franchisor and the franchisee enter into an agreement to grow the concept based on a belief that there are mutual advantages to the alliance. The nature of these advantages is defined by the ability of the partners to execute a particular aspect of the opportunity for which each is respectively better suited than the other. The heart of franchising is entrepreneurship, the pursuit of and intent to gain wealth by exploiting the given opportunity. The unique aspect of franchising is that it brings together two parties that both have individual intentions of wealth creation through opportunity exploitation, but who choose to achieve their goals by working together. Because franchising aligns the different skill sets and capabilities of the franchisor and franchisee as a partnership, the whole of a franchise opportunity is greater than the sum of its parts.

At its most fundamental level, franchising is a large-scale growth opportunity based on a partnership rather than on individual effort. Once a business is operating successfully, then according to the Timmons Model, it is appropriate to think about franchising as a growth tool. The sum of the activities between the partners is manifest in a trademark or brand. The mission of the entrepreneurial alliance is to maintain and build the brand. The brand signals a price–value relationship in the minds of customers. Revenue is driven higher because the marketplace responds to the brand with more purchases or purchases at a higher price than the competition.

JOB CREATION VERSUS WEALTH CREATION

As a franchise entrepreneur, we can control the growth of our franchise opportunity. For those whose life goal is to own a pizza restaurant and earn a comfortable income, the opportunity is there. Franchising allows us to do this, but it also allows us to build 30 pizza restaurants and to participate fully in the wealth-creation process. One strength of franchising is that it provides a wide breadth of options for individuals to customize opportunities to meet their financial goals and business visions, however conservative or grandiose.

The ability to create wealth in any venture starts with the initial opportunity assessment. For example, a franchise company may decide to limit its geographic territories in terms of the number of stores. Therefore, the expansion market is limited from the start for potential franchisees. Even if franchisees work hard and follow all the proven systems, they may be buying a job versus creating wealth.

But some companies are designed to reward successful franchisees with the opportunity to buy more stores in a particular market or region. Franchisees who achieve prosperity with single units are rewarded with additional stores. The entrepreneurial process is encouraged, and wealth is created.

Much of the goal of *New Venture Creation* is to increase the odds for success in a new venture and increase its scope. Franchising can be an excellent vehicle for growth for the franchisor.

FRANCHISING: A STORY OF ENTREPRENEURSHIP

The franchise entrepreneurial spirit in Canada has never been more alive than today. More than 900 different brand names with 76,000 outlets populate the marketplace; these businesses make up 20 percent of all retail sales nationwide, approximately $100 billion. In Canada, a franchise opens every two hours every day of the year.[1] The belief that franchising can be an exciting entrepreneurial venture is supported by the continued success of established franchise systems, the proliferation of new franchises, and the profitability reported by franchisors and franchisees.[2] These statistics hint at the scope and richness that franchising has achieved in a relatively short period. The process of wealth creation through franchising continues to evolve as we witness an increase not only in the number of multiple outlet franchisees,[3] but also in the number of franchisees that operate multiple outlets in different franchise systems. Exhibit 13.1 reveals several aspects of contemporary Canadian franchises.

Shoppers Drug Mart boasts having over 1,000 stores. The franchising concept was to have pharmacists own and operate their own stores. Pharmacist Murray Koffler inherited two stores at the age of 20. In 1962 he had grown to 17 pharmacies and adopted the name Shoppers Drug Mart. Through acquisitions and aggressive expansion the brand grew to the presence it has today.

Home Hardware is another chain whose footprint has grown to a formidable level—over 1,000 stores strong. In 1964, 122 independent Ontario hardware retailers banded together to form a "dealer-owned cooperative—an answer to the challenge posed by 'big box' retailers who enjoyed the advantage of direct-from-manufacturer buying power."[4] Like Shoppers Drug Mart it offers a number of store brands in addition to those of popular manufacturers.

Cara Operations Ltd. provides catering services to airlines and operates Harvey's, Swiss Chalet, Kelsey's, Milestone's, Montana's, and formerly Outback and Second Cup. The corporate vision is to become "Canada's leading branded restaurant and airline services company."[5] Cara was founded by the Phelan family in 1883. The name "Cara" is derived from the first two letters of the words "Canadian Railway"—the enterprise's initial focus. The company went public in 1968 and later was taken private in 2004.

Anyone considering and exploring entrepreneurial opportunities should give serious consideration to the franchising option. As franchisor, this route can be a viable way to share risk and reward, create and grow an opportunity, and raise human and financial capital.

FRANCHISING: ASSEMBLING THE OPPORTUNITY

As we saw in earlier chapters, the Timmons Model identifies the three subsets of opportunity as market demand, market size and structure, and margin analysis. The franchise organization must understand the nature of demand both as it resides in the individual consumer and in society. At the most fundamental level, the primary target audience is the defining quality of the opportunity recognition process. Without a customer, there is no opportunity; without an opportunity, there is no venture; and without a sustainable opportunity, there can be no franchise.

As we discussed earlier in the chapter, our goal is to look at franchising as it presents opportunities for both franchisees and franchisors. We will now investigate several aspects of franchise opportunity recognition: primary target audience identification; service concept;

EXHIBIT 13.1 Canadian Franchise Facts	
Average franchise fee	$27,500
Average renewal fee	$3,000 to $5,000*
Average franchisee investment	$175,000
Typical length of franchise agreement	5 years**
97% of franchises opened in the last 5 years are still in business, 86% are under the original ownership[†]	
Typical royalty rate	5 to 8%
Typical advertising rate	3 %

Source: Canadian Franchise Association, www.cfa.ca.

* www.cfa.ca/print/Publications_Research/Tutorials/tutorial16.aspx.

** 10 and 20 year agreements are also common, www.ca.ca/FAQ/.

† www.franchiseek.com/Canada/Franchise_Canada_Statistics.htm/.

service delivery system design; training and operational support; field support, marketing, advertising, and promotion; and product purchase provision. Prospective franchisors should understand the nature and quality of each of these franchise components. Those considering growth through franchising must pay attention to the detail of their system offering.

Primary Target Audience

Defining the target customer is essential because it dictates many diverse functions of the business. Most important, it measures the first level of demand. Once the primary target audience is defined, secondary targets may be identified. The degree of market penetration in the secondary target is less than that of the primary target. Although measuring market demand is not an exact science, a franchisor must continually collect data about its customers. Even after a franchise is established, the franchisor and franchisee compare local market demographics with national profiles to decide the potential of the local market in terms of the number of outlets that can be developed. Revenue projections are made from the definition of the target audiences and the degree of market penetration that can be expected based on historical information. Three major areas of data collection can be integral to refining the primary target audience.

Demographic Profiles   A demographic profile is a compilation of personal characteristics that enables the company to define the "average" customer. Most franchisors perform market research as a central function, developing customer profiles and disseminating the information to franchisees. That research may include current user and non-user profiles. Typically, a demographic analysis includes age, gender, income, home address (driving or walking kilometres from the store), working address (driving or walking kilometres from the store), marital status, family status (number and ages of children), occupation, race and ethnicity, religion, and nationality. Demographics must be put into context by looking at concept-specific data such as mean number of automobiles for a Jiffy Lube franchise or percentage of disposable income spent on clothes for a Mexx franchise.

Psychographic Profiles   Psychographic profiles segment potential customers based on social class, lifestyle, and personality traits. Economic class and lifestyle address such issues as health consciousness, fashion orientation, or being a "car freak." Personality variables such as self-confident, conservative, and independent are used to segment markets.

Behavioural variables segment potential customers by their knowledge, attitude, and use of products to project usage of the product or service. By articulating a detailed understanding of the target market and why that consumer will buy our product or service, great knowledge of the competitive landscape is gained. Why will a consumer spend their money with us instead of where they currently find value?

Geographic Profiles   The scope of a franchise concept can be local, regional, national, or international. Regions are divided by population density and described as urban, suburban, or rural from under 5,000 to 4 million or more.

The "smart" franchise uses the ever-growing system of franchisees and company outlets to continually gather data about customers. This helps dynamically shape the vision and therefore the opportunity. The analysis of system data must include a link to the vision of the concept and to what seems possible for the vision. For example, if we launched an earring company a generation ago, we could have defined the target market as women ages 21 to 40, and the size of the market as the number of women in this age group in Canada. But perhaps looking beyond the existing data and anticipating the larger market that now exists can shape our vision. The target market for earrings could be defined as women and men ages 12 to 32, with an average of three earrings (or more properly piercings) per individual, not two. The identification of the target market requires that we combine demographic data with our own unique vision for the venture.

Theory into Practice: Market Demand, a Moving Target for Radio Shack

Target markets are dynamic, often metamorphosing very quickly. Radio Shack (later known in Canada as "The Source by Circuit City" and after Circuit City declared bankruptcy in early 2009, became just "The Source" under Bell Canada ownership) had to change its business to reflect the shift in its target market. In the 1970s and 1980s, Radio Shack grew by addressing the needs of technophiles—young men with penchants for shortwave radios, stereo systems, walkie talkies, and the like. The national retail chain supplied this audience with the latest gadgets and did very well.

Then, starting in the early 1990s, technology became more sophisticated. Personal electronic equipment began to include cellphones, handheld computers, and electronic organizers. The market for these products was expanding from a smaller group of technophiles to a larger group of middle-age males who loved gadgets and who had more disposable income. Yet Radio Shack remained Radio Shack. Its audience dwindled while the personal electronics market boomed.

In the early 1990s, Radio Shack refocused its business to target this new demographic. Its advertising addressed the needs of the 44-year-old upper-middle-class male versus the 29-year-old technophile. That 29-year-old who used to shop at Radio Shack was now 44! He was not going to make a radio, but he would buy a cellphone or GPS for his vehicle. Radio Shack made dramatic changes in its marketing and inventory. As a result, it made dramatic changes in its profitability. Under Bell Canada, The Source would drop its exclusivity agreement with Rogers Communications at the end of 2009 and in 2010 begin promoting the Bell line of products and services.

The focus on primary target audience development as the core to franchise opportunity recognition is essential to determine the consumer appeal of a franchise and to establish validity of the opportunity. We will consider a set of criteria that will help define due diligence in assessing how a franchise has exploited the opportunity. This discussion holds value for an overall understanding of franchising for existing franchisors and potential franchisors alike.

EVALUATING A FRANCHISE

Before looking at the detail of a franchise offering, the prospective franchisee must mine an offering from the 900 franchises in Canada. Although the next section is appropriate for prospective franchisees, the savvy franchisor will use this information to better craft his/her franchise offering for potential franchisees.

Exhibit 13.2 provides a franchise screening template designed to make a preliminary assessment of the key variables that constitute a franchise. The exercise is crafted to help map the risk profile of the franchise and highlight areas that will most likely need further due diligence. If the following criteria are important to the potential franchisee, then they also provide a map of the growth and market positioning objectives a stable franchisor should be pursuing.

This exercise is not designed to culminate in a "go or no go" decision. Rather, prospective franchisees should use it to help evaluate if the franchise meets their personal risk/return profile. Franchisors should also review the exercise to examine the risk signals they may be sending to prospective franchisees. It is especially important to understand this risk profile in the context of the alternative investments a prospective franchisee can make.

EXHIBIT 13.2   Franchise Risk Profile Template

Criteria	Low Risk Average Return 15–20%	Acceptable Risk Incremental Return 30%	High Risk Marginal Return 40–50%	Extreme Risk Large Return 60–100%
Multiple Market Presence	National	Regional	Provincial	Local
Outlet Pro Forma Disclosed or Discerned	Yes, 90% + apparently profitable	Yes, 80% apparently profitable	Yes, 70% + apparently profitable	No, less than 70% profitable
Market Share	No. 1 and dominant	No. 1 or 2 with a strong competitor	Lower than No. 2	Lower than No. 3 with a dominant player
National Marketing Program	Historically successful creative process, national media buys in place	Creative plus regional media buys	Creative plus local media buys	Local media buys only
National Purchasing Program	More than 3% + gross margin advantage in national purchasing contract	1–3% gross margin advantage versus independent operators	Regional gross margin advantages only	No discernible gross margin advantages
Margin Characteristics	50% gross + margin 18% + net outlet margin	40–50% gross margin 12–17% net outlet margin	30–40% gross margin less than 12% net outlet margin	Declining gross margin detected, erratic net outlet margin
Business Format	Sophisticated training, documented operations manual, identifiable feedback mechanism with franchisees	Initial training and dynamically documented operations manual, some field support	Training and operations but weak field support	Questionable training and field support and static operations
Term of the Licence Agreement	20 years with automatic renewal	15 years with renewal	Less than 15 years or no renewal	Less than 10 years
Site Development	Quantifiable criteria clearly documented and tied to market specifics	Markets prioritized with general site development criteria	General market development criteria outlined	Business format not tied to identifiable market segment(s)
Capital Required per Unit	$15,000–$25,000 working capital	Working capital plus $50,000–$100,000 machinery and equipment	Working capital plus machinery and equipment plus $500,000–$1,000,000 real estate	Erratic, highly variable, or ill-defined
Franchise Fee and Royalties	PDV* of the fees are less than the demonstrated economic advantages (reduced costs or increased revenue) of the franchise versus stand-alone		PDV of the fees are only projected to be less than the expected economic advantages (reduced costs or increased revenue) of the franchise versus stand-alone	PDV of the fees are not discernibly less than the expected value of the franchise

*PDV is an abbreviation for present discounted value. If franchising is a risk-reduction strategy, then the discount of future revenue should be less. Concurrently, the economies of scale in marketing should increase the amount of revenue a franchise can generate versus a "stand-alone" operation.

FRANCHISOR AS THE HIGH POTENTIAL VENTURE

As Ron Joyce, Tim Horton's partner in their business demonstrates, becoming a franchisor can be a high potential endeavour. Growth and scale are the essence of the franchise mentality. Throughout this chapter we have taken the approach of franchising as entrepreneurial behaviour by the franchisor. In this section, we focus principally on franchisors and their rewards. In a study of *publicly traded franchisors*, the size and scope of the firms that achieved public capital is impressive. The capital marketplace has rewarded many franchisors, which have measured well against the criteria for a high potential venture franchise. They, in turn, have performed well vis-à-vis return to shareholders. The performance of public franchisors generally exceeds that of the TSX index. The relative buoyancy of franchisor performance can be attributed to being heavily weighted in the food category. During a recession, when household budgets are tight, consumers seek out dining establishments that offer the best value, the primary driver of many food-based franchise organizations.

Even more interesting are those exceptional performers among the high achieving franchisors. Take, for example, the quintessential Canadian franchise, Tim Hortons. Surpassing McDonald's, Tim Hortons is the largest Canadian food service organization with more than 3,300 restaurants. Its infrastructure includes a network of suppliers and resources that allows it to achieve economies of scale and offer great value to customers. In 2008, system-wide sales reached nearly $2 billion, operating income approached $500 million, and earnings per share were strong.[6]

KEY COMPONENTS OF A FRANCHISE OFFERING

In this section, we describe the major aspects of delivering a franchise system. It is excellence in both concept and delivery that has created wealth for the franchisors in publicly traded companies. We have analyzed the features that propel the high performance franchisor to exceptional return. The excellent franchisor supports the franchisee, and the symbiotic nature of the relationship leverages return for both partners. After prospective franchisees narrow their search for a franchise (by using the screening guide among other activities), they should begin a detailed analysis of the exact nature of a franchise. Franchisors should note the following in terms of how they might construct their offerings, knowing that prospective franchisees will conduct a detailed due diligence around these franchise components.

Service Delivery System

The road map for marshalling resources for the franchise comes from establishing the service delivery system. The opportunity dictates that certain tasks are performed to meet consumer demand. The assets put into place to meet these demands are largely the resources needed to launch the concept. In the franchise alliance, the franchisor develops a method for delivering the product or service that fills customer demand. In its most basic essence, the service delivery system is the way in which resources are arrayed so that demand can be extracted from the marketplace. This service delivery system has to be well defined, documented, and tested by the company or prototype operation. The end result of the organization, execution, and transfer of the service delivery system is the firm's competitive advantage.

The Timmons Model first looks at opportunity assessment, which demands a clear understanding of the target market and customer. Next it looks at resource marshalling or, in franchising, the establishment of the service delivery system. The service delivery system is the fundamental means by which customers will be served, and the fashion, often proprietary in design, in which the service delivery resources are arrayed can create competitive advantage in the marketplace. In franchising, this aspect is sometimes called the *business format*. A successful service delivery system's form and function will reflect the specific needs of the target customer. Highly successful and visible examples of business format innovations are the drive-through in fast-food restaurants and the bi-level facilities in quick-oil-change facilities. Every franchise has a well-defined service delivery system, however overt or transparent it may seem to an outside observer.

Because the service delivery system is truly the essence of the successful franchise, the detail given to it should not be underestimated. For the concept innovator, the common phrase, "The devil is in the details," never takes on more meaning than when designing the service delivery system for the franchise. Stephen Spinelli can corroborate this fact from experiences while expanding the Jiffy Lube franchise. One particular component of Jiffy Lube's expansion plans paints a vivid picture as to the intricacy of the development of the service delivery system and reveals what a great benefit this design paid over time.

Jiffy Lube franchises must meet specific location criteria: high volume of car traffic, side of the street located for inbound or outbound traffic, high profile retail area, and the far corner of any given street or block, among other requirements. Through trial and error, Jiffy Lube has determined the optimal location of the structure on any given property. Once these aspects are met, the building specifications follow. Structural specifications regarding the angle of the building and the width, depth, and angle of the entrance allow the optimal number of cars to stack in line waiting for the car in front to complete the service. On several occasions, facilities that met location criteria were failing to perform as expected. Analysis of the situation determined the bend in the driveway was too sharp, preventing customers from driving their cars completely into the line and giving the inaccurate impression that the lot was full. Driveways were adjusted to accommodate an increased number of cars waiting for service.

This same level of refinement and detail orientation is encouraged for concept innovators while looking at their conceptual and actual service delivery system. Unless examined under a microscope, essential components of the service delivery system will be missed, deteriorating the value of the franchise. Jiffy Lube's experience also reinforces the benefits of a beta site, providing a real-world laboratory that can be adjusted and modified until the outlet reaches optimal performance.

Another part of the complete Jiffy Lube service delivery system was the design of the maintenance bay. Considering the limitations inherent in the use of hydraulic lifts, Jiffy Lube faced the dilemma of providing 30 minutes of labour in only 10 minutes. To deliver this 10-minute service, three technicians would need to work on a car at once without the use of a lift. This quandary led to the design of having cars drive into the bay and stop above an opening in the floor. This allowed one technician to service the car from below, another to service the car underneath the hood, and a third to service the car's interior. Without developing such a disruptive system, Jiffy Lube would not have been able to succeed as it did.

The soundness of the decision to use the drive-through/bi-level system was confirmed when competitors, gas stations and car dealers, failed to deliver on offering a "quick lube" using hydraulic lifts and traditional bays. The sum of Jiffy Lube's intricately designed parts created the value of the service delivery system. Such is the level of detail needed for a service delivery system to deliver both value to the customer and cost efficiencies to the operator. In much the same way, the following example highlights the specific design components of the service delivery system that create value.

Training and Operational Support

Formal franchisor training programs transfer knowledge of the service delivery system to the franchisees, both managers and line workers. Continuous knowledge gathering and transfer is important both before launch and on an ongoing basis. The licence agreement must define the specific form in which this franchisor responsibility will be performed. It should extend significantly beyond a manual and the classroom. Training will vary with the specifics of the franchise, but it should include organized and monitored on-the-job experience in the existing system for the new franchisee and as many of the new staff members as the franchisor will allow. Established and stable franchise systems such as Jiffy Lube and Tim Hortons require such operational experience in the existing system for as long as a year before the purchase of the franchise; however, this level of dedication to the franchisee's success is not the norm. Once the franchise is operational, the franchisee may be expected to do much or all of the on-site training of new hires. But as we will discuss in the next section, field support from the franchisor is often a signal of franchise stability and a reflection of the strength of the franchise partnership. Manuals, testing, training aids such as videos, and certification processes are often provided by the franchisor as part of this ongoing field support.

> **Theory to Practice: The Service Delivery System**
> **How Wendy's Used Its Business Format to Enter a "Saturated" Market**
>
> In 1972, Dave Thomas entered what many experts called a crowded hamburger fast-food market. His concept was to offer a "Cadillac hamburger" that was hot, fresh, and delivered more quickly than the competitions'. To execute Thomas' mission, Wendy's introduced the first drive-through in a national fast-food chain. Because Wendy's menu offered double and triple patties in addition to the traditional single-patty hamburger, its kitchens were designed to mass-produce hamburgers and deliver them to the front counter or drive-through window with minimal effort. To ensure a cooked just-in-time hamburger, each Wendy's restaurant included a large front window that enabled grill cooks (who were placed in clear view of the customer, not in a rear kitchen) to observe the flow of customers onto the premises.
>
> Notwithstanding the huge market share owned by McDonald's and Burger King, Wendy's was able to successfully enter the fray because of the manner in which it arranged its resources to create a competitive advantage. In Wendy's, the sum of the intricacies—the drive-through window, the position of the cooks and kitchen, and the double and triple patties—allowed the chain to compete and prosper in the fast-food hamburger market.

As discussed previously, the trade name and trademark are the most valuable assets in a franchise system. A franchisee's success rests soundly on the sales of products that are based on the brand equity and strength of the franchisor. As important as a sound service delivery system design is to the concept's foundation for success, the prospective training regimen is equally important. Without appropriately instructed individuals, an exceptional product will never reach the consumer's hands. As such, a poor training program will inevitably dilute the standardized, consistent delivery of the product and eventually erode the brand's value.

Field Support

Akin to the training program mentioned above is ongoing field support. This will take at least two forms, one in which a franchisor's representative will visit the franchisee's location in person, and the other in which the franchisor will retain resident experts in each of the essential managerial disciplines for consultation at the corporate headquarters. Ideally the licence agreement will provide for scheduled visits by the franchisor's agents to the franchisee's outlet with prescribed objectives, such as performance review, field training, facilities inspection, local marketing review, and operations audit. Unfortunately, some franchisors use their field role as a diplomatic or pejorative exercise rather than for training and support. The greater the substance of the field function, the easier it is for the franchisee to justify the royalty cost. Additionally, in the litigious environment in which we presently live, a well-documented field support program will mute franchisee claims of a lack of franchisor support.

One means of understanding the franchisor's field support motive is to investigate the manner in which the field support personnel are compensated. If field staff is paid commensurate with franchisee performance and ultimate profitability, then politics will play a diminished role. Key warning signs in this regard are when bonuses are paid for growth in the number of stores versus individual store growth, or for product usage (supplied by franchisor) by franchisee. Clearly, as with the training program prescribed by the franchisor and agreed to by the franchisee, a quality field support program is another integral factor to success, and a poor support program will eventually become evident.

Marketing, Advertising, and Promotion

Marketing activities are certainly one of the most sensitive areas in the ongoing franchise relationship because they imprint the trade name and trademark in the mind of the consumer to gain awareness—the most important commodity of the franchise. If the delivery of the product validates the marketing message, then the value of the franchise is enhanced, but if it is not congruent, then there can be a detrimental effect at both the local and national level. As outlet growth continues, marketing budgets increase and spread across the growing organization, thereby optimizing the marketing program.

Generally, marketing programs are funded and implemented at three different levels: national, regional, and local. A national advertising budget is typically controlled by the franchisor and each franchisee contributes a percentage of top-line sales to the fund. The franchisor then produces materials (television, radio, and newspaper advertisements; direct-mail pieces; and point-of-sale materials) for use by the franchisees and, depending on the size of the fund, also buys media time or space on behalf of the franchisees. Because it is impossible to allocate these services equally between franchisees of different sizes across different markets, the licence agreement will specify the use of "best efforts" to approximate equal treatment between franchisees. Although "best efforts" will invariably leave some franchisees with more advertising exposure and some with less, over time this situation should balance itself. This is one area of marketing that requires careful monitoring by both parties.

Regional marketing, advertising, and promotion is structured on the basis of an area of dominant influence (ADI). All the stores in a given area of dominant influence (e.g., Winnipeg) would contribute a percentage of their top-lines sales to the area of dominant influence advertising cooperative.[7] The cooperative's primary function is usually to buy media using franchisor-supplied or -approved advertising and to coordinate regional site promotions. If the franchise has a regional advertising cooperative requirement in the licence agreement, it should also have standardized ADI cooperative bylaws. These bylaws will outline such areas as voting rights and expenditure parameters. Often a single-store franchisee can be disadvantaged in a poorly organized cooperative, whereas a major contributor to the cooperative may find his voting rights disproportionately low in any given cooperative.

The third and final scenario for marketing is typically dubbed local advertising or local store marketing. At this level, the franchisee is contractually required to make direct expenditures on advertising. There is often a wide spectrum of permissible advertising expenditures, depending on the franchisor guidelines in the licence agreement; unfortunately, the licence agreement will probably not be specific. Franchisors will try to maintain discretion on this issue for maximum flexibility in the marketplace, while franchisees will vie for control of this area. Company-owned stores should have advertising requirements equal to those for the franchised units to avoid a franchisor having a free ride; in this regard, historical behaviour is the best gauge of reasonableness.

The franchisor should monitor and enforce marketing expenditures. For example, the customer of a franchisee leaving one area of dominant influence and entering another will have been affected by the advertising of adjacent regions. Additionally, advertising expenditures not made are marketing impressions lost to the system. When this happens, the marketing leverage inherent in franchising is not optimized.

Supply

In most franchise systems, one major benefit is bulk purchasing and inventory control. In the licence agreement, there are several ways to account for this economy of scale advantage. Because of changing markets, competitors and antitrust laws make it impossible for the franchisor to be bound to best-price requirements. The franchise should employ a standard of best efforts and good faith to acquire both national and regional supply contracts. According to John Pozios of the University of Manitoba, franchise-specific laws vary significantly from province to province, "Alberta, Ontario, Prince Edward Island and most recently New Brunswick have passed laws targeting franchising. Québec offers limited protection in its Civil Code."⁸ He states that with franchise-specific laws that differ from province to province, and no legislation in many provinces, "the need for uniformity in franchise legislation in Canada is greater than ever." Regulations protect the franchisee with disclosure requirements for the franchisor, obligations for fair dealing, and other duties of good faith. Inconsistency in law and expectations create a burden on the home-grown, developing franchise systems in Canada. The international franchisors have perfected their business models, are accustomed to variety in legal requirements, and have the experience and resources to take advantage of Canada's obstacles.

Depending on the nature of the product or service, regional deals might make more sense than national ones. Regional contact may provide greater advantages to the franchisee because of shipping weight and cost or service requirements. The savvy franchisor will recognize this and implement a flexible purchase plan. When local advantages exist and the franchisor does not act appropriately, the franchisees will fill the void. The monthly area of dominant influence (ADI) meeting then becomes an expanded forum for franchisees to voice their appreciations and concerns. The results of such ad hoc organizations can be reduced control of quality and expansion of franchisee association matters outside the confines of the licence agreement. Advanced activity of this nature can often fractionalize a franchise system and even render the franchisor obsolete. In some cases, the franchisor and franchisee-operated buying cooperatives peaceably coexist, acting as competitors and lowering the costs to the operator. However, the dual buying co-ops usually reduce economies of scale and dilute system resources, not to mention provide fertile ground for conflict within the franchise alliance.

For purposes of quality control, the franchisor will reserve the right to publish a product specifications list. The list will clearly establish the quality standards of raw materials or goods used in the operation. From those specifications, a subsequent list of approved suppliers is generated. This list can evolve into a franchise "tying agreement," which occurs when the business format franchise licence agreement binds the franchisee to the purchase of a specifically branded product. This varies from the product specification list because brand, not product content, is the qualifying specification. The important question here is: does the tying arrangement of franchise and product create an enhancement for the franchisee in the marketplace? If so, then are arm's-length controls in place to ensure that pricing, netted from the enhanced value, will yield positive results? Unfortunately, this is impossible to precisely quantify. However, if the tying agreement is specified in the licence agreement, then the prospective franchise owner is advised to make a judgment before purchasing the franchise. With this sort of decision at hand, the franchisor should prove the value of the tying agreement or abandon it.

Another subtle form of tying agreements occurs when the licence agreement calls for an approved suppliers list that ultimately includes only one supplier. If adding suppliers to the list is nearly impossible, there is a de facto tying arrangement. Additionally, another tying arrangement can occur when the product specification is written so that only one brand can qualify. A franchisor should disclose any remuneration gained by the franchisor or its officers, directly or indirectly, from product purchase in the franchise system. In this case, the franchisor's market value enhancement test is again proof of a credible arrangement.

Food Franchises with An Appetite for Success

1951 was the year that Hélène and René Léger opened their first St-Hubert restaurant in Montréal. The yellow and red rooster is found in approximately 100 locations throughout Québec, with a few more stores in New Brunswick and Ontario today and signals rotisserie chicken served with that delectable sauce. Adding home delivery and takeout increased consumption of their BBQ chicken and the young married couple realized they were really on to something. Their recipe for chicken, sauce, and service delivery system was easy for franchisees to follow. The sauce was then offered to grocery retailers. The Légers served thousands of visitors at the '67 Expo each day and their reputation grew. By 1979 about 50 St-Hubert restaurants were in existence.⁹

1959 was the year that Richard "Rick" Mauran opened the first Harvey's location in Richmond Hill, Ontario. He arrived at the name in his search for "something simple"—"Harvey's" was the name of the sign of a car dealer at 2300 Danforth Avenue (which today is the location of "Toronto Honda"). Franchising began in 1962 and in 1964 Harvey's Foods Ltd. went public and that year expanded from 7 to 17 locations. By 1965 there were 27 locations including Buffalo, New York. A handful of years later Rick's company merged with Industrial Growth Management to become Foodcorp and Rick and Bernie Syron lead expansive growth and in 1979 Foodcorp and the 80 Harvey's locations were acquired by Cara Operations Ltd. In the mid-1990s Harvey's partnered with Home Depot Canada and opened their first in-store kiosk in Whitby, Ontario.[10]

1963 marked the start of Pizza Nova. The Italian-born Primucci brothers opened one Pizza Nova restaurant in Scarborough, Ontario, and demand grew. In 1969 the Primucci family began franchising and today boast over 120 franchises in Ontario, Québec, New York, New Jersey, Cuba, and Romania. Pizza Nova's Web site lists the answers to the most frequently asked questions regarding opening a franchise with them: $20,000 fee; 6 percent royalties and 4 percent advertising; previous experience; financing required; etc.[11]

1968, during the hippie era the first Mr. Sub opened at 130 Yorkville Avenue in downtown Toronto to customers in tie-dyed shirts and bell-bottom jeans. Two friends raised $1,500 and started making fresh submarine sandwiches. After an "overwhelming response" the co-founders opened a second location five months later. In 1972 their first franchise opened. It expanded the menu and operations and today remains privately held with the original owners/directors and now has over 450 locations facing competition from Subway and Quizos.[12]

FRANCHISE RELATIONSHIP MODEL

Now that we have established the nature and components of the franchise relationship, we can connect these principles to the franchise relationship model, which we have developed over the years (see Exhibit 13.3). The franchise relationship model takes the entrepreneurial framework provided by the Timmons Model and connects the specific processes that are unique to franchising. We have argued that franchising is a powerful entrepreneurial alliance because it fits the Timmons Model and because it creates wealth. The franchise relationship model illustrates both how a concept innovator (i.e., potential franchisor) can most efficiently construct a franchising company and how a concept implementer (i.e., potential franchisee) can determine which company to join. The franchise relationship model further helps to distinguish between those tasks best executed under a corporate umbrella and those best done by the individual franchisee. Just as franchising is itself a risk-ameliorating tool for the entrepreneur; the franchise relationship model is also a tool that both franchisors and franchisees can use to judge the efficiency or success potential of a franchise opportunity. By overlaying the franchise relationship model template onto any given franchise, we can forecast to a great extent where the bottlenecks will impede success or where improvements can be made that will offer a competitive advantage.

The franchise relationship model is a puzzle, a series of franchise principles, each of which fit into the others to form a powerful interlocking business concept that solidifies itself as the linkages are implemented more efficiently. While the process starts in the centre with the customer, moves to the service delivery system and follows from there, the outer perimeter of means and mechanisms drives the competitive advantage of a franchise system. The major areas of concern other than the customer and the service delivery system are transaction analysis, financial structure, agency issues, and relational dynamics.

EXHIBIT 13.3 Franchise Relationship Model

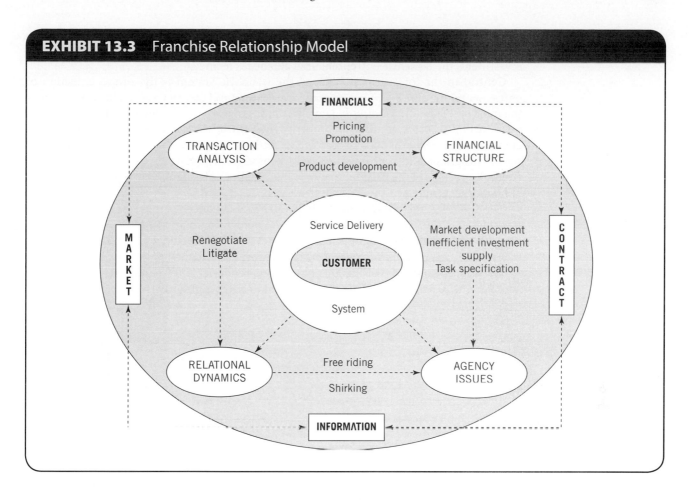

Transaction analysis considers which transactions are better served at a national level by the franchisor and which at the local level by the franchisee.[13] Typically the franchisor functions are centred on economies of scale. Franchisee functions include those that require local knowledge for hiring and local promotion. The financial structure flows from pro forma analysis of customer demand and the cost associated with development and execution of the service delivery system. Agency issues concern delegating responsibility to a partner.[14] No franchisor can know absolutely that the franchisee is "doing the right thing" at the store level. There is always the possibility of shirking, but if incentives are aligned both parties will pursue the same interests for value creation. Franchisees cannot possibly know that the franchisor is always acting in their best interest. Relational dynamics is the area that allows the partnership between franchisor and franchisee to continually change and develop as the business continues to expand.[15] Any partnership that strictly adheres to a contract will end in litigation.

The franchise relationship model (Exhibit 13.3) is dynamic—as events affect one aspect of the model, all other aspects must be reviewed in an iterative process. For example, if renegotiation of the licence agreement were to result in a reduced royalty, the financial model would be altered. A change in royalty could dictate a change in the services that the franchisor provides. Any change creates a cascading effect throughout the system—a reconstruction of the puzzle.

The franchise relationship model begins with opportunity recognition and shaping (customer) and then articulates the competitive advantages and costs of the service delivery system that will extract the demand and create a return on investment. The competitive sustainability of the franchise is embedded in the delineation of responsibilities between franchisor and franchisee and in the conscious design of the service delivery system. The franchisor's tasks are centrally executed and focus on economies of scale; the franchisee concentrates on those responsibilities that require local on-site managerial intensity (transaction analysis). The emergent financial structure is the manifestation of the interaction between the primary target customer and the service delivery system. By sharing both the burden of the service delivery system and the potential for return on investment, the franchise entrepreneurial alliance is formed.

Central to the long-term stability of the franchise system is the proper selection of partners and monitoring of key partner responsibilities (agency issues). However, even in the most stable relationship, a dynamic business environment dictates adjustments in the relationship to ensure continued competitive advantage. Understanding the partner's tolerance zone in performance and reacting to market changes can be standardized by formal review programs and kept unstructured by informal negotiations (relational dynamics). Failure to recognize the need for dynamic management of the relationship can often result in litigation, as noted.

The franchise relationship model illustrates how a concept innovator can construct a franchising company and the pathway for implementing it in the most entrepreneurial way. The model also eliminates those ideas that are best developed using another growth strategy, such as distributorships, licensing, or corporate-owned outlets.

We now understand that franchising is entrepreneurial and we understand the unique components of franchising that enable the building of a high-growth enterprise.

Chapter Summary

1. Franchising is an inherently entrepreneurial endeavour.
2. In this chapter we argue that opportunity, scale, and growth are at the heart of the franchise experience.
3. The success of franchising is demonstrated by the fact that it accounts for more than one-fifth of all Canadian retailing. Equally important is the demonstrated performance of the top franchise companies, outperforming the S&P TSX Composite Index.
4. Franchising shares profits, risk, and strategy between the franchisor and the franchisee.
5. A unique aspect of franchising is the wide spectrum of opportunity that exists and the matching of scale to appetite for a broad spectrum of entrepreneurs.
6. Two tools have been provided in this chapter to help the entrepreneur. For those interested in creating a franchise, the franchise relationship model articulates the dynamic construction of the franchisor–franchisee alliance. The franchise risk profile helps assess the risk-return scenario for any given franchise opportunity.

Study Questions

1. Can you describe the difference between the franchisor and the franchisee? How are these differences strategically aligned to create a competitive advantage?
2. We describe franchising as a "pathway to entrepreneurship" providing a spectrum of entrepreneurial opportunities. What does this mean to you?
3. What are the most important determinants of whether franchising is an appropriate method of rapidly growing a concept?
4. What are the five components of the franchise relationship model? Can you describe the interactive nature of these components?
5. What are the key components of a franchise offering from the franchisor's viewpoint?

Mind Stretchers *Have you considered?*

1. Why do you think that publicly held franchisors consistently outperform the TSX?

2. What would be the most attractive aspects of franchising to you? What is the least attractive part of franchising?

3. Can you list the top 10 franchises in the world? What criteria would you use to make your judgment?

4. Do you know anyone who owns a franchise? Do you think they work more or less hard than a "stand-alone" entrepreneur?

5. Who is franchising for and not for? What sectors are naturals for franchises?

CASE WHICH WAY TO GROW?

Richard Ivey School of Business
The University of Western Ontario

IVEY | Research and Development

Preparation Questions

1. What growth options are available and which one(s) should Eveline Charles pursue?

2. Assess market characteristics and market potential?

3. Will any resources need to be re-deployed? Any change in focus?

Eveline Charles looked pleased as she walked through her beauty salon and spa in Edmonton's Southgate Mall. It was late in the day, most of her staff had gone home, and the shop—one of nine outlets in her eponymous chain—was spic and span, just as she liked it.

Looking out through her storefront window, Charles watched as the last of the day's shoppers wandered towards the exits, bags in hand. Charles, however, wouldn't be heading out like the rest of them. On this mid-December evening, she was staying behind with her chief operating officer, Lina Heath, for a meeting. The subject: where to take the company next.

Turning her attention to that task, Charles sank down into one of the large black chairs in the reception lounge and looked up at Heath. "We've come a long way since we first added spa services to our salon business in 1995," she said. "Most of our stores are doing well. We've improved our decor, introduced new items and special services. And we've stayed true to our formula of offering a luxurious and fashion-forward salon where our clients can be pampered for a few hours."

Heath nodded. Both of the women knew that EvelineCharles was in good shape. Revenue and profit had grown steadily with the business. The company had launched a successful line of beauty products, it had created a training school in partnership with the Northern Alberta Institute of Technology and it had established EvelineCharles as a premium brand in western Canada, with annual sales of $17 million.

Still, Charles was puzzled over where her next phase of growth would come from. At least she had options. For starters, she had a large line of branded products—upwards of 1,800 stock-keeping units (SKUs), including beauty products and salon equipment—which meant she had the potential to become a supplier to other high-end salons. Heath liked this idea. The company had $2 million worth of stock in its inventory, and she reminded Charles that becoming a supplier would increase turnover and generate cash. Charles

agreed. But she had bigger ideas on her mind. "What about our thoughts on franchising our concept?" she asked Heath. "How should we assess that option? This is a unique industry where every operator wants to be an owner. We can give them the tools to build a business. With our school, we can even provide them with business training."

Both Charles and Heath were intrigued by the potential that franchising offered. But neither had experience as franchisors. Was it a good business model for EvelineCharles? They just didn't know and they were wary of pitfalls. Still, the idea was tempting. Growing by opening corporate stores would be time-consuming and expensive. Both women knew that well. But they also had a track record for getting it right. What was their best way forward—franchising or organic growth? Charles and Heath hoped this evening's meeting would shed some light on that question.

If Charles and Heath knew one thing as they pondered their options, it was that they were in a strong business category. The professional beauty-service market in North America was worth more than $60 billion in 2007, encompassing services that ranged from hair cuts and facials to massage and body scrubs. It was also extremely fragmented, with single, owner-operated stores accounting for most of the business.

Charles was such an owner when she opened her first business, a beauty salon in Edmonton, in 1984—but she wasn't content to stay that way. By the early 1990s, she had opened two more salons and, more importantly, had a plan for future growth. Charles had detected an early-stage trend in the industry of adding spa services to the menu of haircuts and manicures offered at traditional salons. She saw promise and, in 1995, launched her first combined salon-spa. She opened a second location in 1998, and set her sights on developing even more.

Part of Charles's strategy centred on developing signature services, such as hot-stone massages and mango body washes. To further differentiate her company, she also began develop-

This case was written by Ken Mark, Eric Morse, and Mary Weil, Pierre L. Morrissette Institute for Entrepreneurship, Richard Ivey School of Business, University of Western Ontario, for purposes of classroom discussion.

ing branded lines of beauty products, like shampoos, lotions and cosmetics, a job she and Heath (who had joined the company by this time) attacked with relish. "Lina and I have spent months in all corners of the world sourcing our products," Charles says. "We have our skin-care products and aromatherapy products sourced in France. Our nail colours come from Italy. We source from the best manufacturers and those with the strongest traditions in beauty care. And every single component is 100 percent customized for us. Everything we offer is unique and very difficult to replicate."

That focus on customization didn't stop at the EvelineCharles product lines. As the chain grew, Charles and Heath paid careful attention the to the details of opening each new store. They oversaw construction at each location, designed the layouts, and picked the colours and the lights to create a feel consistent with the company's high-end positioning. Customers certainly noticed. Many asked if the new stores were part of a U.S. chain making its way into Canada. Industry peers were paying attention, too, and Charles started to win industry awards, including Entrepreneur of the Year for Canada in the Global Salon Business Awards, in both 2004 and 2006. By the middle of this decade, it had become a major player in the salon and spa business, with stores in Edmonton, Calgary, Vancouver and Kelowna, B.C.

Back in the salon, Charles and Heath continued to discuss their options. Their existing growth strategy had taken them a long way. But opening stores themselves was a slow process. Real estate had to be found, leases negotiated and construction managed. Bringing stores to maturity in terms of sales also tied up working capital. And even though EvelineCharles had a source of recruits thanks to its beauty academy, hiring was still a major task.

For these reasons, among others, Charles and Heath were intrigued by the prospect of franchising the EvelineCharles brand. For starters, franchising would help the brand grow quickly, as EvelineCharles would be able to leverage the financial resources of its franchise partners. On the revenue side, the company would earn a percentage from each franchise and create a whole new market for its inventory of branded products.

Of course, franchisees would have to be selected carefully to maintain the quality of the EvelineCharles brand. And they'd have to be committed to growing their locations, keeping a close watch on local trends and ensuring that costs were controlled. Still, the prospects looked very tempting. "One day, EvelineCharles could become a nationwide brand," Heath mused.

But their inexperience as franchisors left Charles and Heath with nagging doubts, no matter how much they liked the idea. Turning to Heath, Charles had only one question: "What do you think we should do?"

Online **LearningCentre**

Find more great exercises and additional study tools on the Online Learning Centre at
www.mcgrawhill.ca/olc/timmons

CHAPTER

14

THE FAMILY AS ENTREPRENEUR[1]

The very elements that foster success, as well as the attitudes bred by success itself, can precipitate failure. The systems that built great companies often work to destroy them.[2]

Danny Miller & Isabelle LeBreton-Miller
HEC Montréal and University of Alberta

Upon completion of this chapter, you will be able to:

1. Describe the significant economic and entrepreneurial contribution families make to communities and countries worldwide.

2. Appreciate the different roles families play as part of the entrepreneurial process.

3. Provide a definition of family enterprising and transgenerational entrepreneurship.

4. Assess a family on the mind-set and methods continua for family enterprising and identify key issues for family dialogue.

4. Explore key questions on the six dimensions for family enterprising.

5. Plot a family's resource and capabilities on the "familiness f+ and f– assessment continuum" and understand their advantages and constraints.

FAMILIES, ENTREPRENEURSHIP, AND THE TIMMONS MODEL

The tension among generations in families can often revolve around the aggressive younger executives seeking to explore new and exciting deals and the older executive who seeks to march forward on the pathway that created the family's fortune. The purpose of this chapter is to help families (and those working with families!) understand that opportunity recognition and balance in the Timmons Model help guide the family's decision-making process. By encouraging the discussion toward the model, we ask, "What is the richest opportunity?" and "Are the opportunity, team, and resources well balanced?" Families have special knowledge, experience, and often resources that bring competitive advantages. We aspire to leverage these special factors to create a "familiness" advantage that creates value. But there also exist pitfalls with which enterprising families need to be aware. As Lloyd Steier of the University of Alberta, James Chrisman of Mississippi State University, and Jess Chua of the University of Calgary indicate, "family based approaches to organizing enterprise might yield advantages or disadvantages."[3]

BUILDING ENTREPRENEURIAL FAMILY LEGACIES[4]

When we hear the phrase *family business*, images of high-flying, harvesting entrepreneurs are not usually the first thoughts that come to our mind. We more often think of the small mom-and-pop businesses, or the large business family fights that hold the potential for reality TV. It is fair to say that family businesses do not always look and act entrepreneurially. They can focus on serving local markets, sustaining the family's lifestyle, or providing jobs to family members. They are often conflicted due to family dynamics, constrained by nepotism, or limited by their conservative risk profile.

But these realities should be held in tension with the corresponding truth that families comprise the dominant form of business organization worldwide and provide more resources for the entrepreneurial economy than any other source.[5] We must be careful that we do not form mental caricatures about either family businesses or entrepreneurs that might keep us from exploring the link between entrepreneurship and family or, more important, keep us from understanding the significance the linkage holds for social and economic wealth creation in our communities and countries worldwide.

The purpose of this chapter is to deepen our understanding of entrepreneurship in the family context. We will explore the entrepreneurial commitments, capabilities, and contributions of families and their businesses. To describe families who leverage the entrepreneurial process in the family context we use the phrase *family enterprising*. As enterprise refers to economic activity, enterprising is the action of generating economic activity. Consistent with earlier definitions of entrepreneurship, families who are enterprising generate new economic activity and build long-term value across generations. We refer to this outcome as *transgenerational entrepreneurship and wealth creation* and it is how to build entrepreneurial family legacies. This chapter will provide families with three sets of assessment and strategy tools to assist them in knowing how to become enterprising and build their family legacy.

Large Company Family Legacies

We must first begin by understanding the economic and entrepreneurial significance of families. It is difficult to walk into a Marriot Hotel, see the father and son picture of J. Willard Marriott Jr. and Sr., and not think about entrepreneurial family legacies. From a small root beer concession stand, who would have expected the emergence of a $13.3-billion and 151,000-employee company? The Marriotts are now operating in their third generation of family leadership and are just one example of the many companies and branded products that are synonymous with family names and legacies.

John Molson founded his brewery in Montreal in 1786. In speaking with employees in 1825, he asserted "We are all members of a larger community which depends on everyone playing a part." In 2004 the Molson family united with the Coors family of Colorado to form the Molson Coors Brewing Company, of which sixth generation, Eric Molson is chairman. Molson is presently North America's oldest beer brand, in Canada it employs 3,000 and has $7 billion in sales. Seventh generation members of the Coors family are engaged in the business including Eric's sons Geoff, a VP and Andrew on the board of Molson Coors Brewing Company.[6]

Robert MacPherson founded Northern Metals and Engineering in 1936. The company became BC Bearing Engineers Ltd. in 1944. Robert died in an airplane crash in 1950 and his wife Wendy took over as president. In 1988, Robby MacPherson was appointed president/COO and Wendy became chairman/CEO, Scott MacPherson continues to play a role in the company. Widowed three times, mother, grandmother, and great grandmother, Wendy has guided the BC Bearing Group for over 50 years to its present global status.[7]

While it is often assumed that family companies cannot play in the technology and telecommunications arena, the Rogers family have shown otherwise and grown one of Canada's largest communications companies with revenues over $10 billion and nearly 30,000 employees.

Many of the popular branded product companies are controlled by families including Tyson Foods, an Arkansas-based $26-billion company in which the family controls 80 percent and the grandson of the founder is the current chairman. Wal-Mart, of course is probably the best-known family firm from Arkansas. Mars, the makers of M&M's, is still 100-percent family owned and the $30-billion company has multiple generations of family members at all levels of top leadership. Cosmetic, fragrance, and skin care products company Estee Lauder generates nearly $7 billion in revenues with the founding family controlling approximately 88 percent of its voting shares with six members in top management bearing the Lauder name. Wrigley's gum, a $6-billion company currently run by the founder's great-grandson, William Wrigley Jr. II, far outperforms its rivals with a 20-percent return on assets. Smucker's Jam—"With a name like Smucker's, it has to be good"—has sales of over $2.2 billion with brothers Tim and Richard continuing to grow the 113-year-old company.

Another interesting category of entrepreneurial family involvement is the investment-holding company. Warren Buffet may be one of the most famous examples. Buffet's company, Berkshire Hathaway, owns many recognizable companies such as GEICO Insurance, Fruit of the Loom, and Dairy Queen. For over 45 years, Buffet's investments in companies have provided an average annual return of 22 percent and have increased the value of Berkshire by over 195,000 percent since 1965. His 38-percent stake in Berkshire Hathaway makes him one of the richest people in the world. Warren's son, Howard G. Buffet, is a director at several Berkshire subsidiaries and currently sits on the board at Berkshire. While succession planning at Berkshire is highly secretive, it is anticipated that Howard Buffet will take over as chairman of the board.

In keeping with this picture of family legacy contributions, a recent survey showed that 35 percent of Fortune 500 companies are controlled and or managed by families. These family-influenced companies consistently outperform non-family businesses on annual shareholder return, return on assets, and both annual revenue and income growth.[8] A study of firms listed on the TSX and included in the S&P/TSX composite index reveals that Canadian family firms "carry more long-term debt than non-family firms."[9] Anthony Markin of Simon Fraser University finds that "stock return volatility is substantially lower for family firms. . . It appears that the family firms long-term perspective translates into a more efficient utilization of the firm's assets." But these large family companies only begin to tell the story of the entrepreneurial and economic contribution made by business families. (See Exhibit 14.1.)

EXHIBIT 14.1   Canada's Family Firms

▶ Employ 4.7 million full-time and 1.3 million part-time
▶ Total annual sales of $1.3 trillion
▶ 27% of family business leaders will retire within 5 years, another 29% will retire in 6 to 10 years
▶ 44% of family firms have an exit strategy, 29% have a succession plan
▶ 3 out of 10 family firms make it to the second generation
▶ 1 out of 10 family firms make it to the third generation

Samuel, Son & Co.: A Growth-Oriented Family Enterprise

Samuel, Son & Co. Limited began in 1855 as "M & L Samuel" by Lewis and Mark Samuel in the metal and hardware business with operations in Toronto and Liverpool, England. In the late 1880s Lewis Samuel's son Sigmund became president and did away with "shelf" hardware and focused on metals and heavy hardware. In 1931, when a non-family partner retired, Sigmund took over that individual's sizeable stake in the company and became a sole proprietor. In 1962 a grandson of Sigmund, Ernest Samuel, became president. Ernest died in 2000, having opened and acquired facilities throughout Canada and the U.S. Having been at the helm for 38 years, Ernest left a strong legacy. Samuel, Son & Co. had become one of the top 10 processors and distributors of metals in North America, "We have a history we can be proud of and a strong future to look forward to."[10]

Smaller and Mid-Size Family Legacies

In many regards, the real heart and often-overlooked segment of the Canadian economy and entrepreneurial activity is the smaller and mid-size companies. This segment is substantively controlled by families, and they are not all your typical "mom and pop" operations.

Vector Construction Group began in 1965 in the earthworks business, building roads. "After several years of highway grading, dam building, site development, and other heavy construction projects, the opportunity came to take on a significant concrete repair project on a hydro-electric facility for Manitoba Hydro. This start in concrete rehabilitation soon led to new opportunities to provide the latest concrete restoration and protection technologies to a broad range of clients." From their home base in Winnipeg, they expanded to Saskatchewan and Sarnia, Ontario. Later they opened branches in Alberta and Fargo, North Dakota. They expanded further to Thunder Bay and Stoney Creek, Ontario, and in the United States to Nebraska, Iowa, Florida, Illinois, and Colorado. Vector Construction Group has been known for its advanced technologies and for itself advancing the technology frontier in its field. In early 2009 it acquired the electrochemical products business to prevent and treat concrete corrosion from a global leader in the field.

Richard Stewart Sr. arrived in the Okanagan Valley in 1908 from Ireland. Having worked in the greenhouses of Lord Guinness in Ireland, with his brother Bill he started Stewart Brothers' Nurseries. "Inspired by Richard, his son Dick ventured out on his own in 1956 and purchased the site on the slopes of Mt. Boucherie, Kelowna, which is now the home of Quails' Gate Winery. As Dick neared retirement, he called on his eldest son Ben to come home to the family farm."[11] They then transformed the family farm from its diverse crops to high-density premium vinifera and became wine producers. Ben, with his siblings Tony, Cynthia, and Andrea have pursued the creation of wonderful wines. And this pursuit has meant looking outside the family to recruit those with expertise in winemaking.

Many family companies may not have brand names consumers recognize, but they are dominant in their industries because of the important part they play in the supply chains of large multinationals. They may make ingredients or inputs for other known wares or may produce goods in their entirety under another's moniker—take Magna for example. The list of these "everyday" family entrepreneurs is endless. They may be a regional or a national distributor behind the scenes, or an unnamed printer.

In this montage of families we have not even mentioned the nascent entrepreneurs and smaller companies that will become the next-generation Marriot, Reitman, Smucker, or Bronfman family company. Nor have we considered the children in existing family firms who will become nascent entrepreneurs. In a recent undergraduate class on family entrepreneurship, more than 80 percent of the students said that they wanted to start *their own company* as an extension of their family business. They were not just looking to run their family company. Students like Toby Donath created a business plan to move his mother's business, Backerhaus Veit, from manufacturing and wholesaling to retailing and branded products. Brothers Colby and Drew West started auctionPAL with their parents as "support investors" based on ideas developed by Drew. Student Jonathan Gelpey had a plan to commercialize a product for which his grandfather holds the patent. All of these young entrepreneurs fulfill our vision for next-generation entrepreneurship and family enterprising.

The Family Contribution and Roles

It is clear from our descriptions of family companies that families still dominate the Canadian economy and even more fully the economies of other countries worldwide.

The most recent economic impact study in Canada reported that family businesses contribute more than 45 percent of Canada's GDP and paycheques for about half of working Canadians.[12] Family-controlled businesses in Canada create nearly 70 percent of new jobs, one-quarter of the top 50 Canadian companies (by market capitalization) are controlled by family, and the top six families generate $100 billion in annual revenues.[13] Worldwide, the economic numbers are similar to those in countries like Italy, reporting 93 percent of their businesses are family controlled, and Brazil, 90 percent.[14] (See Exhibit 14.2.)

Once we acknowledge the economic relevance of families we can better understand the significant pool of resources and potential they represent for entrepreneurial activity. There was a day when "business" meant "family" because the family was understood to be foundational to all socioeconomic progress.[15] Today, however, we must more intentionally categorize the roles families play economically and entrepreneurially. Exhibit 14.3 presents five different roles families can play in the entrepreneurial process and distinguishes between a formal and informal application of these roles.

In this regard the categories are both descriptive and prescriptive. They describe what role families play and how they play them, but also hint at a prescription for a more formal approach to entrepreneurship in the family context. By "formal" we mean establishing individual and organizational disciplines and structure of the entrepreneurial process. We do not mean "bureaucratic." Many family entrepreneurs, particularly senior generation entrepreneurs, embrace the myth that any formalization will constrain their entrepreneurial behaviour. Nothing could be further from the truth. With informed intuition, disciplined processes, clear financial benchmarks, and organizational accountability, family teams can generate higher potential ventures and get the odds in their favour for transgenerational entrepreneurship and wealth creation.

The first and dominant role families play is what we call *family-influenced start-ups*. Data from the Global Entrepreneurship Monitor indicate that worldwide there are about 25 million "new family firms" started every year.[16] Because families are driven by social forces of survival, wealth creation, and progeny, it is natural that start-up businesses think family first. Family-influenced start-ups are new businesses where the family ownership vision and/or leadership influence impacts the strategic intent, decision-making, and financial goals of the company. They may have family involvement in the beginning, intend to have family involvement, or end up having family involvement during the formative stages

---

EXHIBIT 14.2   Worldwide Highlights of Family Businesses

Country	Definition	% of FBs	GNP
Brazil	Middle	90%	63%
Chile	Broad	75%	50–70%
USA	Broad	96%	40%
Belgium	Narrow	70%	55%
Finland	Narrow	80%	40–45%
France	Broad	>60%	>60%
Germany	Middle	60%	55%
Italy	Broad	93%	
Netherlands	Narrow	74%	54%
Poland	Broad	Up to 80%	35%
Portugal	Broad	70%	60%
Spain	Narrow	79%	
UK	Middle	70%	
Australia	Narrow	75%	50%
India	Broad		65%

EXHIBIT 14.3 Roles Families Play in the Entrepreneurial Process

	Family-Influenced Start-ups	Family Corporate Venturing	Family Corporate Renewal	Family Private Cash	Family Investment Funds
Formal	An entrepreneur with no legacy assets/existing business, but who formally launches a new business with family and/or intending to involve family	Family holding companies or businesses that have formal new venture creation and/or acquisition strategies, plans, departments, or capabilities	Family-controlled companies with a formal strategic growth plan for creating new streams of value through change in business strategy, model, or structure	Start-up money from family member or business with a formal written agreement for market-base ROI and or repayment	Stand-alone professional private equity or venture capital fund controlled by family and/or using family generated capital
Informal	An entrepreneur with no legacy assets/existing business who happens to start a new business out of necessity and it begins to involve family members	Family holding companies or businesses that grow through more informal, intuitive, and opportunistic business start-up and acquisitions	Intuitive growth initiatives that result in a change in business strategy, model, or structure and new streams of value for the family company	Start-up money or gift from family member or business with no agreement or conversation about ROI or repayment	Internal capital and/or funds used by family owners to invest in real estate, passive partnerships, or seed new businesses

of the company. Some families begin their collective entrepreneurship experience with a more formal vision and planning process that delineates how the family will capture a new opportunity. This approach often clarifies the role family members will play in the start-up and puts them on a faster path for successfully meeting their family and financial goals.

The *family corporate venturing category* is when an existing family company or group starts new businesses. Families are often, and quite naturally, portfolio entrepreneurs who build numerous businesses under a family umbrella. While they may not always grow each of the businesses to their fullest potential, the new businesses are often synergistic, create jobs for a community, and grow the net worth of the family. Often they are started so that family members have their own business to run. The more formal approach to family corporate venturing makes the new business process part of an overall strategic plan for growing family wealth while leveraging the resources and capabilities of family members.

Family corporate renewal is where the family's entrepreneurial activity is focused on creating new streams of value within the business or group through innovation and transformational change activities. Companies that launch new products or services, enter new markets, or establish new business models are renewing their strategies for the future. This type of strategic or structural renewal is particularly prevalent during family generational transitions or when a family realizes their legacy business can no longer compete. A more formal approach to corporate renewal is proactive, continuous, and institutionalized versus waiting for transitions or competitive triggers to start the renewal processes.

One of the primary roles families play is to provide *family private cash* to family members who want to start a business. More than 63 percent of businesses in the planning stage and up to 85 percent of existing new ventures used family funding. Between 30 and 80 percent of all informal (non-venture capital) funding comes from family. In Canada this amounts to nearly .25 percent of GDP and as high as 3 percent of GDP in South Korea.[17] Most often the family cash is given based upon altruistic family sentiments rather than having more formal investment criteria. While providing seed capital whether it is formal or informal is clearly a significant role in the entrepreneurial process, having some formal investment criteria can avoid future confusion or conflict among family members. It also creates more discipline and accountability for family entrepreneurs, which is a good thing. (See Exhibit 14.4.)

Family investment funds are pools of family capital that families use for entrepreneurial activities. These family funds, both formal and informal, are becoming increasingly more common as families find themselves flush with cash. Most often, the formal family investment funds are created after a family has liquidated all or part of their family group. These

EXHIBIT 14.4   Distribution of Businesses with Family Venture Backing

	Planning Stage Start-ups	New Firms	Established Firms
Number of Cases	1,425	1,594	3,743
Family-Sponsored Ventures	63%	76%	85%

Source: Joseph H. Astrachan, Shaker A. Zahra, and Pramodita Sharma, "Family-Sponsored Ventures" First Annual Global Entrepreneurship Symposium, United Nations, April 29, 2003.

funds are generally formed in conjunction with a family office. Informal family investment funds are pools of money, generally from cash flows, that family leaders invest in entrepreneurial activities as a way to diversify their family portfolios and/or have fun. They often invest within their network of peers and the investments are usually non-operating investments in businesses or real estate deals. These investments are often significant portions of their total wealth.

When we catalogue the wide range of informal and formal roles families can play in the entrepreneurial process, we see the contribution they are capable of making to the entrepreneurial economy. We believe business families who are interested in transgenerational entrepreneurship and wealth creation must cultivate the more formal approach to entrepreneurship. The remainder of this chapter assists families in formalizing their entrepreneurship roles. We present three strategy frames that are based on the Timmons Model introduced in Chapter 2. The frames focus on the controllable components of the entrepreneurial processes that can be assessed, influenced, and altered.

FRAME ONE: THE MIND-SET AND METHOD FOR FAMILY ENTERPRISING

Families who are enterprising are a particular type of family and *not* just a family who is in business. Enterprising families understand that today's dynamic and hypercompetitive marketplace requires families to act entrepreneurially. That is, they must generate new economic activity if they intend to survive and prosper over long periods of time. The Timmons Model shows us that at the heart of the entrepreneurial process is the opportunity. Those families who intend to act entrepreneurially must be opportunity focused. Consistent with this focus, enterprising is seen as the decision that leaders and organizations make to investigate opportunity and seek growth "when expansion is neither pressing nor particularly obvious."[18] The enterprising decision to search for opportunity precedes the economic decision to capture the opportunity. It is when families are faced with a decision (knowingly or unknowingly) to continue along their existing path, versus to expend effort and commit resources to investigate whether there are higher potential opportunities that are not yet obvious, that the "spirit of enterprising" is evidenced. We thus define family enterprising as the proactive and continuous search for opportunistic growth.

12 Challenges To Family Enterprising

Like the gravitational pull that keeps us bound to the earth, families face a number of inherent challenges that may keep them bound to past strategies rather than pursuing new opportunities.

1. Families assume that their past success will guarantee their future success.
2. Family members attribute "legacy value" to their businesses or assets, but that value does not translate into a market value or advantage.
3. Families want a "legacy pass" in the market—"We are 50 years old and we deserve another 50 years since we have been such good citizens."

4. Leaders try to balance the risk profile (risk and reward expectations) of their shareholders with the risk and investment demands of the marketplace.

5. Senior and successor generations have different risk profiles and goals for how the business should grow in the future.

6. Families find it hard to pass the entrepreneurial commitments and capabilities from the senior generation to a less "hungry" successor generation.

7. Families build their first-generation businesses on the founder's intuition, but the business never establishes more intentional entrepreneurial processes to keep the entrepreneurial contributions alive.

8. Families will not use many of the financial strategies that entrepreneurs use to grow businesses—i.e., debt, equity capital, strategic alliances, and partnerships.

9. Families do not "shed" unproductive assets and underperforming businesses to reallocate resources to more productive places.

10. Successor generation family members feel entitled to get a business rather than seek next-generation entrepreneurial opportunity.

11. Senior leaders communicate to the next generation that business planning and entrepreneurial analysis is a waste of time.

12. Family members are given a business to run as part of their legacy and that is viewed as entrepreneurship in the family.

Enterprising families institutionalize the opportunity seeking processes in the mindset and methods of both their family ownership group and their business organizations. Those families who simply try to maintain their local advantage, safeguard their brands, assets, and customers, or hone their operational efficiencies put themselves at a competitive risk in the shorter run. In the longer run, if their strategic planning is mainly focused on how to pass their business from one generation to the next, rather than developing people and strategies for creating new streams of value, their future may be limited. We would certainly not describe these types of families as enterprising or assume that they are transgenerational.

Enterprising Mind-set and Methods

The first assessment and strategy frame for family enterprising is the Mind-set and Methods Model (Exhibit 14.5). The model shows that family enterprising is the combination of a financial ownership mind-set and entrepreneurial strategic methods. The purpose of the model is to ensure that families talk about both the ownership *and* management requirements for carrying out the entrepreneurial process in their family and business. The mind-set and methods assessment instruments[19] for this chapter (see end of chapter exercises) will enable families to determine their level of congruence on the two dimensions. It will also allow them to have a strategic conversation about where they currently are and how they might need to change in order to become more enterprising.

What Enterprising Is Not

It is often useful in defining a concept to understand *what it is not*. Renowned economist, Edith Penrose takes this approach by contrasting the concept of enterprising with three categories of firms that are not necessarily enterprising.[20]

"Just grew firms"—The "just grew" category are those that were in the right place at the right time. They were on the wave of an expanding market and they had to expand to keep up with demand. The decision to grow was automatic, and because they were able to capitalize on the circumstances, they grew. The situation may continue for a long period of time, but because markets do not

EXHIBIT 14.5   Mind-set and Methods Enterprising Model

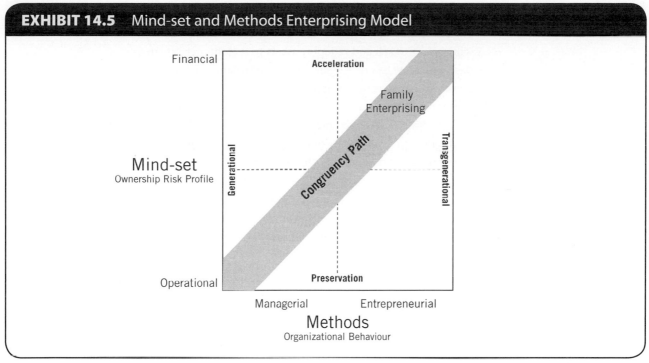

Source: © Habbershon and Pistrui.

expand indefinitely and competitors fill the opportunity gap, firm growth and the firm will come to an end.

"Comfort firms"—This category is often referred to as lifestyle firms. There are firms who refrain from taking full advantage of opportunities for expansion because it would increase their effort and risk. Firms that are comfortable with their income and position have no incentive to grow beyond their acceptable level of profits. These are firms where the goals of the owners to be comfortable are closely aligned with the goals of the firm. Like "just grew firms," comfort firms may continue for decades, but in the end meeting the comfort needs of the owners is not a driver for advantage or renewal.

"Competently managed firms"—Many firms are competently managed and consequently are able to find normal returns for relatively long periods of time by maintaining their operational efficiencies. Competently managed firms are often striving to sustain the entrepreneurial efforts of a founder. They may be competing in more traditional, less dynamic circumstances, have a distinctive market niche, or maintain a regional advantage as a favoured business. While these are exploitable strategies, they are not inherently sustainable and may quickly disappear.

The mind-set continuum is primarily a measure of the financial risk profile of the family owners-shareholders. In general, it reflects the financial premise that entrepreneurial leaders gain strategic advantage and find above normal rents by deploying their resources to points of highest return and by developing strategies that exploit new opportunity. Family leaders who have an operational mind-set predominately focus on management strategies, operational efficiencies, and the perpetuity of a particular business. A financial mind-set moves beyond the operational focus to an investor focus with a view toward the overall capital strategy of the family, creating new streams of value and finding a return on the totality of their assets. While the operational mind-set is a requirement for running an efficient business, the financial focus is a requirement for transgenerational entrepreneurship and wealth creation.

The financial mind-set for enterprising includes the following characteristics[21]

- A proclivity for higher risk and above normal returns.
- A willingness to sell and redeploy assets to seek higher returns.
- A desire to grow by creating new revenue streams with higher returns.
- A commitment to generating next-generation entrepreneurship.
- A willingness to continuously revisit the existing business model.
- An assumption that a percentage of the business will become obsolete.
- A willingness to leverage the business to grow and find higher returns.
- A desire to reinvest versus distribute capital.
- A willingness to enter into partnerships and alliances to grow.
- A strategy to manage the family's wealth for a total return.
- A commitment to innovation in business strategies and structures.
- A belief that bold, wide-ranging acts are necessary to achieve investment objectives in today's environment.

The *methods continuum* is a measure of the entrepreneurial orientation and actions in the business organizations. It assumes that enterprising organizations are taking bold, innovative market leading actions in order to seek a competitive advantage and generate new streams of value. It also reflects the premise that to be enterprising (proactively and continuously seeking new opportunities for growth) organizations must have a collection of individuals who act like an entrepreneur and not just a single leader or small group of family leaders. A single leader acting entrepreneurially might generate entrepreneurial actions in the business during their generation, but it will not create a transgenerational family business or group. Enterprising organizations move beyond managerial methods that focus on maintaining the existing and implementing incremental change. They are seeking and creating "the new" and establishing entrepreneurial renewal processes. While entrepreneurial methods do not replace the need for managerial actions, managerial actions are not sufficient conditions for enterprising and transgenerational wealth creation.

The entrepreneurial methods for enterprising include the following characteristics:[22]

- Allocating disproportionate resources to new business opportunities.
- Systematically searching for and capturing new investment opportunities.
- Seeking new opportunities beyond the core (legacy) business.
- Creating a core competency in innovation at the business unit level.
- Making significant change in products, services, markets, and customers.
- Initiating competitive change to lead our market.
- Investing early to develop or adopt new technology and processes.
- Typically adopting an "undo the competitor" posture in our markets.
- Having institutionalized the entrepreneurial process in the organization.
- Having formal routines for gathering and disseminating market intelligence.
- Having people at every level in the organization "think like competitors."
- Typically adopting a bold, aggressive posture in order to maximize the probability of exploiting potential investment opportunities.

Creating the Dialogue for Congruence

The Mind-set and Methods Model helps families fulfill key process conditions for family enterprising and transgenerational wealth creation:

Creating a healthy *dialogue* in the family ownership group and organization around the mind-set and methods issues.

Establishing *congruence* between the mind-set of the owner-shareholder group and the methods of the business organization(s).

One of the major differences between family enterprising and entrepreneurship as it is normally envisioned is that by definition the team includes the family. Family entrepreneurs are either currently working with family members or planning to work with family members; they are either multigenerational teams or hope to be a multigenerational team; they either have multiple family member shareholders and stakeholders or will have them as they go through time. This inherent familial condition requires families to cultivate effective communication skills to build relationship capital for family enterprising. Families know that it takes financial capital for entrepreneurial activity, but they do not always know that it also requires relationship capital. Relationship capital allows families to have healthy dialogue and find congruence around the mind-set and methods for enterprising.[23]

Sabine Veit, founder of Backerhaus Veit in Toronto, realized the importance of dialogue and congruence when her son came home from university toting a business plan for aggressive growth. She had built her artisan bread manufacturing company into a $24-million force in the industry. When her son Toby won a business planning competition she was definitely proud, but she also knew she was in trouble. The plan was to grow *her* business. Sabine loved the thought of working with Toby and he definitely shared her passion for artisan breads. In fact, during university Toby took every class with the artisan bread industry in mind. How could a parent hope for anything more?

But Toby didn't want to just run her company someday. He wanted to move the business beyond manufacturing and wholesaling into branded products and retailing, and he wanted to do it now. On the Mind-set and Methods Model (Exhibit 14.6), Backerhaus Veit was on the congruency path as an operationally focused, managerially sound business. Sabine had a self-defined lifestyle firm that was competitive in her niche with a clear harvest strategy. But Toby was committed to family enterprising and wanted to be a growth firm. This meant moving beyond their current niche and lifestyle expectations. Clearly Toby had a mind-set for much higher risk than Sabine.

On the methods continuum, Backerhaus Veit did not have the entrepreneurial methods to exploit Toby's plan. Sabine individually had the capabilities and Toby believed he did, but the entrepreneurial team and organization would have to be built. There was clearly significant incongruence as a family and business. The challenge for Sabine and Toby was to establish a plan and process for aligning their mind-set and methods if they want to capture the new opportunity and become an enterprising family.

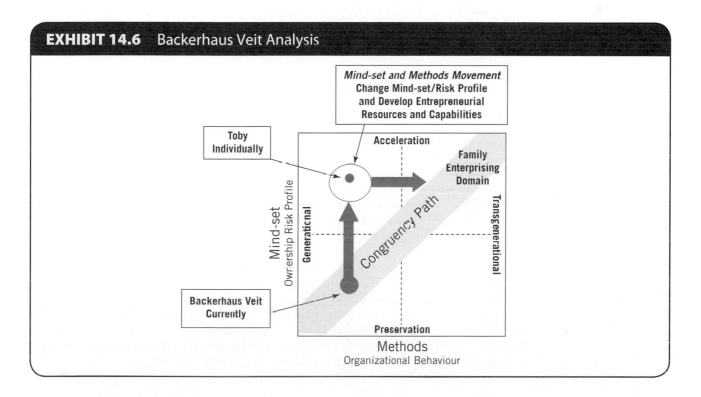

EXHIBIT 14.6   Backerhaus Veit Analysis

Successful Next Generation Entrepreneurship

The challenge for multigenerational family teams like Toby and Sabine is to "keep it in dialogue" rather than letting it turn into a debate or disconnect. Debates become personal and disconnects cut off opportunity. When family members turn the situation into right and wrong, good and bad, winning or losing, there is very little listening, give-and-take, or changing one's position. In contrast, the word dialogue actually means "talking through" an issue. It assumes the ability to challenge each other's assumptions, to keep an open mind, and to test different options. It looks at the big picture, considers the long-term perspective, and discusses the process for getting there. Most important, dialogue does not follow hierarchical roles like parent-child, boss-employee, or the one who owns the business versus the one who does not. The goal of dialogue is to find solutions that are not constrained by the boundaries of either of the original positions.

There are a number of things Toby and Sabine need to do in order to ensure they are an enterprising family. First, they need to develop communication skills to have an effective dialogue. Most families assume they are able to carry on a dialogue simply because they are a family. In actuality the familiarity of a family can make it very difficult to challenge assumptions and talk about differing views. Often families need a facilitator to help them develop communication skill and have a dialogue.

Second, they needed to make sure their views of the future were the same. Families often have a vague notion of "working together" and they assume that they will figure the details out over time. This is a clear formula for future discontent and conflict. In reality, Toby and Sabine had very different visions for their futures. Sabine's vision was to enjoy her passion for breads while balancing growth with her lifestyle interests. Toby's vision was to exploit his passion for breads by building new businesses on the family's reputation and skills.

Third, Toby and Sabine had very different risk profiles. What Sabine was willing to risk for future returns was very different from what Toby was willing to risk and the returns he desired. It is not surprising that the successor generation is willing to risk more than the senior generation. The key is to keep talking until you understand each other's perspective. Once you understand each other you can create a business model and structures that accommodate the risk profiles of both generations. Locking into one generational perspective or the other undermines the collective strengths of a multigenerational team.

Fourth, remember that timing is everything. Usually for the successors the time is now and for the seniors the time is *someday*. Chances are that both generations will end up out of their comfort zones a little. Toby and Sabine realized that timing was really a strategy question of how they would proceed, not just if or when they would proceed.

Fifth, get creative. You can be sure that the final outcome will not look exactly like either of you envisioned. Through dialogue it became clear to Toby and Sabine that the range of options was fairly extensive. We often tell family members to "remember their algebra" when it comes to dialogue. Just because "a equals b" it doesn't mean that "a" might not equal "c, d, or even e, f, and g." The point is that once you start a true dialogue, you may find many more options than you originally envisioned.

Even among entrepreneurs with no family directly involved with their venture, family concerns persist—just as they do for any individual in the workforce. Such work-family conflicts may hit entrepreneurs harder than those who are simply employees.[24] Jennifer Jennings and Megan McDougald both of the University of Alberta suggest "greater work-family conflict is likely to be experienced by female entrepreneurs" and that "growth facilitating" strategies will be more likely with lower levels of work family conflict.[25] The Canadian Association of Family Enterprise regularly features discussions on work/life, multigenerational issues for Canadian family-owned firms.[26]

FRAME TWO: THE SIX DIMENSIONS FOR FAMILY ENTERPRISING

The second assessment and strategy frame for family enterprising addresses the team component of the Timmons Model. In family enterprising "team" is a much broader and complex concept. It encompasses the family ownership group and the family and non-family entrepreneurial capabilities. The entrepreneurial process cannot occur unless there is alignment in the team's ownership mind-set and entrepreneurial methods as described above. When the entrepreneurial leader is a family member there is potentially another layer of team complexity around issues such as parent-child relationships, altruistic versus entrepreneurial decision-making, nepotism and competency, family versus personal equity and compensation, and success measures. In essence, the family as team can create more perfect balance in the Timmons Model or can cause imbalance. One key is to stay focused on the opportunity and stress that the team is in support of exploiting that opportunity.

The six dimensions for family enterprising provide family teams with six areas that they can address to assist them in aligning their mind-set and methods and moving up the congruency path toward the enterprising domain. The six dimensions and the corresponding strategic questions apply key entrepreneurial considerations to the family context. As family owners and leaders answer the questions they are creating unity within the team for entrepreneurial action. The six dimensions are as follows:

- ✓ Leadership
- ✓ Relationship
- ✓ Vision
- ✓ Strategy
- ✓ Governance
- ✓ Performance

There is an internal logic and order to the six dimensions. We begin with the *leadership dimension* because leaders are the catalyst for organizational behaviour and have the responsibility for creating the team. Leaders also set the tone for the relationship commitments and culture in the family and organization. The *relationship dimension* is often overlooked, but it is the foundation for organizational effectiveness and health, especially in family teams and enterprising. The *strategy dimensions* flow out of the leadership and relationship dimensions. At the end of the day, strategy and planning are simply extended organizational conversations. Organizational strategy is only as effective as the leadership and relationships in the family and organization. Governance structures and policies simply enable organizations to carry out their strategies. The *governance dimension* must, therefore, follow both ownership and business strategy formulation. In an interesting way, the *performance dimension* is the last dimension because it is an organizational outcome, but it is also feedback that leaders use to frame their leadership actions.

Leadership Dimension—Does Your Leadership Create a Sense of Shared Urgency for Enterprising and Transgenerational Wealth Creation?

Entrepreneurial leaders create a sense of shared urgency in the organization. The goal is to have everyone, from the owners to those carrying out tasks, thinking and acting like competitors.[27] Families are traditionally and systemically hierarchical in nature—parent-child, older-younger siblings, male-female—and their family organizations often embody these hierarchies in their leadership models. A transgenerational commitment requires families to move beyond the "great leader" model to the "great group."[28] Family leaders who strive to turn their families into a team based upon the great group philosophy overcome many of the negative caricatures often associated with family business leadership and empower the family and organization to be enterprising.

Leadership Dimension Diagnostic Questions

- Do family leaders understand the requirements to be transgenerational?
- Do they develop next-generation leadership?
- Do they move the family beyond the "great leader" model?
- Do they promote a sense of openness and mutuality?
- Do they encourage participation by family members at all levels in the family and organization?
- Do they lead others to think and act like entrepreneurs?
- Do they help the family grow beyond a hierarchical model of leadership to become the "great group"?

Relationship Dimension—Does Your Family Have the Relationship Capital to Sustain Their Transgenerational Commitments?

Effective teams are built upon healthy relationships. We describe healthy relationships as those that build relationship capital and allow efficient interpersonal interactions in the team. Relationship capital is the reserve of attributes such as trust, loyalty, positive feelings, benefit of the doubt, goodwill, forgiveness, commitment, and altruistic motives. Relationship capital is a necessary condition for long-lasting teams and transgenerational families. Now here are two opposite but simultaneously true statements: Families have the natural potential to build relationship capital better than other social groups *and* families have the natural potential to destroy relationship capital more ruthlessly than any other social group. Is this good news or bad news for family enterprising? It depends. Those families who intentionally gain the skills and strive to build relationship capital leverage the natural advantage of family teams. But those families who assume they will always have relationship capital or take their relationships for granted open themselves up to potentially destructive tendencies of families. Families who have relationship capital reserves are more likely to create the dialogue that moves them up the congruence path to the family enterprising domain.

Relationship Dimension Diagnostic Questions

- Is your family intentionally building relationship capital?
- Are you investing in the communication and relationship building skills you need to build relationship capital?
- Are there healthy relationships between family siblings, branches, and across generations?
- Does your family have formal family meetings to discuss family ownership and relationship issues?
- Do you experience synergy in your family relationships?
- Do you have a positive vision for working together as a family?
- Do family members see relationship health as part of their competitive advantage?

Vision Dimension—Does Your Family Have a Compelling Multigenerational Vision That Energizes People at Every Level?

A compelling vision is what creates the shared urgency for family enterprising and mobilizes people to carry out the vision. By compelling we mean that it "makes sense" to people in light of tomorrow's marketplace realities. Often a vision might make sense for the moment, but it does not make sense for the future. For enterprising families, the vision must describe how the family will collectively create new streams of wealth that allow them to be transgenerational. It also has to be multigenerational. It is easy for the different generations to craft their personal visions for the future. Transgenerational families must craft a vision that is compelling to all generations and in a sense transcends generational perspectives. This multigenerational necessity also underscores the importance of establishing participatory leadership and building relationship capital.

Vision Dimension
Diagnostic Questions

- Does your family have a vision that makes sense of tomorrow's marketplace?
- Would all generations describe the vision as compelling?
- Was the vision developed by everyone in the family?
- Does the vision have relevance for your decision making and lives?
- Does your family regularly review and test the vision as an ownership group?
- Is the vision transgenerational?
- Is the vision larger than the personal interests of the family?
- Does the vision mobilize others to create new streams of value?
- Do all family members share in the rewards from the vision?

Strategy Dimension—Does Your Family Have an Intentional Strategy for Finding Their Competitive Advantage as a Family?

We have already said that there is a more intentional and formal application of the entrepreneurial process within the family context. Part of that formal approach is developing strategies for both cultivating and capturing new business opportunities. But for families it means much more. The family's strategic thinking and planning should be based on determining how to exploit their unique family-based resources and capabilities to find advantages in enterprising. While we will address this more specifically in the next section, it includes things like finding synergies with current assets, leveraging their networks of personal relationships, cultivating next-generation entrepreneurs, and extending the power of their family reputation. Because families tend to take their family-influenced resources and capabilities for granted they often fail to see the opportunities they represent for providing them with a long-term advantage for enterprising.

Strategy Dimension
Diagnostic Questions

- How does your family provide you with an advantage in entrepreneurial wealth creation?
- What resources and capabilities are unique to your family?
- Does your family have a formal planning process to direct their enterprising?
- Does your organization have formal systems for cultivating and capturing new opportunities?
- Does your family mentor next-generation family members to become entrepreneurs?
- Does your strategic thinking and planning empower your family to fulfil their trans-generational vision?
- What role does your family play in the strategy process?

Governance Dimension—Does Your Family Have Structures and Policies That Stimulate Change and Growth in the Family and Organization?

Few family leaders would consider that governance structures and policies could actually stimulate growth and change. Most would equate the word *governance* with bureaucracies and, at best, acknowledge that structures and policies are a necessary evil to be tolerated and minimized. But we offer two different perspectives. First the lack of effective governance structures and policies creates significant ambiguity in families and constrains enterprising. Second, when entrepreneurial processes are institutionalized through the governance structures and policies it promotes growth and change activities. For example, when ownership, equity, or value realization is unclear or un-discussable it dis-incentivizes family entrepreneurs. But when financial conversations are part of the professional culture and there are transparent ownership structures, family entrepreneurs are clear on the rules of the game. Governance structures are thus critical to transgenerational entrepreneurship and wealth creation. Danny Miller of HEC Montreal and the University of Alberta, Isabelle Le Breton-Miller of the University of Alberta, and Richard Lester of Texas A&M University find that family owners' ties to one another lead to entrenchment, resource extraction, and conservative strategies, whereas entrepreneur owners without family ties pursue growth priorities and invest more in the firm.[29]

Governance Dimension Diagnostic Questions

- Does your family view governance as a positive part of their family and business lives?
- Are your governance structures static or fluid?
- Do your structures and policies promote family unity?
- Do your governance structures and policies give an appropriate voice to family members?
- Do your governance structures and policies assist you in finding your family advantage?
- Do you have formal processes that institutionalize the entrepreneurial process in your family and businesses?
- Do your governance structures and policies promote next-generation involvement and entrepreneurship?

Performance Dimension—Does Your Performance Meet the Requirements for Transgenerational Entrepreneurship and Wealth Creation?

The performance dimension is where families clarify whether or not they are really committed to family enterprising. Families who are enterprising are market driven and seek to accelerate their wealth creation through their opportunistic entrepreneurial actions. They have clear financial benchmarks and information for assessing their performance against the market. Lifestyle firms often assume that they are performing well because they are sustaining their lifestyles. Enterprising also implies a process of matching the organization's core competencies with external opportunities in order to create new streams of value. Enterprising families do not rely on past performance as an indicator that they will perform well in the future, nor do they define success simply by the preservation of an asset. Their success measures are their ability to fulfill their transgenerational vision for social and economic wealth creation.

Performance Dimension Diagnostic Questions

- Does your family talk openly about financial performance issues or are finances secretive?
- Are you in lifestyle or enterprising mode?
- Are your performance and strategies driven by a clear market orientation?
- Do family owners agree on their risk and return expectations?
- Are performance expectations clear to next-generation entrepreneurs?
- Are there clear transparency and accountability structures in relation to meeting performance expectations?
- Is there family dialogue about performance expectations—growth, dividends, reinvestment, ROE?

FRAME THREE: THE FAMILINESS ADVANTAGE FOR FAMILY ENTERPRISING

All entrepreneurial success and the opportunity to capture above-average returns is premised upon finding an advantage over your competitors. Correspondingly, the potential for finding an advantage is rooted in the distinctive resources and capabilities that an organization possesses. The "resources" aspect of the Timmons Model is where enterprising can get exciting for families. Because every family is unique, they can generate very idiosyncratic bundles of resources and capabilities that can give them an advantage in the entrepreneurial process if they know how to identify and leverage them. We refer to this idiosyncratic bundle of resources and capabilities as their *familiness*.

The Family Systems Model in Exhibit 14.7 shows how the familiness bundle of resources and capabilities is generated. As the vision, history, and capabilities of the collective family interact with the goals, skills, and commitments of the individual family members, and they both in turn interact with the organizational history, culture, and resources of the business entities, it creates this familiness effect or the "f factor" of resources$_f$ and capabilities$_f$. If we think of the four resource categories in Chapter 13—people, financial, assets, and plan—we can explore how the systemic family influence impacts, changes, or somehow reconfigures

EXHIBIT 14.7   Familiness Systems Model

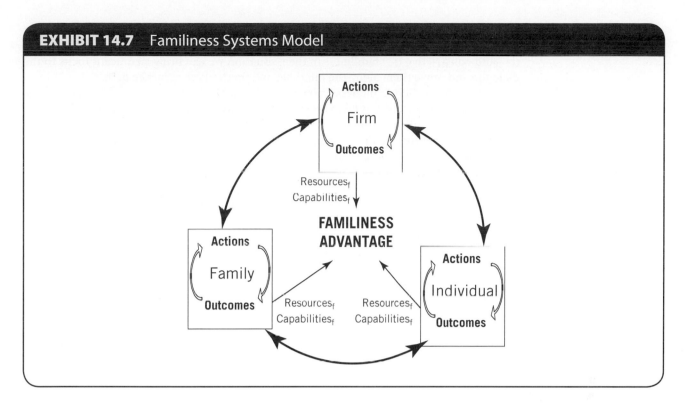

the properties of the resource. We identify familiness resources and capabilities with a subscript "f" such as capital$_f$, leadership$_f$, networking$_f$, knowledge$_f$, reputation$_f$.

The familiness assessment frame helps families become realists. What we mean is the assessment process leads families to realistically evaluate where their family influence might be positive and where it might be negative. One of the key insights from this model is the understanding that family cannot be characterized as either good or bad. Rather, family influence must be viewed as one of the inputs that entrepreneurs need to intentionally manage. As family leaders manage the actions and outcomes within the subsystems—family unit, individuals, and business entities—and between the subsystems, they are managing their bundle of resources$_f$ and capabilities$_f$.

When these familiness resources$_f$ and capabilities$_f$ lead to a competitive advantage for the family we refer to them as "distinctive familiness" or an "f+." When they constrain the competitive enterprising ability of the family we refer to them as "constrictive familiness" or "f−." Exhibit 14.8 allows families to place their resources and capabilities on an assessment continuum. The job of families who desire to be enterprising is to determine how to generate and exploit their distinctive familiness and to minimize or shed their constrictive familiness. When families begin assessing and planning based upon their distinctive and constrictive familiness, they move from an intuitive and informal to the intentional and formal mode of family enterprising.

EXHIBIT 14.8   f+ f− Familiness Advantage

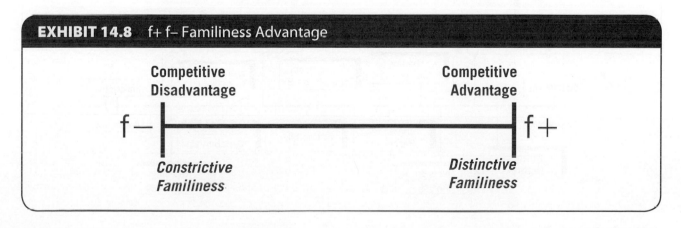

To better understand familiness let's return to the family enterprising decision that Toby and Sabine have to make in regard to Backerhaus Veit (BV). If we analyze the distinctive (f+) and constrictive (f−) familiness in their situation we can bring significant focus to the dialogue and move them along the mind-set and methods congruence path.

Exhibit 14.9 is their familiness resources and capabilities continuum as it relates to the new venture opportunity. When you see the f+ f− assessment it is a comprehensive and revealing picture of their individual and organizational contribution to the new venture. But it is not only the final picture that is useful to families. The conversation to identify the resources and capabilities and to determine where they should be placed is the real learning outcome.

First, there are clear resources and capabilities specifically associated with the senior and successor generations and others that are mixed. While Toby's successor drive is an f+ his business capabilities and lack of experience are an f−. Sabine readily admits that without Toby's drive she would never consider this opportunity. But Sabine's advisors are concerned that Toby may overestimate his capabilities and contribution. This discussion is very natural in next-generation entrepreneurship and families should "normalize" it and not allow it to become personal. Conversely, Sabine's senior capabilities, business networks, and reputation are an f+ for Toby's new venture. Toby readily admits that Sabine's role makes his business plan a much higher potential venture. On the other hand, Sabine's risk profile and lifestyle goals are a significant f− and constraint to enterprising. But we need to remember that they fit very well for her current strategy.

Second, there are resources and capabilities associated with BV, in many ways BV *is* Sabine. Toby's business plan calls for BV to provide valuable shared resources such as wholesale bread supply, bookkeeping, used equipment, repair services, and the like. This opportunity creates a very significant resource advantage that we would call "plan$_{f+}$" because only family members with existing businesses could incorporate these into their plan. The existing management team capabilities are also an f+, but because the existing team is not entrepreneurial (in fact, they see the new venture as a drain on the existing business), we have to give an f− to entrepreneurial team.

Third, there are certain resources that are associated with both Sabine and Toby. Most important is the f+ for tacit bread knowledge. They both know bread making, but the particularly interesting point is to see how advanced Toby is as a young person because he grew up in the bread industry. Correspondingly, the f− for retailing is significant. While Sabine grew up in the retail bread industry (her family has 70 retail bakeries in Germany), she does not know the casual dining bread industry (like Panera Bread Company) and this is the target for Toby's plan. While decision making is an f+, family communication is an f−. The family has great relationships, but in the business setting, they sometimes communicate like mother and son rather than business peers.

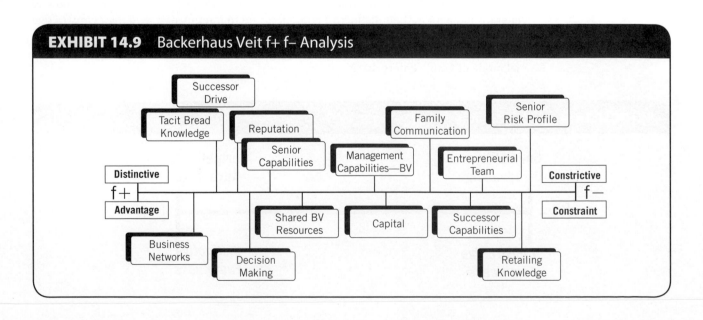

EXHIBIT 14.9   Backerhaus Veit f+ f− Analysis

The f+ to f– continuum makes Toby's and Sabine's "pre-launch" work very clear. Managing the f+ to f– continuum is how families build their resources and capabilities bundle as part of formalizing the entrepreneurial process. It is a critical step in getting the odds more in their favour. Toby and Sabine now need to create a work plan for each of the constraining resources in order to move them to a point of neutrality or advantage.

An additional realization from this analysis is to see the potential synergy between the successor and senior generations for family enterprising. Four things are immediately clear from the analysis. First, as we already noted, Sabine would never explore and/or capture this opportunity if it were not for Toby driving the process. Second, Toby does not have the synergistic familiness resources and capabilities if he tries to do the business on his own. Third, while there are positive reasons to do it together, there are also constraints that must be addressed. Fourth, family enterprising is when they decide to do it together as a family, rather than not doing it, or Toby doing it on his own. That is not to say that one way is right or wrong, but simply that doing it together is a family enterprising approach.

We will provide a final assessment of Sabine and Toby using the Timmons Model to discuss fit and balance. Clearly the opportunity for Backerhaus Veit to move into the retail fast-casual-eating market is very large and growing. In fact, the opportunity is probably greater than the current resources and capabilities of BV, Toby, and Sabine to meet them without outside resources. Currently, the weakest link in the model is the team. While Toby and Sabine have great bread knowledge, they do not have the entrepreneurial team for the retailing initiative. Further the BV leaders and advisors are strongly committed to managing their current assets, rather than launching an entrepreneurial business. Exhibit 14.10 shows that the model is "out of balance" and reaffirms the conclusions from our previous assessment that there is significant pre-launch work to be done to ensure a "fit." If they do this pre-launch work and can get the Timmons Model into balance, however, they have a great high potential venture for the family.

SUCCESSION

Familiness can be an advantage when it comes to succession as well. According to Grant Walsh, Director of KPMG Canada's Centre for Family Business, "History has proven that the influence of the family (active and non-active family members) on the business is too important not to make it one of, if not the major component of the succession process."[30]

Four generations have managed to keep Butler Byers Insurance Ltd. going for 100 years. The Byers family is at the helm of one of the largest family-owned insurance brokers in

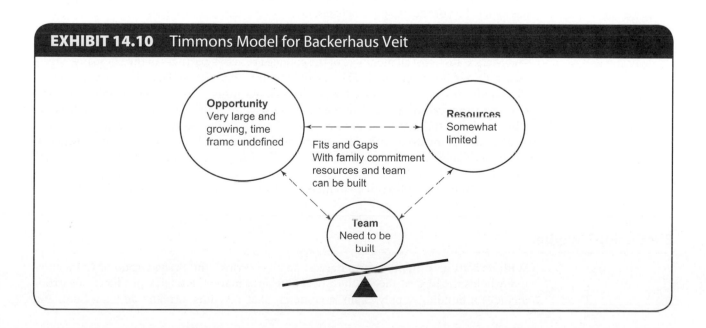

EXHIBIT 14.10   Timmons Model for Backerhaus Veit

Western Canada. Drew Byers, president, indicates that succession was "a very natural process that came about during a restructuring of the companies. . . buying out his father was a natural process with no real drama attached to it." It was Drew's desire to take over not a sense of obligation or duty that led him on a long path to president of the firm. The next handover is "way off," but they are already making certain that the groundwork is "laid early for that process." The Byers family has recently started a "family council to open the lines of communication that they know are vital to healthy business families."[31]

The third generation of Teppermans, Andrew and Noah, transitioned to take charge of the family's four furniture stores in Southwestern Ontario in 2006, becoming president and treasurer respectively. The brothers' parents Rochelle and Bill Tepperman still maintained important roles in the family business, respectively, chair and vice-chair of the board. The brothers knew the family story well and had an appreciation for their grandfather's hard work. In 1925, Nate Tepperman, a Russian immigrant began working as a door-to-door peddler; four years later he opened his first store.[32] With his wife, Bill took over the business in 1970 when his father drowned while swimming in the ocean. In 1992, the one year old store in Chatham, Ontario, burned to the ground, but this did not halt growth and the Teppermans continued to expand. In 1997, Andrew became general manager of the London, Ontario, store and in 2000 Noah became director of Human Resources, overseeing a staff of nearly 300 employees.[33]

The Wilson family has been in business in Nova Scotia for eight generations! Wilson Fuel's original incarnation was as a distributor of wood and coal for home heating. They moved to heating oil and then became a full service home heating company offering equipment sales and leasing, delivery of furnace oil, propane, and biofuel. Today they have nearly 300 retail gas stations throughout Atlantic Canada. Ian Wilson recounts how he got to where he is now:

> I did not see myself working in the family business when I was growing up. I did not grow up sweeping the floors at the business or with any regular involvement. I would occasionally visit the office with my father but never felt any pressure to become involved. I did not work at Wilson Fuel until after achieving a university degree and even then, it was a summer job to earn money for further education. Once I became involved with the business I did not really think about taking a leadership role. After seven years of work and at the age of thirty, I was thrust into the role when my father, the president of the company, died unexpectedly. I was the only family member who was active in a day to day role at the business and I volunteered to become the president of the company.[34]

Family lore has it that Jack Cator started in the meat business with a sledgehammer and knife. He would buy a steer, butcher it in a barn, and sell the meat. His son Ralph Cator founded Cardinal Meat Specialists Ltd. in 1966. From the farm to butcher shops in Bowmanville and Toronto, Ontario, to burger production in Mississauga, Ontario, Cardinal has evolved its products and processes. Jack's sons Mark and Brent have played important roles in the family business.[35] The Cator family has been holding family councils for 15 years—a dozen family members plus spouses; "We even included prospective spouses," said Mark Cator. Not all members of the council are active partners in the company. Meetings last three hours and are held seven to nine times per year and usually end with a meal. Mark indicates that there is no formal agenda, but urgent matters are handled first and business issues rarely occupy half the time. He also notes that personal issues can become a bigger threat than business problems, so discussions on raising children are apropos.[36] Mark Cator is involved with other ventures that leverage his resources: he is owner of Coolinary Connection—"a single source purchasing solution for foodservice operators" and co-owner of Pawsitively Raw Foods—healthy, natural pet foods. Pawsitively Raw Foods is also a family enterprise run by founders Janice and Norm Starr and their daughter Lisa.

Succession? Maybe.

With its start as a "humble farm harvesting blueberries," the Bragg Group of Companies today holds the biggest slice of the global blueberry market, is a large producer of carrots, includes a building-supply chain, a company that reclaims airplane de-icing fluid, and

Canada's largest privately owned cable-TV company. John Bragg is the fifth generation and at age 69 has no succession plan and does not know when he will retire. In fact he has not decided if control will pass to one of his four children, all of whom are involved in the Bragg Group, or an outsider. John Bragg knows he cannot control the fate of the company, but would prefer to see the Bragg Group stay together under family control. Finally he says, "I want them to think of themselves as trustees, rather than inheritors. If it's an inheritance, you think it's for you. If you're a trustee, you know it's for the next generation."[37]

Succession? No.

For Kenneth Levene, the third generation owner of his family's Crescent Furniture, the solution to succession was to exit the business and sell the chain. And he has no regrets, confident that he made the right decision, particularly given the rise of the big box stores and national chains. According to Levene, "Succession planning can be difficult, especially when two adult children who are close in age are involved in the process. . . always expect the unexpected and have some provisions for unanticipated events. In many cases with a family business, those who started the business have a driven personality and are successful at the beginning; however, often the qualities and skills needed to start a business may not be adequate once the business grows and becomes established."[38] Kenneth Levene went on to focus on other matters of interest and 21 years after selling his family's furniture business he donated $4 million to the University of Regina's Graduate School of Business.

Succession Woes

The Avedis Zildjian Company is a cymbal manufacturer founded nearly 400 years ago in Turkey by an Armenian named Avedis Zildjian. For centuries, the family tradition was to keep metallurgical secrets and pass the business to one heir. In 1908 Avedis Zildjian III and his uncle Aram Zildjian began manufacturing cymbals in Quincy, Massachusetts, around 1928 competing with K. Zildjian company back in Turkey! In 1968 Avedis Zildjian Co. bought K. Zildjian Co. and all European trademarks and opened production in Meductic, New Brunswick, to complement production in Massachusetts and Istanbul, Turkey. In early 1977 Armand Zildjian, Avedis Zildjian III's eldest son, was appointed president. Conflict ensued with his brother Robert. Avedis Zildjian III died in 1979 at age 90 and in 1981 Robert started making Sabian cymbals in the Meductic facility. Armand passed the secrets and family namesake to his daughters Craigie and Debbie and now their daughters Cady, Emily, and Samantha are involved in the family enterprise.

Robert Zildjian, son of Avedis Zildjian III carried the family tradition though giving up the name. Avedis broke tradition by passing secrets to both his sons Armand and Robert. After a family feud and legal proceedings Robert became a rival of his older brother. The name Sabian is derived from the first two letters of the names of his three children Sally, Billy, and Andy. Today Andy is the president of Sabian and Robert serves as chairman.

The Phelan family took Cara Operations, which was founded in 1883, public in 1968. But in 2004 sisters Gail and Rosemary along with a deceased sister's daughter Holiday took the company private against the wishes of the sisters' estranged brother Paul. It was the death in 2002 of 84-year-old father of Gail, Rosemary, and Paul that caused the ill feelings. He failed to provide a clear succession plan before his health deteriorated. A full-on family feud ensued. But this is not an isolated case, within Canada, or even within this industry. The McCain family split over control over their empire resulting in one brother breaking off to head Maple Leaf Foods. The Bata family too has squabbled over the family shoe business. Eaton's and Canwest Global's economic woes are tied to family turmoil. Meanwhile the Sobey family and Westons have stuck to business as they battle in the competitive supermarket space. The Comrie and Leon families behind the Brick Warehouse and Leon's Furniture respectively have also managed to keep an eye on economic competition rather than family battles.

CONCLUSION

For those business families who would like to act more entrepreneurially and become an intentional enterprising family that has multiple generations seeking higher potential opportunities we suggest that there are four strategic shifts that may need to occur:

- From lifestyle firm that has the goal of personal comfort to an enterprising family committed to transgenerational entrepreneurship and wealth creation.

- From an intuitive family business that "kicks around" (as one family entrepreneur described it) to see what new opportunities turn up to an intentional entrepreneurial process that seeks to generate and capture new opportunities.

- From a senior-generation entrepreneur who does it to a successor-generation entrepreneurial process and team that create opportunities for others to do it.

- From a "low potential" entrepreneurial family that creates one-off businesses as they can to a "higher potential" entrepreneurial family that mobilizes resources to create transgenerational wealth.

Chapter Summary

1. We began by demonstrating the significant contributions families make to the economy and entrepreneurial process. It is often overlooked that the majority of the businesses worldwide are controlled and managed by families, including many of the very largest businesses that we normally do not associate with family.

2. Families play a diverse number of formal and informal roles in the entrepreneurial process. We described them as (a) the family-influenced start-up, (b) family corporate venturing, (c) family corporate renewal, (d) family private cash, and (e) family investment funds.

3. Family enterprising was defined as the proactive and continuous search for opportunistic growth when expansion is neither pressing nor particularly obvious. The outcome of family enterprising is transgenerational entrepreneurship and wealth creation through balance in the Timmons Model.

4. The mind-set continuum assesses the family's risk profile and those interested in a move from an operational to a financial investor strategy. The methods continuum assesses the organizational behaviour of leaders and organizations and requires a move from managerial to entrepreneurial strategies for enterprising.

5. There are six dimensions for family enterprising that were described as antecedents from the entrepreneurship literature: leadership, relationship, vision, strategy, governance, and performance. The chapter presented key questions on each dimension to assist families in becoming more enterprising.

6. We defined the familiness of an organization as the unique bundle of resources and capabilities that result from the interaction of the family and individual family members with the business entities. Families can have positive and negative family influence, which we described as an f+ or f−.

Study Questions

1. What are the entrepreneurial implications of not appreciating or understanding the role and contribution of families to the economies of our communities and countries?

2. Describe the advantages of a more formal approach on each of the roles families play in the entrepreneurial process. Give a few contrasting examples from a family firm with which you are familiar.

3. Define family enterprising, familiness, and relationship capital and relate each of them to the Timmons Model of the entrepreneurial process.

4. How do the six dimensions for family enterprising relate to one another? How do they enhance family enterprising? Describe how the six dimensions can be used to stimulate positive family dialogue.

5. If a family is trying to find their competitive advantage, how can the familiness assessment approach help them? How is the familiness approach a more formal application of the entrepreneurial process? How can the familiness approach change the family dialogue?

6. Given the familiness assessment of Backerhaus Veit in this chapter, describe why Sabine should or should not partner with Toby to implement his business plan. Describe the familiness action steps that they should take if you say they should launch the business. Describe the familiness reasons for why they possibly should not launch the business.

Mind Stretchers   *Have you considered?*

1. Like a bumblebee that should not be able to fly, it is said that family businesses should not be able to compete. Why might this be a true statement? Why are families so economically dominant worldwide if they are like the bumblebee?

2. How can a lifestyle firm be both a fine choice for a family and a dangerous choice for a family at the same time?

3. Give 10 reasons why dialogue can be harder for families than non-families even though families are supposed to have closer relationships.

4. If you were a Bronfman successor-generation family member, what expectations would you have about your future?

5. Watch the documentary *Born Rich* by Jamie Johnson (heir to the Johnson & Johnson fortune). What did you learn about wealth and entrepreneurship? Are wealthy families the same as entrepreneurial families? Is Jamie Johnson entrepreneurial? Is Paris Hilton entrepreneurial? Is this the same as family enterprising? What are their family legacies?

EXERCISES

Determine where your family is on the mind-set and methods continuum and what familiness advantage you might have for enterprising. Fill out the assessment surveys, plot your family group on the Family Enterprising Model, and fill out the resources and capabilities continuum.

Mind-set Continuum

The mind-set continuum establishes the family's financial risk and return expectations and their competitive posture in relation to the marketplace. There are no right and wrong answers. The point of the assessment is to surface family members' beliefs and fuel the family dialogue.

Using the assessment continuums, have the family member shareholders and future shareholders answer the questions on the mind-set continuum listed below. Circle the number between the two statements that best reflects the strength of your belief about the family as a shareholder group. Total scores are between 12 and 84 reflecting views from the most traditional to the most enterprising.

In general, family member shareholders...

Have a strong proclivity for low-risk businesses and investment opportunities (with normal and certain returns).	1 2 3 4 5 6 7	Have a strong proclivity for high-risk business and investment opportunities (with chances for high returns).
Would sacrifice a higher return to preserve the family's legacy business.	1 2 3 4 5 6 7	Are willing to sell and redeploy their assets to find a higher return in the market.
Tend to think about cultivating our current businesses for current returns.	1 2 3 4 5 6 7	Desire to grow by creating new revenue streams with higher possibilities for returns.
Have a commitment to operating the business and providing job opportunities for family.	1 2 3 4 5 6 7	Have a commitment to mentoring next-generation entrepreneurs to create new streams of value.
Feel we have a good business model that will take us into the future.	1 2 3 4 5 6 7	Feel we should continuously revisit the assumptions of our business model.
Feel that our current businesses and products will serve us well in the future.	1 2 3 4 5 6 7	Assume that a significant percentage of our businesses will become obsolete.

Desire to avoid debt and grow with internally generated cash as they can.	1 2 3 4 5 6 7	Are willing to leverage the businesses to grow and find higher returns in the market.
Desire to increase their financial ability to provide distributions and/or liquidity.	1 2 3 4 5 6 7	Desire to reinvest more aggressively for faster growth and higher returns.
Desire to grow within our current financial and equity structures in order to ensure control over our destiny.	1 2 3 4 5 6 7	Are willing to use alliances, partnerships, share equity, or dilute share positions in order to grow.
Would describe themselves more as a conservative company meeting their family's financial and personal goals.	1 2 3 4 5 6 7	Would describe themselves as a risk taking group seeking higher total returns for the family as investment group.
Would describe our business models and strategy as making us steady rather than opportunistic.	1 2 3 4 5 6 7	Are willing to be innovative in our business models and structures in order to be opportunistic.
Believe that a steady and consistent approach will allow us to fulfill our family's vision and goals for the future.	1 2 3 4 5 6 7	Believe that bold, wide-ranging acts are necessary to achieve our family investment objectives in today's environment.

TOTAL:

Methods Continuum

The methods continuum establishes the organization's entrepreneurial orientation and actions. It reflects the beliefs of the shareholders and stakeholders on how the leaders incite entrepreneurship in the organization.

Using the assessment continuums, have the family member shareholders and future shareholders answer the questions on the methods continuum listed below. Circle the number between the two statements that best reflects the strength of your belief about the family as a shareholder group. Total scores are between 12 and 84 reflecting views from the most traditional to the most enterprising.

In general, senior leaders in our family organization(s)...

Spend their time nurturing the existing businesses.	1 2 3 4 5 6 7	Pay a disproportionate amount of attention to new business opportunities.
Place a strong emphasis on pursing returns by reinvesting in tried and true businesses.	1 2 3 4 5 6 7	Place a strong emphasis on searching for and capturing new business investment opportunities.
Have pursued no new investment opportunities outside of our core operating arena (in last 5 years).	1 2 3 4 5 6 7	Have pursued many new investment opportunities beyond our core operating arena (in the last 5 years).
Believe our core competency is in managing efficient businesses.	1 2 3 4 5 6 7	Believe our core competency is in innovating for opportunistic growth.
Have made minor changes in our businesses, products, services, markets, or business units during the current generation of leaders.	1 2 3 4 5 6 7	Have made significant changes in our products, services, markets, or business units as the market required it.
Typically respond to actions that competitors or the market initiates.	1 2 3 4 5 6 7	Typically initiate actions and competitive change to lead the market and competitors.
Are generally moderate to slow in adopting new technologies and technological processes in our industry.	1 2 3 4 5 6 7	Are often early in investing to develop or adopt new technologies and technological processes in our industries.
Tend to avoid competitive clashes preferring friendly "live and let live" competition.	1 2 3 4 5 6 7	Typically adopt a competitive "undo-the-competitor" posture when making investment decisions.
Are more intuitive and informal in how the organization thinks seeking or capturing new opportunities.	1 2 3 4 5 6 7	Have established formal structures and policies to institutionalize the entrepreneurial process in the organization.
Rely on family leaders to know the markets and customers and get the information to the organization.	1 2 3 4 5 6 7	Have more formal plans and approaches to how they gather and disseminate market intelligence.

Rely on family leaders to set the tone and ensure that the organization is competitive through time.	1 2 3 4 5 6 7	Encourage and empower people at every level of the organization to think and act like competitors.
Typically adopt a cautious "wait and see" posture in order to minimize the probability of making costly investment decisions.	1 2 3 4 5 6 7	Typically adopt a bold, aggressive posture in order to maximize the probability of exploiting potential investment opportunities.

TOTAL:

Family Enterprising Model

Plot your score totals from the mind-set and methods assessment surveys above. The lowest possible score is a 12 and the highest possible score is an 84. Plotting the scores provides you with a visual basis for your family dialogue. Does the plotted score rightly describe your family? Is your family on the "congruence path"? Does everyone agree on where your family is on the model? Develop strategies to move your family on the model if necessary.

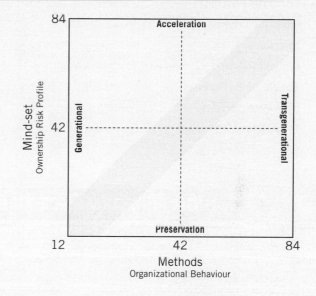

Familiness f + and f– Continuum

Identify where the family influences on your resources and capabilities are part of a competitive advantage (f+) and a competitive constraint (f–). You can conduct this analysis on many levels. The "meta" analysis would be of the larger family group as a whole, while the "micro" analysis would be of a particular business unit, or in relation to a specific innovation or new venture (such as the Backerhaus Veit example in the chapter). Identify the unit of analysis you are assessing and list the f+ and f– resources and capabilities.

Identify Unit of Analysis	
Resources and Capabilities (f+)	**Resources and Capabilities (f–)**

Plot the f+ and f– resources and capabilities from the chart on the continuum below. Place them in position relative to one another so that you see a picture of how the resources and capabilities are related.

A list of potential resources and capabilities to choose from:

Successor Leadership	Experienced leadership	Entrepreneurial processes	Team
Land	Treatment of employees	Firm specific knowledge	Patient capital
Location	Conflict resolution	Firm specific skills	Debt structure
Cash	Effective communication	Leadership development	Strategic alliances
Access to Capital	Decision making	Managerial talent	Compensation
Distribution Systems	Learning environment	Employee productivity	Strategy making and planning
Intellectual Property	Openness to ideas	Network of relationships	Information flow
Raw Materials	Cross functional communication	Employee commitment	Organizational culture
Contracts/Alliances	Reputation of company	Personal values	Unified beliefs and goals
Manufacturing Processes	Market intelligence gathering	Flexible work practices	Time horizons
Innovation Processes	Reporting structures	Trustworthiness	Brand name
Reputation of Company	Coordination and control	Training	Governance structure

---

CASE   HIGH PERFORMANCE TIRE

Richard Ivey School of Business
The University of Western Ontario   **Ivey** | Research and Development

Instruction

Assume the position of Jenny Chen and prepare a two-page memorandum that analyzes the financial condition of High Performance Tire and makes recommendations for the future. Specifically, the memo should be divided into sections describing liquidity, asset management, long-term debt ability, and profitability. A final recommendation section should discuss what Jane Wallace should do to address the problems at High Performance Tire and what might be done in the longer term relating to the management of the company.

High Performance Tire (HPT) Ltd. is a retail tire chain with a network of company-owned stores in the B.C. Interior. It was formed by Harry and Edna Wallace in 1952 and was passed on to their daughter Jane Wallace in the late 1960s. Jane Wallace maintained control of this family-owned business until 2001, at which time she transferred the responsibility for day-to-day management to her son William.

By early 2004, HPT was having difficulties and Jane Wallace decided to become actively involved again in the company to turn things around. Her first action was to hire Jenny Chen, CA, CFA, CMC from the accounting firm of Dexter, Mathews & Jones to review current operations and make recommendations.

William's Tenure

William Wallace had led a privileged and carefree life, and his mother did not feel that he would be able to operate the business successfully, but she had little choice if she wanted to keep the business under family control. Despite his MBA with double concentrations in marketing and finance from a major university, Jane Wallace did not feel that her son had the patience and general business acumen to operate such a sizeable business at this time. She was also fearful that he would recklessly try to expand the business and lose interest once things did not go exactly as planned.

Upon taking over operations in late 2001, William Wallace immediately began to put a major expansion plan into effect that he had worked on as the graduating project in his MBA. This plan had two major focal points. One was to expand the number of retail tire outlets in smaller communities and the other was to diversify the products provided at each of the outlets to include higher margin automotive maintenance services including fluid changes, tune-ups, alignments, batteries and brakes. A number of tire chains in Canada had followed a similar strategy of diversification and were successful.

In 2001, all the outlets were expanded to include bays for maintenance work as well as tire installation. Sales of these

---

new services were poor over the next two years. To have their fluids changed, customers had to leave the vehicle and wait for a considerable period of time in the customer reception area. An appointment was also required. This was not as convenient as other lube stores where patrons did not need either an appointment or to get out of their vehicles and generally could have the work done in less than 20 minutes. For more complicated maintenance work, like tune-ups and alignments, HPT's higher mechanics had a reputation in the community of not being highly qualified. There had been a number of cases that received extensive coverage in the local press, where HPT mechanics had made mistakes that caused major damage to the vehicles they were working on. Instead of admitting they were at fault and keeping public relations damage to a minimum, HPT was taken to court a number of times and forced to pay the repair costs.

In addition to its sales outlets in Kamloops, Kelowna, Penticton, Prince George and Vernon, in 2002/2003 additional stores were added in Revelstoke, Golden, Chase, Williams Lake and Salmon Arm. By early 2004, all outlets were underutilized. Canadian Tire, as well as local service stations with strong ties to the community, lowered their prices and improved their customer service and proved to be formidable competitors.

Prior to 2001, HPT Ltd.'s workforce was composed of a number of experienced tire professionals who had been with the company for years. When William Wallace took over operations, he decided to try to increase profitability by cutting wages and benefits. The result was that most of these professionals left and were replaced by younger, less experienced staff with much poorer customer service skills. The tire sales staff was taken off salary and put on straight commission as a means of increasing sales. The sales staff did become "hungrier," but the more aggressive practices alienated many customers.

In order to increase gross profits, HPT began buying more no-name tires from overseas suppliers. These sales generated a higher gross profit margin for the retailer initially and the customer did receive a lower price, but quality concerns due to shorter tread life and blowouts soon caused sales and margins to fall.

A new accounting system was purchased in 2002 in order to better automate the general accounting, billing, inventory and payroll functions of the company. The low-cost vendor was selected to save cash to help fund the expansion. This vendor provided very poor software installation and training and then went bankrupt. HPT's clerical staff struggled with the new system and matters were made worse by high employee turnover due to low wages and William Wallace's disorganized management style and "short fuse." A lot of overtime had been used to clear the backlog of clerical work, while customers, staff and suppliers were becoming alienated over delays and errors.

In the first quarter of 2003, Jane Wallace suspended all dividend payments. William Wallace had been drawing too much from the company to fund the construction of a new home and to purchase a new luxury car.

Financial Statements

INCOME STATEMENT[1]
For Year Ending December 31

	2003	2002	2001
Sales	6,500,000	5,550,000	4,050,000
Cost of Goods Sold	3,965,000	3,385,500	2,430,000
Gross Profit	2,535,000	2,164,500	1,620,000
Depreciation	485,600	287,200	158,500
Other Operating Expenses	1,690,000	1,387,500	1,012,500
Earnings Before Interest and Taxes	359,400	489,800	449,000
Interest	331,956	160,125	50,645
Earnings Before Taxes	27,444	329,675	398,355
Income Taxes	10,978	131,870	159,342
Net Income	**16,467**	**197,805**	**239,013**

BALANCE SHEET
For Year Ending December 31

	2003	2002	2001
Cash	57,000	110,000	155,000
Accounts Receivable	95,000	59,000	45,000
Inventories	1,050,000	723,000	540,000
Prepaid Expenses	42,000	36,000	25,000
Total Current Assets	1,244,000	928,000	765,000
Property, Plant and Equipment	7,288,800	4,819,200	3,245,000
Less: Accumulative Depreciation	2,432,800	1,947,200	1,660,000
Net Property, Plant, Equipment	4,856,000	2,872,000	1,585,000
Total Assets	6,100,000	3,800,000	2,350,000

[1] All funds in Cdn$ unless otherwise noted.

BALANCE SHEET (continued)
For Year Ending December 31

	2003	2002	2001
Accounts Payable	440,556	165,000	99,000
Line of Credit	570,638	353,000	267,435
Current Portion of Long-term Debt	325,346	162,000	41,461
Total Current Liabilities	1,336,540	680,000	407,895
Long-term Debt	3,256,460	1,620,000	414,605
Equity	1,510,000	1,500,000	1,527,500
Total Liabilities and Equity	6,100,000	3,800,000	2,350,000

Financial Situation

HPT has a $600,000 line-of-credit with the Toronto Dominion Bank. The limit could be extended, but only if the bank has sufficient loanable funds and the company is in good financial condition. The company must maintain a current ratio of 1.5, a times interest earned ratio of 5.0, and can only borrow up to 50 per cent of the value of its accounts receivable and inventory. The company negotiates separate term loans and mortgages to finance its capital purchases. Under Jane Wallace's leadership, HPT had an excellent relationship with its bank, but William's poor management and interpersonal skills had put this relationship in jeopardy.

Retail sales were paid for in cash or by credit card so there were no accounts receivable. Sales to businesses made up about 40 per cent of sales and were on terms 2/10, net 30 with negligible bad debts. HPT bought its tires from the various manufacturers on terms 2/15, net 30, which was the norm in the industry. Interest was charged on overdue accounts at 12 per cent per annum and many retailers who got too far in arrears were put on a cash-and-carry basis.

A slowdown was forecasted in the local economy in 2004 due to the forest fires that took place in the summer of 2003 and the collapse of the Canadian beef industry caused by the discovery of mad cow disease in neighbouring Alberta.

The following industry average ratios (based on year-end figures) were available for companies that sold both tires and automotive maintenance services:

Current Ratio	1.90
Cash Ratio	.51
Inventory Turnover in Days	60 days
Accounts Receivable Turnover in Days	30 days
Accounts Payable Turnover in Days	15 days

Fixed Assets Turnover	3.19
Total Assets Turnover	2.00
Debt Ratio	30.00%
Times Interest Earned	14.63
Cost of Borrowing	6.50%
Gross Profit Margin	42.00%
Operating Profit Margin	12.00%
Net Profit Margin	6.71%
Return on Assets	13.42%
Return on Equity	19.17%

HPT's marginal tax rate was 40 per cent.

Turnaround

Jenny Chen had just returned to her downtown office at Dexter, Mathews & Jones from a meeting with Jane Wallace in February, 2004—Chen was feeling quite sad. Jane Wallace had worked very hard the last 35 years managing the family business as a legacy to her beloved parents who had passed away in a car accident prior to her taking control in the late 1960s. At 64, she was in need of a rest after a long career building HPT, but her son seemed to have mismanaged the business terribly during his short tenure and she now had to take back control before things got even worse.

Jane Wallace asked Chen to prepare a comprehensive review of HPT's operations with a focus on why things had deteriorated so much and what she might do to improve operations. Knowing, quite reasonably, that she could not continue running HPT indefinitely, Jane Wallace also asked Chen to make further recommendations on the future management of the company.

15

LEADING THROUGH TROUBLE, THE HARVEST, AND BEYOND[1]

Another time, we had a cart go up in flames, and we went out on another cart, which we wrecked by running it into the cart that was on fire.

Mike Weir, Golfer

It's better to burn out than it is to rust.

Neil Young, Musician

Upon completion of this chapter, you will be able to:

RESULTS EXPECTED

1. Identify specific signals and clues that can alert entrepreneurial leaders to impending crises, and describe both quantitative (ratio analysis) and qualitative symptoms of trouble.

2. Describe the principal diagnostic methods used to devise intervention and turnaround plans, and identify remedial actions used for dealing with lenders, creditors, and employees.

3. See the importance of first building a great company and thereby creating harvest options.

4. Explain why harvesting is an essential element of the entrepreneurial process and does not necessarily mean abandoning the company.

5. Identify the principal harvest options, including trade sale, going public, and cash flow ("capital cow").

6. Discuss the importance of creating a longer-term legacy from personal and family wealth by pursuing philanthropic activities and contributing to community renewal.

This chapter tackles issues that generally arise in the latter stages of a venture's existence. The first part of this chapter deals with problems after time has elapsed and the venture has made it through growing pains. With experience comes both comfort and an array of problems associated with apathy. Alternatively the entrepreneur may come to the realization that what served the enterprise so well in the past may now be a source of sub-par performance. The second part of this chapter deals with the harvest—the end of one venture—an action that may lead to a foray into another endeavour.

Perhaps the analogy of the automobile serves to demonstrate the service period and final kilometres of a vehicle are similar to events for an enterprise. A new car may require a period of breaking in—any number of things might go wrong early on—but once those bugs are ironed out, it should run fine for quite a while. Later on—depending on how well it's maintained and how hard it's driven—the car comes to the end of its useful life with its owner. The owner may upgrade to a bigger and better car. However, unlike a venture, vehicles seldom increase in value. Finally, tuning-up your vehicle or your venture ensures the highest price when you part ways.

WHEN THE BLOOM IS OFF THE ROSE

We now turn our attention to the entrepreneur and the troubled company. It traces the firm's route into and out of crisis and provides insight into how a troubled enterprise can be rescued by a turnaround specialist.

Many times in history, companies have experienced times of financial troubles. The most recent is the economic downturn in 2009 for instance. Both corporate and personal bankruptcies increased during this period, and entrepreneurs needed a new and special set of skills to lead through the shoals.

There is a saying among horseback riders that the person who has never been thrown from a horse probably has never ridden one! Jim Hindman, founder of Jiffy Lube, is fond of saying, "Ultimately it is not how many touchdowns you score but how fast and often you get up after being tackled." Mike Weir said "Playing hockey, there were a lot of guys bigger than me, so I knew I was going to get hit and have to deal with it. Gotta hit back." These insights capture the essence of the ups and downs that can occur during the growth and development of a new venture.

Getting into Trouble—The Causes

Trouble can be caused by external forces not under the control of management. Among the most frequently mentioned are recession, interest rate changes, changes in government policy, inflation, the entry of new competition, and industry/product obsolescence.

However, those who lead turnarounds find that while such circumstances define the environment to which a troubled company needs to adjust, they are rarely the sole reason for a company's failure. External shocks impact all companies in an industry, and only some of them fail. Others survive and prosper.

Most causes of failure can be found within company leadership. Although there are many causes of trouble, the most frequently cited fall into three broad areas: inattention to strategic issues, general management problems, and poor financial/accounting systems and practices. There is striking similarity between these causes of trouble and the causes of failure for start-ups given in Chapter 2. Exercise 10 "Flaws, Assumptions, and Downside Consequences—Risk Reconsidered" in the Venture Opportunity Screening Exercise that accompanies Chapter 3 and is found on the Online Learning Centre at www.mcgrawhill.ca/olc/timmons is a tool worth visiting.

Strategic Issues

- *Misunderstood market niche.* The first of these issues is a failure to understand the company's market niche and to focus on growth without considering profitability. Instead of developing a strategy, these firms take on low-margin business and add capacity in an effort to grow. They then run out of cash.
- *Mismanaged relationships with suppliers and customers.* Related to the issue of not understanding market niche is the failure to understand the economics of relationships with suppliers and customers. For example, some firms allow practices in the industry to dictate payment terms, when they may be in a position to dictate their own terms.
- *Diversification into an unrelated business area.* A common failing of cash-rich firms that suffer from the growth syndrome is diversification into unrelated business areas. These firms use the cash flow generated in one business to start another without good reason. As one turnaround consultant said, "I couldn't believe it. There was no synergy at all. They added to their overhead but not to their contribution. No common sense!"

- *Mousetrap myopia.* Related to the problem of starting a firm around an idea, rather than an opportunity, is the problem of firms that have "great products" and are looking for other markets where they can be sold. This is done without analyzing the firm's opportunities.

- *The big project.* The company gears up for a "big project" without looking at the cash flow implications. Cash is expended by adding capacity and hiring personnel. When sales do not materialize, or take longer than expected to materialize, there is trouble. Sometimes the "big project" is required by the nature of the business opportunity. An example of this would be the high-technology start-up that needs to capitalize on a first-mover advantage. The company needs to prove the product's "right to life" and grow quickly to the point where it can achieve a public market or become an attractive acquisition candidate for a larger company. This ensures that a larger company cannot use its advantages in scale and existing distribution channels, after copying the technology, to achieve dominance over the start-up.

- *Lack of contingency planning.* As has been stated over and over, the path to growth is not a smooth curve upward. Firms need to be geared to think about what happens if things go sour, sales fall, or collections slow. There need to be plans in place for layoffs and capacity reduction.

Leadership Issues

- *Lack of leadership skills, experience, and know-how.* As was mentioned in Chapter 5, while companies grow, entrepreneurs need to change their leadership mode from doing to leading to leading leaders.

- *Weak finance function.* Often, in a new and emerging company, the finance function is nothing more than a bookkeeper. One company was five years old, with $20 million in sales, before the founders hired a financial professional.

- *Turnover in key management personnel.* Although turnover of key management personnel can be difficult in any firm, it is a critical concern in businesses that deal in specialized or proprietary knowledge. For example, one firm lost a bookkeeper— the only person who really understood what was happening in the business.

- *Big-company influence in accounting.* A mistake that some companies often make is to focus on accruals, rather than cash.

Poor Planning, Financial/Accounting Systems, Practices, and Controls

- *Poor pricing, overextension of credit, and excessive leverage.* These causes of trouble are not surprising and need not be elaborated. Some of the reasons for excess use of leverage are interesting. Use of excess leverage can result from growth outstripping the company's internal financing capabilities. The company then relies increasingly on short-term notes until a cash flow problem develops. Another reason a company becomes overleveraged is by using guaranteed loans in place of equity for either start-up or expansion financing. One entrepreneur remarked, "[The guaranteed loan] looked just like equity when we started, but when trouble came it looked more and more like debt."

- *Lack of cash budgets/projections.* This is a most frequently cited cause of trouble. In small companies, cash budgets/projections are often not done.

- *Poor management reporting.* While some firms have good financial reporting, they suffer from poor management reporting. As one turnaround consultant stated, "[The financial statement] just tells where the company has been. It doesn't help manage the business. If you look at the important management reports—inventory analysis, receivables aging, sales analysis—they're usually late or not produced at all. The same goes for billing procedures. Lots of emerging companies don't get their bills out on time."

- *Lack of standard costing.* Poor management reporting extends to issues of costing, too. Many emerging businesses have no standard costs against which they can compare the actual costs of manufacturing products. The result is they have no variance reporting. The company cannot identify problems in process and take corrective action. The company will know only after the fact how profitable a product is.

  Even when standard costs are used, it is not uncommon to find that engineering, manufacturing, and accounting each has its own version of the bill of material. The product is designed one way, manufactured a second way, and costed a third.

- *Poorly understood cost behaviour.* Companies often do not understand the relationship between fixed and variable costs. For example, one manufacturing company thought it was saving money by closing on Saturday. In this way, management felt it would save paying overtime. It had to be pointed out to the lead entrepreneur by a turnaround consultant that, "He had a lot of high-margin product in his manufacturing backlog that more than justified the overtime."

It is also important for entrepreneurs to understand the difference between theory and practice in this area. The turnaround consultant mentioned above said, "Accounting theory says that all costs are variable in the long run. In practice, almost all costs are fixed. The only truly variable cost is a sales commission."

Getting Out of Trouble

The major protection against and the biggest help in getting out of these troubled waters is to have a set of advisors and directors who have been through this in the past. They possess skills that aren't taught in school or in most corporate training programs. An outside "vision" is critical. The speed of action has to be different; control systems have to be different; and organization generally needs to be different.

Although uncontrollable external factors such as new government regulations do arise, an opportunity-driven firm's crisis is usually the result of management error. Yet in these management errors are found part of the solution to the troubled company's problems. It is pleasing to see that many enterprises—even enterprises that are insolvent or have negative net worth or both—can be rescued and restored to profitability.

Predicting Trouble

Since crises develop over time and typically result from an accumulation of fundamental errors, can a crisis be predicted? The obvious benefit of being able to predict crisis is that the entrepreneur, employees, and significant outsiders, such as investors, lenders, trade creditors—and even customers—could see trouble brewing in time to take corrective actions.

There have been several attempts to develop predictive models. Two are presented below and have been selected because each is easy to calculate and uses information available in common financial reports. Because management reporting in emerging companies is often inadequate, the predictive model needs to use information available in common financial reports.

Each of the two approaches below uses easily obtained financial data to predict the onset of crisis as much as two years in advance. For the smaller public company, these models can be used by all interested observers. With private companies, they are useful only to those privy to the information and are probably only of benefit to such non-management outsiders as lenders and boards of directors.

The most frequently used denominator in all these ratios is the figure for total assets. This figure often is distorted by "creative accounting," with expenses occasionally improperly capitalized and carried on the balance sheet or by substantial differences between tangible book value and book value (i.e., overvalued or undervalued assets).

Net-Liquid-Balance-to-Total-Assets Ratio

The model shown in Exhibit 15.1 was developed to predict loan defaults. This ratio has been shown to predict loan defaults with significant reliability as much as two years in advance. But the science of prediction is ever improving. Marissa Mayer, a Google vice president, points out that credit card companies are generating detailed psychometric profiles and accurately assessing behaviour; the credit card company knows that you will be getting divorced two years before you do.[2]

This approach is noteworthy because it explicitly recognizes the importance of cash. Among current accounts, it distinguishes between operating assets (such as inventory and accounts receivable) and financial assets (such as cash and marketable securities). The same distinction is made among liabilities, where notes payable and contractual obligations are financial liabilities and accounts payable are operating liabilities.

The model then subtracts financial liabilities from financial assets to obtain a figure known as the net liquid balance. Net liquid balance can be thought of as "uncommitted cash," cash the firm has available to meet contingencies. Because it is the short-term margin for error should sales change, collections slow, or interest rates change, it is a true measure of liquidity. The net liquid balance is then divided by total assets to form the predictive ratio.

Non-quantitative Signals

In Chapter 12 we discussed patterns and actions that could lead to trouble, indications of common trouble by growth stage, and critical variables that can be monitored.

Turnaround specialists also use some non-quantitative signals as indicators of the possibility of trouble. As with the signals discussed in Chapter 12, the presence of a single one of these does not necessarily imply an immediate crisis. However, once any of these surfaces and if the others follow, then trouble is likely to mount.

- Inability to produce financial statements on time.
- Changes in behaviour of the lead entrepreneur (such as avoiding phone calls or coming in later than usual).
- Change in management or advisors, such as directors, accountants, or other professional advisors.
- Accountant's opinion that is qualified and not certified.
- New competition.
- Launching of a "big project."
- Lower research and development expenditures.
- Special write-offs of assets and/or addition of "new" liabilities.
- Reduction of credit line.

EXHIBIT 15.1   Net-Liquid-Balance-to-Total-Assets Ratio

Net-Liquid-Balance-to-Total-Assets Ratio = NLB/Total Assets
Where
NLB = (Cash + Marketable securities) − (Notes Payable + Contractual obligations)

Source: Ismael G. Dambolena and Joel M. Shulman, "Primary Rule for Detecting Bankruptcy: Watch the Cash," *Financial Analysts Journal* 44, no. 5 (1988): 74–78.

THE GESTATION PERIOD OF CRISIS

Crisis rarely develops overnight. The time between the initial cause of trouble and the point of intervention can run from 18 months to five years. What happens to a company during the gestation period has implications for the later turnaround of the company. Thus, how the lead entrepreneur reacts to crisis and what happens to morale determine what will need to happen in the intervention. Usually, a demoralized and unproductive organization develops when its members think only of survival, not turnaround, and its entrepreneur has lost credibility. Further, the company has lost valuable time.

In looking backward, the plot of a company's key statistics shows trouble. One can see the sales growth rate (and the gross margin) have slowed considerably. This is followed by an increasing rise in expenses as the company assumes that growth will continue. When the growth doesn't continue, the company still allows the growth rate of expenses to remain high so it can "get back on track."

The Paradox of Optimism

In a typical scenario for a troubled company, the first signs of trouble (such as declining margins, customer returns, or falling liquidity) go unnoticed or are written off as teething problems of the new project or as the ordinary vicissitudes of business. For example, one entrepreneur saw increases in inventory and receivables as a good sign, since sales were up and the current ratio had improved. However, although sales were up, margins were down, and he did not realize he had a liquidity problem until cash shortages developed.

Although the lead entrepreneur may miss the first signs, outsiders usually do not. Banks, board members, suppliers, and customers see trouble brewing. They wonder why the venture team does not respond. Credibility begins to erode.

Soon the venture team has to admit that trouble exists, but valuable time has been lost. Furthermore, requisite actions to meet the situation are anathema. The lead entrepreneur is emotionally committed to people, to projects, or to business areas. Further, to cut back in any of these areas goes against instinct, because the company will need these resources when the good times return.

The company continues its downward fall, and the situation becomes stressful. Turnaround specialists mention that stress can cause avoidance on the part of an entrepreneur. Others have likened the entrepreneur in a troubled company to a deer caught in a car's headlights. The entrepreneur is frozen and can take no action. Avoidance has a basis in human psychology. One organizational behaviour consultant who has worked on turnarounds said, "When a person under stress does not understand the problem and does not have the sense to deal with it, the person will tend to replace the unpleasant reality with fantasy." The consultant went on to say, "The outward manifestation of this fantasy is avoidance." This consultant noted it is common for an entrepreneur to deal with pleasant and well-understood tasks, such as selling to customers, rather than dealing with the trouble. The result is that credibility is lost with bankers, creditors, and so forth. (These are the very people whose cooperation needs to be secured if the company is to be turned around.)

Often, the decisions the entrepreneur does make during this time are poor and accelerate the company on its downward course. The accountant or the controller may be fired, resulting in a company that is then flying blind. One entrepreneur, for example, running a company that manufactured a high-margin product, announced across-the-board cuts in expenditures, including advertising, without stopping to think that cutting advertising on such a product only added to the cash flow problem.

Finally, the entrepreneur may make statements that are untrue or may make promises that cannot be kept. This is the death knell of his or her credibility.

The Bloom Is Off the Rose—Now What?

Generally, when an organization is in trouble some telltale trends appear.

- Ignore outside advice.
- Worse is still yet to come.
- People (including and usually, most especially, the entrepreneur) have stopped making decisions and also have stopped answering the phone.
- Nobody in authority has talked to the employees.
- Rumours are flying.
- Inventory is out of balance. That is, it does not reflect historical trends.
- Accounts receivable aging is increasing.
- Customers are becoming afraid of new commitments.
- A general malaise has settled in while a still high-stressed environment exists (an unusual combination).

Decline in Organizational Morale

Among those who notice trouble developing are the employees. They deal with customer returns, calls from creditors, and the like, and they wonder why management does not respond. They begin to lose confidence in their leader(s).

Despite troubled times, the lead entrepreneur talks and behaves optimistically or hides in the office declining to communicate with employees, customers, or vendors. Employees hear of trouble from each other and from other outsiders. They lose confidence in the formal communications of the company. The grapevine, which is always exaggerated, takes on increased credibility. Company turnover starts to increase. Morale is eroding.

It is obvious there is a problem and that it is not being dealt with. Employees wonder what will happen, whether they will be laid off, and whether the firm will go into bankruptcy. With their security threatened, employees lapse into survival mode. As an organizational behaviour consultant explains:

> The human organism can tolerate anything except *uncertainty*. It causes so much stress that people are no longer capable of thinking in a cognitive, creative manner. They focus on survival. That's why in turnarounds you see so much uncooperative, finger-pointing behaviour. The only issue people understand is directing the blame elsewhere [or in doing nothing].

Crisis can force intervention. The occasion is usually forced by the board of directors, lender, or a lawsuit. For example, the bank may call a loan, or the firm may be put on cash terms by its suppliers. Perhaps creditors try to put the firm into involuntary bankruptcy. Or something from the outside world fundamentally changes the business environment.

THE THREAT OF BANKRUPTCY

Unfortunately the heads of most troubled companies usually do not understand the benefits of bankruptcy law. To them, bankruptcy carries the stigma of failure; however, the law merely defines the priority of creditors' claims when the firm is liquidated.

Although bankruptcy can provide for the liquidation of the business, it also can provide for its reorganization. Bankruptcy is not an attractive prospect for creditors because they stand to lose at least some of their money, so they often are willing to negotiate. The prospect of bankruptcy also can be a foundation for bargaining in a turnaround. Of the late Ted Rogers, the *Globe and Mail* noted: "his greatest expectation-smashing act was escaping bankruptcy, as his flagship Rogers Communications Inc. survived a parade of near-death experiences, buried under the debt amassed by its risk-embracing owner."[3]

Voluntary Bankruptcy

When legal bankruptcy is granted to a business, the firm is given immediate protection from creditors. Payment of interest or principal is suspended, and creditors must wait for their money. Generally the current management (a debtor in possession) is allowed to run the company, but sometimes an outsider, a trustee, is named to operate the company, and creditor committees are formed to watch over the operations and to negotiate with the company.

The greatest benefit of bankruptcy is that it buys time for the firm. The firm has 30 to 90 days to come up with a reorganization plan and time to obtain acceptance of that plan by creditors. Under a reorganization plan, debt can be extended. Debt also can be restructured (composed). Interest rates can be increased, and convertible provisions can be introduced to compensate debt holders for any increase in their risk as a result of the restructuring. Occasionally, debt holders need to take part of their claim in the form of equity. Trade creditors can be asked to take equity as payment, and they occasionally need to accept partial payment. If liquidation is the result of the reorganization plan, partial payment is the rule, with the typical payment ranging from zero to 30 cents on the dollar, depending on the priority of the claim.

Bargaining Power

For creditors, having a firm go into bankruptcy is not particularly attractive. *Bankruptcy, therefore, is a tremendous source of bargaining power for the troubled company.* Bankruptcy is not attractive to creditors because once protection is granted to a firm, creditors must wait for their money. Further, they are no longer dealing with the troubled company but with the judicial system, as well as with other creditors. Even if creditors are willing to wait for their money, they may not get full payment and may have to accept payment in some unattractive form. Last, the legal and administrative costs of bankruptcy, which can be substantial, are paid before any payments are made to creditors.

Faced with these prospects, many creditors conclude that their interests are better served by negotiating with the firm. Because the law defines the priority of creditors' claims, an entrepreneur can use it to determine who might be willing to negotiate.

INTERVENTION

A company in trouble usually will want to use the services of an outside advisor who specializes in turnarounds.

The situation the outside advisor usually finds at intervention is not encouraging. The company is often technically insolvent or has negative net worth. It already may have been put on a cash basis by its suppliers. It may be in default on loans, or if not, it is probably in violation of loan covenants. Call provisions may be exercised. At this point, as the situation deteriorates more, creditors may be trying to force the company into bankruptcy, and the organization is demoralized.

The critical task is to quickly diagnose the situation, develop an understanding of the company's bargaining position with its many creditors, and produce a detailed cash flow business plan for the turnaround of the organization. To this end, a turnaround advisor usually quickly signals that change is coming. He or she will elevate the finance function, putting the "cash person" (often the consultant himself) in charge of the business. Some payments may be put on hold until problems can be diagnosed and remedial actions decided upon.

Diagnosis

Diagnosis can be complicated by the mixture of strategic and financial errors. For example, for a company with large receivables, questions need to be answered about whether receivables are bloated because of poor credit policy or because the company is in a business where liberal credit terms are required to compete.

Diagnosis occurs in three areas: the appropriate strategic posture of the business, the analysis of the venture team, and "the numbers."

Strategic Analysis   This analysis in a turnaround tries to identify the markets in which the company is capable of competing and decide on a competitive strategy. With small companies, turnaround experts state that most strategic errors relate to the involvement of firms in unprofitable product lines, customers, and geographic areas. It is outside the scope of this book to cover strategic analysis in detail.

Analysis of Management   Analysis of management consists of interviewing members of the management team and coming to a subjective judgment of who belongs and who does not. Turnaround consultants can give no formula for how this is done except that it is the result of judgment that comes from experience.

The Numbers   Involved in "the numbers" is a detailed cash flow analysis, which will reveal areas for remedial action. The task is to identify and quantify the profitable core of the business.

- *Determine available cash.* The first task is to determine how much cash the firm has available in the near term. This is accomplished by looking at bank balances, receivables (those not being used as security), and the confirmed order backlog.

- *Determine where money is going.* This is a more complex task than it appears to be. A common technique is called subaccount analysis, where every account that posts to cash is found and accounts are arranged in descending order of cash outlays. Accounts then are scrutinized for patterns. These patterns can indicate the functional areas where problems exist. For example, one company had its corporate address on its bills, rather than the lockbox address at which cheques were processed, adding two days to its dollar days outstanding.

- *Calculate percent-of-sales ratios for different areas of a business and then analyze trends in costs.* Typically, several of the trends will show flex points, where relative costs have changed. For example, for one company that had undertaken a big project, an increase in cost of sales, which coincided with an increase in capacity and in the advertising budget, was noticed. Further analysis revealed this project was not producing enough in dollar contribution to justify its existence. Once the project was eliminated, excess capacity could be reduced to lower the firm's break-even point.

- *Reconstruct the business.* After determining where the cash is coming from and where it is going, the next step is to compare the business as it should be to the business as it is. This involves reconstructing the business from the ground up. For example, a cash budgeting exercise can be undertaken and collections, payments, and so forth determined for a given sales volume. Or the problem can be approached by determining labour, materials, and other direct costs and the overhead required to drive a given sales volume. What is essentially a cash flow business plan is created.

- *Determine differences.* Finally, the cash flow business plan is tied into pro forma balance sheets and income statements. The ideal cash flow plan and financial statements are compared to the business's current financial statements. For example, the pro forma income statements can be compared to existing statements to see where expenses can be reduced. The differences between the projected and actual financial statements form the basis of the turnaround plan and remedial actions.

The most commonly found areas for potential cuts/improvements are these: (1) working capital management, from order processing and billing to receivables, inventory control, and, of course, cash management; (2) payroll; and (3) overcapacity and underutilized assets. More than 80 percent of potential reduction in expenses can usually be found in workforce reduction.

The Turnaround Plan

The turnaround plan not only defines remedial actions but, because it is a detailed set of projections, also provides a means to monitor and control turnaround activity. Further, if the assumptions about unit sales volume, prices, collections, and negotiating success are varied, it can provide a means by which worst-case scenarios—complete with contingency plans—can be constructed.

Because short-term measures may not solve the cash crunch, a turnaround plan gives a firm enough credibility to buy time to put other remedial actions in place. For example, one firm's consultant could approach its bank to buy time with the following: By reducing payroll and discounting receivables, it can improve cash flow to the point where the firm can be current in five months. If it is successful in negotiating extended terms with trade creditors, then the firm can be current in three months. If the firm can sell some underutilized assets at 50 percent off, it can become current immediately.

The turnaround plan helps address organizational issues. The plan replaces uncertainty with a clearly defined set of actions and responsibilities. Since it signals to the organization that action is being taken, it helps get employees out of their survival mode. An effective plan breaks tasks into the smallest achievable unit, so successful completion of these simple tasks soon follows and the organization begins to experience success. Soon the downward spiral of organizational morale is broken.

Finally, the turnaround plan is an important source of bargaining power. By identifying problems and providing for remedial actions, the turnaround plan enables the firm's advisors to approach creditors and tell them in very detailed fashion how and when they will be paid. If the turnaround plan proves that creditors are better off working with the company as a going concern, rather than liquidating it, they will most likely be willing to negotiate their claims and terms of payment. Payment schedules can then be worked out that can keep the company afloat until the crisis is over.

Quick Cash   Ideally, the turnaround plan establishes enough creditor confidence to buy the turnaround consultant time to raise additional capital and turn underutilized assets into cash. It is imperative, however, to raise cash quickly. The result of the actions described below should be an improvement in cash flow. The solution is far from complete, however, because suppliers need to be satisfied.

For the purpose of quick cash, the working capital accounts hold the most promise.

Accounts receivable is the most liquid non-cash asset. Receivables can be factored, but negotiating such arrangements takes time. The best route to cash is discounting receivables. How much receivables can be discounted depends on whether they are securing a loan. For example, a typical bank will lend up to 80 percent of the value of receivables that are under 90 days. As receivables age past the 90 days, the bank needs to be paid. New funds are advanced as new receivables are established as long as the 80 percent and under-90-day criteria are met. Receivables under 90 days can be discounted no more than 20 percent, if the bank obligation is to be met. Receivables over 90 days can be discounted as much as is needed to collect them, since they are not securing bank financing. One needs to use judgment in deciding exactly how large a discount to offer. A common method is to offer a generous discount with a time limit on it, after which the discount is no longer valid. This provides an incentive for the customer to pay immediately.

Consultants agree it is better to offer too large a discount than too small a one. If the discount is too small and needs to be followed by further discounts, customers may hold off paying in the hope that another round of discounts will follow. Generally it is the slow payers that cause the problems and discounting may not help. By getting on the squeaky-wheel list of the particular slow-pay customer, you might get attention. A possible solution is to put on a note with the objective of having the customer start paying you on a regular basis; also, adding a small additional amount to every new order helps to work down the balance.

Inventory is not as liquid as receivables but still can be liquidated to generate quick cash. An inventory "fire sale" gets mixed reviews from turnaround experts. The most common objection is that excess inventory is often obsolete. The second objection is that because much inventory is work in process, it is not in saleable form and requires money to put in saleable form. The third is that discounting finished-goods inventory may generate cash but is liable to create customer resistance to restored margins after the company is turned around. The sale of raw materials inventory to competitors is generally considered the best route. Another option is to try to sell inventory at discounted prices to new channels of distribution. In these channels, the discounted prices might not affect the next sale.

One interesting option for the company with a lot of work-in-process inventory is to ease credit terms. It often is possible to borrow more against receivables than against inventory. By easing credit terms, the company can increase its borrowing capacity to perhaps enough to get cash to finish work in process. This option may be difficult to implement because, by the time of intervention, the firm's lenders are likely following the company very closely and may veto the arrangements.

Also relevant to generating quick cash is the policy regarding current sales activity. Guiding criteria for this needs to include increasing the total dollar value of margin, generating cash quickly, and keeping working capital in its most liquid form. Prices and cash discounts need to be increased and credit terms eased. Easing credit terms, however, can conflict with the receivables policy described above. Obviously, care needs to be taken to maintain consistency of policy. Easing credit is really an "excess inventory" policy. The overall idea is to leverage policy in favour of cash first, receivables second, and inventory third.

Putting all accounts payable on hold is the next option. Clearly, this eases the cash flow burden in the near term. Although some arrangement to pay suppliers needs to be made, the most important uses of cash at this stage are meeting payroll and paying lenders. Lenders are important, but if you do not get suppliers to ship goods you are out of business. Getting suppliers to ship is critical. A company with negative cash flow simply needs to "prioritize" its use of cash. Suppliers are the least likely to force the company into bankruptcy because, under the law, they have a low priority claim.

Dealing with Lenders   The next step in the turnaround is to negotiate with lenders. To continue to do business with the company, lenders need to be satisfied that there is a workable long-term solution.

However, at the point of intervention, the company is most likely in default on its payments. Or, if payments are current, the financial situation has probably deteriorated to the point where the company is in violation of loan covenants. It also is likely that many of the firm's assets have been pledged as collateral. To make matters worse, it is likely that the troubled entrepreneur has been avoiding his or her lenders during the gestation period and has demonstrated that he or she is not in control of the situation. Credibility has been lost.

It is important for a firm to know that it is not the first ever to default on a loan, that the lender is usually willing to work things out, and that it is still in a position to bargain.

Strategically, there are two sources of bargaining power. The first is that bankruptcy is an unattractive result to a lender, despite its senior claims. A low margin business cannot absorb large losses easily. (Recall that banks typically earn 0.5 percent to 1.0 percent total return on assets.)

The second is credibility. The firm that, through its turnaround specialist, has diagnosed the problem and produced a detailed turnaround plan with best-case/worst-case scenarios, the aim of which is to prove to the lender that the company is capable of paying, is in a better bargaining position. The plan details specific actions (e.g., layoffs, assets plays, changes in credit policy, etc.) that will be undertaken, and this plan must be met to regain credibility.

There are also two tactical sources of bargaining power. First, there is the strength of the lender's collateral. The second is the bank's inferior knowledge of aftermarkets and the entrepreneur's superior ability to sell.

The following example illustrates that, when the lender's collateral is poor, it has little choice but to look to the entrepreneur for a way out without incurring a loss. It also shows that the entrepreneur's superior knowledge of his business and ability to sell can get himself and the lender out of trouble. One company in turnaround in the leather business overbought inventory one year, and, at the same time, a competitor announced a new product that made his inventory almost obsolete. Since the entrepreneur went to the lender with the problem, the lender was willing to work with him. The entrepreneur had plans to sell the inventory at reduced prices and also to enter a new market that looked attractive. The only trouble was he needed more money to do it, and he was already over his credit limit. The lender was faced with the certainty of losing 80 percent of its money and putting its customer out of business or the possibility of losing money by throwing good money after bad. The lender decided to work with the entrepreneur. It got a higher interest rate and put the entrepreneur on a "full following mechanism," which meant that all payments were sent to a lockbox. The lender processed the cheques and reduced its exposure before it put money in his account.

Another example illustrates the existence of bargaining power with a lender who is under-collateralized and stands to take a large loss. A company was importing look-alike Cabbage Patch dolls from Europe. This was financed with a letter of credit. However, when the dolls arrived in this country, the company could not sell the dolls because the Cabbage Patch doll craze was over. The dolls, and the bank's collateral, were worthless. The company found that the doll heads could be replaced, and with the new heads, the dolls did not look like Cabbage Patch dolls. It found also that one doll buyer would buy the entire inventory. The company needed $30,000 to buy the new heads and have them put on, so it went back to the bank. The bank said, if the company wanted the money, key members of management had to give liens on their houses. When this was refused, the banker was astounded.

Lenders are often willing to advance money for a company to meet its payroll. This is largely a public relations consideration. Also, if a company does not meet its payroll, a crisis may be precipitated before the lender can consider its options.

When the situation starts to improve, a lender may call the loan. Such a move will solve the lender's problem but may put the company under. While many bankers will deny this ever happens, some will concede that such an occurrence depends on the loan officer.

Dealing with Trade Creditors   In dealing with trade creditors, the first step is to understand the strength of the company's bargaining position. Trade creditors have the lowest priority claims should a company file for bankruptcy and, therefore, are often the most willing to deal. In bankruptcy, trade creditors often receive just a few cents on the dollar.

Another bargaining power boost with trade creditors is the existence of a turnaround plan. As long as a company demonstrates that it can offer a trade creditor a better result as a going concern than it can in bankruptcy proceedings, the trade creditor should be willing to negotiate. It is generally good to make sure that trade creditors are getting a little money on a frequent basis. Remember trade creditors have a higher gross margin than a bank, so their getting paid pays down their "risk" money faster. This is especially true if the creditor can ship new goods and get paid for that, and also get some money toward the old receivables.

Also, trade creditors have to deal with the customer-relations issue. Trade creditors will work with a troubled company if they see it as a way to preserve a market.

The relative weakness in the position of trade creditors has allowed some turnaround consultants to negotiate impressive deals. For example, one company got trade creditors to agree to a 24-month payment schedule for all outstanding accounts. In return, the firm pledged to keep all new payables current. The entrepreneur was able to keep the company from dealing on a cash basis with many of its creditors and to convert short-term payables into what amounted to long-term debt. The effect on current cash flow was very favourable.

The second step is to prioritize trade creditors according to their importance to the turnaround. The company then needs to take care of those creditors that are most important. For example, one entrepreneur told his controller never to make a commitment he could not keep. The controller was told that, if the company was going to miss a commitment, he was to get on the phone and call. The most important suppliers were told that if something happened and they needed payment sooner than had been agreed, they were to let the company know and it would do its best to come up with the cash.

The third step in dealing with trade creditors is to switch vendors if necessary. The lower priority suppliers will put the company on cash terms or refuse to do business. The troubled company needs to be able to switch suppliers, and its relationship with its priority suppliers will help it to do this, because they can give credit references. One firm said, "We asked our best suppliers to be as liberal with credit references as possible. I don't know if we could have established new relationships without them."

The fourth step in dealing with trade creditors is to communicate effectively. "Dealing with the trade is as simple as telling the truth," one consultant said. If a company is honest, at least a creditor can plan.

Workforce Reductions   With workforce reduction representing 80 percent of the potential expense reduction, layoffs are inevitable in a turnaround situation.

A number of turnaround specialists recommend that layoffs be announced to an organization as a onetime reduction in the workforce and be done all at once. They recommend further that layoffs be accomplished as soon as possible, since employees will never regain their productivity until they feel some measure of security. Finally, they suggest that a firm cut deeper than seems necessary to compensate for other remedial actions that may be difficult to implement. For example, it is one thing to set out to reduce capacity by half and quite another thing to sell or sublet half a plant.

Longer-Term Remedial Actions

If the turnaround plan has created enough credibility and has bought the firm time, longer-term remedial actions can be implemented.

These actions will usually fall into three categories:

* *Systems and procedures.* Systems and procedures that contributed to the problem can be improved, or others can be implemented.
* *Asset plays.* Assets that could not be liquidated in a shorter time frame can be liquidated. For example, real estate could be sold. Many smaller companies, particularly older ones, carry real estate on their balance sheet at far below market value. This could be sold and leased back or could be borrowed against to generate cash.
* *Creative solutions.* Creative solutions need to be found. For example, one firm had a large amount of inventory that was useless in its current business. However, it found that if the inventory could be assembled into parts, there would be a market for it. The company shipped the inventory to Jamaica, where labour rates were low, for assembly, and it was able to sell very profitably the entire inventory.

As was stated at the beginning of the chapter, many companies—even companies that are insolvent or have negative net worth or both—can be rescued and restored to profitability.

Although we opened this chapter with the assertion that purchasing an automobile seldom provides a positive financial return—we do know that those who restore cars find great joy in the activity. Rescuing a wreck from the scrapyard or taking a jalopy from a barn and returning it to working condition is rewarding for those who have a passion for it. While diagnosing and overcoming troubles for a venture need not result in harvest, and harvest can be undertaken regardless of the venture's condition, often the two are related. While driving a car into the ground may be prudent with a fully depreciated vehicle, this certainly is not the ideal modus operandi for a viable business. We now turn our attention to exit strategy and execution.

A JOURNEY, NOT A DESTINATION

A common sentiment among successful entrepreneurs is that it is the challenge and exhilaration of the journey that gives them the greatest kick. Actor Jim Carrey captures the spirit: "Desperation is a necessary ingredient to learning anything, or creating anything. Period. If you ain't desperate at some point, you ain't interesting." It is the thrill of the chase that counts. And of course, many entrepreneurial individuals can't sit still—they're always restless. In Jim Carrey's case: "My report card always said, 'Jim finishes first and then disrupts the other students'."[4]

Entrepreneurs also talk of the venture's incredibly insatiable appetite for not only cash but also time, attention, and energy. Some say it is an addiction. Most say it is far more demanding and difficult than they ever imagined. Most, however, plan not to retire and would do it again, usually sooner rather than later. They also say it is more fun and satisfying than any other career they have had.

For the vast majority of entrepreneurs, it takes 10, 15, even 20 years or more to build a significant net worth. According to the popular press and government statistics, there are more millionaires than ever in Canada. One report estimated 315,000 Canadian millionaires in 2001 and predicts 900,000 in 2010.[5] According to Statistics Canada "surging real estate values and a strong economy helped drive up the number of millionaire families in Canada to 1.1 million in 2005."[6] Sadly, a million dollars is not really all that much money today as a result of inflation, and while lottery winners become instant millionaires, entrepreneurs do not. The number of years it usually takes to accumulate such a net worth is a far cry from the instant millionaire, the get-rich-quick impression associated with lottery winners or in either fantasy or "reality" TV shows.

THE JOURNEY CAN BE ADDICTIVE

The total immersion required, the huge workload, the many sacrifices for a family, and the burnout often experienced by an entrepreneur are real. Maintaining the energy, enthusiasm, and drive to get across the finish line, to achieve a harvest, may be exceptionally difficult. For instance, one entrepreneur in the computer software business, after working alone for several years, developed highly sophisticated software. Yet, he insisted he could not stand the computer business for another day. Imagine trying to position a company for sale effectively and to negotiate a deal for a premium price after such a long battle.

Some entrepreneurs wonder if the price of victory is too high. One very successful entrepreneur put it this way:

> What difference does it make if you win, have $20 million in the bank—I know several who do—and you are a basket case, your family has been washed out, and your kids are a wreck?

Entrepreneur Brett Wilson recalls:

> It was hard not to enjoy the success we were having, doing a deal a day. It was enthralling to be at the office. I got as caught up in my career as any investment banker could be. I had always told myself that I worked so hard because of my family. Suddenly, I was facing the possibility of no family at all.[7]

The message is clear: Unless an entrepreneur enjoys the journey and thinks it is worthy, he or she may end up on the wrong train to the wrong destination.

FIRST BUILD A GREAT COMPANY

One of the simplest but most difficult principles for non-entrepreneurs to grasp is that wealth and liquidity are results—not causes—of building a great company. They fail to recognize the difference between making money and spending money. Most successful entrepreneurs possess a clear understanding of this distinction; they get their kicks from growing the company. They know the payoff will take care of itself if they concentrate on proving and building a sustainable venture.

Hard Work and Bad Luck

Sam Tilden bought a Hertz Rent-a-Car franchise for Montréal in 1925. Hertz took the franchise back in 1929 thinking it could make more money, Sam went into the miniature golf business for a few years, and in 1932 Sam reclaimed his old franchise! He expanded to Ottawa and Hamilton, Ontario. In 1953, Sam Tilden and several Hertz franchises walked—and founded Tilden Rent-a-Car. (Hertz had a cancellation policy that allowed them to revoke a franchise without cause on 60-days' notice.) By 1954, they had 100 Tilden locations across Canada.

Sam formed partnerships (50-50 joint ventures) with U.S.-based National Car Rental for Europe and Japanese Nippon Rent-a-Car for Asia. In 1973, at the age of 76 Sam died of a heart attack. His sons Walter and Ted took over and moved headquarters from Montréal to Toronto. In 1991, Ted died of a heart attack. Two months later a Tilden car was involved in a gruesome accident in New York City involving a gasoline tanker truck. Nearly a dozen stores were burned as 200 firefighters fought the blaze. The trucking company did not have insurance and over 20 lawsuits were aimed at Tilden's deeper pockets. For estate planning reasons, Walter looked to sell the company. His niece, Patricia Tilden took over as president and CEO of the family company. Tilden sought protection from potential liability and sought protection under the Companies' Creditor Arrangement (bankruptcy protection) a month before the lawsuits were expected to go to trial. Walter's son, Bruce, witnessed the claims being tossed out of court and within a week National Car Rental paid $115 million for Tilden's fleet with Tilden retaining about $4 million in real estate assets. Walter died in 2008 at age 80.[8]

Source: Anthony J. Patterson, "Canada's Tildens: Waving the Flag That Works for Them," *Financial Times*, March 24, 1975; "Car Rental Industry's Ted Tilden Dies at 60," *Calgary Herald*, March 7, 1991; "Court Clears Way for Tilden Sale," *Financial Post*, June 8, 1996; Sandra Martin, "He Helped Build Tilden Rent-a-Car Into a Thriving, All-Canadian Concern," *Globe and Mail*, July 30, 2008.

CREATE HARVEST OPTIONS

Here is yet another great paradox in the entrepreneurial process: Build a great company but do not forget to harvest. This apparent contradiction is difficult to reconcile, especially among entrepreneurs with several generations in a family-owned enterprise. Perhaps a better way to frame this apparent contradiction is to keep harvest options open and to think of harvesting as a vehicle for reducing risk and for creating future entrepreneurial choices and options, not simply selling the business and heading for the golf course or the beach, although these options may appeal to a few entrepreneurs.

It is not difficult to think of a number of alternative outcomes for those wanting to exit the venture. By stubbornly and steadfastly refusing to explore harvest options and exiting as a natural part of the entrepreneurial process, owners may actually increase their overall risk and deprive themselves of future options. Innumerable examples exist whereby entrepreneurs sold or merged their companies and then went on to acquire or to start another company and pursued new dreams:

- At the age of six Ted Rogers' father died. At the urging of family, his mother sold off industrial assets, including radio station CFRB, which Ted promised his mother he would one day buy back.
- Edgar Bronfman expanded the family fortune as Seagram expanded and then divested ownership in favour of other financial and personal pursuits. The decision to divest the family stake in DuPont Chemical was controversial and received much criticism.
- E.D. Smith & Sons of Winona, Ontario, had been a family business making jams, spreads, marmalades, etc. since 1882. In 2002, Llewellyn S. Smith, chairman of E.D. Smith & Sons Ltd. sold the company to Imperial Capital Corporation. E.D. Smith went on to acquire other food processors. In late 2007, E.D. Smith & Sons was sold to Treehouse Foods Inc.
- While in his early 20s, Stephen Spinelli was recruited by his former college football coach, Jim Hindman, to help start and build Jiffy Lube International. As a captain of the team, Spinelli had exhibited the qualities of leadership, tenacity, and competitive will to win that Hindman knew was needed to create a new company. Spinelli later built the largest franchise in America, and after selling his 49 stores to Pennzoil in 1993, he returned to his MBA alma mater to teach. So invigorated by this new challenge, he even went back to earn his doctorate.

- Dominion Loose Leaf Company was started in 1918, the Nicholds family purchased the company in 1956 creating an exit for the previous owners. The printing services company was renamed Dollco Printing and in 2001 ownership passed to the third generation, cousins Krista Nicholds and Kevin Nicholds co-presidents of an organization that today has 300 employees and operations in Ottawa, Toronto, Québec, Halifax, and the northeastern United States.

These are a tiny representation of the tens of thousands of entrepreneurs that build on their platforms of entrepreneurial success to pursue highly meaningful lives in philanthropy, public service, and community leadership. By realizing a harvest, such options become possible, yet the vast majority of entrepreneurs make these contributions to society while continuing to build their companies (see Jim Pattison). This is one of the best-kept secrets in our culture: The public has very little awareness and appreciation of just how common this pattern of generosity is of their time, their leadership, and their money. One could fill a book with numerous other examples. The entrepreneurial process is endless.

Jim Pattison

Born in Saskatoon, Saskatchewan, Jim Pattison has amassed an amazing empire. At age 81, he is still going strong and making acquisitions one after the other. Forbes lists him as the 6th wealthiest Canadian and like many other high net-worth individuals devotes much time, effort, and money to causes he finds worthy. When CBC Television announced that during the NHL playoffs they could not afford to rent high-definition broadcast trucks during away games, Pattison announced that his Save-On Foods, a western Canadian grocery chain, would cover the costs—$100,000.[9]

Despite his age, Jim Pattison shows no signs of cashing out. As the sole owner of the third-largest privately held Canadian company, he is not required to reveal any "harvest" plans.

Source: www.jimpattison.com.

A HARVEST GOAL

Having a harvest goal and crafting a strategy to achieve it are what separate successful entrepreneurs from the rest of the pack. Many entrepreneurs seek only to create a job and a living for themselves. It is quite different to grow a business that creates a living for many others, including employees and investors, by creating value—value that can result in a capital gain.

Setting a harvest goal achieves many purposes, not the least of which is helping an entrepreneur get after-tax cash out of an enterprise and enhancing substantially his or her net worth. Such a goal also can create high standards and a serious commitment to excellence over the course of developing the business. It can provide, in addition, a motivating force and a strategic focus that does not sacrifice customers, employees, and value-added products and services just to maximize quarterly earnings.

There are other good reasons to set a harvest goal as well. The workload demanded by a harvest-oriented venture versus one in a venture that cannot achieve a harvest may actually be less and is probably no greater. Such a business may be less stressful than managing a business that is not oriented to harvest.

There is a very significant societal reason as well for seeking and building a venture worthy of a harvest. These are the ventures that provide enormous impact and value added in a variety of ways. These are the companies that contribute most disproportionately to technological and other innovations, to new jobs, to returns for investors, and to economic vibrancy.

Also, within the harvest process, the seeds of renewal and reinvestment are sown. Such a recycling of entrepreneurial talent and capital is at the very heart of our system of private responsibility for economic renewal and individual initiative. Entrepreneurial companies organize and manage for the long haul in ways to perpetuate the opportunity creation and recognition process and thereby to ensure economic regeneration, innovation, and renewal.

Thus, a harvest goal is not just a goal of selling and leaving the company. Rather, it is a long-term goal to create real value added in a business. (It is true, however, that if real value added is not created, the business simply will not be worth much in the marketplace.)

CRAFTING A HARVEST STRATEGY: TIMING IS VITAL

Consistently, entrepreneurs avoid thinking about harvest issues. In a survey of the computer software industry, 80 of the 100 companies had only an informal plan for harvesting. The rest of the sample confirmed the avoidance of harvest plans by entrepreneurs—only 15 of the companies had a formal written strategy for harvest in their business plans and the remaining five had a formal harvest plan written after the business plan.[10] When a company is launched, then struggles for survival, and finally begins its ascent, the farthest thing from its founder's mind usually is selling out. Selling is often viewed by the entrepreneur as the equivalent to complete abandonment of his or her very own "baby." But a harvest "makes perfect sense" when the entrepreneur "finds it is the appropriate timing for capturing the value that has been created through the venture."[11]

Thus, time and again, a founder does not consider selling until terror, in the form of the possibility of losing the whole company, is experienced. Usually, this possibility comes unexpectedly: New technology threatens to leapfrog over the current product line, a large competitor suddenly appears in a small market, or a major account is lost. A sense of panic then grips the founders and shareholders of the closely held firm, and the company is suddenly for sale—for sale at the wrong time, for the wrong reasons, and thus for the wrong price. Selling at the right time, willingly, involves hitting a strategic window, one of the many strategic windows that entrepreneurs face.

Entrepreneurs find that harvesting is a non-issue until something begins to sprout, and again there is a vast distance between creating an existing revenue stream of an ongoing business and ground zero. Most entrepreneurs agree that securing customers and generating continuing sales revenue are much harder and take much longer than they could have imagined. Further, the ease with which those revenue estimates can be cast and manipulated on a spreadsheet belies the time and effort necessary to turn those projections into cash.

At some point, with a higher potential venture, it becomes possible to realize the harvest. It is wiser to be selling as the strategic window is opening than as it is closing. Business financier and stock market speculator Bernard Baruch's wisdom is as good as it gets on this matter. He has said, "I made all my money by selling too early." For example, a private candy company with $150 million in sales was not considering selling. After contemplating advice to sell early, the founders recognized a unique opportunity to harvest and sold the firm for 19 times earnings, an extremely high valuation. Another example is that of a cellular phone company that was launched and built from scratch. Only 18 months after purchasing the original rights to build and operate the system, the founders decided to sell the company, even though the future looked extremely bright. They sold because the sellers' market they faced at the time had resulted in a premium valuation—30 percent higher on a per capita basis (the industry valuation norm) than that for any previous cellular transaction to date. The harvest returned over 25 times the original capital in a year and a half. (The founders had not invested a dime of their own money.)

If the window is missed, disaster can strike. Shaping a harvest strategy is an enormously complicated and difficult task. Thus, crafting such a strategy cannot begin too early. Companies declared bankruptcy in the wake of the dot-com bubble burst and stock market crashes. The toll includes large corporations and dozens of lesser-known small and mid-size companies. This is one history lesson that seems to repeat itself. While building a company is the ultimate goal, failure to preserve the harvest option, and utilize it when it is available, can be most disheartening.

In shaping a harvest strategy, some guidelines and cautions can help:

- *Patience.* As has been shown, several years are required to launch and build most successful companies; therefore, patience can be invaluable. A harvest strategy is more sensible if it allows for a time frame of at least three to five years and as long as seven to 10 years. The other side of the patience coin is not to panic as a result of precipitate events. Selling under duress is usually the worst of all worlds.

- *Realistic valuation.* If impatience is the enemy of an attractive harvest, then greed is its executioner. For example, an excellent, small firm, which was nearly 80 years old and run by the third generation of a line of successful family leaders, had attracted a number of prospective buyers and had obtained a bona fide offer for more than $25 million. The owners, however, had become convinced that this "great little company" was worth considerably more, and they held out. Before long, there were no buyers, and market circumstances changed unfavourably. In addition, interest rates skyrocketed. Soon thereafter, the company collapsed financially, ending up in bankruptcy.

- *Outside advice.* It is difficult but worthwhile to find an advisor who can help craft a harvest strategy while the business is growing and, at the same time, maintain objectivity about its value and have the patience and skill to maximize it. A major problem seems to be that people who sell businesses, such as investment bankers or business brokers, are performing the same economic role and function as real estate brokers; in essence, their incentive is their commissions during a quite short time frame, usually a matter of months. However, an advisor who works with a lead entrepreneur for as much as five years or more can help shape and implement a strategy for the whole business so that it is positioned to spot and respond to harvest opportunities when they appear.

HARVEST OPTIONS

There are seven principal avenues by which a company can realize a harvest from the value it has created. Described on the next pages, these most commonly seem to occur in the order in which they are listed. No attempt is made here to do more than briefly describe each avenue, since there are entire books written on each of these, including their legal, tax, and accounting intricacies. As you read through these harvest options consider Roots. Established in 1973, Roots is "Canada's leading lifestyle" brand known worldwide, particularly after outfitting Olympic athletes.[12] But Roots has had ups and downs. Roots is owned by its co-founders Michael Budmand and Don Green who met one summer at camp in Algonquin Park, Ontario. When would you "harvest" Roots and how? What signals would tell you? Exercise 7 "Capital and Harvest—How Will You Realize Dollars from the Venture?" in the Venture Opportunity Screening Exercise that accompanies Chapter 3 and is found on the Online Learning Centre at www.mcgrawhill.ca/olc/timmons is worth visiting.

Capital Cow

A "capital cow" is to the entrepreneur what a "cash cow" is to a large corporation. In essence, the high-margin profitable venture (the cow) throws off more cash for personal use (the milk) than most entrepreneurs have the time and uses or inclinations for spending. The result is a capital-rich and cash-rich company with enormous capacity for debt and reinvestment. Take, for instance, a health care–related venture that realized early success and went public. Several years later, the founders decided to buy the company back from the public shareholders and to return it to its closely held status. Today the company has sales in excess of $100 million and generates extra capital of several million dollars each year. This capital cow has enabled its entrepreneurs to form entities to invest in several other higher potential ventures, which included participation in the leveraged buyout of a $150-million sales division of a larger firm and in some venture capital deals. Sometimes the creation of a capital cow results in substantial real estate holdings by the entrepreneur, off the books of the original firm. This allows for greater flexibility in the distribution of cash flow and the later allocation of the wealth.

Employee Stock Ownership Plan

Employee stock ownership plans have become very popular among closely held companies as a valuation mechanism for stock for which there is no formal market. They are also vehicles through which founders can realize some liquidity from their stock by sales to the plan and other employees. And since an ESOP usually creates widespread ownership of stock among employees, it is viewed as a positive motivational device as well. In General Motors' 2009 restructuring, Magna sought to acquire GM's European product group Opel. The deal called for 10 percent of the shares to be turned over to Opel employees.

Management Buyout

Another avenue, called a management buyout (MBO), is one in which a founder can realize a gain from a business by selling it to existing partners or to other key managers in the business. If the business has both assets and a healthy cash flow, the financing can be arranged via banks, insurance companies, and financial institutions that do leveraged buyouts (LBOs) and MBOs. Even if assets are thin, a healthy cash flow that can service the debt to fund the purchase price can convince lenders to do the MBO.

Usually, the problem is that the managers who want to buy out the owners and remain to run the company do not have the capital. Unless the buyer has the cash up front—and this is rarely the case—such a sale can be very fragile, and full realization of a gain is questionable. MBOs typically require the seller to take a limited amount of cash up front and a note for the balance of the purchase price over several years. If the purchase price is linked to the future profitability of the business, the seller is totally dependent on the ability and integrity of the buyer. Further, management, under such an arrangement, can lower the price by growing the business as fast as possible, spending on new products and people, and showing very little profit along the way. In these cases, it is often seen that after the marginally profitable business is sold at a bargain price, it is well positioned with excellent earnings in the next two or three years. As can be seen, the seller will end up on the short end of this type of deal.

Merger, Acquisition, and Strategic Alliance

Merging with a firm is still another way for a founder to realize a gain. For example, two founders who had developed high-quality training programs consummated a merger with another company. These entrepreneurs had backgrounds in computers, rather than in marketing or general management, and the results of the company's first five years reflected this gap. Sales were under $500,000, based on custom programs and no marketing, and they had been unable to attract venture capital. The firm with which they merged was a $15-million company that had an excellent reputation for its management training programs, had a large customer base, had repeat sales of 70 percent, and had requests from the field sales force for programs to train managers in the use of personal computers. The buyer obtained 80 percent of the shares of the smaller firm, to consolidate the revenues and earnings from the merged company into its own financial statements, and the two founders of the smaller firm retained a 20-percent ownership in their firm. The two founders also obtained employment contracts, and the buyer provided nearly $1.5 million of capital advances during the first year of the new business. Under a put arrangement, the founders will be able to realize a gain on their 20 percent of the company, depending upon performance of the venture over the next few years.[13] The two founders now are reporting to the president of the parent firm, and one founder of the parent firm has taken a key executive position with the smaller company, an approach common for mergers between closely held firms.

In a strategic alliance, founders can attract badly needed capital, in substantial amounts, from a large company interested in their technologies. Such arrangements often can lead to complete buyouts of the founders downstream.

Outright Sale

Most advisors view outright sale as the ideal route to go because up-front cash is preferred over most stock, even though the latter can result in a tax-free exchange.[14] In a stock-for-stock exchange, the problem is the volatility and unpredictability of the stock price of the purchasing company. Many entrepreneurs have been left with a fraction of the original purchase price when the stock price of the buyer's company declined steadily. Often the acquiring company wants to lock key management into employment contracts for up to several years. Whether this makes sense depends on the goals and circumstances of the individual entrepreneur. Recall from Chapter 2 that John W. Sleeman sold his namesake in 2004 and agreed to stay on to serve as CEO under the new owner Sapporo Breweries of Japan.

Public Offering

Probably the most sacred business school cow of them all—other than the capital cow—is the notion of taking a company public.[15] The vision or fantasy of having one's venture listed on one of the stock exchanges arouses passions of greed, glory, and greatness. For many would-be entrepreneurs, this aspiration is unquestioned and enormously appealing. Yet, for all but a chosen few, taking a company public, and then living with it, may be far more time and trouble—and expense—than it is worth. Richard L'Abbé of Med-Eng (end-of-chapter case in Chapter 5) was strongly opposed to taking his company public.

After the stock market crash of October 1987, the market for new issues of stock shrank to a fraction of the robust IPO market of 1986 and earlier years. The number of new issues and the volume of IPOs did not rebound; instead, they declined between 1988 and 1992. Beginning in 1993 the IPO window opened again. During this IPO frenzy, small companies with total assets under $500,000 issued most of the IPOs. Previously, small companies had not been as active in the IPO market. Now most of the firms that go public in Canada have small capitalizations.

This cyclical pattern repeats itself regularly. As the dot.com, telecommunications, and networking explosion accelerated from 1995 to 2000, the IPO markets exploded as well. In 1996, for instance, despite twice the number of IPOs as in 2005, the total dollar value in 2006 was lower than in 2005. In 2008, there were months when not a single IPO occurred on the Toronto Stock Exchange! Few signs of recovery were evident in 2009. The lesson is clear: Depending upon the IPO market for a harvest is a highly cyclical strategy, which can cause both great joy and disappointment. Such is the reality of the stock markets. Exhibits 15.2(A) and 15.2(B) show this pattern vividly.

There are several advantages to going public, many of which relate to the ability of the company to fund its rapid growth. Public equity markets provide access to long-term capital, while also meeting subsequent capital needs. Companies may use the proceeds of an IPO to expand the business in the existing market or to move into a related market. The founders and initial investors might be seeking liquidity, but restrictions limiting the timing and the amount of stock that the officers, directors, and insiders can dispose of in the public market are increasingly severe. As a result, it can take several years after an IPO before a liquid gain is possible. A public offering not only increases public awareness of the company but also contributes to the marketability of the products, including franchises. Tim Hortons went public in 2006 on the New York Stock Exchange and the Toronto Stock Exchange.

However, there are also some disadvantages to being a public company. For example, 50 percent of the computer software companies surveyed in one study agreed that the focus on short-term profits and performance results was a negative attribute of being a public company.[16] Also, because of the disclosure requirements, public companies lose some of their operating confidentiality, not to mention having to support the ongoing costs of public disclosure, audits, and tax filings. With public shareholders, the management of the company has to be careful about the flow of information because of the risk of insider trading. Thus, it is easy to see why companies need to think about the positive and negative attributes of being a public company. When considering this decision, you may find it useful to identify the key components of the IPO process and to assess which investment bankers, accountants, lawyers, and advisors might be useful in making this decision.

EXHIBIT 15.2(A)   Number of Canadian IPOs

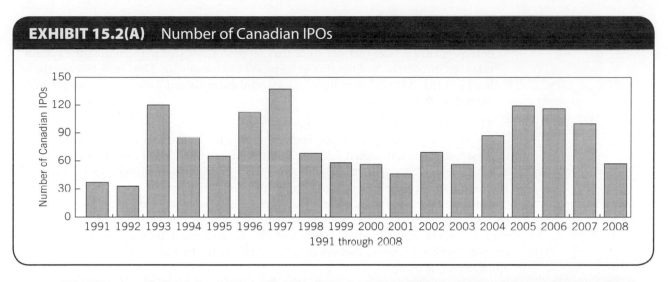

EXHIBIT 15.2(B)   Value of Canadian IPOs ($millions)

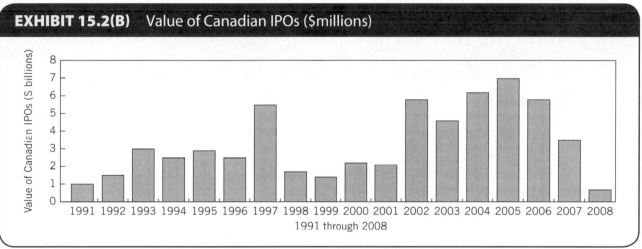

Source: "Survey of IPOs in Canada," PricewaterhouseCoopers (2004, 2006, 2008).

BEYOND THE HARVEST

A majority of highly successful entrepreneurs seem to accept a responsibility to renew and perpetuate the system that has treated them so well. They are keenly aware that our system of opportunity and mobility depends in large part upon a self-renewal process.

There are many ways in which this happens. Some of the following data often surprise people:

- *University endowments*. Entrepreneurs are the most generous regarding larger gifts and the most frequent contributors to school endowments, scholarship funds, and the like. One study showed that eight times as many entrepreneurs, compared to all other *graduates*, made large gifts to the schools that they attended.[17] On college and university campuses across Canada, a huge number of dorms, classroom buildings, arts centres, and athletic facilities are named for the contributor. In virtually every instance, these contributors are entrepreneurs whose highly successful companies enabled them to make major gifts of stock to their alma mater.

- *Community activities*. Entrepreneurs who have harvested their ventures very often reinvest their leadership skills and money in such community activities as symphony orchestras, museums, and local colleges and universities. These entrepreneurs lead fund-raising campaigns, serve on boards of directors, and devote many hours to other volunteer work.

- *Investing in new companies.* Post-harvest entrepreneurs also reinvest their efforts and resources in the next generation of entrepreneurs and their opportunities. Successful entrepreneurs behave this way since they seem to know that perpetuating the system is far too important, and too fragile, to be left to anyone else. They have learned the hard lessons. As angel investors, experienced entrepreneurs are the key source of capital for start-up firms.

The innovation, the job creation, and the economic renewal and vibrancy are all results of the entrepreneurial process. Government does not cause this complicated and little understood process, though it facilitates and/or impedes it. It is not caused by the stroke of a legislative pen, though it can be ended by such a stroke. Rather, entrepreneurs, investors, and hardworking people in pursuit of opportunities create it.

Fortunately, entrepreneurs seem to accept a disproportionate share of the responsibility to make sure the process is renewed. And, judging by the new wave of entrepreneurship in Canada, both the marketplace and society once again are prepared to allocate the rewards to entrepreneurs that are commensurate with their acceptance of responsibility and delivery of results.

THE ROAD AHEAD: DEVISE A PERSONAL ENTREPRENEURIAL STRATEGY

Goals Matter—A Lot!

Of all the anchors one can think of in the entrepreneurial process, two loom above all the rest:

1. A passion for achieving goals.
2. A relentless competitive spirit and desire to win, and the will to never give up!

These two habits drive the quest for learning, personal growth, continuous improvement, and all other development. Without these good habits, most quests will fall short. In Chapter 1 and on the Online Learning Centre, you will find the "Crafting a Personal Entrepreneurial Strategy" exercise. Visit www.mcgrawhill.ca/olc/timmons and the exercise is within the material associated with Chapter 1. Completing this lengthy exercise will help you develop these good habits.

Values and Principles Matter—A Lot!

We have demonstrated, in numerous places throughout the book, that values and principles matter a great deal. We encourage you to consider those of others as you develop your own anchors. This is a vital part of your leadership approach, and who and what you are:

- Treat others as you would want to be treated.
- Share the wealth with those high performers who help you create it.
- Give back to the community and society.

We would add a fourth principle in the Aboriginal spirit of considering every action with the seventh generational impact foremost in mind:

- Be a guardian and a steward of the air, land, water, and environment.

One major legacy of the coming generations of entrepreneurial leaders can be the sustainability of our economic activities. It is possible to combine a passion for entrepreneurship with love of the land and the environment. The work of such organizations as the Nature Conservancy, the World Wildlife Fund, and Direct Relief International, and dozens of others is financially made possible by the contributions of money, time, and leadership from highly successful entrepreneurs. It is also one of the most durable ways to give back. Practising what he preaches, Professor Timmons and his wife made a permanent gift of nearly 500 acres of their New Hampshire farm to a conservation easement. Other neighbours joined in for a combined total of over 1,000 acres of land preserved forever, never to be developed. This has led to a regional movement as well, which involves landowners from a dozen surrounding towns.

Another purposeful environmental action to preserve space for future generations to enjoy is the Trans Canada Trail, which aims to be the longest recreational path in the world when finished. Depending on section, the trail allows a variety of uses: walk, cycle, ski, canoe, horse, ATV, or snowmobile. Much of the trail is former railroad lines donated by provincial, federal, and commercial entities. Kilometres of the trail are sponsored by individuals, families, and corporations. It began on Canada's 125th anniversary in 1992 and upon completion will be 21,500 kilometres connecting 1,000 communities and 33 million Canadians.

SEVEN SECRETS OF SUCCESS

The following seven secrets of success are included for your contemplation and amusement:

1. There are no secrets. Understanding and practising the fundamentals discussed here, along with hard work, will get results.
2. As soon as there is a secret, everyone else knows about it, too. Searching for secrets is a mindless exercise.
3. Happiness is a positive cash flow.
4. If you teach a person to work for others, you feed him or her for a year, but if you teach a person to be an entrepreneur, you feed him or her, and others, for a lifetime.
5. Do not run out of cash.
6. Entrepreneurship is fundamentally a human process, rather than a financial or technological process. You can make an enormous difference.
7. Happiness is a positive cash flow.

Chapter Summary

1. Numerous signals of impending trouble—strategic issues, poor planning and financial controls, and running out of cash—invariably point to a core cause: top management.
2. Crises don't develop overnight. Often it takes 18 months to five years before the company is sick enough to trigger a turnaround intervention. Both quantitative and qualitative signals can predict patterns and actions that could lead to trouble.
3. Bankruptcy, usually an entrepreneur's nightmare, can actually be a valuable tool and source of bargaining power to help a company survive and recover.
4. Turnaround specialists begin with a diagnosis of the numbers—cash, strategic market issues, and management—and develop a turnaround plan.
5. The turnaround plan defines remedial action to generate cash, deal with lenders and trade creditors, begin long-term renewal, and monitor progress.
6. Entrepreneurs thrive on the challenges and satisfactions of the game: It's a journey, not a destination.
7. First and foremost, successful entrepreneurs strive to build a great company; wealth follows that process.
8. Harvest options mean more than simply selling the company, and these options are an important part of the entrepreneur's know-how.
9. Entrepreneurs know that to perpetuate the system for future generations, they must give back to their communities and invest time and capital in the next entrepreneurial generation.

Study Questions

1. What do entrepreneurs need to know about how companies get into and out of trouble? Why?

2. Why do most turnaround specialists invariably discover that it is management that is the root cause of trouble?

3. Why is it difficult for existing management to detect and to act early on signals of trouble?

4. Why can bankruptcy be the entrepreneur's ally?

5. What are the main components of a turnaround plan and why are these so important?

6. Why is it essential to focus first on building a great company, rather than on just getting rich?

7. Why is a harvest goal so crucial for entrepreneurs and the economy?

8. Define the principal harvest options, the pros and cons of each, and why each is valuable?

9. Beyond the harvest, what do entrepreneurs do to give back, and why is this so important to their communities and the nation?

Mind Stretchers   *Have you considered?*

1. General Motors was forced to "harvest" a few of its divisions. Oldsmobile was eliminated in 2004. Saab, founded in 1937 in Sweden, came under GM's full control in 2000. GM placed Saab on the auction block during the economic turmoil of 2009, but is that the best time to sell? And with GM under bankruptcy protection plans were to shrink Pontiac, and Saturn, a fresh new venture within GM created in 1985 was to be folded or sold off—Penske eventually bid on it. After only a decade under GM's control Hummer was sold to a machinery company in China. Meanwhile Magna International was poised to purchase GM's

European lines: Opel and Vauxhall. The deal included a Russian bank and Opel employees taking a 10-percent stake. Please discuss harvest timing.

2. CanWest Global Communications is in financial distress. Is it another brontosaurus heading for a fall? What are the signals and what is the remedy?

3. With so much positive spin on restructuring, has the stigma of bankruptcy (personal and corporate) completely been eliminated?

4. Would you go to work for a troubled company? Why and under what conditions?

CASE   **CAVENDISH COVE COTTAGES**

Preparation Questions:

1. What are the strengths and weaknesses of CCC's current strategy?

2. Should Sherry Noonan make an offer? What is the value of the business?

3. What is the business's financial position now and for the future?

4. What valuation methods can be used to construct an estimate?

"I just don't know if the asking price is fair," Sherry Noonan explained to Martin Heaney, one of her business professors at the University of Prince Edward Island (UPEI). It was December 10, 2008 and Sherry had just finished writing her final exam for the semester. She was now finished with the first half of her fourth and final year of the business program at UPEI. Sherry was considering making an offer on a cottage rental business located in the heart of Cavendish, the very popular tourist destination on Prince Edward Island (PEI). While Sherry would have some financial support from her

family if she bought the cottage business, she knew that a key to ensure the future success of the business was to pay a fair price for it, and to be able to exploit marketing opportunities.

As Sherry left Martin Heaney's office, she reflected on the conversation with her professor. At this point in her university career, Sherry had completed courses in all of the functional areas of business (marketing, operations management, corporate finance, organizational behaviour, and accounting) and she felt that she should be able to analyze the information she had available regarding the cottage property. The work

---

This case was written by Dr. Sean M. Hennessey, University of Prince Edward Island, for purposes of classroom discussion.

required to make an offer on the business, would have to be completed over the next few days. That would allow Heaney and her parents the time to review her work. It would also give Sherry the time to negotiate with the business's owners, Fran and Ted Baker. It was important to get all of this work done before the activities of Christmas began, and before she would begin her final semester of classes. It would also ensure that she would have plenty of time to prepare for the opening of the cottages in May 2009, if her bid was successful.

The price for the cottages was $800,000, and Martin Heaney had asked Sherry whether she thought that was a fair price for the business. Heaney had focused on some of the key questions that had to be answered: How should the value of the cottage business be estimated? Could a new marketing strategy increase the value of the business to Sherry? If so, how would the new marketing strategy differ from the one employed by the current owners? What is the business worth? If a deal was negotiated, how should the purchase be financed? Now all Sherry had to do was answer these questions using the concepts she had learned over the last three-and-a-half years of her business education.

PEI and the Cavendish Area

Prince Edward Island is Canada's smallest province, with a population of just 140,000 and 5,684 square kilometres of land. The Island, as it was known to locals, was often called "the million acre farm," though PEI actually consisted of 1.4 million acres. About 55 percent of the population lived in rural areas. PEI, in the Gulf of St. Lawrence, was separated from its sister provinces of Nova Scotia and New Brunswick by the Northumberland Strait. In 1997, the Confederation Bridge was opened providing PEI with a permanent link to New Brunswick. A ferry service also ran between PEI and Nova Scotia for about eight months of the year. At the turn of the 21st century, PEI continued to rely heavily on three industries that had seen it through the last century: agriculture, tourism, and fishing.

From May 1 to October 31, 2008, 1,105,264 visitors in 393,681 tourist parties spent a total of $345.6 million while vacationing on PEI. Compared to 2007, this was a decrease of 3.8 percent in numbers and 2.1 percent in expenditures. In 2008, 93.9 percent of the visitors and 90.6 percent of the tourist parties visited PEI for pleasure (rather than business), and accounted for 90.6 percent of the expenditures. The average party size was 2.91 people, and they spent an average of 4.5 nights on PEI.

Tourism on PEI was seasonal with mid-July to late-August being the peak of the tourism season. The early season (pre-July) is quite slow in many areas of PEI, and winter tourism is almost non-existent, except when special events are held. These are normally on weekends. The fall season was starting to become popular after many years of marketing by the Provincial Government Tourism Department and individual operators. The primary visitors during the fall were older and retired couples who liked the cooler temperatures and smaller crowds. While some came on bus tours, many were independent travellers who valued quality products and services.

The largest share of visitors (27.8 percent) came from Ontario followed by the United States with 19.4 percent and Nova Scotia was a close third. New Brunswick and Québec accounted for 18 percent of visitors. About 56 percent of the

pleasure visitors were repeat customers, while 47 percent were in the 40–59 age bracket. Over 74 percent reported household incomes greater than $50,000. The primary activities of pleasure visitors in 2008 were: sightseeing (84 percent), soft outdoor adventure (77 percent), beach visits (71 percent), and craft shopping (69 percent). Golf was enjoyed by 15 percent of visitors.

Cavendish was located on the north shore of PEI, on the Gulf of St. Lawrence, in the centre of the province. It was about a 30-minute, very scenic, drive from Charlottetown, the capital city. Cavendish was a favourite destination for many visitors since the area has much to offer in terms of tourist attractions. In the area there were national parks, beaches, amusement parks, and many other types of tourist attractions, eight golf courses within a 15-minute drive and eight more within 30 minutes, numerous restaurants, shopping, a nightclub for night life, miniature golf, as well as beautiful scenery.

In addition, there were all types of accommodations from campgrounds to self-catering cottages, to hotels and resorts, to four-star B&Bs and country inns. A major draw was the famous Cavendish Beach, within the PEI National Park, with its rolling dunes and beautiful sandstone rock facings. The beach attracted many visitors to PEI either to swim in its warm waters, or walk the long stretches of red sandy shoreline. Young and old could always find something to do in the area.

Market research statistics for the 2008 tourism season, as collected by the government agency Tourism PEI, indicated that Cavendish was the main overnight destination for 263,600 pleasure visitors, or 25.4 percent of all pleasure visitors to PEI. Cavendish was the second most popular destination for visitors with Charlottetown being the first (32.9 percent of visitors). Other statistics for the pleasure visitors whose main overnight destination was Cavendish indicated that:

- 95 percent stayed in paid accommodations. Of these, 34 percent rented cottages or cabins.
- 55 percent were repeat customers.
- 46 percent made their decision to come to PEI more than 12 weeks prior to their departure.
- 49 percent of visitors were adult couples, while families with children less than 18 years old accounted for 38 percent.
- They spent an average of 4.1 nights on PEI.
- Expenditures averaged $919 per tourist party, similar to the level in 2007.
- Accommodations, restaurant meals, and souvenirs accounted for 66 percent of total expenditures.
- Total expenditures were $65.5 million in 2008.
- The top activities enjoyed by visitors to Cavendish in 2008 were: sightseeing (85 percent), beach visits (81 percent), souvenir shopping (73 percent), visiting the National Park (63 percent), visiting "Anne attractions" (51 percent), driving tours (50 percent), and lobster suppers (48 percent).[1]

"Anne attractions" referred to the book *Anne of Green Gables* written by the well-known Island author Lucy Maud Montgomery. Montgomery was born and raised in the Cavendish area where she lived until she was 36. *Anne of Green Gables*, published in 1908, was based in Cavendish. It has been translated into 15 different languages, put on film, and was the title of a musical stage production that had been staged at

[1] Data were taken from "Economic impact: Tourism 2008" published by the Province of PEI.

the Confederation Centre of the Arts in Charlottetown since 1965. The production also toured around the world. The story imparted an image of PEI that each year drew thousands of visitors to Cavendish from around the world. As a result, *Anne* was a major focus of the tourism industry in Cavendish with many attractions and names of businesses based on characters and locations in the book.

Cavendish Cove Cottages

Cavendish Cove Cottages (CCC) was located in the heart of the community of Cavendish on Route 6, Cavendish Road, a few hundred metres inland from the shoreline. Route 6 was the main road running along the north coastline of central PEI and was easily reached from all parts of PEI. All of the main tourist attractions in Cavendish and the neighbouring communities were on this main road. Cavendish beach, a significant attraction in its own right, was a four-minute drive away from the main entrance to CCC. Those with more time could easily walk to the beach in less than 15 minutes.

Also within 200 metres of the business, were grocery stores, restaurants, a laundromat, shopping, and numerous family-oriented attractions. These included amusement parks such as Rainbow Valley (water and ride park), Sandspit (roller coasters, racing cars, and other park rides), and Avonlea Village (a re-creation of a village from 1908 that allows visitors to interact with characters from the *Anne of Green Gables* novel). Also close by was the Green Gables heritage site that includes the famous Green Gables House. The house and farm site were once owned by relatives of Lucy Maud Montgomery and were the inspiration for her book. Also on the site were numerous other family-oriented attractions.

Finally, within 10 minutes of the cottages were four championship golf courses, with two of these within walking distance. One was the brand new, five-star, 27-hole, championship Eagles Glenn Golf Course that bordered the cottage complex. The other was the scenic, ocean-side Green Gables golf course, designed and built in 1939 by world-renowned architect Stanley Thompson. The cottage business had been in operation in the same location, under the same name, for over 50 years. The complex was zoned as "resort commercial" and, for property tax purposes, was assessed a value of $417,250 with property taxes of $5,340. On the income statement, this expense was included within licences.

The business was owned and operated by an older couple, Fran and Ted Baker. They started the business in the 1950s when land and building costs were quite low. Fran and Ted each owned half of the common shares of the business. The property consisted of 19 rental units and one owner's unit on 2.4 acres of land. Of the rental units, seven were 1-bedroom, four were 2-bedroom, and eight were 3-bedroom. The units were further divided into standard, deluxe, and executive categories. The rental units ranged in size from 226 to 784 square feet. There were five smaller (226 to 270 square feet) units with the remainder generally between 435 and 784 square feet. Exhibit 1 provides a listing of the cottage complex with rental rates for the 2008 tourism season. Given the low rate of inflation and the need to set rental rates up to a year in advance, the Bakers were quoting and taking bookings for the 2009 season based on the 2008 rental rates.

Seventeen of the units were built many years earlier but, within the past three years, 11 had been upgraded with new interiors, windows, and flooring. Dishwashers and whirlpool tubs were installed in some units. These upgrades were in addition to the yearly outlays for repairs and maintenance. Six of the units still required work. The real estate agent listing the property indicated that these units, while structurally sound, were "looking tired." The two executive 2-bedroom cottages were new additions to the property and were very popular. These units were usually the first to rent. Construction of these 784 square foot units had started in the fall of 2006, and were first rented in the spring of 2007. The owner's unit was 1,170 square feet with 3-bedrooms, and an office and laundry. There was also a 480 square foot garage on the property.

CCC was rated as a three-star rental accommodation by Canada Select. Canada Select was the only national accommodations rating program for all types of properties. Their ratings range from one star to five stars. There were at least 75 other accommodation providers within a five-minute drive of CCC. These included over 50 cottage operations ranging in size from two to three rental units to as many as 40 units. In addition, there were 10 motel properties, 11 B&Bs, and four campgrounds. The ratings of these properties range from 2 to 4 stars. Most properties in the Cavendish area were rated 2.5 to 4 stars. There were no properties that were rated less than two stars or more than four. About half of the properties were rated 3.5 or four stars. Exhibit 2 provides a brief discussion of some of the local competitors.

Many of the local competitors had 3.5 or higher star ratings (see Exhibit 2). As a consequence, CCC's average nightly rates were lower than many of their competitors. In addition to the cottages, the complex had an in-ground heated swimming pool, old-fashioned wooden swing benches, and a playground for children. All cottages had cable television, fridge, stove, microwave, barbeque, picnic table, as well as the other standard amenities normally expected with a rental unit.

Rental rates for cottages were often set six months to one year in advance since many repeat guests booked for the following year when checking out in the current year. Many cottage operators were fully booked for the peak season six to 12 months ahead of time. CCC's long history meant that many of their visitors were repeat. Recently, however, a few long-time clients had been lost to competitors who had newer and additional amenities such as ocean-view rooms, hot tubs, fireplaces, and fitness centres. Many competitors also had very well-designed Web sites featuring attractive pictures and detailed information concerning the property, the area, and PEI, in general.

In the high season CCC employed four workers, three full-time and one part-time. In the low season, this was reduced to one full-time and one part-time employee. They worked as housekeepers and on the front desk. Two of the employees had been on the staff for over 20 years. This provided a consistent vision and level of service for repeat guests. In the Cavendish area, it was relatively easy to hire low-skilled workers. Pay rates were usually $6.50 to $7.50 per hour, including benefits. Long-term employees often received $2 to $3 more per hour. The Bakers actively worked and managed the business and drew a salary.

Exhibit 3 provided income statements for CCC for the 2006-2008 fiscal years. Exhibit 4 provides balance sheets for the same period, while Exhibit 5 is the notes to the statements. The cottages were open from May 17 to September 30. Fran and Ted indicated that CCC's occupancy rate in 2007 and 2008 was 93 percent in the high season and 30 percent in the low. The asking price for CCC was $800,000. In discussions with Sherry, the real estate agent listing the property indicated that this was a reasonable price given that it was essentially a turn-key operation, the location of the property, the goodwill created by the Bakers, and given the high value of the assets.

Martin Heaney had told Sherry that there might be tax consequences for the Bakers from the sale. On the sale of a small business in Canada, each of the owners of the common shares would be exempt from tax on the first $500,000 of capital gains. But, 50 percent of any remaining gain would be taxed at about 45 percent. Sherry wondered if this should be considered in her analysis of the business.

Marketing Issues

Fran and Ted believed that there were two primary target markets for their cottages. The principal market was middle-income families with children residing in the Maritime provinces who came to PEI for sightseeing and rest and relaxation. These customers stayed at CCC because they were close to all the major attractions of Cavendish, there was entertainment for their children, the price was affordable, and the accommodations were clean, friendly, and adequate. These were customers who might return year after year because they were satisfied with the services provided for the price paid, and they did not require luxuries.

The second and newer target market was more upscale consumers who came to PEI with friends for a golfing vacation. These customers were also from the Maritime provinces but tended to have more money to spend and visit primarily with other adults. CCC's location made it a good choice for these visitors since there were two exceptional golf courses within walking distance. CCC also offered their customers golf packages with reduced rates on green fees.

Fran and Ted listed CCC in the *PEI Visitors Guide*, and had brochures and a Web site. These were the only forms of advertising used, but that was the case with many of the smaller accommodation providers on PEI. The current Web site could be best described as "lean." The home page and all linked pages only used about 40 percent of the screen space due to a coding problem in the page design. The site itself provided basic information on the property including a brief description of the units, a list of amenities, rates, contact details, golf package details, four short reviews by guests totalling 24 words, and some pictures of the grounds, pool, and cottages. There was also a virtual tour of the grounds and of two cottages, but this was very slow and one of the cottages used looked very average with poor lighting. Most of the pictures were very small and lacked clarity and excitement. While it was not possible to make reservations online, there was a toll-free number and an email address available.

The competition in the accommodations sector in the Cavendish area was fierce. In the area there were four campgrounds, five hotels, and dozens of cottage rental properties. Exhibit 2 provides a listing of the major accommodation properties in the area, and some facts concerning each. With a short season, all operators aggressively competed for the tourist business.

Conclusion

Sherry Noonan considered all of the information she had collected and knew she had better get to work on trying to determine the amount she should offer for Cavendish Cove Cottages. If she bought the business, Sherry planned to be the manager. Her family had run a very successful hotel operation in Charlottetown for many years and she had worked in the business since she was 12. But still, there were many questions she had to consider: Was this a business worth buying? What marketing strategy would she use if she purchased the cottage? Was the $800,000 asking price fair? How should she determine a fair price? With a fair price calculated, how would she finance the purchase?

Her parents indicated that they would provide a portion of the purchase price as equity. Sherry wondered how large an investment she should request from her parents and what rate of return her parents would require on this investment. From her corporate finance course, Sherry knew that the market risk premium on Canadian common shares over the 69 years to 2006 was 6.7 percent. Sherry also questioned where she would access the remainder of the money required. Borrowing from a bank was a possibility. But, after the courses she took, Sherry knew that a bank would not lend her the full purchase price. All lenders required someone to sign that the owners were committed to the business.

After phoning the bank, Sherry knew that prime rate was currently 4.5 percent, while commercial mortgage rates were 4.75 percent for a one-year term, 5.9 percent for a three-year term, and 6.45 percent for a five-year term. Sherry felt she should develop a monthly amortization schedule for the loan for at least the first five years of the planned loan amortization period so she would know the cash flow required to service the loan. But first she had to decide on the loan amortization period, the number of years she would take to repay the loan in full.

Sherry only had a few days to come up with the answers to these questions and to finalize an offer to Fran and Ted Baker. Martin Heaney had volunteered to review her analysis and Sherry wanted to be sure to take advantage of the free expert advice. Also, before making an offer, her parents had indicated that they wanted to review the work behind the proposed offer price. Sherry knew she had better get to work and develop answers to the ever-expanding list of questions that were popping into her head.

EXHIBIT 1   Cavendish Cove Cottages: Categories and Pricing of Cottages

Cottage Type	Number of Cottages	Daily Rate for 2008[1]	
		High Season	Low Season
1-bedroom Deluxe	7	$131	$76
2-bedroom Standard	1	$131	$76
2-bedroom Deluxe	1	$151	$81
2-bedroom Executive	2	$176	$96
3-bedroom Standard	5	$131	$76
3-bedroom Deluxe	3	$146	$81
Total	19		

Notes:

1. The stated rate for each cottage is for from 1 to 4 people. Extra people cost $8.00 per day. The business is open from about May 17 (the date changes every year since the actual opening date is the Friday of the Victoria Day holiday that falls on the Monday preceding May 25 in Canada) to September 30. High season is from June 25 to Labour Day (the first Monday in September). Low season is before June 25 and after Labour Day. The Bakers were taking bookings and quoting the 2008 rates for the 2009 season. This was due to the need to set rental rates up to a year in advance, and the current low rate of inflation.

EXHIBIT 2   Competition in the Cavendish Area

Green Gables Bungalow Court 2.5*

40 cottages on beautiful treed grounds. Bed-sitting, one- and two-bedroom housekeeping bungalows. Kitchenettes and gas barbecues. Located beside Green Gables House and golf course. Excellent playground and heated pool. Ideal for families, golfers. Popular destination for families of all ages for 50 years. Walking distance to golf, restaurants, and shops. Walk, bike or jog to the beach and trails—less then 1 km by path through the National Park. Daily rate: $65 to $145; weekly rate: $655 to $980; based on cottage type and season.

Cavendish Bosom Buddies Cottages & Suites 3.5*

On Route 6, 1 km east of main route 6 and 13 intersection. Ten modern, heated, spacious, well-equipped deluxe two, three, and four bedroom cottages. Jacuzzi, dishwasher, microwave, skylight, gas barbecues, sun decks, laundromat. Deluxe efficiency suites with double Jacuzzis. Large, well-equipped, safe play area. Panoramic view of ocean and sunsets. Golf course, beach, and other major attractions nearby. Daily rate: $85 to $295; weekly rate: $560 to $2,065; based on cottage type and season.

Get a 2008/09 visitor guide at
www.cavendishbeachresort.com/search_maps_accommodations.php.

EXHIBIT 3	Cavendish Cove Cottages		
	Income Statements for the Year Ended December 31		
	2006	**2007**	**2008***
Rental Income	$158,375	$196,881	$210,499
less: Operating Expenses			
Advertising	4,483	4,221	6,528
Amortization	20,258	25,965	27,573
Cable	1,284	1,095	2,088
Electric	8,753	9,281	10,270
Heat	1,146	1,436	1,183
Insurance	6,729	7,988	10,471
Interest and bank charges	2,216	4,131	3,149
Interest on long-term debt	10,321	14,966	11,700
Licences	6,963	7,159	6,706
Office	879	1,919	1,489
Professional fees	3,583	4,649	3,460
Repairs and maintenance	15,935	20,541	18,955
Supplies	11,586	6,844	8,479
Telephone	3,995	2,914	3,801
Vehicle and travel	1,965	2,911	3,035
Wages and benefits	63,425	49,460	47,388
Total Fixed Expenses	166,519	165,480	166,273
Earnings Before Taxes and Other	−8,144	31,401	44,226
Net Other Income	$0	$6,305	$568
Earnings Before Taxes	−8,144	37,706	44,794
Taxes	1,340	8,174	9,436
Net Income after Tax	**−$6,804**	**$29,533**	**$35,358**

* Note: The results for the 2008 fiscal year have not yet been certified.

EXHIBIT 4

Cavendish Cove Cottages
Balance Sheets as at December 31

	2006	2007	2008*
ASSETS			
Cash	$0	$8,113	$4,084
Marketable securities	0	18,750	6,250
Accounts receivable	2,944	189	1,605
Income taxes receivable	1,340	0	0
Total Current Assets	4,284	27,051	11,939
Land	16,655	16,495	16,495
Gross fixed assets (Note 1)	518,700	580,604	612,986
less: Accum amortization	242,210	268,175	295,748
Net value	276,490	312,429	317,238
Total Fixed Assets	293,145	328,924	333,733
Other assets (Note 2)	1	1,919	1,493
Total Assets	**$297,430**	**$357,894**	**$347,164**
LIABILITIES and EQUITY			
Line of credit (Note 3)	$2,784	$0	$0
Accounts payable	7,223	4,300	4,818
Income taxes payable	0	8,209	8,405
Bonus payable	7,500	10,000	10,000
Demand loan (Note 4)	31,250	31,250	37,500
Curr portion of long-term debt	21,796	22,271	22,271
Total current liabilities	70,553	76,030	82,994
Long-term debt (Note 5)	116,040	149,544	127,273
Payable to shareholder (Note 6)	38,440	30,390	24,610
Total liabilities	225,033	255,964	24,876
EQUITY			
Common shares (Note 7)	3,125	3,125	3,125
Retained earnings	69,273	98,805	109,163
Net equity	72,398	101,930	112,288
Total liabilities & equity	**$297,430**	**$357,894**	**$347,164**

* Note: The results for the 2008 fiscal year have not yet been certified.

EXHIBIT 5

Cavendish Cove Cottages Inc.
Notes to the Financial Statements (unaudited)

The company is incorporated under the Companies' Act of Prince Edward Island, and is primarily engaged in the cottage rental industry. The financial statements have been prepared in accordance with Canadian generally accepted accounting principles and include the following significant accounting policies:

1. Capital Assets

Capital assets are recorded at cost, net of government assistance. Amortization is computed using the declining-balance method at the following annual rates, which were the same as the Capital Cost Allowance (CCA) rates for the applicable asset classes.

Building	5%
Equipment	20%
Vehicle	30%
Pool	8%
Pavement	8%

		2008		2007
	Cost	Accumulated Amortization	Net Book Value	Net Book Value
Buildings	$350,804	$104,636	$246,168	$237,478
Equipment	189,985	128,202	61,783	63,648
Vehicle	43,181	40,281	2,900	4,350
Pool	22,323	19,709	2,614	3,261
Pavement	6,693	2,920	3,773	3,693
Totals	**$612,986**	**$295,748**	**$317,238**	**$312,429**

Government assistance of $27,953 has been deducted from the cost of the buildings while $10,655 has been deducted from the cost of the equipment.

2. Other Assets

	2008			2007
Web site development	$2,131	$639	$1,492	$1,918
Goodwill	1	0	1	1
Totals	**$2,132**	**$639**	**$1,493**	**$1,919**

Web site development costs are being amortized on a straight-line basis over a five year period.

3. Line of Credit

The line of credit is authorized to a maximum of $20,000 and is payable on demand. The interest rate is based on prime plus 1.5%. The line is secured by land and cottages, and the personal guarantee and postponement of claims by shareholders.

4. Demand Loan

The demand loan is payable on demand and bears interest at prime plus 2%. The average prime rate during 2008 was 5% (2007 — 5%, 2006 — 6.5%). The demand loan is secured by a collateral first mortgage on the cottages, and personal guarantees of the shareholders.

EXHIBIT 5 — Cavendish Cove Cottages Inc.
Notes to the Financial Statements (unaudited) [continued]

5. Long-Term Debt

The long-term debt is secured by a mortgage on the land and cottages, personal guarantees of the shareholders, and life insurance on the shareholders.

	2008	2007	2006
Loan at 8.5%, payable to 2010 in annual amounts of $5,000 plus interest	$30,000	$35,000	$40,000
Loan at prime +1.5%, payable to 2012 in annual amounts of $10,000 plus interest	$80,000	$90,000	$43,750
Loan at prime +1.5%, payable to 2011 in annual amounts of $2,271 plus interest	$4,544	$6,815	$9,086
Loan at prime +1.5%, payable to 2011 in annual amounts of $5,000 plus interest	$35,000	$40,000	$45,000
Totals	$149,544	$171,815	$137,836
less: Current portion	22,271	22,271	21,796
	$127,273	$149,544	$116,040

Principal repayments required in each of the next four years are:

2009	2010	2011	2012
$22,271	$22,272	$20,000	$20,000

6. Due to Shareholders

This amount is due on demand without interest. However, the shareholders have indicated they will not request material repayment within the next fiscal year and consequently, the amount has not been classified as current.

7. Common Shares

There are 20,000 common shares at no par value authorized to be issued, 5,000 common shares are issued for a total value of $3,125. No dividends were paid during the 2006 fiscal year.

 Online LearningCentre

Find more great exercises and additional study tools on the Online Learning Centre at
www.mcgrawhill.ca/olc/timmons

END-OF-TEXT CASES

In 1989, having taken losses on a string of real estate plays, Kingston resident Will Hodgskiss found himself close to broke. Entrepreneurial to the end, he leveraged the last few dollars in his savings account and bought a hot dog cart. It wasn't much, but Hodgskiss was convinced that, with the right discipline and vision, he could start with his lowly hot dog cart and build a serious growth business.

He was right. In less than a decade, Hodgskiss's business, Willy Dog, had grown from a one-cart operation to a substantial franchise network with cart owners patrolling North American streets. And—thanks to Hodgskiss's decision in his first years as a vendor to trade in his standard metal cart for one in the shape of an eight-foot-long wiener—it had developed a distinct and instantly recognizable brand.

By 2006, Hodgskiss's company was enjoying annual sales of about $1 million. It had diversified from its roots as a franchiser and had become one of the world's leading manufacturers of specialty carts for street-food vendors. Hodgskiss had travelled a great distance from his humble roots—but he was not yet ready to call it a day. He had set a goal of growing Willy Dog's annual sales to $5 million within three years. When he reached that goal, he planned to step back from the company to either retire or start another business. Meeting that target, however, wouldn't be easy. For all Hodgskiss's success, Willy Dog faced a number of issues. It wasn't growing as quickly as it had in the past, and it was facing heightened competition. On top of that, Hodgskiss was wrestling with staffing issues, customer relations, and breaking into new markets. In short, he needed to develop a fresh strategy to foster growth at his firm. But knowing that he needed a plan wasn't enough. Hodgskiss also needed time—something he didn't have, given the chaotic schedule that managing all the minutiae of his company forced him to keep. And without it, he was left wondering how he could plot a course to carry Willy Dog into the future.

Back in 1999, when Willy Dog was celebrating its 10th anniversary, Hodgskiss was sitting on top of a thriving franchise network. But his company was starting to have problems. The revenue from franchise fees that had fuelled growth during Willy Dog's first decade was starting to dry up, and Hodgskiss's margins were thinning rapidly.

Looking for ways to generate new income, he began to experiment with making and selling his firm's distinctive carts. His revenue growth picked up dramatically. "I was making $2,000 to $5,000 per sale, with none of the follow-up of franchising," Hodgskiss recalls with a grin.

And so, a manufacturer was born: Hodgskiss changed his franchising revenue model to encourage owners to buy the cart rather than the franchise, and he moved production of the carts in-house, hiring a staff of fabricators to operate the production line.

But even though his company was back on a growth footing, Hodgskiss remained a classic founder, involved in every dimension of the firm he started. Three separate hotlines—for support, orders, and other inquiries—were often routed to his cellphone. As a result, that phone was practically glued to his ear.

Hodgskiss felt it was important that Willy Dog customers be able to reach the "top dog" directly; that personal touch had been a hallmark of the company since its inception. But since he was involved in all aspects of Willy Dog's operations, he could be anywhere when a call came in. Customers liked dealing with Hodgskiss directly, but were occasionally frustrated when he didn't have all their information on hand. Hodgskiss, for his part, loved talking with his customers—but hated having to spend time reciting information easily found on the company's Web site. He valued the relationships, but wished that there was a more effective way of handling inquiries.

Part of the problem stemmed from Willy Dog's internal structure. Almost all of the company's 18 employees worked on the shop floor as machinists and fabricators. Under the leadership of the shop foreperson, this staff spent its days producing the company's signature carts. The rest of the operations, from finance to marketing, were handled by Hodgskiss, his general manager, and an office clerk.

For Hodgskiss, this meant he had to keep up a frenzied pace of activity to manage the company's operations. In a typical day, he rose at 5:00 a.m. to tackle his email inbox before breakfast and his morning run. At the office, he would handle everything from clerical work to minor errands, though two-thirds of his usual day would be consumed by supervising staff.

Though Hodgskiss described his ideal leadership approach as "hands-off," he couldn't resist getting involved in the day-to-day details of the business, from staffing to equipment. But his enthusiasm for running the business, he realized, left Willy

This case was written by Lukas Neville, Ph.D. student, Queen's School of Business, and Professor Elspeth J. Murray, CIBC Teaching Fellow in Entrepreneurship, Queen's School of Business, Queen's University. This case was prepared with the assistance of Kimberley Mosher and Gillian Shiau. Developed with the support of the CIBC Curriculum Development Fund at Queen's School of Business, for purposes of classroom discussion.

Dog vulnerable. If he ever took ill, his general manager could handle only some of the company's operations for a limited time. But Hodgskiss knew he was personally still indispensable to the firm.

By this year, cart sales had come to account for 80 percent of Willy Dog's annual revenue. But as the cart business grew, Hodgskiss began running into stiff competition from an entrenched U.S. manufacturer called All-American Hot Dogs Co. With fierce rhetoric on their graphic-saturated Web sites, the two titans clashed over features, quality and, eventually, price. It was war, and the battles bit deep into Hodgskiss's margins. His price woes didn't end with a single competitor. He also competed against a range of small local players, who Hodgskiss described as "backyard mechanics." Worse, his market for high-end carts was being eroded by online marketplaces for used carts. On any given day, dozens of carts could be found for sale on eBay.

Short-handed on sales and marketing staff, and faced with intensifying competition, Willy Dog turned to a distributorship model. Though it involved parcelling out a portion of the company's modest margins, Willy Dog's five American distributors contributed marketing and sales resources, and their high-volume purchases cut down dramatically on the cost of shipping the bulky carts. Finally, the local presence allowed for improved customer service and local regulatory knowledge for new vendors.

But while the distributor network had improved Willy Dog's outlook, Hodgskiss still wondered how to sustain his firm's competitive advantage. With individual vendors accounting for most of his cart sales, the majority of revenue came from one-off purchases. Hodgskiss's customer service and personal touch had built customer loyalty, but it didn't often translate to repeat sales. And while Willy Dog had invested considerable effort in product innovation, customers were highly price-sensitive and often indifferent about the firm's higher-gauge steel or other technical improvements.

Having to fight for every last sale to small-scale customers was an unappealing part of Willy Dog's business model. Over 70 percent of the company's sales came from small-time owner-operators and seasonal "hobby" entrepreneurs—often leaving the company saddled with bad debt from failed clients. The last 30 percent of Willy Dog's sales, by contrast, was to business managers: franchised restaurants and professionally managed local chains. Earlier this year, for instance, Willy Dog completed an order for 10 carts from an ice cream vendor. But how, Hodgskiss wondered, could he go about finding more customers in this appealing segment? His own market research offered clues about how strong the hot dog market was: At major-league baseball parks, hot dog sales had increased by over 13 percent between 2004 and 2005, Hodgskiss learned. And 'curbside takeout,' the market that included Willy Dog-built stands, was growing even more quickly. With street-side vendors propagating rapidly, Hodgskiss knew his market was relatively secure.

At the same time, with increasing health concerns and a globalizing palate, would the lowly hot dog be abandoned in favour of sushi or samosas? The demand for frankfurters was enough to sustain Willy Dog at its present level, but Hodgskiss wanted more than comfortable, flat growth. He wanted to quintuple his annual sales and then make a graceful exit.

To do that, he had to find a growth market, but he wondered how his modest manufacturing operation would scale up. Between resignations and seasonal layoffs, his staff suffered annual turnover of 30 percent. On top of that, it was hard to keep trained staff in a market starved for skilled workers. Earlier in the year, Hodgskiss had to establish employee health and dental plans as a retention measure.

Intermittently starved for production capacity, Hodgskiss had experimented with contracting out production. The strategy worked out exceptionally well—until the contracting firm decided to launch its own cart manufacturing business, directly competing with Willy Dog.

Willy Dog was also highly reliant on steel to build the carts. With slender margins, Hodgskiss wondered whether manufacturing was necessarily the most appealing part of his industry's value chain. With labour and input prices on the rise and mixed experiences with outsourcing, Hodgskiss would need to carefully consider how to grow his manufacturing operations to keep pace with the growth he hoped to foster.

Though growth was a priority for Willy Dog's founder, his schedule didn't afford him much time for strategic planning sessions. Busy revamping his cart models, dealing with his steel suppliers and handling the constant barrage of customer calls, Hodgskiss's days were already a flurry of activity. He had built Willy Dog into a million-dollar enterprise. But with so little time, he had no idea how to begin dealing with eroding margins and stiff competition.

CASE 2 · HANDSHAKE VR INC.: INNOVATING WITH TOUCH

As the senior executives of Handshake VR walked out of the boardroom of their Waterloo, Ontario, office in June 2005, the same thoughts were going through all of their minds. Based on the market analysis, the company had a very promising future. However, it was not exactly clear what the proper evaluation criteria should be, given the very early stage of the markets. Also, it was far from certain how long it would take for each of the markets to develop, and what role Handshake should play in the development of each. Should they continue as a component technology, or middle-ware provider, inventing new technology and looking for ways to license that technology? Or should they help the early stage market break through the commercialization barrier by picking one vertical and developing it to at least the proof-of-concept stage?

The latest financial statements indicated that additional funding for the company to capitalize on new market opportunities would be required sometime between October and December in order to capitalize on "windows of opportunity." The company would need to present its case to potential investors by early August, only two months away, if agreements were to be in place in time. What would potential investors expect if they were going to commit substantial amounts of money to the young company? Different investors might be interested, depending on which strategy was chosen. The choice would also have an impact on how the company developed priorities and allocated resources over the next few years.

Background

Handshake was founded[1] in 2001 to commercialize telehaptic (the sense of touch over networks) technology that Dr. David Wang had developed at the University of Waterloo, where he was an Electrical Engineering professor. To assist him in his business venture, Wang brought in Dr. Kevin Tuer as vice-president of technology and Tim Ellis as vice-president of corporate development. Wang was on leave from the university and took on the role of president. The three partners raised angel financing and spent long hours developing strategy.

The founders of the company resisted the often-suggested strategy of focusing on one or two vertical segments, fearing that a forced choice too early in the product development process might mean that they would be missing out on significant opportunities in the future.

In 2001, the Handshake founders rejected a financing offer from a consortium of venture capital funds, thinking that a more attractive deal would be possible when customers had been signed. As a result, a lack of cash constrained product development and marketing activities for the next few years. In some cases, company stock was used to pay expenses. For example, the landlord at their original offices accepted shares in the company instead of rent payments.

Key sources of funds were the many government programs that encouraged research and development. Some of the programs that provided assistance to Handshake were the Canada Revenue Agency's Scientific Research and Experimental Design (SR&ED) tax credits, the National Research Council of Canada's Industrial Research Assistance Program (IRAP), and the Accelerator Investment program of Communications and Information Technology Ontario (CITO).

The challenge for Handshake was that the need to maintain secrecy around the new technology meant that the Handshake people were the only ones who could make use of it. By its nature, the Handshake technology would be embedded in other applications, but that was going to be very difficult to do, when so few people had access to it. Given resource and time constraints, Handshake would not be building the commercial applications, so they needed to get the technology into the hands of the developers who would be creating the applications. In early 2004, a strategic decision was made to make the Handshake technology available to as many developers as possible. They needed to multiply the number of people with access to the technology, beyond the five Handshake developers.

In June 2004 Handshake secured $3 million in seed financing from Tech Capital Partners Inc. (www.techcapital.com), BDC Venture Capital (www.bdc.ca), and Trellis Capital Corporation (www.trelliscapital.com). Throughout 2004 and early 2005, the company's main focus was on development of a product that would get the Handshake technology into developers' hands without compromising the company's intellectual property (IP). During this time, the management team was strengthened with the addition of several key players, with strong industry experience, and the number of employees grew from eight to 16.

Haptics and Telehaptics

Haptics referred to simulating the sense of touch in human-computer interactions. The most widely known, but very basic application of haptics was the video game controller that vibrated when cars collided or guns were fired. NASA had also employed haptics on the International Space Station, to allow astronauts to control robots outside the station to do repairs. Telehaptics referred to the use of haptics in a network environment, e.g., Internet. In order to demonstrate the concept of telehaptics, a number of science museums contained exhibits where visitors could 'arm wrestle' with opponents over a computer network. The two opponents each pushed against a mechanical 'arm' while watching the other player on a monitor. The pressure applied by one player was transmitted to the mechanical arm of the other player.

The development and commercial application of telehaptic technology required further progress on the software and

---

This case was written by Dave Rose and Hugh Munro, for purposes of classroom discussion.

[1] The original name of the company was Handshake Interactive Technologies Inc. but it was later changed to Handshake VR Inc.

hardware (devices) fronts as well as considerable education and training of potential users. The increasing number of hardware 'feedback' devices that were becoming available was raising the level of interest in the subject. An American company, SensAble, had the largest share of the hardware market so compatibility with SensAble's technology had been a development priority for Handshake's software developers. Several other companies in North America and Europe produced haptics devices for specific applications.

A major issue affecting the use of telehaptics was the effect of network time-delay. Time-delay creates insurmountable problems in more sensitive, precise operations like those in medical training or surgery-based applications. The issue was that time delays over networks caused the devices that people were using to become unstable and behave very erratically—imagine a small robot swinging wildly out of control. The major advantage of Handshake's technology was that it eliminated, or greatly reduced, the problems associated with network time delays. The whole field of telehaptics had become much closer to reality with the development of Handshake's patented technology.

The Role of Venture Capital

For Handshake to grow to a profitable size, significant money would need to be spent on further product development and, more significantly, marketing and business development. Sources of funds for the commercialization of innovative technologies were generally restricted to venture capital firms (VCs). The VC industry used unique terms for investments in each stage of a company's growth, which reflected the fact that multiple rounds of financing were usually required for new technology companies. For example, one well-accepted categorization was: seed-money stage, start-up, and first-round to fourth-round financing.[2] Another way to describe the progression of investment fund sources was Family & Friends, Angel Funds, Seed Funds, Venture Capital Series A,B,C etc. and Initial Public Offering (IPO).[3]

VCs filled the void between sources of funds for innovation, such as the government programs, angel funding and personal investments that had financed Handshake so far, and traditional, lower-cost sources of capital available to ongoing concerns, such as bank loans. Venture capital investments were risky, and VCs expected a sufficient return on investment to compensate for the risk.[4] The successful investments needed to generate large enough returns to make up for the investments that only returned the original investment or nothing at all. For every 10 investments, it was expected that in perhaps two cases the VC's original investment would be lost, six might see the initial investment returned with a modest return on investment and one or two would be winners. The profitable ventures needed to return 10 to 20 times the VC's initial investment for the average return on the portfolio to be within the VC's targeted range.

Typically VCs wanted to see an exit opportunity, through a sale to a larger corporation or a public share offering, within five years. Only certain businesses could grow fast enough and large enough to attract VC funding. Generally VCs concentrated on fast growing industries, where the capacity would be constrained in the next five years[5] and looked for compelling technology, driven founders, and talented entrepreneurs with extraordinary vision.[6,7]

The Launch of proSENSE

In March 2005 Handshake's first product, the Handshake proSENSE Virtual Touch Toolbox, was launched. The proSENSE Toolbox provided researchers and developers of haptic-enabled (sense of touch) applications a dramatic, new approach to product development. With its "drag and drop" functionality, developers could now quickly and easily embed haptic functionality into their applications. With the launch of proSENSE, Handshake had achieved its strategic goal of getting its technology into as many developers' hands as possible, while keeping the IP secure, as developers did not need to understand the 'secret sauce' behind proSENSE to use it. As well, TiDeC, Handshake's patented time delay technology, was instantly available to developers using proSENSE.

Vertical Market Development

While the proSENSE product was attracting considerable interest from the research community and, surprisingly, a couple of commercial developers, the Handshake executives felt there was still a need and an opportunity to get more involved in the development of end-user applications. A well-respected book in the field of high-tech marketing was *Crossing the Chasm*, by Geoffrey Moore. Moore described the chasm as the gap in the market between the adoption of a new technology product by the innovators and early adopters and its acceptance by the broader end-user market. Moore's prescription for crossing the chasm was to develop a 'whole product' that met the needs of a very specific target market. Moore's theory appeared to be very appropriate to Handshake's situation. Despite the broad acceptance proSENSE was receiving from the haptics development community, commercial applications would not gain market acceptance until at least one 'whole product' was developed. Was it Handshake's role to push one or more applications through to a commercially viable product, or at least to proof of concept, so that the chasm could be crossed?

Some of the markets that were currently being considered were:

ONLINE HAPTIC GAMING   Local haptics had been available in the gaming industry for a number of years, but this generally involved fairly basic effects, e.g., rumble packs. More complex activities, such as sword fighting with someone in Tokyo, required telehaptics but this technique had not been developed for online games due to problems with time-delay. Handshake had a viable solution for online haptics, but it was difficult to adapt haptics to existing games. New games had to be written specifically to use haptics. The major game console manufacturers were no longer funding new game development, as they once did, and now required a complete solution before considering a new game. They appeared to be waiting for 'the next big thing.'

[2] Ross, Westerfield, Jaffe, and Roberts, *Corporate Finance*, 3rd Canadian ed. (Toronto: McGraw-Hill Ryerson, 2003), 590.

[3] Timmons and Spinelli, *New Venture Creation: Entrepreneurship for the 21st Century* (New York: McGraw-Hill/Irwin, 2004), 470.

[4] Bob Zider, "How Venture Capital Works," *Harvard Business Review*, November-December 1998.

[5] Ibid.

[6] www.woodsidefund.com.

[7] www.techcapital.com.

This meant that Handshake would need to find a partner willing to create online games that incorporated telehaptics.

LEARNING DISABILITIES The learning disabilities market was very fragmented but represented a substantial opportunity for total customer potential. The use of touch in learning for children with disabilities was proven to be of extreme benefit in their progress. To date, each child was assigned a therapist who worked with them in the classroom on tasks such as learning to write, spatial awareness, and basic skills. In the U.S., law mandated children's rights to therapy—the problem was the demand was outstripping the supply of therapists.

SPORTS REHAB AND FITNESS There were a number of promising applications in the sports rehabilitation and fitness markets. Basically, the concept involved either retrofitting existing exercise equipment or working with manufacturers to develop new equipment that incorporated motors that could drive haptics effects and also connect to the Internet. This would provide a new opportunity in personalization of workouts and sports rehab by allowing the user to take their "exercise card," insert it into the machine and pick up where they last left off.

STROKE AND TRAUMATIC BRAIN INJURY REHAB Stroke rehab was a sub-segment of a general category called traumatic brain injury. The combination of increasing numbers of North Americans requiring rehab, declining therapist resources and pressure from increasing hospital and clinic costs was pointing to a need to establish a more reliable home-based approach. The underlying concept was for a patient to pay a monthly subscription fee for hardware and access to a Web-portal. From there, they could interact with their therapist and other patients and also track their progress.

REMOTE HEALTH DIAGNOSTICS In an effort to address a shortage of doctors, nurses, and other health care providers in remote communities, the Romanow Report advised Canadian politicians to accelerate initiatives in telehealth. Millions of dollars were being spent transporting patients, for example, from places like Yellowknife to medical centres in Edmonton. The industry was still in its infancy but great use was being made of video conferencing for conferring with patients. Ontario had set up a program called North Network, with over 20 centres linking health experts in Southern Ontario and patients in the North.

MEDICAL TRAINING AND SIMULATION Haptic solutions for medical training and simulation already existed with products on the market by at least six companies. What was lacking was the ability to network these devices for remote training opportunities. Early indications were that there was a need for remote training of medical students, medical sales forces, and end customers. Both medical schools and large medical companies were showing interest in developing applications.

TELESURGICAL OPERATIONS Telesurgery sounded like something from Star Wars, but by 2005 a Canadian doctor in Hamilton, Ontario, had already conducted more than 20 telesurgeries to address "acid reflux" conditions in patients located in Ontario and Québec. This success was generating great interest from NASA and the U.S. military. There were about three players developing surgical robots—usually with a price tag of more than US$1 million. Handshake had participated in a joint NASA/U.S. military/

Canadian project in 2004 and was working on new projects to expand the use of haptics.

Current Situation

FINANCIAL POSITION A common metric used to assess the burn-rate for a new technology company was to assume a cost of $100,000 per employee, including salary, expenses, and space for them to work. Revenues from the sale of proSENSE would decrease the burn rate, but with 15 employees and rapidly increasing people requirements, the company's cash was expected to run out within the next year. Further capital from the seed round investors was certainly a possibility, but their $3 million investment had been intended to provide a clear picture of the market potential for Handshake's products. The next round of financing would be expected to fund the targeted development and marketing activities for specific verticals. At an estimated cost of $2 million to $5 million per vertical, on top of the current burn rate, and the cost of filling existing organizational gaps, a very promising market potential would need to be identified. Costs would include marketing, intellectual property, legal and development expenses. Investment from other venture capital firms was also a possibility, but it would be difficult to attract any new investors if the existing ones would not contribute more money.

ORGANIZATIONAL CONSIDERATIONS Attracting talented people had not been a problem for Handshake. The company's close relationship with the University of Waterloo and downsizing at a number of area technology companies had created an excellent pool of developers and executives to choose from. The company had never used a recruiting firm to attract the people they needed. The exciting technology, the talented founders, and the opportunity to be part of a high-potential start-up had led promising candidates to approach Handshake and to join the firm for competitive rates of pay. The main problem the company faced was being able to afford to hire the necessary talent before they were needed rather than after the need had become critical.

MARKETING CHALLENGES The founders of Handshake were convinced of the potential for Wang's technology to revolutionize the field of telehaptics. In many ways, they were creating new markets and acting as visionaries to educate customers on what was now possible with the new technology. As a result, much of the work that had been done so far was based on a theoretical view of what was possible, i.e., a 'technology push' rather than a 'market pull' approach to product development.

THE DECISION While there were viable opportunities for Handshake to remain as a component technology provider, relying on others to develop commercial applications, the Handshake executives looked to Microsoft's development of Windows-based applications for an analogy to the situation facing them: Microsoft's decision to allow others to develop applications based on the Windows platform, resulting in scores of new applications, was similar to Handshake's decision to launch proSENSE. However, Microsoft had seen certain areas where it made sense to get involved in end-user applications, for example, Microsoft Office. So now they were looking at the different verticals where haptics would play a role in the future, and wondering if they should be pushing towards a commercial application in any of them.

The management team had also discussed other possible strategies that might not need another round of venture capital financing, or perhaps a smaller amount of capital. Relying on sales of proSENSE was an option, but it would require more aggressive and devoted attention to rapidly penetrate the global, niche market of developers. Securing funding from the U.S. military for development of specific telehaptic applications was another possibility. The associated intellectual property would be owned by the military for their applications but might be available to Handshake for non-military applications. Selling the technology to a larger firm might also be an option, but the team preferred to focus their energy on building the value of the company through development and commercialization of their technical expertise.

Final thoughts before the executives broke from the boardroom were focused on what needed to go into the presentation to potential venture capital firms. The pitch had to clearly and crisply outline the specific market applications that would be developed, the model for how those applications would be commercialized, how the funds would be used, what kinds of returns (i.e., profits and company value) could be expected and the associated timelines. Financial support would be dependent on how confident investors felt about the plan as well as the ability of Handshake's management to successfully execute the plan.

CASE 3   SWEET SUCCESS

Dairy Queen® is a fast-food restaurant franchise that was founded in 1940. With 5,900 restaurants in 22 countries as of 2008, it is one of the largest chains in the world. Much of its early growth occurred in rural areas of the United States, and references to "DQ®" occur repeatedly in both the popular and literary culture. For many years the franchise's slogan was "We treat you right!" in recent years it has been changed to "DQ® something different." The company is a wholly owned subsidiary of Berkshire Hathaway.

The Dairy Queen® franchisee-franchisor relationship is simple yet effective. Prospective franchisees are required to have a certified operator working in the store. To qualify as a certified operator, one must attend training at Dairy Queen®'s head office. The program offers training in employee and financial management, hiring and recruitment, product training, community involvement, customer service, and Dairy Queen® procedures and policies. To successfully complete the training program operator candidates must complete a set of examinations covering all of these different areas. After completing the program and commencing the operation of a franchise location, operators are required to adhere to DQ® Procedures and Policies, follow national marketing campaigns, pay monthly royalties, and pass quarterly on-site evaluations. DQ® District Managers conduct these evaluations by spending a full day on site examining operations, product consistency, cleanliness, and customer service. Franchise locations that fail these evaluations are given a warning and opportunity to rectify shortcomings. If shortcomings are not remedied by a specified date, the franchisor (Dairy Queen® Inc.) has the right to terminate the contract. As consistency and customer service are of the utmost importance, Quarterly Evaluations are often supplemented by the use of mystery shoppers.

The franchisor-franchisee relationship is facilitated through the use of a DQ® Field Consultant from and to whom the franchisee is encouraged to seek guidance and communicate questions or concerns.

St. Thomas

St. Thomas (population 36,110) ranks 51st in size among 912 Ontario cities. Residents of St. Thomas are mostly upper-middle class to wealthy individuals and families, mostly of French roots and Catholic. The small size of the city allows better acquaintance between its residents and for word of mouth to travel quickly. It is a prosperous city with ample opportunity for business growth and success.

St. Thomas Dairy Queen

The St. Thomas Dairy Queen® was first opened in 1995 by Ted Smith and his wife Ronnie. They opened it as a "full Brazier store," which is the Diary Queen® terminology for a fast food restaurant that serves "hot eats" and "cold treats." Prior to opening the St. Thomas location Ted and Ronnie had gained experience as owners of the Dairy Queen® location in White Oaks mall in neighbouring London, Ontario. With their lease expiring at the mall, the Smiths decided to open up a new DQ® location in the emerging city of St. Thomas. With the assistance of two full-time managers, Ted and Ronnie created a successful business realizing nearly $550,000 in revenue in their second year of operation.

St. Thomas's DQ® was perceived as the "cool" place to work by the local high school students. Each year tens of applicants would apply in hopes of a part-time position. During summer weekends DQ® would open until midnight making it a popular hangout for teens, families, and couples alike. The St. Thomas DQ® also became involved in the community though sponsorship of local baseball and hockey little league teams.

Although Ted was both proud and loyal to the brand, he was very cynical of the Franchisor. He often wanted to do things his way and found it difficult to follow DQ® Policies. He often challenged head office and had developed a very antagonistic relationship. He was also known to be strict and firm in managing his business and employees often viewed him as a tyrant, avoiding him at all costs.

After six successful years of running the St. Thomas DQ®, Ted and Ronnie decided they were ready for retirement and put the store up for sale in 2000.

The Hashem Family

In 1990 Sayed Hashem and his family immigrated to Canada from civil war-torn Lebanon. The Hashem family consisted of Sayed, the patriarch, his wife Nora, and their six children, the

This case was written by Zeina Haidar and Francine K. Schlosser, Odette School of Business, University of Windsor, Canada, for purposes of classroom discussion.

youngest of which was born in Canada shortly after arrival. In January 2001 the Hashem family purchased the St. Thomas Dairy Queen® from the Smiths.

At the time of the Dairy Queen® purchase, Sayed's two eldest children, Yasmine and Khalil, were enjoying living away from home to complete their professional educations. Yasmine, a dentist, and Khalil, a doctor, had always described living at home as "boot camp" living with the discipline of a strict father. Sayed's parenting skills were much like those of parents from any war-torn and dangerous region; where strict discipline was a necessity more than an option.

The four youngest children; Aliya, Mira, Hanna, and Bassil were to become integral parts of the Hashem family Dairy Queen. Nora, on the other hand, had no intention of becoming involved with the newly acquired Dairy Queen®. Past experience had taught the Hashems that Nora and Sayed working together put a tremendous strain on their relationship and created problems and unhappiness.

SAYED—FATHER, MANAGER, BOSS In June 2001, five months after purchasing the St. Thomas Diary Queen®, Sayed Hashem completed his three-week training course and officially became a Dairy Queen® operator. While Sayed had immigrated to Canada in 1990 at the age of 37, he still struggled to perfect the English language and assimilate into the Canadian culture. Although Sayed had previous business experience in Canada, the fast food industry was a completely new venture. Prior to being interested in purchasing a Dairy Queen® franchise, Sayed's only experience with Dairy Queen® had involved a single visit during which he enjoyed a banana split and a sunny day with his children.

In Lebanon, Sayed had simultaneously worked three jobs to support his relatively large family. He was a math teacher, the first sales manager for Lebanon's first and largest super store, and an exporter on the side. Clearly not a stranger to hard work, Sayed would soon learn that the restaurant industry would require much more.

ALIYA—DAUGHTER, EMPLOYEE, MANAGER Aliya, the eldest of the Hashem children remaining at home, had completed the Dairy Queen® training program with her father and was also qualified to operate the franchise. Her father had been concerned about failing the training program due to the language barrier and as such had asked her to attend as a backup. At the time the Hashem family took over the St. Thomas Dairy Queen®, Aliya was a 19-year-old first year university student. Aliya also played a key role in the acquisition of the business as both translator and negotiator for her English-challenged father. Sayed often referred to Aliya as his "right hand man" or his "tongue" because of his less than perfect English.

Having been brought up in Canada, Aliya had several advantages over her father. She was fluent in English and completely understood and fit in with the Canadian culture. At the same time, she had been born in Lebanon and spent the first eight years of her life there. This gave her the ability to appreciate the differences in culture and society and communicate from both perspectives. Aliya was a quick learner who, as a teenager raised in Canada, had far more exposure to the fast food industry. Through school, sports, and extra-curricular activities Aliya had gained experience in group work and leadership.

In contrast to Aliya's perspective, her father considered much of the Dairy Queen® requirements, managerial tasks, roles, and tactics to be "just another way to steal money from the Franchisee." He often expressed his opinion that $10,000 for a transfer of ownership, $8,000 for new menu boards, and $10,000 for a required training course were just a few of the many techniques DQ® was using to gouge the Franchisee. Aliya on the other hand was able to understand, appreciate and explain the necessity and benefits of these and other costs.

With Aliya by his side, Sayed would grow to value the DQ® trademark and operating procedures. More importantly, he would learn to train, manage, and retain approximately 25 employees, 90 percent of which are Caucasian teenagers who in the past would have certainly clashed with Sayed's way of doing things.

MIRA Mira was 16 years old when her father acquired the St. Thomas DQ®. She began working for her father immediately after the end of the 2001 school year. She was a quick study and within a short period of time became a key employee in the store. She disliked working at the family business and avoided taking on any additional responsibility. On a given shift, Mira would come in and get straight to task. She would have little communication with other staff except the occasional reminder to get something done or stop "fooling around." She felt that it was easier to get things done on her own and delegated little to the staff. She constantly complained about the staff being slow and inefficient.

Mira and Sayed were very similar and as such would often bump heads resulting in a low tolerance for one another. Unlike Aliya, Mira had little compassion for issues troubling her father. If he told her that a staff member was underperforming and needed retraining her immediate recommendation was to fire them. When asked to do anything outside her normal shift duties she would conveniently "forget."

Today, Mira is 21 years old. She is an efficient and fast employee that makes excellent products and offers great customer service. She still dislikes her job, mainly because she does not enjoy working with her father, and continues to avoid responsibility. Mira works very flexible hours and covers shifts whenever needed. She feels this is a significant contribution to the family business and to expect anything more of her is unreasonable.

HANNA Hanna was 14 years old at the time her father acquired the St. Thomas DQ®. Working at the family business was her first job. Like her sisters, she was quick to absorb and had perfected her role as a cashier. She displayed great customer service and was often complimented by customers on her attitude.

Today, Hanna is 19 years old. She has a pleasant personality but can also be very stubborn. She insists on doing tasks her own way and on her own schedule. Sayed depends on his children and as such has given them authority over the other employees. Hanna often abuses her authority and uses it to avoid work by ordering the staff around.

Hanna has difficulty taking orders and refuses the authority of her older sisters, Aliya and Mira. Mira and Hanna often get into "sisterly fights" at work. Hanna and Aliya have also butted heads. Hanna has been known to refuse Aliya's orders and display rude behaviour to the point of having to be sent home. Hanna often takes out her frustration by ordering around her younger brother Bassil, which results in countless arguments at work.

After five years of working at DQ®, Hanna refuses to learn supervisory responsibilities, and her capabilities are limited.

BASSIL   Bassil is the youngest member to the Hashem family. He started working at DQ® only a year ago, at the age of 13. When he started working his primary responsibilities were to keep the dining room tables clean and the floors spotless. A year later, he is a top kitchen worker.

Why DQ®?

Prior to 2001, the Hashem family resided in London, Ontario. Sayed had purchased a failed variety store that he remodelled, restocked, and reopened. The business was a success! The store location had failed under the previous management of Becker's and Mac's Milk, but Sayed was able to get it back on its feet.

Sayed and the family operated the store for nearly six years before Sayed decided he had enough. He was unhappy with the nature of the job. He did not enjoy standing on his feet all day in what seemed a mindless job. He detested dealing with his three employees who he felt were unreliable or not worthy of trust. In addition, neither he nor his wife Nora enjoyed living in London. They wanted to relocate to St. Thomas as they had many family and friends in the area. They felt that being near family would benefit the children and their own social life and happiness. With this in mind, Sayed sold the variety store in September of 2000, and with a mere $150,000 travelled to St. Thomas in search of the perfect opportunity.

After nearly nine months of networking and searching for an appropriate business, Sayed began to run out of time. A family of eight with two children in medical school could not sustain itself without a substantial income. Sayed had to move quickly to avoid having to tap into the $150,000 business investment account.

The St. Thomas market made Sayed's business searching task a difficult one. Businesses in the appropriate price range were far too risky and less risky businesses were not for sale. Finally, a realtor approached Sayed about a business for sale in St. Thomas where the owner was willing to finance a mortgage. Immediately, Sayed's interest was piqued.

Sayed met with Ted Smith the owner of the St. Thomas Dairy Queen® that was for sale. Sayed noticed it was a very well run and clean facility that had a constant inflow of customers. He also loved the location and the manageable size of the business. Ted had prepared all of the appropriate financial statements, which he revealed to Sayed as soon as he had communicated his interest and signed a confidentiality agreement. Sayed was impressed by the numbers. Over $550,000 in sales, profits were still healthy even though Ted was paying four managerial salaries each year!

Sayed considered the facts. The St. Thomas Dairy Queen® was already established and in a growing area at a busy intersection. Also the staff was already trained and experienced. In addition, the business had a competitive advantage; it was a fast food restaurant that also served soft serve treats that the competition could not compete with. The financials of the business looked great and with Ted willing to finance a five-year mortgage, Sayed could get the most for his money. He knew he had no experience in the industry, but he was determined to learn quickly.

DQ®'s Senior Staff

SAYED AND ALIYA'S RELATIONSHIP   Sayed became heavily reliant on Aliya. Sayed took care of the ordering, cost control, scheduling, maintenance, and training. He expected Aliya to communicate with head office and to train and manage front counter staff. The DQ® staff generally consists of five kitchen workers and 20 cashiers. Kitchen workers would prepare food while cashiers were responsible for taking orders, preparing soft serve treats, making frozen cakes, stocking, and cleaning. Aliya is also responsible for keeping up to date with policies, rules, and regulations and making sure that staff understands and follows them. Further, she has to ensure that the employees are performing to their fullest potential, providing superior customer service, and keeping their morale up. She was also responsible for disciplining those employees that were not performing to standard.

Often Sayed would express a concern, frustration, or problem to Aliya and expect her to resolve it. If a shift task was not completed (e.g., staff not making enough frozen cakes) then Sayed would confront Aliya. He would often say something along the lines of: "Didn't you tell so-and-so to make 20 cakes last night? Why didn't they? What kind of manager are you if your staff won't listen to you? So-and-so is just good at talking and fooling around! Before her next shift you talk to her!"

Although Sayed was often critical of, and hard on, Aliya, she usually did not let it get to her. She remained task oriented and got the job done. She knew that her father's concerns were valid, but she also knew that he had difficulty expressing them fairly and/or calmly. She adapted to his hostile style and was able to calm him down, make him feel better about a situation and eventually solve it. She also realized that it was not easy for her siblings and other staff to cope with his behaviour. Aliya cared about the well-being of both her father and the business and for that reason could put up with the stress and demand. But she knew that it was unrealistic to expect regular staff to deal with her father's style. Aliya vocalized this concern to her father and he apologized for his behaviour and noted that he should be more careful. In time Sayed learned to better control himself in front of employees, but remained hard on Aliya. She accepted this and assumed the role of "counsellor" to her father. She allowed him to vent to her and after he was done his spiel she would dilute the problem making him feel that "it's not a big deal, we'll take care of it."

In 2006, after five years of working hand in hand with her father, Aliya got married and abruptly distanced herself from the family business. She became a full-time graduate student juggling two other part-time jobs while working on building a career in banking. Career combined with married life left her no time to help with the family business. Sayed was left to pick up all of Aliya's responsibilities. He found himself hiring as many as six cashiers in order to be able to retain two of them. He quickly realized that he needed a more gentle management style, especially with the younger and newer employees. He left the training up to Mira and senior staff members Rose and Meredith but constantly interfered with his own input. For example, Meredith would teach a new employee how to make a certain product one way, and then he would tell that employee that he wants it done another. Sayed attempted to have Mira pick up Aliya's responsibilities, but she was not interested. She made it clear to her father that she was working because he was making her and that she did not want to be there or get involved any further. Soon thereafter, Hanna and

Bassil carried the same attitude towards the family business. Sayed felt that dealing with the employees was not his job. In an attempt to solve his problem, he promoted Meredith to chief of staff and made her responsible for communicating his needs and expectations to the staff while at the same time training and resolving employee problems.

OTHER SENIOR STAFF   Rose and Meredith were two senior employees that had worked at the St. Thomas location for six years even before Sayed had purchased it. They were the most experienced and only full-time employees. They often resisted any change but eventually adapted to the new management and did as asked. They were hard working, dedicated employees that cared about the business as if it were their own. But they often did not see eye to eye with Sayed. They quickly came to respect and follow Aliya, for she proved she was competent and caring as well as a hard worker who always set a good example. Aliya often met with them to discuss new changes or ideas and ask for their opinion. Sayed on the other hand, often met with them to complain about an issue and try to get consensus from them.

ROSE   Sayed and Rose did not always get along. In one incident, Sayed was speaking to Rose about incomplete tasks on a previous shift that she had supervised and he said, "You know Rose, that kitchen staff Adam is terrible. I've told him a million times not to leave the lettuce uncovered. He doesn't listen, he doesn't care. You know there's some stupidity in his head, he doesn't understand."

Rose, clearly upset by Sayed's constant attacks and language replied in a seemingly mocking and patronizing voice, "Sayed, I think he's a great worker and very intelligent, he wants to be a doctor one day. I think he's doing fine."

At this response, Sayed became upset with her lack of support and her inability to accept Adam's underperformance. He responded in an aggressive tone "A doctor? He'll never be a doctor; he can't even make an order correctly. None of the kitchen staff is doing well, even you don't perform the kitchen duties perfectly! You need to see that and make things better, not say 'ohhhh, it's okay!'"

Another issue that often created friction between Rose and Sayed was how Sayed would say "my kids are not to be treated as employees here and they are free to do whatever they want. When I'm not here, they are here in charge in my place." On any given summer afternoon, if business was more than expected, Sayed would simply call one of his children to pop in to work for just an hour or so during the peak period. Often, Mira, Hanna, Bassil and even Aliya would have to leave whatever they were doing just to come in for an hour to help out. In these situations they were likely to come in wearing jeans and a t-shirt and provide the necessary support until things were under control and then head out again.

Rose almost always complained about what they were wearing. Sayed would remind her that his kids were also owners and that they came in unscheduled to help so they could do as they pleased. As owners who were just there as unscheduled help, he felt they could wear and do as they pleased. Rose considered this to be unfair treatment and often voiced her opinion in front of the staff.

In another point of conflict, Rose would often say or imply that the Hashem children were spoiled. It was common for Sayed to instruct Rose to have her staff accomplish certain tasks during her shift. Rose often replied, "Well, what if we're busy? You should have Aliya come in to do the extra work!" Sayed replied, "I always told you customer comes first so if it is busy I'll understand. But it's not busy now, so why are you arguing? Also, Aliya works very hard, she was in earlier today making blanks!" Rose replied, "Well she should work hard, you gave her a car and everything!" Sayed was outraged by her comment and told her to mind her own business, he said "she's my daughter, and it's my responsibility to give her everything she wants. She works harder than everyone here and without her I would have lost the business long ago."

MEREDITH   Meredith and Sayed on the other hand had an easier time communicating because Sayed found it easier to explain things to her. He perceived her as being less cynical, where he felt that Rose just always wanted to disagree first regardless of the issue.

Meredith was a diligent employee. She displayed great customer service and always completed her required tasks. Meredith was very task oriented and had great difficulty planning ahead, forecasting product needs, and disciplining employees. For example, if an employee called in sick multiple times and was frequently late she would accept whatever excuse she was given.

It was not long before Sayed realized that Meredith was not management material, so he began interacting directly with the employees. When business was going well and tasks were being completed as needed Sayed would often compliment the staff and give them free desserts and meals. He attempted to be flexible with the employee needs and scheduled them as conveniently as possible. He encouraged them to talk to him about any concerns or problems they may have at work and reminded them that if they did not understand him because of his English or his accent to please ask him to explain again. He also gave raises as soon as he saw an employee show slight improvement. Things seemed to be going great until an employee would call in sick or a customer would complain. After these mistakes Sayed would often say something like "When you want you can be excellent and other times you are terrible." He would call employees into his office and interrogate them on their mistake. Employees would often respond with an apology. But the mistakes were often repeated.

When Sayed called an employee into the office Meredith would attempt to interfere and try to find out what is going on. Sayed's direct management of the employees and Meredith's disagreement with his approach soon created friction between them as well. Meredith became easily irritable and often voiced her disagreements.

Employee Crisis

With Aliya gone Rose and Meredith were integral despite their relationships with Sayed. Soon, the difficult relationships would create an employee crisis for the St. Thomas Dairy Queen®. Meredith began to come in late, ask for more days off, and stopped returning calls on days she was called to cover a shift. Rose submitted a note saying that she would be retiring in May, which was only six months away. Further, nearly all of the remaining employees were newly hired and not very reliable. Their willingness to work depended on how much money they needed at the time. They often exhibited no sense of responsibility or dedication.

Currently

Aliya discusses the business with her father on a daily basis and visits the DQ® periodically. Lately, she has been consumed with worry. She feels that her father is over worked and has become quite unhappy. For the past five years her father has worked seven days a week every week. He appears to be physically and mentally exhausted. He told Aliya that he was worried about the behaviour of Meredith and Rose, but he felt helpless because without them he cannot develop and retain employees. He also mentioned to her that although a high employee turnover rate is expected in the fast food restaurant industry, he has noticed his turnover rate is excessively high.

There is also a concern about the increasing number of customer complaints being delivered to him through head office. Yearly revenues have remained steady and are not growing at the same rate as in previous years. He confessed that "I feel like I am losing the business and I don't know what more to do. Your sisters and brother don't care about the business. If they don't care how are the employees going to care?"

Aliya knows that by correcting some of the main problems at work she would also be able to ensure her father's health and well being. She realizes that she does not have the time to go back to work at DQ® because her schedule was still being consumed by school, career, and marriage. She feels she has to find a way to pin-point the root of the problems and help her father resolve them. She suspected that part of the problem was her father's expectation that she would solve his problems for him. She knew that the first step was to make him realize that he had to change his ways and take responsibility for his business and actions.

But how does she tell her father he needs to change his ways? How does she tell him that he needs to work on his managerial skills or that he may need outside help? She worries that figuring out the problems and solutions would be the easy part, but implementing them would be near impossible. Regardless, she feels that she must intervene for the sake of the family business and her father's well being.

CASE 4   WYSE DESIGN & DEVELOPMENT INC.

Brian Lundrigan typed his company's name, Wyse Design & Development Inc., into Google. Then he clicked on the link leading to a promotional video for its main product—a portable winch system—that he had posted on YouTube. The clip told a simple story: A man driving an all-terrain vehicle through soggy muskeg suddenly becomes stuck in a deep mud hole. He hops off his vehicle and pulls out a small case holding the winch. He hooks one end of the winch's cable to his ATV, the other to a tree, with the winch's motor slung between the two points. He flips on the motor and, a few moments later, is out of the muck and back on his way.

"Putting the demo on YouTube was a good idea," Lundrigan thought to himself as he watched the clip one more time. It helped him deal with one of the key tasks facing his St. John's, N.L.-based firm—specifically, educating consumers and retailers accustomed to fix-mounted winches about his unique, portable product, dubbed the Wyse Mid-Span Winch System. Instead of listening to him explain it, potential customers could see it in action. Best of all, posting videos on YouTube was free—a major consideration for a young company like Wyse, which had little money to spend on a full-scale advertising campaign yet dearly needed to get word out about its product.

Until this point—approximately three years since he launched Wyse—Lundrigan had built up a small but enthusiastic roster of clients that included individual customers as well as local institutional users such as Fisheries and Oceans Canada, the Newfoundland and Labrador Search and Rescue Association, and the Newfoundland Department of Resources. But long-term success could only be achieved if he extended his reach. On the plus side, Lundrigan was convinced there was a much wider market for his winch, as well as a soon-to-be-launched kit option that would allow owners of fix-mounted winches to convert their units into portable devices using Wyse's design. He saw his biggest opportunity in the

mass retail market, even though it was (and remains) dominated by cheaper imports. He believed his product's quality and flexibility would convince consumers to accept his price.

The problem was, how could he get the word out when he had no resources to invest in a major marketing campaign? Posting videos on YouTube was a start. But Lundrigan knew he'd need to do much more than that. But what?

Lundrigan, who had worked for a major food distributor before founding Wyse, came up with the idea for his winch system in 2003. It happened one day while he was visiting a friend, sitting in the man's garage and talking about a new snowmobile he had bought.

"This man, who was about 50 years old at the time, was telling me about how he had been out in the backcountry by himself and had gotten his new snowmobile stuck," Lundrigan recalls. "He complained that it had taken him an hour to walk back to his cabin, an hour back to the sled, and a third hour to dig the machine out." While the man was talking, Lundrigan found himself staring at an ATV in the corner of the garage that had a fix-mounted winch system. "I'm an avid fan of snowmobiles myself and I'd been in a lot of similar predicaments. I kept looking at the winch on the ATV and thinking: This can be made much more useful."

Inspired, Lundrigan spent the next few months sketching out his idea for what would become the Wyse (an acronym for "When You've Struggled Enough") mid-span winch. In 2004, he pulled some funding together and applied to a local business incubator for technology start-ups called the Genesis Centre, which was affiliated with Newfoundland's Memorial University. The centre believed that Lundrigan's concept had potential to compete in the global market and accepted his fledgling company as a client.

Initially, Lundrigan simply planned to design his winch system and license it to a manufacturer. As it turned out, his

---

This case was written by Eric Morse, Ken Mark, and Mary Weil, Pierre L. Morisette Institute for Entrepreneurship, Richard Ivey School of Business, University of Western Ontario, for purposes of classroom discussion.

timing couldn't have been worse. Since early in the decade, the domestic winch industry had been facing stiff competition in the form of cheap imports from Asia. Mass merchandisers had been selling the imports for as low as $69, much cheaper than the $200 to $600 charged for winches made in North America. The Asian winches were of lesser quality, but they had gained market share rapidly. "The traditional winch manufacturers were going through a particularly hard time trying to recapture market share they had lost to the cheaper Asian products," he says. "It seemed that most were in survival mode and focused primarily on cutting costs, not so much on new product development."

Undaunted, Lundrigan continued to test designs and develop prototypes. In the end, he decided to build the business on his own. In 2006, after sourcing his own components and finding a manufacturer, he went to market with the final version that retailed in the range of $300 to $400. Lundrigan decided to call his product a mid-span winch—not a "portable winch"—because he wanted to avoid being confused with various imported winches, some of which gave the impression of being a portable product. "It can be confusing to the consumer because these 'portable winches' are only portable while you are carrying them from the place of purchase to your home," Lundrigan says. "Then they have to be permanently bolted down to something for it to be used."

The name of Lundrigan's winch system may have been a mouthful for casual consumers, but that didn't stop it from having a successful launch. It scored great reviews and generated decent business, much of it via word of mouth. While that interest alone was enough to convince Lundrigan that he needed to reach a wider market, the issue grew more acute when he came up with the idea of the conversion kit.

From his research and meetings with retailers, Lundrigan knew that many consumers had purchased imported fixed winches on a whim, either due to the low shelf price or for a specific but infrequent use. But industry contacts were also telling Lundrigan that many of these winches were not actually being put to use by the people who bought them, due to their impracticality and the added cost of having them mounted on vehicles.

This insight led him back to the design process to develop a product he would call the Wyse Winch Kit. The final version was essentially his mid-span winch system, minus the winch. The customers he was targeting already owned those. What they lacked was the true portability that came with his midspan concept—and, thus, the motivation to pay to have their inexpensive Asian winches fix-mounted on a single vehicle. Lundrigan was hoping that his solution to the mounting issue would give winch owners a whole new reason to open their pocketbooks.

Lundrigan is now ready to launch the Wyse Winch Kit and is looking for an affordable marketing strategy for both his mounting kit and his mid-span system. "The question is, how do we effectively educate potential customers about our products?" he asks. "If consumers realized how useful their winches—either fix-mounted or sitting unused—could be with our kit, I'm confident that they would look for our products at their local retailers. And if they wanted a full winch system, we'd gladly be able to serve their needs as well."

Lundrigan also faces another, related hurdle—getting his products placed at retailers. "Every major retail chain is offering winches in their product line, but what they seem to forget is that every winch they sell will require a mounting solution," he says. "We think we have the solution with our kit, but I'm having a hard time convincing the retailers. How can I get them to see the potential profit that walks out their door every day?"

Indeed, although word about Wyse products is spreading, Lundrigan needs something more to take his business to the next level—specifically, a marketing strategy that's both high-impact and low-cost. What to do?

CASE 5 QIAOLINX INC.'S CHALLENGE: CONVINCING CANADIAN BUSINESS OF THE IMPORTANCE OF CRACKING CHINA'S BUSINESS CODE

The Birth of QiaoLinx

Luc Fournier and Brian Hobbs, co-founders of QiaoLinx Inc., met while doing their Executive MBAs. Luc had seen evidence of the ill-preparedness of Canadian firms during his time spent in China. He believed there to be an opportunity providing a service that would offer insight to understand the Chinese and prepare companies to do business in China. Upon completion of his EMBA, Luc got into consulting and marketing. He wanted to pursue the aforementioned project relating to China, however, his co-workers did not see the need.

In mid-2005 Luc was presented a chance to use his China expertise to do some work for the National Bank of Canada. His consulting colleagues were not interested, so he decided to ask his former classmate Brian Hobbs to join him. They met with the National Bank's international division. This division handled export financing for Québec-based businesses, and dealt with China on an increasingly frequent basis. They wanted to know what their options were to establish a presence in China—should they open an office and set up shop? Should they simply have an agency there?

The idea for QiaoLinx came to life one afternoon in Luc's backyard. Luc and Brian were trying to define the service that they would provide to Canadian companies. They decided their enterprise would serve as a "bridge" between Canadian business and the Chinese. Brian asked Luc what the Chinese word for bridge was. Luc indicated the translation for bridge was "Qiao" and so was formed the name of the company: QiaoLinx—the bridge that would link Canadian and Chinese business. The core idea of their venture was to help companies understand the Chinese and prepare for dealing with China.

This case was written by Maria Scopelliti, European School of Economics, Milan, Italy, and Prescott C. Ensign, for purposes of classroom discussion.

Their challenge was and continued to be: how to sell this idea. They wanted business people to see their service as something valuable and necessary—something that would guarantee success in China. Thus far, few had responded to this value proposition. Clients remained elusive.

Company Profile

QiaoLinx Inc. was essentially a consulting company. Its primary goal was to allow Canadian companies to become increasingly effective when buying, selling, or establishing operations in China. Luc and Brian used their extensive knowledge of international business and consulting expertise, coupled with a proficient understanding of Chinese business practices, cultural, and regional influences to aid organizations in their quest to establish and successfully continue business relationships in China.

How it Works. QiaoLinx sought to offer companies an unprejudiced and thorough assessment of how various aspects including business culture, regional priority, regulations, and government affects the plans of Canadian organizations. The end-result would allow these companies to analyze this information, and incorporate it in an effort to create more successful business strategies.

QiaoLinx Inc. possessed cultural and regional knowledge in addition to a superior understanding of business planning, market development, legal aspects, operations, and technical know-how. The synergy of all of this knowledge was QiaoLinx's recipe for success for Canadian firms wishing to venture into the economic giant that was China.

Creating Awareness

Workshops. In late 2005, Luc and Brian decided to run workshops entitled "How to Win in China." The goal was to establish a client base, gain some revenue, and create awareness as well as do some marketing. The goal of these workshops was for attending managers to be able to apply their newly expanded knowledge of China to create and/or develop business relationships. Of course the workshops weres simply intended to get companies started, and understand the importance of enlisting QiaoLinx to aid them in their quest for success in doing business with China. The drawback to these workshops was that companies started to see QiaoLinx Inc. as a training company.

Marketing and Advertising. The partners of QiaoLinx had a limited budget for marketing and advertising. As two well-established businessmen they realized the importance of "getting the word out," however, could not afford to risk a great deal for elaborate advertising, which was extremely expensive.

They were able to get an advertisement on the *Ottawa Business Journal* Web site in the Fall of 2006. The ad cost them $750 for two weeks. It generated 30,000 hits per week on the QiaoLinx Web site, in comparison to the average couple of hundred hits the Web site normally got. After the advertisement period, the QiaoLinx Web site was visited more frequently at an average of 300-400 hits per week.

They were able to hire a media consultant, Shaun Markey, who had credibility, contacts, and access to the media. He was able to give them a complimentary hour of his time, and some ideas and insight about media relations. The partners of QiaoLinx Inc. realized that he would be an indispensable contact to have on a permanent basis, however, his services began at a costly price of $2,000.

Brian had taken on the project of designing a Web site. Although he had no prior experience in doing this, he was able to design a respectable Web site that contained all of the information about the company, its partners, and the services it could provide to its customers. The only problem that existed with this Web site was the fact that it was not a fancy, hi-tech, media-enabled experience, which was what people had come to expect. The content of the Web site was top-notch, however, for today's Web-savvy businesspeople a more complex and elaborate Web site might be expected, and would serve to contribute to the credibility of a potential business partner.

Struggle to Provoke a Call to Action

By early 2007, QiaoLinx Inc. had hosted a number of workshops, and had formed links with several organizations in both the private and public sectors. One problem that they were faced with was that though these organizations were very interested in the services provided by QiaoLinx, they were only prepared to enlist the new company for small projects. They did not see the need for continued coaching in the area of China.

Brian and Luc believed in the serious need for their services. Not only that, there was concrete evidence for the need in these types of services due to the significant failure of Canadian business in China. The challenge was "How do we show companies that this is something that is worth investing in; something that they can't afford *not* to do?"

Their cash flow at this point was still limited, covering business expenses, a little advertising, and bringing in a small income from a few projects. Brian's project was to address the question, "why should they call us?" and "why do they need our services?" The reasons mentioned in newspaper and magazine articles as well as the statistics supporting these facts should have been enough; but evidently, more was needed to provoke a call to action.

Realizing the Need for Consulting Services

Luc and Brian wanted to be there to help companies prepare a contingency plan so that the only problems that they would encounter would be those that were beyond their control.

Companies, by contrast simply wanted a channel partner out of QiaoLinx-a company that would help them form relationships in China *not* prepare them to work with the Chinese culture. Channel partners sell products and services on behalf of the brand owner to other businesses or customers. They may resell the product "as is," or they may add value to the product by enhancing it or embedding it into their own products and complementary services. They also go by a number of different names—for example, in financial services and insurance, channel partners are brokers or agents; in retail and distribution, they are often called dealers or wholesalers.

Canadian companies wanted QiaoLinx to help them find these types of contacts in China. What these companies did not realize was that without proper development of relationships with Chinese contacts there was a great possibility that individuals who got their hands on the companies' intellectual property could steal it, and release it to a friend in China, and do business at a much more reasonable price.

To help them, QiaoLinx hired a Chinese Lawyer, Lisa Li, to provide them with increased depth and credibility. She also had contacts in the Beijing Ministry of Justice, some low-key firms, and the communist party.

A number of people and organizations wanted to hire Luc for this knowledge, not really for the consulting part of QiaoLinx.

CASE 6 ROCKY MOUNTAIN SOAP

It was meant to be a coup de grâce. Cam Baty and Karina Birch, owners of Canmore-based Rocky Mountain Soap, were offered an opportunity at a national trade show to create a new packaged-goods brand and were given space to sell it on retail shelves in supermarkets nationwide. They jumped at the chance, buoyed by the success of their own thriving trio of retail shops. After all, they reasoned, in the decade since they first founded their company, Rocky Mountain's all-natural soaps and skin-care products had inspired near-fanatical devotion in their customers and created a vibrant, highly profitable regional brand.

The new packaged-goods line was called Glacier, in a nod to the glacier water used in all of Rocky Mountain's soaps, and it was distributed to large-scale retailers across the country. Based on their initial assumptions, Baty and Birch projected at least $800,000 in annual sales for their new line.

But what began as a victory march onto retail shelves ended in bloody trench warfare. The distribution and logistics involved in serving hundreds of retail locations were challenging. Glacier's packaging and branding, though far more sophisticated than Rocky Mountain's previous products, were nonetheless lost in the visual clutter of crowded retail shelves. And, most importantly, supermarket retailers weren't prepared to engage in the loyalty-building customer-education campaigns that were the daily norm at Rocky Mountain's own stores.

Consumers, unfamiliar with the Glacier brand and unmoved by its presentation, reacted tepidly. Annual sales for the Glacier line fizzled, finishing just shy of $100,000 for the year.

The failed project left Rocky Mountain's owners with a dilemma. In early 2006, after winding down the Glacier brand and returning their focus to their three stores, they had to reconcile their ambitions for the brand with the dissatisfying results of their growth experiment. Baty still longed to build a national brand, and looked with a degree of envy at their competitors in the natural skin-care market. Burt's Bees of Durham, North Carolina, for instance, had grown from a small honey bottler to a $250-million hyper-growth consumer brand, while the U.K.'s Lush Handmade had expanded internationally, ratcheting its annual sales well beyond $100 million. While Baty's and Birch's aspirations for Rocky Mountain weren't quite on that scale, they nonetheless hoped to build their company into a national presence—and add to their sales by an order of magnitude.

They had reason for their enthusiasm. Since the start of 2000, Rocky Mountain's same-store sales had grown at a healthy clip, and per-square-foot sales in its stores (the touchstone metric for all retailers) ranged from an enviable $900 to a staggering $1,700. But the brand's impact on its consumers was even more evident in their correspondence than in their cash-register receipts. Gushing, evangelical testimonials arrived at the company's headquarters almost daily. One eczema sufferer tried their soap once, and then described returning to the store for four more bars the same day. A chemotherapy patient weighed in on the relief afforded by Rocky Mountain's foot butter, and noted that they frequently gave the cream as a gift to others.

Rocky Mountain had also developed a successful brand imprint in Alberta. Their logo was a stylized depiction of the Three Sisters mountain range outside Canmore—Baty's mountain-bike stomping grounds and the company's birthplace. Their slogan, "Be Kind, Be Real, Be Natural," was as much a personal mantra as a corporate motto. Since the company's inception, it had eschewed the usual lineup of chemical cleansers, preservatives and colouring agents. Instead, Rocky Mountain's soaps deployed a range of essential oils, grains, and berries. As natural products moved from a niche market in the 1990s to mainstream consciousness in this decade, enthusiasm picked up for the company's high-priced but all-natural offerings. Once converted, customers would frequently spread the word: "Customers are often our best salespeople," Baty noted with a laugh.

Wasting little time after mothballing Glacier, Rocky Mountain's owners started to ruminate about the potential for another type of expansion. Rather than turning their products over to another retailer, Baty and Birch began to consider the prospect of expanding their own retail chain. After all, they figured, the failing of their Glacier-brand, packaged-goods venture was primarily the result of their lack of control over the retail environment. What they recognized was that a customer visit to one of their stores wasn't mere shopping—it was a well-rounded body and mind experience.

It started with the smells of the company's 27 different soaps. Upon entering a store, you might first catch a whiff, say, of pumpkin patch soap, whose pumpkin pulp was designed to soothe rough, sore skin-or of Citrus Smoother, a soap whose sweet orange essential oils were a panacea for acne-prone faces.

But equally important was the embrace of its service. Rocky Mountain didn't owe its success just to its products; it owed it to the company's staff, its intimate, personal marketing efforts and its unique approach to product development. The small chain's employees were remarkably knowledgeable and conscientious.

They could readily match customers' skin conditions to the right product. Their capability wasn't an accident—nor was it easy to achieve. Throughout this decade, Rocky Mountain had worked hard to build employee talent. It recognized the contributions of individual staffers on their Web site, was in the midst of launching a daycare program, had instituted open-book management, and a profit-sharing plan, and had worked out a sales incentive scheme that rewarded teams for sales achievement without encouraging overzealous commission-chasing.

Employees were also intimately involved with the products. For the dozens of items, staffers could recite ingredients and explain how specific oils, extracts, and grains each affected the skin. The staff were also a conduit for customer knowledge, relaying feedback, suggestions, and requests to the owners. Such customer requests were still at the heart of the company's product-development process. Where a competitor like The

This case was originally written by Peggy Cunningham, R.A. Jodfrey Chair at Dalhousie University and was adapted by Lukas Neville, Ph.D. student, and Professor Elspeth J. Murray, CIBC Teaching Fellow in Entrepreneurship at the Queen's School of Business. The adaptation of this case was supported by the CIBC Curriculum Development Fund at Queen's School of Business, for purposes of classroom discussion.

Body Shop had access to the R&D resources of French parent firm L'Oréal, Rocky Mountain's products sprang forth from small-scale experiments conducted by Birch in the company's Canmore factory. Product ideas came from (and were often tested by) customers and staff. Some, like a salt scrub, went through 17 iterations before the founders settled on the final formulation. Others came about more quickly. Their strong-selling Summer Lemonade Soap, for instance, was the result of a suggestion from a local eighth-grade student.

These tight-knit customer relationships had been reinforced in the decade since Rocky Mountain's inception through its marketing efforts. Customer newsletters read like personal notes from Birch, sharing internal goings-on (their Wednesday morning staff yoga sessions, for instance) and describing new products. As the company grew, it began experimenting with more sophisticated marketing techniques, including opt-in email marketing and custom tailored mailings offering premiums such as a free bar of soap on customers' birthdays. The company's marketing also served to help educate consumers, deepening their clients' commitment to natural products. Alongside product updates and contests, Rocky Mountain's newsletters often contained information about natural products and aromatherapy trends. This type of communication was critical, because consumer education took time, particularly when clients had to adjust to things like unorthodox packaging—the stores' body butters, for instance, were packaged in plastic containers more commonly used for men's deodorant.

The owners had also leveraged the tourist economies of Banff and Canmore to grow their brand. Many local hotels in these tourist hubs offered Rocky Mountain soaps in their guest suites, providing customers with an all-important first trial. And from experience, the owners knew that much of the company's sales came from tourists eager for mountain-themed Canadiana. Their retail locations and branding catered to these distinctly local dynamics.

Traditional marketing at Rocky Mountain wasn't quite an afterthought—but it came close. Print advertising was lim-ited and exclusively local. The company took out small ads in low-circulation local newspapers and often left rack cards in hotel lobbies. In Banff and Canmore, whose small populations were served by a single newspaper each, such advertising was relatively inexpensive. In Edmonton, they had tried to scale up their efforts by purchasing billboards, mall posters, and space in the *Edmonton Journal*—all with limited success. On reflection, Baty and Birch realized that they weren't as comfortable managing high-gloss campaigns as they were building deep relationships with customers, one at a time.

With wholesaling all but ruled out, Rocky Mountain needed a unique strategy if it truly wanted to grow nationally. As Baty and Birch discussed their experiences—both their successes with retailing and setbacks with wholesaling—their aims began to crystallize. They decided they should open 30, perhaps 40 stores, with a rollout schedule of four to seven new company-owned outlets per year.

Envisioning growth was easy—getting there, the owners knew, would be an entirely different story. After the failed Glacier launch, Baty and Birch felt a natural trepidation about entering new markets without answers to a range of questions. Among them: How could they translate their personal marketing techniques to a much larger chain? Would the Rockies-themed brand resonate outside the Canadian West? Could they keep their intuitive and organic approach to product development as they entered the turf of larger competitors like The Body Shop? Could they replicate the personal service provided by their long-serving staff members as the chain grew?

Burt's Bees and Lush had both transformed themselves from tiny start-ups to retailing juggernauts on the strength of their organic and natural product niches. Baty hoped to follow in their footsteps but, as a final question, wondered how much space was left in this already crowded market—particularly for a small company with a limited marketing arsenal. As he and Birch surveyed their factory floor and watched employees carve out blocks of soap, they wondered: Did they have what it takes to build a national retail brand?

CASE 7   RESEARCH IN MOTION'S CHINA ENTRY

Dashing out of his modern Beijing condo, Chang Zhou, hopped into a taxi. Opening a Coach briefcase, Zhou put on a pair of Armani shades, pulled out the Financial Times, grabbed his handheld device and began his morning routine—trading a few stocks wirelessly. The taxi darted in and out of traffic as Zhou thumb-typed, moving a few of those volatile B shares listed on the Shanghai exchange. Now if only he could get a decent cup of western coffee . . .

Zhou was a member of the rapidly growing and increasingly prosperous Chinese middle-class that chose to use PDAs (personal digital assistants) in order to access conveniences that living in one of China's major cities could offer. The specific brand that Zhou used, the GWcom PDA, was just one of many niche players in a Chinese market dominated by home-grown companies that had developed a full range of PDAs and applications—this included everything from devices that allowed full Internet access to simple day planners and electronic dictionaries.

Despite the strength of local brands, such as Lenovo (which had grown to acquire IBM's PC division), Meijin Computer, GSL (Group Sense International Limited), Digital China, Legend, and Hi-Tech Wealth, the most popular devices in China continued to be ones that either incorporated imported technology or were imported altogether. Palm's operating system and Linux based systems both found application in Chinese PDAs, while Palm continued to attempt to market its hardware to Chinese consumers.[1] Other firms such as Research In Motion (RIM) found themselves in a peculiar position as they attempted to navigate a very competitive PDA market surrounded by institutional barriers.

This case was written by Nicholas P. Robinson, Faculty of Law, McGill University, and Prescott C. Ensign, for purposes of classroom discussion. A french version of this case (no. 9 00 2009 002) can be found at http://web.hec.ca/centredecas/catalogue/. HEC Montreal.

[1] Michelle Levander, "Handheld Combat: As China's PDA Makers Battle for Market Share, Cautious Global Giants Play a Waiting Game," *Time Magazine (Asia)*, August 6, 2002.

Despite the obstacles, the Chinese market was not one that could be ignored by any firm. In February 2006 China had a base of over 400 million cellphone users (which had eclipsed land line phone users in late 2003 or early 2004 at the 250 million mark) and the highest growth rates in new cellphone sales in the world making China a destination that could make or break a company and determine its long-term success in an industry that continued to mature.

China Mobile Communications Corporation (China Mobile), RIM's partner in China held two-thirds of the domestic cellphone market with over 250 million customers. In contrast, the entire U.S. wireless market was 204 million subscribers. The latest statistic from the government's official Xinhua News Agency was that Chinese mobile handset users 'thumbed' 22.8 billion text messages in March 2006, 66 percent more than in March 2005. Meanwhile, the Canadian Embassy in Beijing continued to intervene on RIM's behalf to help RIM pass technical tests and finally enter this market.

On April 6, 2006, Jim Balsillie, co-chief executive officer of RIM announced BlackBerry's unveiling in China was imminent. "We are on the verge of launching BlackBerry service with China Mobile and expect to launch by the end of May." A week later Norm Lo, VP of Asia-Pacific for RIM told reporters that mid-summer was more likely: "Our talks with China Mobile are going very well. We are working very tightly with them, and a deal is expected very soon, probably by the middle of this year." But Lo discovered that China Mobile would introduce a rival service "PushMail" in Shanghai next month. It would allow China Mobile customers to receive email on their existing handsets.

Norm Lo learned on April 10, 2006—after an almost two year regulatory delay blocking the introduction of RIM's BlackBerry to mainland China—that a "RedBerry" had just been launched by China Unicom. The state-owned enterprise China Unicom—the second largest mobile operator in mainland China—revealed in a press release "The RedBerry name extends the vivid name of BlackBerrry that people are already familiar with, and it also combines the new red symbol of China Unicom." The RedBerrry was driven by software from Chinese firm Facio. Tony Chan, CEO of Facio Software, believed they could win the battle with RIM: "The RedBerry is not afraid, neither did David fear Goliath!" Norm Lo felt like he was David, RIM was the one going to battle against giants.

Research In Motion aimed to increase sales by forming new "partnerships with up to 10 Asian carriers over the next six months to tap strong demand. 'The market is huge. We have just started,' said Norm Lo, vice president for Asia Pacific at RIM. [RIM] enters markets worldwide by signing agreements with local wireless carriers, which then offer services using the BlackBerry name and signature PDA like devices."[2] As of April 2006 RIM had ties with 21 telecom providers in 11 markets including India, Singapore, Malaysia, Hong Kong, Australia, New Zealand, Indonesia, Sri Lanka, Thailand, and the Philippines.

Despite signing a memorandum of intent in the fall of 2004 with Chinese wireless service provider China Mobile—the largest mobile telecommunications firm in China, and one of six Chinese state-controlled telecommunications firms—RIM had yet to launch its BlackBerry on the mainland. Nevertheless, it was estimated that there were hundreds of BlackBerry devices in mainland China that were paying hefty roaming fees for service all beyond the watchful eye and eavesdropping ability of the Chinese authorities.

Prior Experience in Asian Markets

RIM signed agreements with Hutchison Telecom and CSL of Hong Kong in 2002, but by October 2004 Hutchison Telecom had landed only 500 corporate customers for the BlackBerry device. The deals in Hong Kong, however, gave RIM the opportunity to test its product and business strategy in a Chinese market. Cultural similarities—not to mention language and political attachment—with the mainland made Hong Kong a perfect test market. Analysts concluded that RIM's limited success in Hong Kong was due to the company's "pricing structure" and the fact that demand for product "has been hit by the high licensing fees for the BlackBerry server software in Hong Kong."[3]

Competing with technologically inferior, but cheaper, local PDA products was expected to be the key to succeeding in Hong Kong and would likely also be vital to success in the Chinese market. This said, BlackBerry had been welcomed as a god-send by many Chinese firms, including Hutchison and China Mobile, who stated that the product would help them offer "users higher margin data service" and thus improve profit margins and slow the rapid "decline in average revenue per user."[4] The BlackBerry had been seen similarly in other Asian markets, where anxious telecom companies partnered with RIM to launch the BlackBerry in hopes of improving margins and increasing the value of services provided to customers.

In India, for example, "mobile operators are turning to higher end products such as BlackBerry . . . to capitalize on growth."[5] The Indian market's 43 million mobile phone users were demanding more sophisticated products, and RIM hoped that BlackBerry would be a star in the world's fastest growing wireless market. Three different BlackBerry devices able to receive email messages on the go had been introduced in India since the firm entered the market in October 2004, partnering with mobile service provider AirTel.

The Red Factor

More than 15 months after signing a letter of intent with China's largest mobile telephone company—the state-controlled China Mobile—RIM had yet to see its product launched. A variety of China-specific problems seemed to pose barriers to RIM's entry into the vast market. Of these, the most pressing issues revolved around the fact that the technology used by RIM would make it near impossible for the Chinese government to monitor the communication activities of private citizens and businesses using a BlackBerry.

It was thought that those users from Hong Kong, Singapore, the United States, and elsewhere living in China brought the product into the country and refused to give it up. This led some to argue that the Chinese government could do little to stop the use of new communications technologies in the country as mon-

---

[2] Reuters, "BlackBerry Maker Aims for More Asian Partners," October 19, 2005.

[3] *The Standard*, "Telco Leader Signs Deal for BlackBerry," October 5, 2004.

[4] Ibid.

[5] Dinesh C. Sharma, "RIM Takes BlackBerry to India," ZDNet Asia, October 20, 2004.

itoring the ever-increasing volume of information, and cracking the increasingly complex encryption algorithms was not feasible. In fact, the world-renowned Nobel economist Milton Friedman argued that the threat posed by rapidly advancing technology and a rapidly growing middle class would ultimately lead to "future Tiananmen Squares."[6] Improvements in technology and the general welfare of Chinese citizens may mean democratization, just as an authoritarian government could constitute an economic disadvantage.

Telecommunications Industry in China

The Chinese telecommunications industry was characterized by high government involvement and extraordinarily tight controls on foreign investment and private enterprise. The sector, which had been identified by the Communist Peoples' Party government as being key to China's economic development was controlled by a plethora of provincial and federal organizations, with the State Council ultimately having power to override other decisions in many cases. Adding to this control was that all the major telecommunication companies were, at a minimum, partly government owned.

The Chinese government introduced numerous reforms to the telecommunications sector in the mid-1990s to speed up the development of networks that were seen as critical to economic growth. Though all these firms were state-controlled, this was still a far cry from the days when foreign investment in the telecom sector was barred. These changes began in 1994, when the monopoly of the government-run China Telecom ended with the establishment of China Unicom as a direct competitor in the domestic mobile and fixed markets.

These changes had been spurred on by demands that China open its economy to more investment if it wished to trade with the free-market nations of the world. In the past, "the classification of telecommunications as a restricted industry for foreign investment purposes arose from the central government policy of ensuring that control of vital national industries does not fall into foreign hands."[7]

China's entry into the WTO was forcing the country to give increased access to foreign investors who were anxious to profit from China's booming telecom market. More specifically, in the mobile market, the number of subscribers "continues to increase at the phenomenal rate of 5 million per month" giving China the "mantle of the world's largest mobile phone market."[8] Another reason why China wanted to keep investment in its telecom sector restricted was that telecom had been "an extremely profitable" industry and had been a substantial source of government revenue.[9]

Policies such as these, which hit outsiders like Nortel and Lucent very hard, were representative of the lack of transparency that many foreign businesses saw as a major barrier to investing in China. "Foreign companies noted the difficulty in finding and obtaining copies of regulations and other measures undertaken by various ministries" and the issue had forced China to change its practices and establish a set of national

gazettes to inform the business community of Chinese laws and regulations.[10]

In addition, the prospect of exporting a product to China was largely dependent on the nature of the product and Peoples' Republic policies with regard to the industry in question. The laws on the books stated, "the free import and export of goods and technologies" was wholly allowed "except otherwise provided for by other laws or administrative decrees."[11] However, importers had to first obtain a licence to import and an extraordinary number of government orders and decrees severely limited the range of products that could be brought into China.

In March 2002, preparing for China's accession to the WTO, MOFTEC issued an order identifying mobile phones and mobile communications systems as being sectors in which foreign investment would be encouraged. Although the only outright control on the importation of PDAs and other mobile telecommunications devices was a stipulation that imports be subject to tendering, there were numerous other regulatory, legal, and political barriers that made it possible for the Chinese government to halt imports without any sort of government order. Furthermore, the fact that the industry had been identified as being of national importance to develop could make RIM's entry into China more difficult than initially assumed. RIM's manufacturing and design facilities were almost exclusively located in North America (with a factory at Waterloo, Ontario) and the firm would not invest in China, but rather, simply create new competition for domestic manufacturers of similar products.

Institutional Environment

Entering the Chinese market involved overcoming challenges that were unique to economies that have made, or were in the process of making, a transition from a controlled economy to a more free, market-oriented economy. In China, an immature financial system, weak intellectual property protection, and tight labour controls characterized an economy that was shedding the vestiges of socialism. Though many of these issues might not be of direct concern to RIM, all would likely have impact on the firm's experience in China and Norm Lo gave them consideration as they provided good insight into the Chinese business environment.

Repatriating Profits. China's financial system was tightly controlled by the Peoples' Republic government and contained minimal private involvement. The most pressing concern that an immature financial system raised for RIM or any firm involved with China was getting paid. Given that the Chinese currency, the Renminbi (also known as the Yuan), was fixed to a basket of foreign currencies, predominantly the U.S. dollar, exchange rate risk for RIM would be limited to fluctuations in value between the Canadian and U.S. dollars. Because the rate of exchange was fixed by the People's Bank of China (influenced by the interbank foreign exchange market), transferring funds into and out of the country was expected to be more difficult than in more liberalized markets.

[6] *The Charlie Rose Show*, PBS, December 26, 2005.

[7] Jingzhou Tao and Diarmuid O'Brien, *Non-tariff Trade Barriers in China* (Hong Kong: Sweet & Maxwell, 2003).

[8] Ibid.

[9] Ibid.

[10] Ibid.

[11] Kui Hua Wang, *Chinese Commercial Law* (UK: Oxford University Press, 2000).

The process of repatriating RMB to the home currency typically involved receiving approval from the Foreign Exchange Adjustment Centre, which registered the firm's foreign exchange and completed the transaction. Specific Chinese banks could perform these transactions.

Intellectual Property. China's reputation as a safe haven for companies involved in piracy and other violations of intellectual property was grounded in cultural attitudes toward ownership. After years of socialism, the cultural importance of private property to the Chinese people had been partly eroded and was reflected in weak enforcement of intellectual property laws. Officially, however, China was a party to the Paris Convention and thus recognized patent protection:

> *A foreigner can apply for patent protection in China in accordance with the Patent Law and the Paris Convention. If a foreign patent holder has a residential or business address in China, the foreigner will be treated as the equal of any Chinese citizen in accordance with the National Treatment ... under the Paris Convention, a foreign applicant will enjoy National Treatment in China only if his or her home country is a signatory of the convention or provides Chinese applicants with National Treatment in that country.*[12]

Despite this assurance, other Canadian companies had had difficult experiences protecting their intellectual property in China. For instance, Canadian bomb-suit and riot-gear maker, Med-Eng, was shocked to discover that suits provided for a Chinese government agency had been cloned in near perfect detail and were then being marketed throughout the world by a Chinese company.[13] Med-Eng's response was to take legal action against buyers—a manoeuvre that was both successful and costly. The threat for RIM was incredibly significant as the BlackBerry was valuable precisely because of the intellectual property involved. Any violation of the company's proprietary intellectual property, or patents involving key elements of its technologies (hardware or software), could run the firm out of business.

Cultural Barriers. Business in China was not as impersonal as it was in North American where RIM had seen the majority of its success. As the former CEO of Ericsson, Kurt Hellstrom, put it, "personal relationships based on mutual understanding are the key to success" in the Chinese business environment.[14] From a North American perspective, Chinese attitudes toward relationships almost bordered on corruption, as favouritism and camaraderie took precedence over other factors such as price and quality. In fact, some contemporary Chinese legal scholars theorized that this emphasis on relationships could be partly due to old mind-sets, which were gradually changing in China.

> *Transition from a centrally planned economy to the socialist market economy in China is expressed by many contemporary Chinese legal philosophers as the transition from the rule of man (renzhi) to the rule of law (fazhi) or from supremacy of power to supremacy of law.*[15]

Chinese attitudes toward relationships were reflective of the pre-laissez faire mindset, which some expected would gradually dissipate as Chinese businesspeople were held accountable to their shareholders, partners, and international institutions (like the WTO). The emphasis on "guanxi" (a Chinese word for connections) meant that business in China must cultivate meaningful relationships, which could be the "difference between getting the contract or not."[16] For this reason, many Canadian businesses in China chose to hire Chinese nationals "with contacts in China to help promote their business."[17] RIM was hoping that Norm Lo, the VP for the Asia-Pacific Region would be able to make such inroads.

Man on a Mission

Norm Lo was appointed VP for the Asia-Pacific in July of 2005 after five years with Research In Motion. His mandate was to expand RIM's regional presence and "drive BlackBerry mindshare and market penetration across the Asia-Pacific."[18] RIM had offices in Hong Kong, Singapore, and Australia with a staff of about 50 employees. His initial plan included doubling the number of carriers RIM worked with in Asia. This represented a substantial increase from the 16 alliances RIM had in eight countries, but in the eight months since taking charge Norm Lo moved closer to this goal—the April 2006 tally was 21 partnerships in 11 countries. According to Lo, RIM was just "scratching the surface ... Everything in Asia-Pacific is wide open. We're talking to basically everybody. There isn't one country that we are not currently involved in a business discussion."[19]

Norm Lo's career spanned 20 years in high-tech research, product development, management, sales, and marketing. Prior to his present task, Lo had been responsible for two business units focused on the North American market. Before joining RIM in 2000, he worked at Nortel Networks. He had a B.Sc. in Engineering Physics from the University of British Columbia, M.Eng. and Ph.D. degrees in Electrical Engineering from Carleton University, and an M.B.A. from the University of Ottawa.

Like everyone at RIM, Lo had followed daily accounts of the saga between RIM and NTP. Gartner had placed RIM in the lead (Exhibit 1) but at the same time Gartner had recommended clients not go with BlackBerry devices until legal issues were resolved. Gartner's December 5, 2005 news release suggested BlackBerry users in the U.S. might lose service. While U.S. customers and potential ones were being made nervous, headquarters in Waterloo, Ontario were scrambling. Executive attention had been focused almost exclusively on this issue. Market development and the impasse in China were well off the radar for everyone back in Canada.

---

[12] Ibid.

[13] Richard L'abbe, CEO of Med-Eng, onsite interview Ottawa, Ontario, August 2005.

[14] Martin Krott and Kent Williamsson, *China Business ABC: The China Market Survival Kit* (Denmark: Copenhagen Business School Press, 2003).

[15] Kui Hua Wang, *Chinese Commercial Law* (UK: Oxford University Press, 2000).

[16] Martin Krott and Kent Williamsson.

[17] Ibid.

[18] Vivian Yeo, "New Asia-Pacific Head Drives RIM's Expansion," ZDNet Asia, July 12, 2005.

[19] Ibid.

Norm Lo reviewed recent numbers. Global sales in the fourth quarter of 2005 suggested Palm was ahead of RIM (Exhibit 2). But the yearly totals placed RIM in the lead for the year (Exhibit 3). Norm Lo scrutinized the footnotes to these reports closely. Totals did not include smartphones, such as the Treo 650 and BlackBerrry 7100. Palm shipped 2.77 million PDAs in 2005, down 25 percent from 2004, but these results excluded sales of Palm's Treo smartphone, which amounted to 1.95 million units in 2005. Gartner pointed out that Palm's PDA sales were being cannibalized by its Treo products, which were expected to surpass Palm's PDA sales in 2006. On March 29, 2006 Gartner documented smartphone sales at 16.1 million units in the fourth quarter of 2005—a 139-percent increase over the same quarter in 2004 (figures released by Canalys are reported in Exhibits 4 and 5).

EXHIBIT 1 Worldwide Preliminary PDA Vendor Shipment Estimates 3Q 05 (units)

Company	Q3 2005	Market Share	Q3 2004	Market share	Growth
RIM	862,000	25.0%	565,000	14.8%	52.6%
HP	548,338	16.0%	692,113	30.5%	−20.2%
Palm	478,575	13.9%	748,950	21.0%	−36.1%
T-Mobile	206,800	6.0%	51,000	0.0%	305.5%
Nokia	200,000	5.8%	–	6.0%	N/A
Others	1,149,633	33.3%	801,744	27.7%	43.4%
Total	**3,449,346**	**100.0%**	**2,858,807**	**100.0%**	**20.7%**

Source: Gartner Dataquest (October 2005) Press Release "Gartner Says Worldwide PDA Shipments Increased 21 Percent in the Third Quarter of 2005," www.gartner.com/it/page.jsp?id=492211.

Please note that Gartner research is meant to be viewed historically and may not represent current market trends.

EXHIBIT 2 Worldwide Preliminary PDA Vendor Shipment Estimates 4Q 05 (units)

Company	Q4 2005	Market Share	Q4 2004	Market share	Growth
Palm	1,037,680	23.5%	1,226,525	29.9%	−15.4%
RIM	780,000	17.7%	698,000	17.0%	11.7%
HP	660,463	15.0%	869,000	21.1%	−24.0%
T-Mobile	305,000	6.9%	96,000	2.3%	217.7%
Mio Technology	220,214	5.0%	83,645	2.0%	163.3%
Others	1,405,569	31.9%	1,135,788	27.6%	23.8%
Total	**4,408,926**	**100.0%**	**4,108,958**	**100.0%**	**7.3%**

Source: "Gartner Dataquest (February 2006) Press Release "Gartner Says Worldwide PDA Shipments Reach Record Level in 2005," www.gartner.com/it/page.jsp?id=492242.

Please note that Gartner research is meant to be viewed historically and may not represent current market trends.

EXHIBIT 3 Preliminary PDA Vendor Shipment Estimates 2005 (units)

Company	2005	Market Share	2004	Market Share	Growth
RIM	3,193,000	21.4%	2,178,000	17.4%	46.6%
Palm	2,773,025	18.6%	3,726,172	29.8%	−25.6%
HP	2,264,666	15.2%	2,668,627	21.3%	−15.1%
Nokia	1,010,000	6.8%	250,000	2.0%	304.0%
T-Mobile	812,600	5.5%	191,400	1.5%	324.6%
Others	4,839,701	32.5%	3,499,314	28.0%	38.3%
Total	14,892,992	100.0%	12,513,513	100.0%	19.0%

Source: "Gartner Dataquest (February 2006) Press Release "Gartner Says Worldwide PDA Shipments Reach Record Level in 2005," www.gartner.com/it/page.jsp?id=492242.

Please note that Gartner research is meant to be viewed historically and may not represent current market trends.

EXHIBIT 4 Worldwide Smart Mobile Device by Vendor, Q3 2005

Company	Q3 2005	Market Share	Q3 2004	Market Share	Growth
Nokia	7,130,120	54.8%	2,951,450	39.7%	141.6%
Palm	1,053,390	8.1%	1,076,470	14.5%	−2.1%
RIM	977,940	7.5%	619,020	8.3%	58.0%
Motorola	693,650	5.3%	61,630	0.8%	1025.5%
HP	551,140	4.2%	689,410	9.3%	−20.1%
Others	2,598,440	20.0%	2,031,060	27.3%	27.9%
Total	13,004,680	100.0%	7,429,040	100.0%	75.1%

Source: Canalys estimates, © canalys.com ltd. October 25, 2005.

Smart mobile device market: handhelds, wireless handhelds, smart phones.

EXHIBIT 5 Worldwide Smart Mobile Device Market by Vendor, Q1 2006

Company	Q1 2006	Market Share	Q1 2005	Market Share	Growth
Nokia	8,616,530	51.6%	5,394,900	50.0%	59.7%
RIM	1,399,090	8.4%	758,300	7.0%	84.5%
Palm	1,030,610	6.2%	1,009,040	9.4%	2.1%
Mitsubishi	1,016,320	6.1%	86,420	0.8%	1076.0%
Sharp	951,410	5.7%	31,960	0.3%	2876.9%
Others	3,688,680	22.1%	3,501,760	32.5%	5.3%
Total	16,702,640	100.0%	10,782,380	100.0%	54.9%

Source: Canalys estimates, © canalys.com ltd. 2005–2006. April 25, 2006.

Smart mobile device market: handhelds, wireless handhelds, smart phones.

Norm Lo and the Balance of Probabilities

Riding the elevator to his Hong Kong office, Norm Lo reflected on an increasingly complex web of issues faced by his company. Over the past few years RIM had seen its PDA become the market leader in terms of sales and reputation for quality. The firm had successfully built a multi-billion dollar company out of a start-up, and had managed, against the odds, to conquer a U.S. market filled with competition from companies such as Nokia, Samsung, and Palm. Despite past triumphs, the future of RIM was at stake. The NTP threat had subsided with a US$612 million pay out to prevent the devastation of BlackBerry's existence in the U.S. market, but events had taken their toll. The threat to the BlackBerry network caused some customers to delay purchases and others to defect. More importantly, however, Lo understood that RIM's corporate performance would be dependent on its success overseas.

China had emerged as the largest telecom market in the world, an incredible opportunity seemed to lie ahead for any firm that could make sense of the government's complicated regulatory scheme and win favour with local decision makers and organizations, all of which would be essential in order to put BlackBerrys in the hands of people in mainland China. Considering that rogue users from other markets had already been using their BlackBerrys in China, and considering the modest success the company had experienced in Hong Kong and Singapore, Lo pondered the product's future in the Chinese market.

It was confirmed; Norm Lo had an appointment at the end of the week at China Mobile's office to review technical testing-essentially to determine compliance with government policies. Lo knew that, being responsible for Asia Pacific, he would be accountable for RIM's success or failure in this vital market—a market that could become more important than the North American market. China's admission to the WTO, political concerns, and regulatory hurdles all posed a serious challenge to the BlackBerry's future in this colossal country. Considering China's interest in developing its domestic market and considering the intricacy of political issues (even dragging the U.S. military into the milieu) Lo weighed the balance of probabilities in his mind: Could the Chinese block the introduction of RIM's products through regulatory measures and institutional barriers, and what were the chances that the Chinese would actually cooperate to allow the introduction of BlackBerry to the Chinese market?

The introduction of the "RedBerry" was particularly alarming—though it should not have been entirely surprising. China could be expected to reverse engineer or copy and improve many existing products. The Chinese penchant for borrowing technology and pushing it forward was remarkable. If RIM was to enter this tremendous market, could its technology remain in tact? Should operating system and hardware be equally guarded? What were the next steps RIM should take?

CASE 8   REPOSITBOX

The Dilemma

Jeff McLeod, a graduate of the Master's programme in Electrical Engineering at the University of British Columbia mulled over an issue of serious importance. Only hours earlier, in the late afternoon, he had received a call from a locally based "head hunter" who had earmarked Jeff as a superior candidate for a high-profile job, working as a senior engineer in a well-respected hi-tech firm located in Kanata, Ontario.

The job seemed to be out of a dream for Jeff, who had considerable experience working in both management and engineering positions. Further, Jeff's reputation as a skilled engineer whose involvement in numerous projects had driven the development of innovative technologies made him a specifically attractive catch for any firm. His education, expertise, work experience, and reputation made him an indispensable asset, at least so the recruiter thought. The uniqueness of Jeff's skill set made him one of the few individuals able to fill the position in Kanata leading a product development team.

Altogether, the opportunity seemed like a match made in heaven. Jeff McLeod was out of work and the firm was in need of someone with Jeff's exact capabilities. Ideally, this would have meant that Jeff would have been the successful candidate for the position. However, after hanging up the phone with the

administrative staff at the UBC Registrars and Records Office, Jeff realized that he had a serious dilemma on his hands. "Get me proof of your educational background and credentials by tomorrow morning at 10 a.m." the recruiter had stated. The high-tech firm urgently needed to fill the position, and they needed proper verification of Mr. McLeod's successful completion of the Master's degree and records outlining information on his thesis and academic background.[1]

This evidence, however, could not be obtained within 36 hours. Typically, the university would require a signed letter requesting that confirmation of a degree be sent, and would then mail transcripts directly to those concerned. Communicating confirmation of a degree granted by fax, over the telephone, or any other method besides 'snail-mail' would have violated the university's privacy policy, and could lead to a Pandora's Box of legal issues.

Ultimately, this meant that it would be near impossible for Jeff to provide the information requested by the recruiter by the deadline of 10 the next morning. This meant that Mr. McLeod and the Kanata high-tech firm were both at a loss— a dilemma which one Ottawa businessman and former civic leader thought he could solve.

This case was written by Nicholas P. Robinson, Faculty of Law, McGill University, and Prescott C. Ensign, for purposes of classroom discussion.

[1] Federal and provincial privacy laws, including the Personal Information and Protection of Electronic Documents Act, make sharing personal information in Canada a tricky undertaking. The law stipulates that the subject of the personal information must give clear consent (written preferred) for an organization to share personal information.

Conception of RepositBox

In April 2001, Jamie Fisher, a former Deputy Mayor of the City of Ottawa and business consultant, heard about Jeff's dilemma while casually talking with a colleague. "He would have been perfect for the position," remarked Jamie's friend, but "he just couldn't make the deadline." Listening attentively, Jamie was astonished that, despite the incredible power of software and the Internet, problems of this nature could persist. This realization marked the birth of GradChek, a company that aimed to provide immediate, instantaneous verification for its user base.

However, prior to actually formally registering the firm, Jamie and his friend—and soon to be business partner—Janet Wilkinson decided to consult with Dr. Vernon Sulway, a software specialist at the National Research Council, a research-intensive government science and engineering entity whose mission was to encourage innovation in Canada. With the NRC headquartered in Ottawa, this allowed Jamie to take advantage of the know-how that this organization provided. At the core of Jamie's concerns when he approached Dr. Sulway, was the viability of the business concept and the software product that he wished to be developed. He wanted to know:

1. If the software could be developed to solve Jeff McLeod's dilemma, especially considering security and privacy issues.
2. Whether the innovation would provide a unique service for which a market exists.

After a thorough analysis of the proposed technology, which would allow a user to store a variety of sensitive education related documents (such as transcripts, etc.) in a database, and then grant or deny permission to access these authenticated documents to potential employers and others, Dr. Sulway concluded that the answer to both questions was a resounding "YES."

The GradChek concept was unique and would serve a previously untouched market, and the software could be developed to allow the storage of authenticated documents that could be viewed instantaneously without breaching the privacy or security of the subject of the information. After thinking through the concept a little further, the partners realized that this system could be used for far more than just education, and renamed GradChek "RepositBox." This new product concept was further refined to the following:

RepositBox System is an Internet-based service that will provide certified, secure, personal online records and records management for individuals. The service is national and international in scope, and the technology is compatible with current and future Internet technology and multiple information distribution channels. Subscribers, e.g., businesses and institutions, are sold a kit (RepositStation) that enables them to distribute Internet Credential Storage Files (called RepositBoxes) to employees and clients.

A RepositBox is a private, secure container for individuals to access and manage their documents in a structured collection using the Internet and other Virtual Private Networks (VPN) and communication management systems. An individual can store, aggregate, and self-manage personal records or credentials, and uniquely can share a "warranted authentic" copy with a third party without recourse to the issuing institution.[2] (See Exhibit 1.)

This system would offer full control to the owner of the information and documents placed into the system while enabling this person to share them instantaneously when merited. This meant that, had RepositBox existed in 2001 when Jeff McLeod was identified as a prime candidate for a job in "Silicon Valley North," he would likely be working for the high-tech firm today as a result of RepositBox's document verification system. Jamie Fisher likened the product to "those large glass tubes used to sort rough diamonds—with rubber gloves that protrude in. The diamonds may be manipulated, sorted, viewed, but you can't get your hands on 'em—except through those rubber gloves. Once diamonds are placed in that glass tube you can look but there's no direct contact. It's a very secure system that works well."

EXHIBIT 1 How RepositBox Works[3]

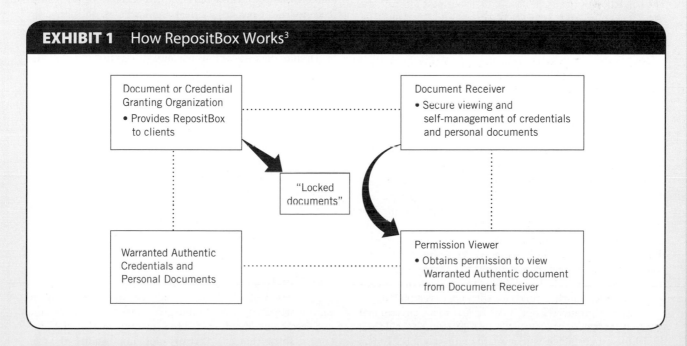

[2] Excerpt from Market Preview Report for the RepositBox System prepared by the Canadian Innovation Centre, Waterloo, Ontario, February 2002.

[3] www.repositbox.com/.

Warranted Authentic Credentials and Personal Documents

However, in order to ensure that this system was feasible, it not only had to be inspected by professional engineers, it also had to be examined by other stakeholders. For precisely this reason, Jamie Fisher chose to contact two other groups:

1. An educational institution: Jamie met and discussed the RepositBox concept with representatives from Algonquin College in Ottawa, Ontario. Jamie met with the Registrar and several members of her team. The response was very positive.
2. Jamie then met with the president of the Canadian Federation of Students, who saw the potential of the innovation to create value for graduates seeking a job. This group also endorsed the RepositBox concept, believing it to be a workable solution to a longstanding problem that graduates faced—verification of educational background.

Having received positive feedback from the previous three sets of people (NRC engineers, college representatives, and student associations) Jamie proceeded to consult with the last key stakeholder. He needed validation of the business concept from a top technology group and decided to approach IBM. Jamie met with John Kutcy, an executive at IBM Canada overseeing the education sector. After several telephone discussions and a meeting, Mr. Kutcy confirmed in a letter that, "if Mr. Fisher and Ms. Wilkinson could build out the software, along the lines discussed, IBM would work with RepositBox to market and sell the product."

After such positive feedback from all these groups, it would have been difficult to not move ahead with the design and development of the software. Potential customers seemed to be lining up, the product solved a previously unaddressed dilemma, and the business partnerships needed to make the concept a reality in the marketplace were being solidified.

Financing the Start-up

The validation of the usefulness of their business idea and the technology supporting it by students, educational institutions, and a major technology firm got Janet Wilkinson thinking of even more elaborate versions of the software that could be used for purposes beyond just verifying documents. In mid-2001, the firm further refined its product idea into something far more expansive. This piece of software, if constructed, would be a layered system where individuals could deposit verified versions of important personal electronic documents (diplomas, insurance documents, birth certificates, etc.). This would further enhance the usefulness of the software but would complicate the marketing, development, and management of the product.

In Jamie Fisher's mind "focusing on what the firm knew best was the wisest approach." This meant ignoring the temptation of a larger market and more broadly appealing product in exchange for honing in on one niche—the education sector. Ultimately, the choice of whether or not to focus on something much larger would be based on constraints. The firm realized that they had few resources and taking on a larger market and larger project would have meant depleting already scarce resources, such as funds for software development.

Despite assurances from IRAP (a Canadian government research incentives program) the firm just simply could not afford to sustain the costs that a large more complex system would entail. That was, until late 2001 when an angel investor entered the picture. This individual, having an interest in seeing some sort of return on his money, offered to finance the development of the software. Only two questions needed to be addressed before RepositBox could get the cash infusion it needed:

1. How much will it cost to build the product?
2. If the product is built, can RepositBox go into business and successfully generate profits?

After having provided convincing arguments to answer both of these questions, the investor signed on and provided RepositBox with a generous injection of cash, to be used in the construction and development of the software. It was now Jamie's responsibility to find a contractor who could put together the system.

The Data Storage Market

RepositBox had commissioned a market review on the potential for the product given the business climate in Canada and the U.S. This review uncovered that at least one other company could compete directly with RepositBox, if it decided to enter the firm's market space, and that several other smaller firms possessed the basic document storage software that would be required to enter the market. This prospect raised the spectre that if RepositBox were to enter the market first, a far larger player with more resources could enter and wipe out the company. The conclusion that the review came to was that relationship-based marketing approaches, such as direct sales would build trust and thus increase customer/user switching costs. This approach, RepositBox hoped, would lead to long-term clients and deter new competition. FleetBoston Financial, a large U.S. bank, had developed a service for its clients that allowed them to store important electronic documents: "customers are given their own personal FileBox." This service, called fileTRUST and initially marketed as "an electronic safe deposit box," could pose a serious challenge to RepositBox if it decided to enter the company's market space. Other smaller California-based firms such as Xdrive Technologies, Anuvio Technologies (formerly i-drive), StoragePoint, and Driveway already produced technologies similar to the one RepositBox had developed and therefore posed a risk as well.

Despite the ease with which any of these firms could enter this market, the review conducted by the Canadian Innovation Centre in February 2002 made it clear that the potential market was large enough to be divvied up between many players. In fact, according to IDC (International Data Corporation) projections, "the U.S. market for Storage Service Providers will grow 360% per year compounded, while worldwide spending will increase to US$10.7 billion in 2005 from US$153 million in 2000." This seemed to indicate that RepositBox was poised to enter an industry (Storage Service Providers) that was in its most premature stages. Many firms would likely enter the market given high profit margins, but it was surmised that few would survive the shakeout. A sound strategy was called for if RepositBox were to survive.

Developing the Product

The question of which firm would construct the software was a particularly delicate one given that the firm had limited cash on hand but wanted to protect its intellectual capital (the software itself). Perhaps more importantly, the firm wanted the software to be completed by professionals who would stand by their work and produce a quality piece of software with few glitches. Given that the hi-tech meltdown had put countless software engineers on the street, it would be relatively easy to recruit a local programmer to perform the work. However, Jamie quickly realized that, "most of these individuals had millionaire dreams and wanted more than they deserved given that they didn't provide the same type and quality of service as a larger firm." Ultimately this led Jamie to decide to go with a consulting firm rather than an individual—but he still had to determine which firm to go with. The following criteria were set:

1. RepositBox had to be able to work with the firm and have a smooth relationship with the principals.

2. The firm would have to be willing to complete the project on a phase-by-phase basis in order to control costs and monitor progress:
   - Relational database would be constructed first
   - Supporting code would be built out
   - An alpha test would be performed[4]
   - A beta test would take place[5]

3. Jamie also wanted to ensure that costs were fixed and that the firm would not charge trailer fees and ongoing consulting fees in the case that the job was not correctly completed.

4. Lastly, Jamie wanted the firm to have constructed a software product in the past that had been commercially successful.

Six months later, after intense searching and analysis of possible options, RepositBox chose Loki Innovations of Toronto, Ontario to build the software. Loki was well established, had great experience in projects similar to RepositBox's and met all the other conditions set by Jamie and Janet. With this completed, they incorporated RepositBox Canada Inc. and issued shares while Loki developed the software. RepositBox's aspiration of becoming the principal provider of warranted authentic online credentials or "the Kleenex of online credential's business" was well underway. As Jamie put it, "RepositBox's technology represents the fifth generation of credentials verification: First there was the stone tablet, then there was papyrus, then parchment, and then paper . . . and now today, finally, RepositBox!" (See Exhibit 2.)

Now that progress was being made on all other fronts, Jamie refocused on strategies for future growth, and concluded that the U.S. market was key for RepositBox and that RepositBox would have to establish a solid U.S. presence before selling into this market. A business school professor at the University of Ottawa and member of RepostiBox's advisory board since

---

EXHIBIT 2 About RepositBox[6]

Overview of Technology

- Thin client Internet application, runs on a Web browser.
- Privacy and authenticity of information are ensured for document and credential grantors, receivers, and viewers.
- Data cannot be compromised.
- The identity of the server and source are verifiable.

Benefits for Grantors

- A significant reduction of paper-based operations.
- Zero payments to RepositBox, plus potential revenue-sharing opportunities.
- Confidence that only the receiver and his/her authorized viewers can view the warranted authentic information.
- Protection of your corporate integrity—assurance that credentials and important personal documents of your clients have not been replicated or tampered with.
- Important, long-term branding and client service opportunities.
- Long-term contact with credential or document receivers.

Benefits for Receivers

- Credentials and important proprietary documents are issued directly from granting organizations to the highly secure RepositBox environment and accessible *only* to you as the document receiver. It's just like paper—only faster and easier!
- You can authorize an unlimited number of third party views of selected credentials, instantly, at one low fixed price per year.
- Your third party viewer can be assured of the authenticity and veracity of your credentials and important documents because with RepositBox, *no one* can touch, tamper, or alter them. They are *Warranted Authentic* by RepositBox.

Benefits for Viewers

- You can view the credential *immediately*, rather than awaiting the arrival of a certified paper copy from a granting organization.
- As a viewer, you can be assured of authenticity. Credentials and documents have been deposited directly by the grantor to the highly secure RepositBox environment.
- You can trust the credentials and important documents you are viewing because with RepositBox, no one can touch, tamper, or alter them.
- RepositBox: credentials and important personal documents are online, accessible, and *Warranted Authentic*.

---

[4] Testing an early version of the software that may not contain all of the features that are planned for the final version. This first stage of testing is often performed only by developers involved in the product's creation.

[5] The second stage of software testing involves a limited number of 'real world' external users.

[6] Information obtained from the company Web site, www.repositbox.com/.

the beginning, David Large, stumbled across a technology that seemed to complete RepositBox's package. Jamie pursued this lead to Rochester, New York and the first U.S. initiative was to enter into a licensing agreement with the University of Rochester to use their patented AuthentImage, digital sealing technology on an exclusive basis in the "virtual credential space." RepositBox would integrate this proprietary technology into the RepositBox solution and also market AuthentImage as a stand-alone security product. In exchange, the University of Rochester would become a minority equity partner in RepositBox's new U.S. corporation and would share a small percentage of the cash flow. Over time the University of Rochester relationship solidified and became a major asset to the new company—providing promising leads.

Financial Fuel and New Connections for RepositBox

It would be through a combination of partnerships with larger organizations in similar industries and a dedicated sales team that RepositBox expected to experience considerable growth soon after the implementation and introduction of its product. In order to ensure this growth, a U.S. partner company was established (jointly owned by a cohort of private New York investors, the University of Rochester, and majority shareholder RepositBox Canada Inc.) and Jamie Fisher decided that aggressively pursuing the U.S. market would be a wise first step given its size. The choice of the University of Rochester was strategic for a few reasons. Most importantly though, upstate New York, where the University of Rochester was situated, had a high concentration of post-secondary higher education institutions-over 300, making it a great target market.

RepositBox's new investors brought substantial relationships and marketing skills to the new company. The new company was invited to present at UNYTECH 2005 (a showcase for technology emanating from upstate New York universities) to be exposed to a variety of different opportunities. All this would not have occurred without the doors opened by the University of Rochester. Jamie was also put in contact with a New York based lawyer who acted as a "rainmaker" for many entrepreneurs seeking venture capital. This individual expressed interest in arranging for substantial funding for RepositBox, but was concerned that a previously unidentified competitor had a similar product in the works. Knowing this information, and knowing that succeeding would be at least partly dependent on economies of scale (and therefore available capital), Jamie tussled with the ways of getting this prominent businessperson onside, and securing even more funding for the firm's future.

Initially, Jamie Fisher's thoughts were to focus on what he felt best prepared for, the education sector. Furthermore, this particular market segment fit into the ideal target profile. Universities and colleges managed enormous amounts of personal information, had large numbers of sensitive documents, could easily afford (yet could cut costs by) investing in the system, and the market was large enough to be lucrative. Furthermore, RepositBox was initially conceptualized in response to a problem that originated from a university's inability to provide expedient verification of official documents. The alternative to this was, of course, to take a more general approach and attack a larger market. Both the insurance industry and the human resources management function looked attractive. This would mean far larger revenues and profits, but could

lead to a weaker brand identity and more complications in terms of managing RepositBox while catering to a wide spectrum of firms. RepositBox wanted to go after larger firms (over 10,000 clients or employees), but could the new venture be all things to all people?

A Critical Inflection Point

It was late August 2005 as Jamie Fisher sat in his office in downtown Ottawa—with air conditioner running full force—he began to question whether he was biting off more than he could realistically chew. "There are so many applications for a product that can verify and maintain the heritage of a document," he thought aloud above the hum of the fan blowing cold air. "We take a document suspended in time and permit access to the glass tube, regulating who looks in and who puts their fingers in those rubber gloves."

Loki Innovations had designed the software to handle a variety of different document types and "big money" might be found in offering RepositBox's verification services to a broader range of clients. Jamie Fisher and Janet Wilkinson started to have second thoughts about which market segment(s) to tackle. Given their background, connections, and the evidence provided by market research, the education sector might be the easiest to crack. However, at the same time, Janet Wilkinson brought up that "this would essentially constitute turning away big business in exchange for a smaller piece of pie." This was purely a question of risk and reward—could RepositBox, a young venture, manage to be a success if it attacked the general document authentication market, which included insurance, health management, and other big-profile markets? Conversely, would it make more sense for the firm to stay on track with the segment it knew best, education? This seemed like the sure thing to do, but the appeal of larger fortunes loomed in front of them.

In any event, a decision had to be made soon; the software was near completion and the firm had to move ahead with its strategy. As the 50-something year-old Ottawa businessman reclined in his chair, he asked himself, given the firm's resources and potential, what direction should be taken in order to make RepositBox the business success story it could be? Jamie turned to Janet, "Do we set our sights on the general credentials verification market or limit ourselves to the education market with the aim of improving chances of success?" Janet replied, "And what did you think of that info I sent you about Ascertia?" Janet had come across a local high-growth company—Med-Eng, a producer of bomb disposal gear-that had been used in endorsements for "PDF Sign&Seal"—an advanced digital signing product from Ascertia in Surrey, England (see Exhibit 3). Janet's investigation of Ascertia turned up IdenTrust of San Francisco (see Exhibit 4). Not knowing if this most recent revelation was bad news or good, Janet bit her lip and murmured, "this market space may not be as vacant as we initially imagined."

Despite the hot dry summer, the "rain" had really come down hard earlier in the month. The rainmaker promised quite a shower of U.S. dollars for RepositBox. This secured capital would provide a foreseeable future for RepositBox. The competitor that was previously unknown, but that had been identified in the nick of time by this astute lawyer/rainmaker had been taken out of the picture—sidelined when a licensing deal had been struck. This serious venture capital would fuel the possibilities.

In less than a month the president of RepositBox USA would have an opportunity to "pitch" to a roomful of several hundred bankers and other potential investors. On September 22 at the UNYTECH 2005 Venture Forum RespositBox could shine among the other 15 or so presenters. These start-ups with no product in hand would be full of wild ambition but empty on cash. Mark Petersen, president of RepositBox USA, would stand up and deliver the script that he and Jamie Fisher had been rehearsing for weeks: "We are RepositBox, we've just come to market with our product—a revolutionary approach to online credential management; we've just completed a round of financing—so we don't need your money today—just your attention for the next few minutes and hopefully your support after that." Jamie had driven his car down to upstate New York a lot lately, but this was one five-hour trip he was really looking forward to making. (See Exhibit 5.)

Things had been going so well lately, that Jamie wondered if he hadn't left anything out. And even if he wasn't forgetting anything, he surmised that despite the sunny skies and smooth sailing that appeared ahead—things could change. Jamie and Janet needed to work on next steps for their new venture if they were going to bring RepositBox to its full potential.

EXHIBIT 3   Ascertia[7]

Ascertia is a privately funded company, managed from the UK with globally located development units. Founded by Industry Professionals to provide services and products for realization of commercial use of cryptography. The company's mission is to provide high quality, cost-effective products and solutions that integrate with existing and widely deployed software products, enhancing their security transparently. The Company uses its own distributed technologies to prove that they provide value for businesses in real world deployments.

Product Line

Secure Desktop: Desktop product range provides the most advanced security functionality imaginable—no other vendor comes close! Together with a revolutionary simple Graphical User Interface (GUI) ensures digital signatures can now become truly as powerful as hand-signatures were in the past!

- PDF Sign&Seal
- Office Sign&Seal
- File Sign&Seal
- Advanced Revocation Provider
- PDF Signer plugin

Server-side Signing: If you require server-side signing, time-stamping and validation of any type of document you have come to the right place. Ascertia's server-side signing products take the hassle out of deploying PKI applications to every end-user; instead users can log on to the server and perform their required security operation on the server. This minimizes the software and cryptographic key material required on the user's desktop.

- PDF Signer Server
- Advanced Digital Signature Service

Management Tools: Ascertia's Management Tools product range is aimed at the administrator, who can now control all aspects of the corporate security policy from one central location. Helping to minimizing the amount of training required for users, helpdesk call costs, and taking the hassle out of deployment as well as dynamic update of all your Ascertia Desktop applications.

- Trust Console
- PolicyUpdate
- Online Certificate Status Protocol Client Tool
- Online Certificate Status Protocol Client Crusher

Infrastructure Products: Ascertia is a recognized, global leader in certificate validation servers. We focus on all aspects of certificate validation with a range of servers which take all the hassle out of certificate path building, certificate path validation and certificate status checking.

- TrustFinder OCSP Server
- TrustFinder Time Stamping Authority Server
- TrustFinder Simple Certificate Validation Protocol Server
- TrustFinder XML Key Management Specification Server
- PureCA

---

[7] Information obtained from the company Web site, www.acertia.com/.

EXHIBIT 4 IdenTrust[8]

IdenTrust is a global leader in trusted identity solutions accepted by global financial institutions, government agencies, and corporations spanning five continents. As the only government regulated, bank-built identity company, IdenTrust provides a worldwide network of trusted credentials based on global standards.

IdenTrust not only addresses the technical aspects of identity management but also provides a legally and globally interoperable environment for using identities. The IdenTrust solution consists of three key components: (a) trusted identity blueprint, (b) proven network and delivery capabilities based on "best of breed" technology, and (c) unmatched expertise in establishing and managing at trusted identity infrastructure.

The IdenTrust platform enables financial institutions, governments and commercial entities to effectively manage the risks associated with identity authentication; minimize investment in creating their own legal frameworks; and deploy a Trusted Identity infrastructure smarter, faster, and more cost effectively.

IdenTrust|DST (formerly Digital Signature Trust Company) is one of the premier providers of digital identity authentication services to the United States federal government, numerous U.S. state governments, the U.S. Department of Defense as well as Energy and supply chain markets.

The U.S. General Services Administration awarded IdenTrust|DST the designation of "Access Certificates for Electronic Services" Certification Authority to issue digital certificates to businesses and consumers to conduct business with the U.S. government electronically. IdenTrust|DST also gained accreditation by the U.S. Department of Defense to issue digital certificates to DoD external contractors under the DoD's Interim External Certification Authority program. IdenTrust|DST has contracts with U.S. state governments such as Washington State.

IdenTrust|DST has been awarded Ernst and Young's WebTrust Seal of Assurance for Certification Authorities.

Key Offerings:

IdenTrust Trust Blueprint

The only government-regulated, bank endorsed, globally interoperable framework for managing identities, including an entire legal, operational and technical framework for trusted identity management.

IdenTrust Trust Infrastructure

A complete set of operational, logistical, network, and technical capabilities for building a foundation of trust across all business applications within an enterprise.

IdenTrust Trust Counsel

Expertise and implementation assistance to design, build, and operate trusted identity infrastructure quickly and cost-effectively.

IdenTrust Trust Sign

Leading collaboration solution for trusted documents, enabling enterprises to prepare, digitally sign and deliver business-authenticated, trusted documents over the Internet.

IdenTrust Trust Financial Applications

A complete set of operational, logistical, network, and technical capabilities to Trust Enable financial applications in order to provide full identity assurance across the financial supply chain.

[8] Information obtained from the company Web site, www.identrust.com.

EXHIBIT 5   Market Opportunity Matrix*: RepositBox System

Using the Market Opportunity Matrix as an illustrative tool, the market opportunity for the *RepositBox System* is represented as follows:

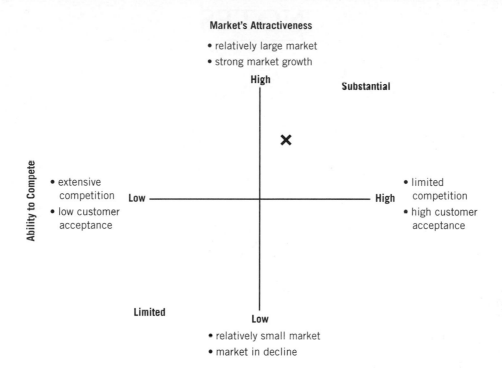

Based on its market size and market growth, market attractiveness is assessed as '**high**', based on the industry's competitive structure, and the market's acceptance of the product, the *RepositBox System.*

* The items that are mapped in the upper right hand quadrant have a relatively high probability of success. Those items mapped in the lower left hand quadrant are characterized as having a relatively low likelihood of success.

NOTES

PART I

1. Arik Hesseldahl, "BlackBerry: Innovation Behind the Icon," *Businessweek*, April 4, 2008.
2. Ibid.

CHAPTER 1

1. The authors would like to thank Frederic M. Alper of Babson College for his insights and contributions to this chapter, in particular the graphic representation of entrepreneurial attributes and the development of the Quicklook Exercise to develop a personal entrepreneurial strategy.
2. Jeffry A. Timmons, *The Entrepreneurial Mind* (Acton, MA: Brick House Publishing, 1989).
3. Graeme Wearden, "The Big Interview: Sir Terry Matthews," ZDNet, November 21, 2006.
4. David Gow, "Terry Matthews: A Well-Connected Celt," *Guardian*, October 28, 2000.
5. Sally Watson, "Terry Matthews: Entrepreneur Extraordinaire," silicon.com, November 14, 2001.
6. Andrew Wahl "VoIP: When Sir Terry Talks..." *Canadian Business*, September 24, 2007.
7. Graeme Wearden, "The Big Interview."
8. L. H. Tiffany Hsieh, "Queen's Students Go Green with Bullfrog," *Kingston This Week*, September 3, 2008.
9. Boyd Cohen, "Sustainable Valley Entrepreneurial Ecosystems," *Business Strategy and the Environment* 15, no. 1 (2006): 1–14.
10. Richard Hudson and Roger Wehrell, "Socially Responsible Investors and the Microentrepreneur: A Canadian Case," *Journal of Business Ethics* 60, no. 3 (2005): 281–292.
11. See John W. Atkinson, *An Introduction To Motivation* (Princeton, NJ: Van Nostrand, 1964); John W. Atkinson, *Motives in Fantasy, Action and Society* (Princeton, NJ: Van Nostrand, 1958); David C. McClelland, *The Achieving Society* (Princeton, NJ: Van Nostrand, 1961).
12. J. Terence Zinger, Rolland Lebrasseur, Yves Robichaud, and Nathaly Riverin, "Stages of Small Enterprise Development: A Comparison of Canadian Female and Male Entrepreneurs," *Journal of Enterprising Culture* 15, no. 2 (2007): 107–131.
13. John B. Miner, Norman R. Smith, and Jeffrey S. Bracker, "Predicting Firm Survival from a Knowledge of Entrepreneur Task Motivation," *Entrepreneurship and Regional Development* 4, no. 2 (1992): 145–154.
14. John B. Miner, Norman R. Smith, and Jeffrey S. Bracker, "Role of Entrepreneurial Task Motivation in the Growth of Techno-logically Innovative Firms: Interpretations from Follow-Up Data," *Journal of Applied Psychology* 79, no. 4 (1994): 627–630.
15. Jeffry A. Timmons and Howard H. Stevenson, "Entrepreneurship Education in the 80s: What Entrepreneurs Say," in *Entrepreneurship: What It Is and How to Teach It*, J. Kao and H. H. Stevenson, eds. (Boston, MA: Harvard Business School, 1985), 115–134.
16. Floyd Norris, "Low-Fat Problem at Ben & Jerry's," *New York Times*, September 9, 1992.
17. Ibid.
18. Donald K. Clifford, Jr., and Richard E. Cavanagh, *The Winning Performance* (New York, NY: Bantam Books, 1991).
19. Determining the attitudes and behaviours in entrepreneurs that are "acquirable and desirable" represents the synthesis of over 50 research studies compiled for the first and second editions

of this book. See extensive references in J. A. Timmons, L. E. Smollen, and A. L. M. Dingee, Jr., *New Venture Creation*, 2nd ed. (Homewood, IL: Irwin, 1985), 139–169.
20. Monica Diochon, Teresa V. Menzies, and Yvon Gasse, "Attri-butions and Success in New Venture Creation Among Canadian Nascent Entrepreneurs," *Journal of Small Business and Entre-preneurship* 20, no. 4 (2007): 335–350; Karen D. Hughes, "Exploring Motivation and Success Among Canadian Women Entrepreneurs," *Journal of Small Business and Entrepreneurship* 19, no. 2 (2006): 107–120; Don A. Moore, John M. Oesch, and Charlene Zietsma, "What Competition? Myopic Self-Focus in Market Entry Decisions," *Organization Science* 18, no. 3 (2007): 440–454.
21. John A. Hornaday and Nancy B. Tieken, "Capturing Twenty-One Heffalumps," *Frontiers of Entrepreneurship Research* (Babson Park, MA: Babson College, 1983).
22. Alan J. Grant, "The Development of an Entrepreneurial Leadership Paradigm for Enhancing New Venture Success," *Frontiers of Entrepreneurship Research* (Babson Park, MA: Babson College, 1992).
23. David L. Bradford and Allan R. Cohen, *Managing for Excellence: The Guide to Developing High Performance in Contemporary Organizations* (New York, NY: John Wiley & Sons, 1997).
24. Thomas Hellmann, "Entrepreneurs and the Process of Obtaining Resources," *Journal of Economics and Management Strategy* 16, no. 1 (2007): 81–109; Yves Robichaud and Egbert McGraw, "Les motivations entrepreneuriales commes facteur explicatif de la taille des enterprises," *Journal of Small Business and Entrepreneurship* 21, no. 1 (2008): 59–73.
25. Paul Kedrosky, "Bless This Mess" *Canadian Business*, January 17, 2005.
26. Daryl G. Mitton, "The Compleat Entrepreneur," *Entrepreneurship Theory and Practice* 13, no. 3 1989): 9–19.
27. John B. Miner, "Entrepreneurs, High Growth Entrepreneurs and Managers: Contrasting and Overlapping Motivational Patterns," *Journal of Business Venturing* 5, no. 4 (1990): 221–234.
28. David E. Gumpert and David P. Boyd, "The Loneliness of the Small-Business Owner," *Harvard Business Review* 62, no. 6 (1984): 18–24.
29. Maria Cook, "Investing in our Future," *Ottawa Citizen*, March 1, 2004.
30. Richard Martin, "Alumni Profile: Entrepreneur Angel," *Carleton University Magazine*, Fall 2006.
31. Timmons and Stevenson, "Entrepreneurship Education in the 80s: What Entrepreneurs Say," 115–34.
32. See Timmons, *The Entrepreneurial Mind* (1989).
33. Dean Tjosvold and David Weicker, "Cooperative and Competitive Networking by Entrepreneurs: A Critical Incident Study," *Journal of Small Business Management* 31, no. 1 (1993): 11–21.
34. Dev K. Dutta and Mary M. Crossan, "The Nature of Entrepre-neurial Opportunities: Understanding the Process Using the 4I Organizational Learning Framework," *Entrepreneurship Theory and Practice* 29, no. 4 (2005): 425–449.
35. Ronald K. Mitchell, J. Brock Smith, Eric A. Morse, Kristie W. Seawright, Ana Maria Peredo, and Brian McKenzie, "Are Entrepreneurial Cognitions Universal? Assessing Entrepreneurial Cognitions Across Cultures," *Entrepreneurship Theory and Practice* 26, no. 4 (2002): 9–32.
36. William Lee, "What Successful Entrepreneurs Really Do," Lee Communications, 2001.
37. John A. Hornaday and Nancy B. Tieken.

38. Jeffry A. Timmons, Daniel F. Muzyka, Howard H. Stevenson, and William D. Bygrave, "Opportunity Recognition: The Core of Entrepreneurship," *Frontiers of Entrepreneurship Research* (Babson Park, MA: Babson College, 1987).

39. G. Page West III and Terry W. Noel, "The Impact of Knowledge Resources on New Venture Performance," *Journal of Small Business Management* 47, no. 1 (2009): 1–22.

40. James J. Chrisman, Ed Mcmullan, and Jeremy Hall, "The Influence of Guided Preparation on the Long-Term Performance of New Ventures," *Journal of Business Venturing* 20, no. 6 (2005): 769–791.

41. "Rodney C. Shrader and Gerald E. Hills, "Opportunity Recognition: Perceptions of Highly Successful Entrepreneurs," *Journal of Small Business Strategy* 14, no. 2 (2003): 92–108.

42. Harvey "Chet" Krentzman, entrepreneur, lecturer, author, and nurturer of at least three dozen growth-minded ventures.

43. Brian O'Reilly and Natasha A. Tarpley, "What It Takes to Start a Startup," *Fortune,* June 7, 1999.

44. Howard H. Stevenson, "Who are the Harvard Self-Employed?" *Frontiers of Entrepreneurship Research* (Babson Park, MA: Babson College, 1983).

45. Henry Mintzberg, *Managers Not MBAs: A Hard Look at the Soft Practice of Managing and Management Development* (San Francisco, CA: Berrett-Koehler, 1992).

46. W. Ed McMullan and Vance Gough, "Developing Entrepreneurs in a Hybrid Management and Entrepreneurship MBA: A Case Study in Calgary," in *Innovation & Entrepreneurship in Western Canada: From Family Business To Multinationals,* J. J. Chrisman, J. A. D. Holbrook, and J. H. Chua, eds. (Calgary, AB: University of Calgary Press, 2002), 225–242.

47. B. Joseph White with Yaron Prywes, *The Nature of Leadership: Reptiles, Mammals, and the Challenge of Becoming a Great Leader* (New York, NY: Amacom Books, 2006).

48. William D. Estbeb, "Your Associate Knows," *Chiropractic Journal,* July 2000.

49. Sarah Scott, "Do Grades Really Matter?" *Maclean's,* September 10, 2007.

50. Stevenson, "Who are the Harvard Self-Employed?"

51. Robert C. Ronstadt, "The Decision Not to Become an Entrepreneur," *Frontiers of Entrepreneurship Research* (Babson Park, MA: Babson College, 1983).

CHAPTER 2

1. Jeffry A. Timmons, Daniel F. Muzyka, Howard H. Stevenson, and William D. Bygrave, "Opportunity Recognition: The Core of Entrepreneurship," in *Frontiers of Entrepreneurship Research* (Babson Park, MA: Babson College, 1987), 409.

2. Ewing M. Kauffman, founder of Marion Laboratories.

3. William J. Dennis, Jr., "Business Starts and Stops," Wells Fargo/NFIB November 1999.

4. Joseph L. Bower and Clayton M. Christensen, "Disruptive Technologies: Catching the Wave," *Harvard Business Review* 73, no. 1: 43–53.

5. Ibid.

6. Ibid.

7. U. Srinivasa Rangan, "Alliances Power Corporate Renewal," Babson College, 2001; Elicia Maine, "Radical Innovation Through Internal Corporate Venturing: Degussa's Commercialization of Nanomaterials," *R&D Management* 38, no. 4 (2008): 359–371.

8. Mike Chiasson and Chad Saunders, "Reconciling Diverse Approaches to Opportunity Research Using the Structuration Theory," *Journal of Business Venturing* 20, no. 6 (2005): 747–767.

9. Library and Archives of Canada, "Joseph (Joey) Smallwood," www.collectionscanada.gc.ca.

10. Paul A. Gompers, Anna Kovner, Josh Lerner, and David S. Scharfstein, "Skill vs. Luck in Entrepreneurship and Venture Capital: Evidence from Serial Entrepreneurs," *NBER Working Paper,* January 22, 2009.

11. Henry Mintzberg takes this metaphor quite far in "Crafting Strategy," *Harvard Business Review* 66, no. 4 (1987): 66–75.

12. See Howard H. Stevenson, *Do Lunch or Be Lunch* (Cambridge, MA: Harvard Business School Press, 1998) for a provocative argument for predictability as one of the most powerful of management tools.

13. Statistics Canada.

14. Harry P. Bowen and Dirk De Clercq, "Institutional Context and the Allocation of Entrepreneurial Effort," *Journal of International Business Studies* 39, no. 4 (2008): 747–767.

15. In response to a student question at Founder's Day, Babson College, April 1983. Pizza Time Theatre (a.k.a. "Chuck E. Cheese's") filed for bankruptcy in 1984.

16. Global Entrepreneurship Monitor 2008 Report, www.gem consortium.org.

17. Summaries of these are reported by Albert N. Shapero and Joseph Giglierano, "Exits and Entries: A Study in Yellow Pages Journalism," *Frontiers of Entrepreneurship Research* (Babson Park, MA: Babson College, 1982) and Arnold C. Cooper, William C. Dunkelberg, and Carolyn Y. Woo, "Survival and Failure: A Longitudinal Study," *Frontiers of Entrepreneurship Research* (Babson Park, MA: Babson College, 1988).

18. Bizminer 2002 Startup Business Risk Index.

19. Monica Diochon, Teresa V. Menzies, and Yvon Gasse, "Exploring the Nature and Impact of Gestation-Specific Human Capital among Nascent Entrepreneurs," *Journal of Developmental Entrepreneurship* 13, no. 2 (2008): 151–165.

20. S. Venkataraman and Murray B. Low, "The Effects of Liabilities of Age and Size on Autonomous Sub-Units of Established Firms in the Steel Distribution Industry," *Journal of Business Venturing* 9, no. 3 (1994): 189–204.

21. Ibid.

22. Dev K. Dutta and Stewart Thornhill, "The Evolution of Growth Intentions: Toward a Cognition-Based Model," *Journal of Business Venturing* 23, no. 3 (2008): 307–332.

23. This reaffirms the exception to the failure rule noted above and in the original edition of this book in 1977.

24. "The Inc. 500 Almanac," *Inc.,* September 1, 2008.

25. Kara Aaserud, "Canada's Hottest Startups," *Profit Magazine,* September 2008

26. Ibid.

27. Ibid.

28. VentureXpert Thompson Financial Data Services, 2001.

29. Jean-Etienne de Bettignies, "Financing the Entrepreneurial Venture," *Management Science* 54, no. 1 (2008): 151–166.

30. Michael S. Malone, "John Doerr's Startup Manual," *Fast Company,* December 18, 2007.

31. Ernie Parizeau, Norwest Venture Partners, June 2001.

32. Eleanor Beaton, "Launch and Learn: Management Lessons from the Profit Hot 50," *Canadian Business,* September 2008.

33. Howard H. Stevenson and Susan S. Harmeling, "Howard Head and Prince Manufacturing, Inc.," Harvard Business School Case, 1992.

34. William D. Bygrave and Jeffry A. Timmons, *Venture Capital at the Crossroads* (Boston, MA: Harvard Business School Press, 1992).

35. Michael Malone, "John Doerr's Startup Manual."

36. Arthur Rock, "Strategy vs. Tactics from a Venture Capitalist," *Harvard Business Review* 65, no. 6 (1987): 63–67.

37. Rob O'Flanagan, "Honorary Degree for Guelph's Beer Baron," *Guelph Mercury,* February 22, 2008.

38. Donald L. Sexton and Forrest I. Seale, *Leading Practices of Fast Growth Entrepreneurs: Pathways to High Performance* (Kansas City, MO: Kauffman Center for Entrepreneurial Leadership, 1997).

CHAPTER 3

1. See www.onset.com/resources/index.html for additional information.

2. See Jeffry A. Timmons, *New Business Opportunities* (Acton, MA: Brick House Publishing, 1989).

3. Prescott C. Ensign, "Small Business Strategy as a Dynamic Process: Concepts, Controversies, and Implications," *Journal of Business and Entrepreneurship* 20, no. 2 (2008): 25–43.

4. Tom Brzustowski, *The Way Ahead: Meeting Canada's Productivity Challenge* (Ottawa, Ontario: University of Ottawa Press, 2008).

5. Barrie McKenna, "More than the Sum of Its Parts," *Globe and Mail,* February 23, 1993.

6. Graham Scott, "From Fat to Fit," *Canadian Business,* October 8, 2006.

7. Allan Lynch, "From Baby Fat to Super-Fit," *Chatelaine,* August 2007.

8. Bill Power, "Exercise Joins Entertainment: Children's TV Producer Buys Chain of Kids' Fitness Centres," *Chronicle Herald,* March 25, 2008.

9. Tracy Corrigan, "Far More than the Viagra Company: Essential Guide to William Steere," *Financial Times*, August 31, 1998.

10. Joline Godfrey, *Our Wildest Dreams: Women Entrepreneurs, Making Money, Having Fun, Doing Good* (New York, NY: Harper Business, 1993).

11. Herbert A. Simon, "What We Know About the Creative Process," in R. L. Kuhn (ed.) *Frontiers in Creative and Innovative Management* (Cambridge, MA: Ballinger Publishing, 1986), 3–20.

12. Alison Stein Wellner, "Creative Control: Even Bosses Need Time to Think," *Inc.*, July 2007.

13. Amar Bhide "Bootstrap Finance: The Art of Start-Ups" *Harvard Business Review* 70, no. 6 (1992): 109–117.

14. Small Business Policy Branch, *Key Small Business Financing Statistics–December 2006* (Industry Canada).

15. Teri Lammers and Annie Longsworth, "Guess Who? Ten Big-Timers Launched from Scratch," *Inc.*, September 1991.

16. Robert A. Mamis, "The Secrets of Bootstrapping," *Inc.*, September 1991.

17. Peter Nowak, "Canadian Cell Phone Bills Double U.S. Counterparts," *Financial Post*, January 30, 2007.

18. Edgar H. Schein, Peter S. Delisi, Paul J. Kampas, and Michael M. Sonduck, *DEC is Dead, Long Live DEC: The Lasting Legacy of Digital Equipment Corporation* (San Francisco, CA: Barrett-Koehler, 2003).

19. Ernie Parizeau, Norwest Venture Partners.

20. Mollie Neal, "Cataloger Gets Pleasant Results," *Direct Marketing*, May 1, 1992.

21. Brian Dumaine, "How to Compete with a Champ," *Fortune*, January 10, 1994.

22. Lionel Perron, "Canadian Fiddler Looks for Quick Payday Via eBay," *Reuters*, July 2, 2008.

23. Scott W. Kunkel and Charles W. Hofer, "The Impact of Industry Structure on New Venture Performance," *Frontiers of Entrepreneurship Research* (Babson Park, MA: Babson College, 1993).

24. Canada's Venture Capital & Private Equity Association, www.cvca.ca.

25. For a more detailed description of free cash flow, see William Sahlman, "Note on Free Cash Flow Valuation Models," Harvard Business School, 2003.

26. William A. Sahlman, "Sustainable Growth Analysis," Harvard Business School, 1984.

27. R. Douglas Kahn, president, Interactive Images, Inc., speaking at Babson College about his experiences as international marketing director at McCormack & Dodge.

28. Dan McLean, "EDS Acquisition Better Late Than Never for HP," *Computerworld Canada*, May 16, 2008.

29. "Bulls, Bears, and Other Animals," *CBC News Online*, June 13, 2006.

30. Kara Aaserud, "Canada's Top Women Entrepreneurs—When Turncoats Attack," *Profit*, November 2006.

31. This point was made by J. Willard Marriott, Jr., at Founder's Day at Babson College, 1988.

32. "Recognizing, Research Results in New Brunswick," hosted by the New Brunswick Innovation Foundation in October 2008.

33. Janet White Bardwell, "Born to Launch," *Profit*, June 2007.

34. Allen C. Bluedorn and Gwen Martin, "The Time Frames of Entrepreneurs," *Journal of Business Venturing* 23, vol. 1 (2008): 1–20.

35. Prescott C. Ensign, "International Channels of Distribution," *Multinational Business Review* 14, no. 3 (2006): 1–26.

36. Largest patent licensor in Canada ("Cash in Your Chips," *Canadian Business*, January 17, 2005.

37. See Steven Flax, "How to Snoop on Your Competitors," *Fortune*, May 14, 1984; and also information such as *Sources of Industry Data* published by Ernst & Young.

38. Leonard M. Fuld, *Secret Language of Competitive Intelligence* (New York, NY: Crown Business, 2006).

39. Ibid.

40. Jonathan Calof, director of the Canadian Institute of Competitive Intelligence.

41. Fuld, *Secret Language of Competitive Intelligence*.

CHAPTER 4

1. Martin L. Martens, Jennifer E. Jennings, and P. Devereaux Jennings, "Do the Stories They Tell Get Them the Money They Need? The Role of Entrepreneurial Narratives in Resource Acquisition," *Academy of Management Journal* 50, no. 5 (2007): 1107–1132.

2. Yuval Deutsch and Thomas W. Ross, "You Are Known by The Directors You Keep: Reputable Directors as a Signalling Mechanism for Young Firms," *Management Science* 49, no. 8 (2003): 1003–1017.

3. Kevin Hindle and Brent Mainprize, "A Systematic Approach to Writing and Rating Entrepreneurial Business Plans," *Journal of Private Equity* 9, no. 3 (2006): 7–21.

4. See also William A. Sahlman, "How to Write a Great Business Plan," *Harvard Business Review* 75, no. 4 (1997): 98–108.

5. Shelley L. MacDougall and Deborah Hurst, "Surviving the Transience of Knowledge: Small High-Technology Businesses Parting Ways with Their Knowledge Workers," *Journal of Small Business & Entrepreneurship* 20, no. 2 (2007): 183–199.

6. Gary G. Gorman, Peter J. Rosa, and Alex Faseruk, "Institutional Lending to Knowledge-Based Businesses," *Journal of Business Venturing* 20, no. 6 (2005): 793–819.

7. These questions were brought forth by Martine Spence of the University of Ottawa.

8. Young Rok Choi, Moren Lévesque, and Dean A. Shepherd, "When Should Entrepreneurs Expedite Or Delay Opportunity Exploitation?" *Journal of Business Venturing* 23, no. 3 (2008): 333–355.

CHAPTER 5

1. George C. Rubenson and Anil K. Gupta, "Replacing the Founder: Exploding the Myth of the Entrepreneur's Disease," *Business Horizons* 35, no. 6 (1992): 53–57.

2. John Kenneth Galbraith, *The New Industrial State* (Princeton, NJ: Princeton University Press, 2007).

3. George C. Rubenson and Anil K. Gupta, "The Initial Succession: A Contingency Model of Founder Tenure," *Entrepreneurship Theory and Practice* 21, no. 2 (1996): 21–36.

4. Gary E. Willard, David A. Krueger, and Henry R. Feeser, "In Order to Grow, Must the Founder Go: A Comparison of Performance between Founder and Non-Founder Managed High-Growth Manufacturing Firms," *Journal of Business Venturing* 7, no. 3 (1996): 181–194.

5. For another useful view of the stages of development of a firm and required management capabilities, see Carroll V. Kroeger, "Management Development and the Small Firm," *California Management Review* 17, no. 1 (1974): 41–47.

6. Larry E. Greiner, "Evolution and Revolution as Organizations Grow," *Harvard Business Review* 50, no. 4 (1972): 37–46; and Herbert N. Woodward, "Management Strategies for Small Companies," *Harvard Business Review* 54, no. 1 (1976): 113–121.

7. David L. Bradford and Allan R. Cohen, *Power Up: Transforming Organizations Through Shared Leadership* (New York, NY: John Wiley & Sons, 1998).

8. Prescott C. Ensign, *Knowledge Sharing Among Scientists: Why Reputation Matters for R&D in Multinational Firms* (New York, NY: Palgrave Macmillan, 2009).

9. Bradford and Cohen.

10. Neil C. Churchill, "Entrepreneurs and Their Enterprises: A Stage Model," *Frontiers of Entrepreneurship Research* (Babson Park, MA: Babson College, 1983).

11. Royston Greenwood and Roy Suddaby, "Institutional Entrepreneurship in Mature Fields: The Big Five Accounting Firms," *Academy of Management Journal* 49, no. 1 (2006): 27–48.

12. Joel West, "Cross-Cultural Differences in Entrepreneurship in the Asia-Pacific PC Industry," Working Paper, University of California, Irvine, 1997.

13. Rosabeth Moss Kanter, *When Giants Learn to Dance* (New York, NY: Simon & Schuster, 1989).

14. Ibid.

15. Ibid.

16. Rosabeth Moss Kanter, *The Change Masters* (New York, NY: Simon & Schuster, 1983).

17. The study was done by McKinsey & Company. See "How Growth Companies Succeed," reported in *Small Business Report*, July 1984, 9.
18. David L. Bradford and Allan R. Cohen, *Managing for Excellence* (New York, NY: John Wiley & Sons, 1984).
19. John Sculley with John A. Byrne, *Odyssey: Pepsi to Apple... A Journey of Adventures, Idea, and the Future* (New York, NY: HarperCollins, 1987).
20. Clayton M. Christensen, *The Innovator's Dilemma* (Boston, MA: Harvard Business School Press, 1997).
21. Geoffrey Moore, *Crossing the Chasm* (New York, NY: Harper-Collins, 2002).
22. Geoffrey Moore, *Inside the Tornado: Marketing Strategies from Silicon Valley's Cutting Edge* (New York, NY: HarperCollins, 1999).
23. Stephen R. Covey, *The 7 Habits of Highly Effective People* (New York, NY: Simon and Schuster, 1989).
24. Donald F. Kuratko, "Entrepreneurial Leadership in the 21st Century," *Journal of Leadership and Organizational Studies* 13, no. 4 (2007): 1–11.
25. Ibid.
26. Donald F. Kuratko and Michael G. Goldsby, "Corporate Entrepreneurs or Rogue Middle Managers: A Framework for Ethical Corporate Entrepreneurship, *Journal of Business Ethics* 55, no. 1 (2004): 13–30.
27. Donald F. Kuratko, "Entrepreneurial Leadership in the 21st Century," *Journal of Leadership and Organizational Studies* 13, no. 4 (2007): 1–11.
28. Don A. Moore, John M. Oesch, and Charlene Zietsma, "What Competition? Myopic Self-Focus in Market-Entry Decisions," *Organization Science* 18, no. 3 (2007): 440–454.
29. Hao Ma and Justin Tan, "Key Components and Implications of Entrepreneurship: A 4-P Framework," *Journal of Business Venturing* 21, no. 5 (2006): 704–725.
30. Bruno Dyck and Frederik A. Starke, "The Formation of Breakaway Organizations: Observations and a Process Model," *Administrative Science Quarterly* 44, no. 4 (1999): 792–822.
31. W. Glenn Rowe, "Creating Wealth in Organizations: The Role of Strategic Leadership," *Academy of Management Executive* 15, no. 1 (2001): 81–94.
32. RBC Royal Bank Canadian Woman Entrepreneur Awards, December 8, 2008.
33. www.buntingcoady.com.
34. RBC Royal Bank Canadian Woman Entrepreneur Awards, December 8, 2008.
35. Jeffry A. Timmons and Howard H. Stevenson, "Entrepreneurship Education in the 80s. What Entrepreneurs Say," in *Entrepreneurship: What It Is and How To Teach It*, John J. Kao and Howard H. Stevenson, eds. (Cambridge, MA: Harvard Business School, 1985), 115–34.

CHAPTER 6

1. Stephen Daze, "Planning Key to Success, Says Tech Vet," *Ottawa Business Journal*, July 14, 2008, 11.
2. Lowell W. Busenitz, Douglas D. Moesel, James O. Fiet, and Jay B. Barney, "The Framing of Perceptions of Fairness in the Relationship between Venture Capitalists and New Venture Teams," *Entrepreneurship Theory and Practice* 21, no. 3 (1997): 5–21.
3. Elicia Maine and Elizabeth Garnsey, "The Commercialization Environment of Advanced Materials Ventures," *International Journal of Technology Management* 39, no. 1/2 (2007): 49–71.
4. David Boyd and David Gumpert, "The Loneliness of the Start-Up Entrepreneur," *Frontiers of Entrepreneurship Research* (Babson Park, MA: Babson College, 1982).
5. Henry Mintzberg, *Tracking Strategies: Towards a General Theory of Strategy Formulation* (London, UK: Oxford University Press, 2008).
6. Michael D. Ensley, James W. Carland, and Joann C. Carland, "Investigating the Existence of the Lead Entrepreneur," *Journal of Small Business Management* 38, no. 4 (2007): 59–77.
7. Stephen Daze.
8. Brett Bundale, "Layoffs at Spheric Technologies seen as 'Right-Sizing,'" *Telegraph Journal*, April 21, 2009.

9. Jean-René Halde, "BDC's Young Entrepreneur Awards," *Canadian Business*, November 24, 2008.
10. See Jeffrey A. Timmons, "The Entrepreneurial Team: An American Dream or Nightmare?" *Journal of Small Business Management* 13, no. 4 (1975): 33–38.
11. Maria Minniti and Moren Lévesque, "Recent Developments in the Economics of Entrepreneurship," *Journal of Business Venturing* 23, no. 6 (2008): 603–612.
12. Jay W. Lorsch and Robert C. Clark, "Leading from the Boardroom," *Harvard Business Review* 86, no. 4 (2008): 104–111.
13. Elicia M. Maine, Daniel M. Shapiro, and Aidan R. Vining, "The Role of Clustering in the Growth of New Technology-Based Firms," *Small Business Economics* 33, no. 4 (2009): 354–367.
14. Tod D. Rutherford and John Holmes, "Entrepreneurship, Knowledge and Learning in Cluster Formation and Evolution: The Windsor Ontario Tool, Die and Mould Cluster," *International Journal of Entrepreneurship & Innovation Management* 7, no. 3/4 (2007): 320–344.
15. Richard Grigonis, "Talking with Mahshad Koohgoli, CEO, Protecode," *TMCcnet.com*, March 11, 2009.
16. Jay W. Lorsch and Edward J. Waitzer, "Corporate Governance in Canada and the United States: A Comparative View," Woodrow Wilson International Center Breakfast, April 28, 2008, New York, NY.
17. See Howard H. Stevenson and William A. Sahlman, "How Small Companies Should Handle Advisers," *Harvard Business Review* 66, no. 3 (1988): 28–34.
18. Reference groups—groups consisting of individuals with whom there is frequent interaction (such as family, friends, and coworkers), with whom values and interests are shared, and from whom support and approval for activities are derived—have long been known for their influence on behaviour. See John W. Thibault and Harold H. Kelley, *The Social Psychology of Groups* (New York, NY: Transaction Publishers, 1986).
19. Jeffry A. Timmons presented a discussion of these entrepreneurial characteristics. See "Entrepreneurial Behavior" Proceedings, First International Conference on Entrepreneurship, Centre for Entrepreneurial Studies, Toronto, November 1973.
20. "Raising Venture Capital" seminar held at Babson College, co-sponsored by *Venture Capital Journal* and Coopers & Lybrand, 1985.
21. Steve Alper, Dean Tjosvold, and Kenneth S. Law, "Conflict Management, Efficacy, and Performance in Organizational Teams," *Personnel Psychology* 53, no. 3 (2000): 625–642.
22. John L. Hayes and Brian Haslett of Venture Founders Corporation have made a major contribution in the area of reward systems, and the following section is based on their work.
23. Ritch L. Sorenson, Cathleen A. Folker, and Keith H. Brigham, "The Collaborative Network Orientation: Achieving Business Success through Collaborative Relationships," *Entrepreneurship Theory and Practice* 32, no. 4 (2008): 615–634
24. Stephen Daze, "Planning Key to Success, Says Tech Vet," *Ottawa Business Journal*, July 14, 2008, 11.
25. See Prescott C. Ensign, "The Concept of Fit in Organizational Research," *International Journal of Organization Theory and Behavior* 4, no. 3 (2001): 287–306.

CHAPTER 7

1. Elizabeth Crawford, "MBA Students Want Programs to Put More Emphasis on Ethics, Survey Finds," *Chronicle of Higher Education*, May 21, 2003.
2. Donald L. McCabe, Kenneth D. Butterfield, and Linda Klebe Treviño, "Academic Dishonesty in Graduate Business Programs: Prevalence, Causes, and Proposed Action," *Academy of Management Learning and Education* 5, no. 3 (2006): 294–305.
3. J.D. Gravenor, "Is Cheating on the Rise?" *Gazette*, March 20, 2007.
4. Cathy Gulli, Nicholas Kohler, and Martin Patriquin, "The Great University Cheating Scandal," *Macleans*, February 9, 2007.
5. Sarath Nonis and Cathy Owens Swift, "An Examination of the Relationship between Academic Dishonesty and Workplace Dishonesty: A Multicampus Investigation," *Journal of Education for Business* 77, no. 2 (2001): 69–77.
6. Associated Press, "Canadian University Rules Against Expelling Student over Facebook Study Group," March 19, 2008.

7. Susan S. Harmeling, Saras D. Sarasvathy, and R. Edward Freeman, "Related Debates in Ethics and Entrepreneurship: Values, Opportunities, and Contingency," *Journal of Business Ethics* 84, no. 3 (2009): 341–365.

8. Olaf Fisscher, David Frenkel, Yotam Lurie, and Andre Nijhof, "Stretching the Frontiers: Exploring the Relationships between Entrepreneurship and Ethics," *Journal of Business Ethics* 60, no. 3 (2005): 207–209.

9. David A. Robinson, Per Davidson, Hennie Van Der Mescht, and Philip Court, "How Entrepreneurs Deal with Ethical Challenges—An Application of the Business Ethics Synergy Start Technique," *Journal of Business Ethics* 71, no. 4 (2007): 411–423.

10. Yves Fassin, "The Reasons Behind Non-Ethical Behaviour in Business and Entrepreneurship," *Journal of Business Ethics* 60, no. 3 (2005): 265–279.

11. Richard Hudson and Roger Wehrell, "Socially Responsible Investors and the Microentrepreneur: A Canadian Case," *Journal of Business Ethics* 60, no. 3 (2005): 281–292.

12. Albert Z. Carr, "Is Business Bluffing Ethical?" *Harvard Business Review* 46, no. 1 (1968): 143–153.

13. Jeannie Macfarlane, "Trio of Alumni Lead Three Canadian Universities," *The University of Western Ontario Alumni Gazette*, Spring 2009.

14. Alistair R. Anderson and Robert Smith, "The Moral Space in Entrepreneurship: An Exploration of Ethical Imperatives and the Moral Legitimacy of Being Enterprising," *Entrepreneurship & Regional Development* 19, no. 6 (2007): 479–497.

15. Kirk Frith and Gerald McElwee "Value-Adding and Value-Extracting Entrepreneurship at the Margins," *Journal of Small Business and Entrepreneurship* 22, no. 1 (2009): 39–54.

16. "New Places to Look for Presidents," *Time*, December 15, 1975.

17. Ibid.

18. Jeremy Hall and Philip Rosson, "The Impact of Technological Turbulence on Entrepreneurial Behavior, Social Norms, and Ethics: Three Internet-Based Cases," *Journal of Business Ethics* 64, no. 3 (2006): 231–248.

19. Andrew Stark, "What's the Matter with Business Ethics?" *Harvard Business Review* 71, no. 3 (1993): 38–48.

20. Ibid.

21. Ibid.

22. Derek Bok, *Universities and the Future of America* (Durham, NC: Duke University Press, 1990), 99–100.

23. Colin Campbell, "M.B.A.s Who Want to Save the World," *Macleans.ca*, September 11, 2008.

24. www.mbaswithoutborders.org.

25. www.rotman.utoronto.ca/nexus.

26. Colin Cambell.

27. Chitra Nayak, "Ethics Under the Microscope," *The Harbus*, 1989.

28. Eva-Maria Hammann, André Habisch, and Harald Pechlaner, "Values that Create Value: Socially Responsible Business Practices in SMEs—Empirical Evidence from German Companies," *Business Ethics: A European Review* 18, no. 1 (2009): 37–51.

29. Lynn Sharp Paine, "Managing for Organizational Integrity," *Harvard Business Review* 72, no. 2 (1994): 105–117.

30. BC Business, "Doing the Right Thing," September 1, 2006.

31. David McClelland, *Achieving Society* (New York, NY: Van Nostrand, 1961), 331.

32. "Letter To Editor," *Wall Street Journal*, October 17, 1975.

33. "The Good, the Bad & the Ugly," *Canadian Business*, March 30, 2009.

34. Wikipedia entry for "Bre-X," www.en.wikipedia.org/wiki/Bre-X.

35. "Theatre Impresario Awaiting Sentencing on Fraud, Forgery," *CBC News*, May 14, 2009.

36. Shannon Kari, "Months, Years before Livent Duo Face Any Prison Time," *Financial Post*, March 25, 2009.

37. Barbara Shecter, "Livent Dazzled Audiences, Investors While Taking on Hollywood," *Financial Post*, May 3, 2009.

38. BC Business, "Doing the Right Thing," September 1, 2006.

CHAPTER 8

1. This definition was developed by Howard H. Stevenson and colleagues at the Harvard Business School.

2. Olivier Torrès, "Le divers types d'entrepreneuriat et de PME dans le monde," *International Management* 6, no. 1 (2001): 1–15.

3. Michael J. Roberts, Howard H. Stevenson, William A. Sahlman, Paul W. Marshall, and Richard G. Hamermesh, *New Business Ventures and the Entrepreneur* (Homewood, IL: McGraw-Hill/Irwin, 2007).

4. Ibid.

5. Emily Barker, "Start With Nothing," *Inc.*, February 2002, 66–72.

6. BDC, "2008 YEA Winners" *BDC etc.*, January 2009.

7. Daryl-Lynn Carlson, "Outlook 2009: Gen Y Takes Recession in Stride," *National Post*, December 29, 2008.

8. www.6nsilicon.com.

9. Howard H. Stevenson and William H. Sahlman, "How Small Companies Should Handle Advisors," in *The Entrepreneurial Venture*, William H. Sahlman, Howard H. Stevenson, Michael J. Roberts, and Amar Bhide (eds.) (Boston, MA: Harvard Business School, 1999).

10. Per Davidsson and Benson L. Honig, "The Role of Social and Human Capital Among Nascent Entrepreneurs," *Journal of Business Venturing* 18, no. 3 (2003): 301–331.

11. Robert A. Baron and Gideon D. Markman, "Beyond Social Capital: The Roles of Entrepreneur's Social Competence in Their Financial Success," *Journal of Business Venturing* 18, no. 1 (2003): 41–60.

12. Olukemi O. Sawyerr, Jeffrey Mcgee, and Mark Peterson, "Perceived Uncertainty and Firm Performance in SMEs: The Role of Personal Networking Activities," *International Small Business Journal* 21, no. 3 (2003): 269–290.

13. Andrew Wahl, "Michael Doesn't Live Here Anymore," *Canadian Business*, October 8, 2007.

14. Ibid.

15. Olivier Torrès.

16. Douglas J. Cumming and Jeffrey G. MacIntosh, "Crowding Out Private Equity: Canadian Evidence," *Journal of Business Venturing* 21, no. 5 (2006): 569–609.

17. James J. Chrisman, Ed McMullan, and Jeremy Hall, "The Influence of Guided Preparation on the Long-Term Performance of New Ventures," *Journal of Business Venturing* 20, no. 6 (2005): 769–791.

18. Jean Lorrain and Sylvie Laferté, "The Support Needs of the Young Entrepreneur," *Journal of Small Business & Entrepreneurship* 19, no. 1 (2006): 37–48.

19. The authors are indebted to Leslie Charm and Carl Youngman formerly of Doktor Pet Centers and Command Performance hair salons, respectively, for insights into and knowledge of boards of directors.

20. Jay W. Lorsch, Andargachew S. Zelleke, and Katharina Pick, "Unbalanced Boards," *Harvard Business Review* 79, no. 2 (2001): 28–30.

21. Ellyn E. Spragins, "Confessions of a Director: Hambro International's Art Spinner Says Most CEOs Don't Know How to Make Good Use of Boards," *Inc.*, April 1991, 119–121.

22. David E. Gumpert, "Tough Love: What You Really Want from Your Advisory Board," www.entrepreneurship.org.

23. Joseph Rosenstein, Albert V. Bruno, William D. Bygrave, and Natalie T. Taylor, "The CEO, Venture Capitalists, and the Board," *Journal of Business Venturing* 8, no. 2 (1993): 99–113.

24. Ellyn E. Spragins.

25. Tara Gray, "Canadian Response to the US Sarbanes-Oxley Act of 2002: New Directions for Corporate Governance," October 4, 2005, Library of Parliament.

26. Monica Diochon, Teresa V. Menzies, and Yvon Gasse, "Exploring the Relationship between Start-Up Activities and New Venture Emergence: A Longitudinal Study of Canadian Nascent Entrepreneurs," *International Journal of Management & Enterprise Development* 2, no. 3/4 (2005): 408–426.

27. James J. Chrisman and W. Ed McMullan, "A Preliminary Assessment of Outsider Assistance as a Knowledge Resource: The Longer-Term Impact of New Venture Counseling," *Entrepreneurship Theory & Practice* 24, no. 3 (2000): 37–53.

28. Craig O. White with Gerda Gallop-Goodman, "Tap Into Expert Input—Learn How a Board of Advisors Can Benefit Your Firm," *Black Enterprise* 30, no. 12 (2000): 47.

29. Justene Adamec, "A Business Owner's Guide to Preventive Law," www.inc.com, January 1997.

30. Bradford W. Ketchum, Jr., "You and Your Attorney," *Inc.,* June 1982, 52.

31. Stevenson and Sahlman, "How Small Companies Should Handle Advisors," 297.

32. Jill Andresky Fraser, "How Many Accountants Does It Take to Change an Industry?" *Inc.,* April 1997, 63, 64, 66–69.

33. Susan Greco and Christopher Caggiano, "How Do You Use Your CPA?" *Inc.,* September 1991, 126.

34. Neil C. Churchill and Louis A. Werbaneth, Jr., "Choosing and Evaluating Your Accountant," in *Growing Concerns*, David E. Gumpert (ed.) (New York, NY: John Wiley & Sons, 1984).

35. Jill Andresky Fraser, "Do I Need a Top-Tier Accounting Firm?" *Inc.,* June 1998, 113.

36. Ibid.

37. Jill Andresky Fraser, "How Many Accountants Does It Take to Change an Industry."

38. The following is excerpted in part from David E. Gumpert and Jeffry A. Timmons, *The Encyclopedia of Small Business Resources* (New York, NY: Harper & Row, 1984).

39. Karl Bayer, "The Impact of Using Consultants during Venture Formation on Venture Performance," *Frontiers of Entrepreneurship Research.* (Babson Park, MA: Babson College, 1991).

40. Ibid.

41. J. Finnegan, "Plug and Pay: The Fine Art of Finding a Consultant" *Inc.,* July 1997, 70–72, 75, 79, 80.

42. Alistair Croll, "6N Silicon Ramps Up Pure Silicon," www.earth2tech.com, February 29, 2008.

43. James McNeill Stancill, "When Is There Cash in Cash Flow?" *Harvard Business Review* 65, no. 2 (1987): 38–49.

44. Ibid.

45. www.springwise.com.

46. www.trendwatching.com.

CHAPTER 9

1. Special appreciation is due to Bert Twaalfhoven, founder and chairman of Indivers, the Dutch firm that compiled this summary and that owns the firm on which the chart is based.

2. See Paul A. Gompers and William A. Sahlman, *Entrepreneurial Finance* (New York, NY: John Wiley & Sons, 2002).

3. Nancy A. Nichols, "Efficient? Chaotic? What's the New Finance?" *Harvard Business Review* 71, no. 2 (1993): 50–60.

4. Ibid., 52.

5. Ibid., 60.

6. Hugh Mackenzie "Timing is Everything: Comparing the Earnings of Canada's Highest Paid CEOs and the Rest of Us," January 2007, www.growinggap.ca.

7. This section is drawn directly from William A. Sahlman, "Note on Free Cash Flow Valuation Models," Harvard Business School, 2003.

8. In addition to the purchase of common shares, equity financing is meant to include the purchase of both shares and subordinated debt, or subordinated debt with shares conversion features or warrants to purchase shares.

9. For lending purposes, commercial banks regard such subordinated debt as equity. Venture capital investors normally subordinate their business loans to the loans provided by the bank or other financial institutions.

10. William H. Wetzel, Jr., of the University of New Hampshire originally showed the different types of equity capital that are available to three types of companies. The exhibit is based on a chart by Wetzel, which the authors have updated and modified. See William H. Wetzel, Jr., "The Cost and Availability of Credit and Risk Capital in New England," in *A Region's Struggling Savior: Small Business in New England*, J. A. Timmons and D. E. Gumpert, eds. (Waltham, MA: Small Business Foundation of America, 1979).

11. Andrew Wahl, "VC Financing: Cold Realities," *Canadian Business*, March 16, 2009.

12. Taken from a lecture on March 4, 1993, at the Harvard Business School, given by Paul A. Maeder and Robert F. Higgins of Highland Capital Partners.

13. Robert A. Mamis, "The Secrets of Bootstrapping," *Inc.,* September 1992, 76.

14. Ibid.

15. Matthew McClearn, "The Good, the Bad & the Ugly," *Canadian Business*, March 30, 2009.

16. Robert Harrison and Colin Mason, eds., *Informal Venture Capital: Evaluating the Impact of Business Introduction Services* (Upper Saddle River, NJ: Prentice Hall, 1996).

17. William H. Wetzel, Jr., "Informal Investors—When and Where to Look," in *Pratt's Guide to Venture Capital Sources*, 6th ed., S. E. Pratt, ed. (Wellesley Hills, MA: Capital Publishing, 1982).

18. New Brunswick Securities Commission, "Venturing Into a New Economy: Developing New Brunswick's Capital Markets," FullSail 2008.

19. Joe Castaldo, "The Next Great Canadian Idea: A Better Mousetrap," *Canadian Business*, July 11, 2008.

20. Sharda Prashad, "The Next Great Canadian Idea: Peripiteia Generator," *Canadian Business*, July 11, 2008.

21. Andrew Wahl, "Semifinalist 3: Drywall Fastener," *Canadian Business*, June 4, 2007.

22. Zena Olijnyk, "Semifinalist 2: Mascara Remover," *Canadian Business*, June 4, 2007.

23. Joe Castaldo, "Semifinalist 1: Trailer Hitch Aligner," *Canadian Business*, June 4, 2007.

24. www.hitchdocker.com.

25. www.easyhitch.net.

26. Unless otherwise noted, this section is drawn from William D. Bygrave and Jeffry A. Timmons, *Venture Capital at the Crossroads* (Boston, MA: Harvard Business School Press, 1992).

27. "Note on the Venture Capital Industry," Harvard Business School Case, 1982.

28. Bygrave and Timmons.

29. Michael Vachon, "Venture Capital Reborn," *Venture Capital Journal*, 1993, 32–36.

30. For more specifics, see Harry A. Sapienza and Jeffry A. Timmons, "Launching and Building Entrepreneurial Companies: Do the Venture Capitalists Build Value?" *Frontiers of Entrepreneurship Research* (Babson Park, MA: Babson College, 1989). See also Jeffry A. Timmons, "Venture Capital: More Than Money," in *Pratt's Guide to Venture Capital Sources*, 13th ed., J. Morris, ed. (Needham, MA: Venture Economics, 1989).

31. The authors express appreciation to Thomas Huseby of Seapoint Ventures for his valuable insights in the following two sections.

32. Geoffrey H. Smart, "Management Assessment Methods in Venture Capital," Ph.D. Thesis (Claremont, CA: Claremont Graduate University, 1998).

33. This section was drawn from Donald P. Remey, "Mezzanine Financing: A Flexible Source of Growth Capital," in *Pratt's Guide to Venture Capital Sources*, D. Schutt, ed. (New York, NY: Venture Economics Publishing, 1993).

34. The following examples are drawn directly from Daniel R. Garner, Robert R. Owen, and Robert P. Conway, *The Ernst & Young Guide to Raising Capital* (New York, NY: Wiley, 1991), 51–52.

35. Garner, Owen, and Conway, 52–54.

36. Ibid., 281.

CHAPTER 10

1. Press Release, "Q1 2009 Private Equity Buyout Industry: Slowdown in Investments and Fundraising," www.cvca.ca, May 5, 2009.

2. Press Release, "Venture Capital Investment Continued to Fall in Q1 2009," www.cvc.ca, May 12, 2009.

3. Ibid.

4. Ibid.

5. The venture capital method of valuation is adapted from William A. Sahlman and Daniel R. Scherlis, "Method for Valuing High-Risk, Long-Term Investments: The 'Venture Capital Method'," Harvard Business School Note, 2009.

6. This paragraph is adapted from Sahlman and Scherlis, "Method for Valuing High-Risk, Long-Term Investments."

7. Ibid., 58–59.

8. Ibid., 24.
9. Jeffry A. Timmons, "Valuation Methods and Raising Capital," lecture at the Harvard Business School.
10. Note that it is WACC, not free cash flow, because of the tax factor.
11. Jeffry A. Timmons, "Deals and Deal Structuring," lecture at the Harvard Business School.
12. William A. Sahlman, "Structure of Venture Capital Organizations," *Journal of Financial Economics* 27, no. 2 (1990): 473–521.
13. www.avrioventures.com/criteria.
14. William A. Sahlman, "Note on Financial Contracting Deals," Harvard Business School Note, 1989.
15. Ibid., 35–36.
16. Ibid., 43.
17. Jeffry A. Timmons, Stephen Spinelli, and Andrew Zacharakis, *How to Raise Capital: Techniques and Strategies for Financing and Valuing Your Small Business* (New York, NY: McGraw-Hill, 2004).
18. Timmons, "Deals and Deal Structuring."
19. Herb Cohen, *You Can Negotiate Anything* (New York, NY: Bantam Books, 1982).
20. Ibid., 16.
21. Roger Fisher and William Ury, *Getting to Yes* (New York, NY: Penguin Books, 1991).
22. See, for example, Harold M. Hoffman and James Blakey, "You Can Negotiate with Venture Capitalists," *Harvard Business Review* 65, no. 2 (1987): 16–24.
23. Fisher and Ury, xviii.
24. Timmons, "Deals and Deal Structuring."
25. Ryan Roberts, "I Got a Term Sheet, Now What?" November 11, 2008, www.thestartuplawyer.com.
26. Mark Davis, "Term Sheets: Exploding Offers," November 10, 2008, www.markpeterdavis.com.
27. Douglass J. Cumming, "Capital Structure in Venture Finance," *Journal of Corporate Finance* 11, no. 3: 550–585.
28. This is a fictional name for an actual company.
29. Timothy Hay, "O Canada VC, We Stand On Guard for Thee," *Wall Street Journal*, April 3, 2009.
30. Ibid.
31. Mark Skapinker, "Say It Like You See It," www.blog.brightspark.com, April 4, 2009.

CHAPTER 11

1. The authors wish to thank Leslie Charm of Babson College for his significant contributions to this chapter.
2. Jean-Etienne De Bettignies and James A. Brander, "Financing Entrepreneurship: Bank Finance Versus Venture Capital," *Journal of Business Venturing* 22, no. 6 (2007): 808–832.
3. Jeffry A. Timmons, *Financing and Planning the New Venture* (Acton, MA: Brick House Publishing, 1990).
4. Ibid., 68.
5. Ibid., 33.
6. Ibid., 68–80.
7. Neelam Jain, "Monitoring Costs and Trade Credit," *Quarterly Review of Economics and Finance* 41, no. 1 (2001): 89–110.
8. Gordon Donaldson, *Corporate Debt Capacity* (New York, NY: Beard Books, 2000)
9. Richard Kinlough and Bill Holy, "The Debt Market," *Private Capital*, Spring 2009.
10. "Canada Will Emerge from Slump Faster, Stronger: PM," *CBC News*, March 10, 2009.
11. Ben S. Bernanke, "Nonmonetary Effects of the Financial Crisis in the Propagation of the Great Depression," *American Economic Review* 73, no. 3 (1983): 257–276.
12. Canada Business, "Online Small Business Workshop," www.canadabusiness.ca.
13. Jain, 81–82.
14. Gordon B. Baty, *Entrepreneurship: Playing to Win* (Reston, VA: Reston Publishing, 1974) and James McNeill Stancill, "Getting the Most from Your Banking Relationship," *Harvard Business Review* 58, no. 2 (1980): 20–28.
15. This section is drawn from Timmons, *Financing and Planning the New Venture* (Action, MA: Brick House Publishing, 1990).
16. Tom Keyser, "Rebel with a Cause," www.albertadventures.com, December 1, 2008.

17. Duncan Cameron, "Needed: The Canadian Investment Bank," www.rabble.ca (accessed May 12, 2009).
18. Timmons, *Financing and Planning the New Venture*, 90–94.
19. Calvin Leung, "The Good, the Bad & the Ugly," *Canadian Business*, March 30, 2009.
20. "Most Actively Traded Companies on Canadian Stock Markets," *Canadian Free Press*, May 30, 2009.
21. "Canwest Media Gets Bondholder Reprieve," *United Press International*, May 21, 2009.
22. Baty, *Entrepreneurship: Playing To Win*.
23. Interview with Anna Maria Tremonti, host of "The Current" *CBC Radio*, May 18, 2009.
24. Christinne Muschi, "'This is Economic War!' Jarislowsky Warns," *Financial Post*, December 29, 2008.

CHAPTER 12

1. Special thanks to Ed Marram, entrepreneur, educator, and friend, for his lifelong commitment to studying and leading growing businesses and sharing his knowledge with the authors.
2. Henry Mintzberg, *Managers Not MBAs: A Hard Look at the Soft Practice of Managing and Management Development* (San Francisco, CA: Berrett-Koehler, 2004).
3. Ellyn Kerr, "Not Another MBA!" *McGill Reporter*, May 13, 2004.
4. Steven M. Dunphy and David Meyer, "Entrepreneur or Manager? A Discriminant Analysis Based on Mintzberg's Managerial Roles," *Journal of Business and Entrepreneurship* 14, no. 2 (2002): 17–36.
5. Special appreciation is given to Ernst & Young LLP and the Kauffman Center for Entrepreneurial Leadership for permission to include the Summary of their research here.
6. Harvey "Chet" Krentzman described this phenomenon to the authors many years ago. The principle still applies.
7. www.bdc.ca/en/business_tools/calculators/salesperemployee.htm.
8. The crises discussed here are the ones the authors consider particularly critical. Usually, failure to overcome even a few can imperil a venture at a given stage. There are, however, many more, but a complete treatment of all of them is outside the scope of this book.
9. Jeffry A. Timmons, "The Entrepreneurial Team: Formation and Development," paper presented at the Academy of Management Annual Meeting, Boston, MA, 1973.
10. "Lina Ball has Yellowknife Dancing! Owner of Bella Dance Academy Wins BDC's Young Entrepreneur Award for the Northwest Territories," *Canadian Newswire*, October 21, 2008.
11. Daron Letts, "Hip Hop is on Top," *Northern News Service*, September 10, 2008.
12. Daron Letts, "Dancer Mum on Results of Her Star Audition," *Northern News Service*, April 24, 2009.
13. David Halabisky, Erwin Dreessen, and Chris Parsley, "Growth in Firms in Canada, 1985–1999," *Journal of Small Business and Entrepreneurship* 19, no. 3 (2006): 255–268.
14. Austin Hill, "Inaugural Blog Post," www.billionswithzero knowledge.com.
15. www.360visibility.com.
16. www.greenlite.ca.
17. Jean-René Halde, "BDC's Young Entrepreneur Awards," *Canadian Business*, November 24, 2008.
18. Ibid.

CHAPTER 13

1. Canadian Franchise Association, www.cfa.ca.
2. Stephen Spinelli, Jr., Benoit Leleux, and Sue Birley, "An Analysis of Shareholder Return in Public Franchisors," Society of Franchising Presentation, 2001.
3. Scott Shane, "Hybrid Organizational Arrangements and Their Implications for Firm Growth and Survival: A Study of New Franchisors," *Academy of Management Journal* 39, no. 1 (1996): 216–34.
4. www.homehardware.ca.
5. www.cara.com.
6. www.timhortons.com.

7. Advertising cooperatives in franchising are common. A cooperative is a contractual agreement whereby franchisees in a geographic area are bound to contribute a percentage of their revenue to a fund that executes a marketing plan, usually including media purchases. The cooperative is typically governed by the participating franchisees and sometimes includes representation from the franchisor and advertising agency.

8. John Pozios, "Canada Needs Uniformity in Franchise Legislation," May 9, 2008, www.lawyersweekly.ca.

9. www.st-hubert.com.

10. www.harveys.com.

11. www.pizzanova.com.

12. www.mrsub.ca.

13. Oliver E. Williamson, "Comparative Economic Organizations: The Analysis of Discrete Structural Alternatives," *Administrative Science Quarterly* 36, no. 2 (1991): 269–296.

14. Francine Lafontaine, "Agency Theory and Franchising: Some Empirical Results," *Rand Journal of Economics* 23, no. 2 (1992): 263–283.

15. Ian R. Mcneil, "Economic Analysis of Contractual Relations: Its Shortfalls and the Need for a 'Rich Classificatory Apparatus,'" *Northwestern University Law Review* 75, no. 6 (1980): 1018–1063.

CHAPTER 14

1. The concepts and models presented in this chapter are based on the research and writing of Timothy Habbershon and colleagues, including Timothy G. Habbershon, Mary L. Williams, and Kenneth Kaye, "A Resource Based Framework for Assessing the Strategic Advantages of Family Firms," *Family Business Review* 12, no. 1 (1999)): 1–25; Timothy G. Habbershon, Mary Williams, and Ian C. Macmillan, "A Unified Systems Perspective of Family Firm Performance," *Journal of Business Venturing* 18, no. 4 (2003): 451–465; Timothy G. Habbershon and Joseph Pistrui, "Enterprising Families Domain: Family-Influenced Ownership Groups in Pursuit of Transgenerational Wealth," *Family Business Review* 15, no. 1 (2002): 223–237.

2. Danny Miller and Isabelle Lebreton-Miller, *Managing for The Long Run: Lessons in Competitive Advantage from Great Family Businesses* (Boston, MA: Harvard Business School Press, 1995).

3. Lloyd P. Steier, James J. Chrisman, and Jess H. Chua, "Entrepreneurial Management and Governance in Family Firms: An Introduction," *Entrepreneurship Theory & Practice* 28, no. 4 (2004): 295–303.

4. Primary financial, performance, and ownership data from Hoovers Online.

5. Joseph H. Astrachan, Shaker A. Zahra, and Pramodita Sharma, "Family-Sponsored Ventures," United Nations. Entrepreneurial Advantage of Nations: Global Entrepreneurship Symposium, 2003.

6. www.molsoncoors.com.

7. www.bearings.com.

8. Joseph Weber, et al., "Family Inc.," *Businessweek*. November 10, 2003.

9. Anthony Markin, "Family Ownership and Firm Performance in Canada," Master's Thesis in Global Asset and Wealth Management, Simon Fraser University, 2004.

10. www.samuel.com.

11. www.quailsgate.com.

12. Peter Leach, Bruce Ball, and Garry Duncan, *Guide to the Family Business*, Canadian ed. (Scarborough, ON: Thomson Carswell, 2003).

13. Ivey Business Families Centre, www.ivey.uwo.ca/entrepreneurship/bfc.

14. "IFERA, Family Businesses Dominate," *Family Business Review* 16, no. 4 (2003):235.

15. Howard E. Aldrich and Jennifer E. Cliff, "The Pervasive Effects of Family on Entrepreneurship: Toward a Family Embeddedness Perspective," *Journal of Business Venturing* 18, no. 5 (2003): 573–596.

16. Global Entrepreneurship Monitor 2002, Special Report on Family Sponsored New Ventures.

17. Ibid.

18. Edith T. Penrose, *The Theory of the Growth of the Firm,* 3rd ed. (New York, NY: Oxford University Press, 1995).

19. The content and questions from the mind-set and methods inventories are based upon the following literature: Jeffrey G. Covin and Dennis P. Slevin, "Strategic Management in Small Firms in Hostile and Benign Environments," *Strategic Management Journal* 10, no. 1 (1989): 75–87; Rita Gunther McGrath and Ian Macmillan, *The Entrepreneurial Mindset: Strategies for Continuously Creating Opportunity in an Age of Uncertainty* (Boston, MA: Harvard Business School Press, 2000); Daniel L. McConaughy, Charles H. Matthews, and Anne S. Fialko, "Founding Family Controlled Firms: Performance, Risk, and Value," *Journal of Small Business Management* 39, no. 1 (2001): 31–49; Danny Miller, "The Correlates of Entrepreneurship in Three Types of Firms," *Management Science* 29, no. 7 (1983): 770–791; Danny Miller and Peter H. Friesen, "Innovation in Conservative and Entrepreneurial Firms: Two Models of Strategic Momentum," *Strategic Management Journal* 3, no. 1 (1982): 1–25; Shaker Zahra "Entrepreneurial Risk Taking in Family Firms," *Family Business Review* 18, no. 1 (2002): 23–40.

20. Edith T. Penrose, *The Theory of the Growth of the Firm,* 3rd ed. (New York, NY: Oxford University Press, 1995).

21. Jeffrey G. Covin and Dennis P. Slevin, "Strategic Management in Small Firms in Hostile and Benign Environments," *Strategic Management Journal* 10, no. 1 (1989): 75–87.

22. Ibid.

23. Ramona K. Z. Heck, Frank Hoy, Panikkos Z. Poutziouris, and Lloyd P. Steier, "Emerging Paths of Family Entrepreneurship Research," *Journal of Small Business Management* 46, no. 3 (2008): 317–330.

24. Nicholas J. Beutell, "Self-Employment, Work-Family Conflict and Work-Family Synergy: Antecedents and Consequences," *Journal of Small Business and Entrepreneurship* 20, no. 4 (2007): 325–334.

25. Jennifer E. Jennings and Megan S. McDougald, "Work-Family Interface Experiences and Coping Strategies: Implications for Entrepreneurship Research and Practice," *Academy of Management Review* 32, no. 3 (2007): 747–760.

26. Bill Fields, "The Art of Delegating: A Critical Approach to Achieving Work/Life Balance," *Canadian Family Business*, November 2008.

27. Rita Gunther McGrath and Ian Macmillan, *The Entrepreneurial Mindset: Strategies for Continuously Creating Opportunity in an Age of Uncertainty* (Boston, MA: Harvard Business School Press, 2000).

28. Duane R. Ireland and Michael A. Hitt, "Achieving and Maintaining Strategic Competitiveness in the 21st Century: The Role of Strategic Leadership," *Academy of Management Executive* 13, no. 1 (1999): 43–57.

29. Danny Miller, Isabelle Le Breton-Miller, and Richard H. Lester, "Divided Loyalties: Governance, Conduct and Performance in Family and Entrepreneur Businesses, *Academy of Management Proceedings*, 2007.

30. Grant Walsh, "Succession Strategy: Managing the All-Important Family Component," *Canadian Family Business*, April 2008.

31. "Sharing Success: Butler Byers Building on Community," *Canadian Family Business*, April 2008.

32. Hank Daniszewski, "Tepperman's Gets Bigger, Better," *London Free Press*, October 2, 2008.

33. www.teppermans.com.

34. "Leadership Insights," *Canadian Family Business*, December 2007.

35. www.cardinalmeats.com.

36. Margot Gibb-Clark, "Family Firms Learn to Share Power," *Globe and Mail Report on Business*, June 25, 1999.

37. Rick Spence, "'Stewards' of a Blueberry Empire: No Special Status for Heirs of Bragg Group Founder," *Financial Post*, June 8, 2009.

38. Jenna Lomas, "Kenneth Levene on Building a Family Legacy," *Small and Medium-Sized Enterprise & Entrepreneur Review*, August 2008.

CHAPTER 15

1. Special credit is due to Robert Bateman, Scott Douglas, and Ann Morgan for contributing material in this chapter. The material is the result of research and interviews with turn-around specialists.

    The authors are especially grateful to two specialists, Leslie B. Charm, who along with his partner has owned three national franchise companies, an entrepreneurial advisory and troubled business management company, and a venture capital company, AIGIS Ventures, LLC; and Leland Goldberg of Coopers & Lybrand, Boston, who contributed enormously to the efforts of Bateman, Douglas, and Morgan and to the material.

2. Charlie Rose, "A Conversation with Marissa Mayer, V.P. of Search Product and User Experience, Google," March 5, 2009.

3. Gordon Pitts, "He was Canada's Master Communicator," *Globe and Mail,* December 3, 2008.

4. www.jimcarreyworld.com.

5. CBC News, "Canada's Super Rich," www.cbc.ca, March 6, 2008.

6. CBC News, "Number of Millionaire Families Rises to 1.1 Million," www.cbc.ca, June 23, 2008.

7. Tom Keyser, "Rebel with a Cause," www.albertadventures.com, December 1, 2008.

8. Sandra Martin, "He Helped Build Tilden Rent-A-Car into a Thriving, All-Canadian Concern," *Globe and Mail,* July 30, 2008.

9. www.jimpattison.com.

10. Steven R. Holmberg, "Value Creation and Capture: Entrepreneurship Harvest and IPO Strategies," *Frontiers of Entrepreneurship Research* (Babson Park, MA: Babson College, 1991).

11. Joao C. Neves, "The Value of Financial Freedom and Ownership in Opportunities of Entrepreneurial Harvest," *International Journal of Entrepreneurship and Innovation Management* 5, no. 5/6 (2005): 469–482.

12. www.roots.com.

13. This is an arrangement whereby the two founders can force (the put) the acquirer to purchase their 20 percent at a predetermined and negotiated price.

14. See several relevant articles on selling a company in *Growing Concerns*, David E. Gumpert, ed. (New York, NY: John Wiley & Sons, 1984).

15. The big accounting firms publish information on deciding to take a firm public, as does the TSX.

16. Holmberg, "Value Creation and Capture."

17. John A. Hornaday, "Patterns of Annual Giving," *Frontiers of Entrepreneurship Research* (Babson Park, MA: Babson College, 1984).

INDEX